Personalized Learning!

In *MyAccountingLab* you are treated as an individual with specific learning needs.

The study and assessment resources that come with your textbook allow you to review content and develop what you need to know, on your own time, and at your own pace.

MyAccountingLab provides

- Quizzes with immediate grades
- A personalized study plan that tells you where to study based on your results
- A gradebook where you can find your grades to see your progress as the term unfolds
- Exercises and problems that correspond to those found in your text
- Help Me Solve This – a step-by-step tutorial tool that helps work through the problem material
- Animations that illustrate important text concepts including the Accounting Cycle
- Animated Demo Doc examples that guide you through specific examples
- Acadia/Pearson Business Insider Videos that contain interviews with industry executives featured in the text
- A section in your study plan for math review, covering the basics to help you in your accounting course
- A multimedia library containing your eText, Audio Chapter Summaries, Glossary Flashcards, Student PowerPoint Slides, Excel templates, and more

Save Time. Improve Results. www.myaccountinglab.com

ACCOUNTING

CANADIAN EIGHTH EDITION

VOLUME TWO

ACCOUNTING

CANADIAN EIGHTH EDITION

CHARLES T. HORNGREN STANFORD UNIVERSITY

WALTER T. HARRISON, JR. BAYLOR UNIVERSITY

M. SUZANNE OLIVER NORTHWEST FLORIDA STATE COLLEGE

PETER R. NORWOOD LANGARA COLLEGE

JO-ANN L. JOHNSTON BRITISH COLUMBIA INSTITUTE OF TECHNOLOGY

WITH CONTRIBUTIONS BY **GEORGE FISHER** DOUGLAS COLLEGE

Pearson Canada
Toronto

VOLUME TWO

Library and Archives Canada Cataloguing in Publication

Accounting / Charles T. Horngren ... [et al.]. — Canadian 8th ed.
  Canadian ed. published under title: Accounting / Charles T. Horngren,
  Walter T. Harrison, W. Morley Lemon ; with Carol E. Dilworth.

Includes index.

ISBN 978-0-13-815601-5 (v. 1).—ISBN 978-0-13-815602-2 (v. 2).

  1. Accounting—Textbooks.   2. Managerial accounting—Textbooks.
I. Horngren, Charles T., 1926- II. Horngren, Charles T., 1926-. Accounting.

HF5636.A32 2011   657'.044   C2009-906520-7

ISBN: 978-0-13-815602-2

Vice-President, Editorial Director: Gary Bennett
Editor-in-Chief: Nicole Lukach
Executive Marketing Manager: Cas Shields
Developmental Editor: Anita Smale
Production Editor: Lila Campbell
Copy Editor: Marg Bukta
Proofreader: Tom Gamblin
Production Coordinator: Andrea Falkenberg
Compositor: MPS Limited, A Macmillan Company
Photo and Permissions Researcher: Sandy Cooke
Art Director: Julia Hall
Cover and Interior Designer: Anthony Leung
Cover Image: Veer.com

2 3 4 5   14 13 12 11 10

Printed and bound in United States of America.

Photo Credits

671 Courtesy Osler, Hoskin & Harcourt LLP; **719** CP PHOTO/Don Denton;
767 CP PHOTO/Jason Kryk; **813** CP PHOTO/Nathan Denette; **874** iStock Photos;
925 CP PHOTO/Larry MacDougal; **999** Courtesy Winpak

BRIEF
Contents

Contents

*In each chapter, Assignment Material includes Questions, Starters, Exercises (including Serial and Challenge Exercises), Beyond
   the Numbers, an Ethical Issue, and Problems (Group A and B, and Challenge Problems).
**Extending Your Knowledge includes Decision Problems and Financial Statement Cases.

CHARLES T. HORNGREN is the Edmund W. Littlefield Professor of Accounting, Emeritus, at Stanford University. A graduate of Marquette University, he received his MBA from Harvard University and his PhD from the University of Chicago. He is also the recipient of honorary doctorates from Marquette University and DePaul University.

A Certified Public Accountant, Horngren served on the Accounting Principles Board for six years, the Financial Accounting Standards Board Advisory Council for five years, and the Council of the American Institute of Certified Public Accountants for three years. For six years, he served as a trustee of the Financial Accounting Foundation, which oversees the Financial Accounting Standards Board and the Government Accounting Standards Board.

Horngren is a member of the Accounting Hall of Fame.

A member of the American Accounting Association, Horngren has been its President and its Director of Research. He received its first annual Outstanding Accounting Educator Award.

The California Certified Public Accountants Foundation gave Horngren its Faculty Excellence Award and its Distinguished Professor Award. He is the first person to have received both awards.

The American Institute of Certified Public Accountants presented its first Outstanding Educator Award to Horngren.

Horngren was named Accountant of the Year, in Education, by the national professional accounting fraternity, Beta Alpha Psi.

Professor Horngren is also a member of the Institute of Management Accountants, from whom he has received its Distinguished Service Award. He was a member of the Institute's Board of Regents, which administers the Certified Management Accountant examinations.

Horngren is the author of other accounting books published by Pearson Prentice Hall: *Cost Accounting: A Managerial Emphasis*, Thirteenth Edition, 2008 (with Srikant Datar and George Foster); *Introduction to Financial Accounting*, Ninth Edition, 2006 (with Gary L. Sundem and John A. Elliott); *Introduction to Management Accounting*, Fourteenth Edition, 2008 (with Gary L. Sundem and William Stratton); *Financial Accounting*, Seventh Edition, 2008 (with Walter T. Harrison, Jr.).

Horngren is the Consulting Editor for Pearson Prentice Hall's Charles T. Horngren Series in Accounting.

WALTER T. HARRISON, JR. is Professor Emeritus of Accounting at the Hankamer School of Business, Baylor University. He received his BBA degree from Baylor University, his MS from Oklahoma State University, and his PhD from Michigan State University.

Professor Harrison, recipient of numerous teaching awards from student groups as well as from university administrators, has also taught at Cleveland State Community College, Michigan State University, the University of Texas, and Stanford University.

A member of the American Accounting Association and the American Institute of Certified Public Accountants, Professor Harrison has served as Chairman of the Financial Accounting Standards Committee of the American Accounting Association, on the Teaching/Curriculum Development Award Committee, on the Program Advisory Committee for Accounting Education and Teaching, and on the Notable Contributions to Accounting Literature Committee.

Professor Harrison has lectured in several foreign countries and published articles in numerous journals, including *Journal of Accounting Research, Journal of Accountancy, Journal of Accounting and Public Policy, Economic Consequences of Financial*

Accounting Standards, Accounting Horizons, Issues in Accounting Education, and *Journal of Law and Commerce*.

He is co-author of *Financial Accounting*, Seventh Edition, 2008 (with Charles T. Horngren), published by Pearson Prentice Hall. Professor Harrison has received scholarships, fellowships, and research grants or awards from PriceWaterhouse Coopers, Deloitte & Touche, the Ernst & Young Foundation, and the KPMG Foundation.

M. SUZANNE OLIVER is an associate professor of accounting at Northwest Florida State College in Niceville, Florida. She received her B.A. in Accounting Information Systems and her Masters in Accountancy from the University of West Florida.

Professor Oliver began her career in accounting in the tax department of a regional accounting firm, specializing in benefit plan administration. She has served as a software analyst for a national software development firm (CPASoftware) and as the Oracle fixed assets analyst for Spirit Energy, formerly part of Union Oil of California (Unocal). A Certified Public Accountant, Oliver is a member of the Florida Institute of Certified Public Accountants.

Professor Oliver has taught financial accounting, managerial accounting, intermediate accounting, tax accounting, accounting software applications, payroll accounting, auditing, accounting systems, advanced accounting, managerial finance, business math, and supervision. She has also taught pension continuing education classes for CPAs, and has developed and instructed online courses using MyAccountingLab, WebCT, and other proprietary software.

Professor Oliver lives in Niceville where she is a member of the First United Methodist Church with her husband Greg and son C.J.

PETER R. NORWOOD is an instructor in accounting and the chair of the Langara School of Management at Langara College in Vancouver. A graduate of the University of Alberta, he received his MBA from the University of Western Ontario. He is a Chartered Accountant, a Fellow of the Institute of Chartered Accountants of British Columbia, a Certified Management Accountant, and a Fellow of the Society of Management Accountants of Canada.

Before entering the academic community, Mr. Norwood worked in public practice and industry for over fifteen years. He is First Vice-President of the Institute of Chartered Accountants of British Columbia (President in 2010–2011) and a member of the board of the Chartered Accountants School of Business (CASB). He is chair of the Chartered Accountants Education Foundation for the British Columbia Institute of Chartered Accountants, for whom he has served on a variety of committees. Mr. Norwood is a past member of the Board of Evaluators of the Canadian Institute of Chartered Accountants. Mr. Norwood is also a sessional instructor in the Sauder School of Business, University of British Columbia. He is a past chair of the Langara College Foundation.

JO-ANN L. JOHNSTON is an instructor in accounting and financial planning in the Financial Management Department at the British Columbia Institute of Technology (BCIT). She obtained her Bachelor in Administrative Studies from British Columbia Open University, her Diploma of Technology in Financial Management from BCIT, and her MBA from Simon Fraser University. She is also a Certified General Accountant and recently completed the Canadian Securities Course.

Prior to entering the field of education, Mrs. Johnston worked in public practice and industry for over 10 years. She is a past member of the Board of Governors of the Certified General Accountants Association of British Columbia and has served on various committees for the Association. She was also a member of the Board of Directors for the BCIT Faculty and Staff Association, and served as Treasurer during that tenure. She currently serves as chair of the CGA Student Advisory Group and is a member of CGA-BC Education Foundation and the Strategic Planning Committee for the Certified General Accountants Association of British Columbia.

In addition to teaching duties and committee work for the British Columbia Institute of Technology, Mrs. Johnston is the financial officer for a family-owned business.

A Letter to Students

Students will "Get It" Anytime, Anywhere with *Accounting's* Student Learning System

Welcome to your introductory accounting course! Accounting is the language of business. Whether you intend to be an accountant or not, you owe it to yourself to develop your skills with this language so that you can give yourself a winning edge in your career.

As instructors, we know that you want to ace your accounting course, and we also know that the volume of material covered in introductory accounting can be overwhelming. To help you develop your skills and understanding of accounting principles—to help you "get it"—we created the *Accounting* **Student Learning System.** All the features of the **student textbook, study resources,** and **online homework system** are designed to work together to provide you with more "I get it!" moments inside the classroom and especially outside the classroom, when you don't have access to your instructor.

We first had to create a really solid textbook, one that covered the material in a way that makes new and possibly intimidating topics easier to understand. To make sure we were on the right track, we held focus groups with first-year accounting students like you. Many of the changes made to the textbook and many of the new study resources were a direct result of suggestions from these students.

We have also created a number of tools and resources to support you, and your portal to these resources is MyAccountingLab. In intro accounting, sometimes the only way to "get it" is to do it—to practise similar questions many times until the concepts are clear, and MyAccountingLab allows you to do this. Sometimes seeing the basics of accounting presented in a slightly different, interactive way will help you "get it," and the Accounting Cycle Tutorials and the Demo Docs in MyAccountingLab help you do this. The tools and the features of MyAccountingLab appear in the fold-out at the front of this book. The tools and the features of this textbook are described in detail in the tour, Helping You "Get" Accounting, which is presented over the next few pages. And reminders appear in Chapter 1 (in Volume 1) to describe how each feature in the text can help you to master accounting.

Best of luck with your course, and much success!

Peter Norwood
Jo-Ann Johnston

Helping You "Get" Accounting

Each chapter of *Accounting* includes a number of tools and features designed to guide you through the process of developing your skills and understanding of key accounting concepts. Please read through the next few pages to learn more about these tools and the many ways in which they will help you learn, understand, and apply accounting concepts.

Learning Objectives are listed on the first page of each chapter. This "roadmap" shows you what will be covered and what is especially important. Each Learning Objective is repeated in the margin where the material is first covered. The Learning Objectives are summarized at the end of the chapter. Notice that the final Learning Objective deals with International Financial Reporting Standards (IFRS).

Chapter openers present a story about a real company or a real business situation, and show why the topics in the chapter are important to real companies. Some of the companies you'll read about include WestJet Airlines, Bombardier Recreational Products Inc., Canadian Tire, and The Forzani Group. Students tell us that using real companies makes it easier for them to learn and remember accounting concepts.

Key questions appear at the beginning of each chapter to highlight the important issues and questions that will be answered in the chapter. Once you read these questions, they will remain in the back of your mind. As you work through the chapter, you'll discover the answers and see why the chapter topics really are important.

Learning Objectives in the margin visually signal the beginning of the section that covers the objective topic. Look for this feature when you are studying and want to review a particular topic.

Exhibits are provided in full colour to make the concepts easier to understand and easier to remember.

Learning Tips in the margin are suggestions for learning or remembering concepts that you might find difficult.

Key Points in the margin highlight important details from the text. These are good review tools for when you prepare for tests or exams.

Real World Examples show how real companies make use of the concepts just discussed in the text. Linking concepts to real companies makes them easier to understand and remember.

Did You Get It? boxes appear at the end of each Learning Objective. The questions allow you to slow down for a moment and test your mastery of the material just covered in the Learning Objective before moving on in the chapter. These serve as an excellent way to check your progress because the answers are provided on MyAccountingLab. Notice the MyAccountingLab reminder!

Decision Guidelines show how the accounting concepts covered in the chapter are used by business people to make business decisions. This feature shows why accounting principles and concepts are important in a broader business context, not just to accountants. The Decision Guidelines also serve as an excellent summary of the chapter topics.

Summary Problem for Your Review pulls together the chapter concepts with an extensive and challenging review problem. Full worked solutions are given so that you can check your progress. Red notes in the margin or in the solution give you hints for how to tackle the solution, reminders of things to watch for, and further explanations about the solutions.

Summary appears at the end of each chapter. It gives a concise description of the material covered in the chapter and is organized by learning objective. Use this summary as a starting point for organizing your review when studying for a test or exam.

Self-Study Questions are multiple-choice questions that allow you to test your understanding of the chapter on your own. Page references are given so that you can review a section quickly if you miss an answer.

Answers to Self-Study Questions appear immediately (but upside down!) so you can check your progress.

Accounting Vocabulary lists all the terms that were defined and appeared in bold type in the chapter. The page references are given so you can review the meanings of the terms. These terms are also collected and defined in the Glossary at the end of the text.

Similar Accounting Terms link the accounting terms used in the chapter to similar terms you might have heard outside your accounting class, in the media, in other courses, or in day-to-day business dealings. Knowing similar terms should make it easier to remember the accounting terms.

While practice may not make you perfect, it is still the best way to make sure you grasp new accounting concepts and procedures. Working through the end of chapter exercises and problems will help you confirm your understanding of accounting concepts and develop your accounting skills. These review and practice materials are described in the following pages.

Questions require short, written answers or short calculations, often on a single topic.

Starters serve as warm-ups and confidence builders at the beginning of the assignment material. They address a single topic from the chapter. A brief description, the learning objectives covered, and **Check figures** appear in the margin beside each Starter. All of the Starters appear on MyAccountingLab in book-match form and algorithmic form (where applicable).

Exercises on a single or a few topics require you to "do the accounting" and, often, to consider the implications of the results in the same way that real companies would. **Check figures** appear in the margin beside each Exercise. All of the Exercises appear on MyAccountingLab in book-match form and algorithmic form (where applicable).

Excel Spreadsheet Template icons appear beside selected Exercises and Problems to remind you that Excel spreadsheets have been created to answer these questions. You can find these spreadsheets on MyAccountingLab. You don't have to use the spreadsheets to answer the questions, but you may find they save you time.

Serial Exercise in each chapter in Volume 1 and Volume 2 follows one company and builds in complexity with each chapter, providing an excellent way to see the big picture and to see how the accounting topics build off one another. Each Serial Exercises appears on MyAccountingLab in book-match form and algorithmic form (where applicable).

Challenge Exercises provide a challenge for those students who have mastered the Exercises, and appear on MyAccountingLab in book-match form and algorithmic form (where applicable).

Beyond the Numbers exercises require analytical thinking and written responses about the topics presented in the chapter.

Ethical Issues are thought-provoking situations that help you recognize when ethics should affect an accounting decision.

Problems are presented in two groups that mirror each other, "A" and "B." Many instructors work through problems from Group A in class to demonstrate accounting concepts, then assign problems from Group B for homework or extra practice. **Check figures** are included for the **"A" Problems only** to make sure you're on the right track. Each Problem appears on MyAccountingLab in book-match form and algorithmic form (where applicable).

Challenge Problems encourage you to consider the effect of accounting information and apply it to decision situations.

Decision Problems allow you to prepare and interpret accounting information and then make recommendations to a business based on this information.

Appendix A — WINNING THE WEST

Appendix B — SUN-RYPE ANNUAL REPORT For the Year Ended December 31, 2008

Financial Statement Cases allow you to use real financial information from a service company and a manufacturer/merchandiser. Canadian Western Bank is Canada's largest publicly traded Schedule I bank headquartered in Western Canada. Sun-Rype Products Ltd. is a leading Canadian manufacturer and marketer of juice-based beverages and fruit-based snacks. Selected financial information from each company's 2008 Annual Report appear in Appendix A and Appendix B of Volume 1 and Volume 2 of *Accounting*. The full annual reports appear on MyAccountingLab.

Comprehensive Problem appears at the end of each part of Volume 1 and Volume 2. It covers the content addressed in the book so far. This is a relatively long problem that provides an excellent review of all of the topics covered in the chapters in that part. See your instructor for the solution to this problem.

Working Papers are available for purchase, and are a set of tear-out forms that you can use to solve all the exercises and problems in Volume 2. Because the forms you need have already been created, you avoid time-consuming set-up and can focus on the accounting right away.

MyAccountingLab Online Homework and Assessment Manager

Experiencing the Power of Practice with MyAccountingLab:
www.myaccountinglab.com

MyAccountingLab is an online homework system that gives students more "I get it!" moments through the power of practice. The power of repetition when you "get it" means learning happens. With MyAccountingLab students can:

- Work on the exact end-of-chapter material and/or similar problems assigned by the instructor.
- Use the Study Plan for self-assessment and customized study outlines.
- Use the Help Me Solve This tool for a step-by-step tutorial.
- View the Demo Docs Example to see an animated demonstration of where the numbers came from.
- View the Flash Animations to understand important text concepts
- Watch a Video to see additional information pertaining to the lecture.
- Open Textbook Pages to find the material they need to get help on specific problems.

Multimedia Library

The **Multimedia Library** provides direct links to all media assets for this course, the eText, Audio Chapter Summaries, Glossary Flashcards, Demo Docs, Accounting Cycle Tutorial, Animations, Excel Templates, Student PowerPoint Slides, Solutions to Did You Get It? Questions, and Acadia Videos.

Multiple Pathways to Learning

Pearson Canada's **Multiple Pathways to Learning Assessment** helps you discover your own personal learning style, including identifying your personal strengths and weaknesses. After completing the survey, you can refer to the "Mapping Guide" to learn which features of your textbook or MyAccountingLab will be most effective for your learning style, ultimately enabling you to develop productive and effective study practices.

StudyLife

Studying can be lonely and difficult—**StudyLife** can help by matching you with your ideal study partner. Using **StudyLife** is simple. It works much like facebook.com or MySpace®. Once you complete our profile, **StudyLife** will match you with ideal study partners—other students taking the same subject with complementary learning styles, study techniques, and skills. They could be your classmates or they could be students on the other side of the country.

To the Instructor

Welcome to *Accounting*! Instructors have told us that their greatest challenges are effectively teaching students with very different business and accounting backgrounds, and motivating students to give accounting the study time and attention it deserves. Add to this an accounting environment that is changing like never before, with new generally accepted accounting principles (GAAP) for private enterprises and new International Financial Reporting Standards (IFRS), and you have teaching challenges like never before. *Accounting*'s approach and features were designed to help you address and overcome these challenges.

Accounting's Approach

With all the changes in the accounting environment, we gave serious thought to all the options before selecting the best approach for presenting the material in *Accounting*. We have chosen **GAAP for private enterprises as the basis for this textbook.** This allows us to base all discussions on the conceptual framework of GAAP for private enterprises, a framework shared in large part with IFRS. GAAP for private enterprises also streamlines some of the material to reduce complexity at the introductory level. One example is the number of categories of investments is reduced, which streamlines recording by focusing on the nature of the investment and its accounting treatment, rather than its label and specific accounting treatment.

We also gave serious thought to **our approach to IFRS.** IFRS will be in effect for all publicly accountable enterprises beginning January 1, 2011, with comparative IFRS figures for 2010 required as well. Given the number of Canadian companies that will have to report results according to IFRS, we thought it was vital for students to be exposed to IFRS and have some understanding of them, even in Introductory Accounting. We thought the "Wait until Intermediate Accounting" approach was *not* an option. However, students can't learn two sets of accounting standards in one introductory-accounting course—many find one set of standards a challenge.

Accounting's approach is to include the description and implications of IFRS as the final Learning Objective in each chapter. It has been designed to stand out from all the other Learning Objectives, but like all the others, it ends with Did You Get It? questions for students and, where applicable, has related Starters, Exercises, or Problems in the end-of-chapter assignment material. While it is integrated with the rest of the chapter's content, its position at the end of the chapter and its self-contained nature make the IFRS Learning Objective "skippable" for those instructors who choose to cover IFRS elsewhere or at another time.

Additional IFRS support materials and updates will be available in the Instructor's section of MyAccountingLab.

A Student-Friendly Textbook Integrated with MyAccountingLab

Instructors have told us that if students miss an accounting class, they must be able to keep up by reading the text. An accounting textbook must help students prepare for class or, should they miss a session, catch up without being overwhelmed. We've taken a two-pronged approach to ensure *Accounting* makes this happen: created a student-friendly textbook and integrated it with a powerful, robust MyAccountingLab.

The biggest change we made to the textbook pedagogy is the introduction of Did You Get It? questions at the end of each Learning Objective. Students have the opportunity to pause at the end of a Learning Objective and check whether they grasped its concepts before moving on to the next Learning Objective. The solutions are provided in MyAccountingLab so students can check their progress immediately and take action if necessary.

We also added examples of documents, such as invoices, cheques, and deposit slips, in Chapter 2. They serve as the source documents for the transactions described there, but they also ensure that all students have the basics covered regardless of their real-life business experience.

The textbook continues to reflect the changes made in previous editions that were well-received by students and that helped them to keep up or catch up if they missed a class:

- The **book design** is colourful, open, and inviting. Bulleted points and more art highlight key ideas and make the layout of explanations less imposing. Features in the margins—Key Points, Learning Tips, and Real World Examples— help students when they study. Artwork is positioned to reduce page flipping. In all, the textbook's design makes it easier to use and makes the concepts more clear. That is encouraging for students.

- **Highlights in Chapter 1** describe each feature of the text and explain how the feature can help students study and learn. A feature can't be effective unless students understand it and use it.

- **Did You Get It?** questions at the end of each Learning Objective, described above, encourage students to be active in their learning.

- We added new **International Financial Reporting Standards (IFRS)** material as the final Learning Objective in every chapter.

- **Worked solutions** for the Summary Problem for Your Review include the full solution as well as red notes in the margin to give students hints for how to tackle the solution, reminders of things to watch for, and further explanations about the solutions. These should help students overcome the "How do I start?" dilemma, as well as the "Why did they do that?" questions that can arise even when a full solution is given.

- **Check figures** in the margins for the Starters, Exercises, and the "A" set of Problems so students can make sure they are on track when they are working on their own. We have not provided check figures for the "B" set of Problems so that they can be assigned for homework or testing. The "B" Problems solutions are available to instructors on MyAccountingLab.

- **Examples from real Canadian companies** enliven the material, make difficult concepts easier to grasp, and illustrate the role of accounting in business. For that reason, we continue to include the **annual reports of two Canadian companies** in the text and on MyAccountingLab—in this edition, we are pleased to present data from the Canadian Western Bank and Sun-Rype Products Ltd. 2008 annual reports.

In those situations where "live" data drawn from real companies would complicate the material for introductory students, we illustrate the accounting with realistic examples from generic companies to give students the clearest examples possible.

- **MyAccountingLab icons and references** appear in the margins or in the headings to remind students of additional materials or resources available on MyAccountingLab, including the solutions to the Did You Get It? questions, reminders of relevant Accounting Cycle Tutorials topics, reminders of Excel Template Spreadsheets to help answer questions, and, of course, opportunities to practise end-of-chapter questions. Seeing a topic presented in a consistent but other, interactive way may help students understand it more fully. MyAccountingLab also includes a complete Study Guide and links to the Acadia Videos, as well as all the material described in the MyAccountingLab spread at the beginning of this book and in the student section of the preface.

Accuracy

As instructors, we know that **accuracy in problems and solutions** is every bit as important as clear writing and effective pedagogy. Tremendous effort has been made to ensure that the solutions to problem materials in *Accounting*, Canadian Eighth Edition are correct.

- The **authors** have developed their own problem and solutions materials.
- Our **Developmental Editor,** Anita Smale, CA, reviewed all problems and solutions.

- As a final stage, **technical checkers** have reviewed all problems and solutions.

We have made every effort to bring you the most accurate text possible. However, if you discover something that is inaccurate, please let us know so we can fix it as soon as possible.

Supplements for Instructors

The primary goal of the Instructor Resources is to help instructors deliver their course with ease, using any delivery method—traditional, self-paced, or online.

www.myaccountinglab.com

MyAccountingLab is web-based tutorial and assessment software for accounting that not only gives students more "I get it!" moments, but also provides instructors the flexibility to make technology an integral part of their course or a supplementary resource for students. And, because practice makes perfect, MyAccountingLab offers exactly the same end-of-chapter material found in the text along with algorithmic options that can be assigned for homework, all auto-graded for unlimited practice. MyAccountingLab also features the same look and feel for exercises and problems so that students are familiar and comfortable working with the material.

It also provides students with rich media assets that are closely integrated with the text including Audio Chapter Summaries, Glossary Flashcards, Demo Docs, Accounting Cycle Tutorial, Animations, Excel Templates, Student PowerPoint Slides, Solutions to Did You Get It? Questions, Acadia Videos, and the eText.

Instructor's Resource CD-ROM or http://vig.pearsoned.ca/

This CD-ROM and password-protected site provide a collection of resources to help you with lecture preparation, presentation, and assessment. It contains the following supplements:

- **Instructor's Solutions Manual** Now provided in both Adobe PDF and MS Word format for ease of use.
- **Instructor's Resource Manual** Also provided in both Adobe PDF and MS Word format, the Instructor's Resource Manual includes Chapter Overviews and Outlines, Assignment Grids, Ten-Minute Quizzes, and other valuable teaching resources including how to integrate MyAccountingLab in your course. In addition there is a new section describing all the supplements that come with *Accounting*, along with suggestions for how and when they can be used, written by an instructor who has used them all!
- **TestGen** This powerful and user-friendly computerized test bank includes well over 100 questions per chapter, ranging from True False, Multiple-Choice, and Matching to Problems and Critical Thinking Exercises.
- **PowerPoint Teaching Transparencies** We provide a comprehensive set of 40 to 50 PowerPoint slides per chapter.
- **Exhibits** We are pleased to provide the exhibits from the text in GIF format for use in the classroom and easy conversion to acetate format.
- **Adapting Your Lecture Notes** These detailed transition notes, including comparison of tables of content, chapter objectives, and chapter content, will facilitate your course preparation if you make the switch to *Accounting* from another introductory accounting text.
- **Personal Response Systems (PRS) Questions** For classrooms that use PRS, this exciting new wireless polling technology makes classrooms even more interactive by enabling instructors to pose questions to the students, record results, and display those results instantly.

Other items include:

- **Group Projects**
- **Solutions to Group Projects**
- **Check Figures**
- **Excel Spreadsheet Templates**
- **Accounting Cycle Tutorials**
- **Canadian Western Bank 2008 Annual Report**
- **Sun-Rype Products Ltd. 2008 Annual Report**

Finally, we want to draw your attention to a great service offered by Pearson to further enhance the use of *Accounting* in your course:

Pearson Custom Publishing We know that not every instructor follows the exact order of a course text. Some may not even cover all the material in a given volume. Pearson Custom Publishing provides the flexibility to select the chapters you need, presented in the order you want, to tailor fit your text to your course and your students' needs. Contact your Pearson Education Canada Sales and Editorial Representative to learn more.

We hope you enjoy *Accounting*!

Peter Norwood
Jo-Ann Johnston

Acknowledgements for the Canadian Eighth Edition

We would like to thank Charles Horngren and Tom Harrison for their encouragement and support.

Thanks are due to the following instructors for reviewing the previous edition of this text during the planning and development of this new edition, and for their excellent suggestions and ideas:

Rod Comrie, *Douglas College*
Vincent Durant, *St. Lawrence College*
Kim Dyke, *Red River College*
Elizabeth Hicks, *Douglas College*
Paul Hurley, *Durham College*
Glen Stanger, *Douglas College*
Selina Tang, *Douglas College*
Richard Wright, *Fanshawe College*

We would also like to thank the following instructors for participating in our accounting focus groups. Your excellent suggestions and feedback helped to shape the development of this textbook and its accompanying MyAccountingLab:

Anita Braaksma, *Kwantlen University College*
Liang Chen, *University of Toronto Scarborough*
Ann Clarke-Okah, *Carleton University*
Douglas Cliff, *Comosun College*
Rod Comrie, *Douglas College*
Cheryl Dyson, *Ryerson University*
Tim Edwards, *British Columbia Institute of Technology*
Erin Egeland, *Comosun College*
Gunter Eisenberg, *Douglas College*
George Fisher, *Douglas College*
Vern Gibson, *British Columbia Institute of Technology*
Elizabeth Hicks, *Douglas College*
Amy Hoggard, *Comosun College*
Gordon Holyer, *Vancouver Island University*
Paul Jeyakumar, *British Columbia Institute of Technology*
Barb Katz, *Kwantlen University College*
Jack Lin, *Douglas College*
Ho Yee Low, *Kwantlen University College*
Carol Meissner, *Georgian College*
Sally Mitzel, *Sheridan College*
Randy Murie, *British Columbia Institute of Technology*
Joe Pidutti, *Durham College*
George Robertson, *Douglas College*
Pat Sauve, *Durham College*
Catherine Seguin, *University of Toronto*
Dave Scott, *Niagara College*
Glen Stanger, *Douglas College*
Carol Stewart, *Kwantlen University College*
Agatha Thalheimer, *Comosun College*
Barry Tober, *Niagara College*
Helen Vallee, *Kwantlen University College*
Victor Waese, *British Columbia Institute of Technology*
Elizabeth Zaleschuk, *Douglas College*

We would like to acknowledge and thank the students who attended focus groups at Douglas College and Kwantlen University College, whose feedback and suggestions helped guide this new edition.

Scott Allen
Karen Fisher
Bradley Head

Matthew Gregory Hunter
Susan Kennedy
Eunji Lee
Kristana Sampang
Nasim Sarafraz-Shekari
Abby Tumak
Marc Andre Villeneuve

These students took the time to give us feedback on what we have been doing well and what we could improve upon with this new edition. As a result of their feedback, many changes were incorporated into the revision. For example, we "chunked" the material in each chapter by inserting Did You Get It? questions at the end of each Learning Objective, giving students the opportunity to check their understanding before moving on in the chapter. New materials have been added to MyAccountingLab as a direct result of these students' suggestions, including animations of important accounting concepts (the links among financial statements; the process of journalizing and posting; creating an accounting work sheet); a business math review; and instructions on using financial calculators. Several students asked for a new design with a fresh and open feel, and we have redesigned this new edition with this in mind.

Thanks are extended to Canadian Western Bank and Sun-Rype Products Ltd. for permission to use their annual reports in Volumes 1 and 2 of this text. Thanks are extended to JVC Canada Inc. for permission to use its invoice in Chapter 5. We acknowledge the support provided by *The Globe and Mail's Report on Business*, the *Financial Post*, the websites of various news organizations, and by the annual reports of a large number of public companies.

The Canadian Institute of Chartered Accountants, as the official promulgator of generally accepted accounting principles in Canada, and the *CICA Handbook*, are vital to the conduct of business and accounting in Canada. We have made every effort to incorporate the most current *Handbook* recommendations in this new edition of *Accounting* for both private enterprises and for publicly accountable enterprises subject to international financial reporting standards (IFRS).

We would like to give special thanks to George Fisher of Douglas College, who provided the new international financial reporting standards (IFRS) material in Volume 2, as well as the related end-of-chapter IFRS questions and solutions. His expertise and contributions are significant and greatly appreciated. We would also like to thank Amy Lam, CA, Senior Director of Member Services, Institute of Chartered Accountants of British Columbia, for her guidance and technical support during this time of great changes in the accounting-standards environment. Her willingness to review and discuss portions of the manuscript was very generous and insightful, and it is gratefully acknowledged.

We would like to acknowledge the people of Pearson Education Canada, in particular President Steve O'Hearn, V-P Editorial Director Gary Bennett, Editor-in-Chief Nicole Lukach, and Marketing Manager Cas Shields. Special thanks to Production Editor Lila Campbell, Production Coordinator Andrea Falkenberg, and their teams for their superior efforts in guiding this edition through the various phases of preparation and production. Special thanks are due to technical checker Michelle Hodgson for her meticulous work on Volume 1 and Volume 2 and the solutions. Special thanks are also due to Helen Vallee (Chapters 12–14) and Debbie Musil (Chapters 15–18) from Kwantlen University College for their thorough review of the end-of-chapter questions and solutions in Volume 2. They added a valuable additional layer of technical checking to these chapters. Finally, we would like to acknowledge the editorial and technical support of Anita Smale, CA.

I would like to thank my wife, Helen, and my family very much for their support, assistance, and encouragement.

Peter R. Norwood

I would like to thank my husband Bill and my family for their encouragement and support.

Jo-Ann L. Johnston

12 Partnerships

What is a partnership, and what are its advantages and disadvantages?

How do you create a partnership?
How are partnership profits and losses shared among partners?

How is a new partner admitted to or withdrawn from a partnership?

These questions and others will be answered throughout this chapter. And the Decision Guidelines at the end of this chapter will provide the answers in a useful summary.

LEARNING OBJECTIVES

1. Identify the characteristics of a partnership

2. Account for partners' initial investments in a partnership

3. Allocate profits and losses to the partners by different methods

4. Account for the admission of a new partner

5. Account for the withdrawal of a partner

6. Account for the liquidation of a partnership

7. Identify the impact on partnerships of international financial reporting standards (IFRS)

Osler, Hoskin & Harcourt LLP (limited liability partnership) is one of Canada's largest law firms. In mid 2009, the firm had over 450 lawyers who provided a variety of legal services to Canadian clients, as well as U.S. and international clients with interests in Canada. The firm has offices in Toronto, Montreal, Ottawa, Calgary, and New York. Osler, Hoskin & Harcourt LLP has a long list of areas of expertise and has been very successful, particularly in the field of mergers and acquisitions, where it acts as an advisor to clients who are either attempting to acquire other companies or are themselves the target of takeover bids from other companies.

Dale Ponder, Managing Partner of Osler, Hoskin & Harcourt LLP, describes the management structure of the firm as "a 'one-firm' model and approach . . . despite our geographic spread. This is an important part of our firm culture." This unified approach to the practice of law is integral to the success of the partnership. "We have a team-based approach to practice at our firm," adds Ms Ponder, "and among the most gratifying things [for me, as managing partner] . . . is seeing how much we can accomplish as a firm and for our clients when we turn our minds to a goal and work at it together."[1]

In this chapter, we will explain the partnership form of business organization and examine many of the issues that affect partnerships.

---

[1] Gail J. Cohen, "Ponder Following On in Osler's Line of Progressive Firm Leaders," *Canadian Lawyer*, June 2008, from http://www.canadianlawyermag.com/index.php/Ponder-following-on-in-Oslers-line-of-progressive-firm-leaders.html, accessed January 14, 2010.

The partnership form of business introduces some complexities that a proprietorship avoids.

- How much cash should a new partner contribute to the business?
- How should the partners divide profits and losses?
- How should a partner who leaves the firm be compensated for her or his share of the business?

A **partnership** is an association of two or more persons who co-own a business for profit. This definition is common to the various provincial partnership acts, which tend to prescribe similar rules with respect to the organization and operation of partnerships in their jurisdictions.

Forming a partnership is easy. It requires no permission from government authorities and involves no legal procedures, with the exception that most provinces require most partnerships to register information such as the names of the partners and the name under which the business will be carried on.[2] When two persons decide to go into business together, a partnership is automatically formed.

A partnership combines the assets, talents, and experience of the partners. Business opportunities closed to an individual may open up to a partnership. As the chapter-opening story illustrates, this is an important characteristic of a partnership. Osler, Hoskin & Harcourt LLP is successful because it is able to combine the skills of its very specialized lawyers and provide its clients with a complete roster of legal services. It is unlikely a lawyer operating as a proprietorship could offer the same level of expertise.

Partnerships come in all sizes. Many partnerships have fewer than 10 partners. Some medical practices may have 10 or more partners, while some of the largest law firms in Canada have more than 300 partners. The largest accounting firms in Canada have up to almost 500 partners.[3] Exhibit 12–1 lists the 10 largest public accounting firms in Canada. Nine of them are partnerships.

Characteristics of a Partnership

OBJECTIVE ①
Identify the characteristics of a partnership

Starting a partnership is voluntary. A person cannot be forced to join a partnership, and partners cannot be forced to accept another person as a partner. Although the partnership agreement may be oral, a written agreement between the partners reduces the chance of a misunderstanding. The following characteristics distinguish partnerships from proprietorships and from corporations.

---

[2] Smyth, J.E., D.A. Soberman, and A.J. Easson, *The Law and Business Administration in Canada,* 11th edition (Toronto: Pearson Education Canada Inc., 2007), pp. 562–567.

[3] "FP 500," *National Post,* Tuesday, June 2, 2009, online at www.nationalpost.com/story.html?id= 1654434, accessed August 25, 2009.

EXHIBIT 12–1 The Ten Largest Accounting Firms in Canada

Rank 2008	Firm	Revenue (Millions)	Number of Partners/ Principals
1	Deloitte & Touche LLP	$1,419	546
2	KPMG LLP	1,122	437
3	PricewaterhouseCoopers LLP	1,062	423
4	Ernst & Young LLP	856	318
5	Grant Thornton Canada	442	416
6	BDO Dunwoody LLP	343	331
7	Meyers Norris Penny LLP	260	197
8	Collins Barrow National Cooperative Inc.	126	153
9	RSM Richter LLP	117	57
10	HLB/Schwartz Levitsky Feldman LLP	48	69

Source: "FP 500," *National Post,* Tuesday, June 2, 2009, online at www.nationalpost.com/story. html?id=1654434, accessed August 25, 2009. Material reprinted with the express permission of: "The National Post Company", a Canwest Partnership.

The Written Partnership Agreement

A business partnership is somewhat like a marriage. To be successful, the partners must cooperate. However, business partners do not vow to remain together for life. To make certain that each partner fully understands how the partnership operates, partners should draw up a **partnership agreement**. This agreement is a contract between the partners, so transactions under the agreement are governed by contract law. The provincial legislatures in Canada have passed their respective versions of a partnership act, the terms of which apply in the absence of a partnership agreement or in the absence of particular matters in the partnership agreement.[4]

The partnership agreement should specify the following points:

1. Name, location, and nature of the business
2. Name, capital investment, and duties of each partner
3. Procedures for admitting a new partner
4. Method of sharing profits and losses among the partners
5. Withdrawals of assets allowed to the partners
6. Procedures for settling disputes among the partners
7. Procedures for settling with a partner who withdraws from the firm
8. Procedures for removing a partner who will not withdraw or retire from the partnership voluntarily
9. Procedures for liquidating the partnership—selling the assets, paying the liabilities, and giving any remaining cash to the partners

As partners enter and leave the business, the old partnership is dissolved and a new partnership is formed. Drawing up a new agreement for each new partnership may be expensive and time-consuming.

KEY POINT

A partnership is not required to have a formal written agreement. But a written agreement prevents confusion as to the sharing of profits and losses, partners' responsibilities, admission of new partners, how the partnership will be liquidated, and so on. However, there can still be disagreements even when there is a written agreement.

---

[4] Smyth, J.E., D.A. Soberman, and A.J. Easson, *The Law and Business Administration in Canada,* 11th edition (Toronto: Pearson Education Canada Inc., 2007), pp. 562–580.

Limited Life

A partnership has a limited life. If one partner withdraws from the business, the partnership dissolves. A new partnership may emerge to continue the same business, but technically the old partnership will have been dissolved. **Dissolution** is the ending of a partnership. The addition of a new partner dissolves the old partnership and creates a new partnership. Large partnerships such as PricewaterhouseCoopers retain the firm name even after partners resign from the firm.

Mutual Agency

Mutual agency means that every partner is a mutual agent of the firm. Any partner can bind the business to a contract within the scope of the partnership's regular business operations. If a partner enters into a contract with a person or another business to provide a service, then the firm—not just the partner who signed the contract—is bound to provide that service. If the partner signs a contract to buy her own car, however, the partnership is not liable because the car is a personal matter. It is not a regular business operation of the partnership.

Unlimited Liability

Each partner has **unlimited personal liability** for the debts of the business. When a partnership cannot pay its debts with business assets, the partners must pay with their personal assets. Proprietors also have unlimited personal liability for the debts of their business.

Suppose the partnership of Willis & Jones cannot pay a $20,000 business debt that Jones created. Willis and Jones each become personally liable (must pay this amount with their personal assets) because each partner has *unlimited liability* for their business debts. If either partner is unable to pay his or her part of the debt, the other partner (or partners) must make payment.

Unlimited liability and mutual agency are closely related. A dishonest partner or a partner with poor judgment may commit the partnership to a contract under which the business loses money. In turn, creditors may force *all* the partners to pay the debt from their personal assets. Hence, a business partner should be chosen with great care.

Co-ownership of Property

Any asset—cash, inventory, machinery, computers, and so on—that a partner invests into the partnership becomes the joint property of all the partners. The partner who invested the asset is no longer its sole owner.

No Partnership Income Tax

A partnership pays no income tax on its business income. Instead, the net income of the partnership is divided and flows through to become the taxable income of the partners. Suppose the Willis & Jones partnership earned net income of $150,000, shared equally by the two partners. The partnership would pay no income tax *as a business entity*. However, each partner would pay income tax *as an individual* on his or her $75,000 share of partnership income.

Partners' Equity Accounts

Recall from Chapter 1, page 13, that owner's equity for a proprietorship has only one account, entitled "Capital." Accounting for a partnership is much like accounting for a proprietorship. We record buying and selling goods and services, collecting and paying cash for a partnership just as we do for a proprietorship. But, because a partnership has more than one owner, the partnership must have a separate owner's equity account for each partner. For example, the equity account for Leslie Willis is "L. Willis, Capital." Just as a proprietor has a drawings or withdrawal account (a temporary account), each partner in a partnership has a withdrawal account, such as "L. Willis, Withdrawals."

Partnership Financial Statements

Partnership financial statements are much like those of a proprietorship. However, as mentioned earlier, a partnership income statement includes a section showing the division of net income to the partners. A partnership balance sheet reports a separate Capital account for each partner. Large partnerships may show one balance, the total for all partners. For example, the Willis & Jones partnership of Leslie Willis and Andrew Jones might report its financial statements for the year ended December 31, 2010, as shown in Panel A of Exhibit 12–2 below. A proprietorship's financial statements are presented in Panel B for comparison.

EXHIBIT 12–2 Financial Statements of a Partnership and a Proprietorship (all amounts in thousands of dollars)

PANEL A—PARTNERSHIP

WILLIS & JONES
Income Statement
For the Year Ended December 31, 2010

Revenues		$460
Expenses		(270)
Net income		$190
Allocation of net income:		
To Leslie Willis	$114	
To Andrew Jones	76	$190

WILLIS & JONES
Statement of Owners' Equity
For the Year Ended December 31, 2010

	Willis	Jones
Capital, January 1, 2010	$ 50	$40
Additional investments	10	—
Net income	114	76
Subtotal	174	116
Withdrawals	(72)	(48)
Capital, December 31, 2010	$102	$68

WILLIS & JONES
Balance Sheet
December 31, 2010

Assets	
Cash and other assets	$170
Partners' Equity	
Leslie Willis, capital	$102
Andrew Jones, capital	68
Total capital	$170

PANEL B—PROPRIETORSHIP

WILLIS CONSULTING
Income Statement
For the Year Ended December 31, 2010

Revenues	$460
Expenses	(270)
Net income	$190

WILLIS CONSULTING
Statement of Owner's Equity
For the Year Ended December 31, 2010

Capital, January 1, 2010	$ 90
Additional investments	10
Net income	190
Subtotal	290
Withdrawals	(120)
Capital, December 31, 2010	$170

WILLIS CONSULTING
Balance Sheet
December 31, 2010

Assets	
Cash and other assets	$170
Owner's Equity	
Leslie Willis, capital	$170

EXHIBIT 12–3   Advantages and Disadvantages of Partnerships

Partnership Advantages	Partnership Disadvantages
Versus Proprietorships:	1. A partnership agreement may be difficult to formulate. Each time a new partner is admitted or a partner leaves the partnership, the business needs a new partnership agreement.
1. A partnership can raise more capital.	2. Relationships among partners may be fragile.
2. A partnership brings together the abilities of more than one person.	3. Mutual agency and unlimited liability create personal obligations for each partner.
3. Partners working well together can achieve more than by working alone: 1 + 1 > 2 in a good partnership.	
Versus Corporations:	
4. A partnership is less expensive to organize than a corporation, which requires articles of incorporation from a province or the federal government.	
5. A partnership is subject to fewer governmental regulations and restrictions than is a corporation.	

Exhibit 12–3 lists the advantages and disadvantages of partnerships (compared with proprietorships and corporations). Most features of a proprietorship also apply to a partnership, most importantly

- Limited life
- Unlimited liability
- No business income tax

Types of Partnerships

There are two basic types of partnerships: general and limited.

General Partnerships

A **general partnership** is the basic form of partnership organization. Each partner is a co-owner of the business with all the privileges and risks of ownership. The general partners share the profits, losses, and the risks of the business. The partnership *reports* its income to the government tax authority (Canada Revenue Agency, or CRA), but the partnership pays *no* income tax. The profits and losses of the partnership pass through the business to the partners, who then pay personal income tax on their income. All the other features just covered also apply to a general partnership.

KEY POINT

Since all partners are personally liable for any debt of the business, it is extremely important to choose a partner carefully. This is one reason some investors/partners prefer the *limited partnership* form of business organization.

Limited Partnerships

Partners can avoid unlimited personal liability for partnership obligations by forming a *limited partnership*. A **limited partnership** has at least two classes of partners. There must be at least one *general partner*, who takes primary responsibility for the management of the business. The general partner also takes most of the risk of failure if the partnership goes bankrupt (liabilities exceed assets). In some limited partnerships, such as real-estate limited partnerships, the general partner often invests little cash in the business. Instead, the general partner's contribution is her or his skill in managing the organization. Usually, the general partner is the last owner to receive a share of partnership profits and losses. But the general partner may earn all excess profits after the limited partners get their share of the income.

The *limited partners* are so named because their personal obligation for the partnership's liabilities is limited to the amount they have invested in the business. Limited partners have limited liability similar to the limited liability that shareholders in a corporation have. Usually, the limited partners have invested the bulk of the partnership's assets and capital. They therefore usually have the first claim to partnership profits and losses, but only up to a specified limit. In exchange for their limited liability, their potential for profits usually has a limit as well.

Most professionals, such as doctors, lawyers, and most public accounting firms in Canada—including almost all of those in Exhibit 12–1—are now organized as **limited liability partnerships** (LLPs). An LLP is designed to protect innocent partners from negligence damages that result from another partner's actions. This means that each partner's personal liability for other partners' negligence is limited to a certain dollar amount, although liability for a partner's own negligence is still unlimited. The LLP must carry an adequate amount of malpractice insurance or liability insurance to protect the public.

DID YOU GET IT?

To check your understanding of the material in this Learning Objective, complete these questions. The solutions appear on MyAccountingLab so you can check your progress.

1. Jerry Fast and John Eddy would like to form a partnership to open up a night club—Fast Eddy's. They each have $100,000 and have decided that since they have been life-long friends, they do not need a written partnership agreement. Detail the contents of a partnership agreement and explain the importance of a written agreement to Fast and Eddy.

2. Suppose you were giving the friends in the previous question advice on their decision to form a partnership. Detail the advantages and disadvantages of their decision.

3. Fast and Eddy may, at some point, want to bring in a partner who does not want any day-to-day responsibility for managing the operations; he or she may simply want to receive a return on his or her investment. Describe the type of partner this person would be.

Forming a Partnership

Let's examine the start up of a partnership. Partners in a new partnership may invest assets and their related liabilities in the business. These contributions are journalized in the same way as for proprietorships, by debiting the assets and crediting the liabilities at their agreed-upon values. Each person's net contribution—assets minus liabilities—is credited to the equity account for that person. Often the partners hire an independent firm to appraise their assets and liabilities at current market value at the time a partnership is formed. This outside evaluation assures an objective valuation for what each partner brings into the business.

OBJECTIVE 2
Account for partners' initial investments in a partnership

Suppose Katie Warren and Dan Rushton form a partnership on June 1, 2010, to develop and sell computer software. The partners agree on the following values based on an independent appraisal:

Warren's contributions

- Cash, $10,000; inventory, $40,000; and accounts payable, $80,000 (The appraiser believes that the current market values for these items equal Warren's book values.)
- Computer equipment: cost, $800,000; accumulated amortization, $200,000; current market value, $450,000

Rushton's contributions

- Cash, $5,000
- Computer software: cost, $50,000; current market value, $100,000

The partnership records receipts of the partners' initial investments at the current market values of the assets and liabilities because, in effect, the partnership is buying the assets and assuming the liabilities at their current market values. The partnership entries are as follows:

Warren's investment

2010

Jun. 1	Cash	10,000	
	Inventory	40,000*	
	Computer Equipment	450,000*	
	Accounts Payable		80,000*
	Katie Warren, Capital		420,000
	To record Warren's investment in the partnership ($500,000 − $80,000).		

Rushton's investment

2010

Jun. 1	Cash	5,000	
	Computer Software	100,000*	
	Dan Rushton, Capital		105,000
	To record Rushton's investment in the partnership.		

*The assets were appraised and their current market values were used.

The initial partnership balance sheet appears in Exhibit 12–4. Note that the asset and liability sections on the balance sheet are the same for a proprietorship and a partnership.

EXHIBIT 12–4 Partnership Balance Sheet

WARREN AND RUSHTON
Balance Sheet
June 1, 2010

Assets		Liabilities	
Cash	$ 15,000	Accounts payable	$ 80,000
Inventory	40,000		
Computer equipment	450,000	**Capital**	
Computer software	100,000	Katie Warren, capital	420,000
		Dan Rushton, capital	105,000
		Total partners' capital	525,000
		Total liabilities	
Total assets	$605,000	and capital	$605,000

DID YOU GET IT?

To check your understanding of the material in this Learning Objective, complete these questions. The solutions appear on MyAccountingLab so you can check your progress.

4. Marty Hicks invests land in a partnership with Lee Manors. Hicks purchased the land in 2007 for $20,000. Three independent real estate appraisers now value the land at $50,000. Hicks wants $50,000 capital in the new partnership, but Manors objects. Manors believes that Hicks' capital investment should be measured by the book value of his land. Manors and Hicks seek your advice. Which value of the land is appropriate for measuring Hicks' capital—book value or current market value? State the reason for your answer.

5. Refer to the previous question. Give the partnership's journal entry to record Hicks' investment in the business.

Sharing Partnership Profits and Losses

Allocating profits and losses among partners can be challenging and can be a major source of disputes. Any division of profits and losses is allowed as long as the partners agree and it is in the partnership agreement. Typical arrangements include the following:

> **OBJECTIVE ③**
> Allocate profits and losses to the partners by different methods

1. Sharing profits and losses based on a stated fraction for each partner, such as 50/50, or 2/3 and 1/3, or 4:3:3 (which means 40 percent to Partner A, 30 percent to Partner B, and 30 percent to Partner C).

2. Sharing based on each partner's investment.

3. Sharing based on each partner's service.

4. Sharing based on a combination of stated fractions, investments, and service.

If the partners have not drawn up an agreement, or if the agreement does not state how the partners will divide profits and losses, then, by law, the partners must share profits and losses equally. If the agreement specifies a method for sharing profits but not losses, then losses are shared in the same proportion as profits. For example, a partner receiving 75 percent of the profits would likewise absorb 75 percent of any losses.

In some cases, an equal division is not fair. One partner may perform more work for the business than the other partner, or one partner may make a larger capital contribution. In the preceding example, Dan Rushton might agree to work longer hours for the partnership than Katie Warren in order to earn a greater share of profits. Warren could argue that she should receive more of the profits because she contributed more net assets ($420,000) than Rushton did ($105,000). Rushton might contend that his computer software program is the partnership's most important asset, and that his share of the profits should be greater than Warren's share. Arriving at fair sharing of profits and losses in a partnership may be difficult. We now discuss some options available in determining partners' shares of profits and losses.

Sharing Based on a Stated Fraction

The partnership agreement may state each partner's fraction of the total profits and losses. Suppose the partnership agreement of Heather Kerry and Ryan Calder allocates two-thirds of the business profits and losses to Kerry and one-third to Calder. This sharing rule can also be expressed as 2:1. If net income for the year is

$60,000, and all revenue and expense accounts have been closed, the Income Summary account has a credit balance of $60,000 prior to it closing:

Income Summary

	Bal. 60,000

The entry to close this account and allocate the net income to the partners' Capital accounts is

Dec. 31	Income Summary	60,000	
	Heather Kerry, Capital...............................		40,000
	Ryan Calder, Capital		20,000
	To allocate net income to partners.		
	(Kerry: $60,000 × ⅔; Calder: $60,000 × ⅓)		

Suppose Kerry's beginning Capital balance was $50,000 and Calder's was $10,000. After posting, the accounts appear as follows:

Income Summary	Heather Kerry, Capital	Ryan Calder, Capital
Clo. 60,000	60,000	Beg. 50,000
		Clo. 40,000
		End. 90,000

Ryan Calder, Capital
Beg. 10,000
Clo. 20,000
End. 30,000

If the partnership had a net loss of $15,000, the Income Summary account would have a debit balance of $15,000. In that case, the closing entry to allocate the loss to the partners' Capital accounts would be

Dec. 31	Heather Kerry, Capital	10,000	
	Ryan Calder, Capital.......................................	5,000	
	Income Summary		15,000
	To allocate net loss to partners.		
	(Kerry: $15,000 × ⅔; Calder: $15,000 × ⅓)		

A profit or loss will increase or decrease each partner's Capital account, but cash will not change hands.

Sharing Based on Capital Investments

Profits and losses are often allocated in proportion to the partners' capital investments in the business. Suppose John Adams, Erica Bennett, and Tony Carter are partners in ABC Company. Their Capital accounts at the end of the first year of business have the following balances, before closing entries. These amounts are equal to the original capital investments for each of the partners, since no earnings or withdrawals have yet been posted to these accounts.

John Adams, Capital...	$120,000
Erica Bennett, Capital...	180,000
Tony Carter, Capital	150,000
Total Capital balances..	$450,000

Assume that the partnership earned a profit of $300,000 for the year. To allocate this amount based on capital investments, each partner's percentage share of the partnership's total capital investment amount must be computed. We simply divide each partner's investment by the total capital investment amount. These figures, multiplied by the $300,000 profit amount, yield each partner's share of the year's profits:

Adams:	($120,000/$450,000) × $300,000	=	$ 80,000
Bennett:	($180,000/$450,000) × $300,000	=	120,000
Carter:	($150,000/$450,000) × $300,000	=	100,000
	Net income allocated to partners	=	$300,000

The closing entry to allocate the profit to the partners' Capital accounts is

Dec. 31   Income Summary..   300,000
                 John Adams, Capital.................................   80,000
                 Erica Bennett, Capital...............................   120,000
                 Tony Carter, Capital.................................   100,000
            To allocate net income to partners.

After this closing entry, the partners' Capital balances are

John Adams, Capital ($120,000 + $80,000)...	$200,000
Erica Bennett, Capital ($180,000 + $120,000)..	300,000
Tony Carter, Capital ($150,000 + $100,000)...	250,000
Total Capital balances after allocation of net income	$750,000

Sharing Based on Capital Investments and on Service

One partner, regardless of his or her capital investment, may put more work into the business than the other partners. Even among partners who log equal service time, one person's superior experience and knowledge may be worth more to the firm. To reward the harder-working or more valuable person, the profit-and-loss-sharing method may be based on a combination of partner capital investments *and* service to the business.

Assume Susan Duke and Carolyn Pax formed a partnership in which Duke invested $60,000 and Pax invested $40,000, a total of $100,000. Pax devotes more time to the partnership and earns the larger payout from the partnership. Accordingly, the two partners have agreed to share profit as follows:

1. The first $50,000 of partnership profit is to be allocated based on partners' capital investments in the business.
2. The next $60,000 of profit is to be allocated based on service, with Duke receiving $24,000 and Pax receiving $36,000.
3. Any remaining profit is allocated equally.

If net income for the first year is $125,000, the partners' shares of this profit are computed as follows:

	Duke	Pax	Total
Total net income..			$125,000
Sharing the first $50,000 of net income, based on capital investments:			
Duke ($60,000/$100,000 × $50,000)	$30,000		
Pax ($40,000/$100,000 × $50,000)..........................		$20,000	
Total..			50,000
Net income remaining for allocation.......................			75,000
Sharing of next $60,000, based on service:			
Duke..	24,000		
Pax		36,000	
Total..			60,000
Net income left for allocation			15,000
Remainder shared equally:			
Duke ($15,000 × ½)...	7,500		
Pax ($15,000 × ½)...		7,500	
Total..			15,000
Net income left for allocation			$ 0
Net income allocated to the partners.......................	$61,500	$63,500	$125,000

On the basis of this allocation, the closing entry is

Dec. 31	Income Summary	125,000	
	Susan Duke, Capital		61,500
	Carolyn Pax, Capital		63,500
	To allocate net income to partners.		

Sharing Based on "Salaries" and Interest

Partners may be rewarded for their service and their capital investments to the business in other ways. In one sharing plan, the partners are allocated "salaries" (which are predetermined sums to be withdrawn, *not* employee salaries) plus interest on their Capital balances. Assume Edward Wright and Pierre Laroque form an oil-exploration partnership. At the beginning of the year, their Capital balances are $200,000 and $250,000, respectively. The partnership agreement allocates an annual "salary" of $107,000 to Wright and $88,000 to Laroque. After these amounts are allocated, each partner earns 8 percent interest on his beginning Capital balance. Any remaining net income is divided equally. Partnership profit of $240,000 for 2010 will be allocated as follows:

	Wright	Laroque	Total
Total net income			$240,000
First, "salaries":			
Wright	$107,000		
Laroque		$88,000	
Total			195,000
Net income remaining for allocation			45,000
Second, interest on beginning capital balances:			
Wright ($200,000 × 0.08)	16,000		
Laroque ($250,000 × 0.08)		20,000	
Total			36,000
Net income remaining for allocation			9,000
Third, remainder shared equally:			
Wright ($9,000 × ½)	4,500		
Laroque ($9,000 × ½)		4,500	
Total			9,000
Net income remaining for allocation			$ 0
Net income allocated to the partners	$127,500	$112,500	$240,000

In the preceding illustration, net income exceeded the sum of "salary" and interest. If the partnership profit is less than the allocated sum of "salary" and interest, a negative remainder will occur at some stage in the allocation process. Even so, the partners use the same method for allocation purposes. For example, assume that Wright and Laroque Partnership earned only $205,000 in 2010.

	Wright	Laroque	Total
Total net income			$205,000
First, "salaries":			
Wright	$107,000		
Laroque		$88,000	
Total			195,000
Net income remaining for allocation			10,000
Second, interest on beginning capital balances:			
Wright ($200,000 × 0.08)	16,000		
Laroque ($250,000 × 0.08)		20,000	
Total			36,000
Net income remaining for allocation			(26,000)

(Continued on next page)

(Continued from previous page)

	Wright	Laroque	Total
Third, remainder shared equally:			
Wright ($26,000 × ½)...............................	(13,000)		
Laroque ($26,000 × ½)...........................		(13,000)	
Total..			(26,000)
Net income remaining for allocation..................			$ 0
Net income allocated to the partners	$110,000	$95,000	$205,000

REAL WORLD EXAMPLE

In some large partnerships, a "units" system of profit and loss allocation is used. Each partner is awarded a particular number of units, which becomes the numerator in the fraction used for allocation. The total number of units awarded is the denominator in the fraction. The units method can allow a partnership to continue even as partners enter and withdraw from the partnership if unit formulas (rather than partner names) are a part of the partnership agreement.

A net loss would be allocated to Wright and Laroque in the same manner outlined for net income. The sharing procedure would begin with the net loss, and then allocate "salary," interest, and any other specified amounts to the partners.

For example, assume that Wright and Laroque Partnership had a loss of $30,000 in 2010.

	Wright	Laroque	Total
Total net income (net loss)...................................			($30,000)
First, "salaries":			
Wright..	$107,000		
Laroque...		$88,000	
Total..			195,000
Net income (loss) remaining for allocation.........			(225,000)
Second, interest on beginning Capital balances:			
Wright ($200,000 × 0.08)..............................	16,000		
Laroque ($250,000 × 0.08).............................		20,000	
Total..			36,000
Net income (loss) remaining for allocation.........			(261,000)
Third, remainder shared equally:			
Wright ($261,000 × ½).................................	(130,500)		
Laroque ($261,000 × ½)...............................		(130,500)	
Total..			(261,000)
Net income remaining for allocation			$ 0
Net income (loss) allocated to the partners	($ 7,500)	($22,500)	($30,000)

We see that partners may allocate profits and losses based on a stated fraction, capital investments, service, interest on Capital balances, or any combination of these factors. Each partnership shapes its profit-and-loss-sharing ratio to fit its own needs.

It is important to remember that the "salaries" and interest amounts discussed above are not the business expenses for salaries and interest in the usual sense. "Salaries" and interest in partnership agreements are ways of expressing the allocation of profits and losses to the partners. The "salary" component rewards service to the partnership. The interest component rewards a partner's investment of cash or other assets in the business. But the partners' "salary" and interest amounts are *not* salary expense and interest expense in the partnership's accounting or tax records.

Partner Withdrawals (Drawings) of Cash and Other Assets

Partners need cash for personal living expenses like anyone else. Partnership agreements usually allow partners to withdraw cash or other assets from the business. These withdrawals are sometimes called *drawings*, and are recorded in a separate Withdrawals or Drawings account for each partner. (Drawings from a

REAL WORLD EXAMPLE

According to the *Income Tax Act*, partners are taxed on their share of partnership income, not on the amount of their withdrawals.

partnership are recorded exactly as for a proprietorship.) Assume that both Edward Wright and Pierre Laroque are allowed a monthly withdrawal of $12,500. The partnership records the March 2010 withdrawal with this entry:

Mar. 31	Edward Wright, Withdrawals	12,500	
	Pierre Laroque, Withdrawals................................	12,500	
	Cash...		25,000
	Monthly partner withdrawals of cash.		

During the year, each partner's Withdrawal account accumulates 12 such amounts, a total of $150,000 ($12,500 × 12). At the end of the year, the general ledger shows the following account balances immediately after net income has been closed to the partners' Capital accounts. Assume the January 1, 2010, balances for Wright and Laroque are shown below, and that $205,000 of profit has been allocated on the basis of the illustration on the bottom of page 682.

Edward Wright, Capital		**Pierre Laroque, Capital**	
	Jan. 1, 2010 Bal. 200,000		Jan. 1, 2010 Bal. 250,000
	Dec. 31, 2010		Dec. 31, 2010
	Net income 110,000		Net income 95,000

Edward Wright, Withdrawals		**Pierre Laroque, Withdrawals**	
Dec. 31, 2010 Bal. 150,000		Dec. 31, 2010 Bal. 150,000	

The Withdrawals accounts must be closed at the end of the period (as must be done for a proprietorship). The closing entry credits each partner's Withdrawals account and debits each partner's Capital account. The amount of the withdrawal does not depend on the partnership's income or loss for the year. In fact, it is possible for a partner to withdraw more than the balance in the Capital account if, for example, profits were expected to be higher than they proved to be and withdrawals were made in anticipation of these high profits. This situation can only occur if the partnership has the cash required for the withdrawal and the other partners agree with the withdrawal and the ending Capital balance.

DID YOU GET IT?

MyAccountingLab

To check your understanding of the material in this Learning Objective, complete these questions. The solutions appear on MyAccountingLab so you can check your progress.

6. List the factors that can influence the way profits and losses are shared.

7. Calculate the net income or net loss to be allocated to each partner under the following partnership agreements:

   (a) Chan and Hannah share profits and losses 60/40. Net partnership income was $50,000.

   (b) Anna, Jones, and Coulter share profits and losses 3:4:3. Net partnership loss was $200,000.

   (c) Locke and Barnel share profits 1/3 and 2/3. The partnership agreement does not address the sharing of losses. Net partnership loss was $60,000.

   (d) Sparks and Kirk do not have a partnership agreement. Sparks does one-third of the work and Kirk does two-thirds of the work. Partnership net income was $90,000.

8. Martin, Cheves, and Close have capital investments of $20,000, $30,000, and $50,000, respectively. The partners share profits and losses as follows:

   (a) The first $40,000 is divided based on the partner's capital investments.

   (b) The next $40,000 is based on service, shared equally by Martin and Cheves.

   (c) The remainder is divided equally.

   Compute each partner's share of the $92,000 net income for the year.

Admission of a Partner

A partnership lasts only as long as its current set of partners remain in the business. Admitting a new partner dissolves the old partnership and begins a new one.

Often the new partnership continues the former partnership's business. In fact, the new partnership may choose to retain the dissolved partnership's name, as is the case with accounting firms. PricewaterhouseCoopers LLP, for example, is an accounting firm that retires and admits partners during the year. Thus the former partnership dissolves and a new partnership begins many times. The business, however, retains the name and continues operations. Other partnerships may dissolve and then re-form under a new name. Let's look at the ways that a new owner can be added to a partnership.

OBJECTIVE 4
Account for the admission of a new partner

Admission by Purchasing a Partner's Interest

A person can become a member of a partnership by purchasing an existing partner's interest in the business. First, however, the new person must gain the approval of the other partners.

Let's assume that Stephanie Fischer and Carlo Rona have a partnership that carries these figures:

Cash	$ 40,000	Total liabilities	$120,000
Other assets	360,000	Stephanie Fischer, capital	170,000
		Carlo Rona, capital	110,000
		Total liabilities	
Total assets	$400,000	and capital	$400,000

Business is so successful that Fischer receives an offer from Linda Drake, an outside party, to buy her $170,000 interest in the business for $200,000. Rona approves Drake as a new partner, and Fischer agrees to accept $200,000. The firm records the transfer of capital with this entry:

Apr. 16	Stephanie Fischer, Capital	170,000	
	Linda Drake, Capital		170,000
	To transfer Fischer's equity to Drake.		

The debit closes Fischer's Capital account because she is no longer a partner in the firm. The credit opens Drake's Capital account because Fischer's equity has been transferred to Drake, as shown in the T-accounts. The entry amount is Fischer's Capital balance ($170,000) and not the $200,000 price that Drake paid Fisher to buy into the business. The full $200,000 goes to Fischer, including the $30,000 difference between her Capital balance and the price received from Drake. In this example, the partnership does not receive cash because the transaction was between Drake and Fischer, not between Drake and the partnership. Suppose Drake pays Fischer less than Fischer's Capital balance. The entry on the partnership books is not affected. Fischer's equity is transferred to Drake at book value ($170,000).

The old partnership of Fischer and Rona has dissolved. Rona and Drake draw up a new partnership agreement, with a new profit-and-loss-sharing ratio, and continue business operations. If Rona does not accept Drake as a partner, the Fischer and Rona partnership might be dissolved, and Drake would be unable to buy Fischer's interest.

Stephanie Fischer, Capital

170,000	170,000

Linda Drake, Capital

	170,000

Carlo Rona, Capital

	110,000

KEY POINT

The profit or loss on the sale of a partnership interest belongs personally to the partner selling the interest and will not appear on the partnership's books.

Admission by Investing in the Partnership

A person may be admitted as a partner by investing directly in the partnership rather than by purchasing an existing partner's interest. The new partner invests assets—for example, cash, inventory, or equipment—in the business. Assume that the partnership of Robin Hardy and Michael May has the following assets, liabilities, and capital:

Cash	$ 20,000	Total liabilities	$ 60,000
Other assets	200,000	Robin Hardy, capital	70,000
		Michael May, capital	90,000
		Total liabilities	
Total assets	$220,000	and capital	$220,000

Let's consider several possible investments by a new partner.

Admission by Investing in the Partnership at Book Value—No Bonus   Lauren Kahn wants to join the Hardy and May partnership. Kahn can invest equipment and land (Other assets) with a market value of $80,000. Hardy and May agree to dissolve their partnership and to start up a new one, giving Kahn one-third interest in exchange for the contributed assets, as follows:

Partnership capital before Kahn is admitted ($70,000 + $90,000)	$160,000
Kahn's investment in the partnership	80,000
Partnership capital after Kahn is admitted	$240,000
Kahn's capital in the partnership ($240,000 × ⅓)	$ 80,000

Notice that Kahn is buying into the partnership at book value because her one-third investment ($80,000) equals one-third of the new partnership's total capital ($240,000). The partnership's entry to record Kahn's investment is

Jul. 18	Other Assets	80,000	
	Lauren Kahn, Capital		80,000
	To admit L. Kahn as a partner with a		
	one-third interest in the business.		

After this entry, the partnership books show:

Cash	$ 20,000	Total liabilities	$ 60,000
Other assets		Robin Hardy, capital	70,000
($200,000 + $80,000)	280,000	Michael May, capital	90,000
		Lauren Kahn, capital	80,000
		Total liabilities	
Total assets	$300,000	and capital	$300,000

Kahn's one-third interest in the partnership does not necessarily entitle her to one-third of the profits. The sharing of profits and losses is a separate element in the partnership agreement.

Admission by Investing in the Partnership—Bonus to the Old Partners   A successful partnership may require a higher payment from a new partner entering the business. The old partners may demand a bonus, which will increase their Capital accounts.

Suppose that Hiro Nagasawa and Lisa Wendt's partnership has earned above-average profits for 10 years. The two partners share profits and losses equally. The balance sheet carries these figures:

Cash	$ 40,000	Total liabilities	$100,000
Other assets	210,000	Hiro Nagasawa, capital	70,000
		Lisa Wendt, capital	80,000
		Total liabilities	
Total assets	$250,000	and capital	$250,000

Nagasawa and Wendt agree to admit Alana Purl to a one-fourth interest in return for Purl's cash investment of $90,000. Purl's Capital balance on the new partnership books is only $60,000, computed as follows:

Partnership capital before Purl is admitted ($70,000 + $80,000)...........	$150,000
Purl's investment in the partnership..	90,000
Partnership capital after Purl is admitted..	$240,000
Purl's capital in the partnership ($240,000 × ¼)......................................	$ 60,000
Bonus to the old partners ($90,000 – $60,000)	$ 30,000

In effect, Purl had to buy into the partnership at a price ($90,000) above the book value of her one-fourth interest ($60,000). Purl's greater-than-book-value investment of $30,000 creates a *bonus* for Nagasawa and Wendt. The entry on the partnership books to record Purl's investment is

Mar. 1	Cash..	90,000	
	Alana Purl, Capital		60,000
	Hiro Nagasawa, Capital.....................................		15,000
	Lisa Wendt, Capital..		15,000
	To admit A. Purl as a partner with a		
	one-fourth interest in the business.		
	Nagasawa and Wendt each receive a		
	bonus of $15,000 ($30,000 × ½).		

Purl's Capital account is credited for her one-fourth interest in the partnership. The bonus is allocated to the original partners (Nagasawa and Wendt) based on their profit-and-loss ratio.

The new partnership's balance sheet reports these amounts:

Cash ($40,000 + $90,000).......	$130,000		Total liabilities.................	$100,000
Other assets	210,000		Hiro Nagasawa, capital	
			($70,000 + $15,000) ...	85,000
			Lisa Wendt, capital	
			($80,000 + $15,000) ...	95,000
			Alana Purl, capital	60,000
			Total liabilities	
Total assets.............................	$340,000		and capital	$340,000

Admission by Investing in the Partnership—Bonus to the New Partner A potential new partner may be so important that the old partners offer a partnership share that includes a bonus to the new partner. A law firm may strongly desire a former premier, cabinet minister, or other official as a partner because of the person's reputation. A restaurant owner may want to go into partnership with a famous sports personality like Wayne Gretzky or a singer like Shania Twain.

Suppose Jan Page and Miko Goh have a restaurant. Their partnership balance sheet appears as follows:

Cash	$140,000		Total liabilities......................	$120,000
Other assets...........................	360,000		Jan Page, capital	230,000
			Miko Goh, capital...............	150,000
			Total liabilities	
Total assets.............................	$500,000		and capital......................	$500,000

The partners admit Martin Hillier, a famous hockey player, as a partner with a one-third interest in exchange for Hillier's cash investment of $100,000. At the time of Hillier's admission, the firm's capital is $380,000—Page, $230,000 plus

Goh, $150,000. Page and Goh share profits and losses in the ratio of two-thirds to Page and one-third to Goh. The computation of Hillier's equity in the new partnership is

Partnership capital before Hillier is admitted ($230,000 + $150,000)...	$380,000
Hillier's investment in the partnership..	100,000
Partnership capital after Hillier is admitted..	$480,000
Hillier's Capital in the partnership ($480,000 × ⅓)	$160,000
Bonus to new partner ($160,000 − $100,000)..	$ 60,000

In this case, Hillier entered the partnership at a price ($100,000) below the book value of his equity ($160,000). The bonus of $60,000 went to Hillier from the other partners. The Capital accounts of Page and Goh are debited for the $60,000 difference between the new partner's equity ($160,000) and his investment ($100,000). The old partners share this decrease in capital, which is accounted for as though it were a loss, based on their profit-and-loss ratio. The entry to record Hillier's investment is

Aug. 24	Cash	100,000	
	Jan Page, Capital ($60,000 × ⅔)	40,000	
	Miko Goh, Capital ($60,000 × ⅓)	20,000	
	Martin Hillier, Capital.....................................		160,000
	To admit M. Hillier as a partner with a		
	one-third interest in the business.		

The new partnership's balance sheet reports these amounts:

Cash		Total liabilities	$120,000
($140,000 + $100,000)	$240,000	Jan Page, capital	
Other assets	360,000	($230,000 − $40,000)....	190,000
		Miko Goh, capital	
		($150,000 − $20,000)....	130,000
		Martin Hillier, capital.......	160,000
		Total liabilities	
Total assets	$600,000	and capital	$600,000

In the next section, we will see how to account for the withdrawal of a partner from a business.

DID YOU GET IT?

To check your understanding of the material in this Learning Objective, complete these questions. The solutions appear on MyAccountingLab so you can check your progress.

9. Mia and Sue are partners with Capital balances of $25,000 and $75,000, respectively. They share profits and losses in a 30:70 ratio. Mia and Sue admit Tab to a 10 percent interest in a new partnership when Tab invests $20,000 in the business.

   (a) Compute the bonus to Mia and Sue.

   (b) Journalize the partnership's receipt of Tab's investment.

   (c) What is each partner's Capital in the new partnership?

10. Refer to the previous question. If Tab had invested only $10,000 into the partnership for a 10 percent interest, journalize the partnership's receipt of Tab's investment.

Withdrawal of a Partner from the Business

A partner may leave the business for many reasons, including retirement or a dispute with the other partners. The withdrawal of a partner dissolves the old partnership. The partnership agreement should specify how to settle with a withdrawing partner.

OBJECTIVE 5
Account for the withdrawal of a partner

In the simplest case, a partner may withdraw by selling his or her interest to another party in a personal transaction. This is the same as admitting a new person who purchases an old partner's interest, as we saw earlier. The journal entry simply debits the withdrawing partner's Capital account and credits the new partner's Capital account. The dollar amount of the entry is the old partner's Capital balance, regardless of the price paid by the purchaser, as illustrated for Fischer and Drake on page 685. The accounting when one current partner buys a second partner's interest is the same as when an outside party buys a current partner's interest.

If the partner withdraws in the middle of the accounting period, the partnership books should be updated to determine the withdrawing partner's Capital balance. The business must measure net income or net loss for the fraction of the year up to the withdrawal date, and allocate profit or loss according to the existing ratio. An alternative is to set an amount in the partnership agreement to be allocated regardless of the final annual results. This could be appropriate in businesses that have seasonal fluctuations, where the selection of withdrawal date could lead to unfair allocations. After the books have been closed, the business then accounts for the change in partnership capital.

KEY POINT

When a partner leaves a partnership, she or he ceases to be an agent and no longer has the authority to bind the business to contracts. Third parties with whom the partnership has dealt should be notified that the exiting partner no longer can bind the partnership. For all other third parties, constructive notice, such as an advertisement in the newspaper, is sufficient.

The withdrawing partner may receive his or her share of the business in partnership assets other than cash. The question then arises of what value to assign the partnership assets—book value or current market value? The settlement procedure often specifies an independent appraisal of the assets to determine their current market value because market values may have changed. In that case, the partnership must revalue the partnership assets. Thus the partners share any market-value changes according to their profit-and-loss ratio.

Suppose Ben Isaac is retiring in midyear from the partnership of Green, Maskluk, and Isaac. After the books have been adjusted for partial-period income but before the asset appraisal, revaluation, and closing entries are recorded, the balance sheet reports the following:

Cash		$ 70,000	Total liabilities	$ 80,000
Inventory		40,000	Joan Green, capital	50,000
Land		50,000	George Maskluk, capital	40,000
Building	$90,000		Ben Isaac, capital	20,000
Less: Accumulated				
amortization	60,000	30,000	Total liabilities	
Total assets		$190,000	and capital	$190,000

An independent appraiser revalues the inventory at $34,000 (down from $40,000), and the land at $100,000 (up from $50,000). The partners share the differences between market value and book value based on their profit-and-loss ratio of 1:2:1.

The entries to record the revaluation of the inventory and land are

Jun. 30	Joan Green, Capital ($6,000 × ¼)	1,500	
	George Maskluk, Capital ($6,000 × ½)	3,000	
	Ben Isaac, Capital ($6,000 × ¼)	1,500	
	Inventory ($40,000 − $34,000)		6,000
	To revalue the inventory and allocate the loss in value to the partners.		

(Continued)

Jun. 30	Land ($100,000 – $50,000)	50,000	
	Joan Green, Capital ($50,000 × ¼)		12,500
	George Maskluk, Capital ($50,000 × ½)..........		25,000
	Ben Isaac, Capital ($50,000 × ¼)		12,500
	To revalue the land and allocate the gain		
	in value to the partners.		

After the revaluations, the partnership balance sheet reports:

Cash............................		$ 70,000	Total liabilities.................	$ 80,000
Inventory....................		34,000	Joan Green, capital ($50,000 –	
Land		100,000	$1,500 + $12,500)........	61,000
Building	$90,000		George Maskluk, capital ($40,000 –	
Less: Accumulated			$3,000 + $25,000)........	62,000
amortization.......	60,000	30,000	Ben Isaac, capital ($20,000 –	
			$1,500 + $12,500)........	31,000
			Total liabilities	
Total assets		$234,000	and capital..................	$234,000

The books now carry the assets at current market value, which becomes the new book value, and the Capital accounts are up to date. As the balance sheet shows, Isaac has a claim to $31,000 in partnership assets. Now we can account for Isaac's withdrawal from the business.

Withdrawal at Book Value

If Ben Isaac withdraws by taking cash equal to the book value of his owner's equity, the entry would be

Jun. 30	Ben Isaac, Capital...	31,000	
	Cash..		31,000
	To record the withdrawal of B. Isaac		
	from the partnership.		

This entry records the payment of partnership cash to Isaac and the closing of his Capital account upon his withdrawal from the business.

Withdrawal at Less Than Book Value

The withdrawing partner may be so eager to depart that she or he is willing to take less than her or his equity. Assume Ben Isaac withdraws from the business and agrees to receive cash of $10,000 and the new partnership's $15,000 note payable. This $25,000 settlement is $6,000 less than Isaac's $31,000 equity in the business. The remaining partners share this $6,000 difference—which is a bonus to them—according to their profit-and-loss ratio.

Because Isaac has withdrawn from the partnership, a new agreement—and a new profit-and-loss ratio—is needed. In forming a new partnership, Maskluk and Green may decide on any ratio they wish.

The entry to record Isaac's withdrawal at less than book value is

Jun. 30	Ben Isaac, Capital...	31,000	
	Cash..		10,000
	Note Payable to Ben Isaac.................................		15,000
	Joan Green, Capital..		2,000
	George Maskluk, Capital		4,000
	To record withdrawal of B. Isaac from		
	the partnership. Green's bonus is		
	$2,000 ($6,000 × ⅓) and Maskluk's		
	bonus is $4,000 ($6,000 × ⅔).		

KEY POINT

Whenever a new partnership is formed, a new partnership agreement and a new profit-and-loss ratio are needed and should be created.

Isaac's account is closed, and Maskluk and Green may or may not continue the partnership.

Withdrawal at More Than Book Value

A withdrawing partner may receive assets worth more than the book value of her or his equity. This situation creates

- A bonus to the withdrawing partner
- A decrease in the remaining partners' Capital accounts, shared in their profit-and-loss ratio

The accounting for this situation follows the pattern illustrated previously for withdrawal at less than book value—with one exception. In this situation, the remaining partners' Capital accounts are debited because they are paying a bonus to the withdrawing partner.

Refer back to our previous example. Suppose Isaac withdraws from the partnership and agrees to receive $40,000 cash. Maskluk and Green agree that Maskluk will get two-thirds of the new partnership's profits and losses, and Green one-third. The entry to record Issac's withdrawal at more than book value is

Jun. 30	Ben Isaac, Capital..	31,000	
	Joan Green, Capital	3,000	
	George Maskluk, Capital	6,000	
	Cash...		40,000

To record withdrawal of B. Isaac from the partnership. Green's Capital is reduced by $3,000 ($9,000 × ⅓) and Maskluk's Capital is reduced by $6,000 ($9,000 × ⅔).

Death of a Partner

As with any other form of partnership withdrawal, the death of a partner dissolves a partnership. The partnership accounts are adjusted to measure net income or loss for the fraction of the year up to the date of death. The accounts are then closed to determine all partners' Capital balances on that date. Settlement with the deceased partner's estate is based on the partnership agreement. There may or may not be an asset revaluation. The estate commonly receives partnership assets equal to the partner's Capital balance. The partnership closes the deceased partner's Capital account with a debit and credits an asset account or a payable to the estate.

Suppose Joan Green (of the partnership on page 689) dies after all accounts have been adjusted to current market value. Green's Capital balance is $61,000. Green's estate may request cash for her final share of the partnership's assets. The partnership's journal entry is

REAL WORLD EXAMPLE

Partners commonly carry life insurance on themselves, with the partners as beneficiaries. In the event of a death, the partners receive the cash flow necessary to settle with the deceased partner's estate, without putting the partnership into financial jeopardy.

Jul. 1	Joan Green, Capital..	61,000	
	Cash...		61,000

To record withdrawal of Green from the business.

Alternatively, a remaining partner may purchase the deceased partner's equity. The deceased partner's Capital account is debited and the purchaser's Capital account is credited. The amount of this entry is the ending Capital balance of the deceased partner.

To check your understanding of the material in this Learning Objective, complete these questions. The solutions appear on MyAccountingLab so you can check your progress.

11. Suppose Linda is withdrawing from the partnership of Linda, Jacob, and Karla. The partners share profits and losses in a 1:2:3 ratio for Linda, Jacob, and Karla, respectively. After the revaluation of assets, Linda's Capital balance is $40,000, and the other partners agree to pay her $50,000. Jacob and Karla agree to a new profit-and-loss ratio of 2:3 for Jacob and Karla, respectively. Journalize the payment to Linda for her withdrawal from the partnership.

12. Refer to the previous question. Suppose the situation is the same except that the other partners agree to pay Linda $30,000. Journalize the payment to Linda for her withdrawal from the partnership.

13. Refer to Question 11 above. Suppose the situation is the same except that Linda died the day after revaluation of the assets, and her estate requests cash for her final share of the partnership's assets. Journalize the payment to Linda's estate for her withdrawal from the partnership.

Liquidation of a Partnership

As we have seen, the admission or withdrawal of a partner dissolves the partnership. However, the business may continue operating with no apparent change to outsiders such as customers and creditors. In contrast, business **liquidation** is the process of going out of business by selling the entity's assets and paying its liabilities. The business shuts down. The final step in liquidation of a business is to *distribute any remaining cash to the owners*. Before the business is liquidated, the books should be adjusted and closed. After closing, only asset, liability, and partners' Capital accounts remain open.

Liquidation of a partnership includes three basic steps:

1. Sell the assets. Allocate the gain or loss to the partners' Capital accounts based on the profit-and-loss ratio.

2. Pay all the partnership liabilities.

3. Pay the remaining cash to the partners in proportion to their Capital balances.

The liquidation of a business can stretch over weeks or months, even years for a large company. Selling every asset and paying every liability of the entity takes time. For example, in one case the liquidation of a law firm of over 75 partners took almost a year.

To avoid excessive detail in our illustrations, we include only two asset categories—Cash and Noncash Assets—and a single liability category—Liabilities. Our examples also assume that the business sells the assets in a single transaction and then pays the liabilities at once. (In actual practice, each asset and its related amortization would be accounted for separately when it is sold, and each liability would be accounted for separately when it is paid.)

Assume that Ryan Aviron, Alexis Bloch, and Scott Zhang have shared profits and losses in the ratio of 3:1:1. (This ratio is equal to 3/5, 1/5, 1/5, or a 60-percent, 20-percent, 20-percent sharing ratio.) The partners decide to liquidate their partnership. After the books are adjusted and closed, these accounts remain:

Cash	$ 10,000	Liabilities	$ 30,000
Noncash assets	90,000	Ryan Aviron, capital	40,000
		Alexis Bloch, capital	20,000
		Scott Zhang, capital	10,000
		Total liabilities	
Total assets	$100,000	and capital	$100,000

Sale of Assets at a Gain

Assume the Aviron, Bloch, and Zhang partnership sells its noncash assets for $150,000 (book value, $90,000). The partnership realizes a gain of $60,000, which is allocated to the partners based on their profit-and-loss-sharing ratio. The entry to record this sale and allocate the gain is

Oct. 31	Cash..	150,000	
	Noncash Assets...		90,000
	Ryan Aviron, Capital		36,000
	Alexis Bloch, Capital..		12,000
	Scott Zhang, Capital		12,000
	To sell noncash assets in liquidation and allocate gain to partners. Aviron's share of the gain is $36,000 ($60,000 × 0.60), Bloch's and Zhang's are $12,000 ($60,000 × 0.20).		

Ryan Aviron, Capital

	40,000
	36,000
	Bal. 76,000

Alexis Bloch, Capital

	20,000
	12,000
	Bal. 32,000

Scott Zhang, Capital

	10,000
	12,000
	Bal. 22,000

Now the partners' Capital accounts have the balances shown in the margin.

This journal entry could be broken down into two steps: recording the gain or loss on liquidation, and recording the allocation of the gain or loss to the partners. If this is done, the journal entries would be

Oct. 31	Cash	150,000	
	Noncash Assets...		90,000
	Gain on Liquidation...		60,000
31	Gain on Liquidation	60,000	
	Ryan Aviron, Capital		36,000
	Alexis Bloch, Capital..		12,000
	Scott Zhang, Capital		12,000

The partnership then pays off its liabilities:

Oct. 31	Liabilities..	30,000	
	Cash		30,000
	To pay liabilities in liquidation.		

The final liquidation transaction pays all remaining cash to the partners *according to their Capital balances*. (By contrast, *gains* and *losses* on the sale of assets are shared by the partners based on their profit-and-loss-sharing ratio.) The amount of cash left in the partnership is $130,000, as follows:

Cash

Beg. bal.	10,000	Payment of liabilities	30,000
Sale of assets	150,000		
End. bal.	130,000		

The partners divide the remaining cash according to their Capital balances:

Oct. 31	Ryan Aviron, Capital	76,000	
	Alexis Bloch, Capital...	32,000	
	Scott Zhang, Capital	22,000	
	Cash		130,000
	To disburse cash to partners in liquidation.		

A convenient way to summarize the transactions in a partnership liquidation is given in Exhibit 12–5. Remember:

- Upon liquidation, gains and losses on the sale of assets are divided according to the *profit-and-loss ratio*.
- The final cash payment to the partners is based on *Capital balances*.

Partnership Liquidation—Sale of Assets at a Gain

	Cash	+ Noncash Assets	= Liabilities	+ Aviron (60%)	+ Bloch (20%)	+ Zhang (20%)
				Capital		
Balances before sale of assets	$ 10,000	$ 90,000	$ 30,000	$ 40,000	$ 20,000	$ 10,000
Sale of assets and sharing of gain	150,000	(90,000)		36,000	12,000	12,000
Balances	160,000	0	30,000	76,000	32,000	22,000
Payment of liabilities	(30,000)		(30,000)			
Balances	130,000	0	0	76,000	32,000	22,000
Disbursement of cash to partners	(130,000)			(76,000)	(32,000)	(22,000)
Balances	$ 0	$ 0	$ 0	$ 0	$ 0	$ 0

LEARNING TIPS

Keep in mind that, upon liquidation, gains and losses on the sale of assets are divided according to the profit-and-loss ratio. The final cash disbursement to the partners is based on Capital balances.

KEY POINT

There are a few ways to deal with a capital deficiency upon liquidation. The decision of which method to use must be made *before* the endline cash is distributed.

After the disbursement of cash to the partners, the business has no assets, liabilities, or equity. All final balances are zero. By the accounting equation, partnership assets *must* equal partnership liabilities plus partnership capital.

Sale of Assets at a Loss

Liquidation of a business often includes the sale of assets at a loss. When a loss occurs, the partners' Capital accounts are debited based on the profit-and-loss-sharing ratio. Otherwise, the accounting follows the pattern illustrated for the sale of assets at a gain.

Suppose the Aviron, Bloch, and Zhang partnership sold its noncash assets for $30,000 and all other details in Exhibit 12–5 remained the same. This creates a loss of $60,000 on the sale of the noncash assets. Exhibit 12–6 summarizes the transactions in a partnership liquidation when the assets are sold at a loss.

Notice that Zhang's Capital account has a negative balance. This is known as a *capital deficiency*. The capital deficiency must be dealt with *before* the ending cash is distributed. One way of dealing with the $2,000 capital deficiency in Zhang's Capital account is for Zhang to contribute $2,000 of assets to the partnership to erase his capital deficiency. If Zhang contributes cash, the journal entry to record this is

Cash	2,000	
Scott Zhang, Capital		2,000

Partnership Liquidation—Sale of Assets at a Loss

	Cash	+ Noncash Assets	= Liabilities	+ Aviron (60%)	+ Bloch (20%)	+ Zhang (20%)
				Capital		
Balances before sale of assets	$ 10,000	$ 90,000	$ 30,000	$ 40,000	$ 20,000	$ 10,000
Sale of assets and sharing of loss	30,000	(90,000)		(36,000)	(12,000)	(12,000)
Balances	40,000	0	30,000	4,000	8,000	(2,000)
Payment of liabilities	(30,000)		(30,000)			
Balances	10,000	0	0	4,000	8,000	(2,000)
Disbursement of cash to partners	(10,000)			(4,000)	(8,000)	2,000
Balances	$ 0	$ 0	$ 0	$ 0	$ 0	$ 0

Another option for dealing with Zhang's $2,000 capital deficiency is for Zhang's partners, Aviron and Bloch, to agree to absorb Zhang's capital deficiency by decreasing their own Capital balances in proportion to their remaining profit-sharing percentages: Aviron, 60/80; Bloch, 20/80. The journal entry to record this is

Ryan Aviron, Capital	1,500	
Alexis Bloch, Capital	500	
Scott Zhang, Capital		2,000

How do partners deal with a situation where two of the three partners have capital deficiencies? Both partners could contribute assets in the amount of their deficiencies to the third partner. However, if the deficient partners cannot contribute personal assets, then the deficits must be absorbed by the remaining partner. If the remaining partner then still has a balance in his or her Capital account, any remaining cash balance would be paid to that partner.

When a business liquidates, there may not be enough cash from the sale of the assets to pay the liabilities. The partners (who are personally liable for the partnership debts) must contribute cash on the basis of their profit-and-loss ratio to cover unpaid debts.

DID YOU GET IT?

MyAccountingLab

To check your understanding of the material in this Learning Objective, complete this question. The solution appears on MyAccountingLab so you can check your progress.

14. Refer to the Aviron, Bloch, and Zhang partnership on page 692. Suppose the partnership sold its noncash assets for $20,000 and all other details in Exhibit 12–5 remained the same.

(a) What is the profit or loss created on the sale of the noncash assets?

(b) Allocate the profit or loss calculated in part (a) to the partners.

(c) How can the partnership deal with any capital deficiencies in this situation?

The Impact on Partnerships of International Financial Reporting Standards (IFRS)

The principles and requirements used to record transactions and prepare financial statements for partnerships, as shown in this chapter, are set out in the "Unincorporated Businesses" section of the CICA *Handbook*. There is no corresponding accounting standard for partnerships reporting under IFRS. However, IFRS require that partnerships disclose information equivalent to that provided by limited companies. Accounting for limited companies will be covered in Chapters 13 and 14. The important point is that IFRS do not include specific guidance on how to account for partnerships.

OBJECTIVE 7

Identifying the impact on partnerships of international financial reporting standards (IFRS)

DID YOU GET IT?

MyAccountingLab

To check your understanding of the material in this Learning Objective, complete this question. The solution appears on MyAccountingLab so you can check your progress.

15. Suppose your partnership prepares its financial statements in accordance with IFRS. How does the IFRS approach for partnerships differ from the approach described in this chapter?

As we conclude this chapter, we return to our opening questions: What is a partnership, and what are its advantages and disadvantages? How do you create a partnership? How are partnership profits and losses shared among partners? How is a new partner admitted to or withdrawn from a partnership? These questions were answered throughout this chapter. And the Decision Guidelines end this chapter with the answers in a useful summary.

DECISION GUIDELINES Accounting for Partnerships

Decision	Guidelines
How should the business be organized?	A partnership offers both advantages and disadvantages in comparison with proprietorships and corporations. (See Exhibit 12–3, page 676.)
On what matters should the partners agree?	See the list on page 673, under the heading "The Written Partnership Agreement."
At what value does the partnership record assets and liabilities?	Current market value on the date of acquisition, because, in effect, the partnership is buying its assets at their current market value.

How are partnership profits and losses shared among the partners?	• Equally if there is no profit-and-loss-sharing agreement.
	• As provided in the partnership agreement. Can be based on the partners'
	  a. Stated fractions
	  b. Capital investments
	  c. Service to the partnership
	  d. "Salaries" and interest on their capital investments
	  e. Any combination of the above

What happens when a partner withdraws from the partnership?	The old partnership ceases to exist (dissolves). The remaining partners may or may not form a new partnership.
How are new partners admitted to the partnership?	• *Purchase a partner's interest.* If the old partners agree to admit the new partner to the partnership, the old partnership is dissolved and a new partnership is created. Close the withdrawing partner's Capital account, and open a Capital account for the new partner. Carry over the old partner's Capital balance to the Capital account of the new partner. • *Invest in the partnership.* Buying in at book value creates no bonus to any partner. Buying in at a price above book value creates a bonus to the old partners. Buying in at a price below book value creates a bonus for the new partner.

How should the withdrawal of a partner from the business be accounted for?	• First, adjust and close the books up to the date of the partner's withdrawal from the business.
	• Second, appraise the assets and the liabilities to determine their current market value. Allocate the gain or loss in value to the partners' Capital accounts based on their profit-and-loss-sharing ratio.
	• Third, account for the partner's withdrawal
	  a. At book value (no change in remaining partners' Capital balances)
	  b. At less than book value (increase the remaining partners' Capital balances)
	  c. At more than book value (decrease the remaining partners' Capital balances)

What happens if the partnership goes out of business?	Liquidate the partnership, as follows:
	  a. Adjust and close the partnership books up to the date of liquidation.
	  b. Sell the partnership's assets. Allocate the gain or loss to the partners' Capital accounts based on their profit-and-loss-sharing ratio.
	  c. Pay the partnership liabilities. (If there is not enough cash to pay partnership liabilities, the partners must pay the liabilities personally in their profit-and-loss ratio.)
	  d. Pay any remaining cash to the partners based on their Capital balances.

How do partnership financial statements differ from those of a proprietorship?	• The partnership income statement may report the allocation of net income or net loss to the partners. • The partnership's statement of owners' (or partners') equity shows the change in each partner's equity during the period. • The partnership balance sheet (or a separate schedule) reports the Capital balance of each partner.

The partnership of Taylor and Uvalde admits Steven Vaughn as a partner on January 2, 2010. The partnership has these balances on that date:

Cash	$ 9,000	Total liabilities	$ 50,000
Other assets	110,000	Debby Taylor, capital	45,000
		Thomas Uvalde, capital ...	24,000
		Total liabilities	
Total assets...........................	$119,000	and capital...................	$119,000

Debby Taylor's share of profits and losses is 60 percent and Thomas Uvalde's share is 40 percent.

Required

(Items 1 and 2 are independent.)

1. Suppose Vaughn pays Uvalde $30,000 to acquire Uvalde's interest in the business after Taylor approves Vaughn as a partner.
   a. Record the transfer of owner's equity on the partnership books.
   b. Prepare the partnership balance sheet immediately after Vaughn is admitted as a partner.

2. Suppose Vaughn becomes a partner by investing $31,000 cash to acquire a one-fourth interest in the business.
   a. Compute Vaughn's Capital balance and determine whether there is any bonus. If so, who gets the bonus?
   b. Record Vaughn's investment in the business.
   c. Prepare the partnership balance sheet immediately after Vaughn is admitted as a partner. Include the appropriate heading.

3. Which way of admitting Vaughn to the partnership increases its total assets? Give your reason.

Name: Taylor and Uvalde
Industry: Partnership admitting a new partner
Date: January 2, 2010

SOLUTION

Requirement 1

a. 2010

Jan. 2	Thomas Uvalde, Capital	24,000		
	Steven Vaughn, Capital		24,000	
	To transfer Uvalde's equity in the partnership to Vaughn.			

b. The balance sheet for the partnership of Taylor and Vaughn is identical to the balance sheet given for Taylor and Uvalde in the problem, except Steven Vaughn's name replaces Thomas Uvalde's name in the title and in the listing of Capital accounts.

When a new partner acquires an old partner's interest, the new partner purchases the old partner's equity balance on the books and *replaces* the old partner. Any amount paid in excess goes to the old partner personally.

Requirement 2

Margin note
When a new partner acquires an interest in a partnership, the new partner *joins the existing partners* by adding cash to the pool of capital, then dividing the pool among the old and new partners. Any amount paid in excess increases the old partners' Capital balances.

a. Computation of Vaughn's Capital balance:

Partnership capital before Vaughn is admitted ($45,000 + $24,000)..	$ 69,000
Vaughn's investment in the partnership	31,000
Partnership capital after Vaughn is admitted	$100,000
Vaughn's capital in the partnership ($100,000 × ¼)	$ 25,000
Bonus to the old partners ($31,000 − $25,000)	$ 6,000

Margin note
Any amount paid in excess increases the old partners' Capital balances by giving each old partner a bonus. The bonus is based on the profit-and-loss percentage in place before the new partner joined.

b. 2010

Jan. 2	Cash	31,000	
	Steven Vaughn, Capital.........................		25,000
	Debby Taylor, Capital............................		3,600
	Thomas Uvalde, Capital.........................		2,400

To admit Vaughn as a partner with a one-fourth interest in the business. Taylor's bonus is $3,600 [($31,000 − $25,000) × 0.60] and Uvalde's bonus is $2,400 [($31,000 − $25,000) × 0.40].

c.

Margin note
The Cash and Capital accounts will change when a new partner joins existing partners. Add the bonus to each of the old partners' Capital balances and add the new partner's Capital balance, all from the January 2, 2010, journal entry.

TAYLOR, UVALDE, AND VAUGHN
Balance Sheet
January 2, 2010

Cash*	$ 40,000	Total liabilities	$ 50,000
Other assets	110,000	Debby Taylor, capital**..........	48,600
		Thomas Uvalde, capital*** ...	26,400
		Steven Vaughn, capital..........	25,000
		Total liabilities	
Total assets	$150,000	and capital	$150,000

```
  *$9,000 + $31,000 = $40,000
 **$45,000 + $3,600 = $48,600
***$24,000 + $2,400 = $26,400
```

Requirement 3

Margin note
A partnership's total assets are increased only when a new partner joins existing partners, not when a new partner "replaces" an old partner by purchasing the old partner's Capital.

Vaughn's investment in the partnership increases its total assets by the amount of his contribution. Total assets of the business are $150,000 after his investment, compared with $119,000 before. By contrast, Vaughn's purchase of Uvalde's interest in the business is a personal transaction between the two individuals. It does not affect the assets of the partnership, regardless of the amount Vaughn pays Uvalde.

Summary

1. **Identify the characteristics of a partnership.** A *partnership* is a business co-owned by two or more persons for profit. The characteristics of this form of business organization are its *ease of formation, limited life, mutual agency, unlimited liability,* and *no partnership income taxes.* In a *limited partnership,* the limited partners have limited personal liability for the obligations of the business.

   A written *partnership agreement* establishes procedures for admission of a new partner, withdrawals of a partner, and the sharing of profits and losses among the partners. When a new partner is admitted to the firm or an existing partner withdraws, the old partnership is *dissolved,* or ceases to exist. A new partnership may or may not emerge to continue the business.

2. **Account for partners' initial investments in a partnership.** Accounting for a partnership is similar to accounting for a proprietorship. However, a partnership has more than one owner. Each partner has an individual Capital account and a Withdrawal account; the Capital accounts for each partner are shown on the balance sheet. The partnership income statement includes a section showing the division of net income to the partners.

3. **Allocate profits and losses to the partners by different methods.** Partners share net income or loss in any manner they choose. Common sharing agreements base the *profit-and-loss ratio* on a stated fraction, partners' capital investments, and/or their service to the partnership. Another allocation of partnership net income to the partners is based on what is called "salaries" and "interest" which, despite their name, are not expenses of the business. Partner withdrawals, also called drawings, reduce the partner capital accounts, but are not a form of net income allocation.

4. **Account for the admission of a new partner.** An outside person may become a partner by purchasing a current partner's interest or by investing in the partnership. In some cases the new partner must pay the current partners a bonus to join. In other situations, the new partner may receive a bonus to join.

5. **Account for the withdrawal of a partner.** When a partner withdraws, partnership assets may be reappraised. Partners share any gain or loss on the asset revaluation on the basis of their profit-and-loss ratio. The withdrawing partner may receive payment equal to, greater than, or less than her or his Capital book value, depending on the agreement with the other partners.

6. **Account for the liquidation of a partnership.** In *liquidation,* a partnership goes out of business by selling the assets, paying the liabilities, and paying any remaining cash to the partners.

7. **Identifying the impact on partnerships of international financial reporting standards (IFRS).** IFRS do not provide specific guidance on how to account for partnerships. The CICA *Handbook* section "Unincorporated Businesses" gives guidance on recording transactions and preparing financial statements for partnerships reporting under GAAP for private enterprises.

SELF-STUDY QUESTIONS

Test your understanding of the chapter by marking the correct answer for each of the following questions:

1. Which of these characteristics identifies a partnership? (*pp. 672–675*)
   a. Unlimited life
   b. No income tax paid by the business entity
   c. Limited personal liability
   d. All of the above

2. A partnership records a partner's investment of assets in the business at (*p. 678*)
   a. The partner's book value of the assets invested
   b. The market value of the assets invested
   c. A special value set by the partners
   d. Any of the above, depending upon the partnership agreement

3. The partnership of O'Connor, LaPlante, and Egly divides profits in the ratio of 4:5:3. There is no provision for losses. During 2010, the business earned $40,000. Egly's share of this income is (*pp. 679–680*)
   a. $10,000   c. $16,000
   b. $13,333   d. $16,667

4. Suppose the partnership of O'Connor, LaPlante, and Egly in the preceding question lost $40,000 during 2010. LaPlante's share of this loss is (*p. 680*)
   a. Not determinable because the ratio applies only to profits
   b. $13,333
   c. $10,000
   d. $16,667

5. The partners of Fraser, Booth, and Craig share profits and losses 1/5, 1/6, and 19/30. During 2010, the first year of their partnership, the business earned $120,000, and each partner withdrew $50,000 for personal use. What is the balance in Craig's Capital account after all closing entries? (*p. 680*)
   a. Not determinable because Craig's beginning Capital balance is not given
   b. Minus $10,000
   c. Minus $50,000
   d. $70,000

6. Barbara Miller buys into the partnership of Quantz and Goodwin by purchasing a one-third interest for

$55,000. Prior to Miller's entry, Edward Quantz's Capital balance was $46,000, and Louisa Goodwin's balance was $52,000; profits and losses were shared equally. The entry to record Miller's buying into the business is (*pp. 685–687*)

a. Cash 55,000
    Barbara Miller, Capital............   55,000

b. Edward Quantz, Capital............... 27,500
    Louisa Goodwin, Capital.............. 27,500
       Barbara Miller, Capital............   55,000

c. Cash 55,000
    Barbara Miller, Capital............   51,000
    Edward Quantz, Capital..........   2,000
    Louisa Goodwin, Capital   2,000

d. Cash 51,000
    Edward Quantz, Capital.............. 2,000
    Louisa Goodwin, Capital.............. 2,000
       Barbara Miller, Capital............   55,000

7. The partners of Tsui, Valik, and Wollenberg share profits and losses equally. Their Capital balances are $40,000, $50,000, and $60,000, respectively, when Brenda Wollenberg sells her interest in the partnership to Brent Valik for $90,000. Raymond Tsui and Valik continue the business. Immediately after Wollenberg's retirement, the total assets of the partnership are (*pp. 689–690*)

a. Increased by $30,000
b. Increased by $90,000

c. Decreased by $60,000
d. The same as before Wollenberg sold her interest to Valik

8. Prior to Bill Hogg's withdrawal from the partnership of Hogg, Han, and Lee, the partners' Capital balances were $140,000, $110,000 and $250,000, respectively. The partners share profits and losses 1/3, 1/4, and 5/12. The appraisal indicates that assets should be written down by $36,000. Arthur Han's share of the write-down is (*pp. 689–690*)

a. $7,920   c. $12,000
b. $9,000   d. $18,000

9. The process of closing the business, selling the assets, paying the liabilities, and disbursing remaining cash to the owners is called (*p. 692*)

a. Dissolution   c. Withdrawal
b. Forming a new   d. Liquidation
   partnership

10. Rick Butterworth and Pamela Coombs have shared profits and losses equally. Immediately prior to the final cash disbursement in a liquidation of their partnership, the books show:

| Cash | = | Liabilities | + | Rick Butterworth, | + | Pamela Coombs, |
| $100,000 | | $0 | | Capital $60,000 | | Capital $40,000 |

How much cash should Butterworth receive? (*p. 693*)

a. $40,000   c. $60,000
b. $50,000   d. None of the above

ACCOUNTING VOCABULARY

Dissolution   *(p. 674)*
General partnership   *(p. 676)*
Limited liability partnership   *(p. 677)*
Limited partnership   *(p. 676)*
Liquidation   *(p. 692)*

Mutual agency   *(p. 674)*
Partnership   *(p. 672)*
Partnership agreement   *(p. 673)*
Unlimited personal liability   *(p. 674)*

SIMILAR ACCOUNTING TERMS

Limited Liability Partnership	LLP
Liquidation	Shutting down the business; going out of business
Owner's equity	Capital
Withdrawals	Drawings

Assignment Material

QUESTIONS

1. List eight items that the partnership agreement should specify.

2. Ron Montgomery, who is a partner in M&N Associates, commits the firm to a contract for a job within the scope of its regular business operations. What term describes Montgomery's ability to obligate the partnership?

3. If a partnership cannot pay a debt, who must make payment? What term describes this obligation of the partners?

4. How is income of a partnership taxed?

5. Identify the advantages and disadvantages of the partnership form of business organization.

6. Robin Randall and Sylvia Smith's partnership agreement states that Randall gets 60 percent of profits and Smith gets 40 percent. If the agreement does not discuss the treatment of losses, how are losses shared? How do the partners share profits and losses if the agreement specifies no profit-and-loss-sharing ratio?

7. What determines the amount of the credit to a partner's Capital account when the partner contributes assets other than cash to the business?

8. Do partner withdrawals of cash for personal use affect the sharing of profits and losses by the partner? If so, explain how. If not, explain why not.

9. Name two events that can cause the dissolution of a partnership.

10. Briefly describe how to account for the purchase of an existing partner's interest in the business.

11. Jeff Malcolm purchases Sheila Wilson's interest in the Wilson & Kareem partnership. What right does Malcolm obtain from the purchase? What is required for Malcolm to become Paula Kareem's partner?

12. Sal Assissi and Barb Carter each have capital of $150,000 in their business. They share profits in the ratio of 55:45. Kathy Denman acquires a one-fifth share in the partnership by investing cash of $100,000. What are the Capital balances of the three partners immediately after Denman is admitted?

13. When a partner resigns from the partnership and receives assets greater than her or his Capital balance, how is the difference shared by the other partners?

14. Distinguish between dissolution and liquidation of a partnership.

15. Name the three steps in liquidating a partnership.

16. The partnership of Ralls and Sauls is in the process of liquidation. How do the partners share (a) gains and losses on the sale of noncash assets, and (b) the final cash disbursement?

17. Compare and contrast the financial statements of a proprietorship and a partnership.

18. Summarize the situations in which partnership allocations are based on (a) the profit-and-loss ratio, and (b) the partners' Capital balances.

STARTERS

Starter 12-1 Marty Stubbs invests land in a partnership with Lee Dix. Stubbs purchased the land in 2001 for $100,000. A real estate appraiser now values the land at $250,000. Stubbs wants $250,000 capital in the new partnership, but Dix objects. Dix believes that Stubbs' capital investment should be measured by the book value of his land.

   Dix and Stubbs seek your advice. Which value of the land is appropriate for measuring Stubbs' Capital—book value or current market value? State the reason for your answer. Give the partnership's journal entry to record Stubbs' investment in the business.

A partner's investment in a partnership.

②

Debit Land for $250,000

Starter 12-2 Abel and Baker had beginning Capital balances of $10,000 and $8,000, respectively. The two partners fail to agree on a profit-and-loss-sharing ratio. For the first month (June 2010), the partnership lost $4,000.

1. How much of this loss goes to Abel? How much goes to Baker?

2. The partners withdrew no assets during June. What is each partner's Capital balance at June 30? Prepare a T-account for each partner's Capital.

Partners' profits, losses, and Capital balances

③

2. Abel, Capital $8,000

Starter 12-3 Lan, Mall, and Nuse have Capital balances of $10,000, $15,000, and $25,000, respectively. The partners share profits and losses as follows:

a. The first $20,000 is divided based on the partners' capital investments.

b. The next $20,000 is based on service, shared equally by Lan and Nuse.

c. The remainder is divided equally.

Compute each partner's share of the $46,000 net income for the year.

Dividing partnership profits based on capital contributions and service

③

Lan $16,000

Admitting a partner who purchases an existing partner's interest

④

Starter 12–4 Todd has a Capital balance of $60,000; Carlson's balance is $50,000. Reynaldo pays $200,000 to purchase Carlson's interest in the Todd & Carlson partnership. Carlson gets the full $200,000.

Journalize the partnership's transaction to admit Reynaldo to the partnership.

Admitting a partner who invests in the business

④

1. No bonus

Starter 12–5 The partnership of Evans and Falconi has these Capital balances:

- Judy Evans $30,000
- Julie Falconi $40,000

Joan Gray invests cash of $35,000 to acquire a one-third interest in the partnership.

1. Does Gray's investment in the firm provide a bonus to the partners? Show your work.
2. Journalize the partnership's receipt of the $35,000 from Gray.

Admitting a new partner; bonus to the old partners

④

Bonus $5,000

Starter 12–6 Bo and Go have partner Capital balances of $115,000 and $75,000, respectively. Bo gets 60 percent of profits and losses, and Go gets 40 percent. Assume Mo invests $70,000 to acquire a 25 percent interest in the new partnership of Bogomo. Is there a bonus? If so, who gets it? Journalize the partnership's receipt of cash from Mo.

Withdrawal of a partner

⑤

Starter 12–7 Adams, Everett, and Caine each have a $50,000 Capital balance. They share profits and losses as follows: 25 percent to Adams, 50 percent to Everett, and 25 percent to Caine. Suppose Caine is withdrawing from the business, and the partners agree that no appraisal of assets is needed. How much in assets can Caine take from the partnership? Give the reason for your answer. What role does the profit-and-loss ratio play in this situation?

Withdrawal of a partner; asset revaluation

⑤

(a) Debit Land $20,000

Starter 12–8 Simpson, Locke, and Job each have a $25,000 Capital balance. Simpson is very old and is retiring from the business. The partners agree to revalue the assets at current market value. A real-estate appraiser values the land at $70,000 (book value is $50,000). The profit-and-loss ratio is 1:2:1. Journalize (a) the revaluation of the land on July 31, and (b) payment of $30,000 to Simpson upon his retirement the same day.

Liquidation of a partnership at a loss

⑥

Starter 12–9 Use the data in Exhibit 12–5. Suppose the partnership of Aviron, Bloch, and Zhang liquidates by selling all noncash assets for $80,000. Complete the liquidation schedule as shown in Exhibit 12–5.

Liquidation of a partnership

⑥

(c) Aviron, $34,000; Bloch, $18,000; Zhang, $8,000 payments of cash

Starter 12–10 This Starter builds on the solution to Starter 12–9. After completing the liquidation schedule in Starter 12–9, journalize the partnership's (a) sale of noncash assets for $80,000 (use a single account for Noncash Assets), (b) payment of liabilities, and (c) payment of cash to the partners. Include an explanation with each entry.

Partnership income statement

② ③

Net income for Bosch $36,000

Starter 12–11 The partnership of Bosch and Cutler had these balances at September 30, 2010:

Cash.............................	$ 20,000	Service Revenue......................	$145,000
Liabilities.....................................	40,000	Bosch, Capital..........................	30,000
Cutler, Capital...........................	10,000	Total expenses	85,000
Other assets..............................	120,000		

Bosch gets 60 percent of profits and losses, and Cutler 40 percent. Prepare the partnership's income statement and ending Capital balances for the year ended September 30, 2010.

EXERCISES

MyAccountingLab All questions in this section appear in MyAccountingLab.

Exercise 12–1

Partnership characteristics

①

Carol Edwards and David Chan are forming a business to imprint T-shirts. Edwards suggests that they organize as a partnership in order to avoid the unlimited liability of a proprietorship. According to Edwards, partnerships are not very risky.

Edwards explains to Chan that if the business does not succeed, each partner can withdraw from the business, taking the same assets that she or he invested at its beginning. Edwards states that the main disadvantage of the partnership form of organization is double taxation: First, the partnership pays a business income tax; second, each partner also pays personal income tax on her or his share of the business's profits.

Correct the errors in Edwards' explanation.

Exercise 12–2

Joanna Volescu, a friend from college, approaches you about forming a partnership to export software. Since graduation, Joanna has worked for the World Bank, developing important contacts among government officials and business leaders in Poland and Hungary. Joanna believes she is in a unique position to capitalize on expanding markets. With your expertise in finance, you would have responsibility for accounting and finance in the partnership.

Organizing a business as a partnership

Required Discuss the advantages and disadvantages of organizing the export business as a partnership rather than a proprietorship. Comment on the way partnership income is taxed.

Exercise 12–3

Laureen Dudra invests a building in a partnership with Jill Swanson. Dudra purchased the building for $600,000. Accumulated amortization on the date of forming the partnership is $160,000. A real estate appraiser states that the building is now worth $800,000. Dudra wants $800,000 capital in the new partnership, but Swanson objects. Swanson believes that Dudra's capital contribution into the partnership should be measured by the book value of her building.

A partner's investment in a partnership

②

Swanson and Dudra seek your advice. Which value of the building is appropriate for measuring Dudra's capital—book value or current market value? State the reason for your answer. Give the partnership's journal entry to record Dudra's investment in the business.

Exercise 12–4

Jackson Cooke and Julia Bamber are forming a partnership to develop an amusement park near Ottawa. Cooke contributes cash of $6 million and land valued at $60 million. When Cooke purchased the land, its cost was $32 million. The partnership will assume Cooke's $12 million note payable on the land. Bamber invests cash of $30 million and construction equipment that she purchased for $28 million (accumulated amortization to date, $12 million). The equipment's market value is equal to its book value.

Investments by partners

②

2. Total assets $112 mil.

Required

1. Journalize the partnership's receipt of assets and liabilities from Cooke and from Bamber. Record each asset at its current market value with no entry to accumulated amortization.

2. Compute the partnership's total assets, total liabilities, and total owners' equity immediately after organizing.

Exercise 12–5

Janice Barnett has operated a management consulting business as a proprietorship. She and Alison Morse have decided to reorganize the business as a partnership, effective April 1. Barnett's investment in the partnership consists of cash, $88,000; accounts receivable, $50,000 less allowance for uncollectibles, $4,000; office furniture, $14,000 less accumulated amortization, $4,000; a small building, $242,000 less accumulated amortization, $120,000; accounts payable, $18,000; and a note payable to the bank, $44,000.

Recording a partner's investment

②

Janice Barnett, Capital $376,000

To determine Barnett's equity in the partnership, she and Morse hire an independent appraiser. This outside party provides the following market values of the assets and liabilities that Barnett is contributing to the business: cash, accounts receivable, office furniture, accounts payable, and note payable—the same as Barnett's book value; allowance for uncollectible accounts, $12,000; building, $310,000; and accrued expenses payable (including interest on the note payable), $8,000.

Required Make the entry on the partnership books to record Barnett's investment.

Exercise 12–6

Ken Danolo and Jim Goldman form a partnership, investing $96,000 and $168,000, respectively. Determine their shares of net income or net loss for each of the following situations:

a. Net loss is $124,800, and the partners have no written partnership agreement.

b. Net income is $105,600, and the partnership agreement states that the partners share profits and losses based on their capital investments.

c. Net income is $264,000. The first $132,000 is shared based on the partner capital investments. The next $100,000 is shared based on partner service, with Danolo receiving 30 percent and Goldman receiving 70 percent. The remainder is shared equally.

Exercise 12–7

Ken Danolo withdrew cash of $148,000 for personal use, and Jim Goldman withdrew cash of $120,000 during the year. Using the data from situation (c) in Exercise 12–6, journalize the entries to close to each Capital account (a) the net income to the partners, and (b) the partners' Withdrawal accounts. Explanations are not required. Indicate the amount of increase or decrease in each partner's Capital balance. What was the overall effect on partnership capital?

Exercise 12–8

Joanna Wang is admitted to a partnership. Prior to the admission of Wang, the partnership books show Tanya Wird's Capital balance at $158,000 and Alan Bales' Capital balance at $79,000. Wird and Bales share profits and losses equally. Compute the amount of each partner's equity on the books of the new partnership under each of the following plans:

a. Wang purchases Bales's interest in the business, paying $94,500 directly to Bales.

b. Wang invests $79,000 to acquire a one-fourth interest in the partnership.

c. Wang invests $143,000 to acquire a one-fourth interest in the partnership.

Exercise 12–9

Make the partnership journal entry to record the admission of Wang under plans a, b, and c in Exercise 12–8. Explanations are not required.

Exercise 12–10

After closing the books, Harley & Raj's partnership balance sheet reports owner's equity of $40,500 for Harley and $54,000 for Raj. Harley is withdrawing from the firm. He and Raj agree to write down partnership assets by $18,000. They have shared profits and losses in the ratio of one-third to Harley and two-thirds to Raj. The partnership agreement states that a partner withdrawing from the firm will receive assets equal to the book value of his owner's equity.

1. How much will Harley receive?

2. Raj will continue to operate the business as a proprietorship. What is Raj's beginning Capital on the proprietorship books?

Exercise 12–11

Alana Bruno is retiring from the partnership of Bruno, Teale, and White on May 31. The partner Capital balances are Bruno, $108,000; Teale, $153,000; and White, $66,000. The partners agree to have the partnership assets revalued to current market values. The independent appraiser reports that the book value of the inventory should be decreased by $24,000, and the book value of the land should be increased by $96,000. The partners agree to these revaluations. The profit-and-loss ratio has been 4:3:3 for Bruno, Teale, and White, respectively. In retiring from the firm, Bruno received $150,000 cash.

Required Journalize (a) the asset revaluations, and (b) Bruno's withdrawal from the firm.

Exercise 12–12

Jonas, Teese, and Moyer are liquidating their partnership. Before selling the noncash assets and paying the liabilities, the Capital balances are Jonas, $115,000; Teese, $69,000; and Moyer, $46,000. The partnership agreement divides profits and losses equally.

Liquidation of a partnership

6

2. Jonas $107,000

Required

1. After selling the noncash assets and paying the liabilities, suppose the partnership has cash of $230,000. How much cash will each partner receive in final liquidation?
2. After selling the noncash assets and paying the liabilities, suppose the partnership has cash of $206,000. How much cash will each partner receive in final liquidation?

Exercise 12–13

Prior to liquidation, the accounting records of Quann, Pel, and Basili included the following balances and profit-and-loss-sharing percentages:

Liquidation of a partnership

6

Payment of cash:
Quann $26,400

		Noncash				Capital		
	Cash	+	Assets	=	Liabilities	+	Quann (40%)	+	Pel (30%)	+	Basili (30%)
Balances before sale of assets	$10,000		$62,500		$26,500		$20,000	$15,000	$11,000

The partnership sold the noncash assets for $78,500, paid the liabilities, and disbursed the remaining cash to the partners. Complete the summary of transactions in the liquidation of the partnership. Use the format illustrated in Exhibit 12–5.

Exercise 12–14

The partnership of Linus, Lebrun, and Beale is liquidating. Business assets, liabilities, and partners' Capital balances prior to dissolution follow. The partners share profits and losses as follows: Shelly Linus, 20 percent; Peter Lebrun, 30 percent; and Cathy Beale, 50 percent.

Liquidation of a partnership

6

Shelly Linus, Capital $29,600

Required Create a spreadsheet or solve manually—as directed by your instructor—to show the ending balances in all accounts after the noncash assets are sold for $280,000. Determine the unknown amounts, represented by (?):

	A	B	C	D	E	F
1			LINUS, LEBRUN, AND BEALE			
2			Sale of Noncash Assets			
3			(For $280,000)			
4				Shelly	Peter	Cathy
5		Noncash		Linus,	Lebrun,	Beale,
6	Cash	Assets	Liabilities	Capital	Capital	Capital
7						
8	$ 12,000	$252,000	$154,000	$24,000	$74,000	$12,000
9	280,000	(252,000)		? +	?	?
10						
11	$292,000	$ 0	$154,000	$?	$?	$?
12						
13					+ ($A9 – $B8)*.2	

Exercise 12–15

Preparing a partnership
balance sheet
②
Total assets $197,427

Carl Haupt has been running Haupt Consulting as a proprietorship but is planning to expand operations in the near future. The Haupt Consulting January 31, 2011, balance sheet appears below, with all amounts reflected at current market value. Carl Haupt is considering forming a partnership with Jill Monroe, who provides the market-value financial information shown below. Create the Haupt and Monroe Consulting partnership balance sheet at January 31, 2011.

Assets	Haupt Consulting	Monroe's Business
Cash	$ 11,700	$100,000
Accounts receivable	5,500	50,000
Inventory	2,713	5,000
Supplies	100	1,000
Prepaid rent	2,000	0
Equipment	2,000	10,000
Accumulated amortization—equipment	(66)	0
Furniture	3,600	4,000
Accumulated amortization—furniture	(120)	0
Total assets	$ 27,427	$170,000

Liabilities and Capital		
Accounts payable	$ 8,200	$ 20,000
Salary payable	1,400	0
Unearned service revenue	600	0
Notes payable	0	50,000
Carl Haupt, capital	17,227	—
Jill Monroe, capital	—	100,000
Total liabilities and capital	$ 27,427	$170,000

CHALLENGE EXERCISE

Exercise 12–16

Preparing a partnership
balance sheet
②
Total assets $1,425,000

On December 31, 2010, Sandra Dunn and Maria Andrews agree to combine their proprietorships as a partnership. Their balance sheets on December 31 are as follows:

Assets	Dunn's Business Book Value	Dunn's Business Current Market Value	Andrews' Business Book Value	Andrews' Business Current Market Value
Cash	$ 30,000	$ 30,000	$ 25,000	$ 25,000
Accounts receivable (net)	110,000	100,000	40,000	35,000
Inventory	255,000	230,000	170,000	180,000
Capital assets (net)	610,000	525,000	270,000	300,000
Total assets	$1,005,000	$885,000	$505,000	$540,000

Liabilities and Capital				
Accounts payable	$ 120,000	$120,000	$ 50,000	$ 50,000
Accrued expenses payable	10,000	10,000	10,000	10,000
Notes payable	275,000	275,000		
Sandra Dunn, capital	600,000	480,000		
Maria Andrews, capital			445,000	480,000
Total liabilities and capital	$1,005,000	$885,000	$505,000	$540,000

Required Prepare the partnership balance sheet at December 31, 2010.

BEYOND THE NUMBERS

Beyond the Numbers 12–1

The following questions relate to issues faced by partnerships.

Partnership issues

① ⑤

1. The text suggests that a written partnership agreement should be drawn up between the partners in a partnership. One benefit of an agreement is that it provides a mechanism for resolving disputes between the partners. What are five areas of dispute that might be resolved by a partnership agreement?

2. The statement has been made that "If you must take on a partner, make sure the partner is richer than you are." Why is this statement valid?

3. Frizzell, Butterworth & Legree is a partnership of lawyers. Butterworth is planning to move to Australia. What are the options open to her to convert her share of the partnership assets to cash?

ETHICAL ISSUE

Leah Rivers and Tanya Ng operate The Party Centre, a party supply store in Red Deer, Alberta. The partners split profits and losses equally, and each takes an annual withdrawal of $90,000. To even out the workload, Ng does the buying and Rivers serves as the accountant. From time to time, they use small amounts of store merchandise for personal use. In preparing for a large private party, Rivers took engraved invitations, napkins, place mats, and other goods that cost $4,000. She recorded the transaction as follows:

Cost of Goods Sold	4,000	
Inventory		4,000

Required

1. How should Rivers have recorded this transaction?
2. Discuss the ethical dimension of Rivers' action.

PROBLEMS (GROUP A)

MyAccountingLab All questions in this section appear in MyAccountingLab.

Problem 12–1A

Adam Lee and Charles Wong formed a partnership on January 1, 2010. The partners agreed to invest equal amounts of capital. Lee invested his proprietorship's assets and liabilities (credit balances in parentheses):

Investments by partners

②

2. Total assets $252,000

	Lee's Book Value	Current Market Value
Accounts receivable	$ 24,000	$20,000
Inventory	86,000	62,000
Prepaid expenses	13,000	12,000
Store equipment...	72,000	52,000
Accounts payable	(40,000)	(40,000)

On January 1, Wong invested cash in an amount equal to the current market value of Lee's partnership capital. The partners decided that Lee would earn 70 percent of partnership profits because he would manage the business. Wong agreed to accept 30 percent of profits. During the period ended December 31, 2010, the partnership earned $432,000. Wong's withdrawals were $128,000 and Lee's withdrawals were $172,800.

Required

1. Journalize the partners' initial investments.
2. Prepare the partnership balance sheet immediately after its formation on January 1, 2010.
3. Calculate the partners' Capital balances on December 31, 2010.

Problem 12–2A

Admitting a new partner

(4)

3. B. Peller, Capital $20,000

SuddenValley Resort is a partnership, and its owners are considering admitting Ben Peller as a new partner. On July 31, 2010, the Capital accounts of the three existing partners and their shares of profits and losses are as follows:

	Capital	Profit-and-Loss Percent
Eleanor Craven	$20,000	20%
Amy Osler	30,000	25
Brian Harmon	40,000	55

Required Journalize the admission of Peller as a partner on July 31, 2010, for each of the following independent situations:

1. Peller pays Harmon $55,000 cash to purchase Harmon's interest.
2. Peller invests $30,000 in the partnership, acquiring a one-quarter interest in the business.
3. Peller invests $30,000 in the partnership, acquiring a one-sixth interest in the business.

Problem 12–3A

Excel Spreadsheet Template

Computing partners' shares of net income and net loss

(3)

1. b. Net income allocated to:
Rogers $53,000

Sheila Rogers, Karen Sharp, and Jim Nas have formed a partnership. Rogers invested $60,000, Sharp $120,000, and Nas $180,000. Rogers will manage the store, Sharp will work in the store three-quarters of the time, and Nas will not work in the business.

Required

1. Compute the partners' shares of profits and losses under each of the following plans:
   a. Net loss is $70,500, and the partnership agreement allocates 45 percent of profits to Rogers, 35 percent to Sharp, and 20 percent to Nas. The agreement does not discuss the sharing of losses.
   b. Net income for the year is $136,500. The first $45,000 is allocated on the basis of partners' Capital investments. The next $45,000 is based on service, with $30,000 going to Rogers and $15,000 going to Sharp. Any remainder is shared equally.
2. Revenues for the year were $858,000 and expenses were $721,500. Under plan (b), prepare the partnership income statement for the year. Assume a year end of September 30, 2010.
3. How will what you have learned in this problem help you manage a partnership?

Problem 12–4A

Recording changes in partnership Capital

(4) (5)

3. Debit
Karen Tenne, Capital $198,000

Trail Equipment is a partnership owned by three individuals. The partners share profits and losses in the ratio of 30 percent to Karen Tenne, 40 percent to Frank Durn, and 30 percent to Erin Hana. At December 31, 2010, the firm has the following balance sheet amounts:

Cash		$ 154,000	Total liabilities	$ 520,000
Accounts receivable	$ 88,000			
Less: Allowance				
for uncollectibles	4,000	84,000		
Inventory		432,000	Karen Tenne, capital	198,000
Equipment	660,000		Frank Durn, capital	260,000
Less: Accumulated			Erin Hana, capital	220,000
amortization	132,000	528,000	Total liabilities	
Total assets		$1,198,000	and capital	$1,198,000

Karen Tenne withdraws from the partnership on this date.

Required Record Tenne's withdrawal from the partnership under the following plans:

1. In a personal transaction, Tenne sells her equity in the partnership to Michael Adams, who pays Tenne $176,000 for her interest. Durn and Hana agree to accept Adams as a partner.

2. The partnership pays Tenne cash of $22,000, and gives her a note payable for the remainder of her book equity in settlement of her partnership interest.

3. The partnership pays Tenne $220,000 cash for her equity in the partnership.

4. The partners agree that the equipment is worth $748,000 (net). After the revaluation, the partnership settles with Tenne by giving her cash of $44,000 and inventory for the remainder of her book equity.

Problem 12–5A

The partnership of Chang, Dixon & Gill has experienced operating losses for three consecutive years. The partners, who have shared profits and losses in the ratio of Lisa Chang, 15 percent, John Dixon, 60 percent, and Brian Gill, 25 percent, are considering the liquidation of the business. They ask you to analyze the effects of liquidation under various assumptions about the sale of the noncash assets. They present the following partnership balance sheet amounts at December 31, 2010:

Liquidation of a partnership

6

1. b. Cash distributed to partners $228,000

Cash	$ 41,000	Liabilities	$151,000
Noncash assets	367,000	Lisa Chang, capital	57,500
		John Dixon, capital	158,500
		Brian Gill, capital	41,000
		Total liabilities	
Total assets	$408,000	and capital	$408,000

Required

1. Prepare a summary of liquidation transactions (as illustrated in the chapter) for each of the following situations:
   a. The noncash assets are sold for $420,000.
   b. The noncash assets are sold for $338,000.

2. Make the journal entries to record the liquidation transactions in requirement 1(b).

Problem 12–6A

The partnership of Yuen, Bachra, and Lang has experienced operating losses for three consecutive years. The partners, who have shared profits and losses in the ratio of Jia Yuen, 60 percent, Denis Bachra, 20 percent, and Alan Lang, 20 percent, are considering the liquidation of the business. They ask you to analyze the effects of liquidation under various possibilities about the sale of the noncash assets. None of the partners have personal assets if they go into a deficit financial position. They present the following partnership balance sheet amounts at December 31, 2010:

Liquidation of a partnership (deficits)

6

1a. Loss allocated to Yuen $49,500

Cash	$ 6,750	Liabilities	$ 28,350
Noncash assets	118,800	Jia Yuen, capital	46,600
		Denis Bachra, capital	30,000
		Alan Lang, capital	20,600
		Total liabilities	
Total assets	$125,550	and capital	$125,550

Required

1. Prepare a summary of liquidation transactions (as illustrated in the chapter) for each of the following situations:
   a. The noncash assets are sold for $36,300.
   b. The noncash assets are sold for $27,600.

2. What legal recourse do the remaining partners have to be reimbursed for deficit balances?

Problem 12–7A

Capital amounts for the balance
sheet of a partnership

② ③

2. K. Fallon, Capital $71,500

FAB & Company is a partnership owned by K. Fallon, R. Anders, and J. Baylor, who share profits and losses in the ratio of 1:3:4. The adjusted trial balance of the partnership (in condensed form) at June 30, 2010, follows.

FAB & COMPANY Adjusted Trial Balance June 30, 2010		
Cash..	$ 166,000	
Noncash assets	800,000	
Liabilities		$ 690,000
K. Fallon, capital..		152,000
R. Anders, capital...		282,000
J. Baylor, capital...		428,000
K. Fallon, withdrawals...................................	96,000	
R. Anders, withdrawals	242,000	
J. Baylor, withdrawals	372,000	
Revenues		748,000
Expenses..	624,000	
Totals...	$2,300,000	$2,300,000

Required

1. Prepare the June 30, 2010, entries to close the revenue, expense, Income Summary, and Withdrawals accounts.

2. Using T-accounts, insert the opening balances in the partners' Capital accounts, post the closing entries to the Capital accounts, and determine each partner's ending Capital balance.

Problem 12–8A

Accounting for partners'
investments; allocating profits
and losses; accounting for the
admission of a new partner;
accounting for the withdrawal
of a partner; preparing a
partnership balance sheet

② ③ ④ ⑤

2. A. Kendall, Capital $381,537

2007

Jun. 10   Adam Kendall and Amber Masters have agreed to pool their assets and form a partnership to be called K&M Consulting. They agree to share all profits equally and make the following initial investments:

	Kendall	Masters
Cash	$15,000	$30,000
Accounts receivable (net)	33,000	27,000
Office furniture...	36,000	24,000

Dec. 31   The partnership's reported net income was $195,000 for the year ended December 31, 2007.

2008

Jan. 1   Kendall and Masters agree to accept Heidi Mooy into the partnership with a $180,000 investment for 30 percent of the business. The partnership agreement is amended to provide for the following sharing of profits and losses:

	Kendall	Masters	Mooy
Annual "salary"........................	$90,000	$120,000	$75,000
Interest on capital balance.......	10%	10%	10%
Balance in ratio of....................	3 :	2 :	5

Dec. 31   The partnership's reported net income was $480,000.

2009

Oct. 10   Kendall withdrew $84,000 cash from the partnership and Masters withdrew $57,000 (Mooy did not make any withdrawals).

Dec. 31   The partnership's reported net income was $255,000.

2010

Jan. 2 After a disagreement as to the direction in which the partnership should be moving, Mooy decided to withdraw from the partnership. The three partners agreed that Mooy could take cash of $300,000 in exchange for her equity in the partnership.

Required

1. Journalize all of the transactions for the partnership.
2. Prepare the partners' equity section of the balance sheet as of January 2, 2010.

Problem 12–9A

Judy Webb, Herb Nobes, and Jean Yee started a partnership to operate a management consulting business. The partnership (WNY Partners) had the following transactions:

Accounting for partners' investments; allocating profits and losses; accounting for the admission of a new partner; accounting for the liquidation of a partnership

②③④⑤⑥

Dec. 31, 2009
Dr. Judy Webb, Capital $90,000

2008

Jan. 2 Webb, Nobes, and Yee formed the partnership by signing an agreement that stated that all profits would be shared in a 3:2:5 ratio and by making the following investments:

	Webb	Nobes	Yee
Cash	$ 24,000	$ 42,000	$138,000
Accounts receivable (net)	84,000	126,000	180,000
Office furniture	0	66,000	0
Computer equipment	156,000	0	54,000

Dec. 31 The partnership reported net income of $252,000 for the year.

2009

Jun. 7 Webb and Yee agreed that Nobes could sell his share of the partnership to André Hughes for $372,000. The new partners agreed to keep the same profit-sharing arrangement (3:2:5 for Webb:Hughes:Yee).

Dec. 31 The partnership reported a net loss of $300,000 for the year.

2010

Jan. 3 The partners agreed to liquidate the partnership. On this date the balance sheet showed the following items:

Cash	$ 78,000
Accounts receivable	1,476,000
Allowance for uncollectible accounts	72,000
Office furniture	360,000
Computer equipment	600,000
Accumulated amortization (total)	180,000
Accounts payable	1,440,000

The assets were sold for the following amounts:

Accounts receivable	$ 720,000
Office furniture	390,000
Computer equipment	360,000

Webb and Hughes both have personal assets, but Yee does not.

Required

Journalize all the transactions for the partnership.

Problem 12–1B

Investments by partners
(2)

On January 1, 2010, Shifra Ahmed and Tonya Baker formed a partnership. The partners agreed to invest equal amounts of capital. Baker invested her proprietorship's assets and liabilities (credit balances in parentheses) as follows:

	Baker's Book Value	Current Market Value
Accounts receivable	$19,200	$19,000
Inventory	44,000	48,000
Prepaid expenses	4,800	4,000
Office equipment	92,000	56,000
Accounts payable	(48,000)	(48,000)

On January 1, 2010, Ahmed invested cash in an amount equal to the current market value of Baker's partnership capital. The partners decided that Baker would earn two-thirds of partnership profits because she would manage the business. Ahmed agreed to accept one-third of profits. During the remainder of the year, the partnership earned $276,000. Baker's withdrawals were $76,000, and Ahmed's withdrawals were $56,000.

Required

1. Journalize the partners' initial investments.
2. Prepare the partnership balance sheet immediately after its formation on January 1, 2010.
3. Calculate the partners' Capital balances at December 31, 2010.

Problem 12–2B

Admitting a new partner
(4)

Pineridge Consulting Associates is a partnership, and its owners are considering admitting Helen Oldham as a new partner. On March 31, 2010, the Capital accounts of the three existing partners and their shares of profits and losses are as follows:

	Capital	Profit-and-Loss Ratio
Jim Zook	$ 50,000	30%
Richard Land	100,000	20
Jennifer Lowe	150,000	50

Required Journalize the admission of Oldham as a partner on March 31, 2010, for each of the following independent situations:

1. Oldham pays Lowe $200,000 cash to purchase Lowe's interest in the partnership.
2. Oldham invests $100,000 in the partnership, acquiring a one-fourth interest in the business.
3. Oldham invests $80,000 in the partnership, acquiring a one-fourth interest in the business.

Problem 12–3B

Excel Spreadsheet Template

Computing partners' shares of net income and net loss
(2) (3)

Alfred Zin, Beth Murray, and Robert Kirk have formed a partnership. Zin invested $30,000, Murray $40,000, and Kirk $50,000. Zin will manage the store, Murray will work in the store half time, and Kirk will not work in the business.

Required

1. Compute the partners' shares of profits and losses under each of the following plans:
   a. Net loss is $100,000, and the partnership agreement allocates 40 percent of profits to Zin, 25 percent to Murray, and 35 percent to Kirk. The agreement does not discuss the sharing of losses.
   b. Net income for the year is $354,000. The first $150,000 is allocated based on partner capital investments. The next $72,000 is based on service, with Zin receiving $56,000 and Murray receiving $16,000. Any remainder is shared equally.

2. Revenues for the year were $1,014,000 and expenses were $660,000. Under plan (b), prepare the partnership income statement for the year. Assume a January 31, 2010, year end.

3. How will what you learned in this problem help you manage a partnership?

Problem 12–4B

Vector Financial Planning is a partnership owned by three individuals. The partners share profits and losses in the ratio of 20 percent to Katherine Nelson, 40 percent to Sam Dune, and 40 percent to Emily Root. At December 31, 2010, the firm has the following balance-sheet amounts:

Recording changes in partnership capital
④ ⑤

Cash..............................		$ 350,400	Total liabilities...................		$ 573,000
Accounts receivable	$ 92,400				
Less: Allowance					
for uncollectibles....	16,800	75,600			
Building..........................	1,102,000		Katherine Nelson, capital		390,600
Less: Accumulated			Sam Dune, capital.............		210,000
amortization	294,000	808,000	Emily Root, capital		260,400
Land...............................		200,000	Total liabilities		
Total assets....................		$1,434,000	and capital....................		$1,434,000

Dune withdraws from the partnership on December 31, 2010, to establish his own consulting practice.

Required Record Dune's withdrawal from the partnership under the following plans:

1. In a personal transaction, Dune sells his equity in the partnership to Rea Patell, who pays Dune $110,000 for one-half of his interest. Nelson and Root agree to accept Patell as a partner.

2. The partnership pays Dune cash of $163,000, and gives him a note payable for the remainder of his book equity in settlement of his partnership interest.

3. The partnership pays Dune cash of $336,000.

4. The partners agree that the building is worth $682,000 (net). After the revaluation, the partnership settles with Dune by giving him cash of $42,000 and a note payable for the remainder of his book equity.

Problem 12–5B

The partnership of Yang, Bell, and Wong has experienced operating losses for three consecutive years. The partners, who have shared profits and losses in the ratio of Jia Yang, 10 percent, Denis Bell, 30 percent, and Alan Wong, 60 percent, are considering the liquidation of the business. They ask you to analyze the effects of liquidation under various possibilities about the sale of the noncash assets. They present the following partnership balance-sheet amounts at December 31, 2010:

Liquidation of a partnership
⑥

Cash................................	$ 70,000	Liabilities...	$316,000
Noncash assets	526,000	Jia Yang, capital..............................	80,000
		Denis Bell, capital	102,000
		Alan Wong, capital	98,000
Total assets......................	$596,000	Total liabilities and capital	$596,000

Required

1. Prepare a summary of liquidation transactions (as illustrated in the chapter) for each of the following situations:
   a. The noncash assets are sold for $552,000.
   b. The noncash assets are sold for $448,000.

2. Make the journal entries to record the liquidation transactions in Requirement 1(b).

Problem 12–6B

Liquidation of a partnership (deficit)
6

The partnership of Lee, Kam, and Chow has experienced operating losses for three consecutive years. The partners, who have shared profits and losses in the ratio of Steven Lee, 60 percent, Eddie Kam, 20 percent, and Kwan Chow, 20 percent, are considering the liquidation of the business. They ask you to analyze the effects of liquidation under various possibilities about the sale of the noncash assets. None of the partners has personal assets if they go into a deficit financial position. They present the following partnership balance-sheet amounts at December 31, 2010:

Cash	$ 27,000	Liabilities...	$ 113,400
Noncash assets	475,200	Steven Lee, capital	186,400
		Eddie Kam, capital	120,000
		Kwan Chow, capital	82,400
Total assets	$502,200	Total liabilities and capital	$502,200

Required

1. Prepare a summary of liquidation transactions (as illustrated in the chapter) for each of the following situations:

   a. The noncash assets are sold for $145,200.

   b. The noncash assets are sold for $110,400.

2. What legal recourse do the remaining partners have to be reimbursed for deficit balances?

Problem 12–7B

Capital amounts for the balance sheet of a partnership
2 3

LH&C is a partnership owned by T. Lonzou, D. Huang, and J. Cong, who share profits and losses in the ratio of 2:3:5. The adjusted trial balance of the partnership (in condensed form) at September 30, 2010, follows.

LH&C
Adjusted Trial Balance
September 30, 2010

Cash..	$ 110,000	
Noncash assets...	389,000	
Liabilities		$ 319,000
T. Lonzou, capital		125,000
D. Huang, capital..		97,000
J. Cong, capital..		46,000
T. Lonzou, withdrawals......................................	99,000	
D. Huang, withdrawals	81,000	
J. Cong, withdrawals..	40,000	
Revenues...		928,000
Expenses	796,000	
Totals...	$1,515,000	$1,515,000

Required

1. Prepare the September 30, 2010, entries to close the revenue, expense, Income Summary, and Withdrawals accounts.

2. Using T-accounts, insert the opening Capital balances in the partner Capital accounts, post the closing entries to the Capital accounts, and determine each partner's ending Capital balance.

Problem 12–8B

Accounting for partners' investments; allocating profits and losses; accounting for the admission of a new partner; accounting for the withdrawal of a partner; preparing partnership balance sheet

2008

Jun. 10 Steven Dai and Sarah Mann have agreed to pool their assets and form a partnership to be called D&M Distributors. They agree to share all profits equally and make the following initial investments:

	Dai	Mann
Cash	$21,000	$36,000
Accounts receivable (net)	42,000	21,000
Office furniture (net)	48,000	27,000

Dec. 31 The partnership's reported net income was $228,000 for the year ended December 31, 2008.

2009

Jan. 1 Dai and Mann agree to accept Myra Pinos into the partnership with a $210,000 investment for 40 percent of the business. The partnership agreement is amended to provide for the following sharing of profits and losses:

	Dai	Mann	Pinos
Annual "salary"........................	$120,000	$90,000	$80,000
Interest on end-of-period caption balance.......................	10%	10%	10%
Balance in ratio of....................	2 :	3 :	5

Dec. 31 The partnership's reported net income is $570,000.

2010

Oct. 10 Dai withdrew $90,000 cash from the partnership and Mann withdrew $60,000 (Pinos did not make any withdrawals).

Dec. 31 The partnership's reported net income is $225,000.

2011

Jan. 2 After a disagreement as to the direction in which the partnership should be moving, Pinos decided to withdraw from the partnership. The three partners agreed that Pinos could take cash of $510,000 in exchange for her equity in the partnership.

Required

1. Journalize all of the transactions for the partnership.
2. Prepare the partners' equity section of the balance sheet as of January 2, 2011.

Problem 12–9B

Accounting for partners' investments; allocating profits and losses; accounting for the admission of a new partner; accounting for the liquidation of a partnership

William Cott, Julie Harris, and Regina Vaz started a partnership to operate a courier service. The partnership (CH&V Couriers) had the following transactions:

2008

Jan. 2 Cott, Harris, and Vaz formed the partnership by signing an agreement that stated that all profits would be shared in a 2:3:5 ratio and by making the following investments:

	Cott	Harris	Vaz
Cash	$12,000	$ 8,000	$14,000
Accounts receivable (net)	20,000	14,500	60,000
Office furniture (net)	0	0	15,000
Vehicles (net)	21,000	38,500	0

Dec. 31 The partnership reported net income of $53,500 for the year.

2009

Jun. 7 Cott and Vaz agreed that Harris could sell her share of the partnership to Ray Ewing for $82,500. The new partners agreed to keep the same profit-sharing arrangement (2:3:5 for Cott:Ewing:Vaz).

Dec. 31 The partnership reported a net loss of $67,000 for the year.

2010

Jan. 3   The partners agreed to liquidate the partnership. On this date the balance sheet showed the following items:

Cash	$ 17,500
Accounts receivable	316,000
Allowance for uncollectible accounts	22,500
Office furniture	74,500
Vehicles	240,000
Accumulated amortization (total)	49,500
Accounts payable	386,500

The assets were sold for the following amounts:

Accounts receivable	$190,000
Office furniture	82,500
Vehicles	106,000

Cott and Ewing both have personal assets, but Vaz does not.

Required   Journalize all of the transactions for the partnership.

CHALLENGE PROBLEMS

Problem 12–1C

Deciding on a capital structure

① ②

Nita Khare and Jason Moon have been in a partnership for five years. The principal business of the partnership is systems design for financial institutions. Gross revenues have increased from $330,000 in 2006 to $3,800,000 in 2010, the year just ended. The number of employees has increased from two in the first year to nine in the most recent year. Khare and Moon realized that they had to build up the partnership's capital and have withdrawn only part of the annual profits. As a result, their Capital accounts have increased from $200,000 (Khare, $140,000; Moon, $60,000) in 2006 to $2,000,000 (Khare, $1,080,000; Moon, $920,000) in 2010.

The two partners realize that they must expand their capital base to expand their operations in order to meet the increasing demand for their systems designs. At the same time, they wish to take personal advantage of the partnership's earnings. They have been trying to determine whether they should continue the partnership and borrow the necessary funds, take on one or more partners (several of their employees have expressed interest and have capital to invest), or incorporate and sell a portion of the business to outsiders. With respect to incorporation, Faisal Jamal, a former classmate of Khare's who works for a stockbroker, has indicated he knows of investors who would be interested in buying a share of the business.

Required   Khare and Moon have come to you to ask for advice. Provide an analysis of the situation and make a recommendation. In response to your questions, they indicate they will need additional capital of $1,600,000 to $2,000,000.

Problem 12–2C

The effects of accounting decisions on profits

③

Valerie Orange, Sara Hills, and Don Lau have been partners in a systems design business for the past eight years. Orange and Lau work full-time in the business; Hills has a public accounting practice and works about five to 10 hours per week on the administrative side of the business. The business has been successful and the partners are considering expansion.

The partnership agreement states that profits will be distributed as follows:

1. Partners will get 6 percent interest on their average Capital balances.

2. Orange will get a "salary" of $75,000; Hills will get a "salary" of $9,375; Lau will get a "salary" of $75,000.

3. The balance remaining will be distributed on the basis of Orange, 40 percent; Hills, 20 percent; and Lau, 40 percent.

The agreement also stipulates that the distributions outlined in parts 1 and 2 of the agreement will be made even if there are not sufficient profits and that any deficiency will be shared on the basis of part 3.

The capital structure was as follows at December 31, 2010, and reflects the average Capital balances for 2010:

Orange..	$ 228,750
Hills	1,091,250
Lau	491,250
Total..	$1,811,250

There has been some stress in the partnership of late because Orange believes that she is contributing a major part of the effort but is earning much less than Lau; Hills is upset because she believes that she is earning the least even though her capital is essentially funding the partnership.

Required   Orange, Hills, and Lau have come to you to ask for advice as to how they might amicably settle the present dispute. Analyze the situation and make a recommendation. Assume net income in 2010 was $400,000.

Extending Your Knowledge

DECISION PROBLEM

Lisa Black invested $30,000 and Erin Radke invested $15,000 in a public relations firm that has operated for 10 years. Neither partner has made an additional investment. They have shared profits and losses in the ratio of 2:1, which is the ratio of their investments in the business. Black manages the office, supervises the 16 employees, and does the accounting. Radke, the moderator of a television talk show, is responsible for marketing. Her high profile generates important revenue for the business. During the year ended December 2009, the partnership earned net income of $75,000, shared in the 2:1 ratio. On December 31, 2009, Black's Capital balance was $152,500 and Radke's Capital balance was $105,000.

Settling disagreements among partners

Required

Respond to each of the following situations:

1. What explains the difference between the ratio of partner Capital balances at December 31, 2009, and the 2:1 ratio of partner investments and profit sharing?

2. Radke believes the profit-and-loss-sharing ratio is unfair. She proposes a change, but Black insists on keeping the 2:1 ratio. What two factors may underlie Radke's unhappiness?

3. During January 2010, Black learned that revenues of $24,000 were omitted from the reported 2009 income. She brings this to Radke's attention, pointing out that her share of this added income is two-thirds, or $16,000, and Radke's share is one-third, or $8,000. Radke believes they should share this added income based on their Capital balances: 60 percent (or $14,400) to Black, and 40 percent (or $9,600) to Radke. Which partner is correct? Why?

4. Assume that an account payable of $18,000 for an operating expense in 2009 was omitted from 2009 reported income. On what basis would the partners share this amount?

FINANCIAL STATEMENT PROBLEM

Fontana, Lo & Romero (FLR) is a regional accounting firm with four offices. Summary data from the partnership's annual report follow:

(Dollars in thousands, except where indicated)	Years Ended June 30				
	2010	2009	2008	2007	2006
Revenues					
Assurance services	$1,234	$1,122	$1,064	$1,093	$1,070
Consulting services	1,007	775	658	473	349
Tax services	743	628	567	515	557
Total Revenues	$2,984	$2,525	$2,289	$2,081	$1,976
Operating Summary					
Revenues	$2,984	$2,525	$2,289	$2,081	$1,976
Personnel costs	1,215	1,004	887	805	726
Other costs	712	630	517	458	415
Income to Partners	$1,057	$ 891	$ 885	$ 818	$ 835
Statistical Data					
Average number of partners	9	9	9	8	8

Required

1. What percentages of total revenues did FLR earn by performing assurance services (similar to audit), consulting services, and tax services during 2006? What were the percentages in 2010? Which type of service grew the most from 2006 to 2010?

2. Compute the average revenue per partner in 2010. Assume each partner works 1,900 hours per year. On average, how much does each partner charge a client for one hour of time?

3. How much net income did each FLR partner earn, on average, in 2010?

13 Corporations: Share Capital and the Balance Sheet

What is a corporation, how do you incorporate, and why are corporations important?

What are shares and dividends, and how are they accounted for?

How do corporation financial statements and taxes differ from those of a proprietorship or a partnership?

These questions and others will be answered throughout this chapter. And the Decision Guidelines at the end of this chapter will provide the answers in a useful summary.

LEARNING OBJECTIVES

1 Identify the characteristics of a corporation

2 Record the issuance of shares and prepare the shareholders' equity section of a corporation's balance sheet

3 Account for cash dividends

4 Use different share values in decision making

5 Evaluate a company's return on assets and return on shareholders' equity

6 Identify the impact on share capital of international financial reporting standards (IFRS)

Tim Hortons® restaurants are a Canadian icon. Founded in 1964 in Hamilton, Ontario, Tim Hortons enjoyed steady growth for the next three decades and, in 1995, was acquired by Wendy's International. The Tim Hortons chain was wholly owned by Wendy's until 2006, when part of the ownership was sold to the investing public through a process known as an initial public offering. However, Tim Hortons, which is currently incorporated in the United States, is moving back to Canada and proposing to reorganize itself as a Canadian public company. It will keep the name Tim Hortons Inc. Canada's falling corporate tax rate is the main lure, although Tim Hortons earns 90 percent of its revenue from its Canadian operations.

"Management and the board believe that the proposed reorganization would be in the best interests of the company and our stockholders by creating operational and administrative efficiencies over the long term, enhancing the company's ability to expand in Canada and internationally, and improving the company's position to take advantage of lower Canadian tax rates commencing in the year following implementation," the company said in a statement.[1]

Tim Hortons will continue to list its shares of stock on the New York Stock Exchange and the Toronto Stock Exchange. The company remains committed to expanding in the U.S. market.

Tim Hortons' success continues. After incurring the costs of reorganizing as a Canadian public company in September 2009, the company's 2009 third quarter operating income was still up 5.4 percent.[2]

---

[1] Galt, Virginia, "Tim Hortons Makes Move Back to Canada," *The Globe and Mail*, July 1, 2009.

[2] "Tim Hortons Inc. Announces 2009 Third Quarter Results," an October 30, 2009, news release from the website www.timhortons.com/ca, accessed January 15, 2010.

Like Canadian Western Bank and Sun-Rype Products Ltd., Tim Hortons Inc. is a corporation. From this point forward, we will focus on corporations, so this chapter marks a turning point. We begin with the start-up of a corporation and also cover the corporate balance sheet. Fortunately, most of the accounting you have learned thus far also applies to corporations. First, however, let's take an overview of corporations with Tim Hortons Inc. as the focus company.

Corporations: An Overview

Corporations dominate business activity in Canada. Tim Hortons Inc. and Magna International Inc. are two familiar examples. Although proprietorships and partnerships are more numerous, corporations transact more business and are larger in terms of total assets, sales revenue, and number of employees. Most well-known businesses, such as sporting goods retailer The Forzani Group Ltd., oil and gas producer EnCana Corporation, and drugstore chain The Jean Coutu Group (PJC) Inc., are corporations. Their full names include *Limited*, *Incorporated*, or *Corporation* (abbreviated *Ltd.*, *Inc.*, or *Corp.*) to show they are corporations. If *Company* is in the name, it is likely a proprietorship or a partnership, not a corporation.

Characteristics of a Corporation

What makes the corporate form of organization so attractive? Several things do. We now discuss corporations' advantages and disadvantages.

OBJECTIVE 1
Identify the characteristics of a corporation

Separate Legal Entity A corporation is a separate legal entity formed under federal or provincial law. The federal or provincial government grants **articles of incorporation**, which consist of a document giving the owners permission to form a corporation. Neither a proprietorship nor a partnership requires federal or provincial approval to do business, because in the eyes of the law the business and the owner(s) are not separate entities. From a legal perspective, a corporation is a distinct entity, an artificial person that exists apart from its owners, who are called **shareholders**.

A corporation has many of the rights that a person has. For example, a corporation may buy, own, and sell property. Assets and liabilities in the business belong to the corporation rather than to the corporation's owners. The corporation may enter into contracts, sue, and be sued, just like an individual.

Continuous Life and Transferability of Ownership The owners' equity of a corporation is divided into **shares** of **stock**. The articles of incorporation specify how many shares the corporation can issue (sell) and lists the other details of its relationships with the federal or provincial government under whose laws it is incorporated. Most corporations have *continuous lives* regardless of changes in the ownership of their shares. In contrast, proprietorships and partnerships end when their ownership changes.

The shareholders of Tim Hortons, EnCana, or any other corporation may sell or trade the shares to another person, give them away, bequeath them in a will, or dispose of them in any other way they desire. The transfer of the shares does not affect the continuity of the corporation.

No Mutual Agency *Mutual agency* means that all the owners act as agents of the business. A contract signed by one owner is binding for the whole company. Mutual agency operates in partnerships, but *not* in corporations. A shareholder of Imperial Oil Limited cannot commit the corporation to a contract (unless the shareholder is also an officer of the corporation).

Limited Liability of Shareholders Shareholders have **limited liability** for corporation debts. That means they have no personal obligation for corporation liabilities. The most that a shareholder can lose on an investment in a corporation's shares is the cost of the investment. In contrast, proprietors and partners are personally liable for all the debts of their businesses, unless the partnership is a limited liability partnership (LLP).

The combination of limited liability and no mutual agency means that persons can invest in a corporation without fear of losing all their personal wealth if the business fails. This feature enables a corporation to raise more money than proprietorships and partnerships can.

Separation of Ownership and Management Shareholders own a corporation, but a *board of directors*—elected by the shareholders—appoints corporate officers to manage the business. Shareholders may invest $100 or $1 million without having to manage the company.

Corporate Taxation Corporations are separate taxable entities. They pay a variety of taxes not borne by proprietorships or partnerships, such as federal and provincial income taxes. Corporate earnings are subject to **double taxation**.

- First, corporations pay their own income taxes on corporate income. For corporations, total revenues minus total expenses, including income tax expense, produces net income. For each period, the corporation calculates income tax expense and also records the related income tax payable.

- The shareholders then pay personal income tax on the dividends (distributions) that they receive from corporations, although the tax rate is usually lower than for regular income to minimize double taxation.

Proprietorships and partnerships pay no business income tax. Instead, the tax falls solely on the owners, who are taxed on their share of the proprietorship or partnership income.

Government Regulation Because of shareholders' limited liability for corporation debts, outsiders doing business with the corporation can look no further than the corporation for payment of its debts. To protect persons who lend money to a corporation or who invest in its shares, the federal and provincial governments monitor the affairs of corporations. This government regulation consists mainly of ensuring that corporations disclose adequate business information for investors and creditors. This government regulation can be expensive for corporations.

Unique Costs for Corporations In Canada, legally, the directors of a corporation (defined below) have unlimited liability. However, insurance is available to cover any costs incurred by directors who may be sued by outsiders doing business with the corporation. If the corporation did not purchase this insurance for its directors, no one would agree to be a director of a corporation. In many small corporations, there may only be one or a few shareholders, who would also be directors of the corporation. The cost for directors' insurance is unique to corporations—proprietorships or partnerships would not incur this cost.

Exhibit 13–1 summarizes the advantages and disadvantages of corporations.

REAL WORLD EXAMPLE

Because of limited shareholder liability, many banks will lend money to a small corporation only if a third party (usually a corporate officer) guarantees payment of the loan personally in the event of default by the corporation.

KEY POINT

Corporations are owned by investors, who usually are not involved in the daily operations. A corporation's financial statements should provide the information for investors and managers to make sound decisions.

EXHIBIT 13–1   Advantages and Disadvantages of a Corporation

Corporation Advantages	Corporation Disadvantages
1. Can raise more money than a proprietorship or partnership.	1. Ownership and management are separated.
2. Has a continuous life.	2. Corporate earnings are subject to some double taxation.
3. Transferring ownership is easy.	3. Government regulation can be expensive.
4. No mutual agency exists among the shareholders.	4. Corporations may incur costs unique to corporations.
5. Shareholders have limited liability.	

Organization of a Corporation

KEY POINT

Most corporations are authorized to issue many more shares of stock than they intend to issue originally. The corporation can raise additional capital by selling shares in the future without having to request government authorization of more shares.

The process of creating a corporation begins when its organizers, called the *incorporators*, submit articles of incorporation to the federal or provincial government for approval. The articles of incorporation include the **authorization of shares** for the corporation to issue a certain number of shares of stock, which are shares of ownership in the corporation. The incorporators pay fees and file the required documents with the incorporating jurisdiction. Then the corporation comes into existence and becomes a legal entity. The incorporators agree to a set of **bylaws**, which act as the constitution for governing the corporation.

The ultimate control of the corporation rests with the shareholders, who usually receive one vote for each voting share they own. The shareholders elect the members of the **board of directors**, which

- sets policy for the corporation
- elects a **chairperson**, who is often the most powerful person in the corporation
- appoints the **president**, who is the chief executive officer in charge of managing day-to-day operations.

Most corporations have a number of vice-presidents. Exhibit 13–2 shows the authority structure in a corporation.

All corporations have an annual meeting at which the shareholders elect directors and make other shareholder decisions such as appointing the external auditors. Shareholders unable to attend this annual meeting may vote on corporation matters by use of a *proxy*, which is a legal document that expresses the shareholder's preference and appoints another person to cast the vote.

KEY POINT

Note the differences between the following terms:

Authorized shares—the maximum number of shares the corporation can issue. This number is specified in the articles of incorporation, but can be increased (although not easily).

Issued and outstanding shares—shares that have been sold to and are held by shareholders. The total number of a corporation's shares issued and outstanding at any time represents 100 percent of its ownership.

Share Capital

A corporation issues *share certificates* to its owners when they invest in the business, although this is now electronic rather than paper-based. Because shares represent the corporation's capital, they are often called *share capital*. The basic unit of share capital is called a *share*. A corporation may issue a share certificate for any number of shares it wishes—one share, 100 shares, or any other number. Exhibit 13–3 depicts an actual share certificate for 200 Intrawest Corporation shares. The certificate shows the

- company name
- type of shares
- shareholder's name
- number of shares owned by the shareholder.

EXHIBIT 13-2 Authority Structure in a Corporation

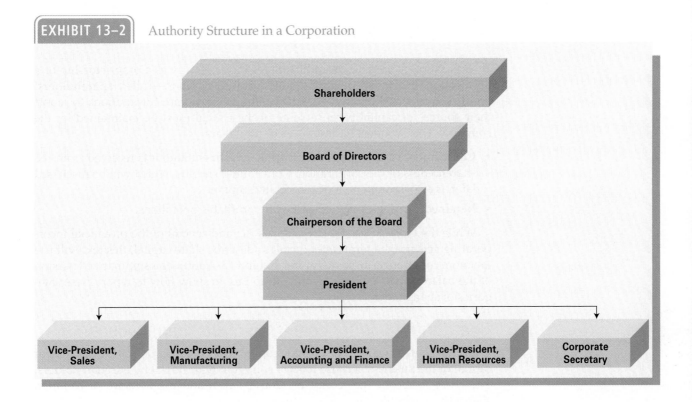

Shareholders rarely see or receive share certificates. Instead, their share purchase and sales transactions are listed on the monthly or annual summary of activity in their brokerage or trading accounts.

Shares held by a shareholder are **outstanding**. The total number of a corporation's shares outstanding at any time represents 100 percent of its ownership.

EXHIBIT 13-3 Share Certificate

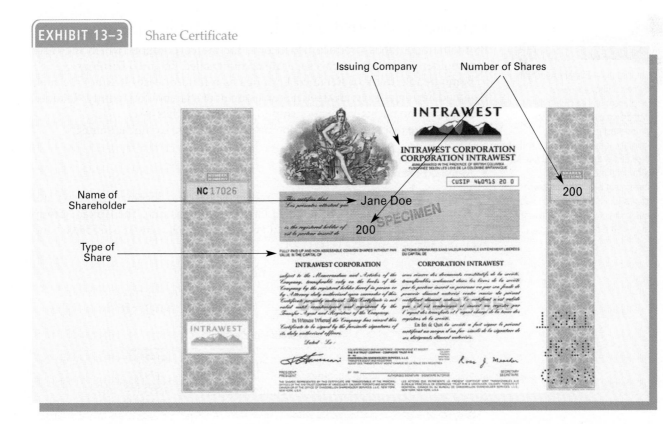

Shareholders' Equity Basics

A corporation reports assets and liabilities the same way as a proprietorship or a partnership. However, owners' equity of a corporation—called **shareholders' equity**—is reported differently. Incorporating acts require corporations to report their sources of capital because some of the capital must be maintained by the company. The two most basic sources of capital are

- **Contributed capital**, which represents investment amounts received from the shareholders of the corporation. Contributed surplus, which will be discussed later, is also a component of contributed capital.
- **Retained earnings** is capital earned by profitable operations.

While the *Canada Business Corporations Act* and several of the provincial incorporating acts use the term *stated capital* to describe share capital, this text will use the more common term, share capital. Exhibit 13–4 outlines a summarized version of the balance sheet of The Forzani Group Ltd. to show how to report these categories of shareholders' equity.

Contributed Capital Comes from the Shareholders

Common shares are one type of share capital. They are regarded as the permanent capital of the business because it is *not* subject to withdrawal by the shareholders. The entry to record the receipt of $200,000 cash and the issuance of common shares to shareholders is

Oct. 20	Cash..	200,000	
	Common Shares...		200,000
	Issued common shares.		

Issuing shares increases both the assets and the shareholders' equity of a corporation.

Retained Earnings Comes from Profitable Operations

KEY POINT

The two main different sources of owners' equity are owner investment and earnings not withdrawn by the owner. In a proprietorship, the owner's investment and earnings are both recorded in the Capital account. In a corporation, the owners' investment is called *contributed capital* and the earnings not paid out to the owners (shareholders) are called *retained earnings*.

Profitable operations produce net income for the corporation, which increases shareholders' equity through a separate account called Retained Earnings.

Some people think of Retained Earnings as a fund of cash. It is not, because Retained Earnings is not an asset; it is an element of shareholders' equity. Retained earnings has no particular relationship to cash or any other asset.

As we have just seen, a corporation needs at least two capital accounts:

- Common Shares
- Retained Earnings

Corporations close their revenues and expenses into Income Summary, and then they close net income to Retained Earnings. To illustrate, The Forzani Group Ltd.'s revenues for the 52 weeks ended February 1, 2009, were $1,346,758,000 and expenses totalled $1,317,433,000.

EXHIBIT 13–4 Summarized Shareholders' Equity at February 1, 2009, of The Forzani Group Ltd. (adapted, amounts in thousands)

Shareholders' equity	
Contributed capital	$153,562
Retained earnings...................................	179,617
Total shareholders' equity	$333,179

724 **Part 3** Accounting for Partnerships and Corporate Transactions

The closing entries would be

```
2009
Feb. 1    Revenue ........................................................  1,346,758,000
              Income Summary .....................................                  1,346,758,000
          To close revenue.
      1   Income Summary .........................................  1,317,433,000
              Expenses (detailed) .................................                  1,317,433,000
          To close expenses.
```

Now, Income Summary holds revenues, expenses, and net income.

<table>
<tr><th colspan="4" align="center">Income Summary</th></tr>
</table>

Expenses	1,317,433,000	Revenues	1,346,758,000
		Balance (net income)	29,325,000

Finally, the Income Summary's balance is closed to Retained Earnings.

```
2009
Feb. 1    Income Summary .........................................   29,325,000
              Retained Earnings ...................................                 29,325,000
          To close net income to Retained
          Earnings.
```

This closing entry completes the closing process. Income Summary is zeroed out, and Retained Earnings now holds net income.

If Forzani had had a net loss, Income Summary would have had a debit balance. To close a $100,000 loss, the closing entry credits Income Summary and debits Retained Earnings as follows:

```
2009
Feb. 1    Retained Earnings ........................................   100,000
              Income Summary ....................................                  100,000
          To close Income Summary by
          transferring net loss to Retained
          Earnings.
```

Negative Retained Earnings Is Called a Deficit   A loss or an accumulation of several years of losses may cause a debit balance in the Retained Earnings account. This condition—called a Retained Earnings or accumulated **deficit**—is reported as a negative amount in shareholders' equity. B2Gold Corp., which has its head office in Vancouver, reported the following (adapted) in its 2008 annual report:

Shareholders' Equity (U.S. dollars)	
Contributed capital..	$157,602,009
Stock options and share purchase warrants...............	11,307,820
Deficit..	(34,190,836)
Total shareholders' equity	$134,718,993

A Corporation May Pay Dividends to Shareholders

A profitable corporation may distribute cash to the shareholders. Such distributions are called **dividends**. Dividends are similar to the withdrawals of cash made by the owner of a proprietorship or by a partner of a partnership. Dividends decrease both the assets and retained earnings (and therefore, shareholders' equity) of the corporation.

LEARNING TIPS

Sometimes accounting students incorrectly view Retained Earnings as an asset, like cash. Remember, Retained Earnings is a part of shareholders' equity and therefore should have a normal *credit* balance. A *debit* balance in Retained Earnings is called a *deficit*.

REAL WORLD EXAMPLE

Public corporations are required to have an audit and file certain reports with the applicable provincial securities commission. These requirements add to a corporation's expenses without increasing its income, but are necessary.

Shareholders' Rights

The owner of a share has certain rights that are set out in the corporation's articles of incorporation; these vary from company to company, and even between classes of shares within a company. In addition, the shareholder may have other rights granted by the legislation under which the corporation receives its articles. While the rights outlined in the articles of incorporation are specific to an individual company, those set forth by legislation are shared by shareholders of all companies incorporated under that legislation. The articles of incorporation, for example, may specify that the shareholder of one class of common shares is entitled to one vote per share at shareholders' meetings, while the shareholder of another class of common shares is not entitled to vote. An example of a shared right is that, under the *Canada Business Corporations Act*, shareholders may require the directors of the company to call a meeting of the shareholders.

Some of the rights normally attached to common shares[3] are:

1. The right to sell the shares.

2. The right to vote at shareholders' meetings.

3. The right to receive a proportionate share of any dividends declared by the directors for that class of shares.

4. The right to receive a proportionate share of any assets on the winding-up of the company, after the creditors and any classes of shares that rank above that class have been paid.

5. A preemptive right—the right to maintain one's proportionate ownership in the corporation. If a shareholder owns 5 percent of the outstanding common shares and the corporation decides to issue 100,000 new shares, the shareholder would be entitled to purchase 5,000 of the new shares. (This right is usually withheld because it is rarely exercised.)

DID YOU GET IT?

MyAccountingLab

To check your understanding of the material in this Learning Objective, complete these questions. The solutions appear on MyAccountingLab so you can check your progress.

1. Compare and contrast the characteristics of proprietorships and corporations.

2. Describe the authority structure of a corporation, starting with the group or position that has the greatest authority.

3. List any three of the five rights typically attached to common shares.

OBJECTIVE 2

Record the issuance of shares and prepare the shareholders' equity section of a corporation's balance sheet

Issuing Shares

Large corporations such as George Weston Limited, BCE Inc., and Nexen Inc. need huge quantities of money to operate. They cannot expect to finance all their operations through borrowing. They need capital that they can raise by issuing shares. The articles of incorporation that the incorporators receive from the federal or provincial government include an *authorization of shares*—that is, a provision giving the government's permission for the business to issue (to sell) a certain number of shares. Corporations may sell their shares directly to the shareholders; however, they typically use the services of an *underwriter* to sell their shares, such as the brokerage firm RBC Dominion Securities or Scotia Capital Inc. The agreement

---

[3] The rights enumerated are basic rights common to incorporating legislation generally. For a more complete listing, the interested reader is referred to the *Canada Business Corporations Act* in *The Revised Statutes of Canada*.

between a corporation and its underwriter will vary, but typically the underwriter will commit to placing all of the share issue it can with its customers, and to buying any unsold shares for its own account. In another form of contract, the underwriter agrees to do its best to sell all of the share issue but makes no guarantees. The underwriter makes its money by selling the shares for a higher price than it pays to the corporation issuing the shares.

The corporation need not issue all the shares that the articles of incorporation allow—the number of authorized shares can, and often does, exceed the number of issued shares. Management may hold some shares back and issue them later if the need for additional capital arises. The shares that the corporation does issue to shareholders are called *issued shares*. Only by issuing shares—not by receiving authorization—does the corporation increase the asset and shareholders' equity amounts on its balance sheet.

The price that the shareholder pays to acquire shares from the corporation is called the *issue price*. A combination of market factors—including the company's comparative earnings record, financial position, prospects for success, and general business conditions—determines issue price. Investors will not pay more than market value for the shares.

Corporations can issue different classes of shares. The shares of a corporation may be either common or preferred. We will examine common shares first.

Common Shares

Every corporation issues *common shares*, the most basic form of share capital. (The U.S. term is *common stock*.) Unless designated otherwise, the word *shares* or *stock* is understood to mean "common shares" or "common stock." Companies may issue different classes of common shares. For example, Rogers Communications Inc. has issued Class A common shares, which carry the right to vote, and Class B common shares, which are nonvoting. (Classes of common shares may also be designated Series A, Series B, and so on, with each series having certain unique features, such as a fixed, stated dividend or a redemption feature.) There is a separate general-ledger account for each class of common shares. In describing a corporation, we would say the common shareholders are the owners of the business.

Investors who buy common shares take the ultimate risk with a corporation. The corporation makes no promises to pay them. If the corporation succeeds, it may distribute dividends to its shareholders, but if retained earnings and cash are too low, the shareholders may receive no dividends. The market value of the shares of successful corporations increase, and investors enjoy the benefit of selling the shares at a gain. The holder of common shares can earn income both from dividends and from increases in the value of the shares.

But share prices can decrease, possibly leaving the investors holding worthless share certificates. Because common shareholders take a risky investment position, they demand increases in share prices, high dividends, or both. If the corporation does not accomplish these goals and many shareholders sell their shares, the market price will fall. Short of bankruptcy, this is one of the worst things that can happen to a corporation because it means that the corporation cannot easily raise capital as needed. The period from the autumn of 2008 to the first part of 2009 highlighted this as most stock markets around the world saw share prices plummet.

Issuing Common Shares

Companies often advertise the issuance of their shares to attract investors. A good source of such information is SEDAR (System for Electronic Document Analysis and Retrieval). SEDAR is the website developed under the authority of the Canadian Securities Administrators and administered by each of the provincial securities regulatory authorities. Exhibit 13–5 is a reproduction of a portion of the prospectus dated March 24, 2006, of Tim Hortons Inc.'s initial public offering of 29,000,000 common shares at $27.00 per share.

KEY POINT

Most corporations are authorized to issue many more shares than they intend to issue originally. If the corporation wants to issue more than the authorized shares, the articles of incorporation must be amended. Amendment of the articles of incorporation requires shareholder approval and may require government approval as well.

KEY POINT

The common shareholders are the owners of the business.

REAL WORLD EXAMPLE

If you looked at the balance sheet of a U.S. corporation, you might see that its common shares had been issued at *par value*. This means the board of directors assigned a value to the common shares. If the shares were sold for more than par value, the difference was credited to Paid-in Capital in Excess of Par, or Additional Paid-in Capital. Most Canadian corporations credit the capital account for common shares for the full amount of the net proceeds from the sale of the shares.

EXHIBIT 13–5 Announcement of Share Issue by Tim Hortons Inc.

Supplemented Prep Prospectus

Initial Public Offering   March 24, 2006

TIM HORTONS INC.
C$783,000,000
29,000,000 Shares of Common Stock

This prospectus qualifies the distribution (the "offering") of 29,000,000 shares of common stock in the capital of Tim Hortons Inc. Unless the context otherwise requires, any reference in this prospectus to "we", "our" and the "Company" refer to Tim Hortons Inc. and its consolidated subsidiaries.

We are offering our common stock for sale concurrently in Canada under the terms of this prospectus and in the United States under the terms of registration statement on Form S-1 filed with the United States Securities and Exchange Commission. Our common stock is being offered in Canada by Goldman Sachs Canada Inc., RBC Dominion Securities Inc., J.P. Morgan Securities Canada Inc., Scotia Capital Inc., BMO Nesbitt Burns Inc., CIBC World Markets Inc., Merrill Lynch Canada Inc. and TD Securities Inc. (the "Canadian Underwriters") and in the United States by Goldman, Sachs & Co., RBC Capital Markets Corporation, J.P. Morgan Securities Inc., Scotia Capital (USA) Inc., Bear, Stearns & Co. Inc., CIBC World Markets Corp., Cowen & Co., LLC, Harris Nesbitt Corp., Lazard Capital Markets LLC, Merrill Lynch, Pierce, Fenner & Smith Incorporated, TD Securities (USA) LLC, Huntington Capital Corp., Loop Capital Markets, LLC, NatCity Investments, Inc. and The Williams Capital Group, L.P. (together with the Canadian Underwriters, the "underwriters"). In connection with this distribution, the underwriters may over-allot or effect transactions which stabilize, maintain or otherwise affect the market price of the common stock at levels other than those which otherwise might prevail on the open market. See "Underwriting". **After the initial offering, the offering price may be changed by the underwriters as described under "Underwriting".**

There is currently no market through which the common stock may be sold and purchasers may not be able to resell shares purchased under this prospectus. The Toronto Stock Exchange has conditionally approved the listing of the common stock under the symbol "THI." Listing is subject to our fulfilling all of the requirements of the Toronto Stock Exchange, including distribution of the common stock to a minimum number of public securityholders. Our common stock has been approved for listing on the New York Stock Exchange under the symbol "THI". An Investment in the common stock is subject to a number of risks that should be considered by a prospective purchaser. Investors should carefully consider the risk factors described under "Risk Factors" before purchasing the common stock.

Price: C$27.00 per Share

	Price to the Public	Underwriters Discounts and Commissions	Net Proceeds to Tim Hortons Inc.
Per Share	C$27.00	C$1.62	C$25.38
Total offering	C$783,000,000	C$46,980,000	C$736,020,000

No-Par-Value Shares   **No-par-value shares** are shares that do not have a value assigned to them by the articles of incorporation. The *Canada Business Corporations Act* (CBCA) requires all shares issued in Canada to be no-par-value. *Par value* is an arbitrary value assigned to each share, and might be seen in Canadian corporations that were established before the CBCA came into effect. We will not be illustrating this concept at this time.

Stated Value of Shares   The board of directors may assign a value to the shares when they are issued; this value is known as the **stated value**. For example, Dajol Inc. has authorization to issue 100,000 common shares, having no par value assigned to them by the articles of incorporation. Dajol Inc. needs $50,000 at incorporation, and might issue 10,000 shares for $5.00 per share, 2,000 shares at $25.00 per share, or 1,000 shares at $50.00 per share, and so on. The point is that Dajol Inc. can assign whatever value to the shares the board of directors wishes; however, the price the shares sell for on the market may be very different from the stated value. To illustrate this, refer to the announcement of the share issue by Tim Hortons Inc. in Exhibit 13–5. The price to the public at the bottom of the announcement of $27.00 per share is the stated value. Once the market opened, the price was $37.00 per share, and at the end of the first day of trading, the price was $33.10 per share.

REAL WORLD EXAMPLE

The financial section of a newspaper and several websites on the Internet often give the market price of a company's shares and the dividend per share, as well as the dividend yield (which is the dividend per share ÷ market price per share).

The full amount of the proceeds from the sale of shares by a company must be allocated to the capital account for those shares, as shown in the next section.

Issuing Common Shares at a Stated Value Suppose Research In Motion Limited (RIM) issues 10,000 common shares for cash, and the directors determine that the shares will be issued with a stated value (selling price) of $95.00 per share. The share issuance entry is

2010			
Jan. 8	Cash	950,000	
	Common Shares		950,000
	To issue common shares at $95.00 per share (10,000 × $95.00).		

We assume RIM received $950,000. The amount invested in the corporation, $950,000 in this case, is called share capital. The credit to Common Shares records an increase in the share capital of the corporation.

The following example shows RIM's shareholders' equity section in its annual report for the year ended February 28, 2009. RIM's annual report in Note 11 (a) "Share Capital" indicates that RIM's articles of incorporation permit it to issue " . . . an unlimited number of voting common shares . . . " At Feb. 28, 2009, RIM had issued 566,218,819 common shares for US$2,208,235,000. The common shares were issued at an average value of $3.90 (calculated as $2,208,235,000 ÷ 566,218,819 common shares). The corporation reported shareholders' equity (adapted) as follows:

Shareholders' Equity (in thousands of U.S. dollars)	
Contributed capital	
Common shares, unlimited number of shares	
authorized, 566,218,819 shares issued	$ 2,208,235
Retained earnings	3,665,893
Total shareholders' equity	$ 5,874,128

The authorized common shares report the maximum number of shares the company may issue under its articles of incorporation. RIM has an unlimited number of authorized common shares.

Issuing Common Shares for Assets Other Than Cash A corporation may issue shares in exchange for assets other than cash. It debits the assets received for their current market value and credits the common shares or preferred shares accounts accordingly. The assets' prior book value does not matter. Suppose Gillan Corporation issued 25,000 common shares for equipment worth $25,000 plus a building worth $125,000. The entry is

Nov. 12	Equipment	25,000	
	Building	125,000	
	Common Shares		150,000
	To issue 25,000 common shares in		
	exchange for equipment and a building.		

Common Shares increases by the amount of the assets' *current market value,* $150,000 in this case; the stated value or value assigned to the shares would be $6.00 ($150,000 ÷ 25,000) per share.

Preferred Shares

Preferred shares have special rights that give their owners certain advantages over common shareholders. Most notably,

1. Preferred shareholders receive dividends before the common shareholders.

2. Preferred shareholders receive assets before the common shareholders if the corporation liquidates.

3. Corporations pay a fixed dividend on preferred shares. Investors usually buy preferred shares to earn those fixed dividends.

Often, preferred shares are cumulative, which means that if the preferred dividend is not paid in a year, the dividend from that year must be paid to the preferred shareholders before the common shareholders can receive a dividend in a later year. Because of the preferred shareholders' priorities, common shares represent the residual ownership in the corporation's assets after the liabilities and the claims of preferred shareholders have been subtracted. Often the right to vote is withheld from preferred shareholders. Companies may issue different classes of preferred shares (Class A and Class B or Series A and Series B, for example). Each class is recorded in a separate account.

Investors who buy preferred shares take less risk than do common shareholders. Why? Because corporations pay a specified amount of dividends on preferred shares. The preferred dividend may be a set amount or a fixed percentage of some number, such as the prime interest rate at the date of declaration of the dividend. For example, Bombardier Inc.'s January 31, 2009, annual report showed the company had three classes of preferred shares outstanding:

- Series 2 Cumulative Redeemable Preferred Shares, paying dividends at 80% of the Canadian prime rate payable monthly
- Series 3 Cumulative Redeemable Preferred Shares, paying dividends of 5.267% or $1.31675 per share payable quarterly
- Series 4 Cumulative Redeemable Preferred Shares, paying dividends of 6.25% or $1.5625 per share payable quarterly

Investors usually buy preferred shares to earn these fixed dividends. Preferred shares' market values do not fluctuate much, so income is mostly from dividends.

Corporations issue preferred shares as opposed to common shares because

- preferred shares usually have no voting rights, unlike most common shares.
- equity (ownership) is not diluted when preferred shares are issued.

Preferred shares may be preferred by corporations to debt because dividends are payable at the discretion of the corporation. As well, the corporation is not compelled to redeem, or buy back, the preferred shares at a certain date, whereas the corporation must repay the debt at a certain date.

Preferred shares operate as a hybrid somewhere between common shares and long-term debt. Like debt, preferred shares pay a specified dividend. But like shares, the dividend becomes a liability only after the board of directors has declared the dividend. Also, there is no obligation to redeem preferred shares in the manner required by debt. Preferred shares that must be redeemed (bought back) by the corporation are a liability masquerading as a stock. Experienced investors treat mandatorily redeemable preferred shares as part of total liabilities, not as part of shareholders' equity. In fact, certain types of preferred shares must be accounted for as debt on the balance sheet. Further discussion of this aspect of preferred shares is covered in advanced accounting texts. While issuing preferred shares is a common way for a corporation to raise funds, not all corporations issue preferred shares. However, all corporations must issue at least one common share.

The method of financing affects net income and income taxes to be paid. Corporations may prefer debt to preferred shares because dividend payments are not tax deductible and interest payments are. Dividends are a distribution of assets created by earnings. On the other hand, individuals might prefer to hold preferred shares because the income tax rate on dividends they receive is lower than the tax rate they pay on interest they receive. It's for that reason that the dividend rate on a company's preferred shares is usually lower than the interest rate on bonds the company issues.

Issuing Preferred Shares

Accounting for preferred shares follows the pattern illustrated for common shares.

Assume Cendant Corporation's articles of incorporation authorize issuance of 10,000 preferred shares with an annual dividend of $10.00 per share. On July 31, the company issues 1,000 shares at a stated price of $100.00 per share and receives a cash payment of $100,000. The issuance entry is

Jul. 31	Cash..	100,000	
	Preferred Shares..		100,000
	To issue 1,000 preferred shares for		
	$100.00 per share (1,000 × $100).		

As was mentioned previously, sometimes preferred shares have characteristics that make them more like debt than equity. Such preferred shares are treated for accounting purposes (and are regarded by investors) as a liability rather than as part of equity, which can affect certain financial ratios. Further discussion of the relevant issues is deferred to a more advanced accounting course.

Convertible Preferred Shares

Convertible preferred shares are preferred shares that may be exchanged by the preferred shareholders, if they choose, for another specified class of shares in the corporation. For example, the preferred shares of Renewal Resources Inc. are convertible into the company's common shares. A note to Renewal's balance sheet describes the conversion terms as follows:

> **The . . . preferred shares are convertible at the rate of
> 7.00 common shares for each preferred share outstanding.**

If you owned 100 Renewal convertible preferred shares, you could convert them into 700 (100 × 7.00) common shares. Under what condition would you exercise the conversion privilege? You would do so if the market value of the common shares that you could receive from conversion was greater than the market value of the preferred shares that you presently held. This way, you as an investor could increase your personal wealth.

Renewal Resources Inc.'s convertible preferred shares were issued at $100.00 per share, and the common shares at $1. The company would record the conversion at the value of the 100 preferred shares on the Renewal Resources Inc. books, or $10,000 (100 × $100). The conversion of the 100 preferred shares into 700 common shares would be recorded as follows:

Mar. 7	Preferred Shares..	10,000	
	Common Shares..		10,000
	Conversion of preferred shares into common.		
	(100 preferred shares converted into		
	700 common shares.)		

KEY POINT

No gain or loss is reported on a conversion of shares.

At this point, the new common shares cannot be converted back to preferred shares.

Ethical Considerations in Accounting for the Issuance of Shares

Issuance of shares for *cash* poses no serious ethical challenge because the value of the asset received (cash) is clearly understood. The company simply receives cash and issues the shares to the shareholders, giving them share certificates as evidence of their purchase. However, issuing shares for assets other than cash can pose an ethical challenge. The company issuing the shares wants to look successful, so it often wishes to record a large amount for the noncash asset received (such as land or a building) and for the shares being issued. Why? Because large asset and equity amounts make the business look prosperous, and financial ratios can be affected in a positive way. This can motivate a company to record a high amount for the assets.

A company is supposed to record an asset received at its current market value. However, one person may appraise land at a market value of $400,000. Another may honestly believe the land is worth only $300,000. A company receiving land in exchange for its shares must decide whether to record the land at $300,000, at $400,000, or at some amount in between based on external, independent evidence.

The ethical course of action is to record the asset at its current market value, as determined by independent appraisers. Corporations are rarely found guilty of *understating* their assets, but companies have been sued for *overstating* asset values.

Incorporation of a Going Business

You may dream of having your own business someday, or you may currently be a business proprietor or partner. Businesses that begin as a proprietorship or a partnership often incorporate at a later date. By incorporating a going business, the proprietor or partners avoid the unlimited liability for business debts. Corporations often pay income tax at a lower rate than individuals. Incorporating makes it easier to raise capital and to achieve a long life for a business.

To account for the incorporation of a going business, we close the owner equity accounts of the prior entity and set up the shareholder equity accounts of the corporation. Suppose SL.com is a partnership owned by Joe Suzuki and Monica Lee. The partnership balance sheet, after all adjustments and closing entries, reports Joe Suzuki, Capital, of $100,000, and Monica Lee, Capital, of $140,000. They incorporate their business as SL.com Inc. with an authorization to issue 1,000,000 common shares. Suzuki and Lee agree to receive common shares equal in stated value to their respective partnership Capital account balances. The Capital account balances represent the net assets of the partnership. If each common share has a stated value of $1.00, the entry to record the incorporation of the business is[4]

Feb. 1	Joe Suzuki, Capital	100,000	
	Monica Lee, Capital	140,000	
	Common Shares...		240,000
	To incorporate the business, close the Capital accounts of the partnership, and issue 240,000 common shares to the incorporators.		

Organization Costs

The costs of organizing a corporation include legal fees for preparing documents and advising on procedures and fees paid to the incorporating jurisdiction, and charges by promoters for selling the company's shares. These costs are grouped in an account titled Organization Costs, which is an asset because these costs contribute to a business's start-up. Suppose BBV Holdings Inc. pays legal fees

---

[4] Other required entries would affect the asset accounts; these entries are discussed in advanced accounting courses.

and incorporation fees of $5,000 to organize the corporation under the *Canada Business Corporations Act* in Newfoundland. In addition, an investment dealer charges a fee of $15,000 for selling 30,000 common shares of BBV Holdings Inc. to investors for $225,000. Instead of being paid in cash, the broker receives 2,000 common shares as payment. BBV Holdings Inc.'s journal entries to record these organization costs are

Mar. 31	Organization Costs..	5,000	
	Cash...		5,000
	Legal fees and incorporation fees to organize the corporation.		
Apr. 3	Cash..	225,000	
	Organization Costs	15,000	
	Common Shares		240,000
	To record receipt of funds from sale of 30,000 common shares and issue of 2,000 shares to investment dealer for selling shares in organization.		

Organization costs is an *intangible asset*, reported on the balance sheet along with patents, trademarks, goodwill, and any other intangibles. We know that intangible assets, with the exception of goodwill and other intangibles with unlimited useful lives, should be amortized over their useful lives, and organization costs will benefit the corporation for as long as the corporation operates. But how long will that be? We cannot know in advance. The *Income Tax Act* allows corporations to expense a portion of organization costs against taxable income. While the *CICA Handbook* does not require them to be amortized, most companies amortize organization costs over a short time period because of their relatively small size. As is true with other intangibles, amortization expense for the year should be disclosed in the financial statements.

The Shareholders' Equity Section of a Corporation's Balance Sheet

The shareholders' equity section of Envoy Corporation's balance sheet at December 31, 2010, appears in Exhibit 13–6. Note the two sections of shareholders' equity: contributed capital and retained earnings. Also observe the order of the contributed capital accounts: preferred shares, then common shares.

LEARNING TIPS

If Envoy Corporation had been a proprietorship rather than a corporation, this shareholders' equity section would be equivalent to Envoy, Capital in the proprietorship—the amount of total shareholders' equity would equal the balance in the Envoy, Capital account.

EXHIBIT 13–6 Part of Envoy Corporation's Balance Sheet

ENVOY CORPORATION
Partial Balance Sheet
December 31, 2010

Shareholders' Equity

Contributed capital	
Preferred shares, $5.00, 10,000 shares authorized, 1,000 shares issued..	$ 50,000
Common shares, 10,000 shares authorized, 4,000 shares issued..	80,000
Total contributed capital	130,000
Retained earnings	55,000
Total shareholders' equity	$185,000

To check your understanding of the material in this Learning Objective, complete these questions. The solutions appear on MyAccountingLab so you can check your progress.

4. Is each of the following statements true or false? For each false statement, explain why it is false.

   a. A shareholder may bind (obligate) the corporation to a contract.

   b. The policy-making body in a corporation is called the board of directors.

   c. The owner of 100 preferred shares has greater voting rights than the owner of 100 common shares.

   d. A company incorporated under the *Canada Business Corporations Act* must assign the proceeds of a share issue to the capital account for that type of share.

   e. All common shares issued and outstanding have equal voting rights.

   f. Issuance of 1,000 common shares at $12.00 per share increases shareholders' equity by $12,000.

   g. The stated value of a share is the value assigned to the shares by the company issuing them at the date issued.

   h. A corporation issues its preferred shares in exchange for land and a building with a combined market value of $200,000. This transaction increases the corporation's shareholders' equity by $200,000 regardless of the assets' prior book value.

   i. Preferred shares are a riskier investment than common shares.

5. Assume WCP Corporation's articles of incorporation authorize issuance of 10,000 convertible preferred shares with an annual dividend of $10.00 per share and an unlimited number of common shares. On July 31, the company issued 1,000 preferred shares at a stated price of $100.00 per share and 2,000 common shares at $50.00 per share, and received total cash of $200,000.

   a. Record the issuance of the shares.

   b. Calculate total contributed capital and total shareholders' equity, assuming retained earnings is now $50,000.

   c. Record the conversion of 10 of the $100.00 convertible preferred shares (now having a market value of $90). Each preferred share is convertible into two common shares.

6. Franklin Technologies Inc., incorporated under the *Canada Business Corporations Act*, had three transactions during the year ended December 31, 2010, involving its common shares. On January 15, 2010, 50,000 Class A voting shares were issued with a stated value of $8.00 per share. On February 28, 2010, 10,000 Class B nonvoting shares with a stated value of $10.00 per share were issued. On August 8, 2010, 15,000 Class B shares were issued in exchange for land with a market value of $165,000. Franklin's articles of incorporation state that 100,000 Class A voting and 200,000 Class B nonvoting common shares are authorized.

   a. Prepare the journal entry to record the transaction of January 15, 2010.

   b. Prepare the journal entry to record the transaction of February 28, 2010.

   c. Prepare the journal entry to record the transaction of August 8, 2010.

   d. Create the shareholders' equity section for Franklin Technologies Inc. after the three transactions have taken place. Assume retained earnings was $100,000 at this time.

   e. What was the average issue price of each Class B common share?

   f. How did Franklin Technologies Inc. withhold the voting privilege from its Class B common shareholders?

Accounting for Cash Dividends

Corporations share their wealth with the shareholders through dividends. Corporations declare dividends from *retained earnings* and usually pay the dividends with *cash*. The corporation must have enough retained earnings to declare the dividend and also have enough cash to pay the dividend.

Dividend Dates

A corporation must declare a dividend before paying it. The board of directors declares the dividend. The corporation has no obligation to pay a dividend until the board declares one. However, once the dividend is declared, it becomes a legal liability. Three dates for dividends are relevant:

1. *Declaration date* On the declaration date, the board of directors announces the intention to pay the dividend. The declaration creates a liability for the corporation.

2. *Date of record* Those shareholders holding the shares on the date of record—a few weeks after declaration—will receive the dividend.

3. *Payment date* Payment of the dividend usually follows the record date by two to four weeks.

Exhibit 13–7 is a "Dividend Notice" for Laurentian Bank of Canada. The announcement states the date of declaration (May 27, 2009), the dividend amount, the date of record (July 2, 2009, for the common shares), and the payment date (August 1, 2009, for the common shares).For the preferred shares Series 9 and the preferred shares Series 10, the announcement states the date of declaration (May 27, 2009), the dividend amount, the date of record (June 8, 2009), and the payment date (June 15, 2009). Dividend announcements are published in the financial press and online to ensure that shareholders or potential shareholders are kept fully aware of the corporation's dividend policy.

EXHIBIT 13–7 Example of a Dividend Notice for Laurentian Bank of Canada

NOTICE OF DIVIDENDS

Laurentian Bank of Canada—Dividend Notice

MONTREAL, May 27 /CNW Telbec/ – At its meeting held on May 27, 2009, the Board of Directors of the Laurentian Bank of Canada (the "Bank") declared the following dividends:

(R) a regular quarterly dividend of 34 cents per share on the common shares payable on August 1, 2009 to the holders on record at the close of business on July 2, 2009;

(R) a dividend of $0.375 on the preferred shares Series 9, payable on June 15, 2009 to shareholders of record at the close of business on June 8, 2009; and

(R) a dividend of $0.328125 on the preferred shares Series 10, payable on June 15, 2009 to shareholders of record at the close of business on June 8, 2009.

For year 2009, all dividends declared will be eligible dividends, unless otherwise indicated. The dividends declared on May 27, 2009, are eligible dividends for income tax legislation purposes.

For further information: Gladys Caron, Vice-President, Public Affairs, Communications and Investor Relations, (514) 284-4500, extension 7511, Cellular: (514) 893-3963, gladys.caron@banquelaurentienne.ca

---

Source: www.newswire.ca/en/releases/archive/May2009/27/c6888.html

Declaring and Paying Dividends

Declaration of a cash dividend is recorded by debiting Retained Earnings and crediting Dividends Payable as follows (amounts assumed):[5]

Oct. 3	Retained Earnings...	20,000	
	Dividends Payable...		20,000
	To declare a cash dividend.		

To pay the dividend on the payment date, the transaction is recorded as follows:

Nov. 15	Dividends Payable...	20,000	
	Cash..		20,000
	To pay a cash dividend.		

Dividends Payable is a current liability. When a company has issued both preferred and common shares, the preferred shareholders receive their dividends first. The common shareholders receive dividends only if the total declared dividend is large enough to satisfy the preferred requirements. Let's see how dividends are divided between preferred and common shares.

Guthrie Industries Inc. has 10,000 shares of $1.50 cumulative preferred shares outstanding plus common shares. Exhibit 13–8 shows the division of dividends between the preferred shares and common shares for two situations.

EXHIBIT 13–8 Dividing a Dividend between the Preferred Shares and Common Shares of Guthrie Industries Inc.

Case A: Total dividend of $15,000

Preferred dividend (The full $15,000 goes to the preferred shares because the annual preferred dividend is $15,000 ($1.50 × 10,000).)	$15,000
Common dividend (None, because the total dividend declared did not exceed the preferred dividend for the year.)	0
	$15,000

Case B: Total dividend of $50,000

Preferred dividend ($1.50 × 10,000)	$15,000
Common dividend ($50,000 – $15,000)	35,000
	$50,000

If Guthrie Industries Inc.'s annual dividend is large enough to exceed the preferred dividend for the year (Case B in Exhibit 13–8), the preferred shareholders receive their regular dividend and the common shareholders receive the remainder. But if the year's dividend is just equal to or less than the preferred dividend (Case A in Exhibit 13–8), the preferred shareholders receive the entire dividend, and the common shareholders receive nothing that year.

We noted that preferred shareholders enjoy the advantage of priority over common shareholders in receiving dividends. The various features or *sweeteners* for preferred shares are explained on pages 729–731. The dividend preference is normally stated as a dollar amount. For example, the preferred shares may be "$3 preferred," meaning that the shareholders are entitled to an annual dividend of $3.00 per share.

---

[5] Some accountants debit a Dividends account, a temporary account that is closed to Retained Earnings, but most businesses debit Retained Earnings directly, as shown here.

When a company has more than one class of preferred shares or common shares, the division of dividends among the various classes of shares follows this same pattern: the most senior preferred shares get the first dividends, and so on.

Dividends on Cumulative and Noncumulative Preferred Shares

The allocation of dividends may be complex if the preferred shares are *cumulative*. A corporation may fail to pay the preferred dividend. The missed dividends are said to be *in arrears*. The owners of **cumulative preferred shares** must receive all dividends in arrears plus the current year's dividend before the corporation pays dividends to the common shareholders. "Cumulative" means that any dividends in arrears will accumulate, or carry over, to the future. The cumulative feature is not automatic to preferred shares but must be assigned to the preferred shares in the articles of incorporation. Common shares are never cumulative.

As noted above, the preferred shares of Guthrie Industries Inc. are cumulative. Suppose the company did not distribute the 2009 preferred dividend of $15,000. Before paying dividends to its common shareholders in 2010, the company must first pay preferred dividends of $15,000 for each of 2009 and 2010, a total of $30,000.

Assume that Guthrie Industries Inc. did not distribute its 2009 preferred dividend. In 2010, the company declares a $100,000 dividend. How much of this dividend goes to the preferred shareholders? How much goes to the common shareholders? The allocation of this $100,000 dividend is

Total dividend		$100,000
Preferred shareholders get		
2009: 10,000 shares × $1.50 per share	$15,000	
2010: 10,000 shares × $1.50 per share	15,000	
Total to preferred $1.50 shareholders		30,000
Common shareholders get the remainder........................		$ 70,000

The entry to record the declaration of this dividend is

2010			
Sept. 6	Retained Earnings..	100,000	
	Dividends Payable, Preferred Shares.......		30,000
	Dividends Payable, Common Shares.......		70,000
	To declare a cash dividend. Preferred		
	dividends are $30,000 ($15,000 × 2); common		
	dividends are $70,000 ($100,000 − $30,000).		

If the preferred shares are not designated as cumulative, the corporation is not obligated to pay any dividends in arrears. Suppose that the Guthrie Industries Inc. preferred shares were not cumulative, and the company did not distribute a dividend in 2009. The preferred shareholders would lose the 2009 dividend forever. Of course, the common shareholders would not receive a 2009 dividend either. Before paying any common dividends in 2010, the company would have to pay only the 2010 preferred dividend of $15,000.

Having dividends in arrears on cumulative preferred shares is *not* a liability to the corporation. (A liability for dividends arises only after the board of directors declares the dividend.) Nevertheless, a corporation must report cumulative preferred dividends in arrears in the notes to the financial statements. This information alerts common shareholders to how much in cumulative preferred dividends must be paid before the common shareholders will receive any dividends.

Note disclosure of cumulative preferred dividends might take the following form. Observe the two references to Note 3 in this section of the balance sheet. The "$1.50" after "Preferred shares" is the dividend rate.

Preferred shares, $1.50, 50,000 shares authorized,
 10,000 shares issued (Note 3)... $ 80,000
Common shares, 100,000 shares authorized, 40,000 shares issued   200,000
Retained earnings (Note 3)...   414,000

> **Note 3: Cumulative preferred dividends in arrears. At December 31, 2010,**
> **dividends on the company's $1.50 preferred shares were in arrears**
> **for 2009 and 2010, in the amount of $30,000 ($1.50 × 10,000 × 2 years).**

DID YOU GET IT?

To check your understanding of the material in this Learning Objective, complete these questions. The solutions appear on MyAccountingLab so you can check your progress.

7. CRS Robotics Inc. was organized on January 1, 2009, with 500,000 shares authorized; 200,000 shares were issued on January 5, 2009. CRS Robotics Inc. earned $250,000 during 2009 and declared a dividend of $0.25 per share on November 30, 2009, payable to shareholders on January 5, 2010.

 a. Journalize the declaration and payment of the dividend.

 b. Compute the balance of Retained Earnings on December 31, 2009.

8. Trivision Corp. has outstanding 20,000 common shares and 10,000 $2.00 cumulative preferred shares. The company has declared no dividends for the past two years but plans to pay $90,000 this year.

 a. Compute the dividends for the preferred and common shares.

 b. By how much will the dividends reduce Retained Earnings?

9. Preferred shares usually have preference over common shares when dividends are distributed. What other alternative features of preferred shares give them an advantage over common shares?

OBJECTIVE ④
Use different share values in decision making

Different Values of Shares

The business community refers to several different *share values*. Market value and book value are used for decision making.

Market Value

REAL WORLD EXAMPLE

A change in the market price of a company's shares does not affect the corporation unless the corporation decides to issue additional shares or repurchase its own shares. Most share transactions are between shareholders and are carried out through a stock exchange.

A share's **market value**, or *market price*, is the price for which a person can buy or sell a share. The issuing corporation's net income, financial position, future prospects, and the general economic conditions determine market value. The Internet and most newspapers report the market price of many shares. Most companies' websites track their share prices. Corporate annual reports generally provide quarterly market price data for the past five or ten years. *In almost all cases, shareholders are more concerned about the market value of a share than any other value.* At September 14, 2009, the common shares of Winpak Ltd., the Winnipeg-based manufacturer of packaging, were *listed at* (an alternative term is *quoted at*) $9.41, which meant they sold for, or could be bought for, $9.41 per share. The purchase of 1,000 common shares of Winpak Ltd. would cost $9,410 ($9.41 × 1,000), plus a commission. If you were selling 1,000 common shares, you would receive cash of $9,410 less a commission. The commission is the fee an investor pays to a stockbroker for buying or selling the shares. If you buy shares in Winpak Ltd. from another investor, Winpak Ltd. gets no cash. The transaction is a sale between investors. Winpak Ltd. records only the change in shareholder name.

Book Value

The **book value** of a share is the amount of shareholders' equity on the company's books for each share. If the company has only common shares outstanding, divide total shareholders' equity by the number of shares *outstanding*. A company with shareholders' equity of $180,000 and 5,000 common shares outstanding has a book value of $36.00 per share ($180,000 ÷ 5,000 shares).

If the company has both preferred and common shares outstanding, the preferred shareholders have the first claim to shareholders' equity. Ordinarily, preferred shares have a specified liquidation, or redemption, or call value. The book value of preferred shares is usually their liquidation, redemption, or call value plus any cumulative dividends in arrears on the shares. The book value *per share* equals the sum of the liquidation, redemption, or call value and any cumulative dividends in arrears divided by the number of preferred shares outstanding. After the corporation computes the preferred share's book value, it computes the book value per common share. The corporation divides the common equity (total shareholders' equity minus preferred equity) by the number of common shares outstanding.

LEARNING TIPS

Book value per share uses the number of shares outstanding, not the number of shares authorized.

Therefore, we subtract preferred equity from total equity to compute the book value of the common shares, and divide this amount by the number of common shares outstanding to determine the book value per common share. To illustrate, Garner Corp. reports the following amounts:

Shareholders' Equity	
Contributed capital	
Preferred shares, $7.00, $100 call price, 5,000 shares authorized,	
1,000 shares issued	$100,000
Common shares, 20,000 shares authorized,	
5,000 shares issued	150,000
Total contributed capital	250,000
Retained earnings	90,000
Total shareholders' equity	$340,000

Suppose that three years of cumulative preferred dividends are in arrears. The current year preferred dividend must also be paid. The book value for the common shares follow:

Total shareholders' equity	$340,000
Less: Shareholders' equity allocated to preferred	128,000*
Shareholders' equity available	
for common shareholders	$212,000
Book value per share ($212,000 ÷ 5,000 shares)	$ 42.40

*$100,000 + ($7.00 × 1,000 × 3) + ($7.00 × 1,000) = $128,000

Using Book Value in Decision Making   How is book value used in decision making? Book value may be a factor in determining the price to pay for a closely held corporation. Also, a company may buy out a shareholder by agreeing to pay the book value of the shareholder's shares.

Some investors compare the book value of a share with its market value. The idea is that shares selling below book value are underpriced and thus are a good buy. But the relationship between book value and market value is far from clear. Other investors believe that, if shares sell at a price below book value, the company must be experiencing difficulty. Exhibit 13–9 contrasts the book values and market prices for the common shares of three well-known companies. In two of the three cases, the share price, which is the market value, exceeds book value—a sign of success. Enbridge Inc.'s market price far exceeds its book value.

EXHIBIT 13–9 | Book Value and Market Value

	Year-End Book Value	Approximate Fourth-Quarter Market-Value Range
Enbridge Inc. (December 31, 2008)	$17.41	$34.50–$42.00
The Forzani Group Ltd. (February 1, 2009)	$10.11	$6.56–$9.51
Winpak Ltd. (December 28, 2008)	US$4.32	C$4.50–$9.50

DID YOU GET IT?

MyAccountingLab

To check your understanding of the material in this Learning Objective, complete these questions. The solutions appear on MyAccountingLab so you can check your progress.

10. Castle Corporation's balance sheet at year end shows the following:

Shareholders' Equity

Contributed capital	
Preferred shares, 7%, $13.00 liquidation value, 5,000 shares authorized, 3,500 shares issued	$ 45,500
Common shares, 140,000 shares authorized and issued	74,500
Total contributed capital	120,000
Retained earnings	260,000
Total shareholders' equity	$380,000

Compute the shareholders' equity allocated to the preferred shareholders. Five years of cumulative preferred dividends are in arrears including the current year.

11. Refer to the Castle Corporation data in the previous question. Compute the shareholders' equity available for the common shareholders and the book value per common share.

OBJECTIVE 5
Evaluate a company's return on assets and return on shareholders' equity

Evaluating Operations

Investors and creditors are constantly comparing companies' profits. The Forzani Group's net income may not be comparable to that of a company in the oil and gas business, such as EnCana Corporation, or of a brewery, such as Sleeman Breweries Ltd. It is difficult to compare an established company, such as Canadian Tire Corporation, Limited, to a relatively young company, such as Infowave Software, Inc. of Burnaby, B.C. To compare companies, investors, creditors, and managers use standard profitability ratios. Two important ratios are the rate of return on total assets and the rate of return on shareholders' equity.

Rate of Return on Total Assets

The **rate of return on total assets**, or simply **return on assets (ROA)**, measures a company's success in using its assets to earn income. Two groups invest money to finance a corporation:

- Shareholders
- Creditors

Net income and interest expense are the returns to these two groups. Shareholders have invested in the corporation's shares and expect the company to earn net income. Creditors have lent money to the corporation to earn interest.

The sum of net income and interest expense is the return to the two groups that have financed the corporation's assets, and this is the numerator of the return on assets ratio. The denominator is average total assets. Return on assets is computed as follows, using the actual data from the Winpak Ltd. December 28, 2008, annual report (amounts in millions of U.S. dollars):

$$\text{Rate of return on total assets} = \frac{\text{Net income} + \text{Interest expense}}{\text{Average total assets}} = \frac{\$29.35 + \$1.13}{(\$417.02 + \$441.60)/2} = \frac{\$30.48}{\$429.31} = 0.071, \text{ or } 7.1\%$$

Net income and interest expense are taken from the income statement. Average total assets are computed from the beginning and ending balance sheets. How is this profitability measure used in decision making? It is used to compare companies. By relating the sum of net income and interest expense to average total assets, we have a standard measure that describes the profitability of all types of companies.

What is a good rate of return on total assets? There is no single answer to this question because rates of return vary widely by industry. For example, consumer products companies earn much higher returns than do utilities or grocery store chains. In most industries, a return on assets of 10 percent is considered very good.

Rate of Return on Common Shareholders' Equity

Rate of return on common shareholders' equity, often called **return on equity (ROE)**, shows the relationship between net income and average common shareholders' equity. The numerator is net income minus preferred dividends. This information is taken from the income statement and statement of retained earnings. Preferred dividends are subtracted because the preferred shareholders have the first claim to dividends from the company's net income. The denominator is average *common shareholders' equity*—total shareholders' equity minus preferred equity. Winpak Ltd.'s rate of return on common shareholders' equity for December 28, 2008, is computed as follows (amounts in millions of U.S. dollars):

$$\text{Rate of return on common shareholders' equity} = \frac{\text{Net income} - \text{Preferred dividends}}{\text{Average common shareholders' equity}} = \frac{\$29.35 - \$0}{(\$280.56 + \$293.40)/2} = \frac{\$29.35}{\$286.98} = 0.102, \text{ or } 10.2\%$$

Observe that the return on equity (10.2 percent) is higher than the return on assets (7.1 percent). This difference results from the interest expense component of return on assets. Companies such as Winpak Ltd. borrow at one rate, say, 7.5 percent, and invest the funds to earn a higher rate, say, 9.5 percent. Borrowing at a lower rate than the return on investments is called *using leverage*. During good times, leverage produces high returns for shareholders. However, too much borrowing can make it difficult to pay the interest on the debt. The company's creditors are guaranteed a fixed rate of return on their loans. The shareholders, conversely, have no guarantee that the corporation will earn net income, so their investments are riskier. Consequently, shareholders demand a higher rate of return than do creditors, and this explains why return on equity should exceed return on assets. If return on assets is higher than return on equity, the company may be in trouble.

Investors and creditors use return on common shareholders' equity in much the same way as they use return on total assets—to compare companies. The higher the rate of return, the more successful the company. A 12-percent return on common shareholders' equity is considered quite good in most industries. Investors also compare a company's return on shareholders' equity to interest rates available in the market. If interest rates are almost as high as return on equity, many investors will lend their money to earn interest or deposit it in a bank rather than invest in common shares. They choose to forego the extra risk of investing in shares when the rate of return on equity is too low.

DID YOU GET IT?

To check your understanding of the material in this Learning Objective, complete these questions. The solutions appear on MyAccountingLab so you can check your progress.

12. The financial statements of Riley Resources Corp. reported the following:

	2010	2009
Net income	$ 80,000	$ 90,000
Interest expense	20,000	24,000
$6.00 Preferred shares (1,000 shares)	100,000	100,000
Common shares	200,000	200,000
Retained earnings	180,000	160,000
Total assets	840,000	760,000

Dividends were paid to preferred shareholders in 2009 and 2010. Dividends of $54,000 were declared and paid to common shareholders in 2010. Compute the return on assets for 2010.

13. Refer to the Riley Resources Corp. financial information in the previous question. Compute the return on common shareholders' equity for 2010.

14. Refer to the previous two questions. Compare the return on assets (ROA) and return on equity (ROE). Is there a favourable or unfavourable relationship between the two ratios?

The Impact on Share Capital of International Financial Reporting Standards (IFRS)

OBJECTIVE 6
Identify the impact on share capital of international financial reporting standards (IFRS)

The principles governing accounting for share capital are essentially the same under GAAP for private enterprises, as described in this chapter, and under IFRS. The primary difference in the two sets of accounting standards has to do with the required disclosure for share capital. Under IFRS, companies must make certain disclosures about *all* classes of shares authorized by the corporation, whether those classes of shares have been issued or not. The requirements under GAAP for private enterprises are less rigorous—they only require that disclosure be made for classes of shares that have actually been issued.

The remaining details of accounting for and reporting share capital under IFRS are highly technical in nature and beyond the scope of this text.

DID YOU GET IT?

To check your understanding of the material in this Learning Objective, complete this question. The solution appears on MyAccountingLab so you can check your progress.

15. How does accounting for share capital under IFRS differ from that required under GAAP for private enterprises as shown in this chapter?

DECISION GUIDELINES

Shareholders' Equity of a Corporation, Dividends, Share Values, and Evaluating Operations

Decision	Guidelines
Shareholders' Equity of a Corporation	
What are the two main segments of shareholders' equity?	• Contributed capital • Retained earnings
Which is more permanent, contributed capital or retained earnings?	Contributed capital is more permanent because corporations may use their retained earnings for distributing dividends to the shareholders.
How are contributed capital and retained earnings • Similar? • Different?	• Both represent the shareholders' equity (ownership) of the corporation. • Contributed capital and retained earnings come from different sources: a. Contributed capital comes from the corporation's shareholders, who invested in the company. b. Retained earnings comes from the corporation's customers and other sources of investment. It was earned by the company's profitable operations and successful investments.
What categories of contributed capital appear most often on corporate financial statements?	• Preferred shares • Common shares
Dividends	
When can a company declare a cash dividend?	• Must have enough retained earnings to declare the dividend. • Must have enough cash to pay the dividend.
What happens with a dividend?	• The corporation's board of directors declares the dividend. The dividend then becomes a liability of the corporation. • The date of record fixes who will receive the dividend. • Payment of the dividend occurs later.
Who receives the dividend?	• Preferred shareholders receive their dividends first. Preferred dividends have a specified rate. • Common shareholders receive the remainder.
Share Values	
How much would an investor pay for a share?	Its market value.
What is book value's role in decision making?	Sometimes used to help determine the market value of a share that is not traded on a stock exchange.
Evaluating Operations	
How can an investor evaluate the operations of a corporation?	Two measures that relate earnings to the amount that shareholders have invested are • Rate of return on assets • Rate of return on common shareholders' equity For a healthy company, return on common shareholders' equity should exceed return on assets.

Presented below are the accounts and related balances for Sault Outfitters Ltd. at September 30, 2010.

Common Shares,		Inventory	$ 85,000
50,000 shares authorized,		Property, Plant, and	
20,000 shares issued	$95,000	Equipment, net	204,000
Salary Payable	3,000	Accounts Receivable, net	25,000
Cash	15,000	Preferred Shares, $6.00, cumulative,	
Accounts Payable	20,000	10,000 shares authorized,	
Retained Earnings	80,000	2,000 shares issued	50,000
Organization Costs, net	1,000	Income Tax Payable	12,000
Long-term Note Payable	70,000		

Required

Name: Sault Outfitters Ltd.
Industry: Corporation with preferred and common shares
Fiscal Period: Year ended September 30, 2010

1. Prepare the classified balance sheet at September 30, 2010. Use the account format of the balance sheet.

2. Are the preferred shares cumulative or noncumulative? How can you tell?

3. What is the total amount of the annual preferred dividend?

4. Assume the common shares were all issued at the same time. What was the selling price per share?

5. Compute the book value per share of the preferred shares and the common shares. No prior-year preferred dividends are in arrears, and Sault Outfitters Ltd. has not declared the current-year dividend.

SOLUTIONS

1. The classified balance sheet must specify current assets and current liabilities. Make sure that Total assets + Total liabilities = Shareholders' equity.

SAULT OUTFITTERS LTD.
Balance Sheet
September 30, 2010

Assets		Liabilities	
Current:		**Current:**	
Cash	$ 15,000	Accounts payable	$ 20,000
Accounts receivable, net	25,000	Salary payable	3,000
Inventory	85,000	Income tax payable	12,000
Total current assets	125,000	Total current liabilities	35,000
Property, plant, and equipment, net	204,000	Long-term note payable	70,000
Intangible assets:		Total liabilities	105,000
Organization costs, net	1,000	**Shareholders' Equity**	
		Contributed capital:	
		Preferred shares, $6.00, cumulative,	
		10,000 shares authorized,	
		2,000 shares issued	50,000
		Common shares,	
		50,000 shares authorized,	
		20,000 shares issued	95,000
		Total contributed capital	145,000
		Retained earnings	80,000
		Total shareholders' equity	225,000
		Total liabilities and	
Total assets	$330,000	shareholders' equity	$330,000

2. The preferred shares are cumulative as is noted in their description.

3. Total annual preferred dividend: $12,000 (2,000 × $6.00)

4. Price per share: $4.75 ($95,000 ÷ 20,000 shares issued)

5. Book values per share of preferred and common shares:

Preferred	
Book value	$ 50,000
Cumulative dividend for current year (2,000 × $6.00)	12,000
Shareholders' equity allocated to preferred	$ 62,000
Book value per share ($62,000/2,000 shares)	$ 31.00

Common	
Total shareholders' equity	$225,000
Less: Shareholders' equity allocated to preferred	62,000
Shareholders' equity available	
for common shareholders	$163,000
Book value per share ($163,000 ÷ 20,000 shares)	$ 8.15

Side notes:

2. All features must be specified in the financial statements.

3. Details are given on the balance sheet.

4. Use the number of shares issued, *not* the number of shares authorized.

5. Preferred: Remember to *add* any dividends in arrears, including the current year's dividends if they were not paid.

5. Common: Book value per common share must exclude any amounts pertaining to preferred shares.

Summary

1. **Identify the characteristics of a corporation.** A corporation is a separate legal and business entity. Continuous life, the ease of raising large amounts of capital and transferring ownership, and limited liability are among the advantages of the corporate form of organization. An important disadvantage is a degree of double taxation: corporations pay income taxes, and shareholders pay tax on dividends. Shareholders are the owners of a corporation. They elect a board of directors, which elects a chairperson and appoints the officers to manage the business.

2. **Record the issuance of shares, and prepare the shareholders' equity section of a corporation's balance sheet.** Corporations may issue different classes of common and preferred shares. Convertible preferred shares may be exchanged for the corporation's common shares. The balance sheet carries the capital raised through share issuance under the heading Contributed Capital in the shareholders' equity section. Retained Earnings is listed last.

3. **Account for cash dividends.** Only when the board of directors declares a dividend does the corporation incur the liability to pay dividends. Preferred shares have priority over common shares as to dividends, which are usually stated as a dollar amount per share. In addition, preferred shares have a claim to dividends in arrears if they are cumulative.

4. **Use different share values in decision making.** A share's *market value* is the price for which a share may be bought or sold. *Book value*—the amount of shareholders' equity per share—is another value that may apply to shares.

5. **Evaluate a company's return on assets and return on shareholders' equity.** *Return on assets* and *return on shareholders' equity* are two standard measures of profitability. A healthy company's return on equity will exceed its return on assets.

6. **Identify the impact on share capital of international financial reporting standards (IFRS).** Accounting for share capital is essentially the same under GAAP for private enterprises, as described in this chapter, and IFRS. The primary difference in the two sets of accounting standards is that IFRS also requires that certain disclosures be made for classes of shares that have been authorized but not issued.

SELF-STUDY QUESTIONS

Test your understanding of the chapter by marking the best answer for each of the following questions:

1. Which characteristic of a corporation is most attractive to an owner (shareholder)? (*pp. 720–722*)
   a. Limited liability
   b. Double taxation
   c. Mutual agency
   d. All of the above

2. The person with the most power in a corporation often is the (*p. 722*)
   a. Accountant
   b. Chairperson of the board
   c. President
   d. Vice-president

3. The dollar amount of the shareholder investments in a corporation is called (*p. 724*)
   a. Outstanding shares
   b. Total shareholders' equity
   c. Contributed capital
   d. Retained earnings

4. The arbitrary value assigned to a share by the board of directors is called (*p. 728*)
   a. Market value
   b. Liquidation value
   c. Book value
   d. Stated value

5. Shares issued by a corporation incorporated under the *Canada Business Corporations Act* normally have (*p. 728*)
   a. No par value
   b. A par value set by management
   c. A par value set by the government
   d. A par value of $10.00

6. Magnum Corporation receives a building for 1,000 common shares. The building's book value is $385,000 and its current market value is $640,000. This transaction increases Magnum's share capital by (*p. 729*)
   a. $0 because the corporation received no cash
   b. $100,000
   c. $385,000
   d. $640,000

7. Organization costs is classified as a(n) (*pp. 732–733*)
   a. Operating expense
   b. Current asset
   c. Contra item in shareholders' equity
   d. None of the above

8. Trade Days Inc. has 10,000 $3.50 cumulative preferred shares and 100,000 common shares issued and outstanding. Two years' preferred dividends are in arrears.

Trade Days Inc. declares a cash dividend large enough to pay the preferred dividends in arrears, the preferred dividend for the current period, and a $1.50 dividend per common share. What is the total amount of the dividend? (p. 737)

a. $255,000
b. $220,000
c. $150,000
d. $105,000

9. The preferred shares of Trade Days Inc. in the preceding question were issued at $55.00 per share. Each preferred share can be converted into 10 common shares. The entry to record the conversion of these preferred shares into common is (p. 731)

a. Cash   550,000
   Preferred Shares   500,000
   Common Shares   50,000

b. Preferred Shares   500,000
   Cash   50,000
   Common Shares   550,000

c. Preferred Shares   550,000
   Common Shares   550,000

d. Common Shares   550,000
   Preferred Shares   550,000

10. When an investor is buying shares as an investment, the value of most direct concern is (p. 738)

a. Par value
b. Market value
c. Liquidation value
d. Book value

ACCOUNTING VOCABULARY

Articles of incorporation   (p. 720)
Authorization of shares   (p. 722)
Board of directors   (p. 722)
Book value   (p. 739)
Bylaws   (p. 722)
Chairperson (of board)   (p. 722)
Common shares   (p. 724)
Contributed capital   (p. 724)
Convertible preferred shares   (p. 731)
Cumulative preferred shares   (p. 737)
Deficit   (p. 725)
Dividends   (p. 725)
Double taxation   (p. 721)
Limited liability   (p. 721)
Market value   (p. 738)
No-par-value shares   (p. 728)

Organization costs   (p. 733)
Outstanding shares   (p. 723)
Preferred shares   (p. 729)
President   (p. 722)
Rate of return on common shareholders' equity   (p. 741)
Rate of return on total assets   (p. 740)
Retained earnings   (p. 724)
Return on assets (ROA)   (p. 740)
Return on equity (ROE)   (p. 741)
Shareholder   (p. 720)
Shareholders' equity   (p. 724)
Shares   (p. 720)
Stated value   (p. 728)
Stock   (p. 720)

SIMILAR ACCOUNTING TERMS

Liquidation value   Redemption value; Call value; Call price
Market value   Market price
Share capital   Capital stock; Stated capital
Shareholder   Stockholder

Assignment Material

QUESTIONS

1. Identify the characteristics of a corporation.

2. Explain how corporate earnings are subject to a degree of double taxation.

3. Briefly outline the steps in the organization of a corporation.

4. Compare the characteristics of a partnership and a corporation.

5. Name the five rights of a common shareholder. Are preferred shares automatically nonvoting?

6. Which event increases the assets of the corporation: authorization of shares or issuance of shares? Explain.

7. Suppose Saskinc Ltd. issued 1,200 shares of its $4.50 preferred shares for $100.00 per share. By how much would this transaction increase the company's contributed capital? By how much would it increase retained earnings? By how much would it increase annual cash dividend payments?

8. Black Bear Inc. issued 150 common shares for $8.00 per share and 250 shares for $9.50 per share. What would be the journal entry to record the combined issue?

9. How does issuance of 1,500 common shares for land and a building, together worth $200,000, affect contributed capital?

10. Journalize the incorporation of the Saxon & Cowle partnership.

11. Rank the following accounts in the order in which they would appear on the balance sheet: Common Shares, Organization Costs, Preferred Shares, Retained Earnings, Dividends Payable. Also, give each account's balance-sheet classification.

12. What type of account is Organization Costs? Briefly describe how to account for organization costs.

13. Briefly discuss the three important dates for a dividend.

14. Banner Inc. has 2,500 shares of its $1.75 preferred shares outstanding. Dividends for 2008 and 2009 are in arrears. Assume that Banner Inc. declares total dividends of $25,000 at the end of 2010. Show how to allocate the dividends to preferred and common (a) if preferred is cumulative, and (b) if preferred is noncumulative.

15. As a preferred shareholder, would you rather own cumulative or noncumulative preferred? If all other factors are the same, would the corporation rather issue cumulative or noncumulative preferred shares? Give your reasons.

16. How are cumulative preferred dividends in arrears reported in the financial statements? When do dividends become a liability of the corporation?

17. Distinguish between the market value of shares and the book value of shares. Which is more important to investors?

18. How is book value per common share computed when the company has both preferred shares and common shares outstanding?

19. Why should a healthy company's rate of return on shareholders' equity exceed its rate of return on total assets?

STARTERS

Authority structure in a corporation
①

Starter 13–1 Answer these questions about corporations.

1. Who is the most powerful person in the corporation?
2. What group holds the ultimate power in a corporation?
3. Who is in charge of day-to-day operations?
4. Who is in charge of accounting?

The balance sheets of a corporation and a proprietorship
①

Starter 13–2 How does a proprietorship's balance sheet differ from a corporation's balance sheet? How are the two balance sheets similar?

Issuing shares
②

Starter 13–3 Lowell Corporation has two classes of shares: common and preferred. Journalize Lowell's issuance of

a. 1,000 common shares for $50.00 per share

b. 1,000 preferred shares for a total of $48,000

Explanations are not required.

Starter 13-4 Slott Inc. issued all its shares during 2010 and reported the following on its balance sheet at December 31, 2010:

Issuing shares and interpreting shareholders' equity

②

Common shares	
Authorized: 5,000 shares	
Issued: 3,000 shares	$ 9,200
Retained earnings	49,000

Journalize the company's issuance of the shares for cash.

Starter 13-5 At December 31, 2010, KD Corporation reported the following on its comparative balance sheet, which included 2009 amounts for comparison:

Issuing shares and analyzing retained earnings

②

1. Increased $11,000

	December 31, 2010	2009
Common shares		
Authorized: 10,000 shares		
Issued: 3,500 shares in 2010	$90,000	
3,490 shares in 2009		$79,000
Retained earnings	49,000	46,800

1. How much did KD Corporation's total contributed capital increase during 2010? What caused total contributed capital to increase? How can you tell?

2. Assuming no dividends were declared during 2010, did KD Corporation have a profit or a loss for 2010? How can you tell?

Starter 13-6 Apex Corporation reported the following accounts (a partial list):

Preparing the shareholders' equity section of a balance sheet

②

Total shareholder's equity $36,500

Cost of Goods Sold	$29,400	Accounts Payable	$3,000	
Common Shares,		Retained Earnings	8,000	
40,000 shares issued	28,500	Unearned Revenue	2,600	
Cash	12,000			
Long-term Note Payable	3,800	Total assets	?	

Prepare the shareholders' equity section of the Apex balance sheet.

Starter 13-7 Use the Apex Corporation data in Starter 13-6 to compute Apex's

a. Total liabilities

b. Total assets

Using shareholders' equity data

②

b. Total assets $45,900

Starter 13-8 Mowli Corporation earned net income of $85,000 during the year ended December 31, 2009. On December 15, Mowli Corporation declared the annual cash dividend on its 5,000 $5.00 preferred shares and a $0.60 per share cash dividend on its 50,000 common shares. Mowli Corporation then paid the dividends on January 4, 2010.

Accounting for cash dividends

③

  Journalize for Mowli Corporation:

a. Declaring the cash dividends on December 15, 2009

b. Paying the cash dividends on January 4, 2010

Starter 13-9 Golda Inc. has the following shareholders' equity:

Dividing cash dividends between preferred and common shares

③

3. Preferred $3,000
Common $12,000

Preferred shares, $0.025, cumulative, liquidating value $0.50, 50,000 shares authorized, 40,000 shares issued	$ 20,000
Common shares, 1,000,000 shares authorized and issued	200,000
Retained earnings	130,000
Total shareholders' equity	$350,000

Answer these questions about Golda's dividends:

1. Are Golda Inc.'s preferred shares cumulative or noncumulative? How can you tell?

2. Suppose Golda Inc. declares cash dividends of $15,000 for 2010. How much of the dividends goes to preferred shares? How much goes to common shares?

3. Suppose Golda Inc. did not pay the preferred dividend in 2008 and 2009. In 2010, the company declares cash dividends of $15,000. How much of the dividends goes to preferred shares? How much goes to common shares?

Book value per common share

(4)

Book value per share $0.305

Computing return on assets and return on equity

(5)

ROA 13.9%

Starter 13–10 Refer to the shareholders' equity information of Golda Inc. in Starter 13–9. Golda Inc. has not declared preferred dividends for five years (including the current year). Compute the book value per share of Golda Inc.'s common shares.

Starter 13–11 Township Corp.'s 2010 financial statements reported the following items—with 2009 figures given for comparison.

	2010	2009
Balance sheet		
Total assets...	$49,000	$44,800
Total liabilities...	$25,400	$22,000
Total shareholders' equity (all common).................................	23,600	22,800
Total liabilities and equity..	$49,000	$44,800
Income statement		
Net sales	$39,130	
Cost of goods sold...	14,210	
Gross margin..	24,920	
Selling and administrative expenses......................................	14,000	
Interest expense	400	
All other expenses, net	4,420	
Net income	$ 6,100	

Compute Township Corp.'s rate of return on total assets and rate of return on common shareholders' equity for 2010. Do these rates of return look high or low?

EXERCISES

Exercise 13–1

Characteristics of a corporation

(1)

Suppose you are forming a business and you need some outside money from other investors. Assume you have decided to organize the business as a corporation that will issue shares to raise the needed funds. Briefly discuss your most important reason for organizing as a corporation rather than as a partnership. If you had decided to organize as a partnership, what would be your most important reason for not organizing as a corporation?

Exercise 13–2

Organizing a corporation

(1)

David Johnston and Lisa Jacobs are opening a decorating business to be named D&L Decor Ltd. They need outside capital, so they plan to organize the business as a corporation. Because your office is in the same building, they come to you for advice. Write a memorandum informing them of the steps in forming a corporation. Identify specific documents used in this process, and name the different parties involved in the ownership and management of a corporation.

Exercise 13–3

Issuing shares

(2)

2. Contributed capital $127,500

East Ltd. made the following share issuance transactions:

Jan. 19   Issued 4,000 common shares for cash of $11.00 per share.
Feb. 3   Sold 1,000 $1.50 Class A preferred shares for $14,000 cash.
   11   Received inventory valued at $27,000 and equipment with market value of $16,500 for 5,800 common shares.
   15   Issued 2,000 $1.00 Class B preferred shares for $13.00 per share.

Required

1. Journalize the transactions. Explanations are not required.
2. How much contributed capital did these transactions generate for East Ltd?

Exercise 13–4

Murphy Supplies Ltd. imports farm equipment. The corporation issues 10,000 common shares for $15.00 per share. Record issuance of the shares.

Recording issuance of common shares

(2)

Exercise 13–5

This exercise shows the similarity and the difference between two ways for Keifer Equipment Ltd. to acquire property, plant, and equipment.

Issuing shares to finance the purchase of assets

(2)

Case A—Issue shares and buy the assets in separate transactions:

Keifer Equipment Ltd. issued 7,000 common shares for cash of $1,260,000. In a separate transaction, Keifer then used the cash to purchase an office building for $900,000 and equipment for $360,000. Journalize the two transactions.

Case B—Issue shares to acquire the assets:

Keifer Equipment Ltd. issued 7,000 common shares to acquire an office building valued at $900,000 and equipment worth $360,000. Journalize this transaction.

Compare the balances in all accounts after making both sets of entries. Are the account balances similar or different?

Exercise 13–6

The articles of incorporation for Mid-way Consulting Inc. authorize the company to issue 500,000 $4 preferred shares and 1,000,000 common shares. During its first year of operations, Mid-way Consulting Inc. completed the following selected transactions:

Issuing shares and preparing the shareholders' equity section of the balance sheet

(2)

2. Total shareholders' equity $440,000

2010

Jan. 4	Issued 5,000 common shares to the consultants who organized the corporation, receiving cash of $120,000.
13	Issued 500 preferred shares for cash of $50,000.
14	Issued 4,000 common shares in exchange for land valued at $120,000.
Dec. 31	Earned a profit for the fiscal year and closed the $150,000 net income into Retained Earnings.

Required

1. Record the transactions in the general journal.
2. Prepare the shareholders' equity section of the Mid-way Consulting Inc. balance sheet at December 31, 2010.

Exercise 13–7

Yippee Corp. has recently organized. The company issued common shares to a lawyer who provided legal services worth $7,500 to help organize the corporation. It issued common shares to another person in exchange for his patent with a market value of $50,000. In addition, Yippee Corp. received cash both for 2,500 of its $1.50 preferred shares at $20.00 per share and for 35,000 of its common shares at $12.50 per share. Without making journal entries, determine the total contributed capital created by these transactions.

Contributed capital for a corporation

(2)

Total contributed capital $545,000

Exercise 13–8

The Coquitlam Adanacs are a semi-professional baseball team that has been operated as a partnership by Sheila Mason and Tom Neilson. In addition to their management responsibilities, Neilson also plays for the team and Mason operates the concession. Journalize the following transactions in the first month of operation as a corporation:

Incorporating a partnership

(2)

Jun. 14	The incorporators paid legal fees of $2,000 and other fees of $500 to obtain articles of incorporation.
14	Issued 4,000 common shares to Mason and 3,000 common shares to Neilson. Mason's Capital balance on the partnership books was $40,000, and Neilson's Capital balance was $30,000.

Exercise 13–9

Shareholders' equity section
of a balance sheet

(2)

2. Total shareholders' equity
$250,000

The articles of incorporation for Lipton Technology Inc. authorize the issuance of 100,000 preferred shares and 250,000 common shares. During a two-month period, Lipton Technology Inc. completed these share-issuance transactions:

Mar. 23	Issued 12,000 common shares for cash of $10.00 per share.
Apr. 12	Received inventory valued at $40,000 and equipment with a market value of $10,000 for 5,000 common shares.
17	Issued 1,500 $2.25 preferred shares. The issue price was cash of $10.00 per share.

Required

1. Journalize the transactions, with explanations.
2. Prepare the shareholders' equity section of the Lipton Technology Inc. balance sheet for the transactions given in this exercise. Retained Earnings has a balance of $65,000.

Exercise 13–10

Excel Spreadsheet Template

Shareholders' equity section
of a balance sheet

(2)

Total shareholders' equity
$277,500

Sunnee Corporation has the following selected account balances at June 30, 2010. Prepare the shareholders' equity section of the company's balance sheet.

Common Shares,			Inventory...	$70,000
500,000 shares authorized,			Machinery and Equipment	82,500
100,000 shares issued	$100,000		Preferred Shares, $1.25,	
Accumulated Amortization—			100,000 shares authorized,	
Machinery and Equipment	32,500		10,000 shares issued..............	87,500
Retained Earnings	90,000		Organization Costs, net	2,500
Cost of Goods Sold.....................	42,500			

Exercise 13–11

Dividing cash dividends between
preferred and common shares

(3)

4. Common $35,000

Refer to the shareholders' equity of Envoy Corporation in Exhibit 13–6, page 733. Answer these questions about Envoy's dividends.

1. How much in dividends must Envoy Corporation declare each year before the common shareholders receive cash dividends for the year?
2. Suppose Envoy Corporation declares cash dividends of $20,000 for 2010. How much of the dividends go to preferred shareholders? How much goes to common shareholders?
3. Are Envoy Corporation's preferred shares cumulative or noncumulative? How can you tell?
4. Suppose Envoy Corporation did not pay the preferred dividend in 2008 and 2009. In 2010, Envoy declares cash dividends of $40,000. How much of the dividends go to preferred? How much goes to common?

Exercise 13–12

Computing dividends on
preferred and common shares

(3)

Common gets $21,000

The following elements of shareholders' equity are adapted from the balance sheet of Barclay Marketing Ltd:

Shareholders' Equity
Preferred shares, $0.10, cumulative, 100,000 shares authorized, 50,000 shares issued .... $ 50,000
Common shares, 2,000,000 shares authorized, 900,000 shares issued .. 1,500,000

The company has paid all dividends through 2008.

Required Compute the dividends paid to preferred shareholders and to common shareholders for 2009 and 2010 if total dividends are $0 in 2009 and $31,000 in 2010. Round your answers to the nearest dollar.

Exercise 13–13

The balance sheet of Nature's Design Technology Inc. reported the following:

Cumulative preferred shares; 300 shares issued, liquidation value $15,000...	$ 15,000
Common shares; 25,000 shares issued...	187,500

Assume that Nature's Design had paid preferred dividends for the current year and all prior years (no dividends in arrears). Retained earnings was $115,000.

Required Compute the book value per share of the preferred shares and the common shares.

Book value per share of preferred and common shares

④

Common $12.10 per share

Exercise 13–14

Refer to Exercise 13–13. Compute the book value per share of the preferred shares and the common shares, assuming that three years of preferred dividends (including dividends for the current year) are in arrears. Assume the preferred shares are cumulative and their dividend rate is $7.00 per share.

Book value per share of preferred and common shares; preferred dividends in arrears

③ ④

Preferred $71.00 per share; common $11.85 per share

Exercise 13–15

Waldy Equipment Inc. reported the figures shown below for 2010 and 2009.

Evaluating profitability

⑤

ROA 8.45%

	2010	2009
Income statement:		
Interest expense	$ 5,200	$ 3,700
Net income	3,250	5,250
Balance sheet:		
Total assets	105,000	95,000
Preferred shares, $1.15, 200 shares issued and outstanding.........................	1,000	1,000
Common shareholders' equity	46,500	43,000
Total shareholders' equity......................................	47,500	44,000

Compute the rate of return on total assets (ROA) and the rate of return on common share-holders' equity (ROE) for 2010. Do these rates of return suggest strength or weakness? Give your reasons.

SERIAL EXERCISE

This exercise continues the Haupt Consulting situation from Chapter 12.

Exercise 13–16

Carl Haupt has been running Haupt Consulting as a proprietorship but is planning to expand operations in the near future. In Chapter 12, Carl Haupt had considered taking on a partner, but decided not to form a partnership. To raise cash for future expansion, Carl Haupt has now decided to incorporate and create Haupt Consulting Corporation. He has gone through all the legal steps to incorporate his business; as of February 1, 2011, Haupt Consulting Corporation is authorized to issue an unlimited number of common shares and 50,000 $2.00 preferred shares.

The Haupt Consulting January 31, 2011, balance sheet appears below. All amounts in the accounting records reflect current market value.

Incorporation of a going business and corporate transactions

① ②

Haupt Consulting	
Assets	
Cash..	$11,700
Accounts receivable...	5,500
Inventory...	2,713
Supplies...	100
Prepaid rent...	2,000
Equipment...	2,000
Accumulated amortization—equipment.............................	(66)
Furniture..	3,600
Accumulated amortization—furniture................................	(120)
Total assets...	$27,427
Liabilities and Capital	
Accounts payable...	$ 8,200
Salary payable...	1,400
Unearned service revenue...	600
Carl Haupt, capital..	17,227
Total liabilities and capital...	$27,427

Required

1. Carl Haupt decides to issue 20,000 common shares to himself to maintain control of the company. Create the journal entry to record the incorporation of the business on February 1, 2011.

2. To raise $50,000 cash, Haupt Consulting Corporation issued 1,000 of the preferred shares for $50.00 per share on February 1, 2011. Journalize this transaction.

3. Haupt Consulting Corporation incurred $1,500 in legal fees and incorporation fees to organize the corporation under the *Canada Business Corporations Act* in Ontario. Prepare the journal entry for these organization costs.

CHALLENGE EXERCISE

Exercise 13–17

Accounting for shareholders' equity transactions
② ③

Mussalem Motors Inc. reported these comparative shareholders' equity data:

	December 31,	
	2010	**2009**
Common shares..	$1,500,000	$ 300,000
Retained earnings..	2,308,000	1,538,000

During 2010, Mussalem Motors Inc. completed these transactions and events:

a. Net income, $1,430,000.

b. Cash dividends, $660,000.

c. Issuance of common shares for cash, 3,000 shares at $50.00 per share.

d. Issuance of common shares to purchase another company (Mussalem Motors debited the Investments account), 15,000 shares at $70.00 per share.

Required   Without making journal entries, show how Mussalem Motors Inc.'s 2010 transactions and events accounted for the changes in the shareholders' equity accounts. For each shareholders' equity account, start with the December 31, 2009 balance and work toward the balance at December 31, 2010.

BEYOND THE NUMBERS

Beyond the Numbers 13–1

Answering the following questions will enhance your understanding of the shareholders' equity of corporations.

Characteristics of corporations' shareholders' equity

 ② ④

1. Why do you think contributed capital and retained earnings are shown separately in the shareholders' equity section?

2. Vivien Chan, major shareholder of VC Inc., proposes to sell some land she owns to the company for common shares in VC Inc. What problem does VC Inc. face in recording the transaction?

3. Preferred shares generally have preference over common shares for dividends and on liquidation. Why would investors buy common shares when preferred shares are available?

4. If you owned 100 shares of Canadian Tire Corporation, Limited and someone offered to buy the shares for their book value, would you accept the offer? Why or why not?

5. What is a convertible preferred share? Why would an investor exercise the conversion privilege?

ETHICAL ISSUE

Note: This case is based on a real situation.

Jason Wertz paid $50,000 for a franchise that entitled him to market Success software programs in the countries of the European Union. Wertz intended to sell individual franchises for the major language groups of Western Europe—German, French, English, Spanish, and Italian. Naturally, investors considering buying a franchise from Wertz asked to see the financial statements of his business.

Believing the value of the franchise to be greater than $50,000, Wertz sought to capitalize his own franchise at $375,000. The law firm of St. Charles and LaDue helped Wertz form a corporation authorized to issue 500,000 common shares. Lawyers suggested the following chain of transactions:

1. A third party borrows $375,000 and purchases the franchise from Wertz.

2. Wertz pays the corporation $375,000 to acquire all its shares.

3. The corporation buys the franchise from the third party, who repays the loan.

In the final analysis, the third party is debt-free and out of the picture. Wertz owns all the corporation's shares, and the corporation owns the franchise. The corporation balance sheet lists a franchise acquired at a cost of $375,000. This balance sheet is Wertz's most valuable marketing tool.

Required

1. What is unethical about this situation?

2. Who can be harmed? How can they be harmed? What role does accounting play?

PROBLEMS (GROUP A)

MyAccountingLab All questions in this section appear in MyAccountingLab.

Problem 13–1A

Mark Mathews and Karen Willamas are opening a software company. They have developed a new and effective software to manage small business operations. Their most fundamental decision is how to organize the business. Mathews thinks the partnership form is best. Willamas favours the corporate form of organization. They seek your advice.

Organizing a corporation

①

Required   Write a memo to Mathews and Willamas to make them aware of the advantages and the disadvantages of organizing the business as a corporation. Use the following format for your memo:

Date:	_____
To:	Mark Mathews and Karen Willamas
From:	Student Name
Subject:	Advantages and disadvantages of the corporate form of business organization

Problem 13–2A

Journalizing corporation transactions and preparing the shareholders' equity section of the balance sheet

(2)

2. Total shareholders' equity
$667,500

The partnership of Nuan Zhang and Jen Phuah needed additional capital to expand into new markets, so the business incorporated as A-1 Services Inc. The articles of incorporation under the *Canada Business Corporations Act* authorize A-1 Services Inc. to issue 500,000 $2.50 preferred shares and 2,000,000 common shares. In its first year, A-1 Services Inc. completed the following transactions:

2010

Aug. 2		Paid incorporation fees of $6,000 and paid legal fees of $16,000 to organize as a corporation.
	2	Issued 20,000 common shares to Zhang and 25,000 common shares to Phuah in return for the net assets of the partnership. Zhang's Capital balance on the partnership books was $150,000, and Phuah's Capital balance was $187,500.
Dec. 10		Issued 1,000 preferred shares to acquire a computer system with a market value of $80,000.
	16	Issued 15,000 common shares for cash of $120,000.

Required

1. Record the transactions in the general journal.

2. Prepare the shareholders' equity section of the A-1 Services Inc. balance sheet at December 31, 2010. The ending balance in Retained Earnings is $130,000.

Problem 13–3A

Issuing shares and preparing the shareholders' equity section of the balance sheet

(2)

5. Total shareholders' equity
$521,250

Riverbend Inc. was organized in 2009. At December 31, 2009, Riverbend Inc.'s balance sheet reported the following shareholders' equity:

Preferred shares, $4.00, 200,000 shares authorized, none issued..................	$ 0
Common shares, 1,000,000 shares authorized, 150,000 shares issued	225,000
Retained earnings (Deficit)	(50,000)
Total shareholders' equity	$175,000

Required

Answer the following questions, making journal entries as needed.

1. What does the $4.00 mean for the preferred shares? If Riverbend Inc. issues 2,000 preferred shares, how much in cash dividends will it expect to pay?

2. At what average price per share did Riverbend Inc. issue the common shares during 2009?

3. Were first-year operations profitable? Give your reason.

4. During 2010, the company completed the following selected transactions:
   a. Issued for cash 1,500 preferred shares at $25.00 per share.
   b. Issued for cash 5,000 common shares at a price of $1.75 per share.
   c. Issued 100,000 common shares to acquire a building valued at $200,000.
   d. Net income for the year was $100,000, and the company declared no dividends. Make the closing entry for net income.
   Journalize each transaction. Explanations are not required.

5. Prepare the shareholders' equity section of the Riverbend Inc. balance sheet at December 31, 2010.

Problem 13–4A

The following summaries for Play-time Equipment Ltd. and Lil-tikes Products Inc. provide the information needed to prepare the shareholders' equity section of each company's balance sheet. The two companies are independent.

Shareholders' equity section of the balance sheet

Play-time Equipment Ltd. total shareholders' equity $590,000

Play-time Equipment Ltd. This company is authorized to issue 200,000 common shares. All the shares were issued at $3.00 per share. The company incurred a net loss of $75,000 in 2007 (its first year of operations) and a net loss of $30,000 in 2008. It earned net incomes of $35,000 in 2009 and $60,000 in 2010. The company declared no dividends during the four-year period.

Lil-tikes Products Inc. Lil-tikes Products Inc.'s articles of incorporation authorize the company to issue 200,000 cumulative preferred shares and 1,000,000 common shares. Lil-tikes Products Inc. issued 2,000 preferred shares at $12.50 per share. It issued 100,000 common shares for $300,000. The company's Retained Earnings balance at the beginning of 2010 was $75,000. Net income for 2010 was $50,000, and the company declared the specified preferred share dividend for 2010. Preferred share dividends for 2009 were in arrears. The preferred dividend was $1.10 per share per year.

Required

For each company, prepare the shareholders' equity section of its balance sheet at December 31, 2010. Show the computation of all amounts. Entries are not required.

Problem 13–5A

Sefton Limited reported the following information in its December 31, 2009 annual report:

Analyzing the shareholders' equity of a corporation

4. Dividends Payable— Common $25,000

Shareholders' Equity	
Preferred shares, $2.75, cumulative;	
600,000 shares authorized; 100,000 shares issued	$ 500,000
Common shares, unlimited number of shares	
authorized, 1,300,000 shares issued	1,850,000
Retained earnings...	5,950,000
Total shareholders' equity	$8,300,000

Required

1. Identify the different issues of shares that Sefton Limited has outstanding.
2. What is the average issue price per preferred share?
3. Make two summary journal entries to record issuance of all the Sefton shares for cash. Explanations are not required.
4. Assume no preferred dividends are in arrears. Journalize the declaration of a $300,000 dividend at June 30, 2010. Use separate Dividends Payable accounts for preferred and common shares. An explanation is not required.

Problem 13–6A

The following accounts and related balances of Etse Manufacturing Inc. are arranged in no particular order.

Preparing a corporation balance sheet; measuring profitability

1. Total assets, Dec. 31, 2010, $659,000

Accounts Payable....................	$ 36,000	Accrued liabilities.....................	$ 23,000
Retained Earnings..................	?	Long-term Note Payable	100,500
Common Shares,		Accounts Receivable, net.........	100,000
100,000 shares		Preferred Shares, $0.15	
authorized,		25,000 shares authorized,	
33,000 shares issued............	165,000	6,000 shares issued..............	30,000
Dividends Payable..................	4,500	Cash...	35,000
Total assets, Dec. 31, 2009	567,500	Inventory	190,500
Net income.............................	40,750	Property, Plant, and	
Common Shareholders'		Equipment, net....................	281,000
Equity, Dec. 31, 2009..........	520,000	Prepaid Expenses	15,500
Interest Expense	10,850	Patent, net...............................	37,000

Required

1. Prepare the company's classified balance sheet in the report format at December 31, 2010.

2. Compute the rate of return on total assets and the rate of return on common shareholders' equity for the year ended December 31, 2010.

3. Do these rates of return suggest strength or weakness? Give your reason.

Problem 13–7A

Everest Corporation has 40,000 $0.50 preferred shares and 600,000 common shares issued and outstanding. During a three-year period, Everest Corporation declared and paid cash dividends as follows: 2007, $0; 2008, $124,000; and 2009, $240,000.

Required

1. Compute the total dividends to preferred shares and common shares for each of the three years if

   a. Preferred shares are noncumulative.
   b. Preferred shares are cumulative.

2. For requirement 1b, record the declaration of the 2009 dividends on December 22, 2009 and the payment of the dividends on January 12, 2010.

Problem 13–8A

The balance sheet of Tulameen Systems Inc. reported the following:

Shareholders' Equity	
Cumulative convertible preferred shares; authorized 25,000 shares	$200,000
Common shares, authorized 50,000 shares; issued 44,000 shares	528,000
Retained earnings	168,000
Total shareholders' equity...	$896,000

Notes to the financial statements indicate that 10,000 $1.20 preferred shares were issued and outstanding. The preferred shares have a liquidation value of $24.00 per share. Preferred dividends are in arrears for two years, including the current year. On the balance sheet date, the market value of the Tulameen Systems Inc. common shares was $28.00 per share.

Required

1. Are the preferred shares cumulative or noncumulative? How can you tell?

2. What is the total contributed capital of the company?

3. What is the total market value of the common shares?

4. Compute the book value per share of the preferred shares and of the common shares.

Problem 13–9A

Tony Wong and Patrick Wu, partners in a small tools business with capital account balances of $60,000 and $95,000, respectively, were considering incorporating and establishing a new manufacturing plant in Brampton. The following transactions then took place:

2008
Jan. 2   Wong and Wu incorporated their partnership into WW Tools Inc. with an authorization to issue 200,000 $0.75 convertible preferred shares and 1,000,000 common shares. Wong received 60,000 common shares and Wu received 95,000 common shares.

     17   Paid $2,500 and gave 4,000 common shares to the corporation's legal firm for incorporating the business. The total legal fee was $8,500.

Mar. 7   Sold 5,000 preferred shares for $12,500. The preferred shares are convertible on the basis of 3 common shares for each preferred share.

Dec. 31   The company reported net income after taxes of $75,000 for the year, and then closed the Income Summary account.

2009

Feb. 14 Declared cash dividends of $17,500, payable on April 11, 2009, to the shareholders of record on March 1, 2009. Indicate the amount that would be payable to the preferred shareholders and to the common shareholders.

Apr. 11 Paid the cash dividend declared on February 14, 2009.

Sept. 7 The preferred shareholders converted 1,000 preferred shares into common shares.

Dec. 31 The company reported net income after taxes of $82,000 for the year, and then closed the Income Summary account.

2010

Dec. 16 Declared cash dividends of $40,000, payable on January 10, 2011, to the shareholders of record on December 31, 2010. Indicate the amount that would be payable to the preferred shareholders and to the common shareholders.

31 The company reported net income after taxes of $100,000 for the year, and then closed the Income Summary account.

Required

1. Record the transactions in the general journal.
2. Prepare the shareholders' equity section of the balance sheet as of the close of business on December 31, 2010.

Problem 13–10A

At January 1, 2008, Red Deer Manufacturing Ltd.'s balance sheet reported the following shareholders' equity:

Shareholders' Equity	
Contributed capital:	
Preferred shares, $0.75, cumulative (2 years in arrears), liquidation price of $25, 100,000 shares authorized, 30,000 shares issued	$ 200,000
Common shares,	
Class A, 20,000 shares authorized and issued	125,000
Class B, unlimited number of shares authorized,	
150,000 shares issued	1,500,000
Total contributed capital	1,825,000
Retained earnings	300,000
Total shareholders' equity	$2,125,000

Recording the issuance of shares; allocating cash dividends; preparing the liability and shareholders' equity sections of the balance sheet

② ③

2. Total shareholders' equity $2,415,000

The company had the following transactions on the dates indicated:

2008

Dec. 1 The company declared dividends of $175,000, payable on January 15, 2009, to the shareholders of record on December 31, 2008. Indicate the amount that would be payable to the preferred shareholders and to the common shareholders. The dividend rate for Class A and Class B shares is the same.

31 The company reported net income after taxes of $60,000 for the year and then closed the Income Summary account.

2009

Jan. 7 The company sold 10,000 preferred shares at $22.50 per share.

15 The company paid the dividend declared on December 1, 2008.

Feb. 14 The company sold 15,000 Class B common shares at $11.00 per share.

Dec. 2 The company declared dividends of $90,000, payable on January 15, 2010, to the shareholders of record on December 31, 2009. Indicate the amount that would be payable to the preferred shareholders and to the common shareholders.

31 The company reported net income after taxes of $105,000 and then closed the Income Summary account.

2010

Jan. 15 Paid the dividend declared on December 2, 2009.

Required

1. Record the transactions in the general journal.

2. Prepare the liability and shareholders' equity sections of the balance sheet as of the close of business on December 31, 2009.

3. Calculate the book value per share of the preferred shares and of the common shares (Class A and Class B combined) on December 31, 2009.

4. What was the average price at which the Class A common shares were issued?

PROBLEMS (GROUP B)

MyAccountingLab All questions in this section appear in MyAccountingLab.

Problem 13–1B

Organizing a corporation

①

Jack Rudd and Pam Kines are opening an office supply store. The area where the store is located is growing, and no competitors are located in the immediate vicinity. Their most fundamental decision is how to organize the business. Rudd thinks the partnership form is best. Kines favours the corporate form of organization. They seek your advice.

Required

Write a memo to Rudd and Kines to make them aware of the advantages and disadvantages of organizing the business as a corporation. Use the following format for your memo:

Date:	_____
To:	Jack Rudd and Pam Kines
From:	[Student Name]
Subject:	Advantages and disadvantages of the corporate form of business organization

Problem 13–2B

Journalizing corporation transactions and preparing the shareholders' equity section of the balance sheet

②

The articles of incorporation from the federal government authorize Intuite Solutions Ltd. to issue 100,000 $2.00 preferred shares and 250,000 common shares. In its first year, Intuite Solutions Ltd. completed the following selected transactions:

2010

Jan. 2   Paid incorporation costs of $1,500 and legal fees of $6,000 to organize as a corporation.

     6   Issued 20,000 common shares for equipment with a market value of $175,000.

   12   Issued 100 preferred shares to acquire software with a market value of $17,500.

   22   Issued 5,000 common shares for $6.00 cash per share.

Required

1. Record the transactions in the general journal.

2. Prepare the shareholders' equity section of the Intuite Solutions Ltd. balance sheet at December 31, 2010. The ending Retained Earnings balance is $50,000.

Problem 13–3B

Sloboda Corporation was organized in 2009. At December 31, 2009, Sloboda Corporation's balance sheet reported the following shareholders' equity:

Issuing shares and preparing the shareholders' equity section of the balance sheet

Preferred shares, $0.20, 50,000 shares authorized, none issued	$ 0
Common shares, 100,000 shares authorized, 10,000 shares issued	87,500
Retained earnings (Deficit)	(20,000)
Total shareholders' equity	$67,500

Required

1. What does the $0.20 mean for the preferred shares? If Sloboda Corporation issued 2,000 preferred shares, how much in cash dividends will Sloboda Corporation expect to pay per year?

2. At what average price per share did Sloboda Corporation issue the common shares?

3. Were first-year operations profitable? Give your reason.

4. During 2010, the company completed the following selected transactions. Journalize each transaction. Explanations are not required.

   a. Issued for cash 10,000 preferred shares at $2.50 per share.
   b. Issued for cash 1,000 common shares at a price of $8.00 per share.
   c. Issued 25,000 common shares to acquire a building valued at $225,000.
   d. Net income for the year was $62,500, and the company declared no dividends. Make the closing entry for net income.

5. Prepare the shareholders' equity section of the Sloboda Corporation balance sheet at December 31, 2010.

Problem 13–4B

Shareholders' equity information is given for AGI Inc. and Canfer Corp. The two companies are independent.

Excel Spreadsheet Template

Shareholders' equity section of the balance sheet

AGI Inc. AGI Inc. is authorized to issue 100,000 common shares. All the shares were issued at $10.00 per share. The company incurred a net loss of $30,000 in 2008, its first year of business. It earned net income of $35,000 in 2009 and $50,000 in 2010. The company declared no dividends during the three-year period.

Canfer Corp. Canfer Corp.'s articles of incorporation authorize the company to issue 50,000 $1.25 cumulative preferred shares and 500,000 common shares. Canfer Corp. issued 3,000 preferred shares at $10.00 per share. It issued 60,000 common shares for a total of $150,000. The company's retained earnings balance at the beginning of 2010 was $75,000, and net income for the year was $62,500. During 2010, the company declared the specified dividend on preferred and a $0.50 per share dividend on common. Preferred dividends for 2009 were in arrears.

Required

For each company, prepare the shareholders' equity section of its balance sheet at December 31, 2010. Show the computation of all amounts. Journal entries are not required.

Problem 13–5B

Basile Fuels Ltd. included the following shareholders' equity on its year-end balance sheet at December 31, 2010:

Analyzing the shareholders' equity of a corporation

Shareholders' Equity	
Preferred shares, $0.25, cumulative, unlimited authorization,	
20,000 shares issued	$ 32,500
Common shares, unlimited authorization, 230,000 shares issued	100,000
Retained earnings	1,000,000
	$1,132,500

Required

1. Identify the different issues of shares that Basile has outstanding.

2. Are the preferred shares cumulative or noncumalative? How can you tell?

3. Give two summary journal entries to record issuance of all the Basile shares. All the shares were issued for cash. Explanations are not required.

4. Assume that preferred dividends are in arrears for 2009. Record the declaration of a $25,000 dividend on December 31, 2010. Use separate Dividends Payable accounts for preferred shares and common shares.

Problem 13–6B

Preparing a corporation balance sheet; measuring profitability

2 5

The accounts and related balances of Labelle Systems Ltd. are arranged in no particular order.

Trademark, net........................	$ 19,000	Common Shareholders'	
Preferred Shares, $0.20,		Equity, June 30, 2009.........	$200,000
10,000 shares		Net income	25,000
authorized and issued........	29,500	Total assets, June 30,	
Cash	15,000	2009.....................................	410,000
Accounts Receivable, net	52,500	Interest Expense.....................	7,200
Accrued Liabilities	30,000	Property, Plant, and	
Long-term Note Payable..........	48,500	Equipment, net	300,000
Inventory	93,500	Common Shares, 500,000	
Dividends Payable	10,500	shares authorized;	
Retained Earnings	?	272,000 shares issued........	300,000
Accounts Payable.....................	36,000	Prepaid Expenses...................	12,000

Required

1. Prepare the company's classified balance sheet in report format at June 30, 2010.

2. Compute the rate of return on total assets and the rate of return on common shareholders' equity for the year ended June 30, 2010.

3. Do these rates of return suggest strength or weakness? Give your reason.

Problem 13–7B

Excel Spreadsheet Template

Computing dividends on preferred and common shares

3

MMT Broadcasting Inc. has 15,000 $2.50 preferred shares and 75,000 common shares outstanding. MMT Broadcasting Inc. declared and paid the following dividends during a three-year period: 2008, $40,000; 2009, $0; and 2010, $120,000.

Required

1. Compute the total dividends on preferred shares and common shares for each of the three years if

   a. Preferred shares are noncumulative.
   b. Preferred shares are cumulative.

2. For requirement 1b, record the declaration of the 2010 dividends on December 28, 2010 and the payment of the dividends on January 17, 2011. Use separate Dividends Payable accounts for preferred shares and common shares.

Problem 13–8B

Analyzing the shareholders' equity of a corporation

3 4

The balance sheet of Cohen Sales Limited reported the following at December 31, 2010:

Shareholders' Equity	
Redeemable, nonvoting, cumulative preferred shares;	
authorized 16,000 shares (liquidation value $375,000)	$350,000
Common shares, authorized 200,000 shares; issued 90,000 shares...........	340,000
Retained earnings	120,000
Total shareholders' equity	$810,000

Notes to the financial statements indicate that 16,000 of the cumulative preferred shares were issued and outstanding. The shares paid a dividend of $1.40. Preferred dividends have not been paid for three years, including the current year. On the balance sheet date, the market value of Cohen Sales Limited's common shares was $3.00 per share.

Required

1. Are the preferred shares cumulative or noncumulative? How can you tell?
2. Which class of shareholders controls the company? Give your reason.
3. What is the total contributed capital of the company?
4. What was the total market value of the common shares?
5. Compute the book value per share of the preferred shares and the common shares.

Problem 13–9B

Greg Sallows and Billy Canovale are partners in an import business. Their Capital account balances are $50,000 and $72,500, respectively. They were considering incorporating and established a new showroom in Belleville. The following transactions then took place:

Accounting for the incorporation of an ongoing business; recording the issuance of shares; allocating cash dividends; preparing the shareholders' equity section of the balance sheet

2007

Jan. 2   Sallows and Canovale incorporated their partnership into Welluck Carpets Corporation, with an authorization to issue 100,000 $0.30 convertible preferred shares and 500,000 common shares. Sallows received 100,000 common shares and Canovale received 145,000 common shares.

15   Paid $2,000 and gave 4,000 common shares to the corporation's legal firm for incorporating the business. The total legal fee was $4,500.

Mar. 5   Sold 4,000 preferred shares for $15,000. The preferred shares are convertible on the basis of 2 common shares for each preferred share.

Dec. 31   The company reported net income after taxes of $55,000 for the year, and then closed the Income Summary account.

2008

Feb. 12   Declared cash dividends of $10,000, payable on April 8, 2008, to the shareholders of record on March 1, 2008. Indicate the amount that would be payable to the preferred shareholders and to the common shareholders.

Apr. 8   Paid the cash dividend declared on February 12, 2008.

Jul. 7   The preferred shareholders converted 1,000 preferred shares into common shares.

Dec. 31   The company reported net income after taxes of $70,000 for the year, and then closed the Income Summary account.

2009

Dec. 31   Declared cash dividends of $30,000, payable on February 11, 2010, to the shareholders of record on January 13, 2010. Indicate the amount that would be payable to the preferred and to the common shareholders.

31   The company reported net income after taxes of $100,000 for the year, and then closed the Income Summary account.

Required

1. Record the transactions in the general journal.
2. Prepare the shareholders' equity section of the balance sheet as of the close of business on December 31, 2009.

Problem 13–10B

Recording the issuance of
shares; allocating cash
dividends; preparing the liability
and shareholders' equity
sections of the balance sheet

② ③

At January 1, 2008, Barton Ltd.'s balance sheet reported the following shareholders' equity:

Shareholders' Equity

Contributed capital:	
Preferred shares, $0.85, cumulative (3 years in arrears),	
liquidation price of $25, 100,000 shares authorized,	
40,000 shares issued...	$ 800,000
Common shares:	
Class A, 15,000 shares authorized and issued.................................	120,000
Class B, unlimited number of shares authorized,	
75,000 shares issued..	375,000
Total contributed capital	1,295,000
Retained earnings..	300,000
Total shareholders' equity	$1,595,000

The company had the following transactions on the dates indicated:

2008

Dec. 1 The company declared dividends of $150,000, payable on January 14, 2009, to the shareholders of record on December 31, 2008. Indicate the amount that would be payable to the preferred shareholders and to the common shareholders. Class A and Class B shares receive the same per-share dividend.

31 The company reported net income after taxes of $70,000 and closed the Income Summary account.

2009

Jan. 7 The company sold 10,000 preferred shares at $22.50 per share.

14 The company paid the dividend declared on December 1, 2008.

Feb. 14 The company sold 15,000 Class B common shares at $6.00 per share.

Dec. 2 The company declared dividends of $75,000, payable on January 13, 2010, to the shareholders of record on December 31, 2009. Indicate the amount that would be payable to the preferred shareholders and to the common shareholders.

31 The company reported net income after taxes of $63,000 and closed the Income Summary account.

2010

Jan. 13 Paid the dividend declared on December 2, 2009.

Required

1. Record the transactions in the general journal.
2. Prepare the shareholders' equity section of the balance sheet as of the close of business on December 31, 2009.
3. Calculate the book value per share of the preferred shares and of the common shares on December 31, 2009.
4. What was the average price at which the Class A common shares were issued?

CHALLENGE PROBLEMS

Problem 13–1C

Your friend Bryan McNair has come to you for advice. He has a very successful antiques store that had sales of more than $800,000 in the year just ended. He would like to expand and will need to borrow $350,000 to finance an enlarged inventory. He has learned that he can buy the store adjoining his for $250,000 and estimates that $60,000 of renovations would be needed to make the store compatible with his present store. Expansion would mean adding three or four employees to the two employees Bryan already has.

Bryan's accountant has suggested that he incorporate his business and that Bryan hold all the shares. He has cited several reasons to Bryan, including the benefits of limited liability. Bryan has talked to his banker about the possibility of incorporating; the banker has pointed out that if Bryan does incorporate, the bank will need personal guarantees for any loans Bryan arranges with the bank.

Required

Consider Bryan's situation and discuss the pros and cons of incorporation for Bryan. What would you suggest?

Problem 13–2C

You have just received a bequest of $2,000 from an aunt and you have decided to invest the money in shares of Electronic Games Inc., a company that develops software for video games and that is listed on the Toronto Stock Exchange. Electronic Games Inc. (EGI) has common shares; cumulative preferred shares; noncumulative, convertible preferred shares; and noncumulative preferred shares. The common shares are trading at $40.00 and currently have been paying a dividend of $2.40 per share. The cumulative preferred shares are selling at $50.00 and have a stated dividend of $3.50. The convertible preferred shares are selling for $78.50 and are convertible at the rate of 2 common for 1 preferred; the dividend rate is $5.30. The noncumulative preferred shares are trading at $25.00 and have a dividend rate of $1.55.

Deciding on an investment in shares; evaluating different types of shares

Required

Evaluate each of the four different shares as an investment opportunity. After performing your analysis, select which shares you will buy and explain your choice.

Extending Your Knowledge

DECISION PROBLEM

Kimberly Carlyle and Erron Friesen have written a spreadsheet program (Viacalc) to rival Excel. They need additional capital to market the product, and they plan to incorporate the business. They are considering the capital structure. Their primary goal is to raise as much capital as possible without giving up control of the business. Carlyle and Friesen plan to sell the Viacalc software to the corporation in exchange for 100,000 common shares. The partners have been offered $100,000 for the software.

Evaluating alternative ways of raising capital
(2)

The corporation's plans for the articles of incorporation include an authorization to issue 10,000 preferred shares and 1,000,000 common shares. Carlyle and Friesen are uncertain about the most desirable features for the preferred shares. Prior to incorporating, the partners have discussed their plans with two investment groups. The corporation can obtain capital from outside investors under either of the following plans:

Plan 1 Group 1 will invest $100,000 to acquire 1,000 shares of $7.50, cumulative preferred shares and $72,000 to acquire 60,000 common shares. Each preferred share will receive 50 votes if preferred dividends are more than two years in arrears.

Plan 2 Group 2 will invest $150,000 to acquire 1,200 shares of $8.50 nonvoting, noncumulative preferred shares.

Required

Assume the corporation receives its articles of incorporation.

1. Journalize the issuance of common shares to Kimberly Carlyle and Erron Friesen.

2. Journalize the issuance of shares to the outsiders under both plans.

3. Assume that net income for the first year is $184,000, and total dividends of $34,800 are properly subtracted from retained earnings. Prepare the shareholders' equity section of the corporation balance sheet under both plans.

4. Recommend one of the plans to Carlyle and Friesen. Give your reasons.

FINANCIAL STATEMENT CASES

Financial Statement Case 1

Shareholders' equity

②

The Canadian Western Bank (CWB) October 2008 financial statements appear in Appendix A. Answer the following questions about the company's share capital.

1. Where can you find information about CWB's share capital? What classes of shares does CWB have issued and outstanding? How many shares are authorized and how many are issued?

2. Were any shares issued during the year? If yes, at what average price were the shares issued?

Financial Statement Case 2

Shareholders' equity

②

2. Book value per share $2.68

The Sun-Rype Products Ltd. December 31, 2008, financial statements appear in Appendix B. Answer the following questions about the company's share capital.

1. What classes of shares has Sun-Rype issued? How many shares are authorized and how many are issued?

2. What is the book value per share at December 29, 2008? The market price of the shares closed at $5.79 on that date. Why is the market price different from the book value per share?

3. What did Sun-Rype earn per common share in 2008? Where did you find that information?

14

Corporations: Retained Earnings and the Income Statement

What is a stock dividend and what is a stock split? Why would a corporation repurchase its own shares?

What are earnings per share, and how are they calculated?

How do you prepare a statement of retained earnings and a statement of shareholders' equity?

These questions and others will be answered throughout this chapter, as well as in the Decision Guidelines at the end of this chapter.

LEARNING OBJECTIVES

1. Account for stock dividends
2. Distinguish stock splits from stock dividends
3. Account for repurchased shares
4. Analyze a corporate income statement
5. Prepare a statement of retained earnings and a statement of shareholders' equity
6. Identify the impact on the income statement and the statement of shareholders' equity of international financial reporting standards (IFRS)

Imperial Oil Limited is one of Canada's largest corporations and one of its largest crude oil and natural gas producers. It is also Canada's largest refiner and marketer of petroleum products, selling primarily under the Esso and Mobil brand names. In 2008, the company's revenues totalled over $31 billion, and it earned a profit of $3.9 billion, or $4.36 per share.

Regular annual per-share dividends were increased for the fourteenth consecutive year and $2.5 billion was distributed to shareholders through dividend payments and share repurchases. The company's dividend record shows that Imperial Oil has paid dividends every year since 1890 and has steadily increased its dividend over time. The company currently has over 859 million shares outstanding.

In June 2008, a 12-month share repurchase program was implemented. During 2008, the company repurchased 44.3 million shares for $2,210 million, including shares repurchased from ExxonMobil. During 2007, Imperial Oil repurchased 50.5 million shares for $2,358 million. Since Imperial Oil initiated its first share repurchase program in 1995, the company has repurchased 890.4 million shares—representing about 51 percent of the total outstanding shares at the start of the program—with resulting distributions to shareholders of over $15 billion.[1]

---

[1] Information from the Imperial Oil Limited website (www.imperialoil.ca) and SEDAR (www.sedar.com), accessed on July 16, 2009.

Chapter 13

introduced corporations and covered the basics of shareholders' equity. We saw that a corporation's balance sheet is the same as that for a proprietorship or a partnership, except for owners' equity, which is shareholders' equity for a corporation. Chapter 13 began with the issuance of common shares, and also covered the declaration and payment of cash dividends. The topics covered in Chapter 13 apply to private corporations, whose shares tend to be held by a small number of shareholders and are not traded on a stock exchange, as well as public corporations, whose shares trade on stock exchanges.

Private corporations are governed by Canadian generally accepted accounting principles (GAAP) for private enterprises, described in this chapter. Public corporations are governed by international financial reporting standards (IFRS), which are discussed in Learning Objective 6 in this chapter. Generally, GAAP for private enterprises is less complicated and requires fewer disclosures than IFRS because it is assumed that private-corporation shareholders and lenders can get access to the information they need directly from the corporation. Typically, shareholders and lenders cannot get this access to information from large, public corporations.

While GAAP for private enterprises forms the basis for this chapter, some examples include public corporations to illustrate concepts more easily and to acknowledge that the accounting information students will see in the business press and in everyday dealings will be generated mainly by public corporations.

This chapter takes corporate equity a few steps further, as follows:

Chapter 13 covered	Chapter 14 covers
Contributed capital	Retained earnings
Issuing shares	Repurchasing shares
Cash dividends	Stock dividends and stock splits
Corporate balance sheet	Corporate income statement

Chapter 14 completes our discussion of corporate equity. We begin with retained earnings, stock dividends, and stock splits—terms you may have heard. Let's see what these terms mean.

Retained Earnings

We have seen that the owners' equity section of a corporation's balance sheet is called *shareholders' equity*. The contributed capital accounts and retained earnings make up the shareholders' equity section. We studied contributed capital in Chapter 13. Now let's focus on retained earnings.

Retained Earnings carries the balance of the business's accumulated lifetime net income less all net losses from operations and less all dividends. *Retained* means "held onto" or "kept." Retained earnings is the shareholders' stake in total assets that come from profits. Successful companies grow by reinvesting the assets they generate from profitable operations. A debit balance in Retained Earnings is called a *deficit*. Retained earnings deficits are not common because they often indicate that the corporation may be facing corporate failure and bankruptcy.

When you see a balance sheet, remember these facts about Retained Earnings:

1. *Credits to the Retained Earnings account arise only from net income.* Retained Earnings shows how much net income a corporation has earned and retained in the business. Its balance is the cumulative, lifetime earnings of the company less all net losses and all dividends.

2. *The Retained Earnings account is not a reservoir of cash.* Instead, Retained Earnings represents no particular asset. In fact, the corporation may have a large balance in Retained Earnings but too little cash to pay a dividend.

   • To *declare* a dividend, the company must have a credit balance in Retained Earnings, both before and after the declaration of dividends.

   • To *pay* the dividend, it must have the cash.

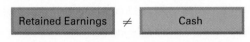

Retained Earnings and Cash are two very
different accounts, unrelated to each other.

3. *Retained Earnings' ending balance is computed as follows* (amounts assumed):

Beginning balance	$ 70,000
Add: Net income for the year	80,000
Less: Net loss* (none this year)	
Dividends for the year	(50,000)
Ending balance	$100,000

*A corporation has a net income *or* a net loss, but not both.

Stock Dividends

A **stock dividend**, also called a **share dividend**, is a distribution of a corporation's own shares to its shareholders. Stock dividends are fundamentally different from cash dividends because stock dividends do not give any assets to the shareholders. Stock dividends

• Affect *only* the accounts within shareholders' equity (including Retained Earnings and Common Shares)

• Have *no* effect on total shareholders' equity

• Have *no* effect on assets or liabilities

A stock dividend increases Common Shares and decreases Retained Earnings. Both of these accounts are elements of shareholders' equity, so total shareholders' equity is unchanged. There is merely a transfer from Retained Earnings to Common Shares. No asset or liability is affected by a stock dividend, as shown in Exhibit 14–1.

EXHIBIT 14–1 Effects of a Stock Dividend

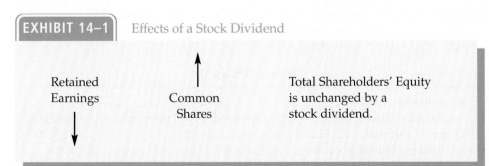

OBJECTIVE ①
Account for stock dividends

KEY POINT

A stock dividend normally applies only to common shares.

The corporation distributes stock dividends to shareholders in proportion to the number of shares they already own. For example, suppose you owned 300 common shares in the Bank of Montreal. If the Bank of Montreal distributed a 10 percent common stock dividend, you would receive 30 (300 × 0.10) additional shares. You would now own 330 common shares. All other Bank of Montreal shareholders also receive additional shares equal to 10 percent of their prior holdings, so you are all in the same relative ownership position after the dividend as you were before.

Reasons for Stock Dividends

Why do companies issue stock dividends? There are several reasons:

1. *To continue dividends but conserve cash.* A company may wish to continue dividends in some form but may need to keep its cash in the business.

2. *To reduce the market price per share of its shares.* For companies whose shares trade on a stock exchange, a stock dividend may cause the market price of a company's shares to fall because of the increased supply of the shares. Canadian Western Bank's common shares traded at $16.36 per share recently. Doubling the number of its shares outstanding by issuing a stock dividend is likely to drop the market price of the shares by approximately half, to $8.18 per share. The objective of such a large stock dividend is to make the shares less expensive and thus more affordable and attractive to investors.

Recording Stock Dividends

A cash dividend involves the payment of a current asset (cash). A stock dividend is a distribution of a company's own shares, which are not an asset.

As with a cash dividend, there are three key dates for a stock dividend:

- Declaration date
- Date of record
- Distribution date (payment date)

The board of directors announces stock dividends on the declaration date. The date of record and the distribution date follow. (This is the same sequence of dates used for a cash dividend.) The declaration of a stock dividend does *not* create a liability because the corporation is not obligated to pay out assets. (Recall that a liability is a claim on *assets*.) Instead, the corporation has declared its intention to distribute its shares.

Never credit a payable account for a stock dividend. No liability is created when a stock dividend is declared, as compared to a cash dividend, which does create a liability.

In 2007, the Canadian Western Bank Board of Directors declared a stock dividend of one additional common share for each common share outstanding, payable on January 18, 2007, to shareholders of record on January 11, 2007. This doubled the number of shares outstanding and reduced the market price to half of its previous value at that time.

One concern about stock dividends is how to determine the amount to transfer from retained earnings to the Common Shares account. The *Canada Business Corporations Act* suggests that the market value of the shares issued is the appropriate amount to transfer, while other incorporating acts allow the directors to set a value on the shares. If market value were to be used, it would be the market value on the date the dividend is declared. This is the valuation used in this text.

Assume General Communications Corporation has the following shareholders' equity prior to a stock dividend:

Shareholders' Equity	
Contributed capital	
Common shares, 100,000 shares authorized, 40,000 shares issued.....	$400,000
Retained earnings	100,000
Total shareholders' equity...	$500,000

Assume General Communications Corporation declares a 10 percent common stock dividend on November 17. The company will distribute 4,000 (40,000 × 0.10) shares in the dividend. On November 17, the market value of its common shares is $16.00 per share. Using the market value approach, Retained Earnings is debited for the market value of the 4,000 dividend shares and Common Stock Dividend Distributable is credited. General Communications Corporation makes the following entry on the declaration date.

Nov. 17	Retained Earnings..	64,000	
	Common Stock Dividend Distributable		64,000
	To declare a 10 percent common stock dividend.		
	(40,000 × 0.10 × $16)		

The accounting equation for this transaction shows that a stock dividend does not affect assets, liabilities, or total shareholders' equity.

Assets	=	Liabilities	+	Shareholders' Equity
				−64,000
0	=	0		+64,000

On the distribution date, the company records issuance of the dividend shares as follows:

Dec. 12	Common Stock Dividend Distributable	64,000	
	Common Shares..		64,000
	To issue common shares in a stock dividend.		

Common Stock Dividend Distributable is a shareholders' equity account. (It is *not* a liability because the corporation has no obligation to pay assets.) If the company prepares financial statements after the declaration of the stock dividend but before issuing it, Common Stock Dividend Distributable is reported in the shareholders' equity section of the balance sheet immediately after Common Shares. However, this account holds the value of the dividend shares only from the declaration date to the date of distribution.

The following tabulation shows the changes in shareholders' equity caused by the stock dividend:

Shareholders' Equity	Before the Dividend	After the Dividend	Change
Contributed capital			
Common shares, 100,000 shares authorized, 40,000 shares issued...	$400,000		
44,000 shares issued		$464,000	Up by $64,000
Total contributed capital	400,000	464,000	**Up by $64,000**
Retained earnings................................	100,000	36,000	**Down by $64,000**
Total shareholders' equity................	$500,000	$500,000	Unchanged

A stock dividend does not affect assets, liabilities, or total shareholders' equity. A stock dividend merely rearranges the shareholders' equity accounts, leaving total equity unchanged.

Amount of Retained Earnings Transferred in a Stock Dividend Stock dividends are said to be *capitalized retained earnings* because they transfer an amount from retained earnings to contributed capital. The contributed capital accounts are more permanent than retained earnings because they cannot be paid out as dividends. Many shareholders view stock dividends as distributions little different from cash dividends.

Stock dividends, like cash dividends, are taxable in the hands of the recipient. The value of the stock dividend is equal to the amount of the increase in the capital of the company paying the dividend. The increase is usually the fair market value of the shares issued.

Stock Splits

A **stock split** is fundamentally different from a stock dividend. A stock split increases the number of authorized and outstanding shares with a proportionate reduction in the book value per share. For example, if the company splits its stock 2 for 1, the number of outstanding shares is doubled and each share's book value is halved. Many large companies in Canada—Imperial Oil, St. Lawrence Cement [which now operates under the name Holcim (Canada) Inc.], Bank of Nova Scotia, Loblaw Companies Limited, and others—have split their stock.

Assume that the market price of one common share of Marcato Corp. is $100 and that the company wishes to decrease the market price to approximately $50. Marcato decides to split the common shares 2 for 1 in the expectation that the share's market price would fall from $100 to $50. A 2-for-1 stock split means that the company would have two times as many shares outstanding after the split as it had before and that each share's book value would be halved. Assume Marcato had 400,000 common shares issued and outstanding before the split. Exhibit 14–2 shows how a 2-for-1 stock split affects Marcato Corp.'s shareholders' equity.

EXHIBIT 14–2	A 2-for-1 Stock Split

Shareholders' Equity before 2-for-1 Stock Split	
Contributed capital	
Common shares, unlimited number of shares authorized,	
400,000 shares issued	$4,000,000
Retained earnings	1,800,000
Total shareholders' equity	$5,800,000
Shareholders' Equity after 2-for-1 Stock Split	
Contributed capital	
Common shares, unlimited number of shares authorized,	
800,000 shares issued	$4,000,000
Retained earnings	1,800,000
Total shareholders' equity	$5,800,000

Exhibit 14–2 shows that a 2-for-1 stock split

- Doubles the number of shares authorized and issued
- Leaves all account balances and total shareholders' equity unchanged

Because the stock split affects no account balances, no formal journal entry is necessary.

Instead, the split is often recorded in a *memorandum entry* such as the following:

Aug. 19 Distributed one new common share for each old share previously outstanding. This increased the number of common shares issued from 400,000 to 800,000.

A company may engage in a reverse split (or consolidation) to decrease the number of shares outstanding and increase the market price per share. If the number of shares outstanding is decreased, then existing shareholders may have a better chance of maintaining control over a corporation's shares. There are fewer shares available to be traded and purchased by new shareholders. For example, Marcato Corp. could consolidate its stock 1 for 4, which would reduce the number of shares issued from 400,000 to 100,000 and increase the share price from, for example, $25.00 per share to $100.00 per share. Reverse splits are rare but are sometimes done to allow companies to continue trading their shares on stock exchanges that require a minimum share price if the company's share price falls below the minimum.

DID YOU GET IT?

To check your understanding of the material in this Learning Objective, complete these questions. The solutions appear on MyAccountingLab so you can check your progress.

1. Answer the following questions to review stock and cash dividends:

   a. How is a stock dividend like a cash dividend?

   b. What happens to total share capital as a result of cash and stock dividends?

   c. What happens to total shareholders' equity as a result of cash and stock dividends?

   d. Which type of dividend gives taxable income to the shareholder?

2. Beachcomber Pool Supply Inc. has 16,000 common shares outstanding for a total contributed capital value of $48,000. Beachcomber declares a 10 percent stock dividend on July 15 when the market value of its shares is $8.00 per share. The date of record is August 15 and the distribution date is August 31.

   a. Journalize the declaration of the stock dividend on July 15 and the distribution on August 31.

   b. What is the overall effect on Beachcomber's total assets?

   c. What is the overall effect on total shareholders' equity?

3. Refer to the information in the previous question.

   a. What would be the journal entry on July 15 if Beachcomber declared a 2-for-1 stock split instead of a stock dividend?

   b. What would be the effect of the stock split on shareholders' equity?

Similarities and Differences between Stock Dividends and Stock Splits

OBJECTIVE 2
Distinguish stock splits from stock dividends

Stock dividends and stock splits both increase the number of shares owned per shareholder. Neither a stock dividend nor a stock split changes the investor's total cost of the shares owned. For example, assume you paid $32,000 to acquire 1,000 common shares of Western AquaCulture Ltd. If Western AquaCulture Ltd. distributes a 100 percent stock dividend, your 1,000 shares increase to 2,000, but your total cost is still $32,000. Likewise, if Western AquaCulture Ltd. performs a 2-for-1 stock split, your shares increase in number to 2,000, but your total cost is unchanged.

Both a stock dividend and a stock split increase the corporation's number of shares issued and outstanding. For example, a 100 percent stock dividend and a 2-for-1 stock split both double the outstanding shares and are likely to cut the stock's market price per share in half.

Where stock dividends and stock splits differ, however, is in the way they are treated for tax purposes. A stock split does not create taxable income to the investor, but a stock dividend does because stock dividends are taxed in the same way as cash dividends. The stock dividend is valued at the market value of the shares on the date the stock dividend is declared, and this amount is included as taxable income. This is one reason why stock dividends are less popular than stock splits; investors must pay income tax on a stock dividend even though no cash is received.

They also differ in that a stock *dividend* shifts an amount from retained earnings to contributed capital, leaving the total book value unchanged. However, the book value per share will decrease because of the increased number of shares outstanding. A stock *split* affects no account balances whatsoever but instead changes the book value of each share.

Exhibit 14–3 summarizes the effects of cash dividends, stock dividends, and stock splits on total shareholders' equity.

EXHIBIT 14–3 Effects of Dividends and Stock Splits

Event	Common Shares	Retained Earnings	Total Shareholders' Equity
Cash dividend	No effect	Decrease	Decrease
Stock dividend	Increase	Decrease	No effect
Stock split	No effect	No effect	No effect

Income Trusts

A new investment vehicle came into being in the mid-1990s. The vehicle is called an **income trust** or **investment trust**. It is quite simply a portfolio of assets that is designed to provide safety of principal and a regular fixed income. An example of an income trust is Big Rock Brewery Income Trust of Calgary. In January 2003, Big Rock Brewery Ltd., which had shareholders but had not paid dividends on common shares, converted Big Rock shares into trust units.[2] The change provides individual unitholders (formerly shareholders) with the opportunity to receive monthly cash payments, but at the same time allows the unitholders to maintain their equity position in the company. The monthly cash payments are roughly equivalent to dividends paid by corporations, but their tax treatment in the hands of unitholders is different.

DID YOU GET IT?

MyAccountingLab

To check your understanding of the material in this Learning Objective, complete this question. The solution appears on MyAccountingLab so you can check your progress.

4. Stutterstep Corp., an Internet service provider, has prospered during the past seven years, and recently the company's share price has shot up to $61.00. Stutterstep's management wishes to decrease the share price to the range of $29.00 to $31.00, which will be attractive to more investors. Should the company issue a 100 percent stock dividend or split the stock? Why? If you propose a stock split, state the split ratio that will accomplish the company's objective. Show your computations.

OBJECTIVE 3
Account for repurchased shares

Repurchase of Its Shares by a Corporation

Corporations may **repurchase shares** from their shareholders for several reasons:

1. The corporation may have issued all its authorized shares and need to recover shares for distributions to officers and employees under bonus plans or share purchase plans.
2. The purchase may help support the share's current market price by decreasing the supply of shares available to the public.
3. Management may gather in the shares to avoid a takeover by an outside party.

[2] Big Rock Brewery Income Trust Annual Report, December 31, 2003.

The *Canada Business Corporations Act* requires a corporation that purchases its own shares to cancel the shares bought; it may do so by treating the purchased shares as authorized but unissued, and it may issue them in the normal way at a later date, or it may cancel them outright. Several of the provincial incorporating acts also require that the shares be treated this way, while other incorporating acts permit the corporation to hold the shares as treasury shares (in effect, the corporation holds the shares in its treasury) and resell them.

Shares that are cancelled outright may not be reissued. The effect of repurchasing an outstanding share is to reduce the number of shares issued; the effect of cancelling a share outright is to reduce the number of shares authorized.

For practical purposes, treasury shares are like unissued shares: neither category of shares is in the hands of shareholders. The company does not receive cash dividends on its treasury shares, and treasury shares do not entitle the company to vote or to receive assets in liquidation. The difference between unissued shares and treasury shares is that treasury shares have been issued and bought back.

The repurchase of its own shares by a company decreases the company's assets and its shareholders' equity. The size of the company literally decreases, as shown on the balance sheet. The *Canada Business Corporations Act* and most of the provincial incorporating acts do not permit a corporation to acquire its own shares if such reacquisition would result in the corporation's putting itself into financial jeopardy and being unable to pay its liabilities as they become due.

For companies incorporated under the *Canada Business Corporations Act* and in jurisdictions where repurchased shares must be cancelled or treated as unissued, the Common Shares account is debited.

In those jurisdictions in Canada where treasury shares are permitted, the entry to record a purchase of treasury shares would include a debit to Treasury Shares and a credit to Cash. The Treasury Shares account has a debit balance, which is the opposite of the other shareholders' equity accounts. Therefore, Treasury Shares is a contra shareholders' equity account; it is deducted from the total of contributed capital and Retained Earnings to compute total shareholders' equity. Treasury shares are permitted in the United States but are rare in Canada. For this reason, the remainder of this text will *not* deal with treasury shares.

Repurchase of Shares

The *CICA Handbook* requires a company that purchases its own shares at a price less than the *average issue price* to debit Common Shares (or Preferred Shares, as the case may be) for the average issue price; the excess of the average issue price over the purchase price should be credited to Contributed Surplus—Share Repurchase. (If the company has more than one class or series of shares, the Contributed Surplus—Share Repurchase account name would include the class or series.) When a company purchases its own shares at a price equal to or greater than the average issue price, the excess should first be debited to Contributed Surplus—Share Repurchase to reduce the balance in this account to $0, and any remaining excess should then be debited to Retained Earnings. Under the *Canada Business Corporations Act*, any subsequent issues of repurchased shares are treated as new share issues, with the proceeds credited to the Common Shares account. The Contributed Surplus—Share Repurchase account is not adjusted.

Suppose Cassie Products Inc. had the following shareholders' equity before repurchasing 10,000 of its own shares. Its 80,000 shares were issued at the same price, as follows:

Shareholders' Equity	
Contributed capital	
Common shares, 100,000 shares authorized, 80,000 shares issued......	$200,000
Retained earnings..	150,000
Total shareholders' equity...	$350,000

On November 22, 2010, Cassie Products Inc. purchases 10,000 of its common shares, paying cash of $7.50 per share; the shares had been issued at $2.50 ($200,000 ÷ 80,000). The shares are to be cancelled. Cassie Products Inc. records the purchase as follows:

2010			
Nov. 22	Common Shares	25,000	
	Retained Earnings...	50,000*	
	Cash		75,000
	Purchased 10,000 shares at $7.50 per share.		

Note: If there is a balance in the Contributed Surplus—Share Repurchase account, it must be debited until it reaches a nil balance; then Retained Earnings is debited.

The shareholders' equity section of Cassie Products Inc.'s balance sheet would appear as follows after the transaction:

Shareholders' Equity	
Contributed capital	
Common shares, 90,000 shares authorized, 70,000 shares issued	$175,000
Retained earnings	100,000
Total shareholders' equity	$275,000

Observe that the purchase of the shares decreased the number of shares authorized and decreased the number of shares issued and outstanding. Only outstanding shares have a vote, receive cash dividends, and share in assets if the corporation liquidates. Notice that the dollar amount shown for Common Shares and Retained Earnings decreased by $25,000 and $50,000 respectively.

Assume the articles of incorporation for Dawson Resources Ltd., issued under the *Canada Business Corporations Act*, authorized it to issue 100,000 common shares. By February 28, 2010, Dawson Resources had issued 9,000 shares at a price of $20.00 per share, and its shareholders' equity appeared as follows:

Shareholders' Equity	
Contributed capital	
Common shares, 100,000 shares authorized, 9,000 shares issued	$180,000
Retained earnings	24,000
Total shareholders' equity	$204,000

On March 20, 2010, Dawson Resources Ltd. repurchases 1,000 shares at $15.00 per share with the intention of reissuing the shares in the future. The company records the transaction as follows:

2010			
Mar. 20	Common Shares..	20,000	
	Contributed Surplus—Share Repurchase...		5,000
	Cash..		15,000
	Purchased 1,000 shares at $15.00 per share.		

Since the common shares repurchased had an issue value of $20,000 (1,000 × $20), the contributed surplus was $5,000 [1,000 × ($20 − $15)].

The shareholders' equity section of Dawson Resources Ltd.'s balance sheet would appear as follows after the transaction:

Shareholders' Equity

Contributed capital

Common shares, 100,000 shares authorized, 8,000 shares issued .... $ 160,000

Contributed surplus—Share Repurchase (Note 6) 5,000

Total contributed capital... 165,000

Retained earnings 24,000

Total shareholders' equity $189,000

Note 6: During the year, the company acquired 1,000 common shares at a price of $15.00 per share; the shares had been issued at $20.00 per share. The company intends to reissue these shares in the future.

Dawson Resources Ltd. now has a balance in the Contributed Surplus—Share Repurchase account. If Dawson repurchased another 1,000 shares at $30.00 per share on April 30, 2009, with the intention of reissuing the shares in the future, the company would reduce the balance in Contributed Surplus—Share Repurchase to nil before reducing the Retained Earnings account, as follows:

2010			
Apr. 30	Common Shares	20,000	
	Contributed Surplus—Share Repurchase	5,000	
	Retained Earnings	5,000	
	Cash		30,000
	Purchased 1,000 shares at $30.00 per share.		

Since the common shares repurchased had an issue value of $20,000 (1,000 × $20), the contributed surplus was reduced to nil and Retained Earnings was debited for the remainder (1,000 × $30 − $20,000 − $5,000 = $5,000).

The shareholders' equity section of Dawson Resources Ltd.'s balance sheet would appear as follows after the transaction:

Shareholders' Equity

Contributed capital

Common shares, 100,000 shares authorized, 7,000 shares

issued (Note 6)... $140,000

Retained earnings 19,000

Total shareholders' equity $159,000

Note 6: During the year, the company acquired 1,000 common shares at a price of $15.00 per share and 1,000 common shares at a price of $30.00 per share; the shares had been issued at $20.00 per share. The company intends to reissue these shares in the future.

Sale of Repurchased Shares

A company incorporated under the *Canada Business Corporations Act* may reissue the shares that it previously had repurchased. The sale would be treated like a normal sale of authorized but unissued shares.

To continue our example, on June 18, 2010, Dawson Resources Ltd. sells 1,000 common shares for $22.00 per share. Exhibit 14–4 tracks the shareholders' equity of Dawson Resources Ltd. to show how these share repurchase and resale transactions affect corporate equity.

No Gain or Loss from Repurchased Share Transactions

The repurchase and sale of its own shares do not affect a corporation's net income. A share repurchase affects *balance sheet accounts*, not income statement accounts.

EXHIBIT 14–4 Shareholders' Equity of Dawson Resources Ltd.

Shareholders' equity before share repurchase transaction	Shareholders' equity after a $20,000 repurchase of shares	Shareholders' equity after a $30,000 repurchase of shares	Shareholders' equity after sale of the repurchased shares for $22,000
	Equity decreases by $15,000	Equity decreases by $30,000	Equity increases by $22,000
$204,000 (Common Shares, $180,000)	$189,000 (Common Shares, $160,000)	$159,000 (Common Shares, $140,000)	$181,000 (Common Shares, $162,000)

The fact that a company may have repurchased shares at a price different from their average issue price and then reissued shares later is not relevant, since the issue of shares is treated in the normal way, as a credit to Common Shares. The sale of 1,000 shares repurchased for $15,000 and resold for $22,000, discussed above, illustrates this point.

Share repurchase transactions have a serious ethical and legal dimension. A company buying its own shares must be extremely careful that its disclosures of information are complete and accurate. Otherwise, a shareholder who sold shares back to the company may claim that he or she was deceived into selling the shares at too low a price. For example, what would happen if a company repurchased its own shares at $17.00 per share and one day later announced a technological breakthrough that would generate millions of dollars in new business? The share price would likely increase in response to the new information. If it could be proved that management withheld the information, a shareholder selling shares back to the company might file a lawsuit to gain the difference per share. The shareholder would claim that, with the knowledge of the technological advance, he or she would have held the shares until after the price increase and been able to sell the shares at a higher price.

Variations in Reporting Shareholders' Equity

Accountants sometimes report shareholders' equity in ways that differ from our examples. We use a detailed format in this book to help you learn the components of shareholders' equity. Companies assume that investors and creditors understand the details.

One of the most important skills you will learn in this course is how to read the financial statements of actual companies. In Exhibit 14–5 we present a side-by-side comparison of our teaching format and the format of the Bank of Nova Scotia, taken from its 2008 annual report. Note the following points with respect to the real-world format illustrated in Exhibit 14–5 and also with regard to actual financial statements:

1. The Bank of Nova Scotia uses the heading Capital Stock. Companies may use Share Capital or other headings instead of Contributed Capital.

2. Some companies combine all classes of contributed capital into a single line item and provide specifics in the notes. The Bank of Nova Scotia has combined

two series of preferred shares in a single line item but does show preferred and common shares separately.

3. The preferred and common shares are described fully in the notes with respect to shares authorized and issued; the information in the balance sheet is limited to a description of the class and total amount for which each of the two classes of shares were issued.

4. Often total shareholders' equity is not specifically labelled.

EXHIBIT 14–5 Formats for Reporting Shareholders' Equity**

Teaching Format		Real-World Format	
Shareholders' Equity **($ amounts in millions)**		**Shareholders' Equity** **($ amounts in millions)**	
Contributed capital		Capital stock (Note 14)*	
Unlimited number of preferred shares authorized		Preferred shares	$2,860
114,400,000 issued	$ 2,860	Common shares	3,829
Unlimited number of common shares authorized			
991,923,631 issued	3,829		
Retained earnings	18,549	Retained earnings	18,549
Accumulated other comprehensive income (loss) (Note 16)	(3,596)	Accumulated other comprehensive income (loss) (Note 16)	(3,596)
Total shareholders' equity	$21,642		$21,642

*Note 14: Capital Stock (adapted)
Authorized
An unlimited number of Preferred Shares without nominal or par value.

An unlimited number of Common Shares without nominal or par value.

Issued and fully paid
Preferred shares   114,400,000 shares
Common shares   991,923,631 shares

**GAAP suggests the presentation of comparative data; in order to simplify the illustration, data are presented for 2008 only.

DID YOU GET IT?

MyAccountingLab

To check your understanding of the material in this Learning Objective, complete these questions. The solutions appear on MyAccountingLab so you can check your progress.

5. Scopis Ltd. reported its shareholders' equity as shown below.

Shareholders' Equity	
Preferred shares, $1.00	
Authorized: 10,000 shares	
Issued: None	$ 0
Common shares	
Authorized: 100,000 shares	
Issued: 14,000 shares	70,000
Retained earnings	84,000
	$154,000

a. What was the average issue price per common share?

b. Journalize the issuance of 1,200 common shares at $8.00 per share. Use Scopis Ltd.'s account titles.

c. After part b, how many Scopis Ltd. common shares are now outstanding?

d. How many common shares would be outstanding after Scopis Ltd. splits its common shares (computed in part c) 3 for 1?

e. Using Scopis Ltd. account titles, journalize the declaration of a 10 percent stock dividend when the market price of Scopis Ltd.'s common shares is $6.00 per share. Use the shares outstanding in part c.

6. Refer to the Scopis Ltd. shareholders' equity information at the beginning of the previous question, which shows 14,000 common shares issued.

a. Journalize the following share repurchase and sale transactions by Scopis Ltd., assuming they occur in the order given.

i. Scopis Ltd. repurchases 500 of its own shares at $16.00 per share.

ii. Scopis Ltd. repurchases 500 of its own shares at $4.00 per share.

iii. Scopis Ltd. sells 100 shares for $18.00 per share.

b. How many Scopis Ltd. common shares would be outstanding after the transactions in part a take place?

7. Anderson Products Inc. issued 100,000 common shares at $10.00 per share. Later, when the market price was $15.00 per share, the company distributed a 10 percent stock dividend. Then Anderson Products Inc. repurchased 500 shares at $20.00 per share. What is the final balance in the Common Shares account?

OBJECTIVE 4
Analyze a corporate income statement

The Corporate Income Statement— Analyzing Earnings

As we have seen, the shareholders' equity of a corporation is more complex than the capital of a proprietorship or a partnership. Also, a corporation's income statement includes some features that don't often apply to a proprietorship or a partnership. Most of the income statements you will see belong to corporations, so we turn now to the corporate income statement.

Net income is probably the most important piece of information about a company. Net income measures how successfully the company has operated. To shareholders, the larger the corporation's profit, the greater the likelihood of dividends. To creditors, the larger the corporation's profit, the better able it is to pay its debts. Net income builds up a company's assets and shareholders' equity. It also helps to attract capital from new investors who hope to receive dividends from future successful operations.

Suppose you are considering investing in the shares of The Toronto-Dominion Bank, The Forzani Group Ltd., the sporting goods retailer, or a private corporation. You would examine these companies' income statements. Of particular interest is the amount of net income they can expect to earn year after year. To understand net income, let's examine Exhibit 14–6, which presents the income statement of Como Technology Inc., a small manufacturer of electronic switching equipment that is owned by a few shareholders who run the company. Its shares do not trade on a stock exchange, so Como Technology Inc. is a private enterprise.

 **EXHIBIT 14–6** | Corporate Income Statement

COMO TECHNOLOGY INC.
Income Statement
For the Year Ended December 31, 2010

Sales revenue		$1,000,000
Cost of goods sold		480,000
Gross margin		520,000
Operating expenses (listed individually)		362,000
Operating income		158,000
Other gains (losses)		
Loss on restructuring operations	($20,000)	
Gain on sale of machinery	42,000	22,000
Income from continuing operations before income tax		180,000
Income tax expense		63,000
Income from continuing operations		117,000
Discontinued operations		
Operating income, $60,000, less income tax of $21,000	39,000	
Gain on disposal, $10,000, less income tax of $3,500	6,500	45,500
Net income		$ 162,500
Earnings per common share		
(60,000 shares outstanding)		
Income from continuing operations		$1.95
Income from discontinued operations		0.76
Net income		$2.71

Continuing operations } (brace beside continuing operations section)
Discontinued operations } (brace beside discontinued operations section)
Earnings per share } (brace beside EPS section)

Continuing Operations

Income from a business's continuing operations helps financial statement users make predictions about the business's future earnings. In the income statement of Exhibit 14–6, the topmost section reports income from continuing operations. This part of the business is expected to continue from period to period. In the absence of other information, we may use this information to predict that Como Technology Inc. will earn income of approximately $117,000 next year.

The continuing operations of Como Technology Inc. include three items deserving explanation:

1. During 2010, the company had a $20,000 loss on restructuring operations. Restructuring costs include severance pay to laid-off workers, moving expenses for employees transferred to other locations, and environmental cleanup expenses. The restructuring loss is part of continuing operations because Como Technology Inc. is remaining in the same line of business. But the restructuring loss is highlighted as an "other" item (unusual item) on the income statement because its cause—restructuring—falls outside Como's main business endeavour, which is selling electronics products.

2. Como Technology Inc. had a gain on the sale of machinery ($42,000), which is also outside the company's core business activity. This explains why the gain is reported separately from Como's sales revenue, cost of goods sold, and gross margin.

The gains or losses from *any* unusual or infrequent transactions that are outside a company's core business activity would be disclosed separately on the income statement as part of income from continuing operations. Other examples in addition to those shown in Exhibit 14–6 include:

- Losses due to lawsuits

KEY POINT

Businesses operate to generate profits; without profits a business will not exist for long. The main source of income for an ongoing business must be from regular, continuing operations, not from sources such as selling off a business segment.

LEARNING TIPS

The first income tax expense— $63,000—listed on the income statement relates solely to income from continuing operations. Therefore, the tax effect of the discontinued segment's operating income (or loss) is not included in income tax expense; rather, it is added or deducted in the discontinued-operations part of the income statement.

- Losses due to employee labour strikes
- Losses due to floods, fire, or other forces of nature

These items are *not* shown net of tax effects.

3. Income tax expense ($63,000) has been deducted in arriving at income before discontinued operations (i.e., income from continuing operations). The tax corporations pay on their income is a significant expense. The combined federal and provincial income tax rates for corporations varies from time to time, for type and size of company, and from province to province; for corporations not eligible for the small business deduction, the current rates range from about 25 percent to a maximum rate of 38 percent. We will use an income tax rate of 35 percent in our illustrations. This is a reasonable estimate of combined federal and provincial income taxes. The $63,000 income tax expense in Exhibit 14–6 equals the pretax income from continuing operations multiplied by the tax rate ($180,000 $\times$ 0.35 = $63,000).

After continuing operations, an income statement may include gains and losses from discontinued operations.

Discontinued Operations

Many corporations engage in several lines of business. For example, The Jim Pattison Group of Vancouver and ATCO Ltd. of Calgary are very diversified conglomerates with several lines of business. Bombardier Inc. owns aerospace companies in Canada, the U.S., and Ireland to serve a world market, and manufactures subway cars for a world market. We call each significant part of a company a **segment of the business**.

A company may sell a segment of its business. Such a sale is not a regular source of income because a company cannot keep on selling its segments indefinitely. The sale of a business segment is viewed as a one-time transaction. Financial analysts and potential investors typically do not include income or loss on discontinued operations to predict a company's future income. The discontinued segments will generate no income in the future.

The income statement presents information on the segment that has been disposed of under the heading Discontinued Operations. This section of the income statement is divided into two components:

1. Operating income (or loss) from the segment that is disposed of.
2. Gain (or loss) on the disposal.

Assume income and gains are taxed at the 35-percent rate. They would be reported as follows:

Discontinued operations	
Operating income $60,000, less income tax, $21,000............................	$39,000
Gain on disposal, $10,000 less income tax, $3,500................................	6,500
	$45,500

This presentation appears in Exhibit 14–6.

It is necessary to separate discontinued operations into these two components because the company may operate the discontinued segment for part of the year. This is the operating income (or loss) component; it should include the results of operations of the segment from the beginning of the period to the disposal date. There is usually also a gain (or loss) on disposal. Both the operating income (or loss) and the gain (or loss) on disposal are shown net of tax. This is because income tax is such a significant component of continuing operations and discontinued operations that investors and analysts need to know the tax effects. Operating losses and losses on disposal generate tax benefits because they reduce net income and thus reduce the amount of tax that needs to be paid.

If the transactions for discontinued operations have not been completed at the company's year end, the gain (or loss) may have to be estimated. To be conservative, the estimated net loss should be recorded in the accounts at year end while an estimated net gain would not be recognized until it was realized.

It is important that the assets, liabilities, and operations of the segment can be clearly identified as separate from those of other operations of the company. The notes to the financial statements should disclose fully the nature of the discontinued operations and other relevant information about the discontinued operations, such as revenue to the date of discontinuance.

Discontinued operations are common in business. A recent example is General Motors' decision to stop producing the Saturn line of vehicles. Another example is Molson Coors Brewing Company's sale of part of its interest in Cervejarias Kaiser, a Brazilian brewing company.

Earnings Per Share (EPS)

For many corporations, the final segment of a corporation income statement presents the company's earnings per share. **Earnings per share (EPS)** is the amount of a company's net income per outstanding common share. While GAAP for private enterprises does not require that corporations disclose EPS figures on the income statement or in a note to the financial statements, many corporations do provide this information because investors and financial analysts sometimes use it to assess a corporation's profitability. EPS is also widely reported in the financial press, so it is important to know how it is calculated and how it is used. EPS is a key measure of a business's success. Basic EPS is computed as follows:

$$\text{Earnings per Share} = \frac{\text{Net income} - \text{Preferred dividends}}{\text{Weighted average number of common shares outstanding}}$$

Consider Plaza Corporation with net income of $200,000, no preferred dividends, and 100,000 common shares outstanding. Its EPS is $2 ($200,000 ÷ 100,000). Quaid Corporation may also have net income of $200,000 and no preferred dividends, but only 50,000 common shares outstanding. Its EPS is $4 ($200,000 ÷ 50,000).

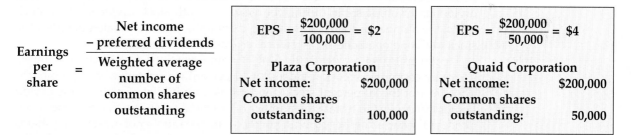

Just as the corporation lists separately its different sources of income from continuing operations and discontinued operations, it should list separately the EPS figure for income before discontinued operations and net income for the period to emphasize the significance of discontinued operations to a company's overall results.

Consider the income statement of Como Technology Inc. shown in Exhibit 14–6; in 2010, it had 60,000 common shares outstanding. Income from continuing operations was $117,000 and income from discontinued operations net of tax was $45,500. Como Technology Inc. could present the following EPS information:

Earnings per common share
Income per share from continuing operations ($117,000 ÷ 60,000) $1.95
Income per share from discontinued operations ($45,500 ÷ 60,000) 0.76
Net income per share [($117,000 + $45,500) ÷ 60,000] $2.71

Note that the details of calculations shown above are for illustrative purposes only. They would not appear in formal financial statements.

The income statement user can better understand the sources of the business's EPS amounts when they are presented in this detail.

Weighted Average Number of Common Shares Outstanding Computing EPS is straightforward if the number of common shares outstanding does not change over the entire accounting period. For many corporations, however, this figure varies as the company issues new shares and repurchases its own shares over the course of the year. Consider a corporation that had 100,000 shares outstanding from January through November, then purchased 60,000 of its own shares for cancellation. This company's EPS would be misleadingly high if computed using 40,000 (100,000 – 60,000) shares. To make EPS as meaningful as possible, corporations use the weighted average number of common shares outstanding during the period.

Let's assume the following figures for IMC Communications Corporation. From January through May, 2010, the company had 240,000 common shares outstanding; from June through August, 200,000 shares; and from September through December, 210,000 shares. We compute the weighted average by considering the outstanding shares per month as a fraction of the year:

Number of Common Shares Outstanding		Fraction of Year				Weighted Average Number of Common Shares Outstanding
240,000	×	$\frac{5}{12}$	(January through May)	=		100,000
200,000	×	$\frac{3}{12}$	(June through August)	=		50,000
210,000	×	$\frac{4}{12}$	(September through December)	=		70,000
			Weighted average number of common shares outstanding during 2010	=		220,000

The 220,000 weighted average would be divided into net income to compute the corporation's EPS.

Stock Dividends and Stock Splits The calculation of weighted average number of common shares outstanding becomes complicated when there have been stock dividends or stock splits during the year. For both stock dividends and stock splits, the number of shares outstanding during the year are restated to reflect the stock dividend or stock split *as if it had occurred at the beginning of the year.*

To illustrate, let's extend the IMC Communications Corporation example above by assuming a stock dividend of 10 percent was effective on September 1. The effect of the 10-percent stock dividend is a multiplier of 1.10 for the period January to August to restate the number of outstanding shares as if the stock dividend had occurred at the beginning of the year. The number of outstanding shares for September to December already reflects the 10-percent stock dividend, so the effect is a multiplier of 1.00 for those months. We compute the weighted average by considering the outstanding shares per month as a fraction of the year:

Number of Common Shares Outstanding		Effect of Stock Dividend		Fraction of Year				Weighted Average Number of Common Shares Outstanding
240,000	×	1.10	×	$\frac{5}{12}$	(January through May)	=		110,000
200,000	×	1.10	×	$\frac{3}{12}$	(June through August)	=		55,000
231,000*	×	1.00	×	$\frac{4}{12}$	(September through December)	=		77,000
					Weighted average number of common shares outstanding during 2010	=		242,000

* Amount includes the 10-percent stock dividend

The 242,000 weighted average number of common shares outstanding would be divided into net income to compute the corporation's EPS.

To illustrate the results of a stock split, change the IMC Communications Corporation example above by assuming a 2-for-1 stock split on September 1, 2010, instead of the 10-percent stock split shown above. The effect of the 2-for-1 stock split is 2.00, to double the number of shares for the period January to August to restate the number of outstanding shares as if the stock split had occurred at the beginning of the year. The number of outstanding shares for September to December already reflects the 2-for-1 stock split, so the effect is 1.00 for those months. Again, we compute the weighted average by considering the outstanding shares per month as a fraction of the year:

Number of Common Shares Outstanding		Effect of Stock Split		Fraction of Year				Weighted Average Number of Common Shares Outstanding
240,000	×	2.00	×	$\frac{5}{12}$	(January through May)	=		200,000
200,000	×	2.00	×	$\frac{3}{12}$	(June through August)	=		100,000
420,000*	×	1.00	×	$\frac{4}{12}$	(September through December)	=		140,000
					Weighted average number of common shares outstanding during 2010	=		440,000

* Amount includes the 2-for-1 stock split

The 440,000 weighted average number of common shares outstanding would be divided into net income to compute the corporation's EPS.

Preferred Dividends   Throughout the EPS discussion we have used only the number of common shares outstanding. Holders of preferred shares have no claim to the business's income beyond the stated preferred dividend. Even though preferred shares have no claims, preferred dividends do affect the EPS figure. Recall: EPS is earnings per common share. Also recall that dividends on preferred shares are paid first if *either* dividends on preferred shares are declared in the current year *or* the preferred shares are cumulative (since the dividends will have to be paid in the current or a future year whether they are declared in the current year or not). Therefore, declared or cumulative preferred dividends must be subtracted from income from continuing operations and net income in the computation of EPS.

If Como Technology Ltd. had 10,000 cumulative preferred shares outstanding, each with a $1.50 dividend, the annual preferred dividend would be $15,000 (10,000 × $1.50). The $15,000 would be subtracted from income from continuing operations and net income, resulting in the following EPS computations:

Income per share from continuing operations [($117,000 – $15,000) ÷ 60,000]	$1.70
Net income per share [($162,500 – $15,000) ÷ 60,000]	$2.46

Dilution   Some corporations make their bonds or preferred shares more attractive to investors by offering conversion privileges, which permit the holder to convert the bond or preferred shares into some specified number of common shares. If in fact the bonds or preferred shares are converted into common shares, then the EPS will be diluted (reduced) because more common shares are divided into net income. Because convertible bonds or convertible preferred shares can be traded for common shares, the common shareholders want to know the amount of the decrease in EPS that would occur if conversion took place. To provide this information, corporations with convertible bonds or preferred shares outstanding present two sets of EPS amounts: EPS based on actual outstanding common shares (basic EPS) and EPS based on outstanding common shares plus the number of additional common shares that would arise from conversion of the convertible bonds and convertible preferred shares into common shares (fully diluted EPS). Fully diluted EPS is always lower than basic EPS. The topic of dilution can be very complex and is covered more fully in intermediate accounting texts.

EPS is one of the most widely used accounting figures. Many income statement users place top priority on EPS. Also, the market price of a share in a company is related to its EPS. By dividing the market price of a company's share by its EPS, we compute a statistic called the *price-to-earnings ratio* or *price–earnings ratio*. Several Internet sites as well as the business press, such as the *Globe and Mail Report on Business*, report the price–earnings ratios (listed as P/E) daily for hundreds of companies listed on the Toronto Stock Exchange (TSX), the Montréal Exchange, the TSX Venture Exchange, the New York Stock Exchange, and NASDAQ. The price–earnings ratio is explored more fully in Chapter 18.

DID YOU GET IT?

To check your understanding of the material in this Learning Objective, complete these questions. The solutions appear on MyAccountingLab so you can check your progress.

8. On September 1, 2010, Acme Equipment Corp. sells its division that manufactures mobile homes. The assets are sold at a taxable gain of $1,700,000. The loss from operations for the year up to the date of sale was $960,000. The tax rate is 30 percent. How would you present the loss for the year and the sale of the division on the income statement for the year ended December 31, 2010?

9. The net income of Hart Corp. amounted to $3,750,000 for the year ended December 31, 2010. Hart Corp. had 200,000 $9.00 cumulative preferred shares throughout the year, and 310,000 common shares at the end of the year. At January 1, 2010, Hart Corp. had 270,000 common shares outstanding, and issued 40,000 common shares on April 1. Calculate Hart Corp.'s EPS.

10. Refer to the Hart Corp. data in the previous question. Assume the same details but, in addition, that a 3-for-1 stock split of the common shares occurred on October 1, 2010. Calculate Hart Corp.'s EPS.

OBJECTIVE 5

Prepare a statement of retained earnings and a statement of shareholders' equity

Statement of Retained Earnings

Retained earnings may be a significant portion of a corporation's shareholders' equity. The year's income increases the Retained Earnings balance, and dividends declared decrease it. Retained earnings is so important that some corporations prepare a separate financial statement outlining the major changes in this equity account. The statement of retained earnings for Como Technology Inc. appears in Exhibit 14–7.

Some companies report income and retained earnings on a single statement. Exhibit 14–8 illustrates how Como Technology Inc. would combine its income statement and its statement of retained earnings.

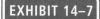

EXHIBIT 14–7

COMO TECHNOLOGY INC.
Statement of Retained Earnings
For the Year Ended December 31, 2010

Retained earnings, January 1, 2010	$260,000
Net income for 2010	162,500
	422,500
Dividends for 2010	(42,000)
Retained earnings, December 31, 2010	$380,500

EXHIBIT 14–8 Statement of Income and Retained Earnings

COMO TECHNOLOGY INC.
Statement of Income and Retained Earnings
For the Year Ended December 31, 2010

Income statement

Sales revenue	$1,000,000
Cost of goods sold	480,000
Gross margin	520,000
Operating expenses (listed individually)	362,000

Statement of Retained Earnings

Net income for 2010	162,500
Retained earnings, January 1, 2010	260,000
	422,500
Dividends for 2010	(42,000)
Retained earnings, December 31, 2010	$ 380,500

Earnings per common share (60,000 shares outstanding)		
Income from continuing operations	$	1.95
Income from discontinued operations		0.76
Net income	$	2.71

Statement of Shareholders' Equity

In addition to the balance sheet and income statement, corporations sometimes also prepare the **statement of shareholders' equity**, or simply **statement of equity**, to present changes in all components of equity, much as the statement of owner's equity presents information on changes in the equity of a proprietorship. Sales and repurchases of shares during the year affect contributed capital. The year's income increases the Retained Earnings balance, and dividends decrease it. The statement of shareholders' equity begins with the previous year's shareholders' equity balances and shows the changes that led to the current year's final balances. The statement of shareholders' equity for Como Technology Inc. appears in Exhibit 14–9, with some details added for illustration. Notice that the information from the statement of retained earnings appears in the Retained Earnings column of the statement of shareholders' equity.

EXHIBIT 14–9 | Statement of Shareholders' Equity

COMO TECHNOLOGY INC.
Statement of Shareholders' Equity
For the Year Ended December 31, 2010

	Common Shares	Contributed Surplus— Share Repurchases	Retained Earnings	Total Share- holders' Equity
Balance, December 31, 2009	$360,000	$ 0	$260,000	$620,000
Issuance of shares	100,000			100,000
Net income			162,500	162,500
Cash dividends			(42,000)	(42,000)
Repurchase of common shares	(40,000)	10,000		(30,000)
Balance, December 31, 2010	$420,000	$10,000	$380,500	$810,500

Accounting for Errors and Changes in Accounting Policy

What happens when a company makes an error in recording revenues or expenses? Detecting the error in the period in which it occurs allows the company to make a correction before preparing that period's financial statements. But failure to detect the error until a later period means that the business will have reported an incorrect amount of income on its income statement. After the revenue and expense accounts are closed, the Retained Earnings account will absorb the effect of the error, and its balance will be wrong until the error is corrected.

To correct an error, the correcting entry includes a debit or credit to Retained Earnings for the error amount and a debit or credit to the asset or liability account that was misstated. The error correction appears on the corporation's statement of retained earnings or in the Retained Earnings column of the statement of shareholders' equity to indicate to readers the amount and the nature of the change in the Retained Earnings balance.

Assume that Paquette Corporation recorded the closing inventory balance for 2009 as $30,000. The correct amount was $40,000. This error resulted in overstating 2009 expenses by $10,000 and understating net income by $10,000. A review of the inventory working papers after the financial statements were issued alerted the Paquette Corporation management to the mistake. The entry to record this error correction in 2010[*] is

```
2010
Jun. 19    Inventory .........................................................    10,000
               Retained Earnings ......................................                10,000
           Correction of prior years' error in
           recording closing inventory in 2009.
```

The credit to Retained Earnings adjusts retained earnings to reflect the understated income in 2009. If Cost of Goods Sold was credited in 2010 when the correcting entry is recorded, income in 2010 would be overstated. The journal entry properly locates the adjustment in the period prior to 2010 (i.e., to 2009, when the error occurred.)

The error correction would appear on the statement of retained earnings as shown below for simplicity, or on the statement of shareholders' equity in the Retained Earnings section (not shown):

---

[*]We disregard the income tax effects to simplify the illustration.

PAQUETTE CORPORATION
Statement of Retained Earnings
For the Year Ended December 31, 2010

Retained earnings, January 1, 2010	
as originally reported	$390,000
Adjustment to correct error	
in recording closing inventory in 2009 (see Note XX)	10,000
Retained earnings, January 1, 2010,	
as adjusted	400,000
Net income for 2010...	114,000
	514,000
Dividends for 2010..	(41,000)
Retained earnings balance, December 31, 2010.................................	$473,000

Our example shows a correction for additional revenue. To make a correction for additional expense, Retained Earnings is debited and the misstated asset or liability is credited.

A change in accounting policy should be applied retrospectively, prior periods should be restated to reflect the change, and the facts of the restatement should be disclosed in the notes. An example would be a change in amortization method. The effect of the change on prior periods' results would appear as an item on the statement of retained earnings or on the statement of shareholders' equity in the Retained Earnings section, the same way as an error would.

Restrictions on Retained Earnings

To ensure that corporations maintain a minimum level of shareholders' equity for the protection of creditors, incorporating acts restrict the amount of its own shares that a corporation may repurchase. This restriction often focuses on the balance of Retained Earnings. Companies usually report their retained earnings restrictions in notes to the financial statements but these are rarely seen in Canada.

Appropriations of Retained Earnings **Appropriations** are restrictions of retained earnings that are recorded by formal journal entries. A corporation may appropriate—that is, segregate in a separate account—a portion of Retained Earnings for a specific use. For example, the board of directors may appropriate part of Retained Earnings for building a new manufacturing plant. A debit to Retained Earnings and a credit to a separate account—Retained Earnings Restricted for Plant Expansion—records the appropriation. Appropriated Retained Earnings is normally reported directly above the regular Retained Earnings account, with a footnote where the appropriation is more fully described. *Retained earnings appropriations are rare.*

Limits on Dividends and Share Repurchases Dividends and repurchases of shares require a cash payment. In fact, repurchases of shares are returns of their investment to the shareholders. These outlays decrease assets, so the corporation has fewer resources to pay liabilities. A bank may agree to lend $500,000 only if the borrowing corporation limits dividend payments and repurchases of its shares. A corporation might agree to restrict dividends as a condition for receiving a loan in order to get a lower interest rate.

This type of restriction on the payment of dividends is more often seen, as shown in the following note:

Restriction on Dividends Certain terms of the Company's preferred shares and debt instruments could restrict the Company's ability to declare dividends on preferred and common shares. At year end, such terms did not restrict or alter the company's ability to declare dividends.

To check your understanding of the material in this Learning Objective, complete these questions. The solutions appear on MyAccountingLab so you can check your progress.

11. Calculate the missing amounts in the following corporation's income statement. Show your calculations.

Golden Goods Ltd.
Income Statement
For the Year Ended December 31, 2010

Sales revenue..	$800,000
Cost of goods sold...	380,000
Gross margin..	a
Operating expenses (listed individually)	342,000
Operating income..	b
Other gains (losses)	
Gain on sale of land..	($80,000)
Loss due to labour dispute...	20,000 c
Income from continuing operations before income tax	d
Income tax expense..	51,000
Income from continuing operations.....................................	e
Discontinued operations	
Operating loss, $60,000, plus	
income tax saving of $21,000	f
Gain on disposal, $21,000, less	
income tax of $7,000..	14,000 g
Net income	$ h
Earnings per common share	
(20,000 shares outstanding)	
Income from continuing operations....................................	$ i
Income from discontinued operations.................................	j
Net income..	$ k

12. Refer to the Golden Goods Ltd. data in the previous question. Retained earnings were $240,000 at December 31, 2009, and dividends paid during 2010 totalled $60,000. Create the December 31, 2010 statement of retained earnings for this company.

13. Refer to the Golden Goods Ltd. data in the previous two questions. Calculate the missing amounts in the company's statement of shareholders' equity. Show your calculations.

GOLDEN GOODS LTD.
Statement of Shareholders' Equity
For the Year Ended December 31, 2010

	Common Shares	Contributed Surplus— Share Repurchases	Retained Earnings	Total Share-holders' Equity
Balance, December 31, 2009	$160,000	$ 0	$ a	$400,000
Issuance of shares	e			e
Net income			b	b
Cash dividends			c	c
Repurchase of common shares	(20,000)	5,000		f
Balance, December 31, 2010	$240,000	$5,000	$ d	$ g

The Impact of IFRS on the Income Statement and the Statement of Shareholders' Equity

When it comes to preparing the income statement, Canadian GAAP for private enterprises and IFRS are very similar; however, there are some differences. One of the main differences is that IFRS requires companies to disclose EPS information on the income statement, whereas GAAP for private enterprises does not. However, many private corporations do provide EPS information for current and potential investors.

IFRS also requires corporations to report other comprehensive income, whereas GAAP for private enterprises does not. Other comprehensive income arises from a number of sources including unrealized gains and losses on certain classes of investment securities. Under IFRS, other comprehensive income is recorded on the Statement of Comprehensive Income. Other comprehensive income is covered in more advanced accounting courses.

Likewise, the two sets of standards governing retained earnings are very comparable. IFRS requires companies to prepare a Statement of Changes in Equity, rather than a Statement of Retained Earnings. The Statement of Changes in Equity is similar to the Statement of Shareholders' Equity described in this chapter.

> **OBJECTIVE 6**
>
> Identify the impact on the income statement and the statement of shareholders' equity of international financial reporting standards (IFRS)

DID YOU GET IT?

MyAccountingLab

To check your understanding of the material in this Learning Objective, complete these questions. The solutions appear on MyAccountingLab so you can check your progress.

14. Companies reporting under IFRS are required to provide two types of information in their financial statements that are not required for companies reporting under GAAP for private enterprises. Describe each type of information and the financial statement on which it is reported.

15. Companies reporting under GAAP for private enterprises, as described in this chapter, sometimes create a Statement of Shareholders' Equity. What is the name of the same statement for companies reporting under IFRS?

As we conclude this chapter, we return to our opening questions: What is a stock dividend and what is a stock split? Why would a corporation repurchase its own shares? What are earnings per share, and how are they calculated? How do you prepare a statement of retained earnings and a statement of shareholders' equity? These questions were answered throughout this chapter. And the following Decision Guidelines provide the answers in a useful summary.

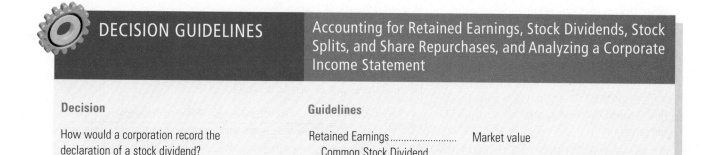

DECISION GUIDELINES
Accounting for Retained Earnings, Stock Dividends, Stock Splits, and Share Repurchases, and Analyzing a Corporate Income Statement

Decision	Guidelines	
How would a corporation record the declaration of a stock dividend?	Retained Earnings........................	Market value
	Common Stock Dividend	
	Distributable............................	Market value

Decision	Guidelines

How would a corporation record a stock split?

Memorandum only: Split the common stock 3 for 1. Distributed two new common shares for each one old share outstanding.

What are the effects of stock dividends and stock splits on each of the following?

	Effects of	
	Stock Dividend	**Stock Split (for example, a 2-for-1 split)**
• Number of shares authorized	No effect	Increase (however, for unlimited authorized, no effect)
• Shares issued	Increase	Increase
• Shares outstanding	Increase	Increase
• Total assets, total liabilities, and total shareholders' equity	No effect	No effect
• Common Shares account	Increase	No effect
• Retained Earnings account	Decrease	No effect

How would a corporation record repurchase of shares:

• At issue price?

Common Shares	Issue price	
Cash		Issue price

• Above issue price (with no relevant Contributed Surplus)?

Common Shares..........................	Issue price	
Retained Earnings.......................	Excess*	
Cash		Amount paid

*Excess of amount paid over issue price

• Below issue price?

Common Shares..........................	Issue price	
Contributed Surplus—Share Repurchase		Gain**
Cash		Amount paid

**Gain is equal to issue price minus amount paid.

What are the effects of the repurchase and subsequent sale of the repurchased shares on:

	Effects of	
	Repurchase of Shares	**Sale of Repurchased Shares**
• Total assets?	Decrease by full amount of cash paid	Increase by full amount of cash received
• Total shareholders' equity?	Decrease by full amount of cash paid	Increase by full amount of cash received

What are the main sections of the income statement?

Continuing operations
• Continuing operations, including unusual gains and losses, less income tax expense

Discontinued operations
• Discontinued operations—income or loss, and gain or loss on sale—less the income tax effects

Net income (or net loss)

Earnings per share (not required but often provided)
• Earnings per share—applies only to net income (or net loss) and its components

What earnings per share (EPS) figures can a corporation report?

May compute basic EPS figures for
• Income from continuing operations
• Discontinued operations
• Net income (or net loss)

Fully diluted EPS should be presented by corporations that have bonds or preferred shares with conversion privileges.

How is basic EPS for net income computed?

$$\text{Earnings per share} = \frac{\text{Net income} - \text{Preferred dividends}}{\text{Weighted average number of common shares outstanding}}$$

The following information was taken from the ledger of Caravale Inc. at December 31, 2010:

Loss on sale of discontinued operations	$ 20,000	Selling expenses	$ 78,000
Prior-year error—credit to Retained Earnings	5,000	Common shares, 40,000 shares issued	155,000
		Sales revenue	620,000
Gain on sale of property	61,000	Interest expense	30,000
Income tax expense (saving)		Cost of goods sold	380,000
Continuing operations	42,000	Operating income, discontinued operations	30,000
Discontinued operations		Loss due to lawsuit	11,000
Operating income	10,500	General expenses	62,000
Loss on sale	(7,000)	Preferred shares, $4.00, cumulative, 1,000 shares issued	50,000
Total dividends	16,000	Retained earnings, January 1, 2010, as originally reported	103,000

Required

Prepare a single-step income statement first, then a statement of retained earnings, then a statement of shareholders' equity for Caravale Inc. for the year ended December 31, 2010. Include the EPS presentation and show computations. Assume no changes in the share accounts during the year, and assume a 35-percent tax rate.

Name: Caravale Inc.
Industry: Corporation with common and preferred shares
Fiscal Period: Year ended December 31, 2010

SOLUTION

Sort the ledger items into those that appear on the various statements. Selected items are highlighted in the margins.

Note: The statement of retained earnings is presented here first, then the income statement is presented. Reverse this order when you complete this question.

CARAVALE INC.
Statement of Retained Earnings
For the Year Ended December 31, 2010

Retained earnings, January 1, 2010, as originally reported	$103,000
Correction of prior-year error—credit (Note X)	5,000
Retained earnings, January 1, 2010, as adjusted	108,000
Net income for current year	84,500
	192,500
Dividends for 2010	(16,000)
Retained earnings, December 31, 2010	$176,500

Prior-period adjustments must be disclosed in a separate line in the statement of retained earnings.

Given in the list of data

Revenue includes gain on sale of property in a single-step income statement.

Expenses include all normal operating costs related to the revenue reported. Income tax expense is included here.

This is reported net of income tax of 35 percent.

The EPS are calculated by using net income from various parts of the income statement less preferred dividends. Use the common shares and preferred shares information from the data given to calculate preferred dividends and the number of common shares outstanding.

The Retained Earnings column of the statement of shareholders' equity contains the same information as the statement of retained earnings created earlier.

CARAVALE INC.
Income Statement
For the Year Ended December 31, 2010

Revenue and gains			
Sales revenue			$ 620,000
Gain on sale of property			61,000
Total revenues and gains			681,000
Expenses and losses			
Cost of goods sold		$380,000	
Selling expenses		78,000	
General expenses		62,000	
Interest expense		30,000	
Loss due to lawsuit		11,000	
Income tax expense		42,000	
Total expenses and losses			603,000
Income from continuing operations			78,000
Discontinued operations (Note A)			
Operating income	$30,000		
Less income tax	10,500	19,500	
Loss on sale of discontinued operations	(20,000)		
Less income tax saving	7,000	(13,000)	6,500
Net income			$ 84,500

Earnings per share

Income from continuing operations

[($78,000 − $4,000) ÷ 40,000 shares] .... $ 1.85

Income from discontinued operations ($6,500 ÷ 40,000 shares) 0.16

Net income [($84,500 − $4,000) ÷ 40,000 shares] .... $ 2.01

Computations:

$$\text{Earnings per share} = \frac{\text{Net income} - \text{Preferred dividends}}{\text{Weighted average number of common shares outstanding}}$$

Preferred dividends: 1,000 × $4.00 = $4,000

CARAVALE INC.
Statement of Shareholders' Equity
For the Year Ended December 31, 2010

	Common Shares	Preferred Shares	Retained Earnings	Total Shareholders' Equity
Balance, December 31, 2009	$155,000	$50,000	$103,000	$308,000
Adjustment to correct error			5,000	5,000
Net income			84,500	84,500
Cash dividends			(16,000)	(16,000)
Balance, December 31, 2010	$155,000	$50,000	$176,500	$381,500

Summary

1. **Account for stock dividends.** *Retained Earnings* carries the balance of the business's net income accumulated over its lifetime, less all declared dividends and net losses. *Cash dividends* are distributions of corporate assets made possible by earnings. *Stock dividends*, or *share dividends*, are distributions of the corporation's own shares to its shareholders.

2. **Distinguish stock splits from stock dividends.** *Stock dividends* shift amounts from retained earnings to contributed capital. *Stock splits* do not change any account balances. Stock splits and stock dividends increase the number of shares outstanding and thus lower the market price per share.

3. **Account for repurchased shares.** *Repurchased shares* are the corporation's own shares that have been issued and reacquired. The corporation may issue repurchased shares in the normal way or may cancel the repurchased shares.

4. **Analyze a corporate income statement.** The corporate *income statement* lists separately the various sources of income—*income from continuing operations* (which includes unusual gains and losses), and *discontinued operations*—as well as related *income tax expense*. The bottom line of the income statement reports *net income* or *net loss* for the period. *Earnings-per-share* figures may also appear on the income statement, or may be calculated by investors.

5. **Prepare a statement of retained earnings and a statement of shareholders' equity.** A corporation must prepare a statement of retained earnings, which reports the changes in the Retained Earnings account, including prior-period adjustments, net income or net loss, and dividends paid. This statement may be combined with the income statement. Retained earnings may be *restricted* by law or contract or by the corporation itself. An *appropriation* is a restriction of retained earnings that is recorded by formal journal entries and appears on the balance sheet as a separate Retained Earnings item. Corporations may prepare a statement of shareholders' equity, which reports the changes in all the shareholders' equity accounts, including sales and repurchases of a corporation's own shares, cash and stock dividends paid, and net income or loss.

6. **Identify the impact on the income statement and the statement of shareholders' equity of international financial reporting standards (IFRS).** Unlike companies that report under GAAP for private enterprises, companies that report under IFRS must present EPS information on their income statement and must report comprehensive income in a statement of comprehensive income. Under IFRS, the statement of shareholders' equity is called the statement of changes in equity.

SELF-STUDY QUESTIONS

Test your understanding of the chapter by marking the best answer for each of the following questions:

1. A corporation has total shareholders' equity of $200,000, including Retained Earnings of $38,000. The Cash balance is $70,000. The maximum cash dividend the company can declare and pay is (*pp. 768–769*)
   - a. $38,000
   - c. $130,000
   - b. $70,000
   - d. $200,000

2. A stock dividend, or share dividend, (*p. 769*)
   - a. Decreases shareholders' equity
   - b. Decreases assets
   - c. Leaves total shareholders' equity unchanged
   - d. Does none of the above

3. Acres Ltd. has 10,000 common shares outstanding. The shares were issued at $20.00 per share, and now their market value is $40.00 per share. Acres' board of directors declares and distributes a common stock dividend of one share for every 10 held. Which of the following entries shows the full effect of declaring and distributing the dividend? (*pp. 770–771*)
   - a. Retained Earnings 40,000
     Common Stock Dividend
     Distributable...................... 40,000

   - b. Retained Earnings 20,000
     Common Shares................... 20,000
   - c. Retained Earnings 20,000
     Cash 20,000
   - d. Retained Earnings 40,000
     Common Shares................... 40,000

4. Lang Real Estate Investment Corporation declared and distributed a 50 percent stock dividend. Which of the following stock splits would have the same effect on the number of Lang shares outstanding? (*p. 773*)
   - a. 2 for 1
   - c. 4 for 3
   - b. 3 for 2
   - d. 5 for 4

5. Deer Lake Outfitters Ltd. purchased 10,000 of its common shares that had been issued at $1.50 per share, paying $6.00 per share. This transaction (*p. 776*)
   - a. Has no effect on company assets
   - b. Has no effect on shareholders' equity
   - c. Decreases shareholders' equity by $15,000
   - d. Decreases shareholders' equity by $60,000

6. A restriction of retained earnings (*p. 789*)
   - a. Has no effect on total retained earnings
   - b. Reduces retained earnings available for the declaration of dividends

c. Is usually reported by a note

d. Does all of the above

7. Which of the following items is not reported on the income statement? (*p. 781*)

a. Issue price of shares

b. Unusual gains and losses

c. Income tax expense

d. Earnings per share

8. The income statement item that is likely to be most useful for predicting income from year to year is (*pp. 780–783*)

a. Unusual items

b. Discontinued operations

c. Income from continuing operations

d. Net income

9. In computing earnings per share (EPS), dividends on cumulative preferred shares are (*p. 785*)

a. Added because they represent earnings to the preferred shareholders

b. Subtracted because they represent earnings to the preferred shareholders

c. Ignored because they do not pertain to the common shares

d. Reported separately on the income statement

10. A corporation accidentally overlooked an accrual of property tax expense at December 31, 2009. Accountants for the company detect the error early in 2010 before the expense is paid. The entry to record this correction in 2010 for a prior year's error is (*pp. 788–789*)

a. Retained Earnings..................... XXX
    Property Tax Expense.......... XXX

b. Property Tax Expense.............. XXX
    Property Tax Payable XXX

c. Retained Earnings..................... XXX
    Property Tax Payable XXX

d. Property Tax Payable XXX
    Property Tax Expense.......... XXX

Answers to Self-Study Questions

1.a 2.c 3.d 4.b 5.d 6.d 7.a 8.c 9.b 10.c

ACCOUNTING VOCABULARY

Appropriations   (*p. 789*)
Earnings per share (EPS)   (*p. 783*)
Income trust   (*p. 774*)
Investment trust   (*p. 774*)
Segment of the business   (*p. 782*)
Share dividend   (*p. 769*)

Repurchase of own shares   (*p. 774*)
Stock dividend   (*p. 769*)
Stock split   (*p. 772*)
Statement of equity   (*p. 787*)
Statement of shareholders' equity   (*p. 787*)

SIMILAR ACCOUNTING TERMS

Contributed capital	Share capital; Capital stock
Income Statement	Statement of Earnings
Income Trust	Investment Trust
Price-to-earnings ratio	Price–earnings ratio; P/E ratio
Shareholders' equity	Stockholders' equity
Statement of shareholders' equity	Statement of equity; Statement of changes in equity

Assignment Material

QUESTIONS

1. Identify the two main parts of shareholders' equity and explain how they differ.

2. Identify the account debited and the account credited from the last closing entry a corporation makes each year. What is the purpose of this entry?

3. Tam Logistics Ltd. reported a Cash balance of $3 million and a Retained Earnings balance of $18 million. Explain how Tam Logistics Ltd. can have so much more retained earnings than cash. In your answer, identify the nature of retained earnings and state how it ties to cash.

4. Give two reasons for a corporation to distribute a stock dividend.

5. A friend of yours receives a stock dividend on an investment. She believes stock dividends are the same as cash dividends. Explain why the two are not the same.

6. Csordas Properties Inc. declares a stock dividend on June 21 and reports Stock Dividend Payable as a liability on the June 30 balance sheet. Is this correct? Give your reason.

7. What value is normally assigned to shares issued as a stock dividend?

8. Explain the similarity and difference between a 100-percent stock dividend and a 2-for-1 stock split to the corporation issuing the stock dividend and the stock split.

9. Give three reasons why a corporation may repurchase its own shares.

10. What effect does the repurchase of shares have on the (a) assets and (b) issued and outstanding shares of the corporation?

11. What effect does the repurchase and cancellation of common shares have on the (a) assets, (b) authorized shares, and (c) issued and outstanding shares of the corporation?

12. What does the *Canada Business Corporations Act* (CBCA) require a company to do when it repurchases its own shares?

13. Are there any exceptions to the requirement of the CBCA mentioned in question 12? If so, what are they?

14. Incorporating legislation frequently has a prohibition on a corporation's purchasing its own shares in certain circumstances. What are those circumstances? Why does the prohibition exist?

15. Why do creditors wish to restrict a corporation's payment of cash dividends and repurchases of the corporation's shares?

16. What are two ways to report a retained earnings restriction? Which way is more common?

17. Identify two items on the income statement that generate income tax expense. What is an income tax saving, and how does it arise?

18. Why is it important for a corporation to report income from continuing operations separately from discontinued operations?

19. Give four examples of gains and losses that are unusual and reported separately in the continuing operations section of the income statement.

20. What is the most widely used of all accounting statistics? What is the price–earnings ratio? Compute the price–earnings ratio for a company with EPS of $2.25 and a market price of $18.00 per common share.

21. What is the earnings per share of Singh Realty Ltd., which had net income of $63,000 and a weighted average number of common shares of 18,000?

22. What account do all corrections made for errors in prior periods affect? On what financial statement are these corrections reported?

STARTERS

MyAccountingLab All questions in this section appear in MyAccountingLab.

Starter 14–1 Bayline Boats Ltd. has 10,000 common shares outstanding. Bayline distributes a 20 percent stock dividend when the market value of its shares is $15.00 per share.

1. Journalize Bayline's declaration and distribution of the stock dividend on September 30, 2010. Explanations are not required.
2. What is the overall effect of the stock dividend on Bayline's total assets? On total shareholders' equity?

Recording a stock dividend
①

1. Dr Retained Earnings $30,000

Starter 14–2 Compare and contrast the accounting for cash dividends and stock dividends. In the space provided, insert either "Cash dividends," "Stock dividends," or "Both cash dividends and stock dividends" to complete each of the following statements:

1. _____ decrease Retained Earnings.
2. _____ have no effect on a liability.

Comparing and contrasting cash dividends and stock dividends
①

3. _____ increase contributed capital by the same amount that they decrease Retained Earnings.

4. _____ decrease both total assets and total shareholders' equity, resulting in a decrease in the size of the company.

Accounting for a stock split

②

1. Total shareholders' equity $332,000

Starter 14–3 Angelo Imports Inc. recently reported the following shareholders' equity:

Common shares,	
250,000 shares authorized, 101,000 shares issued.............	$121,500
Retained earnings...	210,500
Total shareholders' equity...	$332,000

Suppose Angelo Imports split its common shares 2 for 1 in order to decrease the market price of its shares. The company's shares were trading at $10.00 immediately before the split.

1. Prepare the shareholders' equity section of Angelo Imports Inc.'s balance sheet after the stock split.
2. Which account balances changed after the stock split? Which account balances were unchanged?

Accounting for the repurchase and sale of common shares

③

Starter 14–4 Dan's Discount Furniture Inc. completed the following share repurchase and sale transactions:

a. Repurchased 1,000 common shares paying cash of $10.00 per share. The shares were originally issued for $6.00 per share.
b. Sold 500 of the repurchased shares for cash of $16.00 per share.

Journalize these transactions. Explanations are not required.

Interpreting a restriction of retained earnings

④

Starter 14–5 BLT Corporation's agreement with its bank lender restricts BLT's dividend payments. Why would a bank lender restrict a corporation's dividend payments and share repurchases?

Preparing a corporate income statement

④

Starter 14–6 List the major parts of a multi-step corporate income statement for Fitness Plus Athletic Clubs Inc. for the year ended December 31, 2010. Include all the major parts of the income statement, starting with net sales revenue and ending with net income (net loss). You may ignore dollar amounts and earnings per share.

Explaining the items on a complex corporate income statement

④

Starter 14–7 Answer these questions about a corporate income statement:

1. How do you measure gross margin?
2. What is the title of those items that are unusual, infrequent, and over which management has no influence or control?
3. Which income number is the best predictor of future net income?
4. What is the "bottom line"?
5. What does *EPS* abbreviate?

Preparing a corporate income statement

④

Net income $12,000

Starter 14–8 EPR Corp's accounting records include the following items, listed in no particular order, at December 31, 2010.

Other gains (losses)..................	$(12,500)	Net sales revenue........	$90,000
Cost of goods sold....................	35,000	Operating expenses....	30,000
Gain on discontinued		Accounts receivable....	9,500
operations..............................	7,500		

Income tax of 40 percent applies to all items.
    Prepare EPR Corp.'s multi-step income statement for the year ended December 31, 2010. Omit earnings per share.

Reporting earnings per share

④

EPS for net income $0.88

Starter 14–9 Return to the EPR Corp. data in Starter 14–8. EPR had 10,000 common shares outstanding on January 1, 2010. EPR declared and paid preferred dividends of $1,500 during 2010. In addition, EPR paid a 20 percent stock common dividend on June 30.
    Show how EPR Corp. reported EPS data on its 2010 income statement.

Interpreting earnings-per-share data

④

Starter 14–10 Figero Inc. has preferred shares outstanding.

1. Give the basic equation to compute earnings per common share for net income.
2. List all the income items for which Figero Inc. must report EPS data.

Starter 14–11 Census Research Inc. (CRI) ended 2009 with Retained Earnings of $37,500. During 2010, CRI earned net income of $45,000 and declared dividends of $15,000. Also during 2010, CRI got a $10,000 tax refund from Canada Revenue Agency. A tax audit revealed that CRI in error paid too much income tax in 2008.

Prepare CRI's statement of retained earnings for the year ended December 31, 2010 to report the correction of the prior-period error.

Reporting the correction of a prior-period error

Retained Earnings, Dec. 31, 2010, $77,500

Starter 14–12 Return to the Census Research Inc. (CRI) data in Starter 14–11. CRI ended 2009 with $20,000 in common shares and $15,000 in $0.50 preferred shares. No shares were sold or repurchased during 2010. Create CRI's statement of shareholders' equity for the year ended December 31, 2010.

Creating a statement of shareholders' equity

⑤

Total shareholders' equity, December 31, 2010, $112,500

EXERCISES

MyAccountingLab All questions in this section appear in MyAccountingLab.

Exercise 14–1

The shareholders' equity for Pagliano Bros. Paving Inc. on June 30, 2010 (end of the company's fiscal year), follows:

Journalizing dividends and reporting shareholders' equity

②

2.Total shareholders' equity $680,000

Common shares, 800,000 shares authorized, 60,000 shares issued.........	$300,000
Retained earnings	380,000
Total shareholders' equity	$680,000

On August 8, 2010, the market price of Pagliano Bros. Paving Inc.'s common shares was $12.00 per share and the company declared a 20 percent stock dividend. Pagliano Bros. Paving Inc. issued the dividend shares on August 31, 2010.

Required

1. Journalize the declaration and distribution of the stock dividend.
2. Prepare the shareholders' equity section of the balance sheet after the stock dividend distribution.

Exercise 14–2

Poco Travel Ltd. is authorized to issue 500,000 common shares. The company issued 70,000 shares at $7.50 per share. On June 10, 2010, when the Retained Earnings balance was $360,000, Poco Travel Ltd. declared a 10 percent stock dividend, using the market value of $4.00 per share. It distributed the stock dividend on July 20, 2010. On August 5, 2010, Poco Travel Ltd. declared a $0.45 per share cash dividend, which it paid on September 15, 2010.

Journalizing a stock dividend and reporting shareholders' equity

①

3. Total shareholders' equity $850,350

Required

1. Journalize the declaration and distribution of the stock dividend.
2. Journalize the declaration and payment of the cash dividend.
3. Prepare the shareholders' equity section of the balance sheet after both dividends.

Exercise 14–3

Delta Metal Products Ltd. had the following shareholders' equity at October 31, 2010:

Reporting shareholders' equity after a stock split

②

Total shareholders' equity $500,000

Common shares, unlimited shares authorized, 60,000 shares issued.....	$150,000
Retained earnings	350,000
Total shareholders' equity	$500,000

On November 14, 2010, Delta Metal Products Ltd. split its common shares 2 for 1. Make the memorandum entry to record the stock split, and prepare the shareholders' equity section of the balance sheet immediately after the split.

Exercise 14–4

Examine Delta Metal Products Ltd.'s shareholders' equity section for October 31, 2010, in Exercise 14–3. Suppose Delta Metal Products Ltd. consolidated its common shares 1 for 2 (a reverse stock split) in order to increase the market price of its shares. The company's shares were trading at $4.00 immediately before the reverse split. Make the memorandum entry to record the share consolidation, and prepare the shareholders' equity section of Delta Metal Products Ltd.'s balance sheet after the share consolidation. What would you expect the market price to be, approximately, after the reverse split?

Accounting for a reverse stock split

②

Total shareholders' equity $500,000

Using a stock split or a stock dividend to decrease the market price of a share

Exercise 14–5

Usurp Corp., an Internet service provider, has prospered during the past seven years, and recently the company's share price has shot up to $244.00.Usurp's management wishes to decrease the share price to the range of $116.00 to $124.00, which will be attractive to more investors. Should the company issue a 100-percent stock dividend or split the stock? Why? If you propose a stock split, state the split ratio that will accomplish the company's objective. Show your computations.

Effects of share issuance, dividends, and share repurchase transactions

(1)(2)(3)

Exercise 14–6

Identify the effects of these transactions on shareholders' equity. Has shareholders' equity increased, decreased, or remained the same? Each transaction is independent.

a. A 10-percent stock dividend. Before the dividend, 300,000 common shares were outstanding; market value was $7.50 at the time of the dividend.

b. A 2-for-1 stock split. Prior to the split, 60,000 common shares were outstanding.

c. Repurchase of 3,000 common shares at $7.00 per share. The average issue price of these shares was $5.00.

d. Sale of 1,000 repurchased common shares for $6.50 per share.

Journalizing share repurchase transactions

(3)

Exercise 14–7

Journalize the following transactions that Apex Technologies Ltd. conducted during 2010:

Feb.	19	Issued 8,000 common shares at $15.00 per share.
Apr.	24	Repurchased 2,000 common shares at $13.00 per share. The average issue price of the shares was $14.00.
Jun.	30	Repurchased 2,000 common shares at $18.00 per share. The average issue price of the shares was $14.00.
Nov.	12	Sold 400 repurchased shares at $11.50 per share.
Dec.	6	Sold 300 repurchased shares at $8.00 per share.

Journalizing repurchase of company shares and reporting shareholders' equity

(3)

1. Total shareholders' equity $877,500

Exercise 14–8

Debon Ltd. had the following shareholders' equity on March 26, 2010:

Common shares, unlimited shares authorized, 140,000 shares issued...	$420,000
Retained earnings	475,000
Total shareholders' equity...	$895,000

On May 3, 2010, the company repurchased and retired 5,000 common shares at $3.50 per share.

1. Journalize this transaction and prepare the shareholders' equity section of the balance sheet at June 30, 2010.

2. How many common shares are outstanding after the share repurchase?

Accounting for the retirement of preferred shares

(3)

(b) Reduced by $2,860 million

Exercise 14–9

Study Exhibit 14–5 on page 779. Suppose the Bank of Nova Scotia retired its preferred shares. What would be the amount of the reduction of the company's total shareholders' equity if the cost to retire the preferred shares was (a) $2,800 million? (b) $2,860 million? (c) $3,000 million?

Reporting a retained earnings restriction

a. Total shareholders' equity $587,500

Exercise 14–10

The agreement under which Karset Transport Ltd. issued its long-term debt requires the restriction of $150,000 of the company's Retained Earnings balance. Total Retained Earnings is $337,500, and total contributed capital is $250,000.

Required Show how to report shareholders' equity (including retained earnings) on Karset Transport Ltd.'s balance sheet at December 31, 2010, assuming:

    a. Karset Transport Ltd. discloses the restriction in a note. Write the note.

    b. Karset Transport Ltd. appropriates retained earnings in the amount of the restriction and includes no note in its statements.

Exercise 14–11

The ledger of Doe Plastics Inc. contains the following information for operations for the year ended September 30, 2010.

Excel Spreadsheet Template

Preparing a multiple-step income statement

(4)

Net income $17,500

Sales revenue	$350,000	Income tax expense—gain on		
Operating expenses		discontinued operations...	$ 5,000
(excluding income tax).........	77,500	Other loss.................................	22,500
Cost of goods sold	230,000	Income tax expense—	
Gain on discontinued		operating income...............	10,000
operations	12,500		

Required Prepare a multiple-step income statement for the year ended September 30, 2010. Omit earnings per share. Was 2010 a good year or a bad year for Doe Plastics Inc.? Explain your answer in terms of the outlook for 2011.

Exercise 14–12

Computing earnings per share

EPS = $0.78

BMO Solutions Inc. earned net income of $84,000 in 2010. The ledger reveals the following figures:

Preferred shares, $1.50, 4,000 shares issued and outstanding .... $ 50,000
Common shares, unlimited shares authorized, 100,000 shares issued... 300,000

Required Compute BMO Solutions Inc.'s EPS for 2010, assuming no changes in the share accounts during the year.

Exercise 14–13

Computing earnings per share

EPS for net income $0.40

Balfour Construction Ltd. had 60,000 common shares and 20,000 $0.75 preferred shares outstanding on December 31, 2009. On May 31, 2010, the company issued 6,000 additional common shares and split the common shares 2 for 1 on December 1, 2010. There were no other share issuances and no share repurchases during the year ended December 31, 2010. Income for the year from continuing operations was $70,000, and loss on discontinued operations (net of income tax) was $4,000.

Required Compute Balfour Construction Ltd.'s EPS amounts for the year ended December 31, 2010.

Exercise 14–14

Pacific Hotels Inc., a large hotel chain, had Retained Earnings of $250.0 million at the beginning of 2010. The company showed these figures at December 31, 2010:

	($ millions)
Net income	$75.0
Cash dividends—preferred	1.5
common	44.5
Debit to retained earnings due to repurchase of preferred shares	4.0

Excel Spreadsheet Template

Preparing a statement of retained earnings

Retained earnings, Dec. 31, 2010, $275.0 million

Required Prepare the statement of retained earnings for Pacific Hotels Inc. for the year ended December 31, 2010.

Exercise 14–15

Howren Concrete Products Ltd. reported the correction of an error made in the year ended December 31, 2010. An inventory error caused net income of the prior year to be overstated by $50,000. Retained Earnings at January 1, 2010, as previously reported, stood at $2,408,000. Net income for the year ended December 31, 2010 was $448,000, and dividends were $61,000.

Excel Spreadsheet Template

Preparing a statement of retained earnings with a correction of a prior-period error

Retained earnings, Dec. 31, 2010, $2,745,000

Required Prepare the company's statement of retained earnings for the year ended December 31, 2010.

Exercise 14–16

For the year ended December 31, 2009, Evans Inc. reported the following shareholders' equity:

Preparing a statement of shareholders' equity

Total shareholders' equity, Dec. 31, 2010, $2,252,000

Common shares, 400,000 shares authorized,
140,000 shares issued.. $1,400,000
Retained earnings 672,000
$2,072,000

During 2010, Evans Inc. completed these transactions and events (listed in chronological order):

a. Declared and issued a 20-percent stock dividend. At the time, Evans Inc.'s common shares were quoted at a market price of $11.50 per share.
b. Sold 1,000 common shares for $12.50 per share.
c. Sold 1,000 common shares to employees at $10.00 per share.
d. Net income for the year was $297,500.
e. Declared and paid cash dividends of $140,000.

Required Prepare Evans Inc.'s statement of shareholders' equity for 2010.

Journalizing share repurchase
and sale transactions

(3)

2. Common Shares ending
balance, $28,597

Exercise 14–17

To raise cash for future expansion, Carl Haupt incorporated his proprietorship and created Haupt Consulting Corporation. Haupt Consulting Corporation is authorized to issue an unlimited number of common shares and 50,000 $2.00 preferred shares. On February 1, 2010, Carl Haupt purchased 20,000 common shares for his proprietorship equity of $17,227 to maintain control of the company and issued 1,000 of the preferred shares for $50.00 per share.

In March 2010, Haupt Consulting Corporation has the following transactions related to its common shares:

Mar. 3 The company sold 1,000 of its common shares for $10.00 per share to a small number of people who believed in the company's potential for profit.

20 The company repurchased 100 of its common shares for $12.00 per share from a shareholder who was having financial difficulties. The shares will be resold in the near future, so they will not be cancelled.

30 The company sold the 100 shares repurchased on March 20 for $15.00 per share.

Required

1. Journalize the entries related to the transactions.
2. Calculate the ending balance in the Common Shares account.

CHALLENGE EXERCISE

Recording a stock dividend and
preparing a statement of
retained earnings

(1)(5)

2. Retained Earnings, Dec. 31,
2010, $4,200,000

Exercise 14–18

Tillay Environmental Products Inc. (TEPI) began 2010 with 1.6 million common shares issued and outstanding for $4.0 million. Beginning Retained Earnings was $4.5 million. On February 26, 2010, TEPI issued 100,000 common shares at $3.50 per share. On November 16, 2010, when the market price was $5.00 per share, the board of directors declared a 10 percent stock dividend, which was paid on December 20, 2010. Net income for the year was $550,000.

Required

1. Make the journal entries for the issuance of shares for cash and for the 10 percent stock dividend.
2. Prepare the company's statement of retained earnings for the year ended December 31, 2010.

BEYOND THE NUMBERS

Reporting special items

(3)(4)

Beyond the Numbers 14–1

The following accounting issues have arisen at Tri-City Computers Corp.:

1. An investor noted that the market price of shares seemed to decline after the date of record for a cash dividend. Why do you think that would be the case?

2. Corporations sometimes repurchase their own shares. When asked why, Tri-City Computers Corp.'s management responded that the shares were undervalued. What advantage would Tri-City Computers Corp. gain by buying and selling its own shares under these circumstances?

3. Tri-City Computers Corp. earned a significant profit in the year ended June 30, 2010, because land that it held was expropriated for a low-rental housing project. The company proposes to treat the sale of land to the government as operating revenue. Why do you think Tri-City Computers Corp. is proposing such treatment? Is this treatment appropriate?

ETHICAL ISSUE

Blackberry Gold Mine Ltd. is a gold mine in Ontario. In February 2010, company geologists discovered a new vein of gold-bearing ore that tripled the company's reserves. Prior to disclosing the new vein to the public, top managers of the company quietly bought most of the outstanding Blackberry Gold Mine Ltd. shares for themselves personally. After the discovery announcement, Blackberry Gold Mine Ltd.'s share price increased from $4.00 to $30.00.

Required

1. Did Blackberry Gold Mine Ltd. managers behave ethically? Explain your answer.
2. Who was helped and who was harmed by management's action?

PROBLEMS (GROUP A)

 All questions in this section appear in MyAccountingLab.

Problem 14–1A

Journalizing shareholders' equity transactions

Assume Frelix Construction Ltd. completed the following selected transactions during the year 2010:

Apr. 19	Declared a cash dividend on the $8.50 preferred shares (3,000 shares outstanding). Declared a $1.00 per share dividend on the 100,000 common shares outstanding. The date of record was May 2, and the payment date was May 25.
May 25	Paid the cash dividends.
Jun. 7	Split the company's 100,000 common shares 2 for 1; one new common share was issued for each old share held.
Jul. 29	Declared a 10-percent stock dividend on the common shares to holders of record on August 22, with distribution set for September 9. The market value was $36.00 per common share.
Sept. 9	Issued the stock dividend shares.
Oct. 26	Repurchased 5,000 of the company's own common shares at $40.00 per share. They had an average issue price of $28.00 per share.
Nov. 8	Sold 1,500 common shares for $42.00 per share.
Dec. 13	Sold 1,000 common shares for $38.00 per share.

Required Record the transactions in the general journal.

Problem 14–2A

 Excel Spreadsheet Template

The balance sheet of Gailey Ltd. at December 31, 2009, reported 250,000 common shares authorized, with 75,000 shares issued and a Common Shares balance of $187,500. Retained Earnings had a credit balance of $150,000. During 2010, the company completed the following selected transactions:

Journalizing dividend and share-repurchase transactions, and reporting shareholders' equity

① ② ③

2. Total shareholders' equity $451,500

Mar. 15	Repurchased 10,000 of the company's own common shares at $2.75 per share. These shares will *not* be cancelled.
Apr. 29	Declared a 5-percent stock dividend on the 65,000 outstanding common shares to holders of record on May 2, with distribution set for May 16. The market value of Gailey Ltd. common shares was $5.00 per share.
May 16	Issued the stock dividend shares.
Oct. 7	Sold 3,000 repurchased common shares for $5.50 per share.
Dec. 19	Split the common shares 2 for 1 by issuing one new share for each old share held on December 30, 2010.
31	Earned net income of $125,000 during the year.

Required

1. Record the transactions in the general journal. Explanations are not required.
2. Prepare the shareholders' equity section of the balance sheet at December 31, 2010.
3. Calculate the average issue price per common share on December 31, 2010. Assume no shares were issued or repurchased after December 19, 2010.

Problem 14–3A

Skiptrace Software Inc. is positioned ideally in the manufacturing and distribution sectors. It is the only company providing highly developed inventory tracking software. The company does a brisk business with companies such as Home Hardware and Roots. Skiptrace Software Inc.'s success has made the company a prime target for a takeover. Against the wishes of Skiptrace Software Inc.'s board of directors, an investment group is attempting to buy 55 percent of Skiptrace Software Inc.'s outstanding shares. Board members are convinced that the investment group would sell off the most desirable pieces of the business and leave little of value.

At the most recent board meeting, several suggestions were advanced to fight off the hostile takeover bid. One suggestion was to increase the shares outstanding by splitting the company's shares two for one.

Required   As a significant shareholder of Skiptrace Software Inc., write a short memo to the board advising how a stock split would affect the investor group's attempt to take over Skiptrace Software Inc. Include in your memo a discussion of the effect that the stock split would have on assets, liabilities, and total shareholders' equity; that is, the split's effect on the size of the corporation.

Problem 14–4A

The balance sheet of Lumiere Vision Ltd. at December 31, 2009 reported the following shareholders' equity:

Common shares, 200,000 shares authorized, 50,000 shares issued	$ 750,000
Retained earnings	250,000
Total shareholders' equity	$1,000,000

During 2010, Lumiere Vision Ltd. completed the following selected transactions:

Apr. 29	Declared a 10-percent stock dividend on the common shares. The market value of Lumiere Vision Ltd.'s common shares was $14.00 per share. The record date was May 20, with distribution set for June 3.
Jun. 3	Issued the stock dividend shares.
Jul. 29	Repurchased 5,000 of the company's own common shares at $13.50 per share; average issue price was $14.91.
Nov. 10	Sold 1,000 repurchased common shares for $14.50 per share.
25	Declared a $0.25 per share dividend on the common shares outstanding. The date of record was December 16, and the payment date was January 6, 2011.
Dec. 31	Closed the $105,000 credit balance of Income Summary to Retained Earnings.

Required

1. Record the transactions in the general journal.
2. Prepare a statement of shareholders' equity at December 31, 2010.

Problem 14–5A

The information below was taken from the ledger and other records of Hudson Steelworks Corp. at September 30, 2010.

Cost of goods sold................	$157,500	Preferred shares, $1.00,	
Loss on sale of property	17,500	15,000 shares authorized ...	
Sales returns	3,500	7,500 shares issued............	$ 93,750
Income tax expense (saving)		Retained earnings,	
Continuing operations ...	13,500	October 1, 2009..................	30,500
Discontinued segment:		Selling expenses	50,750
Operating loss..............	(1,800)	Common shares, 50,000 shares	
Gain on sale	600	authorized and issued......	165,000
Gain on sale of of discontinued		Sales revenue	315,000
segment............................	1,750	Dividends................................	11,000
Interest expense	4,250	Operating loss,	
General expenses.................	42,000	discontinued segment......	5,250
Interest revenue	1,750	Loss on insurance settlement	4,000

Required Prepare a single-step income statement, including earnings per share, for Hudson Steelworks Corp. for the fiscal year ended September 30, 2010. Evaluate income for the year ended September 30, 2010, in terms of the outlook for 2011. Assume 2010 was a typical year and that Hudson Steelworks Corp.'s managers hoped to earn income from continuing operations equal to 10 percent of net sales.

Problem 14–6A

Muriel Thomas, accountant for Phizor Ltd., was injured in a hiking accident. Another employee prepared the income statement shown below for the fiscal year ended December 31, 2010.

The individual amounts listed on the income statement are correct. However, some accounts are reported incorrectly, and others do not belong on the income statement at all. Also, income tax (40 percent) has not been applied to all appropriate figures. Phizor Ltd. issued 64,000 common shares in 2006 and has not issued or repurchased common shares since that time. The Retained Earnings balance, as originally reported at December 31, 2009 was $242,500. There were no preferred shares outstanding at December 31, 2010.

Preparing a corrected combined statement of income and retained earnings

Net income $43,800

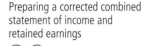

PHIZOR LTD. Income Statement 2010		
Revenue and gains		
Sales		$295,000
Proceeds from sale of repurchased preferred shares		66,000
Gain on retirement of preferred shares		
(issued for $76,000; repurchased for $66,500)		9,500
Total revenues and gains		370,500
Expenses and losses		
Cost of goods sold	$ 73,000	
Selling expenses	54,000	
General expenses	58,500	
Sales returns	7,500	
Dividends	5,500	
Sales discounts	4,500	
Income tax expense	29,200	
Total expenses and losses		232,200
Income from operations		138,300
Other gains and losses		
Loss on sale of discontinued operations	$ (2,500)	
Flood loss	(15,000)	
Operating loss on discontinued segment	(7,000)	
Correction for 2009 due to an inventory error	(3,000)	
Total other losses		(27,500)
Net income		$110,800
Earnings per share		$ 1.92

Required Prepare a corrected combined statement of income and retained earnings for the year ended December 31, 2010; include earnings per share. Prepare the income statement portion in single-step format.

Problem 14–7A

The capital structure of Revel Marketing Inc. at December 31, 2009 included 50,000 $0.50 preferred shares and 74,000 common shares. The 50,000 preferred shares were issued in 2006. Common shares outstanding during 2010 were 74,000 January through April and 80,000 May through September. A 20-percent stock dividend was paid on October 1. Income from continuing operations during 2010 was $122,000. The company discontinued a segment of the business at a gain (net of tax) of $9,250. The Revel Marketing Inc. board of directors restricts $125,000 of retained earnings for contingencies.

Computing earnings per share and reporting a retained earnings restriction

1. EPS for net income $1.14

Required

1. Compute Revel Marketing Inc.'s earnings per share. Start with income from continuing operations. Income of $122,000 is net of income tax.

2. Show two ways of reporting Revel Marketing Inc.'s retained earnings restriction. Retained Earnings at December 31, 2009 was $145,500, and total contributed capital at December 31, 2010 is $375,000. The company declared dividends of $49,500 in 2010.

Accounting for stock dividends, stock splits, share transactions, and the statement of shareholders' equity

2. Total shareholders' equity $1,209,750

Problem 14–8A

Cisco Communication Inc. had the following shareholders' equity on January 1, 2010:

Preferred shares, $2.00, cumulative (1 year in arrears), liquidation price of $20, 100,000 shares authorized, 15,000 shares issued and outstanding	$240,000
Common shares, unlimited number of shares authorized, 25,000 shares issued and outstanding..................	200,000
Total contributed capital..	440,000
Retained earnings	512,000
Total shareholders' equity...	$952,000

The following transactions took place during 2010:

Jan.	14	Declared a $80,000 cash dividend, payable on March 1 to the shareholders of record on February 1. Indicate the amount payable to each class of shareholder.
Feb.	28	Issued 10,000 common shares for $6.00 per share.
Mar.	1	Paid the cash dividend declared on January 14.
Apr.	1	Declared a 10 percent stock dividend on the common shares, distributable on May 2 to the shareholders of record on April 15. The market value of the shares was $6.40 per share.
May	2	Distributed the stock dividend declared on April 1.
Jul.	4	Repurchased 3,000 of the company's own common shares at $7.00 per share.
Sept.	2	Issued 2,500 repurchased common shares for $7.50 per share.
Nov.	2	Split the common shares 2 for 1.
Dec.	31	Reported net income of $280,000. Closed the Income Summary account.

Required

1. Record the transactions in the general journal. Explanations are not required.

2. Prepare the statement of shareholders' equity for the year ended December 31, 2010.

Accounting for stock dividends, stock splits, and errors from a prior period; preparing a combined statement of income and retained earnings; calculating earnings per share

①②④⑤

2. Net income $730,600

Problem 14–9A

ArtnMotion Inc. specializes in truck tires and had the following shareholders' equity on January 1, 2010:

Preferred shares, $2.50, convertible to common on a 2-for-1 basis, 100,000 shares authorized, 50,000 shares issued and outstanding	$1,500,000
Common shares, unlimited number of shares authorized, 150,000 shares issued	1,500,000
Total contributed capital..	3,000,000
Retained earnings	1,200,000
Total shareholders' equity...	$4,200,000

The following information is available for the year ending December 31, 2010:

Feb.	1	Declared a cash dividend of $275,000, payable on March 1 to the shareholders of record on February 15. Indicate the amount payable to each class of shareholder.
Mar.	1	Paid the cash dividend declared on February 1.
May	2	Declared a 20-percent stock dividend on the common shares, distributable on July 4 to the shareholders of record on June 15. The market value of the shares was $11.00 per share.
Jul.	4	Distributed the common shares dividend declared on May 2.

Aug. 8 The company discovered that amortization expense recorded in 2007 was understated in error by $30,000.

Dec. 31 ArtnMotion Inc.'s records show the following:

Sales for the year	$3,150,000
Cost of goods sold	1,290,000
Operating expenses	792,000
Income from discontinued operations	132,000
Loss on sale of discontinued operations	76,000

Close the Income Summary account, assuming the company pays taxes at the rate of 35 percent.

Required

1. Record the transactions in the general journal. Explanations are not required.

2. Prepare a combined statement of income and retained earnings for the year ended December 31, 2010. Include earnings-per-share information. For purposes of the earnings-per-share calculation, the weighted average number of common shares is 180,000.

PROBLEMS (GROUP B)

 MyAccountingLab All questions in this section appear in MyAccountingLab.

Problem 14–1B

ICN Corporation Inc. completed the following selected transactions during 2010:

Journalizing shareholders' equity transactions

①③

Feb. 4 Declared a cash dividend on the 30,000 $1.40 preferred shares. Declared a $0.30 per share cash dividend on the 40,000 common shares outstanding. The date of record was February 15, and the payment date was February 18.

18 Paid the cash dividends.

Apr. 18 Declared a 15 percent stock dividend on the common shares to holders of record on April 29, with distribution set for May 31. The market value of the common shares was $14.00 per share.

May 31 Issued the stock dividend shares.

Jun. 17 Repurchased 3,000 shares of the company's own common shares at $10.00 per share; average issue price was $8.00 per share. The shares will be reissued in the future.

Nov. 14 Issued 1,000 repurchased common shares for $9.00 per share.

Dec. 22 Issued 900 repurchased common shares for $13.50 per share.

Required Record the transactions in the general journal.

Problem 14–2B

 **Excel Spreadsheet Template**

The balance sheet of Investtech Inc. at December 31, 2009 reported 2,000,000 common shares authorized with 250,000 shares issued at an average price of $4.00 each. Retained Earnings had a balance of $700,000. During 2010, the company completed the following selected transactions:

Journalizing dividend and share-repurchase transactions and reporting shareholders' equity

①②③

Feb. 15 Repurchased 20,000 of the company's own common shares at $4.00 per share.

Mar. 8 Sold 8,000 repurchased common shares for $4.25 per share.

Sept. 28 Declared a 5-percent stock dividend on the 238,000 outstanding common shares to holders of record on October 15, with distribution set for October 31. The market value of Investtech Inc. common shares was $4.50 per share.

Oct. 31 Issued the stock dividend shares.

Nov. 5 Consolidated the common shares 1 for 2 (reverse split); one new common share was issued for every two existing shares held. Prior to the split, the corporation had 249,900 shares issued and outstanding.

Dec. 31 Earned net income of $230,000 during the year.

Required

1. Record the transactions in the general journal. Explanations are not required.

2. Prepare the shareholders' equity section of the balance sheet at December 31, 2010.

3. Calculate the average issue price per common share on December 31, 2010.

Problem 14–3B

Fundybay Corporation is positioned ideally in its industry. Located in Nova Scotia, Fundybay Corporation is the only company with a reliable record for its locally managed transport company. The company does a brisk business with local major corporations. Fundybay Corporation's recent success has made the company a prime target for a takeover. An investment group from Halifax is attempting to buy 51 percent of the company's outstanding shares against the wishes of Fundybay Corporation's board of directors. Board members are convinced that the Halifax investors would sell off the most desirable pieces of the business and leave little of value.

At the most recent board meeting, several suggestions were advanced to fight off the hostile takeover bid. The suggestion with the most promise is to purchase and retire a huge quantity of shares. Fundybay Corporation has the cash to carry out this plan.

Required

1. As a significant shareholder of Fundybay Corporation, write a memorandum to explain for the board how the repurchase and retirement of shares might make it more difficult for the Halifax group to take over Fundybay Corporation. Include in your memo a discussion of the effect that repurchasing shares would have on shares outstanding and on the size of the corporation.

2. Suppose Fundybay Corporation management is successful in fighting off the takeover bid and later issues shares at prices greater than the purchase price. Explain what effect the sale of these shares will have on assets, shareholders' equity, and net income.

Journalizing dividends and
stock-repurchase transactions;
reporting shareholders' equity

① ③ ⑤

Problem 14–4B

The balance sheet of Marconi International Inc. at December 31, 2009 presented the following shareholders' equity:

Contributed capital

Common shares, 2,000,000 shares authorized, 500,000 shares issued	$3,000,000
Retained earnings...	720,000
Total shareholders' equity	$3,720,000

During 2010, Marconi International Inc. completed the following selected transactions:

Mar.	29	Declared a 10 percent stock dividend on the common shares. The market value of Marconi International Inc. common shares was $5.00 per share. The record date was April 19, with distribution set for May 19.
May	19	Issued the stock dividend shares.
Jul.	13	Repurchased 30,000 of the company's own common shares at $5.00 per share; average issue price was $5.91.
Oct.	4	Sold 20,000 common shares for $6.50 per share.
Dec.	27	Declared a $0.20 per share dividend on the common shares outstanding. The date of record was January 17, 2011, and the payment date was January 31, 2011.
	31	Closed the $660,000 net income to Retained Earnings.

Required

1. Record the transactions in the general journal.

2. Prepare the statement of shareholders' equity for the year ended December 31, 2010.

Problem 14–5B

The information below was taken from the ledger and other records of Make a Statement Inc. at September 30, 2010.

General expenses.......................	$220,000	Sales revenue...............................	$1,000,000
Loss on sale of		Operating income, discontinued	
discontinued segment	18,000	segment.................................	8,000
Cost of goods sold.....................	570,000	Loss on sale of property,	
Income tax expense (saving)		plant, and equipment.........	5,000
Continuing operations	44,000	Dividends on preferred	
Discontinued segment:		shares....................................	12,500
Operating income............	2,000	Preferred shares, $0.50, cumulative,	
Loss on sale	(6,000)	50,000 shares authorized,	
Interest expense	27,000	25,000 shares issued	350,000

Gain on settlement of lawsuit	27,000	Dividends on common shares		25,000
Sales returns	23,000	Retained earnings,		
Contributed surplus from retirement of preferred shares	18,000	October 1, 2009		197,000
		Selling expenses		33,000
		Common shares,		
Sales discounts	7,000	unlimited shares authorized, 40,000 shares issued		433,000

Required Prepare a single-step income statement, including earnings per share, for Make a Statement Inc. for the fiscal year ended September 30, 2010. Evaluate income for the year ended September 30, 2010 in terms of the outlook for 2011. Assume 2010 was a typical year and that Make a Statement's managers hoped to earn income from continuing operations equal to 12 percent of net sales.

Problem 14–6B

Preparing a corrected combined statement of income and retained earnings

Thomas Wong, accountant for Maaco Bikes Ltd., was injured in a biking accident. Another employee prepared the income statement shown below for the fiscal year ended September 30, 2010.

The individual amounts listed on the income statement are correct. However, some accounts are reported incorrectly, and others do not belong on the income statement at all. Also, income tax (35 percent) has not been applied to all appropriate figures. Maaco Bikes Ltd. issued 30,000 common shares in 2005 and has not issued or repurchased common shares since that date. The Retained Earnings balance, as originally reported at September 30, 2009 was $660,000. There were no preferred shares outstanding at September 30, 2010.

MAACO BIKES LTD.
Income Statement
September 30, 2010

Revenues and gains		
Sales		$1,000,000
Gain on retirement of preferred shares (issued for $60,000; purchased for $48,000)		12,000
Total revenues and gains		1,012,000
Expenses and losses		
Cost of goods sold	$478,000	
Selling expenses	133,000	
General expenses	60,000	
Sales returns	13,000	
Correction of an error from a prior period— understated income tax for 2009 due to error	10,000	
Dividends	14,000	
Sales discounts	18,000	
Income tax expense	98,700	
Total expenses and losses		824,700
Income from operations		187,300
Other gains and losses		
Operating income on discontinued segment	16,000	
Loss on sale of discontinued operations	(32,000)	
Total other gains		(16,000)
Net income		$ 171,300
Earnings per share		$ 5.71

Required Prepare a corrected combined statement of income and retained earnings for fiscal year 2010; include earnings per share. Prepare the income statement portion in single-step format.

Problem 14–7B

Computing earnings per share and reporting a retained earnings restriction

The capital structure of Calgary Design Ltd. at December 31, 2009 included 15,000 $1 preferred shares and 420,000 common shares. Common shares outstanding during 2010 were

330,000 in January through March; 348,000 during April; 385,000 May through September; and 420,000 during October through December. Income from continuing operations during 2010 was $446,000. The company discontinued a segment of the business at a gain of $61,500. The board of directors of Calgary Design Ltd. has restricted $82,500 of retained earnings for expansion of the company's office facilities.

Required

1. Compute Calgary Design Ltd.'s earnings per share. Start with income from continuing operations. Income and loss amounts are net of income tax.

2. Show two ways of reporting Calgary Design Ltd.'s retained earnings restriction. Retained Earnings at December 31, 2009 was $172,000, and total contributed capital at December 31, 2010 is $575,000. Calgary Design Ltd. declared cash dividends of $250,000 during 2010.

Accounting for stock dividends, stock splits, share transactions, and the statement of shareholders' equity

Problem 14–8B

Barrier Outfitters Ltd. had the following shareholders' equity on January 1, 2010:

Preferred shares, $0.75, cumulative (1 year in arrears), liquidation price of $5.00, 50,000 shares authorized, 15,000 shares issued and outstanding......................	$150,000
Common shares, unlimited number of shares authorized, 25,000 shares issued and outstanding...	125,000
Total contributed capital	275,000
Retained earnings	225,000
Total shareholders' equity..	$500,000

The following transactions took place during 2010:

Jan.	28	Declared a $25,000 cash dividend, payable on March 1 to the shareholders of record on February 15. Indicate the amount payable to each class of shareholder.
Feb.	25	Issued 8,000 common shares for $7.00 per share.
Mar.	1	Paid the cash dividend declared on January 28.
Apr.	4	Declared a 10-percent stock dividend on the common shares, distributable on May 15 to the shareholders of record on April 15. The market value of the shares was $8.00 per share.
May	15	Distributed the stock dividend declared on April 4.
Jul.	6	Repurchased 10,000 of the company's own common shares at $8.50 per share.
Sept.	3	Issued 5,000 common shares for $8.50 per share.
Nov.	2	Split the common shares 2 for 1.
Dec.	31	Reported net income of $100,000. Closed the Income Summary account.

Required

1. Record the transactions in the general journal. Explanations are not required.

2. Prepare the statement of shareholders' equity for the year ended December 31, 2010.

Accounting for stock dividends, stock splits, and prior-period adjustments; preparing a combined statement of income and retained earnings; calculating earnings per share

Problem 14–9B

Red Deer Hardware Ltd. had the following shareholders' equity on January 1, 2010:

Preferred shares, $0.50 cumulative, convertible to common on a 2-for-1 basis, 50,000 shares authorized, 20,000 shares issued and outstanding...	$ 55,000
Common shares, unlimited number of shares authorized, 50,000 shares issued and outstanding...	62,500
Total contributed capital	117,500
Retained earnings	110,000
Total shareholders' equity...	$227,500

The following information is available for the year ending December 31, 2010:

Mar. 7 Declared a cash dividend of $12,500, payable on April 1 to the shareholders of record on March 15. Indicate the amount payable to each class of shareholder.

Apr. 1 Paid the cash dividend declared on March 7.

Jun. 6 Declared a 5-percent stock dividend on the common shares, distributable on August 5 to the shareholders of record on July 4. The market value of the shares was $1.50 per share.

Aug. 5 Distributed the common shares dividend declared on June 6.

Sept. 15 Received notification from Canada Revenue Agency that Red Deer Hardware Ltd. had made an error in filing 2008 taxes. The reassessment showed that the company had reported and overpaid $4,000 in taxes.

Dec. 31 Red Deer Hardware Ltd.'s records show the following:

Sales for the year	$212,500
Cost of goods sold	95,000
Operating expenses	65,000
Income from discontinued operations	4,000
Loss on sale of discontinued operations	(2,500)

Close the Income Summary account, assuming the income tax on all types of income is 40 percent.

Required

1. Record the transactions in the general journal. Explanations are not required.

2. Prepare a combined multi-step statement of income and retained earnings for the year ended December 31, 2010. Include earnings-per-share information.

CHALLENGE PROBLEM

Problem 14–1C

Explaining the effects of a share repurchase

Assume Wat Inc., a private corporation with a small number of shareholders, had issued 20,000 common shares at incorporation at a price of $22.00. The book value per share was $34.00 at the most recent year end. The company has been paying an annual dividend of $1.56 per share.

Recently, the company had offered to repurchase 3,000 shares at $28.00 per share.

You and a friend bought 100 shares each when the shares were issued. Your friend wonders whether she should sell her shares back to Wat Inc. since the company was offering 27 percent more than she had paid.

Required Analyze the information provided to help your friend decide whether or not she should sell her shares back to the company.

Extending Your Knowledge

DECISION PROBLEM

Fraser Valley Technologies Inc. had the following shareholders' equity on December 31, 2010:

Analyzing cash dividends and stock dividends

①

2. 2008 dividends $20,000; 2010 dividends $16,500

Common shares, 200,000 shares issued and outstanding	$2,000,000
Retained earnings	1,200,000
Total shareholders' equity	$3,200,000

In the past, Fraser Valley Technologies Inc. has paid an annual cash dividend of $2.00 per share. In 2009, despite a large Retained Earnings balance, the board of directors wished to conserve cash for expansion and did not pay a cash dividend but distributed a 10 percent stock dividend. During 2010, the company's cash position improved, so the board declared and paid a cash dividend of $1.50 per share.

Suppose you own 10,000 Fraser Valley Technologies Inc. common shares, acquired January 2, 2008. The market price was $25.00 per share before any of the above dividends.

Required

1. How did the stock dividend affect your proportionate ownership in the company? Explain.

2. What amount of cash dividends did you receive in 2008? What amount of cash dividends did you receive in 2010? Would you expect the dividend per share to remain unchanged?

3. Immediately after the stock dividend was distributed, the market value of Fraser Valley Technologies Inc. shares decreased from $25.00 per share to $22.72 per share. Does this represent a loss to you? Explain.

4. Suppose Fraser Valley Technologies Inc. announces at the time of the stock dividend that the company will continue to pay the annual $2.00 cash dividend per share, even after the stock dividend. Would you expect the market price of the shares to decrease to $22.72 per share as in Requirement 3 above? Explain.

FINANCIAL STATEMENT CASES

Corporate income statement and earnings per share
④

Financial Statement Case 1

Use the Canadian Western Bank (CWB) financial statements in Appendix A to answer the following questions.

1. Which income statement format—single-step or multi-step—does CWB's consolidated statement of income more closely resemble?

2. CWB is restricted from paying dividends by two types of restrictions. What are the two types of restrictions and give details of each. *Hint:* The details are contained in the notes of the financial statements, in the Capital Stock note.

3. CWB's basic earnings per share at August 31, 2008 was $ 1.61 per share. For purposes of this calculation, what was the weighted average number of shares outstanding?

Repurchased shares and retained earnings
③ ④ ⑤

Financial Statement Case 2

Use the Sun-Rype Products Ltd. financial statements in Appendix B to answer the following questions.

1. Sun-Rype's 2008 financial statements reveal that the company had the same amount of contributed surplus at December 31, 2008 and at December 31, 2007. What is the balance of contributed surplus at December 31, 2008?

2. Retained earnings has a restatement in 2008 regarding the adoption of a new accounting standard. Briefly explain this change.

3. The company paid $433,000 in dividends in 2008, which is a quarter of what Sun-Rype paid in 2007. What is the reason for this reduction?

4. Should a company with losses pay dividends? Explain.

15 Long-Term Liabilities

What are bonds payable, and why are they important? How are bond prices determined?

How do you account for bonds and report them in the financial statements?

How do bonds compare with shares? How do you account for other long-term liabilities?

These questions and others about long-term liabilities will be answered throughout this chapter. And the Decision Guidelines at the end of this chapter will provide the answers in a useful summary.

LEARNING OBJECTIVES

1. Define bonds payable and the types of bonds

2. Determine the price of a bond, and account for basic bond transactions

3. Amortize a bond discount and premium by the straight-line amortization method and the effective-interest amortization method

4. Account for retirement and conversion of bonds

5. Show the advantages and disadvantages of borrowing

6. Report lease liabilities

7. Identify the effects on long-term liabilities of international financial reporting standards (IFRS)

CHAPTER 15 APPENDIX

A1. Compute the future value of an investment

A2. Compute the present value of a single future amount and the present value of an annuity

A3. Determine the cost of an asset acquired through a capital lease

Canwest Global Communications Corp. is a large Canadian company that owns various businesses in the field of communications. The company has grown through acquisition—that is, it has purchased other companies—over the years. At the time of writing, Canwest was a dominant competitor in the field of media communications.

How do companies like Canwest finance the acquisition of other companies? They could issue shares of Canwest in exchange for shares of the other company; however, many of the acquired companies would prefer to be paid in cash. Canwest could issue more shares and use the proceeds to purchase shares of the acquired company. It might borrow from financial institutions and other investors by issuing bonds. Many companies prefer this approach because it doesn't dilute the shares of the acquiring company and it locks in principal and interest payments, which allows a company like Canwest to manage its cash flow. Canwest used this strategy so much that it had amassed almost $4 billion of debt by the summer of 2009.

Using debt to fund company growth is a double-edged sword, however. When the economy is buoyant and things are going well, it is a good strategy because your payments are set and once they are covered, profits earned stay with the company and its shareholders. However, when the economy is performing poorly, as it was through 2008 and 2009, financing with bonds and other debt instruments is more of a problem. Canwest found itself in such a predicament that it has had to restructure its borrowings and has had trouble doing so. It has missed several payment dates. An analyst summed up Canwest's problems as follows:

" 'We've seen so many delays up until now that my gut tells me there's going to be yet another one,' said Carmi Levy, an analyst at AR Communications Inc.

'I don't think creditors have reached the end of their patience with Canwest. They're getting there—the thread is getting shorter but you don't just rearrange hundreds of millions of dollars worth of credit on a dime, and you certainly don't do it under the gun.'

Even if it resolves the April deadlines, Canwest won't be in the clear. Overall, the company has $3.9 billion in debt, which it is trying to recapitalize.

'The question is when will the economy pick up to the point that Canwest will be able to work itself out of the hole it has dug for itself through cash flow,' Levi said."[1]

This chapter discusses long-term liabilities in general and bonds in great detail. Corporate bonds are a very common form of financing, and it is important to understand not only how to account for them but also how they can be beneficial to companies. As Canwest has learned, this kind of financing is risky as well.

---

[1] "Canwest Faces Tuesday Deadline for Restructuring Debt Agreement," April 5, 2009, as cited at cbc.ca. *Source:* CBC.CA.

Chapters 13 and 14 covered two ways of financing operations: contributed capital and profitable operations (retained earnings). This chapter discusses the third way to finance a company—borrowing money on long-term liabilities, including bonds and debentures payable (and notes payable) and lease liabilities. The chapter appendix provides background on the valuation of long-term liabilities.

Before launching into bonds payable, let's compare bonds with shares, which were covered in Chapters 13 and 14.

Shares	Bonds
1. Shares represent *ownership* (equity) of the corporation. Each shareholder is an *owner*.	1. Bonds represent a *debt* (liability) of the corporation. Each bondholder is a *creditor*.
2. The corporation is *not* obligated to repay the amount invested by the shareholders.	2. The corporation *must* repay the bonds at maturity.
3. The corporation may or may not pay dividends on the shares.	3. The corporation *must* pay interest on the bonds.
4. Dividends are *not* an expense and are not tax deductible by the corporation.	4. Interest is a tax-deductible expense of the corporation.

OBJECTIVE 1
Define bonds payable and the types of bonds

Bonds: An Introduction

Large companies, such as Canwest, Canadian National Railway Company (CN), and Westjet, cannot borrow billions from a single lender because no lender will risk lending that much money to a single company. Even for smaller companies, it may be impossible to borrow all they need from a bank. Banks and other lenders diversify their risk by lending relatively small amounts to numerous customers. That way, if a borrower cannot repay, the lender is not devastated.

How, then, do large corporations borrow a huge amount? They may issue bonds to the public. A **bond** is a formal arrangement between the issuer of the bond and the holder of the bond. The bondholder (the person or company that buys the bond) lends a fixed amount of money to the issuer. The issuer promises to pay the fixed amount at some future time and to pay regular payments of interest to the bondholder over the life of the bond. A bond is a debt of the company that issued the bond. **Bonds payable** are groups of notes payable issued to multiple lenders, called bondholders. TELUS Communications Inc. can borrow large amounts from thousands of individual investors, each investor buying a modest amount of TELUS Communications Inc. bonds.

Purchasers of bonds receive a bond certificate, which shows the name of the company that borrowed the money, exactly like a note payable. The certificate also states the *principal*, which is the amount that the company has borrowed from the bondholder. The bond's principal amount is also called the bond's *maturity value*, *par value*, or *face value*. The issuing company must pay each bondholder the principal amount at a specific future date, called the maturity date, which also appears on the certificate. In Chapter 11, we saw how to account for short-term notes payable. There is a lot of similarity between accounting for short-term notes payable and long-term notes payable.

Bondholders lend their money to earn interest. The bond certificate states the interest rate that the issuer will pay the bondholder and the dates that the interest payments are due (generally twice a year). Some bond certificates name the bondholder (the investor). Exhibit 15–1 shows a bond certificate issued by XYZ Corporation.

EXHIBIT 15–1   Bond Certificate

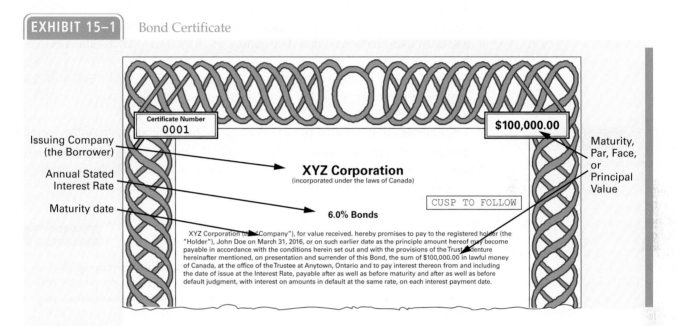

Review these bond fundamentals in Exhibit 15–1.

- **Principal value** (also called maturity value, face, or par value)—the amount the borrower must pay back to the bondholders at maturity.
- **Maturity date**—the date on which the borrower must pay the principal amount to the lender.
- **Stated interest rate**—the annual rate of interest that the borrower pays the lender.

Types of Bonds

There are various types of bonds, including the following:

- **Term bonds** all mature at the same time.
- **Serial bonds** mature in instalments at regular intervals. For example, a $500,000, five-year serial bond may mature in $100,000 annual instalments over a five-year period.
- **Secured bonds** give the bondholder the right to take specified assets of the issuer (called collateral) if the issuer *defaults*, that is, fails to pay principal or interest. A **mortgage** is an example of a secured bond.
- **Debentures** are unsecured bonds backed only by the good faith of the issuer.

The discussion in this chapter will generally refer to bonds and include secured bonds and debentures. When reference is made to a debenture, the instrument will be treated in the same way as a bond.

KEY POINT

A debenture is unsecured and, therefore, is riskier than a bond, which is secured.

DID YOU GET IT?

MyAccountingLab

To check your understanding of the material in this Learning Objective, complete this question. The solution appears on MyAccountingLab so you can check your progress.

1. Refer to the bond certificate illustrated in Exhibit 15–1 and answer the following questions:
   a. What is the name of the corporation issuing the bond?
   b. What is the face value of the bond?
   c. What is the maturity date of the bond?
   d. What is the name of the bondholder?
   e. What is the stated interest rate the issuer will pay the bondholder?

OBJECTIVE ②

Determine the price of a bond, and account for basic bond transactions

Bond Prices

A bond can be issued at any price agreed upon by the issuer and the bondholders. There are three basic categories of bond prices. A bond can be issued at

- **Maturity (par, face, or principal) value**. Example: A $1,000 bond issued for $1,000. A bond issued at par has no discount or premium.
- **Discount**, a price below maturity (par) value. Example: A $1,000 bond issued for $980. The discount is $20 ($1,000 – $980).
- **Premium**, a price above maturity (par) value. Example: A $1,000 bond issued for $1,015. The premium is $15 ($1,015 – $1,000).

The issue price of a bond does not affect the required payment at maturity. In all cases, the issuer must pay the maturity value of the bonds when they mature.

Bonds sell at a premium or a discount when the interest rate that will be paid on the bond is different from the interest rate available to investors elsewhere in the market at the time of the bond issuance. This will soon be explained more fully. As a bond nears maturity, its market price moves toward its maturity value. On the maturity date, the market value of a bond equals exactly its maturity value because the company that issued the bond pays that amount to retire the bond.

After a bond is issued, investors may buy and sell it through bond markets. The bond market in Canada is called the over-the-counter (OTC) market. It is a network of investment dealers who trade bonds issued by the Government of Canada and Crown corporations, the provinces, municipalities, regions, and corporations.

Bond prices are quoted at a percentage of their maturity value, using $100 as a base. For example,

- A $1,000 bond quoted at 100 is bought or sold for 100 percent of maturity value ($1,000).

- A $1,000 bond quoted at 101.5 has a price of $1,015 ($1,000 × 1.015).

- A $1,000 bond quoted at 98.5 has a price of $985 ($1,000 × 0.985).

Exhibit 15–2 contains actual price information for a Fairfax Financial Holdings bond, as quoted on the website http://www.pfin.ca/canadianfixedincome/Default. aspx on October 8, 2009. On that date, Fairfax Financial Holding's 7.5-percent par-value bond maturing August 19, 2019, was quoted at 106.27, which was a bid price of $1,062.70 for a $1,000.00 bond. This bid price provided a yield of 6.62 percent (the yield rate of a bond is influenced by the market interest rate and time to maturity).

EXHIBIT 15–2   Bond Price Information

Bonds	Coupon	Eff. Maturity	Price	Yield
Fairfax Financial Holdings	7.50	Aug. 19/19	106.27	6.62

Present Value[2]

A dollar received today is worth more than a dollar received in the future. Why? Because you can invest today's dollar and earn income from it. Likewise, deferring any payment until later gives your money a period of time to grow. Money earns income over time, a concept called the *time value of money*. Let's examine how the time value of money affects the pricing of bonds.

Assume a $1,000 bond reaches maturity three years from today and carries no interest. Would you pay $1,000 to purchase this bond? No, because paying $1,000 today to receive the same amount in the future provides you with no income on the investment. You would not be taking advantage of the time value of money. Just how much would you pay today in order to receive $1,000 at the end of three years? The answer is some amount less than $1,000. Suppose $850 is a fair price. By investing $850 now to receive $1,000 later, you earn $150 interest revenue over the three years. The diagram below shows the relationship between a bond's price (present value) and its maturity amount (future value).

KEY POINT

Present value is always less than future value. You should be able to invest today's money (present value) so that its value will increase (future value). The difference between present value and future value is interest earned.

Present Value + Interest Earned = Future Value

or

Future Value − Interest Earned = Present Value

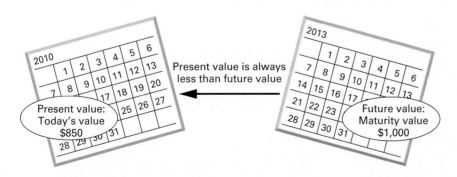

The amount that a person would invest *at the present time* to receive a greater amount at a future date is called the **present value** of the investment or payment.

---
[2] The Chapter 15 Appendix covers present value in more detail.

The present value is the bond's market price. In our example, $850 is the present value (bond price), and the $1,000 maturity value to be received in three years is the future value.

The exact present value of any future amount depends on (1) the amount of the future payment (or receipt), (2) the length of time from the date of the investment to the date when the future amount is to be received (or paid), and (3) the interest rate during the period. We show how to compute present value in this chapter's appendix. We need to be aware of the present-value concept, however, in the discussion of bond prices that follows. If your instructor so directs you, please study the appendix now.

Bond Interest Rates

KEY POINT

When you buy a bond, you are really "buying" two future cash flows: principal and interest. The principal is a single sum received at maturity, and the interest is a series of receipts received each period until maturity.

Bonds are sold at their market price, which is the amount that investors are willing to pay at any given time. Market price is the bond's present value, which equals the present value of the principal payment plus the present value of the cash interest payments (which are made quarterly, semiannually, or annually over the term of the bond).

Two interest rates work to set the price of a bond:

- The **stated interest rate**, or **contract interest rate**, determines the amount of cash interest the borrower pays—and the investor receives—each year. The stated interest rate is printed on the bond and is set by the bond contract. It may be fixed or adjustable. If the rate is fixed, it *does not change* during the life of the bond. For example, XYZ Corporation's 6-percent bonds have a stated interest rate of 6 percent (Exhibit 15–1). Thus, XYZ Corporation pays $6,000 of interest annually on each $100,000 bond. Each semiannual interest payment is $3,000 ($100,000 × 0.06 × ½).

KEY POINT

Because market interest rates fluctuate daily, the stated interest rate will seldom equal the market interest rate on the date the bonds are sold.

- The **market interest rate**, or **effective interest rate**, is the rate that investors demand for lending their money. The market interest rate varies, sometimes daily. A company may issue bonds with a stated interest rate that differs from the prevailing market interest rate. XYZ Corporation may issue its 6-percent bonds when the market rate for bonds issued by companies with a similar level of risk has risen to 7 percent. Will the XYZ Corporation bonds attract investors in this market? No, because investors can earn 7 percent on other bonds with a similar level of risk. In order to receive a 7-percent return on their investment, investors will purchase XYZ Corporation bonds only at a price less than the maturity value. The difference between the lower price and the bonds' maturity value is a *discount*. Conversely, if the market interest rate is 5 percent, XYZ Corporation's 6-percent bonds will be so attractive that investors will pay more than maturity value for them. The difference between the higher price and the maturity value is a *premium*.

Exhibit 15–3 shows how the stated (contract) interest rate and the market interest rate interact to determine the issue, or selling price, of a bond.

EXHIBIT 15–3 How the Stated Interest Rate and the Market Interest Rate Interact to Determine the Issue Price of a Bond

Example: Bond with a Stated (Contract) Interest Rate of 8%				
Bond's Stated Interest Rate		**Market Interest Rate**		**Issue Price of the Bond**
8%	=	8%	⇒	Maturity value of the bond (face or par value)
8%	<	9%	⇒	Discount (price below maturity value)
8%	>	7%	⇒	Premium (price above maturity value)

Issuing Bonds to Borrow Money

KEY POINT

Bonds sell at a *premium* if the market rate drops below the stated (contract) rate. Bonds sell at a *discount* if the market rate rises above the stated (contract) rate.

The basic journal entry to record the issuance of bonds debits Cash and credits Bonds Payable. The company may issue bonds for three different bond prices:

- At *maturity (par)* value
- At a *discount*
- At a *premium*

We begin with the simplest case: issuing bonds at maturity (par) value.

Suppose that UVW Corporation has $100 million in 6 percent bonds that mature in 10 years. Assume that UVW Corporation issued these bonds at par on January 2, 2010. The issuance entry is

```
2010
Jan. 2   Cash............................................................   100,000,000
              Bonds Payable.....................................                   100,000,000
         To issue 6%, 10-year bonds at par.
```

UVW Corporation, the borrower, makes this one-time entry to record the receipt of cash and issuance of bonds. Afterward, investors buy and sell the bonds through the bond markets, in a similar way to buying and selling shares through the stock market. Many of these transactions can be completed online. The buy-and-sell transactions between investors do not involve the company that issued the bonds. The company does not keep records of these transactions, except for the names and addresses of the bondholders. (This information is needed for mailing the interest and principal payments.)

Interest payments for these bonds occur each January 2 and July 2. UVW Corporation's entry to record the first semiannual interest payment is

```
2010
Jul. 2   Interest Expense .........................................   3,000,000
              Cash.....................................................                    3,000,000
         To pay semiannual interest on bonds
         payable ($100,000,000 × 0.06 × 1/2).
```

Each semiannual interest payment follows this same pattern.

At maturity, UVW Corporation will record payment of the bonds as follows:

```
2020
Jan. 2   Bonds Payable ............................................   100,000,000
              Cash.....................................................                    100,000,000
         To pay bonds payable at maturity.
```

Issuing Bonds and Notes Between Interest Dates

The foregoing entries to record UVW Corporation's bond transactions are straightforward because the company issued the bonds on an interest payment date (January 2). However, corporations often issue bonds between interest dates because they may not need the funds in one lump sum or the bonds may take longer to sell than originally planned.

Suppose Manitoba Hydro issues $200 million of 5 percent bonds due June 15, 2020. These bonds are dated June 15, 2010, and carry the price "100 plus accrued interest." An investor purchasing the bonds after the bond date must pay market value *plus accrued interest*. The issuing company will pay the full semiannual interest amount to the bondholder at the next interest payment date. Companies do not split semiannual interest payments among two or more investors who happen to hold the bonds during a six-month interest period since the recordkeeping for this would be difficult.

Assume that Manitoba Hydro sells $100,000 of its bonds on July 15, 2010, one month after the bond date of June 15. Also assume that the market price of the bonds on July 15 is the face value. Manitoba Hydro receives one month's accrued interest in addition to the bond's face value, as shown on the following timeline:

June 15	July 15		Dec. 15
Interest accrued from issue date to purchase date	Interest earned from purchase date to interest-payment date ($2,500 interest paid on Dec. 15)		
$417	$2,083		

Manitoba Hydro's entry to record issuance of the bonds payable is

2010
Jul. 15 Cash 100,417
     Bonds Payable 100,000
     Interest Payable... 417
    To issue 5%, 10-year bonds at par, one
    month after the original issue date. Interest
    payable is $417 ($100,000 × 0.05 × ½).

Manitoba Hydro has collected one month's interest in advance. On December 15, 2010, Manitoba Hydro's entry to record the first semiannual interest payment on this $100,000 is

2010
Dec. 15 Interest Expense... 2,083
    Interest Payable 417
     Cash... 2,500
    To pay semiannual interest on bonds
    payable. Interest expense is $2,083
    ($100,000 × 0.05 × 5⁄₁₂); cash paid is
    $2,500 ($100,000 × 0.05 × 6⁄₁₂).

The debit to Interest Payable eliminates the credit balance in that account from July 15. Manitoba Hydro has now paid that liability.

Note that Manitoba Hydro pays a full six months' interest on December 15. After subtracting the one month's accrued interest received at the time of issuing the bond, Manitoba Hydro has recorded interest expense for five months ($2,083). This interest expense is the correct amount for the five months that the bonds have been outstanding.

If Manitoba Hydro prepared financial statements immediately after December 15, 2010, it would report nothing on the balance sheet because Interest Payable is $0 and would report Interest Expense of $2,083 on the income statement.

KEY POINT

In addition to including the premium or discount in the selling price, all transactions also include accrued interest.

Sale of Bonds and Debentures Between Interest Dates—"Plus Accrued Interest"

Selling bonds and debentures between interest dates at market value plus accrued interest simplifies the borrower's accounting. Manitoba Hydro pays the same amount of interest on each bond regardless of the length of time the investor has held the bond. Manitoba Hydro need not compute each bondholder's interest payment on an individual basis.

When an investor sells bonds or debentures to another investor, the price is always "plus accrued interest."

Suppose you hold Manitoba Hydro bonds as an investment for two months of a semiannual interest period and sell the bonds to another investor before you receive your interest. The person who buys the bonds will receive your two months of interest on the next specified interest date. Business practice dictates that you must collect your share of the interest from the buyer when you sell your investment. For this reason, all bond or debenture transactions are "plus accrued interest."

Issuing Bonds at a Discount

Unlike shares, bonds are often issued at a discount. We know that market conditions may force a company like UVW Corporation to accept a discount price for its bonds. Suppose UVW Corporation issues $1,000,000 of its 6-percent, 10-year bonds when the market interest rate is slightly above 6 percent. As a result, the market price of the bonds drops to 98.00, which means 98 percent of face or par value. UVW Corporation receives $980,000 ($1,000,000 × 0.98) at issuance and makes the following journal entry:

2010
Jan. 2   Cash   980,000
         Discount on Bonds Payable   20,000
             Bonds Payable   1,000,000
         To issue 6%, 10-year bonds at a discount.
         Cash received was $980,000 ($1,000,000 × 0.98).

After posting, the bond accounts have the following balances:

Main Account: Bonds Payable	**Contra Account:** Discount on Bonds Payable
1,000,000	20,000

Bond carrying amount = $980,000

Discount on Bonds Payable is a contra account to Bonds Payable. Bonds Payable *minus* the discount gives the book value, or carrying value, of the bonds. The relationship between Bonds Payable and the Discount account is similar to the relationships between Equipment and Accumulated Amortization, and between Accounts Receivable and Allowance for Doubtful Accounts. Thus, UVW Corporation's liability is $980,000, which is the amount the company borrowed. UVW Corporation's balance sheet immediately after issuance of the bonds reports:

Long-term liabilities
     Bonds payable, 6%, due 2020 .... $1,000,000
     Less: Discount on bonds payable 20,000 $980,000

If UVW Corporation were to pay off the bonds immediately (an unlikely occurrence), the company's required outlay would be $980,000 because the market price of the bonds is $980,000.

Interest Expense on Bonds Issued at a Discount   We saw earlier that a bond's stated interest rate may differ from the market interest rate. Suppose the market rate is 6.27 percent when UVW Corporation issues its 6-percent bonds. The 0.27 percent interest rate difference creates the $20,000 discount on the bonds. UVW Corporation borrows $980,000 cash but must pay $1,000,000 cash when the bonds mature 10 years later. What happens to the $20,000 balance of the discount account over the life of the bond issue?

Borrows in 2010	Pays backs in 2020	Discount	
			How do we account for this?
$980,000	$1,000,000	$20,000	

The $20,000 is in reality an additional interest expense to the issuing company. That amount is a cost—beyond the stated interest rate—that the business pays for borrowing the investors' money. The discount has the effect of raising the interest expense on the bonds to the market interest rate of 6.27 percent.

The discount amount is an interest expense not paid until the bond matures. However, the borrower—the bond issuer—benefits from the use of the investors' money each accounting period over the full term of the bond issue. The matching objective directs the business to match an expense against its revenues on a period-by-period basis, so the discount is allocated to interest expense through amortization for each accounting period over the life of the bonds. We will examine this in more detail shortly.

Issuing Bonds at a Premium

Why are bonds issued at a premium less common than bonds issued at a discount? Because companies prefer to issue bonds that pay a lower stated interest rate than the market interest rate, so they price the bonds to sell at a discount. To illustrate issuing bonds at a premium, let's change the UVW Corporation example. Assume that the market interest rate is 5.5 percent when the company issues its 6-percent, 10-year bonds. These 6-percent bonds are attractive in a 5.5-percent market, so investors will pay a premium price to acquire them. If the bonds are priced at 103.77 (103.77 percent of par value), UVW Corporation receives $1,037,700 cash upon issuance. The entry is

2010				
Jan. 2	Cash	1,037,700		
	Bonds Payable		1,000,000	
	Premium on Bonds Payable		37,700	
	To issue 6%, 10-year bonds at a premium.			
	Cash received is $1,037,700 ($1,000,000 × 1.0377).			

After posting, the bond accounts have the following balances:

Main Account: Bonds Payable		Companion Account: Premium on Bonds Payable	
	1,000,000		37,700

Bond carrying amount = $1,037,700

UVW Corporation's balance sheet immediately after issuance of the bonds reports:

Long-term liabilities
Bonds payable, 6%, due 2020 .... $1,000,000
Premium on bonds payable....................................... 37,700 $1,037,700

Premium on Bonds Payable is added to Bonds Payable to show the book value, or carrying value, of the bonds. UVW Corporation's liability is $1,037,700, which is the amount that the company borrowed. Immediate payment of the bonds would require an outlay of $1,037,700 because the market price of the bonds at issuance is $1,037,700. The investors would be unwilling to give up bonds for less than their market value.

Interest Expense on Bonds Issued at a Premium   The 0.5-percent difference between the 6-percent contract rate on the bonds and the 5.5-percent market interest rate creates the $37,700 premium. UVW Corporation borrows $1,037,700 cash but must pay only $1,000,000 cash at maturity.

Borrows in 2010	Pays back in 2020	Premium	
			How do we account for this?
$1,037,700	$1,000,000	$37,700	

We treat the premium as a reduction of interest expense to UVW Corporation. The premium reduces UVW Corporation's cost of borrowing the money and reduces the company's interest expense to an effective interest rate of 5.5 percent, the market rate. We account for the premium much as we handled the discount. We amortize the bond premium as a *decrease* in interest expense over the life of the bonds.

To check your understanding of the material in this Learning Objective, complete these questions. The solutions appear on MyAccountingLab so you can check your progress.

2. In each of the following situations, will the bonds sell at par, at a premium, or at a discount?
   a. 4-percent bonds sold when the market rate is 4.5 percent
   b. 4-percent bonds sold when the market rate is 3.8 percent
   c. 3.5-percent bonds sold when the market rate is 3.5 percent
   d. 3.25-percent bonds sold when the market rate is 3.15 percent
   e. 3.15-percent bonds sold when the market rate is 3.2 percent

3. Blackwell Insurance Corp. issued $1,000,000 of 3.75-percent, 10-year bonds at the market price of 99.00.
   a. Were the bonds issued at par, at a discount, or at a premium?
   b. How much did Blackwell receive on issuance of the bonds?
   c. Make the journal entry for the issuance of the bonds. Include an explanation.
   d. What is the carrying value of the bonds?

4. Redmond Insurance Corp. issued $1,000,000 of 3.75-percent, 10-year bonds at the market price of 101.50.
   a. Were the bonds issued at par, at a discount, or at a premium?
   b. How much did Redmond receive on issuance of the bonds?
   c. Make the journal entry for the issuance of the bonds. Include an explanation.
   d. What is the carrying value of the bonds?

Amortization of a Bond Discount and a Bond Premium

> **OBJECTIVE 3**
> Amortize a bond discount and premium by the straight-line amortization method and the effective-interest amortization method

There are two methods for amortizing a bond discount and a bond premium: the straight-line method and the effective-interest method. Each of these will be discussed in turn.

Straight-line Method of Amortization of a Bond Discount and a Bond Premium

We can amortize a bond discount or a bond premium by dividing the discount or premium into equal amounts for each interest period. This method is called **straight-line amortization**. (This is very similar to the straight-line method of amortizing assets that we studied in Chapter 10.)

Straight-line Amortization of a Bond Discount   In our UVW Corporation example on page 821, the beginning discount is $20,000, and there are 20 semiannual interest periods during the bonds' 10-year life. Therefore, $\frac{1}{20}$ of the $20,000 bond discount ($1,000) is amortized each interest period. UVW Corporation's semiannual interest entry on July 2, 2010, is

2010			
Jul. 2	Interest Expense	31,000	
	Cash...		30,000
	Discount on Bonds Payable.........................		1,000

To pay semiannual interest of $30,000 ($1,000,000 × 0.06 × ½) and amortize discount on bonds payable $1,000 ($20,000 ÷ 20).[3]

---

[3] Some accountants record the payment of interest and the amortization of the discount in two separate entries, as follows:

2010			
Jul. 2	Interest Expense...	30,000	
	Cash		30,000
	Paid semiannual interest ($1,000,000 × 0.06 × ½).		
2	Interest Expense	1,000	
	Discount on Bonds Payable.....................................		1,000
	Amortized discount on bonds payable ($20,000 ÷ 20).		

Interest expense of $31,000 for each six-month period is the sum of

- The stated interest ($30,000, which is paid in cash)
- *Plus* the amortization of the discount ($1,000)

Discount on Bonds Payable has a debit balance. Therefore, we credit the Discount account to amortize (reduce) its balance. Since Discount on Bonds Payable is a contra account, each reduction in its balance increases the book value or carrying value of Bonds Payable. Twenty amortization entries will decrease the discount balance to zero, which means that the Bonds Payable book value will have increased by $20,000 up to its face value of $1,000,000 by the maturity date. The entry to pay the bonds at maturity is

2020			
Jan. 2	Bonds Payable	1,000,000	
	Cash..		1,000,000
	To pay the bonds payable at maturity.		

KEY POINT

When bonds sell at a premium we collect additional revenue. However, to amortize this amount we reduce interest expense rather than set up a separate revenue account.

Straight-line Amortization of a Bond Premium   In our example on page 822, the beginning premium is $37,700, and there are 20 semiannual interest periods during the bonds' 10-year life. Therefore, $\frac{1}{20}$ of the $37,700 ($1,885) of bond premium is amortized each interest period. UVW Corporation's semiannual interest entry on July 2, 2010, is

2010			
Jul. 2	Interest Expense	28,115	
	Premium on Bonds Payable............................	1,885	
	Cash..		30,000
	To pay semiannual interest ($1,000,000 × 0.06 × $\frac{6}{12}$) and amortize premium on bonds payable ($37,700 ÷ 20).[4]		

Interest expense of $28,115 is

- The stated interest
- *Minus* the amortization of the premium ($1,885)

The debit to Premium on Bonds Payable reduces its normal balance, which is a credit.

At July 2, 2010, immediately after amortizing the bond premium, the bonds have this carrying amount:

$1,035,815 [calculated as $1,000,000 + ($37,700 − $1,885)]

At January 2, 2011, the bonds' carrying amount will be

$1,033,930 [calculated as $1,000,000 + ($37,700 − $1,885 − $1,885)]

---

[4] The payment of interest and the amortization of the bond premium can be recorded in two separate entries as follows:

2010			
Jul. 2	Interest Expense..	30,000	
	Cash		30,000
	Paid semiannual interest ($1,000,000 × 0.06 × $\frac{6}{12}$).		
2	Premium on Bonds Payable	1,885	
	Interest Expense..		1,885
	Amortized premium on bonds payable ($37,700 ÷ 20).		

At maturity on January 2, 2020, the bond premium will have been fully amortized, and the bonds' carrying amount will be $1,000,000.

Effective-Interest Method of Amortization of a Bond Discount and a Bond Premium

The straight-line amortization method has a theoretical weakness. Each period's amortization amount for a premium or discount is the same dollar amount over the life of the bonds. However, over that time, the bonds' carrying value continues to increase (with a discount) or decrease (with a premium). Thus the fixed dollar amount of amortization changes as a percentage of the bonds' carrying value, making it appear that the bond issuer's interest rate changes over time. This appearance is misleading because in fact the issuer locked in a fixed interest rate when the bonds were issued. The stated (contract) interest *rate* on the bonds does not change.

The **effective-interest amortization** method keeps each interest expense amount at the same percentage of the bonds' carrying value or book value for every interest payment over the bonds' life. The total amount of bond discount or bond premium amortized over the life of the bonds is the same under both methods. Canadian GAAP for private enterprises specifies that the effective-interest method should be used because it does a better job of matching. However, the straight-line method is popular because of its simplicity, and, in practice, if there is no material difference, then the cost/benefit constraint results in companies using straight-line amortization.

Effective-Interest Method of Amortizing a Bond Discount Assume that on January 2, 2010, UVW Corporation issues $1,000,000 of 5-percent bonds at a time when the market rate of interest is 6 percent. Also assume that these bonds mature in five years and pay interest semiannually, so there are 10 semiannual interest payments. The issue price of the bonds is $957,349.[5] The discount on these bonds is $42,651 ($1,000,000 − $957,349). Exhibit 15–4 illustrates amortization of the discount by the effective-interest method.

Recall that we want to present interest expense amounts over the full life of the bonds at a fixed percentage of the bonds' carrying value. The 3-percent rate—the effective-interest rate (6 ÷ 2)—*is* that percentage. We have calculated the cost of the money borrowed by the bond issuer—the interest expense—as a constant percentage of the carrying value of the bonds. The *dollar amount* of interest expense varies from period to period but the interest percentage applied to the carrying value remains the same.

The *accounts* debited and credited under the effective-interest amortization method and the straight-line method are the same. Only the amounts differ. We may take the amortization *amounts* directly from the table in Exhibit 15–4. We assume that the first interest payment occurs on July 2 and use the appropriate amounts from Exhibit 15–4, reading across the line for the first interest payment date:

Jul. 2 Interest Expense (column B)...................................... 28,720
          Discount on Bonds Payable (column C) 3,720
          Cash (column A) 25,000
        To pay semiannual interest and amortize
        discount on bonds payable.

On page 827, Exhibit 15–5, Panel A diagrams the interest expense over the life of bonds issued at a discount. Panel B shows how the carrying amount of the bonds rises to the maturity date. All amounts are taken from Exhibit 15–4. Focus on the highlighted items to understand the main points of Exhibit 15–5.

KEY POINT

The amount of *cash* paid each semiannual interest period is calculated with the formula:
Interest paid = Par value × (Stated rate ÷ 2). This amount does not change over the term of the bond.

KEY POINT

The amount of semiannual interest expense is calculated with the formula:
Interest expense = Bond carrying value × (Market interest rate ÷ 2)
This amount will change each period as the carrying value changes over the term of the bond.

---

[5] We show how to compute this amount in the Chapter 15 Appendix. The calculation shown here was made with a calculator. In the Chapter 15 Appendix, the amount is computed using the present-value tables that appear in the Appendix.

EXHIBIT 15-4 Effective-Interest Method of Amortizing a Bond Discount

Panel A: Bond Data

Maturity value—$1,000,000
Stated (contract) interest rate—5%
Interest paid—2.5% semiannually—$25,000 ($1,000,000 × 0.025)
Market interest rate at time of issue—6% annually, 3% semiannually
Issue price—$957,349

Panel B: Amortization Table

	A	B	C	D	E
Semiannual Interest Period	Interest *Payment* (2.5% of Maturity Value)	Interest *Expense* (3% of Preceding Bond Carrying Amount)	Discount Amortization (B − A)	Discount Account Balance (D − C)	Bond Carrying Amount ($1,000,000 − D)
Issue Date				$42,651	$957,349*
1	$25,000	$28,720	$3,720	38,931	961,069
2	25,000	28,832	3,832	35,099	964,901
3	25,000	28,947	3,947	31,152	968,848
4	25,000	29,065	4,065	27,087	972,913
5	25,000	29,187	4,187	22,900	977,100
6	25,000	29,313	4,313	18,587	981,413
7	25,000	29,442	4,442	14,145	985,855
8	25,000	29,576	4,576	9,569	990,431
9	25,000	29,713	4,713	4,856	995,144
10	25,000	29,856	4,856	0	1,000,000

*Minor differences because of the effect of rounding.

Notes

Column A The semiannual interest payments are constant because they are fixed by the stated interest rate and the bonds' maturity value.

Column B The interest expense each period is computed by multiplying the preceding bond carrying amount by the market interest rate. The effect of this *effective-interest rate* determines the interest expense each period. The amount of interest each period increases as the effective-interest rate, a constant, is applied to the increasing bond carrying amount (E).

Column C The excess of each interest expense amount (B) over each interest payment amount (A) is the discount amortization for the period.

Column D The discount balance decreases by the amount of amortization for the period (C) from $42,651 at the bonds' issue date to zero at their maturity. The balance of the discount plus the bonds' carrying amount equals the bonds' maturity value at all times.

Column E The bonds' carrying amount increases from $957,349 at issuance to $1,000,000 at maturity.

Effective-Interest Method of Amortizing a Bond Premium Let's modify the UVW Corporation example above to illustrate the effective-interest method of amortizing a bond premium. Assume that, on April 1, UVW Corporation issues $1,000,000 of five-year, 5-percent bonds that pay interest semiannually. If the bonds are issued when the market interest rate is 4 percent, their issue price is $1,044,913.[6]

---

[6] Again, we compute the present value of the bonds using a calculator. In the Chapter 15 Appendix, the amount is computed using present-value tables.

Panel A—Interest Expense on Bonds Issued at a Discount

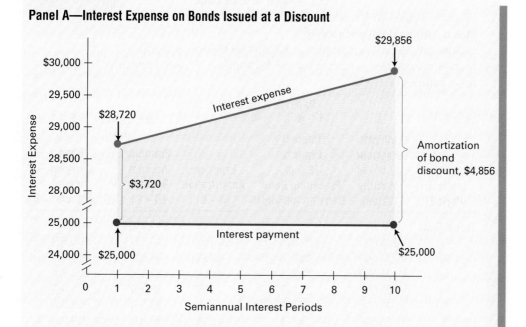

Panel B—Carrying Amount of Bonds Issued at a Discount

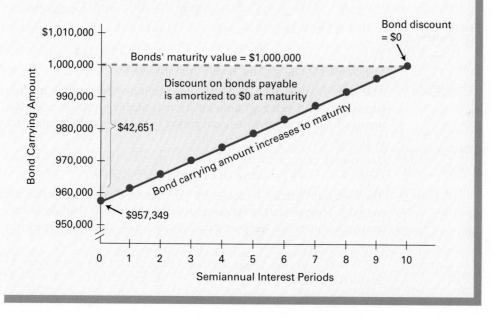

The premium on these bonds is $44,913, and Exhibit 15–6 (on page 828) illustrates amortization of the premium by the effective-interest method.

Assuming that the first interest payment occurs on October 31, we read across the line in Exhibit 15–6 for the first interest payment date and pick up the appropriate amounts.

Oct. 31	Interest Expense (column B)............................	20,898	
	Premium on Bonds Payable (column C)	4,102	
	Cash (column A)..		25,000
	To pay semiannual interest and amortize premium on bonds payable.		

EXHIBIT 15–6   Effective-Interest Method of Amortizing a Bond Premium

Panel A: Bond Data

Maturity value—$1,000,000
Stated (contract) interest rate—5%
Interest paid—2.5% semiannually, $25,000 ($1,000,000 × 0.025)
Market interest rate at time of issue—4% annually, 2% semiannually
Issue price—$1,044,913

Panel B: Amortization Table

Semiannual Interest Period	A Interest Payment (2.5% of Maturity Value)	B Interest Expense (2% of Preceding Bond Carrying Amount)	C Premium Amortization (A – B)	D Premium Account Balance (D – C)	E Bond Carrying Amount ($1,000,000 + D)
Issue Date				$44,913	$1,044,913
1	$25,000	$20,898	$4,102	40,811	1,040,811
2	25,000	20,816	4,184	36,627	1,036,627
3	25,000	20,733	4,267	32,360	1,032,360
4	25,000	20,647	4,353	28,007	1,028,007
5	25,000	20,560	4,440	23,567	1,023,567
6	25,000	20,471	4,529	19,038	1,019,038
7	25,000	20,381	4,619	14,419	1,014,419
8	25,000	20,288	4,712	9,707	1,009,707
9	25,000	20,194	4,806	4,901	1,004,901
10	25,000	20,099	4,901	0	1,000,000

Notes:

Column A   The semiannual interest payments are a constant amount fixed by the stated interest rate and the bonds' maturity value.

Column B   The interest expense each period is computed by multiplying the preceding bond carrying amount by the effective-interest rate. The amount of interest decreases each period as the bond carrying amount decreases.

Column C   The excess of each interest payment (A) over the period's interest expense (B) is the premium amortization for the period.

Column D   The premium balance decreases by the amount of amortization for the period (C) from $44,913 at issuance to zero at maturity. The bonds' carrying amount minus the premium balance equals the bonds' maturity value.

Column E   The bonds' carrying value decreases from $1,044,913 at issuance to $1,000,000 at maturity.

On page 829, Exhibit 15–7, Panel A diagrams the interest expense over the life of the bonds issued at a premium. Panel B shows how the carrying amount of the bonds decreases to maturity. All amounts are taken from Exhibit 15–6. Focus on the highlighted items.

Does the method of amortizing a bond premium or discount affect the amount of cash interest paid on a bond? No. The amortization method for a bond premium or discount has *no effect* on the amount of cash interest paid on a bond. The amount of cash interest paid depends on the contract interest rate stated on the bond. That interest rate, and the amount of cash interest paid, are fixed and therefore remain constant over the life of the bond. To see this, examine column A of Exhibits 15–4 and 15–6.

Panel A—Interest Expense on Bonds Issued at a Premium

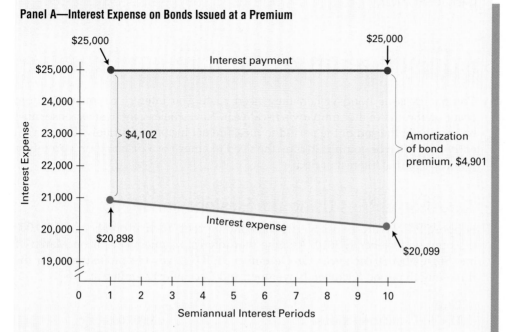

Panel B—Carrying Amount of Bonds Issued at a Premium

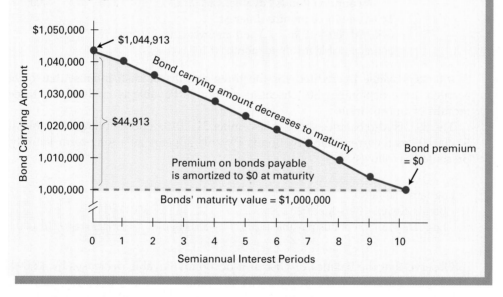

Reporting Bonds Payable

Bonds payable are reported on the balance sheet at their maturity amount plus any unamortized premium or minus any unamortized discount. For example, consider the UVW Corporation example on page 824. At December 31, 2011, UVW Corporation would have amortized the Premium on Bonds Payable for three semiannual periods ($1,885 × 3 = $5,655). The issue date is January 2, 2010, first payment is July 2, 2010, second payment is January 2, 2011, and third payment is July 2, 2011. The UVW Corporation balance sheet would show the bonds payable as follows:

Long-term liabilities		
Bonds Payable, 6% due 2020	$1,000,000	
Premium on bonds payable [$37,700 − (3 × $1,885)]	32,045	$1,032,045

Over the life of the bonds, 20 amortization entries will decrease the premium balance to zero. The payment at maturity will debit Bonds Payable and credit Cash for $1,000,000.

Adjusting Entries for Interest Expense

Companies issue bonds when they need cash. The interest payments seldom occur on the end of the company's fiscal year. Nevertheless, interest expense must be accrued at the end of the period to measure net income accurately. The accrual entry may often be complicated by the need to amortize a discount or a premium for only a partial interest period.

Adjusting Entries Using the Straight-line Method

Suppose B.C. Hydro issues $50,000,000 of 8 percent, 10-year bonds at a $200,000 discount on October 1, 2010. Assume that interest payments occur on March 31 and September 30 each year. On December 31, B.C. Hydro records interest for the three-month period (October, November, and December) as follows:

2010			
Dec. 31	Interest Expense..	1,005,000	
	Interest Payable		1,000,000
	Discount on Bonds Payable...................		5,000
	To accrue three months' interest		
	($50,000,000 × 0.08 × 3⁄12) and amortize the discount on		
	bonds payable for three months ($200,000 ÷ 10 × 3⁄12).		

Interest Payable is credited for the three months of cash interest that have accrued since September 30. Discount on Bonds Payable is credited for three months of amortization.

The B.C. Hydro balance sheet at December 31, 2010, reports Interest Payable of $1,000,000 as a current liability. Bonds Payable appears as a long-term liability, presented as follows:

Long-term liabilities		
Bonds payable, 8%, due 2020	$50,000,000	
Less: Discount on bonds payable ($200,000 – $5,000) ...	195,000	$49,805,000

Observe that the balance of Discount on Bonds Payable decreases by $5,000. The bonds' carrying value increases by the same amount. The bonds' carrying value continues to increase over their 10-year life, reaching $50,000,000 at maturity when the discount will be fully amortized.

The next semiannual interest payment occurs on March 31, 2011, as follows:

2011			
Mar. 31	Interest Expense..	1,005,000	
	Interest Payable	1,000,000	
	Cash..		2,000,000
	Discount on Bonds Payable........................		5,000
	To pay semiannual interest		
	($50,000,000 × 0.08 × 6⁄12), part of which was		
	accrued, and amortize three months' discount		
	on bonds payable ($200,000 ÷ 10 × 3⁄12).		

Amortization of a premium over a partial interest period is similar except that Premium on Bonds Payable is debited.

Adjusting Entries Using the Effective-Interest Method

At year end, it is necessary to make an adjusting entry for accrued interest and amortization of the bond premium for a partial period. In our example on page 826, the last interest payment occurred on October 31. The adjustment for November and December must cover two months, or one-third of a semiannual period.

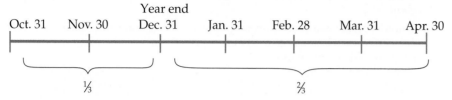

Year end

Oct. 31   Nov. 30   Dec. 31   Jan. 31   Feb. 28   Mar. 31   Apr. 30

⅓   ⅔

Accrual at year end

The entry, with amounts drawn from line 2 in Exhibit 15–6 on page 828, is

Dec. 31	Interest Expense	6,939	
	Premium on Bonds Payable	1,395	
	Interest Payable		8,334
	To accrue two months' interest expense ($20,816 × ⅓), amortize the premium on bonds payable for two months ($4,184 × ⅓), and record interest payable ($25,000 × ⅓).		

The second interest payment occurs on April 30 of the following year. The payment of $25,000 includes interest expense for four months (January through April), the interest payable at December 31, and premium amortization for four months. The payment entry is the following:

Apr. 30	Interest Expense	13,877	
	Interest Payable	8,334	
	Premium on Bonds Payable	2,789	
	Cash		25,000
	To pay semiannual interest ($13,877 = $20,816 × ⅔), some of which was accrued ($8,334), and amortize the premium on bonds payable for four months ($4,184 × ⅔).		

If these bonds had been issued at a discount, procedures for these interest entries would be the same, except that Discount on Bonds Payable would be credited.

DID YOU GET IT?

To check your understanding of the material in this Learning Objective, complete these questions. The solutions appear on MyAccountingLab so you can check your progress.

5. Assume that Hydro-Québec has 6-percent, 10-year bonds that mature on May 1, 2020. Further, assume that $10,000,000 of the bonds are issued at 94.00 on May 1, 2010 and that Hydro-Québec pays interest each April 30 and October 31.

   a. Record issuance of the bonds on May 1, 2010.

   b. Record the interest payment and straight-line amortization of the premium or discount on October 31, 2010.

   c. Accrue interest and amortize the premium or discount on December 31, 2010.

   d. Show how the company would report the bonds on the balance sheet at December 31, 2010.

   e. Record the interest payment on April 30, 2011.

6. Refer to the example of the bonds issued at a premium illustrated in Exhibit 15–6. Use the data in Exhibit 15–6 to accrue interest and amortize the bond premium at the end of the second year, December 31, 2011. Then record the April 30, 2012 payment of interest.

7. Refer to Exhibits 15–4 and 15–6 to answer the following questions.

a. Will the periodic amount of interest expense increase or decrease over the life of a bond issued at a *discount*, under the effective-interest amortization method?

b. Will the periodic amount of interest expense increase or decrease for a bond issued at a *premium*? Assume the effective-interest method of amortizing the premium.

c. Consider bonds issued at a discount. Which will be greater, the cash interest paid per period or the amount of interest expense? Answer the same question for bonds issued at a premium.

Additional Bond Topics

Companies that issue bonds payable face additional issues such as:

- Retirement of bonds payable
- Convertible bonds payable
- Balance sheet presentation of bonds payable
- Advantages and disadvantages of issuing bonds versus shares

Retirement of Bonds

OBJECTIVE ④
Account for retirement and conversion of bonds

KEY POINT

Callable bonds may be paid off at the corporation's option. The bondholder does not have the choice of refusing but must surrender the bond for retirement.

Normally, companies wait until maturity to pay off, or retire, their bonds payable. All the bond discount or premium has been amortized, and the retirement entry debits Bonds Payable and credits Cash for the bonds' maturity value, as we saw earlier. But companies sometimes retire their bonds prior to maturity. The main reason for retiring bonds early is to relieve the pressure of making interest payments. Interest rates fluctuate. The company may be able to borrow at a lower interest rate and use the proceeds from new bonds to pay off the old bonds, which bear a higher rate.

Some bonds are **callable**, which means that the company may *call* or pay off those bonds at a specified price whenever it so chooses. The call price is usually a few percentage points above the face value or par, perhaps 104.00 or 105.00, to make the bonds attractive to lenders. Callable bonds give the issuer the benefit of being able to take advantage of low interest rates by paying off the bonds at the most favourable time. An alternative to calling the bonds is to purchase them in the open market at their current market price. Whether the bonds are called or purchased in the open market, the journal entry is the same.

Suppose XYZ Corporation has $10,000,000 of bonds outstanding with an unamortized discount of $40,000. Lower interest rates in the market may convince management to retire these bonds now. Assume that the bonds are callable at 103.00. If the market price of the bonds is 99.50, will XYZ Corporation call the bonds or purchase them in the open market? The market price is lower than the call price, so market price is the better choice. Retiring the bonds at 99.50 results in a gain of $10,000, computed as follows:

Face value of bonds being retired	$10,000,000
Unamortized discount	40,000
Book value, or carrying value...	9,960,000
Market price ($10,000,000 × 0.9950) paid to retire the bonds.........	9,950,000
Gain on retirement of bonds	$ 10,000

The following entry records retirement of the bonds immediately after an interest date:

Jun. 30	Bonds Payable	10,000,000	
	Discount on Bonds Payable..................		40,000
	Cash...		9,950,000
	Gain on Retirement of		
	Bonds Payable		10,000
	To retire bonds payable before maturity.		

After posting, the bond accounts have zero balances.

Bonds Payable	
Retirement 10,000,000	Prior balance 10,000,000

Discount on Bonds Payable	
Prior balance 40,000	Retirement 40,000

The entry removes the bonds payable and the related discount from the accounts and records a gain on retirement. Of course, any existing premium would be removed with a debit.

When bonds are retired before maturity, follow these steps:

1. Record a partial-period amortization of the premium or discount, if the date is other than an interest payment date.

2. Write off the portion of the premium or discount that relates to the portion of bonds being retired.

3. Calculate any gain or loss on retirement.

If XYZ Corporation had retired only half of these bonds, the accountant would remove half of the discount or premium. Likewise, if the price paid to retire the bonds exceeded their carrying value, the retirement entry would record a loss with a debit to the account Loss on Retirement of Bonds. GAAP for private enterprises requires that gains and losses on early retirement of debt that are both abnormal in size and unusual be reported separately as a line item on the income statement before the line items for income tax and discontinued operations.

Convertible Bonds and Notes

Corporations often add *sweeteners* to their bonds—features to make the bonds more attractive to potential investors. Many corporate bonds, debentures, and notes payable have the feature of being convertible into the common shares of the issuing company at the option of the investor. These bonds and notes, called **convertible bonds** (or **convertible notes**), combine the safety of assured receipts of principal and interest on the bonds with the opportunity for large gains on the shares. The conversion feature is so attractive that investors usually accept a lower stated, or contract, interest rate than they would on nonconvertible bonds. The lower interest rate benefits the issuer. Convertible bonds are recorded like any other debt at issuance.

If the market price of the issuing company's shares gets high enough, the bond-holders will convert the bonds into shares. The corporation records conversion by debiting the bond accounts and crediting the shareholders' equity accounts. Normally, the carrying value of the bonds becomes the book value of the newly issued shares, and no gain or loss is recorded.

Assume that XYZ Corporation bondholders converted $100,000 of XYZ Corporation bonds into 20,000 common shares on May 1, 2010. The bonds were issued at par. XYZ Corporation's entry to record the conversion would be:

2010
May 1   Bonds Payable   100,000
                Common Shares   100,000
            To record conversion of $100,000 bonds
            outstanding into 20,000 common shares.

The entry brings the Bonds Payable account to zero, exactly the same as for a bond retirement. The carrying value of the bonds ($100,000) becomes the amount of increase in shareholders' equity.

Current Portion of Long-Term Debt

Reporting Liabilities on the Balance Sheet

Companies report their bonds payable and notes payable among the liabilities on the balance sheet. As we have seen throughout, there are two categories of liabilities: current and long-term.

Many companies have several issues of long-term debt outstanding where each issue has a different maturity date. Suppose XYZ Corporation had 10 different issues of debt outstanding amounting to $1,643 million and that $97 million of that total was due in one year. XYZ Corporation would report the debt as follows on its year-end balance sheet:

	$ millions
Current liabilities	
Current portion of long-term debt...	$ 97
Long-term debt, excluding amounts payable within one year	1,546

The principal portion of long-term debt that is due within the next year is reclassified as a current liability, and the long-term debt is reduced by the same amount.

DID YOU GET IT?

To check your understanding of the material in this Learning Objective, complete these questions. The solutions appear on MyAccountingLab so you can check your progress.

8. Suppose McMeeken Corporation has $5,000,000 of bonds outstanding with an unamortized premium of $30,000. The call price is 105.00. To reduce interest payments, the company retires half of the bonds at the 100.50 market price. Calculate the gain or loss on retirement, and record the retirement immediately after an interest date.

9. Suppose McMeeken Corporation has $5,000,000 of bonds outstanding with an unamortized premium of $30,000. The bonds are convertible. Assume bondholders converted half of the bonds into 1,000,000 common shares on September 1, 2010. Record the conversion of these bonds into common shares.

10. Suppose McMeeken Corporation has $5,000,000 of bonds outstanding that were issued on different dates, with a total unamortized premium of $30,000. Of these amounts, $1,500,000 of the bonds and $5,000 of the unamortized premium are due in one year. How would McMeeken Corporation report the debt on its year-end balance sheet?

Advantages and Disadvantages of Issuing Bonds versus Shares

OBJECTIVE 5

Show the advantages and disadvantages of borrowing

Businesses acquire assets in different ways. Management may decide to purchase or to lease equipment. If management decides to purchase, the money to pay for the asset may be financed by the business's retained earnings, a note payable, a share issue, or a bond issue. Each financing strategy has its advantages and disadvantages, as follows:

Advantages of Financing Operations by	
Issuing Shares	**Issuing Notes or Bonds**
• Creates no liabilities or interest expense, which must be paid even during bad years; is less risky to the issuing corporation. • Raises capital without increasing debt and adversely affecting some key ratios. • Carries no obligation to pay dividends.	• Does not dilute share ownership or control of the corporation. • May result in higher earnings per share because interest expense is tax-deductible and ownership is not diluted. • Can create greater returns for the shareholders if leveraged profitably.

Exhibit 15–8 illustrates the earnings-per-share (EPS) advantage of borrowing. Recall that earnings per share (EPS) is a company's net income per common share outstanding. EPS may be the most important figure on the income statement. Suppose XYZ Corporation has net income of $600,000 and 200,000 common shares outstanding before a new project. The company needs $1,000,000 for expansion, and management is considering two financing plans:

• Plan 1 is to issue $1,000,000 of 10-percent bonds.

• Plan 2 is to issue 100,000 common shares for $1,000,000.

XYZ Corporation management believes the new cash can be invested in operations to earn income of $300,000 before interest and taxes.

The EPS amount is higher if the company borrows (Plan 1). The business earns more on the investment ($120,000) than the interest it pays on the bonds

EXHIBIT 15–8   Earnings-per-Share Advantage of Borrowing versus Issuing Shares

	Plan 1: Borrow $1,000,000 at 10%	Plan 2: Issue $1,000,000 of Common Shares
Net income after interest and income tax, before expansion...	$600,000	$600,000
Project income before interest and income tax..	300,000	300,000
Less: interest expense ($1,000,000 × 0.10).......	100,000	0
Project income before income tax.....................	200,000	300,000
Less: income tax expense (40%)........................	80,000	120,000
Project net income	120,000	180,000
Total company net income................................	$720,000	$780,000
Earnings per share including expansion:		
Plan 1 ($720,000 ÷ 200,000 shares)	$ 3.60	
Plan 2 ($780,000 ÷ 300,000 shares)		$ 2.60

($100,000). Earning more income than the cost of borrowing increases the earnings for common shareholders, and is called **trading on the equity**. It is widely used in business to increase earnings per common share.

Borrowing has its disadvantages. Debts must be paid during bad years as well as during good years. Interest expense may be high enough to eliminate net income and lead to a cash crisis and even bankruptcy. This has happened to many Internet startups. In contrast, a company that issues shares can omit paying dividends during a bad year.

Computer spreadsheets are useful in evaluating financing alternatives such as issuing common shares, preferred shares, or bonds. This assessment is often called "what if" analysis—for instance, "what if we finance with common shares?" The answers to "what if" questions can be modelled on a spreadsheet to project the company's financial statements over the next few years.

DID YOU GET IT?

To check your understanding of the material in this Learning Objective, complete these questions. The solutions appear on MyAccountingLab so you can check your progress.

11. If trading on the equity can improve EPS, how might it be to the corporation's *disadvantage* to finance with debt?

12. Suppose JKL Corporation has net income of $600,000 and 200,000 common shares outstanding before a new project. The company needs $1,000,000 for expansion, and management is considering two financing plans:

   - Plan 1 is to issue $1,000,000 of 12 percent bonds.
   - Plan 2 is to issue 50,000 common shares for $1,000,000.

   JKL Corporation management believes the new cash can be invested in operations to earn income of $300,000 before interest and taxes. Which plan seems more favourable given the corporation's tax rate of 40 percent? Why?

OBJECTIVE 6
Report lease liabilities

Lease Liabilities

A **lease** is an agreement in which the tenant (**lessee**) agrees to make regular, periodic payments to the property owner (**lessor**) in exchange for the exclusive use of the asset. Leasing is the way the tenant or lessee avoids having to make the large initial cash down payment that purchase agreements require. Accountants divide leases into two types when considering the lease from the lessee's perspective: operating and capital. From the lessor's perspective, there are again two categories of leases, operating and capital, with capital leases further divided into two kinds: *sales-type leases*, in which the lessor is usually a manufacturer or dealer, and *direct financing leases*, in which the lessor is usually not a manufacturer or dealer but provides financing. This text will consider the broader term, *capital lease*, and not the kinds of capital leases.

In a recent survey of 189 Canadian companies, 104 or 55 percent had operating leases only, 6 or 3 percent had capital leases only, and 70 or 37 percent had both operating and capital leases.[7]

Operating Leases

Operating leases are usually short-term or cancellable. Many apartment leases and most short-term car-rental agreements extend a year or less. These operating

---

[7] Lavigne, A., D. Paul, and J. Tang, *Financial Reporting in Canada 2008*, 33rd Edition. (Toronto: Canadian Institute of Chartered Accountants, 2009), online edition, Chapter 9—Leases, Analysis and Discussion section.

leases give the lessee the right to use the asset, but provide the lessee with no continuing rights to the asset. The lessor retains the usual risks and rewards of owning the leased asset. To account for an operating lease, the lessee debits Rent Expense (or Lease Expense) and credits Cash for the amount of the lease payment. The lessee's books report neither the leased asset nor any lease liability (except perhaps a prepaid rent amount or a rent accrual at the end of the period). However, the future lease payments for each of the next five years should be given in the notes to the financial statements. The nature of the lease commitments should also be stated in the notes.

Capital Leases

Many businesses use capital leasing to finance the acquisition of some assets. A capital lease is long-term, noncancellable financing that is a form of debt.

How do you distinguish a capital lease from an operating lease? Section 3065 of the *CICA Handbook* defines a **capital lease** as one that substantially transfers all the benefits and risks incident to ownership of property to the lessee. The section goes on to suggest that a lease is a capital lease from the perspective of the lessee if one or more of the following conditions are present at the beginning of the lease:

1. There is reasonable assurance that the lessee will obtain ownership of the leased asset at the end of the lease term.
2. The lease term is of such a length that the lessee will obtain almost all (usually 75 percent or more) of the benefits from the use of the leased asset over its life.
3. The lessor will both recover the original investment and earn a return on that investment from the lease.

A lease that does not meet any of the above conditions is probably an operating lease and should be accounted for as such.

A lease is a capital lease from the perspective of the lessor if any one of the three conditions outlined above is present and *both* of the following are present:

1. The credit risk associated with the lease is normal.
2. The amounts of any unreimbursable costs to the lessor are estimable.

Accounting for a Capital Lease Accounting for a capital lease is much like accounting for a purchase. The lessor removes the asset from his or her books. The lessee enters the asset into his or her accounts and records a lease liability at the beginning of the lease term. Thus, the lessee capitalizes the asset on its own financial statements even though the lessee may never take legal title to the property.

Sierra Wireless, Inc. has its head office in Vancouver. Suppose Sierra leases a building on January 2, 2010, agreeing to pay $200,000 annually for a 20-year period, with the first payment due immediately and all subsequent payments due at the beginning of the year. This meets the second condition for a capital lease given above; this arrangement is similar to purchasing the building on an instalment plan. In an instalment purchase, Sierra would debit Building and credit Cash and Instalment Note Payable. The company would then pay interest and principal on the note payable and record amortization on the building. Accounting for a capital lease follows this same pattern.

Sierra records the building at cost, which is the sum of the $200,000 initial payment plus the present value of the 19 future lease payments of $200,000 each.[8] The company credits Cash for the initial payment and credits Lease Liability for the present value of the future lease payments. Assume the interest rate on Sierra's lease is 10 percent and the present value (PV) of the future lease payments (19 more

---

[8] The Chapter 15 Appendix explains present value.

payments) is $1,672,974.[9] At the beginning of the lease term, Sierra Wireless, Inc. makes the following entry:

2010			
Jan. 2	Building under Capital Lease	1,872,974	
	Cash...		200,000
	Capital Lease Liability...........................		1,672,974
	To lease a building ($200,000 + $1,672,974) and make the first annual lease payment on the capital lease ($200,000). The lease liability is $1,672,974, the present value of the future lease payments.		

Sierra's lease liability at January 2, 2010, is for 19 payments of $200,000 each on January 2, 2011, to January 2, 2029. However, included in those payments is interest calculated at 10 percent. The lease liability is

Cash payments January 2, 2011, to January 2, 2029 (19 × $200,000)...	$3,800,000
Interest embedded in the lease payments	2,127,026
Present value of future lease payments	$1,672,974

If Sierra Wireless, Inc. were to record the liability at $3,800,000, it would also have to record the interest included in that amount as a contra amount. Most companies net the interest against the cash payments and show the liability as the net amount (principal).

Because Sierra has capitalized the building, the company records amortization (straight-line). Assume the building has an expected life of 25 years. It is amortized over the lease term of 20 years because the lessee has the use of the building only for that period. No residual value enters into the amortization computation because the lessee will have no residual asset when the building is returned to the lessor at the expiration of the lease. Therefore, the annual amortization entry is

2010			
Dec. 31	Amortization Expense.......................................	93,649	
	Accumulated Amortization— Building under Capital Lease		93,649
	To record amortization on leased building of $93,649 ($1,872,974 ÷ 20).		

Note that a lessee, such as Sierra, might obtain ownership of the leased asset at the end of the lease term. In such a situation, the lessee would amortize the leased asset over its useful life instead of over the term of the lease. At year end, Sierra must also accrue interest on the lease liability. Interest expense is computed by multiplying the lease liability by the interest rate on the lease. The following entry credits Capital Lease Liability (not Interest Payable) for this interest accrual:

2010			
Dec. 31	Interest Expense	167,297	
	Capital Lease Liability....................................		167,297
	To accrue interest on the lease liability ($1,672,984 × 0.10).		

[9] The formula for this computation appears in the Chapter 15 Appendix. The calculation shown here was made with a calculator. In the Chapter 15 Appendix, the amount is computed using the present-value tables that appear in the Appendix.

The balance sheet at December 31, 2010, reports:

Assets

Capital assets:
Building under capital lease.................................... $1,872,974
Less: Accumulated amortization 93,649 $1,779,325

Liabilities

Current liabilities:
Lease liability (next payment due on Jan. 2, 2011)* .... $ 200,000

Long-term liabilities:
Lease liability... 1,640,271**

---

* The information in brackets is for student reference only. It would not appear on the balance sheet.
** $1,640,271 = [Beginning balance ($1,672,974) + Interest accrual ($167,297) − Current portion ($200,000)]

In addition, the lessee must report the minimum capital lease payments for the next five years in the notes to the financial statements.

The lease liability is split into current and long-term portions because the next payment ($200,000) is a current liability and the remainder is long-term. The January 2, 2011, lease payment is recorded as follows:

```
2011
Jan. 2   Lease Liability................................................... 200,000
             Cash............................................................            200,000
         To make second annual lease payment on building.
```

Off-Balance-Sheet Financing

An important part of business is obtaining the funds needed to acquire assets. To finance operations, a company may issue shares, borrow money, or retain earnings in the business. All three of these financing plans affect the right-hand side of the balance sheet. Issuing shares affects preferred or common shares. Borrowing creates notes or bonds payable. Internal funds come from retained earnings.

Off-balance-sheet financing is the acquisition of assets or services whose resulting debt is not reported on the balance sheet. A prime example is an operating lease. The lessee has the use of the leased asset, but neither the asset nor any lease liability is reported on the balance sheet. In the past, most leases were accounted for by the operating method. More recently, however, Section 3065 of the *CICA Handbook* has required businesses to account for an increasing number of leases by the capital lease method. Also, Section 3065 has brought about detailed reporting of operating lease payments in the notes to the financial statements; minimum operating lease payments for the next five years must be reported. The inclusion of more lease information, whether for capital or operating leases, makes the accounting information for decision making more complete. Much useful information is reported only in the notes. Experienced investors study them carefully.

DID YOU GET IT?

To check your understanding of the material in this Learning Objective, complete these questions. The solutions appear on MyAccountingLab so you can check your progress.

13. Bedrock Construction Inc. acquired equipment under a capital lease that requires six annual lease payments of $30,000. The first payment is due when the lease begins, on January 2, 2010. Future payments are due on January 2 of each year of the lease term. The interest rate in the lease is 12 percent and the present value of the five future lease payments is $108,150. Journalize (a) the acquisition of the equipment, (b) the amortization for 2010, (c) the accrued interest at December 31, 2010, and (d) the second lease payment on January 2, 2011.

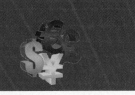

The Effects on Long-Term Liabilities of International Financial Reporting Standards (IFRS)

OBJECTIVE ⑦

Identify the effects on long-term liabilities of international financial reporting standards (IFRS)

Two types of long-term liabilities are discussed in this chapter: bonds payable and leases. We will discuss each item in turn as the accounting treatment for each type of indebtedness does differ.

The two sets of standards governing accounting for bond indebtedness—GAAP for private enterprises and IFRS—are comparable in many key areas. Under GAAP for private enterprises, the liability for bonds is measured at amortized cost. Under IFRS, the liability for bonds is measured at amortized cost as well, but companies are also allowed the option of recording the liability for bonds at fair value. While the fair value option is the primary difference between the IFRS and GAAP for private enterprises, there are a number of other differences as well. Variations such as the IFRS requirement to report separately the components of compound financial instruments on the balance sheet are beyond the scope of this text and are covered in more advanced accounting courses.

The principles governing accounting for leases are basically the same under GAAP for private enterprises and IFRS. The only material difference is that companies reporting under IFRS are required to disclose more supplementary information than those reporting under GAAP for private enterprises.

DID YOU GET IT?

MyAccountingLab

> To check your understanding of the material in this Learning Objective, complete these questions. The solutions appear on MyAccountingLab so you can check your progress.
>
> 14. When accounting for bonds, what is the primary difference between GAAP for private enterprises and IFRS?
>
> 15. When accounting for leases, what is the primary difference between GAAP for private enterprises and IFRS?

As we conclude this chapter, we return to our opening questions: What are bonds payable, and why are they important? How are bond prices determined? How do you account for bonds and report them in the financial statements? How do bonds compare with shares? How do you account for other long-term liabilities? These questions were answered throughout this chapter. The following Decision Guidelines provide the answers in a useful summary.

Decision	Guidelines
Types of bonds:	
a. When will you pay off the bonds?	
• All at maturity?	• Term bonds
• In instalments?	• Serial bonds
b. Are the bonds secured?	Then they are
• Yes	• Secured bonds (for example, mortgages)
• No	• Unsecured bonds (for example, debentures)
How are bond prices	
• Quoted?	• As a percentage of maturity value or face value (Example: A $500,000 bond priced at $510,000 would be quoted at 102 ($510,000 ÷ $500,000 = 1.02)
• Determined?	• Present value of the future principal amount to pay plus present value of the future periodic interest payments (see the Chapter 15 Appendix).
What are the two interest rates used for bonds?	• *Stated (contract) interest rate* determines the amount of cash interest the borrower pays. This interest rate is set by contract and does not change during the life of the bonds.
	• *Market (effective) interest rate* is the rate that investors demand for lending their money. This interest rate determines the bonds' market price and varies, sometimes daily.
What causes a bond to be priced at	When the bonds are issued,
• Maturity (face, principal, or par) value?	• Stated interest rate on the bond *equals* the market interest rate.
• A discount?	• Stated interest rate on the bond is *less than* the market interest rate.
• A premium?	• Stated interest rate on the bond is *greater than* the market interest rate.
What is the relationship between interest expense and interest payments when bonds are issued at	
• Maturity (face, principal, or par) value?	• Interest expense *equals* interest payment.
• A discount?	• Interest expense is *greater than* interest payment.
• A premium?	• Interest expense is *less than* interest payment.
How are bonds payable reported on the balance sheet?	Maturity (face, principal, or par) value ⎰ + Premium on bonds / or / − Discount on bonds
What happens to the bonds' carrying amount when bonds payable are issued at	
• Maturity (face, principal, or par) value?	• Carrying amount *stays* at maturity (face, principal, or par) value during the life of the bonds.
• A discount?	• Carrying amount *increases* gradually to the bonds' maturity value on their maturity date.
• A premium?	• Carrying amount *decreases* gradually to the bonds' maturity value on their maturity date.

How do companies account for the retirement of bonds?

At maturity date:

Bonds Payable...........................	Maturity value
Cash	Maturity value

Before maturity date (assume a discount on the bonds and a gain on retirement):

Bonds Payable...........................	Maturity value
Discount on Bonds Payable ..	Balance
Cash	Amount paid
Gain on Retirement of Bonds Payable	Excess

How do companies account for the conversion of convertible bonds payable into common shares (assume a bond premium)?

Bonds Payable	Maturity value
Premium on Bonds Payable	Balance
Common Shares	Total

Note that there is no gain or loss on the conversion.

What are the advantages of financing operations with
- Shares?

- Bonds (or notes) payable?

- Creates no liability or interest expense; is less risky to the issuing corporation.
- Does not dilute share ownership or control of the corporation.
- Results in higher earnings per share—under normal conditions.

How to account for
- An operating lease?
- A capital lease?

- Debit lease (or rent) expense when making each lease payment.
- At the beginning of the lease period, record
  a. Asset (as though it were purchased).
  b. Capital lease liability—present value of future lease payments.

Each period thereafter, record
a. Lease payment as a debit to the Capital Lease Liability account, a credit to Cash.
b. Interest expense on the lease liability.
c. Amortization expense on the asset.

Summary Problem for Your Review

Astoria Inc. has outstanding an issue of 8-percent convertible bonds that mature in 2020. Suppose the bonds were dated October 1, 2010 and pay interest each April 1 and October 1.

Required

Name: Astoria Inc.
Accounting Period:
The years 2010, 2011, 2012

1. Complete the following effective-interest amortization table through October 1, 2012.

   Bond data: Maturity value—$2,000,000

   Contract interest rate—8%

   Interest paid—4% semiannually, $80,000 ($2,000,000 × 0.04)

   Market interest rate at time of issue—9% annually, 4.5% semiannually

   Issue proceeds—$1,869,921

Amortization table:

	A	B	C	D	E
Semiannual Interest Period	**Interest Payment (4% of Maturity Value)**	**Interest Expense (4.5% of Preceding Bond Carrying Amount)**	**Discount Amortization (B – A)**	**Discount Account Balance (D – C)**	**Bond Carrying Amount ($2,000,000 – D)**
Oct. 1, 2010					
Apr. 1, 2011					
Oct. 1, 2011					
Apr. 1, 2012					
Oct. 1, 2012					

2. Using the amortization table, record the following transactions:

   a. Issuance of the bonds on October 1, 2010.

   b. Accrual of interest and amortization of discount on December 31, 2010.

   c. Payment of interest and amortization of discount on April 1, 2011.

   d. Conversion of one-third of the bonds payable into common shares on October 2, 2012.

   e. Retirement of two-thirds of the bonds payable on October 2, 2012. Purchase price of the bonds was 102.00.

SOLUTION

Requirement 1

Amortization table:

	A	B	C	D	E
Semiannual Interest Period	Interest Payment (4% of Maturity Value)	Interest Expense (4.5% of Preceding Bond Carrying Amount)	Discount Amortization (B – A)	Discount Account Balance (D – C)	Bond Carrying Amount ($2,000,000 – D)
Oct. 1, 2010				$130,079	$1,869,921
Apr. 1, 2011	$80,000	$84,146	$4,146	125,933	1,874,067
Oct. 1, 2011	80,000	84,333	4,333	121,600	1,878,400
Apr. 1, 2012	80,000	84,528	4,528	117,072	1,882,928
Oct. 1, 2012	80,000	84,732	4,732	112,340	1,887,660

The semiannual interest payment is constant ($80,000). The interest expense is calculated as 4.5 percent of the previous period's carrying value. The discount account balance reflects that the issue proceeds of $1,869,921 are less than the maturity value of the bonds.

Requirement 2

a. The bonds were issued for less than $2,000,000, reflecting a discount. Use the amounts from columns D and E for Oct. 1, 2010 from the amortization table.

2010
a. Oct. 1 Cash 1,869,921
        Discount on Bonds Payable 130,079
            Bonds Payable 2,000,000
        To issue 8%, 10-year bonds at a discount.

b. The accrued interest is calculated, and the bond discount is amortized. Use 3/6 of the amounts from columns A, B, and C for Apr. 1, 2011.

b. Dec. 31 Interest Expense ($84,146 × ³⁄₆) 42,073
        Discount on Bonds Payable ($4,146 × ³⁄₆) ... 2,073
        Interest Payable ($80,000 × ³⁄₆) 40,000
        To accrue interest and amortize bond discount for three months.

c. The semiannual interest payment is made ($80,000 from Column A). Only the January–March 2011 interest expense is recorded, since the October–December interest expense was already recorded in Requirement 2b. The same is true for the discount on bonds payable. Reverse Interest Payable from Requirement 2b, since cash is paid now.

2011
c. Apr. 1 Interest Expense 42,073
        Interest Payable 40,000
            Discount on Bonds Payable ($4,146 × ³⁄₆) ... 2,073
            Cash 80,000
        To pay semiannual interest, part of which was accrued, and amortize three months' discount on bonds payable.

d. When converting bonds to common shares, retire the full amount of the bonds (1/3 × $2,000,000) and the discount account balance (1/3 × $112,240 from column D for Oct. 1, 2012).

2012
d. Oct. 2 Bonds Payable ($2,000,000 × ⅓) 666,667
            Discount on Bonds Payable ($112,340 × ⅓) ... 37,447
            Common Shares ($1,887,660 × ⅓) 629,220
        To record conversion of bonds payable.

e. The cash paid on retirement was $102 for every $100 of bonds. Use 2/3 of the amount from column D for Oct. 1, 2012 to calculate Discount on Bonds Payable. The loss on retirement reflects the excess of the book value over the cash received and is the "plug" figure in the journal entry.

e. Oct. 2 Bonds Payable ($2,000,000 × ⅔) 1,333,333
        Loss on Retirement of Bonds 101,560
            Discount on Bonds Payable ($112,340 × ⅔) ... 74,893
            Cash ($2,000,000 × ⅔ × 1.02) 1,360,000
        To retire bonds payable before maturity.

Summary

1. **Define bonds payable and the types of bonds.** A corporation may borrow money by issuing long-term notes and *bonds*. A bond contract specifies the maturity value of the bonds, the *stated (contract) interest rate*, and the dates for paying interest and principal. Bonds may be secured (for example, a *mortgage*) or unsecured (e.g. *debentures*). Bonds and debentures are accounted for similarly.

2. **Determine the price of a bond, and account for basic bond transactions.** Bonds are traded through organized markets, such as the over-the-counter market. Bonds are typically divided into $1,000 units. Their prices are quoted at the price per $100.00 bond. *Market interest rates* fluctuate and may differ from the stated rate on a bond. If a bond's stated rate exceeds the market rate, the bond sells at a *premium*. A bond with a stated rate below the market rate sells at a *discount*.

   Money earns income over time, a fact that gives rise to the *present-value concept*. An investor will pay a price for a bond equal to the present value of the bond principal plus the present value of the stream of bond interest.

3. **Amortize a bond discount and premium by the straight-line amortization method and the effective-interest amortization method.** *Straight-line amortization* allocates an equal *dollar amount* of premium or discount to each interest period. In the *effective-interest method* of amortization, the market rate at the time of issuance is multiplied by the bonds' carrying amount to determine the interest expense for each period and to compute the amount of discount or premium amortization. This method allocates a *constant percentage* of premium or discount to each interest period.

4. **Account for retirement and conversion of bonds.** Companies may retire their bonds payable before

maturity. *Callable* bonds give the borrower the right to pay off the bonds at a specified call price; otherwise, the company may purchase the bonds in the open market.

   Convertible bonds and notes give the investor the privilege of trading the bonds in for shares of the issuing corporation. The carrying amount of the bonds becomes the book value of the newly issued shares.

5. **Show the advantages and disadvantages of borrowing.** A key advantage of raising money by borrowing versus issuing shares is that interest expense on debt is tax-deductible. Thus, borrowing is less costly than issuing shares. If the company can earn more income than the cost of borrowing, EPS will increase. Borrowing's disadvantages result from the fact that the company *must* repay the loan and its interest, unlike issuing shares, where dividends do not have to be declared and paid.

6. **Report lease liabilities.** A *lease* is an agreement between the *lessee* and the *lessor*. In an *operating lease*, the lessor retains the usual risks and rights of owning the asset. The lessee debits Rent Expense and credits Cash when making lease payments. A *capital lease* is long-term, noncancellable, and similar to an instalment purchase of the leased asset. In a capital lease, the lessee capitalizes and amortizes the leased asset, and reports a lease liability.

7. **Identify the effects on long-term liabilities of international financial reporting standards (IFRS).** Under GAAP for private enterprises, liabilities for bond indebtedness are reported at amortized cost. Under IFRS, the liability may be reported at amortized cost or fair value. Under IFRS, companies are required to disclose more lease information than under GAAP for private enterprises.

SELF-STUDY QUESTIONS

Test your understanding of the chapter by marking the best answer for each of the following questions:

1. Which type of bond is unsecured? (*p. 816*)
   a. Serial bond   c. Debenture bond
   b. Common bond   d. Mortgage bond

2. How much will an investor pay for a $200,000 bond priced at 102.5? (*p. 817*)
   a. $200,000   c. $205,000
   b. $204,000   d. $202,500

3. A bond with a stated interest rate of 6.5 percent is issued when the market interest rate is 6.75 percent. This bond will sell at (*p. 818*)
   a. Par value   c. A premium
   b. A discount   d. A price minus accrued interest

4. Imported Cars Inc. has $1,000,000 of 10-year bonds payable outstanding. These bonds had a discount of $80,000 at issuance, which was five years ago. The company uses the straight-line amortization method. The carrying amount of the Imported Cars Inc. bonds payable is (*pp. 823–825*)
   a. $920,000   c. $1,000,000
   b. $960,000   d. $1,040,000

5. Imported Cars issued its 8-percent bonds payable at a price of $880,000 (maturity value is $1,000,000). The market interest rate was 10 percent when Imported Cars issued its bonds. The company uses the effective-interest method for the bonds. Interest expense for the first year is (*pp. 825–826*)
   a. $70,400   c. $88,000
   b. $80,000   d. $100,000

6. Bonds payable a with face value of $1,800,000 and carrying value of $1,728,000 are retired before their scheduled maturity with a cash outlay of $1,752,000. Which of the following entries correctly records this bond retirement? (pp. 832–833)

a. Bonds Payable 1,800,000
    Discount on Bonds Payable..... 72,000
        Cash... 1,752,000
        Gain on Retirement of
            Bonds Payable 120,000

b. Bonds Payable 1,800,000
    Loss on Retirement of
        Bonds Payable 24,000
        Discount on Bonds Payable. 72,000
        Cash... 1,752,000

c. Bonds Payable 1,800,000
    Discount on Bonds Payable. 36,000
    Cash... 1,752,000
        Gain on Retirement of
            Bonds Payable 12,000

d. Bonds Payable 1,728,000
    Discount on Bonds Payable..... 72,000
        Gain on Retirement of
            Bonds Payable 48,000
        Cash... 1,752,000

7. YYZ Corporation has $3,450,000 of debt outstanding at year end, of which $990,000 is due in one year. What will this company report on its year-end balance sheet? (p. 834)
    a. Long-term debt of $3,450,000
    b. Current liability of $990,000 and long-term debt of $3,450,000
    c. Current liability of $990,000 and long-term debt of $2,460,000
    d. None of the above

8. An advantage of financing operations with debt versus shares is (pp. 835–836)
    a. The tax deductibility of interest expense on debt
    b. The legal requirement to pay interest and principal
    c. Lower interest payments compared to dividend payments
    d. All of the above

9. In a capital lease, the lessee records (pp. 837–839)
    a. A leased asset and a lease liability
    b. Amortization on the leased asset
    c. Interest on the lease liability
    d. All of the above

10. Which of the following is an example of off-balance-sheet financing? (p. 839)
    a. Operating lease
    b. Current portion of long-term debt
    c. Debenture bonds
    d. Convertible bonds

Answers to Self-Study Questions
1. c   2. c [$200,000 × 1.025 = $205,000]   3. b   4. b   5. c   6. b   7. c   8. a   9. d   10. a

ACCOUNTING VOCABULARY

Bond (p. 814)
Bonds payable (p. 814)
Callable bond (p. 832)
Capital lease (p. 837)
Contract interest rate (p. 818)
Convertible bond (p. 833)
Convertible note (p. 833)
Debenture (p. 816)
Discount (p. 816)
Effective-interest amortization (p. 825)
Effective interest rate (p. 818)
Face value (p. 816)
Lease (p. 836)
Lessee (p. 836)
Lessor (p. 836)
Market interest rate (p. 818)

Maturity date (p. 816)
Maturity value (p. 816)
Mortgage (p. 816)
Off-balance-sheet financing (p. 839)
Operating lease (p. 836)
Par value (p. 816)
Premium (p. 816)
Present value (p. 817)
Principal value (p. 816)
Secured bond (p. 816)
Serial bond (p. 816)
Stated interest rate (p. 818)
Straight-line amortization (p. 823)
Term bond (p. 816)
Trading on the equity (p. 836)

SIMILAR ACCOUNTING TERMS

Bond	Secured bond; Mortgage bond
Bond principal	Maturity value; Face value; Par value; Principal value
Stated interest rate	Contract interest rate; Indenture rate
Debenture	Unsecured bond
Market interest rate	Effective interest rate
Capital lease liability	Obligation under capital lease

Assignment Material

QUESTIONS

1. How do bonds payable differ from a note payable?

2. How does an underwriter assist with the issuance of bonds?

3. Compute the price to the nearest dollar for the following bonds with a face value of $10,000:
   a. 93.00   c. 101.375   e. 100.00
   b. 88.75   d. 122.50

4. In which of the following situations will bonds sell at par? At a premium? At a discount?
   a. 9-percent bonds sold when the market rate is 9 percent.
   b. 9-percent bonds sold when the market rate is 10 percent.
   c. 9-percent bonds sold when the market rate is 8 percent.

5. Identify the accounts to debit and credit for transactions (a) to issue bonds at *par*, (b) to pay interest, (c) to accrue interest at year end, and (d) to pay off bonds at maturity.

6. Identify the accounts to debit and credit for transactions (a) to issue bonds at a *discount*, (b) to pay interest, (c) to accrue interest at year end, and (d) to pay off bonds at maturity.

7. Identify the accounts to debit and credit for transactions (a) to issue bonds at a *premium*, (b) to pay interest, (c) to accrue interest at year end, and (d) to pay off bonds at maturity.

8. Why are bonds sold for a price "plus accrued interest"? What happens to accrued interest when bonds are sold by an individual?

9. How does the straight-line method of amortizing a bond discount (or premium) differ from the effective-interest method?

10. A company retires 10-year bonds payable of $100,000 after five years. The business issued the bonds at 104.00 and called them at 103.00. Compute the amount of gain or loss on retirement. How is this gain or loss reported on the income statement? The straight-line method of amortization is used.

11. Bonds payable with a maturity value of $200,000 are callable at 102.50. Their market price is 101.25. If you are the issuer of these bonds, how much will you pay to retire them before maturity?

12. Why are convertible bonds attractive to investors? Why are they popular with borrowers?

13. Ingoldby Corp. has $156 million of bonds outstanding at December 31, 2010. Of the total, $26 million are due in 2011, and the balance in 2012 and beyond. How would Ingoldby Corp. report its bonds payable on the balance sheet?

14. Contrast the effects on a company of issuing bonds versus issuing shares.

15. Identify the accounts a lessee debits and credits when making operating lease payments.

16. What characteristics distinguish a capital lease from an operating lease?

17. A business signs a capital lease for the use of a building. What accounts are debited and credited (a) to begin the lease term and make the first lease payment, (b) to record amortization, (c) to accrue interest on the lease liability, and (d) to make the second lease payment? The lease payments are made on the first day of the fiscal year.

18. Show how a lessee reports on the balance sheet any leased equipment and the related lease liability under a capital lease.

19. What is off-balance-sheet financing? Give an example.

STARTERS

MyAccountingLab All questions in this section appear in MyAccountingLab.

Starter 15–1 Determine whether the following bonds payable will be issued at maturity value, at a premium, or at a discount:

   a. The market interest rate is 7 percent. Canuck Corp. issues bonds payable with a stated rate of 6.5 percent.

   b. Oiler Inc. issued 7-percent bonds payable when the market rate was 6.75 percent.

   c. Leaf Corporation issued 8 percent bonds when the market interest rate was 8 percent.

   d. Canadien Corp. issued bonds payable that pay stated interest of 7 percent. At issuance, the market interest rate was 8.25 percent.

Determining if bond price is at par, at a discount, or at a premium
(2)

Starter 15–2 Compute the price of the following 7-percent bonds of Allied Telecom:

   a. $100,000 issued at 98.5
   b. $100,000 issued at 103.8
   c. $100,000 issued at 92.6
   d. $100,000 issued at 102.5

Pricing bonds
(2)

c. $92,600
d. $102,500

Starter 15–3 For which bond in Starter 15–2 will Allied Telecom have to pay the most at maturity? Explain your answer.

Starter 15–4 Hunter Corp. issued a $500,000, 6.5-percent, 10-year bond payable on January 1, 2010. Journalize the following transactions for Hunter Corp. Include an explanation for each entry.

   a. Issuance of the bond payable at par on January 1, 2010.
   b. Payment of semiannual cash interest on July 1, 2010. (Round to the nearest dollar.)
   c. Payment of the bonds payable at maturity. (Give the date.)

Starter 15–5 Sonic Drive-Ins Ltd. borrowed money by issuing $2,000,000 of 6-percent bonds payable at 96.5.

   1. How much cash did Sonic receive when it issued the bond payable?
   2. How much must Sonic pay back at maturity?
   3. How much cash interest will Sonic pay each six months?

Starter 15–6 A 7-percent, 10-year bond was issued at a price of 93. Was the market interest rate per annum at the date of issuance closer to 6 percent, 7 percent, or 8 percent? Explain.

Starter 15–7 Ogden Inc. issued a $500,000, 8-percent, 10-year bond payable at a price of 90 on January 1, 2010. Journalize the following transactions for Ogden Inc. Include an explanation for each entry.

   a. Issuance of the bond payable on January 1, 2010.
   b. Payment of semiannual interest and amortization of bond discount on July 1, 2010. Ogden uses the straight-line method to amortize the bond discount.

Starter 15–8 Solar Corp. issued a $400,000, 7-percent, 10-year bond payable at a price of 105 on January 1, 2010. Journalize the following transactions for Solar Corp. Include an explanation for each entry.

   a. Issuance of the bond payable on January 1, 2010.
   b. Payment of semiannual interest and amortization of bond premium on July 1, 2010. Solar uses the straight-line method to amortize the premium.

Starter 15–9 Reliable Limited issued $800,000 of 6-percent, 10-year bonds payable on October 1, 2010, at par value. Reliable's accounting year ends on December 31. Journalize the following transactions. Include an explanation for each entry.

   a. Issuance of the bonds on October 1, 2010.
   b. Accrual of interest expense on December 31, 2010.
   c. Payment of the first semiannual interest amount on April 1, 2011.

Starter 15–10 EMU Inc. issued $1,500,000 of 5-percent, 10-year bonds payable and received cash proceeds of $1,388,419 on March 31, 2010. The market interest rate at the date of issuance was 6 percent, and the bonds pay interest semiannually.

   1. Did the bonds sell at a premium or a discount?
   2. Prepare an effective-interest amortization table for the bond discount, through the first two interest payments. Use Exhibit 15–4 as a guide, and round amounts to the nearest dollar.
   3. Record EMU Inc.'s issuance of the bonds on March 31, 2010, and on September 30, 2010, payment of the first semiannual interest amount and amortization of the bond discount. Explanations are not required.

Starter 15–11 Jones Inc. issued $400,000 of 8-percent, 10-year bonds payable at a price of 115 on May 31, 2010. The market interest rate at the date of issuance was 6 percent, and the Jones Inc. bonds pay interest semiannually.

   1. How much cash did Jones Inc. receive upon issuance of the bonds payable?
   2. Prepare an effective-interest amortization table for the bond premium, through the first two interest payments. Use Exhibit 15–6 as a guide, and round amounts to the nearest dollar.

3. Record issuance of the bonds on May 31, 2010 and, on November 30, 2010, payment of the first semiannual interest amount and amortization of the bond premium. Explanations are not required.

Starter 15–12 Simm Corp. issued $750,000 of 8-percent, 10-year bonds at par value on May 1, 2010, four months after the bond's original issue date of January 1, 2010. Journalize the following transactions. Include an explanation for each entry.

a. Issuance of the bonds payable on May 1, 2010.
b. Payment of the first semiannual interest amount on July 1, 2010.

Issuing bonds payable between interest dates and then paying the interest

(2)

b. Interest Expense $10,000

Starter 15–13 On January 1, 2010, Rogerson Inc. issued $500,000 of 9-percent, five-year bonds payable at 104. Rogerson has extra cash and wishes to retire all the bonds payable on January 1, 2011, immediately after making the second semiannual interest payment. Rogerson uses the straight-line method of amortization. To retire the bonds, Rogerson pays the market price of 98.

1. What is Rogerson's carrying amount of the bonds payable on the retirement date?
2. How much cash must Rogerson pay to retire the bonds payable?
3. Compute Rogerson's gain or loss on the retirement of the bonds payable.

Accounting for the retirement of bonds payable

(4)

3. Gain $26,000

Starter 15–14 Newmarket Corp. has $3,000,000 of convertible bonds payable outstanding, with a bond premium of $60,000 also on the books. The bondholders have notified Newmarket that they wish to convert the bonds into shares. Specifically, the bonds may be converted into 400,000 of Newmarket's common shares.

1. What is Newmarket's carrying amount of its convertible bonds payable prior to the conversion?
2. Journalize Newmarket's conversion of the bonds payable into common shares. No explanation is required.

Accounting for the conversion of bonds payable

(4)

1. Carrying amount, $3,060,000

Starter 15–15 Suburban Inc. includes the following selected accounts in its general ledger at December 31, 2010:

Reporting liabilities

(4)

Total current liabilities, $33,000

Notes Payable, Long-term	$100,000	Accounts Payable....................	$32,000
Bonds Payable............................	200,000	Discount on Bonds Payable...	6,000
Interest Payable (due next year)	1,000		

Prepare the liabilities section of Suburban Inc.'s balance sheet at December 31, 2010 to show how the company would report these items. Report a total for current liabilities.

Starter 15–16 Speegle Marina needs to raise $2 million to expand. Speegle's president is considering two plans:

- Issue Plan A: $2,000,000 of 8 percent bonds payable to borrow the money
- Issue Plan B: 200,000 common shares at $10.00 per share

Before any new financing, Speegle expects to earn net income of $600,000, and the company already has 200,000 common shares outstanding. Speegle believes the expansion will increase income before interest and income tax by $400,000. The income tax rate is 35 percent.

Prepare an anlaysis similar to Exhibit 15–8 to determine which plan is likely to result in higher earnings per share. Which financing plan would you recommend?

Earnings-per-share effects of financing with bonds versus shares

(5)

EPS: Plan A $3.78

Starter 15–17 Best Corp. agrees to lease a store in a mall and open a coffee shop. On January 2, 2010 the company pays a non-refundable $10,000 deposit to secure the store and agrees to a lease amount of $5,000 per month for two years. Journalize the initial lease deposit, the first monthly lease payment, and the December 31 year-end adjustment of the $10,000 deposit. Explanations are not required. Would Best Corp. report the lease information in the notes to the financial statements? Why or why not?

Reporting lease liabilities

Determining whether the bond price will be at par, at a discount, or at a premium

Issuing bonds and paying interest

b. Interest Expense $80,000

Issuing bonds; paying and accruing interest

b. Interest Expense $600,000

Issuing bonds between interest dates; paying and accruing interest

b. Interest Expense $166,667

Issuing bonds between interest dates

Issuing bonds, paying and earning interest, and amortizing discount by the straight-line method

b. Interest Expense $177,500

Issuing bonds, paying and accruing interest, and amortizing premium by the straight-line method

b. Interest Expense $592,500

 Excel Spreadsheet Template

Preparing an effective-interest amortization table; recording interest payments and the related discount amortization

2. Interest Expense on June 30, $133,288

 Excel Spreadsheet Template

Exercise 15–1

Dylan Corp. is planning to issue long-term bonds payable to borrow for a major expansion. The chief executive, Robert Dylan, asks your advice on some related matters, as follows:

a. At what type of bond price will Dylan have total interest expense equal to the cash interest payments?

b. Under which type of price will Dylan's total interest expense be greater than the cash interest payments?

c. The stated interest rate on the bonds is 7 percent, and the market interest rate is 8 percent. What type of price can Dylan expect for the bonds?

d. Dylan could raise the stated interest rate on the bonds to 9 percent (market rate is 8 percent). In that case, what type of price can Dylan expect for the bonds?

Exercise 15–2

Sea-Link Distributors Inc. issues $2,000,000 of 8-percent, semiannual, 20-year bonds dated on April 30. Record (a) the issuance of bonds at par on April 30 and (b) the next semiannual interest payment on October 31.

Exercise 15–3

On February 1, Island Logistics Inc. issues 20-year, 6-percent bonds payable with a maturity value of $20,000,000. The bonds sell at par and pay interest on January 31 and July 31. Record (a) the issuance of the bonds on February 1, (b) the semiannual interest payment on July 31, and (c) the interest accrual on December 31.

Exercise 15–4

Lightening Corp. issues 20-year, 8-percent bonds with a maturity value of $5,000,000 on April 30. The bonds sell at par and pay interest on March 31 and September 30. Record (a) issuance of the bonds on April 30, (b) payment of interest on September 30, and (c) accrual of interest on December 31.

Exercise 15–5

Refer to the data for Lightening Corp. in Exercise 15–4. If Lightening Corp. issued the bonds on June 30, how much cash would Lightening Corp. receive upon issuance of the bonds?

Exercise 15–6

On February 1, Harvard Logistics Inc. issued 20-year, 7-percent bonds with a maturity value of $5,000,000. The bonds sell at 98.00 and pay interest on January 31 and July 31. Harvard Logistics Inc. amortizes bond discounts by the straight-line method. Record (a) issuance of the bonds on February 1, (b) the semiannual interest payment on July 31, and (c) the interest accrual on December 31.

Exercise 15–7

Cornell Corp. issues $15,000,000 of 20-year, 8-percent bonds on March 31, 2010. The bonds sell at 102.00 and pay interest on March 31 and September 30. Assume Cornell Corp. amortizes the premium by the straight-line method. Record (a) the issuance of the bonds on March 31, 2010, (b) payment of interest on September 30, 2010, (c) accrual of interest on December 31, 2010, and (d) payment of interest on March 31, 2011.

Exercise 15–8

FirstStar Sports Ltd. is authorized to issue $6,000,000 of 5-percent, 10-year bonds. On January 2, 2010, the contract date, when the market interest rate is 6 percent, the company issues $4,800,000 of the bonds and receives cash of $4,442,941. FirstStar Sports Ltd. amortizes bond discounts by the effective-interest method.

Required

1. Prepare an amortization table for the first four semiannual interest periods. Follow the format of Panel B in Exhibit 15–4 on page 826.

2. Record the first semiannual interest payment on June 30 and the second payment on December 31.

Exercise 15–9

On September 30, 2010, when the market interest rate is 7 percent, Yale Ltd. issues $8,000,000 of 8-percent, 20-year bonds at 110.625. The bonds pay interest on March 31 and September 30. Yale Ltd. amortizes bond premium by the effective-interest method.

Required

1. Prepare an amortization table for the first four semiannual interest periods. Follow the format of Panel B in Exhibit 15–6 on page 828.

2. Record the issuance of the bonds on September 30, 2010, the accrual of interest at December 31, 2010, and the semiannual interest payment on March 31, 2011.

Exercise 15–10

On January 2, 2010, Tennant Industries Inc. issued $4,000,000 of 8.5-percent, 5-year bonds when the market interest rate was 10 percent. Tennant Industries pays interest annually on December 31. The issue price of the bonds was $3,772,553.

Required   Create a spreadsheet model to prepare a schedule to amortize the discount on these bonds. Use the effective-interest method of amortization. Round to the nearest dollar, and format your answer as follows:

Preparing an effective-interest amortization table; recording interest accrual and payment, and the related premium amortization

(3)

2. Interest Expense on Dec. 31, $154,875

Excel Spreadsheet Template

Debt payment and discount amortization schedule using a spreadsheet

(3)

Interest payment $340,000

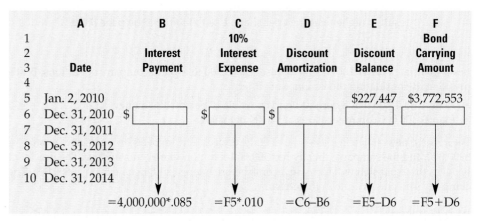

Exercise 15–11

Tide Management Inc. issued 8-percent bonds with a maturity value of $6,000,000 at 97.00 on October 1, 2010. These bonds mature on October 1, 2018, and are callable at 101.00. Tide Management Inc. pays interest each April 1 and October 1. On October 1, 2015, when the bonds' market price is 104.00, Tide Management Inc. retires the bonds in the most economical way available.

Required   Record the payment of interest and the amortization of the bond discount at October 1, 2015; also record the retirement of the bonds on that date. Tide Management Inc. uses the straight-line method to amortize the bond discount.

Recording retirement of bonds payable

(4)

Interest Expense Oct. 1, 2015, $251,250

Exercise 15–12

Kellogg Imaging Ltd. issued $7,500,000 of 8.5-percent, 15-year convertible bonds payable on July 1, 2010 at a price of 98.50. Each $1,000 face amount of bonds is convertible into 50 common shares. On December 31, 2013 bondholders exercised their right to convert the bonds into common shares.

Recording conversion of bonds payable

(4)

2. Carrying amount at Dec. 31, 2013, $7,413,750

Required

1. What would cause the bondholders to convert their bonds into common shares?

2. Without making journal entries, compute the carrying amount of the bonds payable at December 31, 2013. Kellogg Imaging Ltd. uses the straight-line method to amortize bond premium or discount on an annual basis.

3. All amortization has been recorded properly. Journalize the conversion transaction at December 31, 2013.

Exercise 15–13

Statton Products Ltd. reported the following at September 30, 2010:

Recording early retirement and conversion of bonds payable

(4)

1. Cr Cash $808,000

Long-term liabilities
  Convertible bonds payable, 9%,
    due September 30, 2016.. $1,600,000
  Discount on bonds payable 60,000 $1,540,000

Required

1. Record the retirement of one-half of the bonds on October 1, 2010, at the call price of 101.00.

2. Record the conversion of one-fourth (of the original $1,600,000) of the bonds into 10,000 common shares of Statton Products Ltd. on October 1, 2010.

Analyzing alternative plans for raising money

(5)

EPS: Plan A $5.72

Exercise 15–14

Hazelmere Transport Ltd. is considering two plans for raising $8,000,000 to expand operations. Plan A is to borrow at 9 percent, and Plan B is to issue 800,000 common shares. Before any new financing, Hazelmere Transport Ltd. has net income after interest and income tax of $4,000,000 and 800,000 common shares outstanding. Management believes the company can use the new funds to earn income of $1,680,000 per year before interest and taxes. The income tax rate is 40 percent.

Required   Analyze Hazelmere Transport Ltd.'s situation to determine which plan will result in higher earnings per share. Use Exhibit 15–8 on page 835 as a guide.

Earnings-per-share effects of financing with bonds versus shares

(5)

EPS: Plan A $3.72

Exercise 15–15

Best Financial Services Ltd. needs to raise $3,000,000 to expand company operations. Best's president is considering the issuance of either

- Plan A: $3,000,000 of 8 percent bonds payable to borrow the money
- Plan B: 150,000 common shares at $20.00 per share

Before any new financing, Best Financial Services Ltd. expects to earn net income of $900,000, and the company already has 300,000 common shares outstanding. The president believes the expansion will increase income before interest and income tax by $600,000. The company's income tax rate is 40 percent.

Required   Prepare an analysis similar to Exhibit 15–8, page 835, to determine which plan is likely to result in the higher earnings per share. Which financing plan would you recommend for Best Financial Services Ltd.? Give your reasons.

Reporting long-term debt on the balance sheet

(6)

Exercise 15–16

The chief accounting officer of Kenora Productions Ltd. is considering how to report long-term notes.

The company's financial accountant has assembled the following for long-term notes payable:

Note 5: Long-Term Debt

Total	$2,400,000
Less: Current portion	300,000
Less: Unamortized discount	6,000
Long-term debt	$2,094,000

None of the unamortized discount relates to the current portion of long-term debt. Show how Kenora Productions Ltd.'s balance sheet would report these liabilities.

Reporting liabilities, including capital lease obligations

(6)

Total liabilities $1,590,000

Exercise 15–17

HMR Associates Inc. includes the following selected accounts in its general ledger at December 31, 2010:

Bonds Payable	$1,040,000	Current Obligation under Capital Lease		$ 24,000
Equipment under Capital Lease	350,000	Accounts Payable		57,000
Interest Payable (due March 1, 2011)	21,000	Long-term Capital Lease Liability		126,000
Current Portion of Bonds Payable	150,000	Discount on Bonds Payable (all long-term)		18,000
Notes Payable, Long-term	190,000			

Required   Prepare the liabilities section of HMR Associates Inc.'s balance sheet at December 31, 2010 to show how the company would report these items. Report a total for both current and long-term liabilities.

Exercise 15-18

A capital lease agreement for equipment requires Salmon Equipment Ltd. to make 10 annual payments of $40,000, with the first payment due on January 2, 2010, the date of the inception of the lease. The present value of the nine future lease payments at 10 percent is $230,360.

Journalizing capital lease and operating lease transactions

6

2. Dec. 31, 2010 Amortization Expense $27,036

Required

1. Calculate the present value of the lease at 10 percent if your instructor has taught present value.

2. Journalize the following lessee transactions:

   2010
   Jan. 2   Beginning of lease term and first annual payment.
   Dec. 31   Amortization of equipment.
       31   Interest expense on lease liability.
   2011
   Jan. 2   Second annual lease payment.

3. Assume now that this is an operating lease. Journalize the January 2, 2010 lease payment.

SERIAL EXERCISE

This exercise continues the Haupt Consulting situation from Chapter 14.

Exercise 15-19

Haupt Consulting Corporation is considering raising capital for a planned business expansion to a new market. Carl Haupt believes the company will need $500,000 and plans to raise the capital by issuing 6-percent, 10-year bonds on April 1, 2011. The bonds pay interest semiannually on April 1 and October 1. On April 1, 2011, the market rate of interest required by similar bonds by investors is 8 percent, causing the bonds to sell for $431,850.

Bonds transactions

2

3. Oct. 1, 2011, Interest Expense $17,274

Required

1. Were the Haupt Consulting Corporation's bonds issued at par, a premium, or a discount?

2. Record the cash received on the bond issue date.

3. Journalize the first interest payment on October 1, 2011, and amortize the premium or discount using the effective-interest method.

4. Journalize the entry required, if any, on December 31, 2011, related to the bonds.

CHALLENGE EXERCISE

Analyzing bond transactions

② ③

2. Interest payment $9,000,000

Exercise 15–20

The (partial) advertisement below appeared in *The Financial Post*.

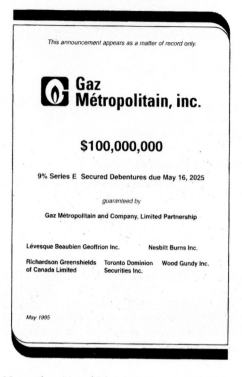

Interest is payable on November 16 and May 16.

Required Answer these questions about Gaz Métropolitain, Inc.'s secured debentures (bonds):

1. Suppose investors purchased these securities at 98.50 on May 16, 2010. Describe the transaction in detail, indicating who received cash, who paid cash, and how much.

2. Compute the annual cash interest payment on the Gaz Métropolitain, Inc. bonds.

3. Prepare an effective-interest amortization table for Gaz Métropolitain, Inc.'s first two payments, on November 16, 2010 and May 16, 2011. Assume the market rate at the date of issuance was 9.2 percent.

4. Compute Gaz Métropolitain, Inc.'s interest expense for the first full year ended May 16, 2011 under the effective-interest amortization method.

5. Another company's issue of unsecured bonds for $20,000,000 was issued the same day; it bore an interest rate of 12 percent. Why was the rate so much higher for this issue than for the Gaz Métropolitain, Inc. issue?

Analyzing bond transactions

② ③

2. c. $98,563,426

Exercise 15–21

Refer to the bond situation of Gaz Métropolitain, Inc. in Exercise 15–20. Assume Gaz Métropolitain, Inc. issued the bonds at a price of 98.50 and that the company uses the effective-interest amortization method. The company's year end is December 31.

Required

1. Journalize the following bond transactions of Gaz Métropolitain, Inc.:

2010

May 16   Issuance of the bonds.

Nov. 16   Payment of interest expense and amortization of discount on bonds payable. The market rate on the date of issuance was 9.2 percent.

Dec. 31   Accrual of interest expense and amortization of discount on bonds payable.

2. What is Gaz Métropolitain, Inc.'s carrying amount of the bonds payable at
   a. November 16, 2010?
   b. December 31, 2010?
   c. May 16, 2011?

BEYOND THE NUMBERS

Beyond the Numbers 15–1

Questions about long-term debt
(2) (6)

The following questions are not related.

1. IMAX Corporation obtains the use of most of its theatre properties through leases. IMAX Corporation prefers operating leases over capital leases. Why is this a good idea? Consider IMAX Corporation's debt ratio.

2. IMAX Corporation likes to borrow for longer periods when interest rates are low and for shorter periods when interest rates are high. Why is this a good business strategy?

3. Suppose IMAX Corporation needs to borrow $2,000,000 to open new theatres. The company can borrow $2,000,000 by issuing 8 percent, 20-year bonds at a price of 96. How much will IMAX Corporation actually be borrowing under this arrangement? How much must the company repay at maturity?

ETHICAL ISSUE

Cavell Products Inc., a manufacturer of electronic devices, borrowed heavily during the 1990s to exploit the advantage of financing operations with debt. At first, Cavell Products Inc. was able to earn operating income much higher than its interest expense and was therefore quite profitable. However, when the business cycle turned down, Cavell Products Inc.'s debt burden pushed the company to the brink of bankruptcy. Operating income was less than interest expense.

Required Is it unethical for managers to commit a company to a high level of debt? Or is it just risky? Who could be hurt by a company's taking on too much debt? Discuss.

PROBLEMS (GROUP A)

MyAccountingLab | All questions in this section appear in MyAccountingLab.

Problem 15–1A

Journalizing bond transactions (at par) and reporting bonds payable on the balance sheet
(2)
1. b. Interest Expense $400,000

The board of directors of Metcalfe Production Co. Ltd. authorizes the issuance of 8-percent, 10-year bonds with a maturity value of $12,000,000. The semiannual interest dates are May 31 and November 30. The bonds are issued through an underwriter on June 30, 2010 at par plus accrued interest. Metcalfe's year end is December 31.

Required

1. Journalize the following transactions:
   a. Issuance of the bonds on June 30, 2010.
   b. Payment of interest on November 30, 2010.
   c. Accrual of interest on December 31, 2010.
   d. Payment of interest on May 31, 2011.

2. Report interest payable and bonds payable as they would appear on the Metcalfe Production Co. Ltd. balance sheet at December 31, 2010.

Problem 15–2A

Issuing bonds at a discount, amortizing by the straight-line method, and reporting bonds payable on the balance sheet
(2) (3)
3. b. Interest Expense $216,250

On March 1, 2010, Nugent Systems Ltd. issues 8.5-percent, 20-year bonds payable with a maturity value of $5,000,000. The bonds pay interest on February 28 and August 31. Nugent Systems Ltd. amortizes premium and discount by the straight-line method.

Required

1. If the market interest rate is 8 percent when Nugent Systems Ltd. issues its bonds, will the bonds be priced at par, at a premium, or at a discount? Explain.

2. If the market interest rate is 8.875 percent when Nugent Systems Ltd. issues its bonds, will the bonds be priced at par, at a premium, or at a discount? Explain.

3. Assume the issue price of the bonds is 97.00. Journalize the following bond transactions:
   a. Issuance of the bonds on March 1, 2010.
   b. Payment of interest and amortization of discount on August 31, 2010.
   c. Accrual of interest and amortization of discount on December 31, 2010, Nugent Systems Ltd.'s year end.
   d. Payment of interest and amortization of discount on February 28, 2011.

4. Report interest payable and bonds payable as they would appear on the Nugent Systems Ltd. balance sheet at December 31, 2010.

Excel Spreadsheet Template

Analyzing a company's long-term debt, journalizing its transactions, and reporting the long-term debt on the balance sheet

② ③

4. Interest Expense $25,200

Problem 15–3A

The notes to Joyce Biotech Inc.'s financial statements recently reported the following data on September 30, 2010:

> NOTE 4: INDEBTEDNESS
> Long-term debt at September 30, 2010 included the following:
>
> | | |
> |---|---:|
> | 6.00-percent debentures due September 30, 2029 with an effective interest rate of 7.00 percent, net of unamortized discount of $206,712 .... | $1,793,288 |
> | Other indebtedness with an interest rate of 6.30 percent, due $204,000 in 2014 and $196,000 in 2015.................................. | 400,000 |

Assume Joyce Biotech Inc. amortizes discount by the effective-interest method.

Required

1. Answer the following questions about Joyce Biotech Inc.'s long-term liabilities:
   a. What is the maturity value of the 6-percent debentures?
   b. What are Joyce Biotech Inc.'s annual cash interest payments on the 6-percent debentures?
   c. What is the carrying amount of the 6-percent debentures at September 30, 2010?
   d. How many years remain in the life of the 6-percent debentures?

2. Prepare an amortization table through September 30, 2013, for the 6-percent debentures. Round all amounts to the nearest dollar, and assume Joyce Biotech Inc. pays interest annually on September 30.

3. Record the September 30, 2012 and 2013, interest payments on the 6-percent debentures.

4. There is no premium or discount on the other indebtedness. Assuming annual interest is paid on September 30 each year, record Joyce Biotech Inc.'s September 30, 2011, interest payment on the other indebtedness.

5. Show how Joyce Biotech Inc. would report the debentures payable and other indebtedness on September 30, 2013.

Excel Spreadsheet Template

Issuing convertible bonds at a premium, amortizing by the effective-interest method, retiring bonds early, converting bonds, and reporting the bonds payable on the balance sheet

② ③ ④

2. b. Interest Expense $161,693

Problem 15–4A

On December 31, 2010, Wynn Holdings Ltd. issues 6-percent, 10-year convertible bonds with a maturity value of $6,000,000. The semiannual interest dates are June 30 and December 31. The market interest rate is 5 percent and the issue price of the bonds is 107.795. Wynn Holdings Ltd. amortizes any bond premium and discount by the effective-interest method.

Required

1. Prepare an effective-interest-method amortization table for the first four semiannual interest periods.

2. Journalize the following transactions:
   a. Issuance of the bonds on December 31, 2010. Credit Convertible Bonds Payable.
   b. Payment of interest on June 30, 2011.

c. Payment of interest on December 31, 2011.

d. Retirement of bonds with maturity value of $2,000,000 on July 2, 2011. Wynn Holdings Ltd. pays the call price of 102.00.

e. Conversion by the bondholders on July 2, 2012 of bonds with maturity value of $3,000,000 into 20,000 of Wynn Holdings Ltd. common shares.

3. Prepare the balance sheet presentation of the bonds payable that are outstanding at December 31, 2012.

Problem 15–5A

Journalizing bonds payable and capital lease transactions

② ⑥

July 2, 2010, Interest Expense $182,500

Journalize the following transactions of Whitecourt Technologies Inc.:

2010		
Jan.	2	Issued 7-percent, 10-year bonds with a maturity value of $5,000,000 at 97.00.
Jan.	2	Signed a five-year capital lease on equipment. The agreement requires annual lease payments of $400,000, with the first payment due immediately. The present value of the four future lease payments is $1,324,851.
Jul.	2	Paid semiannual interest and amortized discount by the straight-line method on the 7-percent bonds.
Dec. 31		Accrued semiannual interest expense, and amortized discount by the straight-line method on the 7-percent bonds.
	31	Recorded amortization on leased equipment, using the straight-line method.
	31	Accrued interest expense at 8 percent on the lease liability.
2020		
Jan.	2	Paid the 7-percent bonds at maturity.

Problem 15–6A

Financing operations with debt or with shares

⑤

Two businesses must consider how to raise $10,000,000.

Windmill Inc. is in the midst of its most successful period since it began operations 48 years ago. For each of the past 10 years, net income and earnings per share have increased by 15 percent. The outlook for the future is equally bright, with new markets opening up and competitors unable to manufacture products of Windmill Inc.'s quality. Windmill Inc. is planning a large-scale expansion.

Valleyview Limited has fallen on hard times. Net income has remained flat for five of the last six years, even falling by 10 percent from last year's level of profits. Top management has experienced unusual turnover, and the company lacks strong leadership. To become competitive again, Valleyview Limited desperately needs $10,000,000 for expansion.

Required

1. Propose a plan for each company to raise the needed cash. Which company should borrow? Which company should issue shares? Consider the advantages and disadvantages of raising money by borrowing and by issuing shares, and discuss them in your answer.

2. How will what you have learned in this chapter help you manage a business?

Problem 15–7A

Reporting liabilities on the balance sheet

⑥

The accounting records of Gold River Resources Inc. include the following items:

Capital Lease Liability,		Mortgage Note Payable,		
Long-term	$438,000	long-term	$ 402,000
Bonds Payable, Long-term	960,000	Building acquired under	
Premium on Bonds Payable....	78,000	capital lease	1,200,000
Interest Expense	300,000	Bonds Payable, Current	
Interest Payable.........................	98,820	Portion	96,000
Interest Revenue	61,800	Accumulated Amortization,	
Capital Lease Liability,		Building	648,000
Current	54,000		

Required Show how these items would be reported on the Gold River Resources Inc. balance sheet, including headings for property, plant, and equipment, current liabilities, long-term liabilities, and so on. Note disclosures are not required.

Amortizing bond discount and premium by the effective-interest method; retirement of bonds; conversion of bonds

② ③ ④

1. June 30, 2010, Interest Expense $221,209

Problem 15–8A

Shield Transport Ltd. is authorized to issue 10-year, 6 percent convertible bonds with a maturity value of $16,000,000. Interest is payable on June 30 and December 31. The bonds are convertible on the basis of 50 common shares for each $1,000 bond. The following bond transactions took place:

2010

Jan. 2   Sold (issued) bonds with $6,400,000 maturity value. Since the market rate of interest on this date was 8 percent, the bonds had a present value of $5,530,219.

Jun. 30   Paid the interest and amortized the discount using the effective-interest amortization method.

Dec. 31   Paid the interest and amortized the discount using the effective-interest amortization method.

2011

Apr. 1   Sold (issued) $1,280,000 (maturity value) of bonds at par plus accrued interest. The market rate of interest on this date was 6 percent.

Jun. 30   Paid the interest and amortized the discount using the effective-interest amortization method.

Jul. 2   Retired $4,800,000 (maturity value) of the bonds issued on January 2, 2010 at a rate of 96.00.

      2   Bondholders converted $1,600,000 (maturity value) of bonds issued on January 2, 2010 into common shares.

Required Round all amounts to the nearest whole dollar.

1. Journalize the transactions.

2. Show the balance sheet presentation of the bonds payable on July 2, 2011.

Amortizing bond premium by the effective-interest method; accounting for lease transactions

③ ⑥

1. Apr. 2, 2011, Interest Expense $102,020

Problem 15–9A

Selkirk Systems Inc. had the following information available on bonds payable outstanding at December 31, 2010, its year end:

- $5,000,000—Bonds Payable, 9-percent, interest paid on April 2 and October 2. The bonds had been sold April 2, 2009, when the market rate of interest was 8 percent, and were due April 2, 2013.

- $101,022—Premium on Bonds Payable

The following transactions took place after December 31, 2010:

2011

Jan. 2   Selkirk Systems Inc. signed a lease to rent a warehouse for expansion of its operations. The lease is five years, with an option to renew, and calls for annual payments of $50,000 per year payable on January 2. Selkirk Systems Inc. gave a cheque for the first year upon signing the contract.

      2   Selkirk Systems Inc. signed a lease for equipment. The lease is for 10 years with payments of $40,000 per year payable on January 2 (first year's payment was made at the signing). At the end of the lease the equipment will become the property of Selkirk Systems Inc. The future payments on the lease have a present value (at 10 percent) of $230,361. The equipment has a 10-year useful life and zero residual value.

Apr. 2   Paid the interest on the bonds payable and amortized the premium using the effective-interest method. Assume interest payable of $112,500 had been accrued on December 31, 2010.

Oct. 2   Paid the interest on the bonds payable and amortized the premium using the effective-interest method.

Dec. 31   Recorded any adjustments required at the end of the year for the bonds payable and the lease(s).

2012

Jan. 2   Made the annual payments on the leases.

Apr. 2   Paid the interest on the bonds payable and amortized the premium using the effective-interest method.

Oct. 2 Paid the interest on the bonds payable and amortized the premium using the effective-interest method.

Dec. 31 Recorded any adjustments required at the end of the year for the bonds payable and the lease(s).

Required Round all amounts to the nearest whole dollar.

1. Prepare the general journal entries required to record the transactions of 2011 and 2012.

2. Show the liabilities section of the balance sheet on December 31, 2012.

PROBLEMS (GROUP B)

MyAccountingLab | All questions in this section appear in MyAccountingLab.

Problem 15–1B

The board of directors of Dolan Communications Ltd. authorizes the issuance of 6-percent, 20-year bonds with a maturity value of $10,000,000. The semiannual interest dates are March 31 and September 30. The bonds are issued through an underwriter on April 30, 2010 at par plus accrued interest. Dolan's year end is December 31.

Required

1. Journalize the following transactions:
   a. Issuance of the bonds on April 30, 2010.
   b. Payment of interest on September 30, 2010.
   c. Accrual of interest on December 31, 2010.
   d. Payment of interest on March 31, 2011.

2. Report interest payable and bonds payable as they would appear on the Dolan Communications Ltd. balance sheet at December 31, 2010.

Journalizing bond transactions (at par) and reporting bonds payable on the balance sheet
②

Problem 15–2B

On April 1, 2010, Sunray Corp. issues 7-percent, 10-year bonds payable with a maturity value of $3,000,000. The bonds pay interest on March 31 and September 30, and Sunray Corp. amortizes premium and discount by the straight-line method.

Required

1. If the market interest rate is 7.75 percent when Sunray Corp. issues its bonds, will the bonds be priced at par, at a premium, or at a discount? Explain.

2. If the market interest rate is 6.5-percent when Sunray Corp. issues its bonds, will the bonds be priced at par, at a premium, or at a discount? Explain.

3. Assume the issue price of the bonds is 103.00. Journalize the following bonds payable transactions:
   a. Issuance of the bonds on April 1, 2010.
   b. Payment of interest and amortization of premium on September 30, 2010.
   c. Accrual of interest and amortization of premium on December 31, 2010, the year end.
   d. Payment of interest and amortization of premium on March 31, 2011.

4. Report interest payable and bonds payable as they would appear on the Sunray Corp. balance sheet at December 31, 2010.

Issuing bonds at a premium, amortizing by the straight-line method, and reporting bonds payable on the balance sheet
② ③

Problem 15–3B

Assume that the notes to Lytton Ltd.'s financial statements reported the following data on September 30, 2010:

NOTE E: LONG-TERM DEBT
5-percent debentures due 2029, net of unamortized
   discount of $223,162 (effective interest rate of 6.0 percent) $1,776,838
Lytton Ltd. amortizes the discount by the effective-interest method.

Excel Spreadsheet Template

Analyzing a company's long-term debt, journalizing its transactions, and reporting the long-term debt on the balance sheet
② ③

Required

1. Answer the following questions about Lytton Ltd.'s long-term liabilities:
   a. What is the maturity value of the 5-percent debentures?
   b. What is the carrying amount of the 5-percent debentures at September 30, 2010?
   c. What are Lytton Ltd.'s annual cash interest payments on these debentures?

2. Prepare an amortization table through September 30, 2012, for the 5-percent debentures. Lytton Ltd. pays interest annually on September 30.

3. Record the September 30, 2012, interest payments on the 5-percent debentures.

4. What is Lytton Ltd.'s carrying amount of the 5-percent debentures at September 30, 2012, immediately after the interest payment?

Excel Spreadsheet Template

Issuing convertible bonds at a discount, amortizing by the effective-interest method, retiring bonds early, converting bonds, and reporting the bonds payable on the balance sheet
② ③ ④

Problem 15–4B

On December 31, 2010, Monashee Corp. issues 4-percent, 10-year convertible bonds with a maturity value of $4,500,000. The semiannual interest dates are June 30 and December 31. The market interest rate is 5 percent, and the issue price of the bonds is 92.200. Monashee Corp. amortizes bond premium and discount by the effective-interest method.

Required

1. Prepare an effective-interest method amortization table for the first four semiannual interest periods.

2. Journalize the following transactions:
   a. Issuance of the bonds on December 31, 2010. Credit Convertible Bonds Payable.
   b. Payment of interest on June 30, 2011.
   c. Payment of interest on December 31, 2011.
   d. Retirement of bonds with maturity value of $200,000 on July 2, 2012. Monashee Corp. purchases the bonds at 96.00 in the open market.
   e. Conversion by the bondholders on July 2, 2012, of bonds with maturity value of $400,000 into 5,000 Monashee Corp. common shares.

3. Prepare the balance sheet presentation of the bonds payable that are outstanding at December 31, 2012.

Journalizing bonds payable and capital lease transactions
② ⑥

Problem 15–5B

Journalize the following transactions of Khalil Communications Inc.:

2010
Jan. 2   Issued $8,000,000 of 7-percent, 10-year bonds payable at 97.00.
      2   Signed a five-year capital lease on machinery. The agreement requires annual lease payments of $80,000, with the first payment due immediately. The present value of the four future lease payments is $253,589.
Jul. 2   Paid semiannual interest and amortized discount by the straight-line method on the 7-percent bonds payable.
Dec. 31   Accrued semiannual interest expense and amortized discount by the straight-line method on the 7-percent bonds.
      31   Recorded amortization on leased machinery, using the straight-line method.
      31   Accrued interest expense at 10 percent on the lease liability.

2020
Jan. 2   Paid the 7-percent bonds at maturity.

Financing operations with debt or with shares
⑤

Problem 15–6B

Marketing studies have shown that consumers prefer upscale restaurants, and recent trends in industry sales have supported the research. To capitalize on this trend, Orca Ltd. is embarking on a massive expansion. Plans call for opening five new restaurants within the next 18 months. Each restaurant is scheduled to be 30 percent larger than the company's existing restaurants, furnished more elaborately, with more extensive menus. Management estimates that company operations will provide $15 million of the cash needed for expansion. Orca Ltd. must raise the remaining $15 million from outsiders. The board of directors is considering obtaining the $15 million either through borrowing or by issuing common shares.

Required

1. Write a memo to company management. Discuss the advantages and disadvantages of borrowing and of issuing common shares to raise the needed cash. Use the following format for your memo:

Date:	
To:	Management of Orca Ltd.
From:	Student Name
Subject:	Advantages and disadvantages of borrowing and issuing shares to raise $15 million for expansion

Advantages and disadvantages of borrowing:

Advantages and disadvantages of issuing shares:

2. How will what you have learned in this problem help you manage a business?

Problem 15–7B

The accounting records of Carter Technologies Inc. include the following items:

Equipment Acquired under Capital Lease..........................	$561,000	Interest Expense......................	$171,000
Bonds Payable—Current Portion......................................	225,000	Mortgage Note Payable— Long-term.............................	238,000
Capital lease liability— Long-term................................	162,000	Accumulated Amortization— Equipment............................	123,000
Discount on Bonds Payable— Long-term................................	21,000	Capital Lease Liability— Current..................................	54,000
Interest Revenue.........................	15,000	Mortgage Note Payable— Current..................................	69,000
Interest Payable	54,000	Bonds Payable—Long-term ..	900,000

Required Show how these items would be reported on the Carter Technologies Inc. balance sheet, including headings for property, plant, and equipment, current liabilities, long-term liabilities, and so on. Note disclosures are not required.

Problem 15–8B

JarvisVentures Inc. is authorized to issue 10-year, 5-percent convertible bonds with a maturity value of $9,000,000. Interest is payable on June 30 and December 31. The bonds are convertible on the basis of 40 common shares for each $1,000 bond. The following bond transactions took place:

2010
Jan. 2   Sold bonds with $5,400,000 maturity value. Since the market rate of interest on this date was 4 percent, the bonds had a present value of $5,841,500.
Jun. 30   Paid the interest and amortized the premium using the effective-interest method.
Dec. 31   Paid the interest and amortized the premium using the effective-interest method.

2011
Apr. 1   Sold $3,000,000 of bonds at par plus accrued interest. The market rate of interest on this date was 5 percent.
Jun. 30   Paid the interest and amortized the premium using the effective-interest method.
Jul. 2   Retired $600,000 (maturity value) of the bonds issued on January 2, 2010, at a rate of 101.
       2   Bondholders converted $600,000 (maturity value) of bonds issued on January 2, 2010, into common shares.

Required Round all amounts to the nearest whole dollar.

1. Journalize the transactions.
2. Show the balance sheet presentation of the bonds payable on July 2, 2011.

Reporting liabilities on the balance sheet
(6)

Amortizing bond discount and premium by the effective-interest method; retirement of bonds; conversion of bonds

Amortizing bond discount by the
effective-interest method;
accounting for lease
transactions

③ ⑥

Problem 15–9B

Moncton Manufacturing Ltd. had the following information available on bonds payable outstanding at December 31, 2009, its year end:

- $7,500,000—Bonds Payable, 6 percent, interest paid on April 2 and October 2. The bonds had been sold April 2, 2007, when the market rate of interest was 7 percent. The bonds mature on April 2, 2012.
- $153,529—Discount on Bonds Payable.

The following transactions took place after December 31, 2009:

2010
Jan. 2   Moncton Manufacturing Ltd. signed a lease to rent a building for expansion of its operations. The lease is for six years, with an option to renew, and calls for annual payments of $37,500 per year payable on January 2. Moncton Manufacturing Ltd. gave a cheque for the first year upon signing the lease.

      2   Moncton Manufacturing Ltd. signed a lease for equipment. The lease is for 10 years with payments of $22,500 per year payable on January 2 (first year's payment was made at the signing). At the end of the lease the equipment will become the property of Moncton Manufacturing Ltd. The future payments on the lease have a present value (at 10 percent) of $129,578. The equipment has a 10-year useful life and zero residual value.

Apr. 2   Paid the interest on the bonds payable and amortized the discount using the effective-interest method. Assume interest payable of $112,500 had been accrued on December 31, 2009.

Oct. 2   Paid the interest on the bonds payable and amortized the discount using the effective-interest method.

Dec. 31   Recorded any adjustments required at the end of the year for the bonds payable and the lease(s).

2011
Jan. 2   Made the annual payments on the leases.
Apr. 2   Paid the interest on the bonds payable and amortized the discount using the effective-interest method.
Oct. 2   Paid the interest on the bonds payable and amortized the discount using the effective-interest method.
Dec. 31   Recorded any adjustments required at the end of the year for the bonds payable and the lease(s).

Required Round all amounts to the nearest whole dollar.

1. Prepare the general journal entries required to record the transactions of 2010 and 2011.
2. Show the liabilities section of the balance sheet on December 31, 2011.

CHALLENGE PROBLEMS

Problem 15–1C

A friend tells you that she always buys bonds that are at a discount because "You always get more than you paid when the bond matures."

Required Discuss your friend's understanding of present value.

Problem 15–2C

You have just inherited $50,000 and have decided to buy shares. You have narrowed your choice down to QT Logistics Inc. and Compulogic Systems Ltd. You carefully read each company's annual report to determine which company's shares you should buy. Your research indicates that the two companies are very similar. QT Logistics Inc.'s annual report states "The Company has financed its growth through long- and short-term borrowing," while the Compulogic report contains the statement "The Company has financed its growth out of earnings retained in the business."

QT's shares are trading at $25.00 while Compulogic's shares are trading at $13.00. You wonder if that is because QT has been paying an annual dividend of $2.00 per share while Compulogic has been paying a dividend of $1.10.

You recall that the morning newspaper had an article about the economy that predicted that interest rates were expected to rise and stay at a much higher rate than at present for the next two to three years.

Required Explain which shares you would buy and indicate why you have selected them.

Extending Your Knowledge

DECISION PROBLEMS

Decision Problem 1

Analyzing alternative ways of raising $10,000,000

⑤

1. EPS: Plan A $9.84

Business is going well for Valley Forest Products Inc. The board of directors of this family-owned company believes that the company could earn an additional $9,000,000 in income after interest and taxes by expanding into new markets. However, the $30,000,000 that the business needs for growth cannot be raised within the family. The directors, who strongly wish to retain family control of Valley Forest Products Inc., must consider issuing securities to outsiders. They are considering three financing plans.

Plan A is to borrow at 8 percent. Plan B is to issue 300,000 common shares. Plan C is to issue 300,000 nonvoting, $7.50 cumulative preferred shares. The company presently has net income before tax of $18,000,000 and has 1,500,000 common shares outstanding. The income tax rate is 40 percent.

Required

1. Prepare an analysis similar to Exhibit 15–8 to determine which plan will result in the highest earnings per common share.

2. Recommend one plan to the board of directors. Give your reasons.

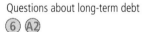

Decision Problem 2

Questions about long-term debt

⑥ Ⓐ②

The following questions are not related.

a. Why do you think corporations prefer operating leases over capital leases? How do you think a shareholder would view an operating lease?

b. If you were to win $3,000,000 from Lotto 649, you would receive the $3,000,000 today, whereas if you were to win $3,000,000 in one of the U.S. lotteries, you would receive 20 annual payments of $150,000. Are the prizes equivalent? If not, why not?

FINANCIAL STATEMENT CASES

Financial Statement Case 1

Long-term debt

① ② ⑥

The Canadian Western Bank (CWB) income statement and balance sheet in Appendix A provide details about the company's long-term debt. Use the data to answer the following questions:

1. How much did CWB owe to the holders of its subordinated debentures at October 31, 2008? On a net basis, how much more cash was raised from issuing subordinated debentures in 2008?

2. How much interest expense did CWB accrue for the subordinated debentures on the fiscal 2008 income statement?

3. What types of shares is CWB authorized to issue? Which types of shares were outstanding at October 31, 2008? Were dividends paid during the year ended October 31, 2008? If so, how much were they?

4. Does CWB have any operating leases? If so, what payments are due in the year ended October 31, 2009? How much is due in the years beyond 2010?

Long-term debt
① ② ⑥

Financial Statement Case 2

The Sun-Rype Products Ltd. income statement and balance sheet in Appendix B provide details about the company's long-term debt and equity. Use the data to answer the following questions:

1. How much cash did Sun-Rype borrow on bank and long-term debt during the year ended December 31, 2008? How much long-term debt did Sun-Rype repay during 2008? During 2007?

2. What was the change in interest expense for Sun-Rype for the year ended December 31, 2008? Why did the expense increase?

3. What is the long-term total amount owing to banks and others at December 31, 2008? What types of debt are included in this total?

4. What types of shares are outstanding? How was the contributed surplus created? If dividends were paid this year, what was the amount of the dividends paid?

5. Does Sun-Rype have any operating leases? If so, what payments are due in the year ended December 31, 2009? How much is due in the years beyond 2010?

CHAPTER 15 APPENDIX

Time Value of Money: Future Value and Present Value

The following discussion of future value lays the foundation for present value but is not essential. For the valuation of long-term liabilities, some instructors may wish to begin on page 868.

The phrase *time value of money* refers to the fact that money earns interest over time. Interest is the cost of using money. To borrowers, interest is the expense of renting money. To lenders, interest is the revenue earned from lending. When funds are used for a period of time, we must recognize the interest. Otherwise we overlook an important part of the transaction. Suppose you invest $4,545 in corporate bonds that pay interest of 10 percent each year. After one year, the value of your investment has grown to $5,000. The difference between your original investment ($4,545) and the future value of the investment ($5,000) is the amount of interest revenue you will earn during the year ($455). If you ignored the interest, you would fail to account for the interest revenue you have earned. Interest becomes more important as the time period lengthens because the amount of interest depends on the span of time the money is invested.

Let's consider a second example, but from the borrower's perspective. Suppose you purchase a machine for your business. The cash price of the machine is $8,000, but you cannot pay cash now. To finance the purchase, you sign an $8,000 note payable. The note requires you to pay the $8,000 plus 10-percent interest one year from date of purchase. Is your cost of the machine $8,000, or is it $8,800 [$8,000 plus interest of $800 ($8,000 × 0.10)]? The cost is $8,000. The additional $800 is interest expense and not part of the cost of the machine.

Future Value

OBJECTIVE A1

Compute the future value of an investment

The main application of future value is to calculate the accumulated balance of an investment at a future date. In our first example above, the investment earned 10 percent per year. After one year, $4,545 grew to $5,000, as shown in Exhibit 15A–1.

EXHIBIT 15A–1 Future Value

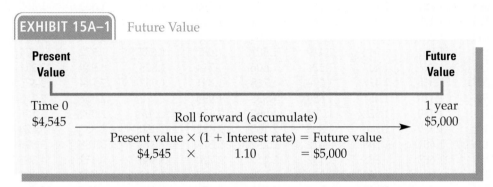

If the money were invested for five years, you would have to perform five such calculations. You would also have to consider the compound interest that your investment is earning. Compound interest is the interest you earn not only on your principal amount but also the interest you receive on the interest you have already earned. Most business applications include compound interest. The table below shows the interest revenue earned each year at 10 percent:

End of Year	Interest	Future Value
0	—	$4,545
1	$4,545 × 0.10 = $455	5,000
2	5,000 × 0.10 = 500	5,500
3	5,500 × 0.10 = 550	6,050
4	6,050 × 0.10 = 605	6,655
5	6,655 × 0.10 = 666	7,321

Earning 10 percent, a $4,545 investment grows to $5,000 at the end of one year, to $5,500 at the end of two years, and so on. Throughout this discussion we round off to the nearest dollar.

Future Value Tables

KEY POINT

The formula for future value is:

$FV = PV(1 + i)^n$

where
FV = future value
PV = present value
i = interest rate per period
n = number of compounding periods

The process of computing a future value is called *accumulating* because the future value is *more* than the present value. Mathematical tables ease the computational burden. You can also use financial calculators and functions in spreadsheet programs to calculate future value. Exhibit 15A–2, Future Value of $1, gives the future value for a single sum (a present value), $1, invested to earn a particular interest rate for a specific number of periods. Future value depends on three factors: (1) the amount of the investment, (2) the length of time between investment and future accumulation, and (3) the interest rate.

The heading in Exhibit 15A–2 states $1. Future value tables and present value tables are based on $1 because unity (the value 1) is so easy to work with. Observe the Periods column and the Interest Rate columns 2% through 12%. In business applications, interest rates are always stated for the annual period of one year unless specified otherwise. In fact, an interest rate can be stated for any period, such as 3 percent per quarter or 5 percent for a six-month period. The length of the period is arbitrary. For example, an investment may promise a return (income) of 3 percent per quarter for six months (two quarters). In that case you would be working with 3 percent interest for two periods. It would be incorrect to use 6 percent for one period because the interest is 3 percent compounded quarterly, and

Future Value of $1

Periods	2%	3%	4%	5%	6%	7%	8%	9%	10%	12%
1	1.020	1.030	1.040	1.050	1.060	1.070	1.080	1.090	1.100	1.120
2	1.040	1.061	1.082	1.103	1.124	1.145	1.166	1.188	1.210	1.254
3	1.061	1.093	1.125	1.158	1.191	1.225	1.260	1.295	1.331	1.405
4	1.082	1.126	1.170	1.216	1.262	1.311	1.360	1.412	1.464	1.574
5	1.104	1.159	1.217	1.276	1.338	1.403	1.469	1.539	1.611	1.762
6	1.126	1.194	1.265	1.340	1.419	1.501	1.587	1.677	1.772	1.974
7	1.149	1.230	1.316	1.407	1.504	1.606	1.714	1.828	1.949	2.211
8	1.172	1.267	1.369	1.477	1.594	1.718	1.851	1.993	2.144	2.476
9	1.195	1.305	1.423	1.551	1.689	1.838	1.999	2.172	2.358	2.773
10	1.219	1.344	1.480	1.629	1.791	1.967	2.159	2.367	2.594	3.106
11	1.243	1.384	1.539	1.710	1.898	2.105	2.332	2.580	2.853	3.479
12	1.268	1.426	1.601	1.796	2.012	2.252	2.518	2.813	3.138	3.896
13	1.294	1.469	1.665	1.886	2.133	2.410	2.720	3.066	3.452	4.363
14	1.319	1.513	1.732	1.980	2.261	2.579	2.937	3.342	3.797	4.887
15	1.346	1.558	1.801	2.079	2.397	2.759	3.172	3.642	4.177	5.474
16	1.373	1.605	1.873	2.183	2.540	2.952	3.426	3.970	4.595	6.130
17	1.400	1.653	1.948	2.292	2.693	3.159	3.700	4.328	5.054	6.866
18	1.428	1.702	2.026	2.407	2.854	3.380	3.996	4.717	5.560	7.690
19	1.457	1.754	2.107	2.527	3.026	3.617	4.316	5.142	6.116	8.613
20	1.486	1.806	2.191	2.653	3.207	3.870	4.661	5.604	6.727	9.646

that amount differs somewhat from 6 percent compounded semiannually. Take care in studying future value and present value problems to align the interest rate with the appropriate number of periods.

Let's use Exhibit 15A–2. The future value of $1.00 invested at 4 percent for one year is $1.04 ($1.00 × 1.040, which appears at the junction under the 4% column and across from 1 in the Periods column). The figure 1.040 includes both the principal (1.000) and the compound interest for one period (0.040).

Suppose you deposit $5,000 in a savings account that pays annual interest of 4 percent. The account balance at the end of the year will be $5,200. To compute the future value of $5,000 at 4 percent for one year, multiply $5,000 by 1.040 to get $5,200. Now suppose you invest in a 10-year, 6-percent certificate of deposit (CD). What will be the future value of the CD at maturity? To compute the future value of $5,000 at 6 percent for 10 periods, multiply $5,000 by 1.791 (from Exhibit 15A–2) to get $8,955. This future value of $8,955 indicates that $5,000 earning 6 percent interest compounded annually grows to $8,955 at the end of 10 years. In this way, you can find any present amount's future value at a particular future date. Future value is especially helpful for computing the amount of cash you will have on hand for some purpose in the future.

Future Value of an Annuity

In the preceding example, we made an investment of a single amount. Other investments, called annuities, include multiple investments of an equal periodic amount at fixed intervals over the duration of the investment. Consider a family investing for a child's education. The Dietrichs can invest $4,000 annually to accumulate a college fund for 15-year-old Helen. The investment can earn 7 percent annually until Helen turns 18—a three-year investment. How much will be available for Helen on the date of the last investment? Exhibit 15A–3 shows the accumulation—a total future value of $12,860.

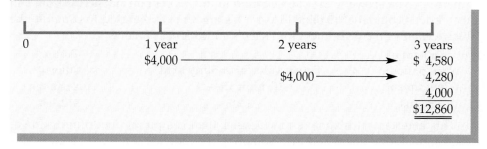

The first $4,000 invested by the Dietrichs grows to $4,580 over the investment period. The second amount grows to $4,280, and the third amount stays at $4,000 because it has no time to earn interest. The sum of the three future values ($4,580 + $4,280 + $4,000) is the future value of the annuity ($12,860), which can be computed as follows:

End of Year	Annual Investment	Interest	Increase for the Year	Future Value of Annuity
0	—	—	—	0
1	$4,000	—	$4,000	$4,000
2	4,000 + ($4,000 × 0.07 = $280) =	4,280		8,280
3	4,000 + ($8,280 × 0.07 = $580) =	4,580		12,860

These computations are laborious. As with the Future Value of $1 (a lump sum), mathematical tables ease the strain of calculating annuities. Exhibit 15A-4, Future Value of Annuity of $1, gives the future value of a series of investments, each of equal amount, at regular intervals.

Future Value of Annuity of $1

Periods	2%	3%	4%	5%	6%	7%	8%	9%	10%	12%
1	1.000	1.000	1.000	1.000	1.000	1.000	1.000	1.000	1.000	1.000
2	2.020	2.030	2.040	2.050	2.060	2.070	2.080	2.090	2.100	2.120
3	3.060	3.091	3.122	3.153	3.184	3.215	3.246	3.278	3.310	3.374
4	4.122	4.184	4.246	4.310	4.375	4.440	4.506	4.573	4.641	4.779
5	5.204	5.309	5.416	5.526	5.637	5.751	5.867	5.985	6.105	6.353
6	6.308	6.468	6.633	6.802	6.975	7.153	7.336	7.523	7.716	8.115
7	7.434	7.663	7.898	8.142	8.394	8.654	8.923	9.200	9.487	10.089
8	8.583	8.892	9.214	9.549	9.897	10.260	10.637	11.028	11.436	12.300
9	9.755	10.159	10.583	11.027	11.491	11.978	12.488	13.021	13.579	14.776
10	10.950	11.464	12.006	12.578	13.181	13.816	14.487	15.193	15.937	17.549
11	12.169	12.808	13.486	14.207	14.972	15.784	16.645	17.560	18.531	20.655
12	13.412	14.192	15.026	15.917	16.870	17.888	18.977	20.141	21.384	24.133
13	14.680	15.618	16.627	17.713	18.882	20.141	21.495	22.953	24.523	28.029
14	15.974	17.086	18.292	19.599	21.015	22.550	24.215	26.019	27.975	32.393
15	17.293	18.599	20.024	21.579	23.276	25.129	27.152	29.361	31.772	37.280
16	18.639	20.157	21.825	23.657	25.673	27.888	30.324	33.003	35.950	42.753
17	20.012	21.762	23.698	25.840	28.213	30.840	33.750	36.974	40.545	48.884
18	21.412	23.414	25.645	28.132	30.906	33.999	37.450	41.301	45.599	55.750
19	22.841	25.117	27.671	30.539	33.760	37.379	41.446	46.018	51.159	63.440
20	24.297	26.870	29.778	33.066	36.786	40.995	45.762	51.160	57.275	72.05255

What is the future value of an annuity of three investments of $1 each that earn 7 percent? The answer 3.215 can be found in the 7% column and across from 3 in the Periods column of Exhibit 15A–4. This amount can be used to compute the future value of the investment for Helen's education, as follows:

Amount of each periodic investment	×	Future value of annuity of $1 (Exhibit 15A–4)	=	Future value of investment
$4,000	×	3.215	=	$12,860

This one-step calculation is much easier than computing the future value of each annual investment and then summing the individual future values. In this way, you can compute the future value of any investment consisting of equal periodic amounts at regular intervals. Businesses make periodic investments to accumulate funds for equipment replacement and other uses—an application of the future value of an annuity.

Present Value

Often a person knows a future amount and needs to know the related present value. Recall Exhibit 15A–1, in which present value and future value are on opposite ends of the same time line. Suppose an investment promises to pay you $5,000 at the *end* of one year. How much would you pay *now* to acquire this investment? You would be willing to pay the present value of the $5,000, which is a future amount.

Present value also depends on three factors: (1) the amount of payment (or receipt), (2) the length of time between investment and future receipt (or payment), and (3) the interest rate. The process of computing a present value is called *discounting* because the present value is *less* than the future value.

In our investment example, the future receipt is $5,000. The investment period is one year. Assume that you demand an annual interest rate of 10 percent on your investment. With all three factors specified, you can compute the present value of $5,000 at 10 percent for one year. The computation is

$$\frac{\text{Future value}}{1 + \text{Interest rate}} = \frac{\$5,000}{1.10} = \$4,545$$

By turning the problem around, we verify the present value computation:

Amount invested (present value)	$4,545
Expected earnings ($4,545 × 0.10)	455
Amount to be received one year from now (future value)	$5,000

This example illustrates that present value and future value are based on the same equation:

$$\text{Present value} \times (1 + \text{Interest rate}) = \text{Future value}$$

$$\text{Present value} = \frac{\text{Future value}}{1 + \text{Interest rate}}$$

If the $5,000 is to be received two years from now, you will pay only $4,132 for the investment, as shown in Exhibit 15A–5.

EXHIBIT 15A–5   Two-Year Investment

Present Value		Future Value

Time 0   1 year   2 years

retreat in time (discount)

?   ← $5,000

$4,132   ← $4,545   ← $5,000

$$\frac{\$4,545}{1.10} = \$4,132 \qquad\qquad \frac{\$5,000}{1.10} = \$4,545$$

By turning the data around, we verify that $4,132 accumulates to $5,000 at 10 percent for two years.

Amount invested (present value)	$4,132
Expected earnings for first year ($4,132 × 0.10)	413
Amount invested after one year	4,545
Expected earnings for second year ($4,545 × 0.10)	455
Amount to be received two years from now (future value)	$5,000

You would pay $4,132—the present value of $5,000—to receive the $5,000 future amount at the end of two years at 10 percent per year. The $868 difference between the amount invested ($4,132) and the amount to be received ($5,000) is the return on the investment, the sum of the two interest receipts: $413 + $455 = $868.

Present-Value Tables

We have shown the simple formula for computing present value. However, calculating present value "by hand" for investments spanning many years presents too many opportunities for arithmetical errors. Present-value tables ease our work. Let's re-examine our examples of present value by using Exhibit 15A–6: Present Value of $1.

For the 10 percent investment for one year, we find the junction under 10% and across from 1 in the Period column. The table figure of 0.909 is computed as follows: 1 ÷ 1.10 = 0.909. This work has been done for us, and only the present values are given in the table. The heading in Exhibit 15A–6 states present value for $1. To calculate present value for $5,000, we multiply 0.909 by $5,000. The result is $4,545, which matches the result we obtained by hand.

For the two-year investment, we read down the 10% column and across the Period 2 row. We multiply 0.826 (computed as 0.909 ÷ 1.10 = 0.826) by $5,000 and get $4,130, which confirms our earlier computation of $4,132 (the difference is due to rounding in the present-value table). Using the table we can compute the present value of any single future amount.

EXHIBIT 15A–6 Present Value of $1

Present Value of $1

Periods	2%	3%	4%	5%	6%	7%	8%	10%	12%
1	0.980	0.971	0.962	0.952	0.943	0.935	0.926	0.909	0.893
2	0.961	0.943	0.925	0.907	0.890	0.873	0.857	0.826	0.797
3	0.942	0.915	0.889	0.864	0.840	0.816	0.794	0.751	0.712
4	0.924	0.889	0.855	0.823	0.792	0.763	0.735	0.683	0.636
5	0.906	0.863	0.822	0.784	0.747	0.713	0.681	0.621	0.567
6	0.888	0.838	0.790	0.746	0.705	0.666	0.630	0.564	0.507
7	0.871	0.813	0.760	0.711	0.665	0.623	0.583	0.513	0.452
8	0.854	0.789	0.731	0.677	0.627	0.582	0.540	0.467	0.404
9	0.837	0.766	0.703	0.645	0.592	0.544	0.500	0.424	0.361
10	0.820	0.744	0.676	0.614	0.558	0.508	0.463	0.386	0.322
11	0.804	0.722	0.650	0.585	0.527	0.475	0.429	0.350	0.287
12	0.789	0.701	0.625	0.557	0.497	0.444	0.397	0.319	0.257
13	0.773	0.681	0.601	0.530	0.469	0.415	0.368	0.290	0.229
14	0.758	0.661	0.577	0.505	0.442	0.388	0.340	0.263	0.205
15	0.743	0.642	0.555	0.481	0.417	0.362	0.315	0.239	0.183
16	0.728	0.623	0.534	0.458	0.394	0.339	0.292	0.218	0.163
17	0.714	0.605	0.513	0.436	0.371	0.317	0.270	0.198	0.146
18	0.700	0.587	0.494	0.416	0.350	0.296	0.250	0.180	0.130
19	0.686	0.570	0.475	0.396	0.331	0.277	0.232	0.164	0.116
20	0.673	0.554	0.456	0.377	0.312	0.258	0.215	0.149	0.104

While we focus on tables in this text, you can also use financial calculators and functions in spreadsheet programs to calculate present value.

Present Value of an Annuity

Return to the investment example beginning on the previous page. That investment provided the investor with only a single future receipt ($5,000 at the end of two years). Annuity investments provide multiple receipts of an equal amount at fixed intervals over the investment's duration.

Consider an investment that promises *annual* cash receipts of $10,000 to be received at the end of each of three years. Assume that you demand a 12-percent return on your investment. What is the investment's present value? What would you pay today to acquire the investment? The investment spans three periods, and you would pay the sum of three present values. The computation is as follows:

Year	Annual Cash Receipt	Present Value of $1 at 12% (Exhibit 15A–6)	Present Value of Annual Cash Receipt
1	$10,000	0.893	$ 8,930
2	10,000	0.797	7,970
3	10,000	0.712	7,120
Total present value of investment			$24,020

The present value of this annuity is $24,020. By paying this amount today, you will receive $10,000 at the end of each of three years while earning 12 percent on your investment.

The example illustrates repetitive computations of the three future amounts, a time-consuming process. One way to ease the computational burden is to add the three present values of $1 (0.893 + 0.797 + 0.712) and multiply their sum (2.402) by the annual cash receipt ($10,000) to obtain the present value of the annuity ($10,000 × 2.402 = $24,020).

An easier approach is to use a present value of an annuity table. Exhibit 15A–7 shows the present value of $1 to be received periodically for a given number of

KEY POINT

The formula for the present value of an annuity is:

$$A_n = R[(1 - (1 + i)^{-n})/i]$$

Where

A_n = present value of a simple annuity

R = the periodic payment (rent)

i = interest rate per period

n = number of periodic payments

EXHIBIT 15A–7 Present Value of Annuity of $1

Present Value of Annuity of $1

Periods	2%	3%	4%	5%	6%	7%	8%	10%	12%
1	0.980	0.971	0.962	0.952	0.943	0.935	0.926	0.909	0.893
2	1.942	1.914	1.886	1.859	1.833	1.808	1.783	1.736	1.690
3	2.884	2.829	2.775	2.723	2.673	2.624	2.577	2.487	2.402
4	3.808	3.717	3.630	3.546	3.465	3.387	3.312	3.170	3.037
5	4.714	4.580	4.452	4.329	4.212	4.100	3.993	3.791	3.605
6	5.601	5.417	5.242	5.076	4.917	4.767	4.623	4.355	4.111
7	6.472	6.230	6.002	5.786	5.582	5.389	5.206	4.868	4.564
8	7.326	7.020	6.733	6.463	6.210	5.971	5.747	5.335	4.968
9	8.162	7.786	7.435	7.108	6.802	6.515	6.247	5.759	5.328
10	8.983	8.530	8.111	7.722	7.360	7.024	6.710	6.145	5.650
11	9.787	9.253	8.760	8.306	7.887	7.499	7.139	6.495	5.938
12	10.575	9.954	9.385	8.863	8.384	7.943	7.536	6.814	6.194
13	11.348	10.635	9.986	9.394	8.853	8.358	7.904	7.103	6.424
14	12.106	11.296	10.563	9.899	9.295	8.745	8.244	7.367	6.628
15	12.849	11.938	11.118	10.380	9.712	9.108	8.559	7.606	6.811
16	13.578	12.561	11.652	10.838	10.106	9.447	8.851	7.824	6.974
17	14.292	13.166	12.166	11.274	10.477	9.763	9.122	8.022	7.120
18	14.992	13.754	12.659	11.690	10.828	10.059	9.372	8.201	7.250
19	15.679	14.324	13.134	12.085	11.158	10.336	9.604	8.365	7.366
20	16.351	14.878	13.590	12.462	11.470	10.594	9.818	8.514	7.469

periods. The present value of a three-period annuity at 12 percent is 2.402 (the junction of the Period 3 row and the 12% column). Thus, $10,000 received annually at the end of each of three years, discounted at 12 percent, is $24,020 ($10,000 × 2.402), which is the present value.

Present Value of Bonds Payable

Using a financial calculator:*

Key	Amount to enter
FV	1,000,000
PMT	25,000
I	3
n	10
COMP	
PV	957,348.99

*Financial calculator keys and results may differ from those shown. Financial calculator results will also differ from those obtained with tables because of the rounding in present-value and future-value tables.

The present value of a bond—its market price—is the present value of the future principal amount at maturity plus the present value of the future contract interest payments. The principal is a single amount to be paid at maturity. The interest is an annuity because it occurs periodically.

Let's compute the present value of 5-percent, five-year bonds of UVW Corporation. The face value of the bonds is $1,000,000, and they pay 2.5 percent contract (cash) interest semiannually. At issuance the market interest rate is 6 percent, but it is computed at 3 percent semiannually. Therefore, the effective-interest rate for each of the 10 semiannual periods is 3 percent. We use 3 percent in computing the present value of the maturity and of the interest. The market price of these bonds is $957,250, as follows:

	Effective annual interest rate ÷ 2	Number of semiannual interest payments	
PV of principal:			
$1,000,000 × PV of single amount at	3%	for 10 periods	
($1,000,000 × 0.744—Exhibit 15A–6) ..			$744,000
PV of interest:			
($1,000,000 × 0.025) × PV of annuity at 3%		for 10 periods	
($25,000 × 8.530—Exhibit 15A–7)			213,250
PV (market price) of bonds			$957,250

The market price of the UVW Corporation bonds shows a discount because the contract interest rate on the bonds (5 percent) is less than the market interest rate (6 percent). We discuss these bonds in more detail on page 821.

Let's consider a premium price for the UVW Corporation bonds. Assume that UVW Corporation issues $1,000,000 of 5 percent bonds when the market interest rate is 4 percent at issuance. The effective-interest rate is 2 percent for each of the 10 semiannual periods.

	Effective annual interest rate ÷ 2	Number of semiannual interest payments	
PV of principal:			
$1,000,000 × PV of single amount at	2%	for 10 periods	
($1,000,000 × 0.820—Exhibit 15A–6) ..			$ 820,000
PV of interest:			
($1,000,000 × 0.025) × PV of annuity at 2%		for 10 periods	
($25,000 × 8.983—Exhibit 15A–7)			224,575
PV (market price) of bonds			$1,044,575

We discuss accounting for these bonds on page 822.

Many calculators and spreadsheet software packages can quickly and accurately perform present value calculations for bonds and leases.

Capital Leases

OBJECTIVE A3
Determine the cost of an asset acquired through a capital lease

How does a lessee compute the cost of an asset acquired through a capital lease? Consider that the lessee gets the use of the asset but does *not* pay for the leased asset in full at the beginning of the lease. A capital lease is therefore similar to borrowing money to purchase the leased asset. The lessee must record the leased asset at the present value of the lease liability. The time value of money must be weighed.

The cost of the asset to the lessee is the sum of any payment made at the beginning of the lease period plus the present value of the future lease payments. The lease payments are equal amounts occurring at regular intervals—that is, they are annuity payments.

Consider a 20-year building lease of Sierra Wireless, Inc. The lease starts on January 2, 2010, and requires 20 annual payments of $200,000 each, with the first payment due immediately. The interest rate in the lease is 10 percent, and the present value of the 19 future payments is $1,673,000 ($200,000 PV of annuity at 10 percent for 19 periods, or 8.365 from Exhibit 15A–7). Sierra's cost of the building is $1,873,000 (the sum of the initial payment, $200,000, plus the present value of the future payments, $1,673,000). The entries for a capital lease are illustrated on pages 837–839.

APPENDIX PROBLEMS

Computing the future value of an investment

A1

b. At 6%, $56,370

Problem 15A–1

For each situation, compute the required amount using the tables in this Appendix.

a. Summit Enterprises Ltd. is budgeting for the acquisition of land over the next several years. The company can invest $800,000 at 9 percent. How much cash will Summit Enterprises Ltd. have for land acquisitions at the end of five years? At the end of six years?

b. Alton Associates Inc. is planning to invest $10,000 each year for five years. The company's investment adviser believes that Alton Associates Inc. can earn 6 percent interest without taking on too much risk. What will be the value of Alton's investment on the date of the last deposit if Alton can earn 6 percent? If Alton can earn 8 percent?

Relating the future and present values of an investment

A1 A2

a. $16,080,000

Problem 15A–2

For each situation, compute the required amount using the tables in this Appendix.

a. XS Technologies Inc.'s operations are generating excess cash that will be invested in a special fund. During 2010, XS Technologies Inc. invests $12,000,000 in the fund for a planned advertising campaign for a new product to be released six years later, in 2016. If XS Technologies Inc.'s investments can earn 5 percent each year, how much cash will the company have for the advertising campaign in 2016?

b. XS Technologies Inc. will need $20 million to advertise a new product in 2016. How much must XS Technologies Inc. invest in 2010 to have the cash available for the advertising campaign? XS Technologies Inc. investments can earn 5 percent annually.

c. Explain the relationship between your answers to (a) and (b).

Computing the present values of various notes and bonds

A2

3. $254,280
4. $200,040

Problem 15A–3

Determine the present value of the following notes and bonds using the tables in this Appendix (notes are accounted for in the same way as bonds):

1. $100,000, five-year note payable with contract interest rate of 9 percent, paid annually. The market interest rate at issuance is 10 percent.

2. Ten-year bonds payable with maturity value of $200,000 and contract interest rate of 12 percent, paid semiannually. The market rate of interest is 10 percent at issuance.

3. Same bonds payable as in number 2, but the market interest rate is 8 percent.

4. Same bonds payable as in number 2, but the market interest rate is 12 percent.

Computing a bond's present value; recording its issuance at a discount and interest payments

A2

1. $569,183

Problem 15A–4

On December 31, 2010, when the market interest rate is 8 percent, Churchill Land Corporation issues $600,000 of 10-year, 7.25-percent bonds payable. The bonds pay interest semiannually.

Required

1. Determine the present value of the bonds at issuance using the tables in this Appendix.

2. Assume that the bonds are issued at the price computed in Requirement 1. Prepare an effective-interest method amortization table for the first two semiannual interest periods.

3. Using the amortization table prepared in Requirement 2, journalize issuance of the bonds and the first two interest payments.

Problem 15A–5

Deciding between two payment plans

(A2)

Ontario Children's Choir needs a fleet of vans to transport the children to singing engagements throughout Ontario. Ford offers the vehicles for a single payment of $120,000 due at the end of four years. Toyota prices a similar fleet of vans for four annual payments of $28,000 each. The children's choir could borrow the funds at 6 percent, so this is the appropriate interest rate. Which company should get the business, Ford or Toyota? Base your decision on present value, and give your reason.

Problem 15A–6

Computing the cost of equipment acquired under a capital lease; recording the lease transactions

(A3)

1. $92,100

Lorus Industries Inc. acquired equipment under a capital lease that requires six annual lease payments of $20,000. The first payment is due when the lease begins, on January 2, 2010. Future payments are due on January 2 of each year of the lease term. The interest rate in the lease is 12 percent.

Required

1. Compute Lorus Industries Inc.'s cost of the equipment using the tables in this Appendix.

2. Journalize (a) the acquisition of the equipment, (b) the amortization for 2010, (c) the accrued interest at December 31, 2010, and (d) the second lease payment on January 2, 2011.

16 Investments and International Operations

What are the different types of investments a company can have in another company, and why are the investment types important?

How do you account for different types of investments?
What is consolidation, and how do you perform a simple consolidation?

What are foreign-currency transaction gains and losses, and how do you account for them?

These questions and others about investments and international operations will be answered throughout this chapter. And the Decision Guidelines at the end of this chapter will provide the answers in a useful summary.

LEARNING OBJECTIVES

1. Account for short-term investments

2. Account for long-term share investments

3. Use the equity method to account for investments

4. Describe and create consolidated financial statements

5. Account for investments in bonds

6. Describe how foreign-currency exchange rates are determined, and account for foreign-currency transactions

7. Identify the impact on accounting for investments of international financial reporting standards (IFRS)

"Fairfax Financial Holdings Ltd. is making its first foray into China with the purchase of a 15-percent stake in Alltrust Insurance Co. of China for about $66 million (U.S.) . . . .Yesterday's deal is a significant investment for Toronto-based Fairfax and follows a pattern of entering various foreign markets by way of joint venture . . . . Fairfax CEO Prem Watsa said Alltrust has had tremendous and profitable growth since its inception, and is one of the leading private insurers in China.

Fairfax earned $275.4 million (Canadian) in its latest quarter, up from $27.6 million a year ago, on large gains in its stock portfolio."[1]

Fairfax Financial Holdings Limited is a financial services holding company that, through its subsidiaries, is engaged in property and casualty insurance, reinsurance, and investment management. As a holding company, Fairfax owns shares in other companies in the insurance and financial services industry. For example, Fairfax owns 100 percent of the shares of Northbridge Financial. From the story above, you can see that it has acquired 15 percent of the common shares of Alltrust. For Fairfax to continue to grow, it must improve the performance of the companies it owns and then continue to acquire other companies.

Accounting for the acquisition of other companies can be complex. An acquirer, such as Fairfax, buys common shares of another company (the acquiree), such as Alltrust Insurance. The accounting treatment for the acquisition will vary depending on the percentage of ownership acquired (based on the number of shares purchased) and management's intention for the acquired company. The first part of this chapter will explain the various accounting treatments for investments in the shares and debt of other companies. The remainder of the chapter provides a brief look at some of the transactions that result when a company operates internationally, as Fairfax does with a number of its investments.

---

[1] Tara Perkins, "Fairfax Makes a Move in China," *The Globe and Mail*, September 1, 2009, posted at globeandmail.com on September 1, 2009, and accessed September 7, 2009.

Throughout this course, you have become increasingly familiar with the financial statements of companies such as Tim Hortons Inc., Imperial Oil Limited, Candian Western Bank, and Sun-Rype Products Ltd. This chapter continues to examine the real world of accounting by discussing investments and international operations. We begin with investments. Investments extend from owning a few shares in another company to the acquisition of an entire company. In earlier chapters we discussed how companies issue shares and bonds. Here we examine shares and bonds from the perspective of an investor who would buy them.

Why do individuals and corporations invest in shares and bonds? You would probably make an investment in order to earn dividend revenue and to sell the shares at a higher price than you paid for them. Investment companies such as pension funds, mutual funds, insurance companies, and bank trust departments buy shares and bonds for this same reason.

Many companies invest in shares and bonds for a second reason: to influence or to control the other company. Fairfax Financial Holdings Ltd. holds 100 percent of the shares of Northbridge Financial and can exert complete control over the affairs of that company. It owns 67.9 percent of the shares of Ridley Inc., a feed producer located in Canada and the United States. While Fairfax doesn't own all the shares of Ridley, it owns more than half of the shares and, therefore, it has control over the affairs of that company. By contrast, Fairfax only holds 15 percent of the shares of Alltrust, which makes Fairfax a minority shareholder. Fairfax may have some input into the business decisions of Alltrust, but there are other shareholders who own more shares and might be in a better position to influence the operations of Alltrust.

Different accounting methods apply to different types of investments. We begin with investments in the shares of other companies (typically referred to as equity investments) and then move to investments in bonds and notes.

Share Investments: An Overview

Share Prices

Investors buy more shares in transactions among themselves than in purchases directly from the issuing company. Each share is issued only once, but it may be traded among investors multiple times thereafter. People and businesses buy shares from and sell shares to each other in markets, such as the Toronto Stock Exchange (TSX) and the TSX Venture Exchange. Recall that share ownership is transferable. Investors trade millions of shares each day. Brokers like RBC Dominion Securities and Raymond James handle share transactions for a commission.

A broker may "quote a share price," which means the broker states the current market price per share. The financial community quotes share prices in dollars and cents. For example, Exhibit 16–1 shows WestJet Airlines Ltd. common shares trading at $12.29 at the close of trading. This information is available instantaneously during the trading day from a variety of websites (such as the website for the Toronto Stock Exchange—tmx.com). Many financial publications and many newspapers also carry daily information on the shares of thousands of corporations. These one-line summaries carry information as of the close of trading the previous day.

EXHIBIT 16–1 Share Price Information for WestJet Airlines Ltd.

52 Weeks High	52 Weeks Low	Stock	Daily High	Daily Low	Cls or Latest	% Chge	Vol 100s	P/E Ratio
15.92	8.34	WestJet Airlines Ltd.	12.38	12.20	12.29	+1.15	1930	10.876

Exhibit 16–1 presents information for the common shares of WestJet Airlines Ltd. just as it appeared on the Toronto Stock Exchange (TSX) website.[2]

At some point during the previous 52 weeks, WestJet common shares reached a high of $15.92 and, at some other point, a low of $8.34. The TSX website continually updates this information while the stock market is open and then provides a summary at the end of each trading day. The closing price was 1.15 percent higher than the closing price one trading day earlier. From this information, we also learn that approximately 193,000 shares of WestJet stock were traded. The P/E ratio (ratio of the share price to earnings per share) is 10.876 for WestJet shares on this day.

Investors and Investees

A person or a company that owns shares in a corporation is an *investor*. The corporation that issued the shares is the *investee*. If you own common shares of WestJet, you are an investor and WestJet is the investee.

A business may purchase another corporation's shares if it has extra cash in the hope of earning dividend revenue and making gains on the sale of the shares. Such investments are rare, however. Most entities prefer to invest in inventory, employees, and capital assets in their own line of business. However, entities do buy the shares of other corporations to gain a degree of control over the investee's operation. An investor holding 25 percent of the outstanding common shares of the investee owns one-fourth of the business. This one-quarter voice in electing the directors of the corporation is likely to give the investor influence over the conduct of the investee's business. An investor holding more than 50 percent of the outstanding common shares controls the investee.

Classifying Investments

KEY POINT

Short-term investments include treasury bills, certificates of deposit, money market funds, and shares and bonds of other companies.

Investments are assets to the investor. The investments may be held for a short term or a long term. **Short-term investments** may also be described as marketable securities or temporary investments, and are current assets. Short-term investments typically are actively traded, with the primary objective being to make a profit from changes in short-term market values. To be listed on the balance sheet as current assets, investments must be liquid (readily convertible to cash). Generally, the investor intends to convert the investments to cash within one year but may continue to hold the investments for a longer period.

---

[2] *Source:* Toronto Stock Exchange website tmx.com for closing information on August 28, 2009. The website was accessed August 31, 2009.

According to Canadian GAAP for private enterprises, an investment in the equity of another publicly traded company that is *not* a short-term investment is categorized as being a *long-term investment*. The different types of long-term equity investments are discussed on pages 881 to 887. Investments are categorized as current or long term based on the length of time management intends to hold them. **Long-term investments** are those investments the investor intends to convert to cash in more than one year. Investments in debt instruments of other companies, such as bonds, can be either short-term or long-term investments. These will be discussed in this chapter.

Exhibit 16–2 provides an example of the presentation of the investment accounts on the balance sheet. We report assets in order of their liquidity, starting with cash. Short-term investments are shown as current assets, while long-term investments and investments subject to significant influence are reported as long-term assets.

EXHIBIT 16–2	Reporting Investments on the Balance Sheet

Current assets
Cash..	$x
Short-term investments...	x
Accounts receivable	x
Inventories..	x
Prepaid expenses...	x
Total current assets	$x
Long-term investments (or simply **Investments**)—Note X	x
Property, plant, and equipment	x

Note X—Long-Term Investments
Details of the long-term investments in shares where there is no significant influence, long-term investments in shares where there is significant influence, and long-term investments in bonds would be given in this note.

Accounting for Short-Term Investments

OBJECTIVE ①
Account for short-term investments

Investments in Shares

The **fair-value method**, or **market-value method**, is used to account for short-term investments in shares where the company does not have significant influence. If there is an available market price for the investment, cost is used only as the initial amount for recording investments and as the basis for measuring gains and losses on their sale. These investments are reported on the balance sheet at their fair values. (If there is not an available market price for the investment, it is recorded and reported on the balance sheet at cost. Unless otherwise stated, we assume all short-term investments in this chapter have an available market price.)

All investments are recorded initially at cost. Cost is the price paid for the shares. Section 3856 of the *CICA Handbook* states that brokerage commission and other transaction costs are expensed. Suppose that Elk Valley Ltd. purchases 1,000 common shares of Finning International Inc. at the market price of $16.00 per share and pays a $500 commission. Elk Valley Ltd. intends to sell this investment within one year or less and, therefore, classifies it as a short-term investment. Elk Valley Ltd.'s entry to record the investment is

Aug. 22	Short-Term Investments......................................	16,000	
	Brokerage Commissions Expense	500	
	Cash		16,500
	Purchased 1,000 common shares of Finning		
	International Inc. at $16.00 per share		
	(1,000 × $16.00 = $16,000) plus commission		
	of $500.		

Assume Elk Valley Ltd. receives a $0.25 per share cash dividend on the Finning shares. Elk Valley Ltd.'s entry to record receipt of the dividends is

Oct. 14	Cash...	250	
	Dividend Revenue..		250
	Received $0.25 per share cash dividend (1,000 × $0.25)		
	on Finning International Inc. common shares.		

Dividends do not accrue with the passage of time (as interest does). The investee has no liability for dividends until the dividends are declared. An investor makes no accrual entry for dividend revenue at year end in anticipation of a dividend declaration.

However, if a dividend declaration does occur before year end, say, on December 28, the investor *may* debit Dividend Receivable and credit Dividend Revenue on that date. The investor would then report this receivable and the revenue in the December 31 financial statements. Receipt of the cash dividend in January would be recorded by a debit to Cash and a credit to Dividend Receivable. The more common practice, however, is to record the dividend as income when it is received.

Receipt of a stock dividend is not income to the investor, and no formal journal entry is needed. As we have seen, a stock dividend increases the number of shares held by the investor but does not affect the total cost of the investment. The *cost per share* of the share investment therefore decreases. The investor usually makes a memorandum entry of the number of stock dividend shares received and the new cost per share. Assume that Elk Valley Ltd. receives a 10-percent stock dividend on its 1,000-share investment in Finning International Inc. that cost $16,000. Elk Valley Ltd. would make a memorandum entry like this:

KEY POINT

Receipt of stock dividends and stock splits is recorded in a memorandum entry. However, for income tax purposes a stock dividend is deemed to be income received by the investor, and tax must be paid on this deemed income.

Nov. 22	Received 100 Finning International Inc. common shares in
	a 10-percent stock dividend. New cost per share is $14.55
	($16,000 ÷ 1,100 shares).

Any gain or loss on the sale of the investment is the difference between the sale proceeds and the carrying value of the investment. Assume that Elk Valley Ltd. sells 400 shares of Finning International Inc. for $20.00 per share, less a $300 commission. The entry to record the sale is

Dec. 18	Cash...	7,700	
	Brokerage Commissions Expense......................	300	
	Short-Term Investments		5,820
	Gain on Sale of Investment..........................		2,180
	Sold 400 common shares of Finning International Inc.		
	Cash received was $7,700 [(400 × $20) − $300].		
	Carrying value of common shares sold was		
	$5,820 (400 × $14.55).		

Observe that the carrying value per share of the investment ($14.55) is based on the total number of shares held, including those received as a stock dividend.

It should be noted that while we have assumed that the Elk Valley investment in the shares of Finning International was a short-term investment, the journal entries to record the transactions noted above would be the same for a long-term investment without significant influence. The only difference would be the presentation on the balance sheet. Short-term investments are classified as current assets. All other equity investments are long term.

Reporting Investments Without Significant Influence at Fair Value

Canadian GAAP for private enterprises require that equity investments where there is no significant influence be reported at their fair value, or current market value, at year end. This approach is referred to as *fair-value accounting* and is applicable to investments where the market value of the equity investment can be readily determined. Thus these investments would appear on the balance sheet at their fair values. Any gain or loss resulting from the change in fair value is recognized in net income for the period in which it arises. The gain or loss is recorded as an unrealized gain or loss in the non-operating section of the company's income statement, under "Other gains and losses."

In our previous example, Elk Valley Ltd. had purchased 1,000 shares of Finning International Inc. for $16.00 per share. Ignoring the stock dividend and the December 18 sale, assume that the fair value of the shares at the December 31 year end had increased to $18.00 per share. Elk Valley Ltd. must adjust the value of the short-term investment to $18,000 (1,000 shares × $18.00) from its carrying value of $16,000, which is an increase of $2,000 ($18,000 – $16,000).

To record this adjustment, companies normally follow a valuation-allowance method. A Fair-Value Valuation Allowance account is created and it is a companion account to the Short-Term Investments or Long-Term Investments account. Using this method, the following journal entry is recorded to increase the short-term investments value by $2,000:

Dec. 31	Fair-Value Valuation Allowance................................... 2,000	
	Unrealized Gain on Fair-Value Adjustment.......	2,000
	Adjusted Finning International Inc. investment	
	to fair value.	

Elk Valley Ltd.'s balance sheet would report short-term investments as follows:

Balance Sheet (partial) Current Assets	
Cash	$ xxx
Short-term investments, at fair value......................................	18,000
Accounts receivable, net of allowance of $xxx	xxx

Elk Valley Ltd.'s income statement would report the increase in the short-term investments as follows:

Income Statement (partial)	
Other gains and losses:	
Unrealized gain on short-term investments	$2,000
Income before income taxes...	xxx
Income tax expense	xxx
Net income (or net loss)...	$ xxx

Now assume instead that the Finning International Inc. shares decreased in value, and at the December 31 year end, Elk Valley Ltd.'s investment in the Finning shares is worth $13,000 ($3,000 less than the carrying value of $16,000).

Using the valuation-allowance method, the following journal entry is recorded to decrease the short-term investment's value by $3,000:

Dec. 31	Unrealized Loss on Fair-Value Adjustment	3,000	
	Fair-Value Valuation Allowance		3,000
	Adjusted Finning International Inc.		
	investment to fair value.		

Elk Valley Ltd.'s balance sheet would report short-term investments as follows:

Balance Sheet (partial) Current Assets	
Cash	$ xxx
Short-term investments, at fair value	13,000
Accounts receivable, net of allowance of $xxx	xxx

Elk Valley Ltd.'s income statement would report the decrease in the short-term investments as follows:

Income Statement (partial)	
Other gains and losses:	
Unrealized loss on short-term investments	$3,000
Income before income taxes	xxx
Income tax expense	xxx
Net income (or net loss)	$ xxx

Selling an Equity Investment (When There Is No Significant Influence)   When a company sells an equity investment, the gain or loss on the sale is the difference between the sale proceeds and the last carrying amount. If Elk Valley Ltd. sells the Finning International Inc. shares after year end for $12,000, Elk Valley Ltd. would record the sale and the $1,000 loss ($12,000 selling price – $13,000 carrying value) as follows:

Jan. 19	Cash	12,000	
	Loss on Sale of Short-Term Investments	1,000	
	Fair-Value Valuation Allowance	3,000	
	Short-Term Investments		16,000
	Sold Finning International Inc. shares at a loss.		

Notice that the Short-Term Investments account is credited for the original cost of the investment. In addition, the Fair-Value Valuation Allowance account is debited, in this case, for the change in fair value since the investment was purchased. These entries remove the fair value of the investment from the books. Companies would normally account for each investment separately, which can be done quite easily with computerized record keeping. Elk Valley Ltd.'s income statement would report the loss on the sale of the short-term investment in the "Other gains and losses" section.

Reporting Short-Term Bond Investments

The fair-value method is used to account for short-term investments in bonds. Like shares, short-term bond investments are valued at fair value, or market value. Premiums or discounts are not amortized as the intent is to hold the bonds for only a short period.

DID YOU GET IT?

To check your understanding of the material in this Learning Objective, complete these questions. The solutions appear on MyAccountingLab so you can check your progress.

1. Calculate the price per share immediately after each of the following actions. This is a short-term investment and the investor does not have a significant influence on the investee.

   a. 1,000 shares were purchased for $18,700 plus commission of $300.

   b. The stocks were split 2 for 1 one month later.

   c. The shares' total market value at year end was $16,000.

   d. All the shares were sold after year end for $20,000 plus commission of $250.

2. Levon Ltd. completed the following investment transactions during 2009 and 2010. Journalize the transactions, providing explanations.

   2009
Sept. 30	Purchased 1,200 of the 50,000 outstanding common shares of Betam Ltd. at a price of $36.00 per share, intending to sell the investment within the next year. Commissions were $125.
Dec. 21	Received a cash dividend of $0.09 per share on the Betam Ltd. shares.
31	At Levon Ltd.'s year end, adjusted the investment to its fair value of $33.50 per share.

   2010
Apr. 13	Sold the Betam Ltd. shares for $31.00 per share. Commissions were $120.

3. At what amount should the following investment portfolio be reported on the December 31 year-end balance sheet? All the investments are less than 5 percent of the investee's shares. Journalize any adjusting entry required by these data.

Shares	Carrying Value	Current Fair Value
All Seasons Hotels	$ 88,000	$ 97,000
Tangerine Manufacturing Corp.	140,000	124,000
Prairie Grocers Inc.	74,000	76,000

Accounting for Long-Term Share Investments

OBJECTIVE 2
Account for long-term share investments

An investor may own numerous investments, some to be held for a short term and others for a long term. For accounting purposes, the two investment portfolios are not mixed. They are reported separately on the balance sheet, as shown in Exhibit 16–2 on page 877. "Long-term" is not often used in the account title. An investment is understood to be long-term unless specifically labelled as short-term and included with current assets.

Long-term investments may be of several different types, depending on the purpose of the investment and thus the percentage of voting interest acquired. Each of the three types is introduced in the following paragraphs and discussed more fully in turn below. Joint ventures are also discussed on page 885.

An investor may make a long-term investment in the shares of another corporation where the purpose is similar to that of short-term investing—the investor will hold the investment to earn dividend revenue but has no significant involvement in the business activities of the investee. In such a situation, the investor will generally hold less than 20 percent of the voting interest of the investee and would normally play no important role in the investee's operations. Such an investor would normally account for the investment using the *fair-value method* (*market-value method*), if the market value for the shares of the investee is readily available.

An investor may also make an investment in the investee by purchasing from 20 to 50 percent of the investee's voting shares. The investor will likely be able to exert a *significant influence* over the investee and how the investee operates the business. Such an investor can likely affect the investee's decisions on dividend policy, product lines, sources of supply, and other important matters. An investor holding from 20 to 50 percent of the voting shares would likely account for the investment using the *equity method* (depending on the circumstances).

The investor may make an investment in the investee that exceeds 50 percent of the voting interest and thus is able to control the operations and activities of the investee. Such investees are called subsidiaries; the financial statements of subsidiaries are normally *consolidated* with those of the parent.

Long-Term Equity Investments Without Significant Influence

Accounting for long-term equity investments where there is no significant influence follows the procedures outlined for short-term equity investments, that is, the fair-value method. The beginning accounting value is cost, which is debited to the Long-Term Investments account at the date of purchase. Dividends are treated as income. Brokerage commission fees are expensed. Gains and losses are recorded on sales.

Suppose Elm Corporation purchases 1,000 common shares of Molson Coors Brewing Company at the market price of $48.00 per share, plus a brokerage commission of $1,000. Elm plans to hold these shares for longer than a year and classifies them as a long-term investment. Elm's entry to record the investment is

Feb. 23	Long-Term Investments 48,000	
	Brokerage Commission Expense 1,000	
	Cash..	49,000
	Purchased investment (1,000 × $48).	
	Paid brokerage commission fee $1,000.	

Assume that Elm receives a $1.00 per share cash dividend on the Molson Coors Brewing Company shares. Elm's entry for receipt of the dividend is

Jul. 14	Cash.. 1,000	
	Dividend Revenue	1,000
	Received dividend on the Molson Coors	
	Brewing Company shares (1,000 × $1.00).	

Long-term investments without significant influence are accounted for at fair value. This requires an adjustment to current market value on the balance sheet date. Assume that the fair value of Elm's investment in Molson Coors Brewing Company shares has increased to $50,000 on December 31, its year end. In this case, Elm makes the following adjustment:

Dec. 31	Fair-Value Valuation Allowance 2,000	
	Unrealized Gain on Fair-Value Adjustment ...	2,000
	Adjusted long-term investment to fair value	
	($50,000 – $48,000).	

Fair-Value Valuation Allowance is a companion account to the Long-Term Investments account. The Allowance account brings the investment to current fair (market) value. Cost ($48,000) plus the Allowance ($2,000) equals the investment carrying amount ($50,000).

Long-Term Investments	Fair-Value Valuation Allowance
48,000	2,000

Investment carrying amount = Market value of $50,000

Here the Fair-Value Valuation Allowance account has a debit balance because the investment has increased in value. If the investment's value declines, the allowance is credited. In that case, the investment carrying amount is cost *minus* the allowance. Fair-Value Valuation Allowance with a credit balance becomes a contra account.

Reporting Long-Term Investments (Where There Is No Significant Influence) The other side of the December 31 adjustment credits Unrealized Gain on Fair-Value Adjustment. If the investment declines, the company debits an Unrealized Loss. *Unrealized* means that the gain or loss resulted from a change in fair value, not from a sale of the investment. A gain or loss on the sale of an investment is said to be *realized* when the company receives cash. For long-term investments where there is no significant influence, the Unrealized Gain (or Loss) is reported in the same manner as the short-term investment gain (or loss): in the non-operating section of the company's income statement, under "other gains and loses."

If there is not an available market price for the long-term investment, it is recorded and reported on the balance sheet at cost, just as short-term investments are. Unless otherwise stated, in this chapter we assume all long-term investments where there is no significant interest have an available market price.

Selling a Long-Term Investment Where There Is No Significant Influence The sale of a long-term investment where there is no significant influence usually results in a *realized* gain or loss. Suppose Elm Corporation sells its investment in the Molson Coors Brewing Company shares for $52,000 during the next year, with brokerage commissions of $1,050. Elm would record the sale as follows:

Cash...	50,950	
Brokerage Commissions Expense.......................	1,050	
Gain on Sale of Long-Term Investment.......		2,000
Long-Term Investments.................................		48,000
Fair-Value Valuation Allowance		2,000
Sold Molson Coors Brewing Company shares at a gain.		

Elm Corporation would report the Gain on Sale of Investment as an "Other gain or loss" in the non-operating section of the income statement.

DID YOU GET IT?

To check your understanding of the material in this Learning Objective, complete this question. The solution appears on MyAccountingLab so you can check your progress.

4. Locus Ltd. completed the following investment transactions during 2009 and 2010. Journalize the transactions, providing explanations.

2009

Oct. 16   Purchased 10,000 of the 60,000 outstanding common shares of Levell Inc. at a price of $45.00 per share; Levell Inc. is known for its generous dividends, so Locus Ltd. plans to hold the investment for more than one year. Commissions were $425.

Dec. 1   Received a cash dividend of $2.00 per share on the Levell Inc. shares.

31   At Locus Ltd.'s year end, adjusted the investment to its fair value of $46.00 per share.

2010

Feb. 15   Suddenly needing cash, Locus Ltd. sold half the Levell Inc. shares for $49.00 per share. Commissions were $260.

Long-Term Share Investments Accounted for by the Equity Method

An investor with a holding of from 20 to 50 percent of the investee's voting shares may significantly influence how the investee operates the business. Since the investor has a voice in shaping business policy and operations, accountants believe that some measure of the business's success and failure should be included in accounting for the investment. We use the **equity method for investments** to account for investments in which the investor can significantly influence the decisions of the investee. (Note that, in certain circumstances, an investor with less than a 20-percent holding may still exert significant influence if there are many other shareholders who all own a small number of shares. In another case, a shareholder with a larger holding, such as a 30-percent holding, may exert no significant influence if another shareholder owns 51 percent of the shares and thus has control of the corporation. In this situation, the cost method would be used to account for this investment rather than the equity method.)

Investments accounted for by the equity method are recorded initially at cost. Suppose Saturna Corp. pays $4,000,000 for 30 percent of the common shares of Galiano Corporation. Brokerage commissions are $5,000. Saturna Corp.'s entry to record the purchase of this investment is

2010				
Jan. 6	Investment in Galiano Corporation			
	Common Shares		4,000,000	
	Brokerage Commissions Expense		5,000	
	Cash			4,005,000
	To purchase a 30% investment in Galiano Corporation common shares.			

KEY POINT

A simple T-account illustrates how to account for equity-method investments:

Equity Method

Original cost	Share of losses
Share of income	Share of dividends

Under the equity method, Saturna Corp., as the investor, applies its percentage of ownership, 30 percent in our example, in recording its share of the investee's net income and dividends. If Galiano Corporation reports net income of $1,000,000 for the year, Saturna Corp. records 30 percent of this amount as an increase in the investment account and as equity-method investment revenue, as follows:

2010				
Dec. 31	Investment in Galiano Corporation			
	Common Shares		300,000	
	Equity-Method Investment Revenue			300,000
	To record 30% of Galiano Corporation net income, $300,000 ($1,000,000 × 0.30).			

The Investment Revenue account carries the Equity-Method label to identify its source. This labelling is similar to distinguishing Sales Revenue from Service Revenue.

The investor increases the Investment account and records Investment Revenue when the investee reports income because of the close relationship between the two companies. As the investee's shareholders' equity increases, so does the Investment account on the books of the investor.

KEY POINT

An investor who holds 20% of a company's shares can usually influence some decisions of the board of directors and gain influence in company decisions. With more than 50% ownership (majority ownership), the investor can usually control the affairs of the company.

Saturna Corp. records its proportionate part of cash dividends received from Galiano Corporation. Assuming Galiano Corporation declares and pays a cash dividend of $600,000, Saturna Corp. receives 30 percent of this dividend, recording it as follows:

2010				
Dec. 31	Cash		180,000	
	Investment in Galiano Corporation			
	Common Shares			180,000
	To record receipt of 30% of Galiano Corporation cash dividend, $180,000 ($600,000 × 0.30).			

Observe that the Investment account is credited for the receipt of a dividend on an equity-method investment. Why? It is because the dividend decreases the investee's shareholders' equity and so it also reduces the investor's investment. In effect, the investor received cash for this portion of the investment.

After the above entries are posted, Saturna Corp.'s Investment account reflects its equity in the net assets of Galiano Corporation (also known as its *carrying value*):

Investment in Galiano Corporation Common Shares					
2010					
Jan. 6	Purchase	4,000,000	Dec. 31	Dividends	180,000
Dec. 31	Net income	300,000			
2010					
Dec. 31	Balance	4,120,000			

Gain or loss on the sale of an equity-method investment is measured as the difference between the sale proceeds and the carrying value of the investment. For example, sale of one-tenth of the Galiano Corporation common shares owned by Saturna Corp. for $400,000 with brokerage fees of $500 would be recorded as follows:

2011			
Feb. 13	Cash...	399,500	
	Brokerage Commissions Expense	500	
	Loss on Sale of Investment....................................	12,000	
	Investment in Galiano Corporation		
	Common Shares		412,000
	Sold one-tenth of investment in Galiano		
	Corporation common shares at a loss		
	of $12,000 [$400,000 – ($4,120,000 × ⅒)].		

Companies with investments accounted for by the equity method often refer to the investee as an affiliated company. The account titles Investments in Affiliated Companies or Investments Subject to Significant Influence refer to investments that are accounted for by the equity method.

Sometimes a company must write down an investment accounted for by the equity method. These write-downs are rare. In its *2008 Annual Report*, Barrick Gold Corporation reported the following information about its 20.4-percent investment in Highland Gold Mining Ltd. in its Note 12—Investments:

> In 2008, we recorded an impairment charge of $140 million against the carrying value at December 31, 2008, of Highland following an other-than-temporary decline in the market value of its publicly traded shares.

Joint Ventures—Accounted for by Proportionate Consolidation

A *joint venture* is a separate entity or project owned and operated by a small group of businesses. Joint ventures are common in risky endeavours such as the petroleum and construction industries. Moreover, they are widely used in regions with developing economies. Many Canadian and U.S. companies that do business abroad enter into joint ventures. For example, Barrick Gold Corporation reports in its December 31, 2008 annual report that it is participating in joint ventures with companies in some of its gold-mine projects.

Section 3055 of the *CICA Handbook* requires the use of proportionate consolidation when accounting for a joint venture. Proportionate consolidation means the venturer consolidates its proportionate interest in the assets, liabilities, revenues, and expenses of a joint venture with its own assets, liabilities, revenues, and expenses. For example, assume the venturer, V Ltd., has inventory of $500,000 and a 40-percent interest in a joint venture. The joint venture has inventory of $200,000. V Ltd. would report inventory on its consolidated financial statements of $580,000 ($500,000 + 40% of $200,000).

Private enterprises can choose to use the equity method or the cost method to account for joint ventures and would typically choose either the equity or cost method if the costs of using proportionate consolidation outweighed the benefits.

Long-Term Share Investments Accounted for by the Consolidation Method

Most large corporations own controlling interests in other corporations. A **controlling** (or **majority**) **interest** is normally the ownership of more than 50 percent of the investee's voting shares. Such an investment enables the investor to elect a majority of the investee's board of directors and so control the investee. The investor is called the **parent company**, and the investee company, as mentioned earlier, is called the **subsidiary**. For example, Loblaw Companies Limited, the grocery store chain, is 62 percent owned by George Weston Limited. Galen Weston and the other shareholders of George Weston Limited own that company and, because George Weston Limited owns 62 percent of Loblaw Companies Limited, they also control Loblaw Companies Limited, as diagrammed in Exhibit 16–3.

EXHIBIT 16–3	Ownership Structure of Loblaw Companies Limited

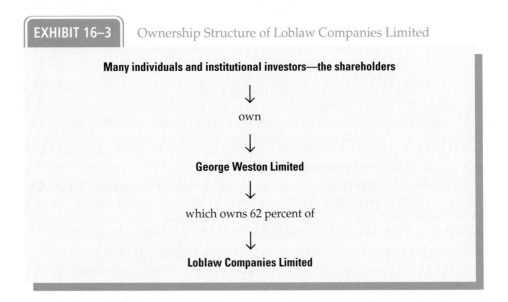

Why have subsidiaries? Why not have the corporation take the form of a single legal entity? Subsidiaries may limit the parent's liabilities in a risky venture; may make mergers, acquisitions, and sales easier; and may ease expansion into foreign countries. For example, Maple Leaf Foods Inc., the processed meat and bakery company, has a U.K. subsidiary, Maple Leaf Bakery U.K., that produces baked goods in the United Kingdom (U.K.) for sale there and in Europe. Exhibit 16–4 shows selected subsidiaries of three major Canadian companies.

Consolidation accounting is a method of combining the financial statements of two or more companies that are controlled by the same owners. This method implements the entity concept by reporting a single set of financial statements for the consolidated entity, which carries the name of the parent company.

GAAP for private interprises allows parent companies to account for their subsidiaries using the equity method or the cost method if the cost of providing consolidated financial statements is greater than the benefits for users who are able to

EXHIBIT 16–4
Selected Subsidiaries of Three Canadian Companies

Parent Company	Selected Subsidiaries
ATCO Ltd.	ATCO Structures Inc.
	Canadian Utilities Limited and its subsidiaries
	ATCO Pipelines
	ATCO Electric Ltd.
	ATCO Travel
	ATCO Power Ltd.
Rogers Communications Inc.	Rogers Cable Communications Inc.
	Rogers Media Inc.
	Rogers Wireless Alberta Inc.
Bombardier Inc.	Bombardier Transportation (Holdings) U.K. Ltd.
	Bombardier Transportation GmbH (Germany)
	Learjet Inc. (U.S.)
	Bombardier Transport France (S.A.S)

gain access to financial information directly from the parent company. However, the *CICA Handbook* emphasizes consolidation for companies with controlling interest, so we focus on consolidation accounting in such situations.

Exhibit 16–5 illustrates the accounting method used generally for share investments according to the percentage of the investor's ownership in the investee company.

EXHIBIT 16–5
Accounting Methods for Share Investment by Percentage of Ownership

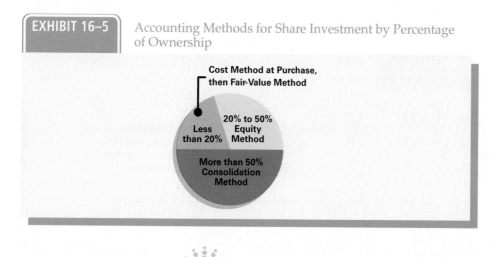

DID YOU GET IT?

To check your understanding of the material in this Learning Objective, complete these questions. The solutions appear on MyAccountingLab so you can check your progress.

5. Identify the appropriate accounting method for each of the following situations involving investments in common shares:

   a. Purchase of 25 percent and investor plans to hold as a long-term investment

   b. Investor intends to sell three months after year end

   c. Purchase of more than 50 percent of investee's shares

6. Investor Ltd. paid $140,000 to acquire 40 percent of the common shares of Investee Ltd. The investment is subject to significant influence. At the end of the first year, Investee Ltd.'s net income was $180,000, and Investee Ltd. declared and paid cash dividends of $140,000. Journalize Investor Ltd.'s (a) purchase of the investment, (b) share of Investee Ltd.'s net income, (c) receipt of dividends from Investee Ltd., and (d) sale of all the Investee Ltd. shares for $160,000.

Consolidated Financial Statements

OBJECTIVE (4)
Describe and create consolidated financial statements

Almost all published financial reports include consolidated statements. To understand the statements you are likely to encounter, you need to know the basic concepts underlying consolidation accounting. **Consolidated statements** combine the balance sheets, income statements, and other financial statements of the parent company with those of the subsidiaries into an overall set as if the parent and its subsidiaries were a single entity. The goal is to provide a better perspective on operations than could be obtained by examining the separate reports of each of the individual companies. The assets, liabilities, revenues, and expenses of each subsidiary are added to the parent's accounts. The consolidated financial statements present the combined account balances. For example, the balance in the Cash account of Loblaw Companies Limited is added to the balance in the George Weston Limited Cash account, and the sum of the two amounts is presented as a single amount in the consolidated balance sheet of George Weston Limited. Each account balance of a subsidiary loses its identity in the consolidated statements. George Weston Limited financial statements are entitled "George Weston Limited and Consolidated Subsidiaries." Loblaw Companies Limited and the names of all other George Weston Limited subsidiaries do not appear in the statement titles. But the names of the subsidiary companies are listed in the parent company's annual report. A reader of corporate annual reports cannot hope to understand them without knowing how consolidated statements are prepared. Exhibit 16–6 diagrams a corporate structure where the parent corporation owns controlling interests in five subsidiary companies and an equity-method investment in another investee company.

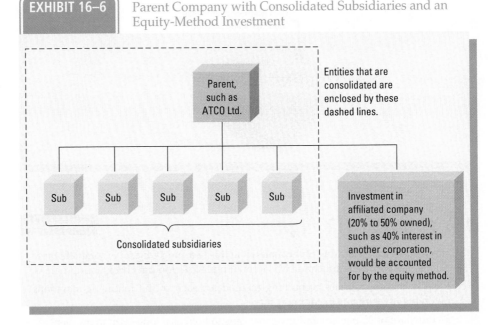

EXHIBIT 16–6 Parent Company with Consolidated Subsidiaries and an Equity-Method Investment

Consolidated Balance Sheet—Parent Owns All Subsidiary's Shares Suppose that Parent Corporation purchased all the outstanding common shares of Subsidiary Corporation at its book value of $1,200,000. In addition, Parent Corporation lent Subsidiary Corporation $640,000. The $1,200,000 is paid to the *former* owners (the shareholders) of Subsidiary Corporation as private investors. The $1,200,000 *is not* an addition to the existing assets and shareholders' equity of Subsidiary Corporation. *That is, the books of Subsidiary Corporation are completely unaffected by Parent Corporation's initial investment and Parent's subsequent accounting for that investment.*

Subsidiary Corporation is not dissolved. It lives on as a separate legal entity but with a new owner, Parent Corporation.

Parent Corporation Books		Subsidiary Corporation Books	
Investment in Subsidiary			
Corporation 1,200,000		No entry	
Cash	1,200,000		
Note Receivable from		Cash 640,000	
Subsidiary Corp. 640,000		Note Payable	
Cash	640,000	to Parent Corp. ...	640,000

Each legal entity has its individual set of books. The consolidated entity does not keep a separate set of books. Instead a work sheet is used to prepare the consolidated statements. A major concern in consolidation accounting is this: Do not double-count—that is, do not include the same item twice.

Companies may prepare a consolidated balance sheet immediately after acquisition. The consolidated balance sheet shows all the assets and liabilities of the parent and the subsidiary. The Investment in Subsidiary account on the parent's books represents all the assets and liabilities of Subsidiary Corporation. The consolidated statements cannot show both the investment account and the amounts for the subsidiary's assets and liabilities. Doing so would count the same net resources twice. To avoid this double-counting, we eliminate (a) the $1,200,000 Investment in Subsidiary Corporation on the parent's books, and the $1,200,000 shareholders' equity on the subsidiary's books ($800,000 Common Shares and $400,000 Retained Earnings), and (b) the intercompany $640,000 note.

Explanation of Elimination-Entry (a) Exhibit 16–7 shows the work sheet for consolidating the balance sheet. Consider the elimination entry for the parent–subsidiary ownership accounts, which are intercompany accounts. Entry (a) credits the parent's Investment account to eliminate its debit balance. It also eliminates the subsidiary's shareholders' equity accounts by debiting Common Shares for $800,000 and Retained Earnings for $400,000. The resulting consolidated balance sheet reports no Investment in Subsidiary Corporation account, and the Common Shares and Retained Earnings are those of Parent Corporation only. The consolidated amounts are in the final column of the consolidation work sheet.

KEY POINT

Each subsidiary company keeps its own set of books and pays its own taxes, just as the parent company does; however, for reporting purposes, the parent and subsidiary companies are treated as one economic unit when they are consolidated. Intercompany receivables and payables must be eliminated.

EXHIBIT 16–7 Work Sheet for Consolidated Balance Sheet—Parent Corporation Owns All Subsidiary Corporation's Shares

	Parent Corporation	Subsidiary Corporation	Eliminations Debit	Eliminations Credit	Consolidated Amounts
Assets					
Cash.......................................	96,000	144,000			240,000
Notes receivable					
from Subsidiary Corp....................	640,000	—		(b) 640,000	—
Inventory	832,000	728,000			1,560,000
Investment in Subsidiary Corp.........	1,200,000	—		(a) 1,200,000	—
Other assets.......................................	1,744,000	1,104,000			2,848,000
Total	4,512,000	1,976,000			4,648,000
Liabilities and Shareholders' Equity					
Accounts payable.............................	344,000	136,000			480,000
Notes payable...................................	1,520,000	640,000	(b) 640,000		1,520,000
Common shares................................	1,408,000	800,000	(a) 800,000		1,408,000
Retained earnings	1,240,000	400,000	(a) 400,000		1,240,000
Total	4,512,000	1,976,000	1,840,000	1,840,000	4,648,000

Explanation of Elimination-Entry (b)   Parent Corporation lent $640,000 to Subsidiary Corporation, and Subsidiary Corporation signed a note payable to Parent Corporation. Therefore, Parent Corporation's balance sheet includes a $640,000 note receivable and Subsidiary Corporation's balance sheet reports a note payable for this amount. This loan was entirely within the consolidated entity and so must be eliminated. Entry (b) accomplishes this. The $640,000 credit in the elimination column of the work sheet offsets Parent Corporation's debit balance in Notes Receivable from Subsidiary Corporation. After this work sheet entry, the consolidated amount for notes receivable is zero. The $640,000 debit in the elimination column offsets the credit balance of Subsidiary Corporation's notes payable, and the resulting consolidated amount for notes payable is the amount owed to those outside the consolidated entity.

Examine Exhibit 16–7. Why does the consolidated shareholders' equity ($1,408,000 + $1,240,000) exclude the equity of Subsidiary Corporation? This is because the shareholders' equity of the consolidated entity is that of the parent only, and because the subsidiary's equity and the parent company's investment balance represent the same resources. Therefore, including them both would amount to double-counting.

Parent Buys Subsidiary's Shares and Pays for Goodwill   A company may acquire a controlling interest in a subsidiary by paying a price above the fair value of the subsidiary's net assets (assets minus liabilities), which we assume is equal to the book value of the subsidiary's shareholders' equity. This excess is called goodwill. Accounting for goodwill was introduced in Chapter 10 on page 522. What drives a company's market value up? The company may create goodwill through its superior products, service, or location.

The subsidiary does not record goodwill; only the purchaser does. The goodwill is identified in the process of consolidating the parent and subsidiary financial statements.

Suppose Parent Corporation paid $2,700,000 to acquire 100 percent of the common shares of Subsidiary Corporation, which had Common Shares of $1,200,000 and Retained Earnings of $1,080,000. Parent's payment included $420,000 for goodwill ($2,700,000 − $1,200,000 − $1,080,000 = $420,000).[3] Parent Corporation would record this purchase as follows:

Parent Corporation Books

Investment in Subsidiary Corporation..............................	2,700,000	
Cash		2,700,000

Exhibit 16–8 shows the work sheet for consolidating the balance sheet in this situation. The entry to eliminate Parent Corporation's Investment account against Subsidiary Corporation's equity accounts is:

Common Shares, Subsidiary Corporation.........................	1,200,000	
Retained Earnings, Subsidiary Corporation	1,080,000	
Goodwill	420,000	
Investment in Subsidiary Corporation...........................		2,700,000

To eliminate cost of investment in Subsidiary Corporation against Subsidiary Corporation's equity balances and to recognize Subsidiary Corporation's unrecorded goodwill.

In *actual* practice, this entry would be made only on the consolidation work sheet. Here we show it in general journal form for instructional purposes.

---

[3] For simplicity, we are assuming the fair market value of the subsidiary's net assets (Assets − Liabilities) equals the book value of company's shareholders' equity. Advanced courses consider other situations.

	Parent Corporation	Subsidiary Corporation	Eliminations Debit	Eliminations Credit	Consolidated Amounts
Assets					
Cash..	880,000	100,000			980,000
Inventory	500,000	1,500,000			2,000,000
Investment in Subsidiary Corp...............	2,700,000	—		2,700,000	0
Goodwill...	—	—	420,000		420,000
Other assets..	816,000	785,000			1,601,000
Total..	4,896,000	2,385,000			5,001,000
Liabilities and Shareholders' Equity					
Accounts payable	426,000	25,000			451,000
Notes payable	1,000,000	80,000			1,080,000
Common shares......................................	1,280,000	1,200,000	1,200,000		1,280,000
Retained earnings..................................	2,190,000	1,080,000	1,080,000		2,190,000
Total..	4,896,000	2,385,000	2,700,000	2,700,000	5,001,000

The asset goodwill is reported as a separate line item on the consolidated balance sheet. For example, Maple Leaf Foods Inc.'s December 31, 2008, consolidated balance sheet includes goodwill of $876.3 million as a separate line item in the non-current-assets section of the balance sheet.

Consolidated Balance Sheet—Parent Owns Less Than 100 Percent of Subsidiary's Shares

When a parent company owns more than 50 percent (a majority) of the subsidiary's shares but less than 100 percent of them, a new category of balance sheet account, called *non-controlling interest*, must appear on the consolidated balance sheet. Suppose Parent Corporation buys 75 percent of Subsidiary Corporation's common shares. The non-controlling interest is the remaining 25 percent of Subsidiary Corporation's equity. Thus, **non-controlling interest** (sometimes called *minority interest*) is the subsidiary's equity that is held by shareholders other than the parent company. While the *CICA Handbook* is silent on where non-controlling interest should be disclosed on the balance sheet, accepted practice is to list it as a liability between liabilities and shareholders' equity.

Assume P Ltd. buys 75 percent of S Ltd.'s common shares for $1,440,000 and there is no goodwill. Also, P Ltd. owes $600,000 on a note payable to S Ltd. P Ltd. would record this purchase as follows:

Parent Corporation Books

Investment in S. Ltd	1,440,000	
Cash		1,440,000

Exhibit 16–9 is the consolidation work sheet. Again, focus on the Eliminations columns and the Consolidated Amounts.

Entry (a) eliminates P Ltd.'s Investment balance of $1,440,000 against the $1,920,000 shareholders' equity of S Ltd. Observe that all S Ltd.'s equity is eliminated even though P Ltd. holds only 75 percent of S Ltd.'s shares. The remaining 25 percent interest in S Ltd.'s equity is credited to Non-controlling Interest ($1,920,000 × 0.25 = $480,000). Thus, entry (a) reclassifies 25 percent of S Ltd.'s equity as non-controlling interest. Entry (b) in Exhibit 16–9 eliminates S Ltd.'s $600,000 note receivable against P Ltd.'s note payable of the same amount. The consolidated amount of notes payable ($504,000) is the amount that S Ltd. owes to outsiders.

The consolidated balance sheet of P Ltd., shown in Exhibit 16–10, is based on the work sheet of Exhibit 16–9. The consolidated balance sheet reveals that ownership of P Ltd. and its consolidated subsidiary is divided between P Ltd.'s shareholders (common shares and retained earnings totalling $4,056,000) and the non-controlling shareholders of S Ltd. ($480,000).

LEARNING TIPS

The accounts that would appear on consolidated financial statements:
Non-Controlling Interest—the non-controlling shareholders' share of the company
Goodwill—excess of the purchase price of the subsidiary over the fair value of its net assets
The investment account, intercompany transactions, and the shareholders' equity of the subsidiary are not on the consolidated statements.

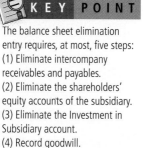

KEY POINT

The balance sheet elimination entry requires, at most, five steps:
(1) Eliminate intercompany receivables and payables.
(2) Eliminate the shareholders' equity accounts of the subsidiary.
(3) Eliminate the Investment in Subsidiary account.
(4) Record goodwill.
(5) Record non-controlling interest.

EXHIBIT 16–9 Work Sheet for Consolidated Balance Sheet: Parent (P Ltd.) Owns Less Than 100 Percent of Subsidiary's (S Ltd.'s) Shares

	P Ltd.	S Ltd.	Eliminations		Consolidated Amounts
			Debit	Credit	
Assets					
Cash..	396,000	216,000			612,000
Notes receivable from P Ltd..............	—	600,000		(b) 600,000	—
Accounts receivable, net	648,000	468,000			1,116,000
Inventory	1,104,000	792,000			1,896,000
Investment in S Ltd............................	1,440,000	—		(a) 1,440,000	—
Property, plant, and equipment, net...	2,760,000	1,476,000			4,236,000
Total..	6,348,000	3,552,000			7,860,000
Liabilities and Shareholders' Equity					
Accounts payable	1,692,000	1,128,000			2,820,000
Notes payable	600,000	504,000	(b) 600,000		504,000
Non-controlling interest	—	—		(a) 480,000	480,000
Common shares....................................	2,040,000	1,200,000	(a) 1,200,000		2,040,000
Retained earnings................................	2,016,000	720,000	(a) 720,000		2,016,000
Total	6,348,000	3,552,000	2,520,000	2,520,000	7,860,000

EXHIBIT 16–10 Consolidated Balance Sheet of P Ltd.

P LTD.
Consolidated Balance Sheet
December 31, 2010

Assets

Current assets
Cash..	$ 612,000	
Accounts receivable, net	1,116,000	
Inventory	1,896,000	
Total current assets		$3,624,000
Property, plant, and equipment, net................................		4,236,000
Total assets		$7,860,000

Liabilities and Shareholders' Equity

Current liabilities
Accounts payable...		$2,820,000
Long-term liabilities		
Notes payable..		504,000
Total liabilities		3,324,000
Non-controlling interest..		480,000
Shareholders' equity		
Common shares...	$2,040,000	
Retained earnings	2,016,000	
Total shareholders' equity		4,056,000
Total liabilities and shareholders' equity		$7,860,000

Income of a Consolidated Entity The income of a consolidated entity is the net income of the parent plus the parent's proportion of the subsidiaries' net income. Suppose Parent Inc. owns all the shares of Subsidiary S-1 Inc. and 60 percent of the shares of Subsidiary S-2 Inc. During the year just ended, Parent Inc. earned net income of $1,980,000, Subsidiary S-1 Inc. earned $900,000, and Subsidiary S-2 Inc.

had a net loss of $600,000. Parent Inc. would report net income of $2,520,000, computed as follows:

	Net Income (Net Loss)	Parent Inc. Shareholders' Ownership	Parent Inc. Net Income (Net Loss)
Parent Inc..........................	$1,980,000	100%	$1,980,000
Subsidiary S-1 Inc............	900,000	100	900,000
Subsidiary S-2 Inc............	(600,000)	60	(360,000)
Consolidated net income			$2,520,000

The parent's net income is the same amount that would be recorded under the equity method. However, the equity method stops short of reporting the investee's assets and liabilities on the parent balance sheet because, with an investment in the range of 20 to 50 percent, the investor owns less than a controlling interest in the investee company.

The procedures for preparation of a consolidated income statement parallel those outlined above for the balance sheet. The consolidated income statement is discussed in an advanced accounting course.

DID YOU GET IT?

To check your understanding of the material in this Learning Objective, complete these questions. The solutions appear on MyAccountingLab so you can check your progress.

7. Answer these questions about consolidated financial statements:

   a. Whose name appears on the consolidated statements—the parent company's, the subsidiary company's, or both?

   b. Why does consolidated shareholders' equity (contributed capital + retained earnings) exclude the equity of a subsidiary corporation?

   c. Suppose A Ltd. owns 90 percent of B Ltd. What are the remaining 10 percent of B Ltd.'s shares called, and where do they appear, if at all, in A Ltd.'s consolidated financial statements?

   d. Suppose C Ltd. paid $2,000,000 to acquire D Ltd., whose shareholders' equity (which has the same fair value as net assets) totalled $1,400,000. What is the $600,000 excess called? Which company reports the excess? Where in the consolidated financial statements is the excess reported?

8. Parent Corp. paid $400,000 for all the common shares of Subsidiary Corp., and Parent Corp. owes Subsidiary Corp. $60,000 on a note payable. Assume the fair value of Subsidiary Corp.'s net assets is equal to book value. Complete the following consolidation work sheet:

	Parent Corp.	Subsidiary Corp.	Eliminations Debit	Eliminations Credit	Consolidated Amounts
Assets					
Cash..	28,000	36,000			
Note receivable from Parent Corp............	—	60,000			
Investment in Subsidiary Corp.	400,000	—			
Goodwill..................................	—	—			
Other assets	432,000	396,000	—	—	—
Total	860,000	492,000	=	=	=
Liabilities and Shareholders' Equity					
Accounts payable	60,000	32,000			
Notes payable	60,000	120,000			
Common shares...........................	560,000	240,000			
Retained earnings	180,000	100,000	—	—	—
Total	860,000	492,000	=	=	=

Investments in Bonds and Notes[4]

OBJECTIVE 5
Account for investments in bonds

Industrial and commercial companies invest far more in shares than they do in bonds. The major investors in bonds are financial institutions, such as pension plans, trust companies, and insurance companies. The relationship between the issuer and the investor may be diagrammed as follows:

Issuing Corporation	Investor (Bondholder)
Bonds payable	Investment in bonds
Interest expense	Interest revenue

The dollar amount of a bond transaction is the same for the issuer and the investor, but the accounts debited and credited differ. For example, the issuer's interest expense is the investor's interest revenue.

Short-term investments in bonds are rare, since the purpose of investing in bonds is to provide a stream of investment income over the life of the bonds, and bonds typically have a life that is longer than one year. Therefore, we focus here on long-term investments in bonds and notes.

Long-term bond investments are recorded at cost, that is, at their purchase price. Brokerage fees, if any, are expensed. The accounting treatment of long-term bond investments is typically referred to as the amortized cost method. The discount or premium is amortized to account more precisely for interest revenue over the period the bonds will be held. The amortization of the discount or the premium on a bond investment affects Interest Revenue and the carrying amount of the bonds in the same way as for the company that issued the bonds. Long-term investments in bonds are reported at their *amortized cost*, which determines the carrying amount. At maturity the investor will receive the face value of the bonds.

The accountant records amortization on the cash interest dates and at year end, along with the accrual of interest receivable. Accountants rarely use separate discount and premium accounts for investments. Amortization of a *discount* is recorded by directly *debiting* the Investment in Bonds account and *crediting* Interest Revenue. Amortization of a *premium* is recorded by directly *crediting* the Investment in Bonds account. This entry *debits* Interest Revenue. These entries bring the investment balance to the bonds' face value on the maturity date and record the correct amount of interest revenue each period.

Suppose $100,000 of 6-percent Xpress Trucking Ltd. bonds were purchased on April 1, 2010. Interest dates are April 1 and October 1. These bonds mature on April 1, 2014, so they will be outstanding for 48 months. The price of 98 (meaning 98 percent of par value) does not include brokerage charges of $800; the cost of the bonds is $98,000 and brokerage charges of $800 are expensed. Assume amortization of the discount by the straight-line method. Straight-line amortization of premium or discount on a bond investment is calculated the same way as it is calculated for bonds payable (see Chapter 15,

---

[4] Section 3856 of the *CICA Handbook* addresses the disclosure and presentation of financial instruments. Much of the discussion in Section 3861 is beyond the scope of this text and is covered in advanced accounting courses.

pages 823–824). The following entries illustrate accounting for this bond investment:[5]

2010

Apr. 1	Investment in Bonds..	98,000	
	Brokerage Charges Expense.................................	800	
	Cash...		98,800
	To purchase long-term bond investment ($100,000 × 0.98).		

Oct. 1	Cash	3,000	
	Interest Revenue		3,000
	To receive semiannual interest ($100,000 × 0.06 × 6/12).		

1	Investment in Bonds...	250	
	Interest Revenue.......................................		250
	To amortize discount on bond investment for six months ([($100,000 − $98,000) ÷ 48] × 6).		

At December 31, 2010, the year-end adjustments are:

Dec. 31	Interest Receivable..	1,500	
	Interest Revenue.......................................		1,500
	To accrue interest revenue for three months ($100,000 × 0.06 × 3/12).		

31	Investment in Bonds...	125	
	Interest Revenue.......................................		125
	To amortize discount on bond investment for three months ([($100,000 − $98,000) ÷ 48] × 3).		

The financial statements at December 31, 2010, report the following effects of this long-term investment in bonds, where $98,375 = $98,000 + $250 + $125 (assume the bonds' market price is 102):

Balance sheet at December 31, 2010:
    Current assets:

	Interest receivable	$ 1,500
	Total current assets..	x,xxx
	Investments in bonds—Note 6..	98,375

———————
Note 6: Investments in Bonds
Investments in bonds are reported at their amortized cost. At December 31, 2010, the current market value of the investments in bonds was $102,000.

———————
[5] If the company were to record the investment at par value and the premium or discount in a separate contra account, the April 1 entry would be:

Investment in Bonds...		100,000	
Brokerage Charges Expense		800	
Discount on Investment in Bonds.....................................			2,000
Cash			98,800

The entry on October 1 would be:

Discount on Investment in Bonds		250	
Interest Revenue			250
Cash..		3,000	
Interest Revenue			3,000

> **Income statement (multiple-step) for the year ended December 31, 2010:**
>   Other revenues:
>   Interest revenue $4,875

Interest revenue is $4,875 = $3,000 + $250 + $1,500 + $125.

If the market value of a long-term bond investment declines below cost and the decline is considered to be other than temporary, the investment should be written down to market.

DID YOU GET IT?

To check your understanding of the material in this Learning Objective, complete these questions. The solutions appear on MyAccountingLab so you can check your progress.

9. On April 30, 2010, Cana Corp. paid 97.50 for 4-percent bonds of Starr Limited as an investment. The maturity value of the bonds is $100,000 at October 31, 2015; they pay interest on April 30 and October 31. At December 31, 2010, the bonds' market value is 98.25. Cana Corp. plans to hold the bonds until they mature.

   a. How should Cana Corp. account for the bonds?

   b. Using the straight-line method of amortizing the discount, journalize all transactions on the bonds for 2010.

10. Refer to the data in the previous question. Show how the investment in Starr Limited bonds would be reported on the Cana Corp. balance sheet at December 31, 2010.

OBJECTIVE (6)

Describe how foreign-currency exchange rates are determined, and account for foreign-currency transactions

Accounting for International Operations

Accounting for business activities across national boundaries makes up the field of *international accounting*. Did you know that Bombardier earns more than 90 percent and Fairfax Financial Holdings over 70 percent of their revenues outside Canada? It is common for Canadian companies to do a large part of their business abroad. Alcan Aluminum, McCain Foods, and others are very active in other countries, as shown in Exhibit 16–11.

EXHIBIT 16–11   Extent of International Business

	Percent That Is International	
Company	Revenue	Capital Assets
CAE Inc.	94%	87%
Bombardier Inc.	96	70
Teck Resources Limited	91	29

The economic environment varies from country to country. Canada may be booming while other countries may be depressed economically. International accounting must deal with such differences.

Foreign Currencies and Foreign-Currency Exchange Rates

Each country uses its own national currency. Assume Research In Motion Ltd. (RIM) sells 1,000 of its Blackberry wireless devices to a U.S. retailer. Will RIM receive Canadian dollars or U.S. dollars? If the transaction takes place in Canadian dollars, the U.S. retailer must buy Canadian dollars in order to pay RIM in Canadian currency. If the transaction takes place in U.S. dollars, RIM will receive U.S. dollars and then exchange them for Canadian dollars. In either case, a step has been added to the transaction: one company must convert domestic currency into foreign currency, or the other company must convert foreign currency into domestic currency.

The price of one nation's currency can be stated in terms of another country's monetary unit. The price of a foreign currency is called the **foreign-currency exchange rate**. In Exhibit 16–12, the dollar value of a Japanese yen is $0.01172. This means that one Japanese yen could be bought for approximately one cent. Other currencies, such as the pound and the euro (also listed in Exhibit 16–12), are similarly bought and sold.

EXHIBIT 16–12   Foreign-Currency Exchange Rates

Country	Monetary Unit	Cost in Canadian Dollars	Country	Monetary Unit	Cost in Canadian Dollars
United States	Dollar	$ 1.0891	Britain	Pound	$1.78312
European			Japan	Yen	0.01172
Union	Euro	1.5571	Denmark	Krone	0.20962

Source: OANDA.com, The Currency Site, accessed September 7, 2009.

We use the exchange rate to convert the price of an item stated in one currency to its price in a second currency. We call this conversion a *translation.* Suppose an item costs 200 euros. To compute its cost in dollars, we multiply the amount in euros by the conversion rate: 200 euros × $1.5571 = $311.42.

To aid the flow of international business, a market exists for foreign currencies. Traders buy and sell Canadian dollars, U.S. dollars, euros, and other currencies in the same way that they buy and sell other commodities such as beef, corn, cotton, and automobiles. And just as supply and demand cause the prices of these other commodities to shift, so supply and demand for a particular currency cause exchange rates to fluctuate daily. When the demand for a nation's currency exceeds the supply of that currency, its exchange rate rises. When supply exceeds demand, the currency's exchange rate falls.

Two main factors determine the supply and demand for a particular currency: (1) the ratio of a country's imports to its exports, and (2) the rate of return available in the country's capital markets.

The Import/Export Ratio   Traditionally, Canada has exported more goods than it imports. However, in the last year, Canada recorded a trade deficit. For exports, customers of Canadian companies must buy the Canadian dollar in the international currency market to pay for their purchases in Canadian dollars. This strong demand drives up the price—the foreign exchange rate—of the Canadian dollar. The United States, on the other hand, imports more goods than it exports. U.S. businesses must sell U.S. dollars in order to buy the foreign currencies needed to acquire the foreign goods. The supply of the U.S. dollar increases and so its price decreases.

The Rate of Return   The rate of return available in a country's capital markets affects the amount of investment funds flowing into the country. When rates of return are relatively high in a politically stable country such as Canada, international investors buy shares, bonds, and real estate in that country. This increases the demand for the nation's currency and drives up its exchange rate.

Currencies are often described in the financial press as "strong" or "weak." What do these terms mean? The exchange rate of a **strong currency** is rising relative to other nations' currencies. The exchange rate of a **weak currency** is falling relative to other currencies.

On March 1, 2001, the exchange rate for the U.S. dollar was $1.5480. On September 7, 2009, the rate had changed to $1.0891. The Canadian dollar has risen against the U.S. dollar; the U.S. dollar has become cheaper, so the Canadian dollar now buys more U.S. dollars. A stronger Canadian dollar makes travel to the United States more attractive to Canadians than when the U.S. dollar was at $1.5480.

OANDA.com reported a rise in the exchange rate of the euro from $1.4321 on May 20, 2006, to $1.5571 on September 7, 2009. This indicates that the euro was strengthening against the Canadian dollar. European Union products are more expensive because each Canadian dollar buys fewer euros.

In our example, we would describe the Canadian dollar as *stronger* than the U.S. dollar because the U.S. dollar's exchange rate fell between March 1, 2001 and September 7, 2009. For the same reason, the Canadian dollar was weakening against the euro. To determine whether the U.S. dollar is stronger than the euro, you would have to compare the euro's exchange in U.S. dollars on two different days to see whether the euro fell against the U.S. dollar.

Foreign-Currency Transactions

When a Canadian company transacts business with a foreign company, the transaction price can be stated either in Canadian dollars or in the national currency of the other company or in any other currency that is stipulated by contract. For example, a number of markets conduct all transactions in U.S. dollars, although neither the seller nor the buyer is located in the United States. If the price is stated in Canadian dollars, the Canadian company has no special accounting difficulties. The transaction is recorded and reported in dollars exactly as though the other company were also Canadian.

Paying Cash in a Foreign Currency

If the transaction price is stated in units of the foreign currency, the Canadian company encounters two accounting steps. First, the transaction price must be translated into Canadian dollars for recording in the accounting records. Second, these transactions usually cause the Canadian company to experience a **foreign-currency transaction gain** or **loss**. This type of gain or loss occurs when the exchange rate changes between the date of the purchase or sale on account and the date of the subsequent payment or receipt of cash.

If a company purchases products from a supplier in another country, Accounts Payable is created. It is recorded at the prevailing exchange rate. Later, when the company pays the invoice, the exchange rate has almost certainly changed. Accounts Payable is debited for the amount recorded earlier, and Cash is credited for the amount paid at the current exchange rate. A debit difference is a loss, and a credit difference is a gain.

Suppose on December 13, 2009 The Bay imports Shalimar perfume from a French supplier at a price of 75,000 euros. If the exchange rate is $1.56 per euro, the Bay records this credit purchase as follows:

Dec. 13	Inventory	117,000	
	Accounts Payable		117,000
	To record a purchase on credit (75,000 × $1.56).		

The Bay translates the euro price of the merchandise (75,000 euros) into Canadian dollars ($117,000) for recording the purchase and the related account payable.

If The Bay were to pay this account immediately (which is unlikely in international commerce), The Bay would debit Accounts Payable and credit Cash for $117,000. Suppose, however, that the credit terms specify payment within 60 days and suppose as well that The Bay's year end is January 31, 2010. It is almost certain that the exchange rate for the euro will be different on the year-end and payment dates.

On January 31, 2010, the payable must be reported at its current dollar value—Canadian GAAP for private enterprises requires current dollar values for receivables and payables at year end. Suppose the exhange rate at January 31, 2010 has changed to $1.57 per euro. The Bay's payable would be $117,750 (75,000 euros × $1.57 per euro), which is $750 higher than the amount of the payable recorded originally. The entry to record this change in the euro exchange rate at year end is

```
2010
Jan. 31   Foreign-Currency Transaction Loss ................      750
             Accounts Payable..........................................               750
          To record the change in the exchange rate of
          the euro at year end (75,000 × ($1.57 – $1.56)).
```

On February 2, 2010, when The Bay pays this debt, suppose the exchange rate has changed to $1.58 per euro. The Bay's payment entry is

```
Feb. 2    Accounts Payable............................................   117,750
          Foreign-Currency Transaction Loss ................       750
             Cash ...........................................................            118,500
          To record payment of a credit purchase (75,000 × $1.58).
```

The Bay has a loss because the company has settled the debt with more dollars than the amount of the original account payable. If on the payment date the exchange rate of the euro was less than $1.56, The Bay would have paid fewer dollars than the $117,750 year-end valuation of the payable. The company would have recorded a gain on the transaction as a credit to Foreign-Currency Transaction Gain.

Collecting Cash in a Foreign Currency

International sales on account also may be measured in foreign currency. Suppose Bombardier sells some products to an American customer on January 30, 2010. The price of the products is US$140,000, and the exchange rate is $1.10. Bombardier's sale entry is

```
Jan. 30   Accounts Receivable.........................................   154,000
             Sales Revenue...............................................            154,000
          To record a sale on account
          (US$140,000 × $1.10).
```

Assume Bombardier collects from the American customer on March 2, 2010, when the exchange rate has fallen to $1.08. Bombardier receives fewer Canadian dollars than the recorded amount of the receivable and so experiences a foreign-currency transaction loss. The collection entry is

```
Mar. 2    Cash ..................................................................   151,200
          Foreign-Currency Transaction Loss ................     2,800
             Accounts Receivable.....................................            154,000
          To record collection of a receivable
          (US$140,000 × $1.08).
```

KEY POINT

When a subsidiary prepares financial statements in a currency other than Canadian dollars, the subsidiary must translate the financial statements into Canadian dollars for the consolidated financial statements.

Foreign-currency transaction gains and losses are combined for each accounting period. The net amount of gain or loss can be reported as Other Revenue and Expense on the income statement.

Hedging—A Strategy to Avoid Foreign-Currency Transaction Losses

One way for Canadian companies to avoid foreign-currency transaction losses is to insist that international transactions be settled in Canadian dollars. This requirement puts the burden of currency translation on the foreign party. However, such a strategy may alienate customers and decrease sales, or it may cause customers to demand unreasonable credit terms. Another way for a company to protect itself from the effects of fluctuating foreign-currency exchange rates is by hedging.

Hedging means protecting oneself from losing money in one transaction by engaging in a counterbalancing transaction. A Canadian company selling goods to be paid for in Mexican pesos expects to receive a fixed number of pesos in the future. If the peso is losing value, the Canadian company would expect the pesos to be worth fewer dollars than the amount of the receivable—an expected loss situation.

The Canadian company may have accumulated payables stated in a foreign currency in the normal course of its business, such as the amount payable by The Bay to the French supplier. Losses on the receipt of pesos may be approximately offset by gains on the payment of euros to the French supplier. Most companies do not have equal amounts of receivables and payables in foreign currency, so offsetting receivables and payables is imprecise. To obtain a more precise hedge, some companies buy *futures contracts*, which are contracts for foreign currencies to be received in the future. Futures contracts can effectively create a payable to exactly offset a receivable, and vice versa. Many companies that do business internationally use hedging techniques.

Further discussion of foreign-currency and international transactions is beyond the scope of this text and will be covered in more advanced accounting courses.

DID YOU GET IT?

MyAccountingLab

To check your understanding of the material in this Learning Objective, complete these questions. The solutions appear on MyAccountingLab so you can check your progress.

11. In each of the following situations, determine whether the Canadian company will experience a foreign-currency transaction gain or loss, and explain why.

   a. A Canadian company purchased car parts from a German supplier at a price of 200,000 euros. On the date of the credit purchase, the exchange rate of the euro was $1.0891. On the payment date, the exchange rate of the euro is $1.0723. The payment is in euros.

   b. A Canadian company sold merchandise to a Danish company at a price of 500,000 krones. On the date of the credit sale, the exchange rate of the krone was $0.20962. On the day the payment is received in krones, the exchange rate of the krone is $0.21325.

   c. A Canadian company purchased electronics from a Japanese supplier at a price of 1,200,000 yen. On the date of the credit purchase, the exchange rate of the yen was $0.01172. On the payment date, the exchange rate of the yen is $0.01221. The payment is in yen.

   d. A Canadian company sold merchandise to a U.S. company at a price of US$15,000. On the date of the credit sale, the exchange rate of the U.S. dollar was $1.0891. On the day the payment is received in U.S. dollars, the exchange rate of the U.S. dollar is $1.0624.

12. In each of the situations in the previous question, did the Canadian dollar strengthen or weaken against the foreign currency?

13. Suppose Zippy Ltd. sells maple syrup to a British company on May 16. Zippy agrees to accept 80,000 British pounds sterling. On the date of sale, the pound is quoted at $1.7831. Zippy collects half the receivable on June 19, when the pound is worth $1.7614. Then, on July 16, when the price of the pound is $1.7792, Zippy collects the final amount. Journalize these three transactions for Zippy; include an explanation. Overall, did Zippy have a net foreign-currency gain or loss?

The Impact on Accounting for Investments of International Financial Reporting Standards (IFRS)

There are a number of diverse topics included in this chapter that can be roughly categorized as:

OBJECTIVE 7

Identify the impact on accounting for investments of international financial reporting standards (IFRS)

- Investments in shares of stock and bonds that are passive, where there is no significant influence
- Investments in equity securities where there is significant influence
- Joint ventures
- Consolidated financial statements
- Foreign currency transactions

The principal differences between the requirements of GAAP for private enterprises and IFRS to account for each of these items are explored separately below.

There are significant differences between IFRS and GAAP for private enterprises when accounting for passive investments in shares and debt (bonds). While a full discussion of the differences is beyond the scope of this text, the main differences stem from the IFRS requirement that most financial instruments must be measured at fair value (market value). In many cases, determining the fair value can be difficult and costly. Under GAAP for private enterprises, fair value is used to value shares traded in an active market, but if fair value is difficult or impossible to determine, the shares are measured at cost.

Accounting for significantly influenced investments using the equity method is substantially the same under IFRS and GAAP for private enterprises. However, GAAP for private enterprises additionally permits the option of accounting for these types of investments using the cost method, an alternative not available under IFRS.

For companies with a controlling interest, the requirements for preparing consolidated financial statements are essentially the same under GAAP for private enterprises and IFRS. GAAP for private enterprises differs substantially from IFRS, though, allowing a company to either consolidate its subsidiaries or account for them using either the cost or the equity method. Under IFRS, the parent company must consolidate its subsidiaries' financial results.

The principles for accounting for joint ventures using the proportionate consolidation method and equity methods are very similar under IFRS and GAAP for private enterprises. However, IFRS does not give companies the option of using the cost method, as GAAP for private enterprises does.

Accounting for foreign-currency transactions is basically the same under IFRS and GAAP for private enterprises. While the two sets of standards differ somewhat in their requirements for accounting for hedges, discussion of hedges is an advanced topic beyond the scope of this textbook.

DID YOU GET IT?

MyAccountingLab

To check your understanding of the material in this Learning Objective, complete these questions. The solutions appear on MyAccountingLab so you can check your progress.

14. For short-term investments, what is the main difference between IFRS and GAAP for private enterprises?

15. For equity investments where there is significant influence, what is the main difference between IFRS and GAAP for private enterprises?

16. For investments in subsidiaries, what is the major variance between IFRS and GAAP for private enterprises?

As we conclude this chapter, we return to our opening questions: What are the different types of investments a company can have in another company, and why are the investment types important? How do you account for different types of investments? What is consolidation, and how do you perform a simple consolidation? What are foreign-currency transaction gains and losses, and how do you account for them? These questions were answered throughout this chapter. And the following Decision Guidelines provide the answers in a useful summary.

DECISION GUIDELINES — Accounting Method to Use for Each Type of Investment, and Foreign-Currency Transactions

Investment Type	Guidelines
Short-term investment in *shares* or *bonds*	**Accounting Method**
Short-term investment	Fair-value, or market-value, method The change in fair value is an unrealized gain or loss in the non-operating section of the income statement.
Long-term investment: **In shares**	
Investor owns less than 20 percent of investee shares	Fair-value, or market-value, method The change in fair value is an unrealized gain or loss in the non-operating section of the income statement.
Investor owns 20 to 50 percent of investee shares	Equity
Investor owns greater than 50 percent of investee shares	Consolidation
In bonds	
Investment in bonds	Amortized cost

Decision	Guidelines
When should a company record a	
• Foreign-currency transaction gain?	• When it receives foreign currency worth *more* in Canadian dollars than the amount of the receivable recorded earlier • When it pays foreign currency that costs *less* in Canadian dollars than the amount of the payable recorded earlier.
• Foreign-currency transaction loss?	• When it receives foreign currency worth *less* in Canadian dollars than the amount of the receivable recorded earlier. • When it pays foreign currency that costs *more* in Canadian dollars than the amount of the payable recorded earlier.

1. Journalize the following transactions of Canada Corp.:

2009

Nov. 16   Purchased equipment on account for US$40,000 when the exchange rate was $1.07 per U.S. dollar.

27   Sold merchandise on account to a Swiss company for 700,000 Swiss francs. Each Swiss franc is worth $0.81.

Dec. 22   Paid the U.S. company when the U.S. dollar's exchange rate was $1.05.

31   Adjusted for the change in the exchange rate of the Swiss franc. Its current exchange rate is $0.80.

2010

Jan. 4   Collected from the Swiss company. The exchange rate is $0.82.

2. In the 2009 transactions, did the following currencies become stronger or weaker by the end of the year? Did they strengthen or weaken during 2010?

    a. U.S. dollar   b. Swiss franc   c. Canadian dollar

> **Name:** Canada Corp.
> **Industry:** Corporation with international purchases and sales
> **Accounting Period:** Partial years 2009 and 2010

SOLUTIONS

1. Entries for transactions stated in foreign currencies:

2009

Nov. 16	Equipment (40,000 × $1.07)	42,800	
	Accounts Payable		42,800
27	Accounts Receivable (700,000 × $0.81)	567,000	
	Sales Revenue		567,000
Dec. 22	Accounts Payable	42,800	
	Cash (40,000 × $1.05)		42,000
	Foreign-Currency Transaction Gain		800
31	Foreign-Currency Transaction Loss		
	[700,000 × ($0.81 − $0.80)]	7,000	
	Accounts Receivable		7,000

2010

Jan. 4	Cash (700,000 × $0.82)	574,000	
	Accounts Receivable ($567,000 − $7,000)		560,000
	Foreign-Currency Transaction Gain		
	[700,000 × ($0.92 − $0.90)]		14,000

2. During 2009:

    a. U.S. dollar—weaker   b. Swiss franc—weaker   c. Canadian dollar—stronger

During 2010, the Swiss franc strengthened and the Canadian dollar weakened.

> Always use the exchange rates in effect on the date of a transaction. When journalizing the payment or receipt for a foreign-currency transaction, calculate the cash payment or receipt amount first. Then,
> Cash payment > Payable → F-C trans. loss
> Cash payment < Payable → F-C trans. gain
> Cash receipt > Receivable → F-C trans. gain
> Cash receipt < Receivable → F-C trans. loss

> If an exchange rate expressed in Canadian $ declines over time → foreign currency is getting weaker
> If an exchange rate expressed in Canadian $ increases over time → foreign currency is getting stronger

Summary

1. **Account for short-term investments.** Investments are classified as short term or long term. *Short-term investments* are liquid, and, generally, the investor intends to convert them to cash within one year or less, or to use them to pay a current liability. All other investments are *long term*. In all cases, brokerage commissions or fees are expensed immediately—they are not included in the cost or selling price of an investment.

   Different methods are used to account for share investments, depending on the investor's degree of influence over the investee. All investments are recorded initially at *cost*. Short-term investments are accounted for by the fair-value method and are reported on the balance sheet at their fair (current market) value at year end. The change in fair value is an unrealized gain or loss, and is reported in the non-operating section of the company's income statement under "other gains and losses." Dividends or interest received are recorded as income.

2. **Account for long-term share investments.** Long-term investments of less than 20 percent of the investee's shares are also accounted for using the fair-value method. Dividends received are recorded as income. The same as for short-term investments at year end, a long-term share investment is recorded at its fair value. The change in fair value is considered to be an unrealized gain or loss, and is reported in the non-operating section of the company's income statement under "other gains and losses."

3. **Use the equity method to account for investments.** The *equity* method is used to account for investments of 20 to 50 percent of the investee company's shares. Such an investment generally enables the investor to significantly influence the investee's activities. Investee income is recorded by the investor by debiting the Investment account and crediting the Equity-Method Investment Revenue account. The investor records the receipt of dividends from the investee by crediting the Investment account.

4. **Describe and create consolidated financial statements.** Ownership of more than 50 percent of the voting shares creates a *parent–subsidiary* relationship and the *consolidation* method must be used. Because the parent has control over the subsidiary, the subsidiary's financial statements are included in the consolidated statements of the parent company. Two features of consolidation accounting are (1) addition of the parent and subsidiary accounts to prepare the parent's consolidated statements, and (2) elimination of intercompany items. When a parent owns less than 100 percent of the subsidiary's shares, the portion owned by outside investors is called a *non-controlling interest*. Purchase of a controlling interest at a cost greater than the fair value of the subsidiary's net assets creates an intangible asset called *goodwill*. A consolidation work sheet is used to prepare the consolidated financial statements.

5. **Account for investments in bonds.** Long-term investments in bonds are recorded at cost. They are reported at their *amortized cost*, which means the discount or premium is amortized to account more precisely for interest revenue over the period the bonds will be held. The amortization of the discount or premium on a bond investment affects Interest Revenue and the carrying amount of the bonds in the same way as for the company that issued the bonds. At maturity the investor will receive the face value of the bonds.

6. **Describe how foreign-currency exchange rates are determined, and account for foreign-currency transactions.** *International accounting* deals with accounting for business activities across national boundaries. A key issue is the translation of foreign-currency accounts into Canadian dollars, accomplished through a *foreign-currency exchange rate*. Changes in exchange rates cause companies with foreign-currency transactions to experience *foreign-currency transaction gains and losses*.

7. **Identify the impact on accounting for investments of international financial reporting standards (IFRS).** In general, IFRS and GAAP for private enterprises require the same or similar treatment of investments and foreign-currency transactions. In many cases, however, GAAP for private enterprises allows companies more options for accounting for their investments.

SELF-STUDY QUESTIONS

Test your understanding of the chapter by marking the best answer for each of the following questions:

1. Short-term investments are reported on the balance sheet (*p. 877*)
   a. Immediately after cash
   b. Immediately after accounts receivable
   c. Immediately after inventory
   d. Immediately after current assets

2. Byforth Inc. distributes a stock dividend. An investor who owns Byforth Inc. shares as a short-term investment should (*p. 878*)
   a. Debit Short-Term Investments and credit Dividend Revenue for the book value of the shares received in the dividend distribution
   b. Debit Short-Term Investments and credit Dividend Revenue for the market value of the shares received in the dividend distribution

c. Debit Cash and credit Short-Term Investments for the market value of the shares received in the dividend distribution

d. Make a memorandum entry to record the new cost per share of Byforth Inc. shares held

3. Short-term investments are reported at the (*pp. 879–880*)

a. Total cost of the portfolio

b. Total fair value of the portfolio

c. Lower of total cost or total fair value of the portfolio, or lower of cost or fair value on an investment-by-investment basis

d. Total equity value of the portfolio

4. Mulgarvey Corporation owns 30 percent of the voting shares of Turner Inc. Turner Inc. reports net income of $200,000 and declares and pays cash dividends of $80,000. Which method should Mulgarvey Corporation use to account for this investment? (*p. 884*)

a. Cost

b. Fair value

c. Equity

d. Consolidation

5. Refer to the facts of the preceding question. What effect do Turner Inc.'s income and dividends have on Mulgarvey Corporation's net income? (*pp. 884–885*)

a. Increase of $24,000

b. Increase of $36,000

c. Increase of $60,000

d. Increase of $84,000

6. In applying the consolidation method, elimination entries are (*pp. 888–892*)

a. Necessary

b. Required only when the parent has a receivable from or a payable to the subsidiary

c. Required only when there is a minority interest

d. Required only for the preparation of the consolidated balance sheet

7. Parent Corp. reports net income of $200,000. Sub A Ltd., of which Parent Corp. owns 90 percent, reports net income of $80,000, and Sub B Ltd., of which Parent Corp. owns 60 percent, reports net income of $100,000. What is Parent Corp.'s consolidated net income? (*p. 892–893*)

a. $200,000

b. $332,000

c. $335,000

d. $380,000

8. On May 16, the exchange rate of the euro was $1.50. On May 20, the exchange rate is $1.52. Which of the following statements is true? (*p. 898*)

a. The Canadian dollar has risen against the euro.

b. The Canadian dollar has fallen against the euro.

c. The Canadian dollar is weaker than the euro.

d. The Canadian dollar and the euro are equally strong.

9. A strong Canadian dollar encourages (*p. 898*)

a. Travel to Canada by foreigners

b. Purchase of Canadian goods by foreigners

c. Canadians to travel abroad

d. Canadians to save dollars

10. Canadian Furniture Inc. purchased dining room suites from an English supplier at a price of 400,000 British pounds sterling. On the date of the credit purchase, the exchange rate of the British pound was $1.75. On the payment date, the exchange rate of the pound is $1.77. If payment is in pounds, Canadian Furniture experiences (*pp. 898–899*)

a. A foreign-currency transaction gain of $8,000

b. A foreign-currency transaction loss of $8,000

c. Neither a transaction gain nor loss because the debt is paid in Canadian dollars

d. None of the above

Answers to Self-Study Questions

1. a 2. d 3. b 4. c 5. c [$200,000 × 0.30 = $60,000; dividends have no effect on investor net income under the equity method] 6. a 7. b [$200,000 + ($80,000 × 0.90) + ($100,000 × 0.60) = $332,000] 8. b 9. c 10. b [400,000 × ($1.77 − $1.75) = $8,000; a loss since cash payment > payable]

ACCOUNTING VOCABULARY

Consolidated statements (*p. 888*)
Controlling interest (*p. 886*)
Equity method for investments (*p. 884*)
Fair-value method (*p. 877*)
Foreign-currency exchange rate (*p. 897*)
Foreign-currency transaction gain (*p. 898*)
Foreign-currency transaction loss (*p. 898*)
Hedging (*p. 900*)
Long-term investments (*p. 877*)

Majority interest (*p. 886*)
Market-value method (*p. 877*)
Non-controlling interest (*p. 891*)
Parent company (*p. 886*)
Short-term investments (*p. 876*)
Strong currency (*p. 898*)
Subsidiary (*p. 886*)
Weak currency (*p. 898*)

SIMILAR ACCOUNTING TERMS

Controlling interest	Majority interest
Fair-value method	Market-value method
Non-controlling interest	Minority interest
Short-term investments	Marketable securities; Temporary investments

Assignment Material

QUESTIONS

1. How are share prices quoted in the securities market? What is the investor's cost of 1,000 Royal Bank of Canada non-cumulative preferred shares at $20.50 with a brokerage commission of $300?

2. What distinguishes a short-term investment in shares from a long-term investment in shares?

3. Show the positions of short-term investments and long-term investments on the balance sheet.

4. At the end of a fiscal period, all equity investments that are traded on public stock exchanges must be re-valued on the balance to their market value. Does this policy provide better information for the investor?

5. How does an investor record the receipt of a cash dividend on an investment accounted for by the fair-value method? How does this investor record receipt of a stock dividend?

6. An investor paid $30,000 for 1,000 common shares and later that same year received a 10-percent stock dividend. Compute the gain or loss on sale of 500 common shares for $15,000 before the year end.

7. Are the short-term and long-term equity investment portfolios mixed, or are they kept separate?

8. When is an investment accounted for by the equity method? Outline how to apply the equity method. Include in your answer how to record the purchase of the investment, the investor's proportion of the investee's net income, and receipt of a cash dividend from the investee. Indicate how a gain or loss on the sale of the investment would be measured.

9. Identify three transactions that cause debits or credits to an equity-method investment account.

10. What are two special features of the consolidation method for investments?

11. Why are intercompany items eliminated from consolidated financial statements? Name two intercompany items that are eliminated.

12. Name the account that expresses the excess of cost of an investment over the fair market value of the sub-sidiary's net assets. What type of account is this, and where in the financial statements is it reported?

13. When a parent company buys more than 50 percent but less than 100 percent of a subsidiary's shares, a certain type of equity is created. What is it called and how do most companies report it?

14. How would you measure the net income of a parent company with three subsidiaries? Assume that two subsidiaries are wholly (100 percent) owned and that the parent owns 60 percent of the third subsidiary.

15. Jane Mathers purchases Canadian Utilities Inc. bonds as a long-term investment. Suppose the face amount of the bonds is $200,000 and the purchase price is 101.30. The bonds pay interest at the stated annual rate of 8 percent. How much did Mathers pay for the bonds? How much principal will Mathers collect at maturity?

16. The purchase date of the bond investment in the preceding question was August 1, 2010. The bonds pay semiannual interest on January 31 and July 31. How much cash interest will Mathers earn during the year ended December 31, 2010?

17. Mentacos Inc. purchased inventory from a French company, agreeing to pay 150,000 euros. On the purchase date, the euro was quoted at $1.55. When Mentacos Inc. paid the debt, the price of a euro was $1.57. What account does Mentacos Inc. debit for the $3,000 difference between the cost of the inventory and the amount of cash paid?

18. Which of the following situations results in a foreign-currency transaction gain for a Canadian business? Which situation results in a loss?

    a. Credit purchase denominated in pesos, followed by weakness in the peso

    b. Credit purchase denominated in pesos, followed by weakness in the dollar

    c. Credit sale denominated in pesos, followed by weakness in the peso

    d. Credit sale denominated in pesos, followed by weakness in the dollar

Starter 16–1 Compute the cost of each of the following short-term investments. Round to the nearest dollar.

a. 500 shares of Grey Ltd. at $16.50 per share. Brokerage fees were $175.

b. 600 shares of Red Corp. at $87.00 per share. Red Corp. pays a cash dividend of $0.60 per year. Brokerage fees were $550.

c. 1,000 shares of White Inc. at $55.90 per share. Brokerage fees were $560.

d. 70 shares of Tangerine Ltd. at $35.50 per share. Brokerage fees were $150.

Computing the cost of an investment in shares

① ②

a. $8,250
b. $52,200

Starter 16–2 Baines Corp. purchased 1,000 common shares in each of three companies:

a. Investment in Cullen Corp. to be sold within the next 9 to 12 months.

b. Investment in Gerson Canada Ltd. to be sold within the next 90 days.

c. Investment in Arnold Ltd. to be sold within the next two years.

Classify each investment as a current asset or a long-term asset. None of these investments is subject to significant influence.

Classifying investments as short term or long term

① ②

Starter 16–3 Heat Publishing Ltd. completed the following transactions during 2009 and 2010.

2009

Dec. 6   Purchased 1,000 shares of Hope Mines Inc. at a price of $42.50 per share, intending to sell the investment within three months. Brokerage fees were $350.

     23   Received a cash dividend of $1.10 per share on the Hope Mines Inc. shares.

     31   Adjusted the investment to its fair value of $45.00 per share.

2010

Jan. 27   Sold the Hope Mines Inc. shares for $46.00 per share, less brokerage fees of $370.

Journalize Heat Publishing Ltd.'s investment transactions. Explanations are not required.

Accounting for a short-term investment

①

Jan 27, 2010, gain on sale $1,000

Starter 16–4 McBain Electronics completed the following investment transactions during 2009 and 2010.

2009

Dec. 12   Purchased 1,500 shares of Delta Logistics Ltd. at a price of $62.00 per share, intending to sell the investment within the next year. Commissions were $510.

     21   Received a cash dividend of $0.48 per share on the Delta Logistics Ltd. shares.

     31   Adjusted the investment to its fair value of $60.50 per share.

2010

Jan. 16   Sold the Delta Logistics Ltd. shares for $59.00 per share, less commissions of $490.

1. Classify McBain's investment as short term or long term.
2. Journalize McBain's investment transactions. Explanations are not required.

Accounting for a short-term investment

①

2. Jan. 16, 2010, loss on sale $2,250

Starter 16–5 Grist Ltd. buys 2,000 of the 100,000 shares of Efron Inc., paying $35.00 per share. Suppose Efron distributes a 10-percent stock dividend. Later the same year, Grist Ltd. sells the Efron shares for $30.00 per share. Disregard commissions on the purchase and sale.

1. Compute Grist Ltd.'s new cost per share after receiving the stock dividend.
2. Compute Grist Ltd.'s gain or loss on the sale of this long-term investment.

Measuring gain or loss on the sale of a share investment after receiving a stock dividend

①

2. Loss on sale $4,000

Starter 16–6 Marsland Inc. completed these long-term investment transactions during 2010. Disregard commissions.

2010

Jan. 14   Purchased 500 shares of Crew Ltd., paying $41.00 per share. Marsland intends to hold the investment for the indefinite future.

Aug. 22   Received a cash dividend of $3.28 per share on the Crew Ltd. shares.

Dec. 31   Adjusted the Crew Ltd. investment to its current fair value of $20,750.

1. Journalize Marsland's investment transactions. Explanations are not required. Marsland Inc. exerts no significant influence on Crew Ltd.

Accounting for a long-term investment's unrealized gain or loss

②

2. Unrealized gain $250

2. Show how to report the investment and any unrealized gain or loss on Marsland's balance sheet at December 31, 2010.

Accounting for the sale of a
long-term investment

②

1. Gain on sale $750

Starter 16–7 Use the data given in Starter 16–6. On August 4, 2011, Marsland Inc. sold its investment in Crew Ltd. for $43.00 per share. Disregard commissions.

1. Journalize the sale. No explanation is required.
2. How does the gain or loss that you recorded differ from the gain or loss that was recorded at December 31, 2010 (in Starter 16–6)?

Accounting for a 40-percent
investment in another company

③

3. Bal. $5,400,000

Starter 16–8 Suppose on January 6, 2010, Ling Corp. paid $5,000,000 for its 40-percent investment in True World Inc. Assume True World earned net income of $1,800,000 and paid cash dividends of $800,000 during 2010. Disregard commissions.

1. What method should Ling Corp. use to account for the investment in True World Inc.? Give your reason.
2. Journalize these three transactions on the books of Ling Corp. Include an explanation for each entry.
3. Post to the Investment in True World Inc. Common Shares T-account. What is its balance after all the transactions are posted?

Understanding consolidated
financial statements

④

Starter 16–9 Answer these questions about consolidation accounting:

1. Define "parent company." Define "subsidiary."
2. Which company's name appears on the consolidated financial statements? How much of the subsidiary's shares must the parent own before reporting consolidated statements?
3. How do consolidated financial statements differ from the financial statements of a single company?

Working with a bond investment

⑤

3. Annual interest revenue
$132,000

Starter 16–10 Nagel Ltd. owns vast amounts of corporate bonds. Suppose the company buys $2,000,000 of Yuzawa Corporation bonds on January 2, 2010 at a price of 97. The Yuzawa bonds pay cash interest at the annual rate of 6 percent and mature on December 31, 2014.

1. How much did Nagel Ltd. pay to purchase the bond investment? How much will Nagel Ltd. collect when the bond investment matures?
2. How much cash interest will Nagel Ltd. receive each year from Yuzawa Corporation?
3. Compute Nagel Ltd.'s annual interest revenue on this bond investment. Use the straight-line method to amortize the discount on the investment.

Recording bond investment
transactions

⑤

b. Cash Interest received
$120,000

Starter 16–11 Return to Starter 16–10, the Nagel Ltd. investment in Yuzawa Corporation bonds. Journalize the following transactions on Nagel Ltd.'s books, along with an explanation:

a. Purchase of the bond investment on January 2, 2010. As Nagel Ltd. expects to hold the investment to maturity, it is classified as a long-term investment.
b. Receipt of the annual cash interest on December 31, 2010.
c. Amortization of the discount on December 31, 2010.
d. Collection of the investment's face value at its maturity date on December 31, 2014. (Interest and amortization of discount for 2014 have already been recorded, so you may ignore these entries.)

Accounting for transactions
stated in a foreign currency

⑥

Net foreign-currency gain
$10,000

Starter 16–12 Suppose Fletcher Ltd. sells athletic shoes to a German company on March 14. Fletcher agrees to accept 2,000,000 euros. On the date of sale, the euro is quoted at $1.56. Fletcher collects half the receivable on April 19, when the euro is worth $1.55. Then, on May 10, when the price of the euro is $1.58, Fletcher collects the final amount.

Journalize these three transactions for Fletcher; include an explanation. Overall, did Fletcher have a net foreign-currency gain or loss?

EXERCISES

Classifying equity investments

① ②

Exercise 16–1

Cummins Corp. reports its annual financial results on June 30 each year. Cummins Corp. purchased 1,000 shares in each of three companies. Classify each investment as a short-term or long-term investment.

a. Investment to be sold within the next 9 to 12 months.
b. Investment to be sold within the next 90 days.
c. Investment to be sold within the next two years.

Exercise 16–2

Journalize the following investment transactions of Russell Corp.:

Accounting for a short-term investment

①

June 14, 2011 gain on sale
$3,300

2010

Nov.	6	Purchased 1,200 common shares of Aveda Corporation at $77.00 per share, with brokerage commission of $2,000. The shares will be sold early in 2011.
	30	Received a cash dividend of $3.85 per share on the Aveda Corporation investment.
Dec.	31	The share price for Aveda Corporation's common shares was $76.25 on December 31, 2010.

2011

Jun.	14	Sold the Aveda Corporation shares for $79.00 per share. Brokerage fees were $1,800.

Exercise 16–3

ATCO Ltd. reported the following information in the notes accompanying its 2008 financial statements:

Reporting investments at fair value

①

Current Assets	(dollars in millions)
Short-term investments (fair value)	$59.7

Assume that the carrying value of ATCO's short-term investments is $55 million prior to the year-end adjustment to fair value.

Required Write a note to identify the method used to report short-term investments, and to disclose cost and fair value. Show the journal entry that would have been made by ATCO if you determine that a journal entry was needed at year end.

Exercise 16–4

Suppose Carlton Ltd. completed the following investment transactions in 2010 and 2011:

Accounting for a short-term investment

①

Jan. 20, 2011 gain on sale
$1,000

2010

Nov.	6	Purchased 2,000 McGill Corporation common shares for $60,000. Carlton plans to sell the shares in the near future to meet its operating-cash-flow requirements. Commissions on the purchase were $800.
	30	Received a quarterly cash dividend of $1.50 per share on the McGill Corporation shares.
Dec.	31	Current fair value of the McGill common shares is $62,000.

2011

Jan.	20	Sold the McGill Corporation shares for $63,000, less commissions on the sale of $900.

Required

1. Make the entries to record Carlton Ltd.'s investment transactions. Explanations are not required.
2. Show how Carlton Ltd. would report its investment in the McGill Corporation shares on the balance sheet at December 31, 2010.

Exercise 16–5

Journalize the following investment transactions of VenturesEast Inc.:

Journalizing transactions for a long-term investment

②

Dec. 4, 2010 gain on sale
$6,120

2010

Aug.	6	Purchased 900 Rhodes Corporation common shares as a long-term investment, paying $90.00 per share. VenturesEast Inc. exerts no significant influence on Rhodes Corporation. Commissions on the purchase were $900.
Sept.	12	Received cash dividends of $1.60 per share on the Rhodes Corporation investment.
Nov.	23	Received 90 Rhodes Corporation common shares in a 10-percent stock dividend.
Dec.	4	Unexpectedly sold all the Rhodes Corporation shares for $88.00 per share, less commissions on the sale of $750.

Journalizing transactions under
the equity method

(3)

Exercise 16–6

Fairfax Financial Holdings Ltd., introduced in the chapter-opening story, owns equity-method investments in several companies. Suppose Fairfax paid $12,000,000 to acquire a 40-percent investment in First Financial Services Ltd. Further, assume First Financial Services Ltd. reported net income of $1,860,000 for the first year and declared and paid cash dividends of $1,100,000. Record the following entries in Fairfax's general journal: (a) purchase of the investment, (b) Fairfax's proportion of First Financial Services Ltd.'s net income, and (c) receipt of the cash dividends. Disregard commissions on the purchase.

Recording equity-method
transactions in the accounts

(3)

Gain on sale $1,196,000

Exercise 16–7

Using the information from Exercise 16–6, calculate the balance in the Investment in First Financial Services Ltd. Common Shares account. Assume that after all the above transactions took place, Fairfax sold its entire investment in First Financial Services Ltd. common shares for $13,500,000 cash. Journalize the sale of the investment. Disregard commissions on sale.

Applying the appropriate
accounting method for
investments

(2) (3)

Exercise 16–8

Windsor Corporation paid $760,000 for a 35-percent investment in the common shares of Ventura Systems Inc. For the first year, Ventura Systems Inc. reported net income of $360,000 and at year end declared and paid cash dividends of $105,000. On the balance sheet date, the fair value of Windsor Corporation's investment in Ventura Systems Inc. shares was $780,000.

Required

1. Which method is appropriate for Windsor Corporation to use in accounting for its investment in Ventura Systems Inc.? Why?

2. Show everything that Windsor Corporation would report for the investment and any investment revenue in its year-end financial statements.

3. What role does the fair value of the investment play in this situation?

Excel Spreadsheet Template

Completing a consolidation
work sheet

(4)

Total consolidated assets
$7,942,000

Exercise 16–9

Penfold Ltd. owns all the common shares of Simmons Ltd. Prepare a consolidation work sheet, using the following information. Assume that the fair value of the assets and liabilities of Simmons Ltd. are equal to their book values.

Assets	Penfold Ltd.	Simmons Ltd.
Cash	$ 225,000	$ 55,000
Accounts receivable, net	360,000	264,000
Note receivable from Simmons Ltd.	66,000	—
Inventory	258,000	159,000
Investment in Simmons Ltd.	2,350,000	—
Property, plant, and equipment, net	3,600,000	2,900,000
Total	$6,859,000	$3,378,000
Liabilities and Shareholders' Equity		
Accounts payable	$ 357,000	$ 180,000
Notes payable	462,000	759,000
Other liabilities	78,000	210,000
Common shares	1,980,000	660,000
Retained earnings	3,982,000	1,569,000
Total	$6,859,000	$3,378,000

Completing a consolidation
work sheet with non-controlling
interest

(4)

Total consolidated assets
$2,086,800

Exercise 16–10

Petticoat Holdings Ltd. owns an 80-percent interest in Shorthouse Inc. Prepare a consolidation work sheet using the information below. Assume that the fair values of Shorthouse Inc.'s assets and liabilities are equal to their book values.

	Petticoat Holdings Ltd.	Shorthouse Inc.
Assets		
Cash	$ 96,000	$ 36,000
Accounts receivable, net	210,000	144,000
Note receivable from Shorthouse Inc.	60,000	—
Inventory...	246,000	216,000
Investment in Shorthouse Inc.	228,000	—
Property, plant, and equipment, net	720,000	312,000
Other assets..	48,000	42,000
Total	$1,608,000	$750,000
Liabilities and Shareholders' Equity		
Accounts payable......................................	$ 108,000	$ 66,000
Notes payable..	120,000	96,000
Other liabilities..	204,000	324,000
Non-controlling interest..............................	—	—
Common shares..	780,000	204,000
Retained earnings	396,000	60,000
Total	$1,608,000	$750,000

Exercise 16–11

Working with a bond investment

(5)

4. Annual interest revenue $312,000

Summit Securities Ltd. has a large investment in corporate bonds. Suppose Summit Securities Ltd. buys $6,000,000 of Government of Alberta bonds at a price of 98. The Government of Alberta bonds pay cash interest at the annual rate of 5.0 percent and mature in 10 years. Summit Securities Ltd. plans to hold the bonds until maturity.

1. How much did Summit Securities Ltd. pay to purchase the bond investment? How much will Summit Securities Ltd. collect when the bond investment matures?

2. How much cash interest will Summit Securities Ltd. receive each year from the Government of Alberta?

3. Will Summit Securities Ltd.'s annual interest revenue on the bond investment be more or less than the amount of cash interest received each year? Give your reason.

4. Compute Summit Securities Ltd.'s annual interest on this bond investment. Use the straight-line method to amortize the discount on the investment.

Exercise 16–12

Recording bond investment transactions

(5)

2. Dec. 31, 2010 bond discount amort. amount $97

On March 31, 2010, Kerr Corp. paid 98.25 for 8-percent bonds of Quest Limited as an investment. The maturity value of the bonds is $100,000 at September 30, 2014; they pay interest on March 31 and September 30. At December 31, 2010, the bonds' market value is 99.25. The company plans to hold the bonds until they mature.

Required

1. How should Kerr Corp. account for the bonds?

2. Using the straight-line method of amortizing the discount, journalize all transactions on the bonds for 2010.

3. Show how the investment would be reported by Kerr Corp. on the balance sheet at December 31, 2010.

Exercise 16–13

Journalizing foreign-currency transactions

(6)

Dec. 31, 2010, foreign-currency transaction loss $2,400

Journalize the following foreign-currency transactions for Knight Import Inc.:

2010
Nov. 17   Purchased goods on account from a Japanese company. The price was 500,000 yen, and the exchange rate of the yen was $0.0117.
Dec. 16   Paid the Japanese supplier when the exchange rate was $0.0120.
     19   Sold merchandise on account to a French company at a price of 80,000 euros. The exchange rate was $1.57.
     31   Adjusted for the decrease in the value of the euro, which had an exchange rate of $1.54.

2011
Jan. 14   Collected from the French company. The exchange rate was $1.58.

Exercise 16–14

Investment transactions

① ② ③ ⑤

2. Dec. 11, 2010 balance,
$59,000

After issuing bonds in Chapter 15, Haupt Consulting Corporation has some excess cash on hand. Carl Haupt, the Corporation's major shareholder, intends to invest some of the cash for different time periods to get better returns than from the bank and to have cash available when needed to expand the business into a new market. Assume Haupt Consulting Corporation completed the following investment transactions:

2011

Apr. 15 Purchased 300 common shares of Canadian Tire Corporation, Limited for $74.00 per share. Carl Haupt intends to hold this investment for less than a year. He thinks the share value will increase and knows Haupt Consulting will need the cash for operations in less than a year.

Jun. 2 Purchased 2,000 of the 6,000 common shares of Landers Consulting Ltd. at a cost of $40,000. Landers Consulting is a company formed by a colleague of Haupt, so Haupt hopes the investment will lead to future business opportunities for Haupt Consulting.

15 Purchased $10,000 of 6-percent, four-year bonds of Consulting Suppliers Inc. at 115. Haupt intends to hold these to maturity since the effective interest rate is still better than other investments he assessed.

Jul. 1 Received the quarterly cash dividend of $0.05 per share on the Canadian Tire investment.

Dec. 10 Received an annual dividend of $0.50 per share from Landers Consulting Ltd. Also received word that at November 30, Landers' year end, net income was $60,000.

15 Received semiannual interest of $300 on the Consulting Suppliers Inc. bonds. Amortized the premium using the straight-line method.

Required

1. Record the transactions in the general journal of Haupt Consulting Corporation. Disregard any commissions on purchases and sales of investments.
2. Post entries to the Investment in Landers Consulting Ltd. Common Shares T-account. Determine its balance at December 10, 2011 after the transaction shown on that date.

CHALLENGE EXERCISE

Exercise 16–15

Analyzing long-term investments

③

2010 dividends $640

Canfor Corporation is a major integrated forest products company based in Vancouver. Suppose Canfor's financial statements reported the following items for affiliated companies whose shares Canfor owns in various percentages between 20 and 50 percent:

	(In thousands of dollars)	
	2010	2009
Balance Sheet (adapted)		
Equity-method investments	$6,950	$6,600
Cash Flow Statement		
Increase in equity-method investments	350	325
Income Statement		
Equity earnings in affiliates	640	400

Assume no sales of equity-method investments during 2009 or 2010.

Required

Prepare a T-Account for Equity-Method Investments to determine the amount of dividends Canfor Corporation received from investee companies during 2010. The company's year end is December 31. Show your calculations.

BEYOND THE NUMBERS

Beyond the Numbers 16–1

Analyzing long-term investments

④

Lynn Jackson inherited some investments, and she has received the annual reports of the companies in which the funds are invested. The financial statements of the companies are puzzling to Jackson, and she asks you the following questions:

a. The companies label their financial statements as *consolidated* balance sheet, *consolidated* income statement, and so on. What are consolidated financial statements?

b. Notes to the statements indicate that "certain intercompany transactions, loans, and other accounts have been eliminated in preparing the consolidated financial statements." Why does a company eliminate transactions, loans, and accounts? Jackson states that she thought a transaction was a transaction and that a loan obligated a company to pay real money. She wonders if the company is juggling the books to defraud Canada Revenue Agency.

c. The balance sheet lists the asset Goodwill. What is goodwill? Does this mean that the company's shares have increased in value?

Required

Respond to each of Lynn Jackson's questions.

ETHICAL ISSUE

Sherman Inc. owns 18 percent of the voting shares of Arbor Corporation. The remainder of the Arbor Corporation shares are held by numerous investors with small holdings. Ken Tung, president of Sherman Inc. and a member of Arbor Corporation's Board of Directors, heavily influences Arbor Corporation's policies.

Under the fair-value method of accounting for investments, Sherman Inc.'s net income increases if or when it receives dividends from Arbor Corporation. Sherman Inc. pays Mr. Tung, as president, a bonus computed as a percentage of Sherman Inc.'s net income. Therefore, Tung can control his personal bonus to a certain extent by influencing Arbor Corporation's dividends.

Sherman Inc. has a bad year in 2010, and corporate income is low. Tung uses his power to have Arbor Corporation pay a large cash dividend. This action requires Arbor Corporation to borrow a substantial sum one month later to pay operating costs.

Required

1. In getting Arbor Corporation to pay the large cash dividend, is Tung acting within his authority as a member of the Arbor Corporation Board of Directors? Are Tung's actions ethical? Whom can his actions harm?

2. Discuss how using the equity method of accounting for investments would decrease Tung's potential for manipulating his bonus.

PROBLEMS (GROUP A)

MyAccountingLab All questions in this section appear in MyAccountingLab.

Problem 16–1A

Journalizing transactions under the fair-value and equity methods

① ② ③

Feb. 6, 2011 loss on sale $24,171

Reynolds Corp., the conglomerate, owns numerous investments in the shares of other companies. Assume Reynolds Corp. completed the following investment transactions:

2010

May 1   Purchased 12,000 common shares (total issued and outstanding common shares, 50,000) of Silverstorm Corp. at a cost of $960,000. Commissions on the purchase were $20,000.

Jul. 2   Purchased 2,000 Silverstorm Corp. common shares at a cost of $164,000. Commissions on the purchase were $1,500.

Sept. 15   Received semiannual cash dividend of $3.20 per share on the Silverstorm Corp. investment.

Oct. 12   Purchased 1,000 Brighton Ltd. common shares as a short-term investment, paying $32.00 per share plus brokerage commission of $1,000.

Dec.	14	Received semiannual cash dividend of $1.60 per share on the Brighton Ltd. investment.
	31	Received annual report from Silverstorm Corp. Net income for the year was $900,000. Of this amount, Reynolds Corp.'s proportion is 28 percent. The current market value for 1,000 Brighton Ltd. shares is $31,000.
2011		
Feb.	6	Sold 2,000 Silverstorm Corp. shares for cash of $166,000, less commissions of $1,550.

Required

Record the transactions in the general journal of Reynolds Corp.; the company's year end is December 31.

Applying the fair-value method
and the equity method

① ② ③

2. Dec. 31, 2010 balance
$3,395,000

Problem 16–2A

The balance sheet of Rutherford Inc. recently included:

Investments in significantly
influenced and other companies $2,500,000

Rutherford Inc. included its short-term investments among the current assets; the investments described above were long-term. Assume the company completed the following investment transactions during 2010:

Mar.	3	Purchased 8,000 common shares as a short-term investment, paying $25.00 per share plus brokerage commission of $1,500.
	4	Purchased additional shares in a company that is significantly influenced by Rutherford Inc. at a cost of $600,000 plus brokerage commission of $4,500.
May	14	Received semiannual cash dividend of $1.70 per share on the short-term investment purchased March 3.
Jun.	15	Received cash dividend of $75,000 from a significantly influenced company.
Aug.	28	Sold the short-term investment (purchased on March 3) for $24.00 per share, less brokerage commission of $1,000.
Oct.	24	Purchased other short-term investments for $275,000, plus brokerage commission of $5,000.
Dec.	15	Received cash dividend of $50,000 from a significantly influenced company.
	31	Received annual reports from significantly influenced companies. Their total net income for the year was $1,400,000. Of this amount, Rutherford Inc.'s proportion is 30 percent.

Required

1. Record the transactions in the general journal of Rutherford Inc.

2. Post entries to the Investments in Significantly Influenced and Other Companies T-account, and determine its balance at December 31, 2010.

3. Assume the beginning balance of Short-Term Investments was at a cost of $250,000. Post entries to the Short-Term Investments T-account and determine its balance at December 31, 2010.

4. Assuming the market value of the short-term investment portfolio is $510,000 at December 31, 2010, show how Rutherford Inc. would report short-term investments and investments in significantly influenced and other companies on the December 31, 2010 balance sheet. Use the following format:

Cash..	$XXX
Short-term investments, at fair value...	☐
Accounts receivable (net)..	XXX
Total current assets	XXX
Investments in significantly influenced and other companies	☐

Problem 16–3A

Pluto Corp. paid $750,000 to acquire all the common shares of Saturn Inc., and Saturn Inc. owes Pluto Corp. $170,000 on a note payable. The fair market value of Saturn Inc.'s net assets equalled the book value. Immediately after the purchase on May 31, 2010, the two companies' balance sheets were as follows:

Excel Spreadsheet Template

Preparing a consolidated balance sheet; goodwill; no non-controlling interest

④

Total consolidated assets $2,420,000

	Pluto Corp.	Saturn Inc.
Assets		
Cash	$ 60,000	$ 100,000
Accounts receivable, net	210,000	150,000
Note receivable from Saturn Inc.	170,000	—
Inventory	300,000	440,000
Investment in Saturn Inc.	750,000	—
Property, plant, and equipment, net	600,000	500,000
Total	$2,090,000	$1,190,000
Liabilities and Shareholders' Equity		
Accounts payable	$ 250,000	$ 40,000
Notes payable	400,000	210,000
Note payable to Pluto Corp.	—	170,000
Other liabilities	156,000	80,000
Common shares	800,000	500,000
Retained earnings	484,000	190,000
Total	$2,090,000	$1,190,000

Required

Prepare a consolidation work sheet.

Problem 16–4A

On July 18, 2010, Peterborough Holdings Ltd. paid $1,920,000 to purchase 90 percent of the common shares of Sheridan Inc., and Sheridan Inc. owes Peterborough Holdings Ltd. $280,000 on a note payable. All historical cost amounts are equal to their fair market value on July 18, 2010. Immediately after the purchase, the two companies' balance sheets were as follows:

Excel Spreadsheet Template

Preparing a consolidated balance sheet with goodwill and non-controlling interest

④

Total consolidated assets $8,299,600

	Peterborough Holdings Ltd.	Sheridan Inc.
Assets		
Cash	$ 200,000	$ 340,000
Accounts receivable, net	720,000	480,000
Note receivable from Sheridan Inc.	280,000	—
Inventory	1,480,000	960,000
Investment in Sheridan Inc.	1,920,000	—
Property, plant, and equipment, net	2,150,000	1,540,000
Goodwill	—	—
Total	$6,750,000	$3,320,000
Liabilities and Shareholders' Equity		
Accounts payable	$1,060,000	$ 680,000
Notes payable	1,680,000	320,000
Note payable to Peterborough Holdings Ltd.	—	280,000
Other liabilities	260,000	384,000
Common shares	1,540,000	1,060,000
Retained earnings	2,210,000	596,000
Total	$6,750,000	$3,320,000

Required

Prepare a consolidation work sheet.

Problem 16–5A

Accounting for a long-term
bond investment purchased at
a discount

(5)

2. Carrying value $1,019,500

Financial institutions such as insurance companies and pension plans hold large quantities of bond investments. Suppose Sun Life Insurance Company purchases $1,000,000 of 6.00 percent bonds of Hydro-Québec at 102.00 on July 1, 2010. These bonds pay interest on January 1 and July 1 each year. They mature on July 1, 2030. At December 31, 2010, the market price of the bonds is 101.00. Sun Life plans to hold these bonds to maturity. Disregard commissions.

Required

1. Journalize Sun Life's purchase of the bonds as a long-term investment in bonds on July 1, 2010 and accrual of interest revenue and amortization of the discount for six months at December 31, 2010. Assume the straight-line method is appropriate for amortizing the discount.

2. Calculate the carrying value of the Hydro-Québec bonds at December 31, 2010.

Problem 16–6A

Computing the cost of a bond
investment and journalizing
its transactions using the
effective-interest method of
amortizing a discount

(5)

Carrying amount at Dec. 31,
2011, $651,863

On December 31, 2010, when the market interest rate is 6 percent, an investor purchases $700,000 of Solar Ltd. 10-year, 5-percent bonds at issuance for $647,929. Interest is paid semi-annually. Assume that the investor plans to hold the investment to maturity. Disregard commissions.

Required

Prepare a schedule for amortizing the discount on the bond investment through December 31, 2011. The investor uses the effective-interest amortization method. Use Exhibit 15-4 on page 826 as a guide. Journalize the purchase on December 31, 2010, the first semiannual interest receipt on June 30, 2011, and the year-end interest receipt on December 31, 2011.

Problem 16–7A

Journalizing foreign-currency
transactions and reporting the
transaction gain or loss

(6)

1. Foreign-currency transaction
loss at Dec. 31, 2010, $6,700

Planet Corporation completed the following transactions:

2010
Dec. 1 Sold equipment on account to a Japanese company for $45,000. The exchange rate of the Japanese yen is $0.0113, and the Japanese company agrees to pay in Canadian dollars.
10 Purchased supplies on account from a U.S. company at a price of US$125,000. The exchange rate of the U.S. dollar is $1.08, and payment will be in U.S. dollars.
17 Sold equipment on account to an English firm for 210,000 British pounds. Payment will be in pounds, and the exchange rate of the pound is $1.61.
22 Collected from the Japanese company. The exchange rate of the yen has not changed since December 1.
31 Adjusted the accounts for changes in foreign-currency exchange rates. Current rates: U.S. dollar, $1.10; British pound, $1.59.

2011
Jan. 18 Paid the U.S. company. The exchange rate of the U.S. dollar is $1.09.
24 Collected from the English firm. The exchange rate of the British pound is $1.63.

Required

1. Record these transactions in Planet Corporation's general journal, and show how to report the transaction gain or loss on the income statement for the fiscal year ended December 31, 2010.

2. How will what you have learned in this problem help you structure international transactions?

Problem 16–8A

Accounting for short-term
investments using the fair-value
method and long-term
investments in bonds

(1) (5)

Dec. 31, 2010 fair-value valuation allowance $125,727

Friedman Holdings Ltd. had the following short-term investments in marketable securities at fair value at December 31, 2009:

Alberta Energy Co.	$300,000
Finning Ltd.	180,000
Canadian National Railway	275,000
Total short-term investments......................	$755,000

Friedman Holdings Ltd. had the following investment transactions during 2010:

2010

Jan. 5   Purchased 5,000 shares (2 percent) of CFG Ltd. as a short-term investment. The shares were purchased at $51.00 and the commission was $2,500.

     31   CFG Ltd. reported net income of $7,000,000 and declared a cash dividend of $2,100,000.

Feb. 15   Received $42,000 from CFG Ltd. as a cash dividend.

Apr. 1   Purchased $500,000 (face value) of bonds at 99 as a long-term investment. The bonds pay 5 percent interest (2.5 percent semiannually) on October 1 and April 1. Friedman Holdings Ltd. plans to hold the bonds until maturity in two years.

Aug. 31   Received a 10-percent stock dividend from CFG Ltd.

Oct. 1   Received the interest on the bonds.

Nov. 1   CFG Ltd. declared and distributed a 2-for-1 stock split.

Dec. 15   Sold 4,000 shares of CFG Ltd. for $28.00 per share and the commission was $1,500.

     31   Recorded the adjustment for accrued interest on the bonds.

     31   The fair values of the investments were:

Alberta Energy Co.	$ 280,000
Finning Ltd.	185,000
Canadian National Railway	290,000
CFG Ltd.	288,000
Total short-term investments......................	$1,043,000

Required

Prepare the general journal entries required to record the transactions of 2010.

Problem 16–9A

Parker Corp. had the following investment transactions:

2010

Jan. 14   Parker Corp. purchased 20,000 (25 percent) of Jarvis Ltd. common shares as a long-term investment. The shares were purchased for $62.00.

May   1   Purchased US$600,000 (face value) of UGG Ltd. bonds at 100 as a long-term investment. The bonds pay interest of 6 percent (3 percent semiannually) each May 1 and November 1, and mature in five years. The exchange rate at the time of the transaction was $1.06 Canadian.

Jun. 20   Received 2,000 Jarvis Ltd. common shares as a 10-percent stock dividend.

Oct. 1   Jarvis Ltd. declared and distributed a 3-for-1 common stock split.

Nov. 1   Received the interest on the UGG bonds when the exchange rate was $1.05.

Dec. 20   Sold 10,000 Jarvis Ltd. common shares at $24.00.

     31   Jarvis Ltd. reported net income of $750,000 and declared and paid a dividend of $190,000.

     31   Adjusted for the accrued interest on the UGG Ltd. bonds. The exchange rate was $1.09. The current value of the bonds is 101.50 (U.S. dollars). Parker Corp.'s year end is December 31.

2011

May   1   Received the interest on the UGG Ltd. bonds when the exchange rate was $1.07.

Accounting for share investments using the equity method; accounting for investments in bonds; and accounting for transactions stated in a foreign currency

③ ⑤ ⑥

Dec. 20, 2010 gain on sale of investment $52,100

Required

Prepare the general journal entries required to record these transactions. Disregard commissions.

Journalizing transactions under the fair-value and equity methods

(1) (2) (3)

Problem 16-1B

Circle Six Investments Ltd. owns numerous investments in the shares of other companies. Assume Circle Six Investments Ltd. completed the following investment transactions:

2010

Feb.	12	Purchased 30,000 (total issued and outstanding common shares, 120,000) common shares of Baines Mfg. Ltd. at a cost of $2,550,000. Commissions on the purchase were $25,000.
Jul.	2	Purchased 6,000 additional Baines Mfg. Ltd. common shares at a cost of $88.00 per share. Commissions on the purchase were $4,000.
Aug.	9	Received the annual cash dividend of $7.00 per share on the Baines Mfg. Ltd. investment.
Oct.	16	Purchased 2,000 Mylora Ltd. common shares as a short-term investment, paying $65.00 per share plus brokerage commission of $2,100.
Nov.	30	Received the semiannual cash dividend of $2.50 per share on the Mylora Ltd. investment.
Dec.	31	Received the annual report from Baines Mfg. Ltd. Net income for the year was $1,160,000. Of this amount, Circle Six Investments Ltd.'s proportion is 30 percent.
	31	The current value of the Mylora shares is $140,000.

2011

Jan.	14	Sold 5,000 Baines Mfg. Ltd. shares for $460,000, less commissions of $2,800.

Required

Record the transactions in the general journal of Circle Six Investments Ltd. The company's year end is December 31.

Applying the fair-value method and the equity method

(1) (2) (3)

Problem 16-2B

The December 31, 2010 balance sheet of Hazelmere Networks Corporation included:

Investments—Associated Companies at Equity............ $15,000,000

Suppose the company completed the following investment transactions during the year:

2011

Mar.	2	Purchased 2,000 common shares as a short-term investment, paying $38.00 per share plus brokerage commission of $2,000.
	5	Purchased additional shares in an associated company at a cost of $1,600,000. Commissions on the purchase were $30,000.
Jul.	21	Received the semiannual cash dividend of $1.90 per share on the short-term investment purchased March 2.
Aug.	17	Received a cash dividend of $160,000 from an associated company.
Oct.	16	Sold 1,600 shares of the short-term investment (purchased on March 2) for $36.00 per share, less brokerage commission of $600.
Nov.	8	Purchased short-term investments for $310,000, plus brokerage commission of $5,000.
	17	Received a cash dividend of $280,000 from an associated company.
Dec.	31	Received annual reports from associated companies. Their total net income for the year was $7,200,000. Of this amount, Hazelmere's proportion is 24 percent.

Required

1. Record the transactions in the general journal of Hazelmere Networks Corporation.

2. Post entries to the Equity Investments T-account and determine its balance at December 31, 2011.

3. Assume the beginning balance of Short-Term Investments was cost of $104,000. Post entries to the Short-Term Investments T-account and determine its balance at December 31, 2011.

4. Assuming the market value of the short-term investment portfolio is $425,000 at December 31, 2011, show how Hazelmere Networks Corporation would report short-term investments and investments in associated companies on the ending balance sheet. Use the following format:

Cash .... $XXX

Short-term investments, at fair value ....

Accounts receivable (net) XXX

Total current assets... XXX

Investments—Associated companies at equity ....

Problem 16–3B

Excel Spreadsheet Template

Preparing a consolidated balance sheet; goodwill, no non-controlling interest

④

Pisa Inc. paid $1,040,000 to acquire all the common shares of Sienna Ltd., and Sienna Ltd. owes Pisa Inc. $120,000 on a note payable. The fair market value of Sienna's net assets equalled the book value. Immediately after the purchase on June 30, 2010, the two companies' balance sheets were as shown below.

	Pisa Inc.	Sienna Ltd.
Assets		
Cash	$ 80,000	$ 72,000
Accounts receivable, net	288,000	144,000
Note receivable from Sienna Ltd.	120,000	—
Inventory...	480,000	388,000
Investment in Sienna Ltd.	1,040,000	—
Property, plant, and equipment, net	608,000	720,000
Total	$2,616,000	$1,324,000
Liabilities and Shareholders' Equity		
Accounts payable.....................................	$ 192,000	$ 128,000
Notes payable..	588,000	224,000
Note payable to Pisa Inc.	—	120,000
Other liabilities...	204,000	12,000
Common shares..	880,000	440,000
Retained earnings	752,000	400,000
Total	$2,616,000	$1,324,000

Required
Prepare a consolidation work sheet.

Problem 16–4B

Excel Spreadsheet Template

Preparing a consolidated balance sheet; goodwill with non-controlling interest

④

On March 22, 2010, Ponderosa Investments Corp. paid $1,575,000 to purchase 70 percent of the common shares of Shuckson Products Inc., and Ponderosa Investments Corp. owes Shuckson Products Inc. $450,000 on a note payable. The fair market value of Shuckson

Products Inc.'s net assets equalled the book value. Immediately after the purchase, the two companies' balance sheets were as follows:

	Ponderosa Investments Corp.	Shuckson Products Inc.
Assets		
Cash	$ 270,000	$ 150,000
Accounts receivable, net	540,000	440,000
Note receivable from Ponderosa		
Investments Corp.	—	450,000
Inventory	750,000	540,000
Investment in Shuckson Products Inc. .	1,575,000	—
Property, plant, and equipment, net	1,797,000	1,520,000
Total	$4,932,000	$3,100,000
Liabilities and Shareholders' Equity		
Accounts payable	$ 480,000	$ 420,000
Notes payable...	1,077,000	270,000
Note payable to Shuckson Products Inc.	450,000	—
Other liabilities.......................................	105,000	280,000
Non-controlling interest	—	—
Common shares	870,000	540,000
Retained earnings....................................	1,950,000	1,590,000
Total..	$4,932,000	$3,100,000

Required

Prepare a consolidation work sheet.

Accounting for a bond investment purchased at a premium
⑤

Problem 16–5B

Financial institutions such as insurance companies and pension plans hold large quantities of bond investments. Suppose VanCity Savings purchases $3,000,000 of 6.0-percent bonds of the Province of British Columbia at 105 on January 1, 2010. These bonds pay interest on January 1 and July 1 each year. They mature on January 1, 2020. VanCity Savings plans to hold the bonds to maturity. Disregard commissions.

Required

1. Journalize VanCity's purchase of the bonds as a long-term investment on January 1, 2010, receipt of cash interest and amortization of premium on July 1, 2010, and accrual of interest revenue and amortization of premium at October 31, 2010, the fiscal year end. Assume the straight-line method is appropriate for amortizing the premium as there is no material difference from the effective-interest method.

2. Calculate the book value of the investment in the Province of British Columbia bonds at October 31, 2010.

Computing the cost of a long-term bond investment and journalizing its transactions using the effective-interest method of amortizing a discount
⑤

Problem 16–6B

Suppose, on December 31, 2010, when the market interest rate is 6 percent, an investor purchases $5,000,000 of Belmont Products Inc.'s six-year, 5.5-percent bonds at issuance. Interest is payable semiannually. Disregard commissions.

Required

1. Determine the cost (present value) of this long-term bond investment. The investor uses the effective-interest amortization method. The investor plans to hold these bonds to maturity.

2. Prepare a schedule for amortizing the discount on bond investment through December 31, 2011. Use Exhibit 15-4 on page 826 as a guide. Journalize the purchase on December 31, 2010; the first semiannual interest receipt on June 30, 2011; and the year-end interest receipt on December 31, 2011.

Problem 16–7B

Journalizing foreign-currency transactions and reporting the transaction gain or loss

(6)

Suppose Homestead Corp. completed the following transactions:

2010

Dec. 4 Sold product on account to a Mexican company for $100,000. The exchange rate of the Mexican peso was $0.078, and the customer agreed to pay in Canadian dollars.

13 Purchased inventory on account from a U.S. company at a price of US$240,000. The exchange rate of the U.S. dollar was $1.05, and payment will be in U.S. dollars.

20 Sold goods on account to an English firm for 180,000 British pounds. Payment will be in pounds, and the exchange rate of the pound was $1.66.

27 Collected from the Mexican company. The exchange rate of the Mexican peso was $0.075.

31 Adjusted the accounts for changes in foreign-currency exchange rates. Current rates: U.S. dollar, $1.07; British pound, $1.64.

2011

Jan. 21 Paid the American company. The exchange rate of the U.S. dollar was $1.06.

Feb. 17 Collected from the English firm. The exchange rate of the British pound was $1.69.

Required

1. Record these transactions in Homestead Corp.'s general journal, and show how to report the transaction gain or loss on the income statement for the year ended December 31, 2010.

2. How will what you have learned in this problem help you structure international transactions?

Problem 16–8B

Accounting for short-term investments using the fair-value method; investments in bonds

(1) (5)

Portal Holdings Ltd. had the following short-term investments in marketable securities on December 31, 2009, at fair value and book value:

Canadian Utilities Limited...	$310,000
TELUS Communications Inc.	425,000
Talisman Energy Ltd.	160,000
Total short-term investments...	$895,000

Portal Holdings Ltd. had the following investment transactions during 2010:

Jan. 5 Purchased 5,000 shares (2 percent) of Salmon Ltd. as a short-term investment. The shares were purchased at $50.00 and the commission was $3,000.

31 Salmon Ltd. reported net income of $1,500,000 and declared a cash dividend of $900,000.

Feb. 15 Received $18,000 from Salmon Ltd. as a cash dividend.

Apr. 1 Purchased $300,000 (face value) of bonds at 98 as a long-term investment. The bonds pay 6 percent interest (3 percent semiannually) on October 1 and April 1 and mature in two years.

Aug. 31 Received a 10-percent stock dividend from Salmon Ltd.

Oct. 1 Received the interest on the bonds.

Nov. 1 Salmon Ltd. declared and distributed a 2-for-1 stock split.

Dec. 15 Sold 3,300 shares of Salmon Ltd. at $48.00 and the commission was $2,000.

31 Recorded the adjustment for accrued interest on the bonds.

31 The fair values of the investments were:

Canadian Utilities Limited	$ 290,000
TELUS Communications Inc.	420,000
Salmon Ltd...	270,000
Talisman Energy Ltd...	175,000
Total short-term investments...	$1,155,000

Required

Prepare the general journal entries required to record the transactions of 2010.

Accounting for share investments using the equity method;
accounting for investments in
bonds; accounting for transactions stated in a foreign currency
③ ⑤ ⑥

Problem 16–9B

Rivershore Ltd. had the following investment transactions:

2010

Jan.	2	Rivershore Ltd. purchased 30,000 (35 percent) Harvest Ltd. common shares as a long-term investment. The shares were purchased for $50.00 per share.
Apr.	1	Purchased US$750,000 (face value) of Padden Ltd. bonds at 100 (U.S. dollars) as a short-term investment. The bonds pay annual interest of 5 percent each April 1 and October 1, and mature in five years. The exchange rate at the time of the transaction was $1.04.
Jun.	10	Received 3,000 Harvest Ltd. common shares as a 10-percent stock dividend.
Sept.	1	Harvest Ltd. declared and distributed a 3-for-1 common stock split.
Oct.	1	Received the interest on the Padden Ltd. bonds when the exchange rate was $1.06.
Dec.	31	Harvest Ltd. reported net income of $650,000 and declared and paid a common share dividend of $260,000.
	31	Adjusted for the accrued interest on the Padden Ltd. bonds. The exchange rate was $1.05. The current value of the bonds is 97.50 (U.S. dollars).

2011

Feb.	10	Sold 39,600 Harvest Ltd. common shares at $17.00 per share.
Apr.	1	Received the interest on the Padden Ltd. bonds when the exchange rate was $1.07.

Required

1. Prepare the general journal entries required to record these transactions. Rivershore Ltd.'s year end is December 31. Disregard commissions.

2. Calculate the December 31, 2010 balances of the investment accounts.

CHALLENGE PROBLEMS

Accounting for ownership of
shares in another company
① ② ③ ④

Problem 16–1C

The text lists general rules for accounting for long-term investments in the voting shares of another corporation. However, the management of the investing company may decide that, in their judgment, the rules do not apply in a particular situation.

Required

1. Identify a situation where an investing company that owns less than 20 percent might believe that the equity method was appropriate.

2. Identify a situation where an investing company that owns between 20 percent and 50 percent might believe that the fair-value method was appropriate.

3. Identify a situation where an investing company that owns more than 50 percent might believe that the fair-value method was appropriate.

Problem 16–2C

Canadian exporters are pleased when the Canadian dollar weakens against the U.S. dollar, while the federal and provincial ministers of finance are likely not happy when this happens.

Required

Explain why a weakening Canadian dollar makes Canadian exporters happy. Why would a weaker Canadian dollar make the finance ministers unhappy?

Extending Your Knowledge

DECISION PROBLEM

Margaret Joyce is the owner of Trickle Music Holdings Ltd., a newly formed company whose year end is December 31. The company made two investments during the first week of January 2010. Both investments are to be held for at least the next five years as investments. Information about each of the investments follows:

a. Trickle Music Holdings Ltd. purchased 30 percent of the common shares of Old Times Ltd. for its book value of $600,000. During the year ended December 31, 2010, Old Times Ltd. earned $240,000 and paid a total dividend of $150,000.

b. Trickle Music Holdings Ltd. purchased 10 percent of the common shares of Mountain Music Inc. for its book value of $150,000. During the year ended December 31, 2010, Mountain Music Inc. paid Trickle Music Holdings Ltd. a dividend of $10,000. Mountain Music Inc. earned a profit of $225,000 for that period. The market value of Trickle Music Holdings Ltd.'s investment in Mountain Music Inc. was $204,000 at December 31, 2010.

   Joyce has come to you as her auditor to ask you how to account for the investments. Trickle Music Holdings Ltd. has never had such investments before. You attempt to explain the proper accounting to her by indicating that different accounting methods apply to different situations.

Understanding the fair-value and equity methods of accounting for investments
① ② ③

Required

Help Joyce understand by

1. Describing the methods of accounting applicable to investments such as these.
2. Identifying which method should be used to account for the investments in Old Times Ltd. and Mountain Music Inc.

FINANCIAL STATEMENT CASES

Financial Statement Case 1

Canadian Western Bank's 2008 financial statements appear in Appendix A.

Investments and foreign-currency transactions
① ② ③ ④ ⑥

Required

1. The financial statements are labelled "consolidated." What evidence can you find in the financial statements that reveals how Canadian Western Bank accounts for its subsidiaries?
2. How does Canadian Western Bank account for goodwill?
3. Does Canadian Western bank have any foreign-currency transactions? How do you know?

Financial Statement Case 2

The Sun-Rype Products Ltd. December 31, 2008, financial statements appear in Appendix B.

Investments and foreign-currency transactions
① ② ③ ④ ⑥

Required

1. What information can you find about Sun-Rype's policy on foreign-currency transactions?
2. Does Sun-Rype have any subsidiaries as of December 31, 2008? How can you tell?

1. ACCOUNTING FOR CORPORATE TRANSACTIONS

Greyhawk Investments Inc.'s articles of incorporation authorize the company to issue 1,000,000 common shares and 400,000 $9.00 preferred shares. During the first quarter of operations, Greyhawk Investments Inc. completed the following selected transactions:

2010

Oct.	1	Issued 50,000 common shares for cash of $30.00 per share.
	4	Signed a capital lease for equipment. The lease requires a down payment of $600,000, plus 20 quarterly lease payments of $60,000. The present value of the future lease payments is $981,086 at an annual interest rate of 8 percent.
	6	Issued 2,000 preferred shares, receiving cash of $300,000.
	22	Purchased land from the Province of Manitoba for $300,000 cash.
	30	Purchased 5,000 (25 percent) of the outstanding common shares of Big Sky Ltd. as a long-term investment, $270,000.
Nov.	1	Issued $1,000,000 of 6-percent, 10-year bonds payable at 98.
	16	Purchased short-term investments in the common shares of TELUS Communications Inc., $85,000, and ATCO Ltd., $87,000.
	19	Experienced a loss of inventory that cost $158,000. Cash received from the insurance company was $85,000.
	20	Repurchased 2,000 of the company's common shares at $15.00 per share for cancellation.
Dec.	1	Received cash dividends of $1,800 on the TELUS investment.
	16	Sold 1,000 of the company's common shares for cash of $24.00 per share.
	29	Received a report from Big Sky Ltd. indicating the combined net income for November and December was $25,000.
	30	Sold merchandise on account, $2,148,000. Cost of the goods was $945,000. Operating expenses totalled $557,000, with $498,000 of this amount paid in cash. Greyhawk Investments Inc. uses a perpetual inventory system.
	31	Accrued interest and amortized discount (straight-line method) on the bonds payable.
	31	Accrued interest on the capital lease liability.
	31	Amortized the equipment acquired by the capital lease. The company uses the double-declining-balance method.
	31	Market values of short-term investments: TELUS Communications Inc. shares, $84,000 and ATCO Ltd. shares, $93,000.
	31	Accrued income tax expense of $240,000. Credit the Income Tax Payable account.
	31	Closed all revenues, expenses, and losses to Retained Earnings in a single closing entry.
	31	Declared a quarterly cash dividend of $2.25 per share on the preferred shares. Record date is January 11, 2011, with payment scheduled for January 19.

Required

1. Record these transactions in the general journal. Explanations are not required. Disregard commissions.

2. Prepare a single-step income statement for the quarter ended December 31, 2010, including earnings per share.

3. Report the liabilities and the shareholders' equity as they would appear on the balance sheet at December 31, 2010.

17 The Cash Flow Statement

What is the cash flow statement, and what information does it show that the other financial statements do not show? What are operating, investing, and financing activities, and are they equally important to a company's continued success?

How do the direct and indirect methods of calculating cash flows from operations differ?

How do you calculate the amounts that appear on the cash flow statement?

How do investors and creditors use cash flow and related information?

These questions and others about the cash flow statement will be answered throughout this chapter. The Decision Guidelines at the end of this chapter will summarize how investors and creditors use cash flow and related information.

LEARNING OBJECTIVES

1. Identify the purposes of the cash flow statement

2. Identify cash flows from operating, investing, and financing activities

3. Prepare a cash flow statement by the direct method

4. Compute the cash effects of a wide variety of business transactions

5. Prepare a cash flow statement by the indirect method

6. Describe the impact on the cash flow statement of international financial reporting standards (IFRS)

CHAPTER 17 APPENDIX

A1. Prepare a spreadsheet for the cash flow statement—indirect method

The *CICA Handbook* states in Section 1540 that an enterprise's cash flow information allows users of its financial statements to assess the enterprise's ability to generate cash and cash equivalents and to determine the enterprise's need for cash.

The income statement indicates to users whether an enterprise is profitable; the cash flow statement indicates whether or not the enterprise is generating enough cash to pay the bills.

WestJet Airlines Ltd. is a national air carrier based in Calgary, Alberta. During its 2008 fiscal year, it generated approximately $461 million in cash from its operations, down from $541 million in the previous fiscal year. There were many factors that caused the generation of cash from operations to decline. "This year-over-year decrease related primarily to the higher cost of fuel in 2008 as compared to 2007, as well as a decrease in noncash working capital due to an increase in prepaid expenses and short-term deposits, mainly resulting from deposits for aircraft fuel and other operating costs."[1]

Companies like WestJet raise cash in different ways. As we have discussed in earlier chapters, a company can raise cash by issuing shares if it is a corporation or by issuing debt in the form of bonds. However, a company's most important ongoing source of cash to run its business needs to come from successfully operating its business.

---

[1] WestJet Airlines Ltd. *2008 Annual Report*, from the Management Discussion and Analysis (MD&A) section, p. 35.

The cash flow statement, a required financial statement, reports where cash came from and how the company spent it. Like the income statement and the balance sheet, the cash flow statement provides important information about an organization. For WestJet Airlines Ltd., the results seem positive overall because operations are generating positive cash flow, even though the company did not generate as much cash from operations as it had during the previous year (see Exhibit 17–1). Positive cash flow from operations is a positive signal about any company because operations should be the main source of cash. We begin this chapter by explaining the cash flow statement format preferred by the Accounting Standards Board as stated in Section 1540 of the *CICA Handbook*. It is very clear and is called the *direct approach*. We end the chapter with the more common format of the cash flow statement, the *indirect approach*. The method used by WestJet in the chapter-opening vignette is the indirect approach. By the time

 **EXHIBIT 17–1** WestJet Airlines Ltd.'s 2008 Cash Flow Statement (Adapted) (Indirect Method for Operating Activities)

WESTJET AIRLINES LTD.
Consolidated Statement of Cash Flows (Adapted)
For the Year Ended December 31, 2008

	(In thousands)
Cash flows from operating activities:	
Net income	$ 178,135
Add transactions not involving cash outlays (e.g., amortization)	198,297
Change in noncash working capital	84,154
Net cash inflow from operating activities	460,586
Cash flows from investing activities:	
Aircraft additions	(114,470)
Other property and equipment additons	(90,663)
Aircraft, property, and equipment disposals	256
Change in noncash working capital	5,147
Net cash outflow from investing activities	(199,730)
Cash flows from financing activities:	
Increase in long-term debt	101,782
Repayment of long-term debt	(179,397)
Decrease in obligations under capital lease	(375)
Increase in other assets	(4,135)
Shares repurchased	(29,420)
Issuance of common shares	227
Change in noncash working capital	(4,111)
Net cash outflow from financing activities	(115,429)
Cash and cash equivalents:	
Cash flow from operating, investing and financing activities	145,427
Effect of exchange rate on cash and cash equivalents	21,229
Net change in cash and cash equivalents	166,656
Cash and cash equivalents, beginning of year	653,558
Cash and cash equivalents, end of year	$820,214

you have worked through this chapter, you will feel more confident in your ability to analyze the cash flows of any company you might encounter. This chapter's Appendix shows how to use a spreadsheet to prepare the cash flow statement (by the indirect method).

The cash flow statement reports where cash came from and how it was spent. We learned in Chapter 1 (pp. 20–23) that the cash flow statement is a required financial statement. Like the other two major financial reports—the income statement and the balance sheet—the cash flow statement enables investors and creditors to make informed decisions about a company. The income statement might present one picture of the company: relatively high income; while the cash flow statement might present a different picture: not enough cash. This example underscores the challenge of financial analysis: that a company's signals may point in different directions. Astute investors and creditors know what to look for; increasingly they are focusing on cash flows.

The Cash Flow Statement: Basic Concepts

OBJECTIVE 1
Identify the purposes of the cash flow statement

The balance sheet reports a company's cash balance at the end of the period. By comparing the beginning and ending balance sheets, you can tell whether cash increased or decreased during the period. However, the balance sheet does not indicate *why* the cash balance changed. The income statement reports revenues, expenses, and net income (or net loss)—clues about the sources and uses of cash—but does not tell *why* cash increased or decreased.

The **cash flow statement** reports the entity's **cash flows**—cash receipts and cash payments—during the period. It

- Shows where cash came from (receipts) and how cash was spent (payments),
- Reports why cash increased or decreased during the period, and
- Covers a period of time and is dated "For the Month Ended xxx" or "For the Year Ended xxx," the same as the income statement.

The cash flow statement is a summary of all the transactions that affected the Cash account for a period of time. Exhibit 17–2 shows the Cash T-account and some of the types of transactions that affect its balance during a period.

Exhibit 17–3 illustrates the relationships among the balance sheet, the income statement, and the cash flow statement, and the time periods covered by each.

EXHIBIT 17–2   Some Transactions that Affect the Cash Account

Cash (and cash equivalents)	
Beginning cash balance	Payments to suppliers
Collections from customers	Payments to employees
Interest received on notes	Payments for income tax
Issuance of shares	Payments for assets
Issuance of bonds	Loan to another company
Receipt of dividends	Payment of dividends
	Repayment of a bank loan
	Repayment of long-term loans
Ending cash balance	

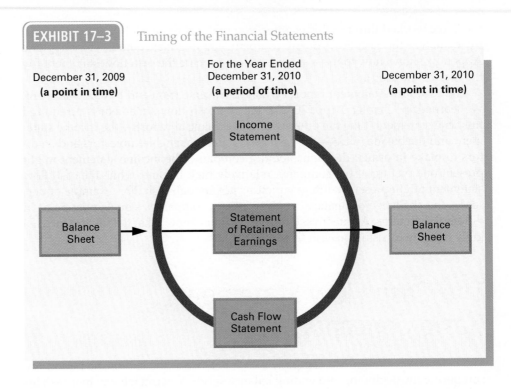

EXHIBIT 17–3 Timing of the Financial Statements

Purpose of the Cash Flow Statement

How do people use cash flow information? The cash flow statement helps to:

1. *Predict future cash flows.* It takes cash to pay the bills or take advantage of opportunities. In many cases, past cash receipts and cash payments help predict future cash flows.

2. *Evaluate management decisions.* Wise decisions lead to profits and strong cash flows. Unwise decisions often bring bankruptcy. One of the areas that the cash flow statement reports on is the investments a company is making.

3. *Determine the company's ability to pay dividends and debts.* Shareholders are interested in receiving dividends on their investments in the company's shares. Creditors want to receive their principal and interest amounts on time. The cash flow statement helps investors and creditors predict whether the business can make dividend and debt payments.

4. *Show the relationship between net income and cash flow.* Usually, cash and net income move together. High profits tend to lead to increases in cash, and vice versa. However, a company's cash balance can decrease when net income is high, and cash can increase when net income is low. The failures of companies that were earning net income but had insufficient cash have pointed to the need for cash flow information.

KEY POINT

A business operates for profit, and it must operate profitably to be a going concern. Information about net income (using the accrual basis) is found on the income statement. However, a business must have cash to pay suppliers, employees, and so on. Information about cash flows is found on the cash flow statement.

Cash and Cash Equivalents

On the financial statements, *Cash* has a broader meaning than just cash on hand and cash in the bank. It includes **cash equivalents** (discussed in Chapter 8), which are highly liquid short-term investments convertible into cash with little delay. Because their liquidity is one reason for holding these investments, they are treated as cash. Examples of cash equivalents are investments in money-market funds and investments in Government of Canada treasury bills. Businesses invest their extra cash in these types of liquid assets to earn interest income rather than let cash remain idle. Throughout this chapter, the term *cash* refers to cash and cash equivalents.

DID YOU GET IT?

To check your understanding of the material in this Learning Objective, complete these questions. The solutions appear on MyAccountingLab so you can check your progress.

1. Refer to the WestJet Airlines Ltd. cash flow statement illustrated in Exhibit 17–1 and answer the following questions:

   a. What is the period of time covered by WestJet's cash flow statement?

   b. What was WestJet's net income during the period covered by the cash flow statement?

   c. In the "investing activities" section, on what did WestJet spend most of its cash? How much cash did the company spend on this category of investment? (Note that cash outflows, or cash payments, are indicated by dollar amounts in parentheses.)

   d. In the "financing activities" section, on what did WestJet spend most of its cash? How much cash did the company spend on this category?

   e. What amount of cash and cash equivalents did WestJet report on its balance sheet at December 31, 2008?

2. Indicate whether each of the following items would increase (I) or decrease (D) the balance of cash and cash equivalents.

   ____ Payment of dividends

   ____ Issuance of shares

   ____ Payment to employees

   ____ Collections from customers

   ____ Payments for assets

   ____ Repayment of a bank loan

   ____ Issuance of bonds

Operating, Investing, and Financing Activities

OBJECTIVE ②
Identify cash flows from operating, investing, and financing activities

A business engages in three basic categories of business activities:

- Operating activities
- Investing activities
- Financing activities

Once the business is up and running, *operations* are the most important activity, followed by *investing activities* and *financing activities*. Investing activities are generally more important than financing activities because *what* a company invests in is usually more important than *how* the company finances the investment.

The cash flow statement has a section for each category of cash flows. Here is what each section reports:

Operating Activities

- Create revenues, expenses, gains, and losses
- Affect net income on the income statement
- Affect current assets and current liabilities on the balance sheet
- Are the most important category of cash flows because they reflect the day-to-day operations that determine the future of an organization

Investing Activities

- Increase and decrease long-term assets, such as computers, software, land, buildings, and equipment
- Include purchases and sales of these long-term assets, plus loans to others and collections of loans
- Are next most important after operating activities

Financing Activities

- Increase and decrease long-term liabilities and owners' equity
- Include issuing shares, paying dividends, and repurchasing a company's own shares
- Include borrowing money and paying off loans
- Are least important of all the activities because what a company invests in is usually more important than how the company finances the investment

Exhibit 17–4 shows the relationships among operating, investing, and financing cash flows and the various parts of the balance sheet.

EXHIBIT 17–4 Operating, Investing, and Financing Cash Flows and the Balance-Sheet Accounts

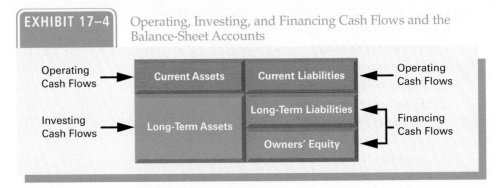

As you can see, operating cash flows affect the current accounts. Investing cash flows affect the long-term assets. Financing cash flows affect long-term liabilities and owners' equity.

The cash flow statement in Exhibit 17–5 shows how cash receipts and payments are divided into operating activities, investing activities, and financing activities for Capilano Ltd., a small manufacturer of glass products and the company we will refer to throughout this chapter. Exhibit 17–5 shows that each set of activities includes both cash inflows (receipts) and cash outflows (payments). Outflows have parentheses to indicate that payments are subtracted. Each section of the statement reports a net cash inflow (net cash receipt) or a net cash outflow (net cash payment).

Exhibit 17–5 shows that Capilano Ltd.'s net cash inflow from operating activities is $168,000. A large positive cash inflow from operations is a good sign about a company. *In the long run, operations must be the main source of a business's cash.* The acquisition of long-term assets dominates Capilano Ltd.'s investing activities, which produce a net cash outflow of $612,000. Financing activities of Capilano Ltd. brought in net cash receipts of $400,000. One thing to watch among financing activities is whether the business is borrowing heavily. Excessive borrowing has been the downfall of many companies. Overall, Capilano Ltd.'s cash decreased by $44,000 during 2010. The company began the year with cash of $101,000 and ended with $57,000.

Each of these categories of activities—operating, investing, and financing—includes both cash receipts and cash payments, as shown in Exhibit 17–6. The exhibit lists the more common cash receipts and cash payments that appear on the cash flow statement.

KEY POINT

If the revenues and expenses on the income statement are converted to the cash basis, then cash flow from operations is complete. Operating activities include all cash inflows and outflows not associated with investing or financing.

Cash Flow Statement (Direct Method for Operating Activities)

CAPILANO LTD.
Cash Flow Statement
For the Year Ended December 31, 2010

		(In thousands)
Cash flows from operating activities		
Receipts:		
Collections from customers..	$ 650	
Interest received on notes receivable.............................	24	
Dividends received on investments in shares.................	22	
Total cash receipts		$ 696
Payments:		
To suppliers for merchandise for resale	(270)	
To suppliers for operating expenses..............................	(44)	
To employees..	(140)	
For interest...	(38)	
For income tax..	(36)	
Total cash payments...		(528)
Net cash inflow from operating activities		168
Cash flows from investing activities		
Acquisition of property, plant, and equipment,		
and intangible assets	(735)	
Loan to another company	(26)	
Cash received from selling property, plant, and		
equipment, and intangible assets.................................	149	
Net cash outflow from investing activities......................		(612)
Cash flows from financing activities		
Cash received from issuing common shares	242	
Cash received from issuing long-term notes payable.....	226	
Payment of long-term debt*..	(27)	
Payment of dividends..	(41)	
Net cash inflow from financing activities....................		400
Net increase (decrease) in cash and cash equivalents...........		(44)
Cash and cash equivalents at beginning of 2010		101
Cash and cash equivalents at end of 2010		$ 57

* This would also include the current portion of long-term debt payable, which is NIL in this case.

LEARNING TIPS

When preparing the cash flow statement, compare beginning and ending cash. Has it increased or decreased? An increase during the period means the statement will show a "net increase in cash."

Discontinued Operations

Just as discontinued operations are to be shown separately on the income statement, they are to be shown separately on the cash flow statement. The cash inflow or outflow resulting from discontinued operations should be shown as part of operating, investing, or financing activities, as is appropriate.

Interest and Dividends as Operating Activities

You may be puzzled by the inclusion of cash receipts of interest and dividends as operating activities. After all, these cash receipts result from investing activities. Interest comes from investments in loans, and dividends come from investments in shares. Equally puzzling is listing the payment of interest as part of operations. Interest expense results from borrowing money—a financing activity. *However, interest and dividends are included as operating activities because they affect the computation of net income.* Interest revenue and dividend revenue increase net income, and interest expense decreases income. Therefore, cash receipts of interest and dividends and cash payments of interest are reported as operating activities on the cash flow statement.

In contrast, note that dividend payments are reported as a financing activity. This is because they do not enter into the computation of net income but rather are payments to the entity's shareholders, who finance the business by purchasing its shares.

EXHIBIT 17–6 Cash Receipts and Payments on the Cash Flow Statement

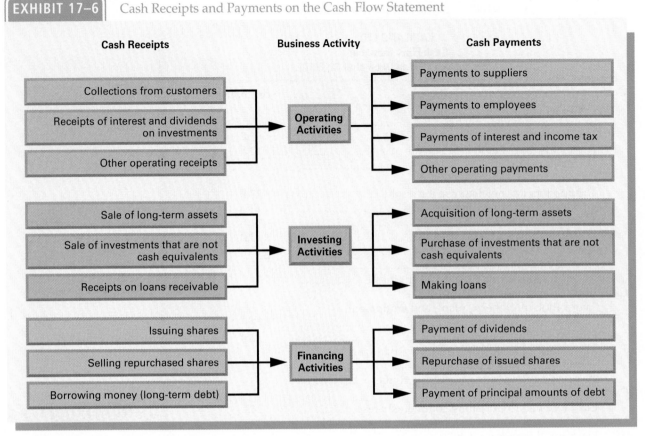

Format of the Cash Flow Statement

There are two ways to format operating activities on the cash flow statement:

- The **direct method**, which reports all the cash receipts and all the cash payments from operating activities
- The **indirect method**, which reconciles net income to net cash provided by operating activities

In the *CICA Handbook*, Section 1540, the Accounting Standards Board (AcSB) approved these two formats for reporting cash flows from operating activities. Section 1540 encourages the direct method, illustrated in Exhibit 17–5, because it reports where cash came from and how it was spent on operating activities.

In keeping with GAAP, companies' accounting systems are designed for accrual, rather than cash-basis, accounting. To use the direct method, a company must be able to access information on cash inflows and cash outflows. However, accrual-based accounting systems make it easy for companies to compute cash flows from operating activities using the indirect method, which starts with net income and reconciles to cash flows from operating activities. Exhibit 17–7 gives an overview of the process of converting from accrual-basis income to the cash basis for the cash flow statement.

The direct method is easier to understand, and it provides better information for decision making, and the Accounting Standards Board and most financial analysts prefer it. However, accounting systems often don't produce the cash flow data easily. By learning how to compute the cash flow amounts for the direct method, you will be learning something far more important: how to determine the cash effects of business transactions. This is a critical skill for analyzing financial statements because accrual-basis accounting often hides cash effects. Then, after you have a firm foundation in cash flow analysis, it is easier to learn the indirect

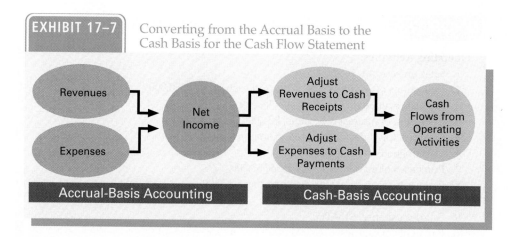

EXHIBIT 17–7   Converting from the Accrual Basis to the Cash Basis for the Cash Flow Statement

method. If your instructor chooses to focus solely on the indirect method, you can study that method, which begins on page 948, with a minimum of references to earlier sections of this chapter.

The indirect and direct methods

- Use different computations but produce the same amount of cash flow from operations, and

- Have no effect on investing activities or financing activities—they show the same net change in cash for the period.

DID YOU GET IT?

MyAccountingLab

To check your understanding of the material in this Learning Objective, complete these questions. The solutions appear on MyAccountingLab so you can check your progress.

3. Identify each of the following transactions as either an operating activity (O), an investing activity (I), a financing activity (F), or an activity that is not reported on a cash flow statement (N). Assume the direct method is used to report cash flows from operating activitties.

_____ Payment of income taxes

_____ Issuance of preferred shares

_____ Amortization of equipment

_____ Payment of employee salaries

_____ Collections of accounts receivable

_____ Payment for a delivery truck

_____ Repayment of a bank loan (principal only)

_____ Receipt of loan interest

_____ Payment of accounts payable

4. For the items listed in the previous question, indicate whether the transaction would increase (+), decrease (–), or have no effect (N) on cash.

The Cash Flow Statement: The Direct Method

OBJECTIVE ③
Prepare a cash flow statement by the direct method

Let's see how to prepare the cash flow statement by the direct method illustrated in Exhibit 17–5. Suppose Capilano Ltd. has assembled the summary of 2010 transactions in Exhibit 17–8. These transactions give data for both the income statement and the cash flow statement. Some transactions affect one statement, some the

EXHIBIT 17–8 | Summary of Capilano Ltd.'s 2010 Transactions

Operating Activities:
1. Sales on account, $682,000.
*2. Collections of accounts receivable and cash sales, $650,000.
3. Interest revenue on notes receivable, $29,000.
*4. Collection of interest receivable, $24,000.
*5. Cash receipt of dividend revenue on investments in shares, $22,000.
6. Cost of goods sold, $360,000.
7. Purchases of inventory on credit, $353,000.
*8. Payments to suppliers for merchandise, $270,000, and operating expenses, $44,000.
9. Salaries expense, $134,000.
*10. Payments of salaries, $140,000.
11. Amortization expense, $43,000.
12. Other operating expense, $41,000.
*13. Interest expense and payments, $38,000.
*14. Income tax expense and payments, $36,000.

Investing Activities:
*15. Cash payments to acquire property, plant, and equipment, and intangible assets, $735,000.
*16. Loan to another company, $26,000.
*17. Cash receipts from sale of property, plant, and equipment, and intangible assets, $149,000, including a $19,000 gain.

Financing Activities:
*18. Cash receipts from issuing common shares, $242,000.
*19. Cash receipts from issuing a long-term note payable, $226,000.
*20. Payment of long-term debt, $27,000.
*21. Declaration and payment of cash dividends, $41,000.

*Indicates a cash flow transaction is to be reported on the cash flow statement.

other. Sales, for example, are reported on the income statement, but cash collections appear on the cash flow statement. Other transactions, such as the cash receipt of dividend revenue, affect both. *The cash flow statement reports only those transactions with cash effects* (those with an asterisk in Exhibit 17–8).

To prepare the cash flow statement, follow these three steps:

1. Identify the activities that increased cash or decreased cash—those items with asterisks in Exhibit 17–8.
2. Classify each cash increase and each cash decrease as an operating activity, an investing activity, or a financing activity.
3. Identify the cash effect of each transaction.

Cash Flows from Operating Activities

Operating cash flows are listed first because they are the most important source of cash for most businesses. The failure of operations to generate the bulk of cash inflows for an extended period may signal trouble for a company. Exhibit 17–5 shows that Capilano Ltd. is sound; its operating activities generated the greatest amount of cash, $696,000 in operating receipts.

Let's apply the three steps listed above to the transactions shown in Exhibit 17–8.

Cash Collections from Customers Cash sales bring in cash immediately. Credit sales bring in cash later, when cash is collected. "Collections from customers" in Exhibit 17–5 include both cash sales and collections of accounts receivable from credit sales—$650,000.

Cash Receipts of Interest Interest revenue is earned on notes receivable. The income statement reports interest revenue. As time passes, interest revenue accrues, but *cash* interest is received only on specific dates. Only the cash receipts of interest appear on the cash flow statement—$24,000 in Exhibit 17–5.

Cash Receipts of Dividends Dividends are earned on share investments. Dividend revenue is ordinarily recorded on the income statement when cash is received. This cash receipt is reported on the cash flow statement—$22,000 in Exhibit 17–5. (Dividends *received* are part of operating activities, but dividends *paid* are a financing activity.)

    These cash receipts add to the total cash receipts of $696,000 in Exhibit 17–5.

Cash Payments to Suppliers Payments to suppliers include all cash payments for inventory and most operating expenses, but not for interest, income taxes, and employee compensation expenses. *Suppliers* are entities that provide the business with its inventory and essential services. For example, a clothing store's payments to Levi Strauss & Co., Nygard International, and Stanfield are payments to suppliers. Other suppliers provide advertising, utilities, and other services. Payments to suppliers *exclude* payments to employees, payments for interest, and payments for income taxes because these are separate categories of operating cash payments. In Exhibit 17–5, Capilano Ltd.'s payments to suppliers are $270,000 for merchandise for resale and $44,000 for operating expenses.

Cash Payments to Employees Salaries, wages, commissions, and other forms of employee compensation require payments to employees. Accrued amounts are excluded because they have not yet been paid. The income statement reports the expense, including accrued amounts. The cash flow statement in Exhibit 17–5 reports only the cash payments $(140,000).

Cash Payments for Interest Expense and Income Tax Expense These cash payments are reported separately from the other expenses. In the Capilano Ltd. example, interest and income tax expenses equal the cash payments. Therefore, the same amount appears on the income statement and the cash flow statement. In practice, this is rarely the case. Year-end accruals and other transactions usually cause the expense and cash payment amounts to differ. The cash flow statement in Exhibit 17–5 reports the cash payments for interest $(38,000) and income tax $(36,000).

Amortization Expense This expense is not listed on the cash flow statement in Exhibit 17–5 because it does not affect cash. Amortization is recorded by debiting the expense and crediting Accumulated Amortization (there is no debit or credit to the Cash account).

Cash Flows from Investing Activities

Investing activities are important because a company's investments determine its future. Purchases of tangible assets such as property, plant, and equipment, as well as intangible assets such as patents, indicate the company is expanding, which is usually a good sign about the company. Low levels of investing activities over a lengthy period mean the business is not replenishing its property, plant, and equipment, or intangible assets. Knowing the cash flows from investing activities helps investors and creditors evaluate the direction that managers are charting for the business.

Cash Payments for Property, Plant, and Equipment, and Intangible Assets, Investments, and Loans to Other Companies All these cash payments acquire a long-term asset. The first investing activity reported by Capilano Ltd. on its cash flow statement is the purchase of property, plant, and equipment, and intangible assets, such as land, buildings, equipment, and patents $(735,000), shown in Exhibit 17–5. The second transaction is a $26,000 loan; Capilano Ltd. obtains a note receivable. These are investing activities because the company is investing in assets for business use rather than for resale. These transactions have no direct effect on revenues or expenses and thus are not reported on the income statement. The other transaction in this category—not shown in Exhibit 17–5—is a purchase of long-term investments.

Cash Received from the Sale of Property, Plant, and Equipment, and Intangible Assets, Investments, and the Collection of Loans   These transactions are the opposite of making acquisitions of property, plant, and equipment, acquisitions of intangible assets, investments, and loans. They are cash receipts from investment transactions.

The sale of the property, plant, and equipment, and intangible assets needs explanation. The cash flow statement in Exhibit 17–5 reports that Capilano Ltd. received $149,000 cash on the sale of these assets. The income statement shows a $19,000 gain on this transaction. What is the appropriate amount to show on the cash flow statement? It is $149,000, the cash received from the sale. If we assume Capilano Ltd. sold equipment that cost $155,000 and had accumulated amortization of $25,000, the following journal entry would record the sale:

Cash..	149,000	
Accumulated Amortization..	25,000	
Equipment..		155,000
Gain on Sale of Equipment (from income statement).....		19,000

The analysis indicates that the book value of the equipment was $130,000 ($155,000 – $25,000). However, the book value of the asset sold is not reported on the cash flow statement. Only the cash proceeds of $149,000 are reported on the cash flow statement. For the income statement, only the gain is reported.

Because a gain occurred, you may wonder why this cash receipt is not reported as part of operations. Operations consist of buying and selling merchandise or rendering services to earn revenue. Investing activities are the acquisition and disposition of assets used in operations. Therefore, the cash received from the sale of property, plant, and equipment, and intangible assets and the sale of investments should be viewed as cash inflows from investing activities. Any gain or loss on the sale is not cash, but rather an accounting amount based on the asset's book value in the accounting records.

Investors and creditors are often critical of a company that sells large amounts of its property, plant, and equipment, and intangible assets. Such sales may signal an emergency need for cash and negative news. But selling property, plant, and equipment or tangible assets may be positive news if the company is selling an unprofitable division or a useless property, plant, and equipment asset. Whether sales of property, plant, and equipment or intangible assets are positive news or negative news should be evaluated in light of a company's net income (or net loss), financial position, and other cash flows.

Cash Flows from Financing Activities

Readers of the financial statements want to know how the entity obtains its financing. Cash flows from financing activities include several specific items. The majority are related to obtaining money from investors and lenders and paying them back.

Cash Received from Issuing Shares and Debt   Issuing shares (preferred and common) and debt are two common ways to finance operations. In Exhibit 17–5, Capilano Ltd. issued common shares for cash of $242,000 and long-term notes payable for cash of $226,000.

Payment of Debt and Repurchases of the Company's Own Shares   The payment of debt decreases Cash, which is the opposite of borrowing money. Capilano Ltd.

reports debt payments of $27,000. Other transactions in this category are repurchases of the company's shares.

Payment of Cash Dividends   The payment of cash dividends decreases Cash and is therefore reported as a cash payment. Capilano Ltd.'s $41,000 payment in Exhibit 17–5 is an example. A dividend in another form—such as a stock dividend—has no effect on Cash and is either *not* reported on the cash flow statement or is reported in the noncash financing and investing section, explained later in this chapter.

DID YOU GET IT?

To check your understanding of the material in this Learning Objective, complete these questions. The solutions appear on MyAccountingLab so you can check your progress.

5. Suppose Markham Corp. sold land at a $3 million gain. The land cost Markham Corp. $2 million when it was purchased in 1995. What amount will Markham Corp. report as an investing activity on the cash flow statement?

6. Shediac Corporation's accounting records include the information shown below for the year ended December 31, 2010. Prepare Shediac Corporation's income statement and cash flow statement for the year ended December 31, 2010. Follow the cash flow statement format of Exhibit 17–5, using the direct method for operating cash flows and follow the single-step format for the income statement (grouping all revenues together and all expenses together, as shown in Exhibit 17–9 on page 938).

   a. Salary expense, $290,000.
   b. Amortization expense on property, plant, and equipment, $104,000.
   c. Cash received from issuing common shares, $87,000.
   d. Declaration and payment of cash dividends, $62,000.
   e. Collection of interest on notes receivable, $20,000.
   f. Payments of salaries, $308,000.
   g. Collections from credit customers, $1,030,000.
   h. Loan to another company, $118,000.
   i. Cash received from selling property, plant, and equipment, $50,000, including a $3,000 loss.
   j. Payments to suppliers, $893,000.
   k. Income tax expense and payments, $45,000.
   l. Credit sales, $1,005,000.
   m. Cash sales, $258,000.
   n. Interest revenue, $22,000.
   o. Cash received from issuing short-term debt, $106,000.
   p. Payments of long-term debt, $160,000.
   q. Interest expense and payments, $31,000.
   r. Loan collections, $143,000.
   s. Cash received from selling investments, $61,000, including a $36,000 gain.
   t. Purchase of inventory on credit, $832,000.
   u. Dividends received in cash, on investments in shares, $8,000.
   v. Cash payments to acquire property, plant, and equipment, $232,000.
   w. Cost of goods sold, $795,000.
   x. Cash balance: December 31, 2009—$230,000

          December 31, 2010—$144,000

   Note that, for simplicity, uncollectible accounts have been ignored.

Computing Individual Amounts for the Cash Flow Statement

How do we compute the amounts for the cash flow statement? We use the income statement and *changes* in the related balance sheet accounts. For the *operating* cash flow amounts, the adjustment process follows this basic approach:

Revenue or expense from the income statement	±	Adjustment for the change in the related balance sheet account(s)	=	Amount for the cash flow statement

This is called the T-account approach. Learning to analyze T-accounts is one of the most useful accounting skills you will acquire. It will enable you to measure the cash effects of a wide variety of transactions.

The following discussions use Capilano Ltd.'s income statement in Exhibit 17–9, comparative balance sheet in Exhibit 17–10, and cash flow statement in Exhibit 17–11 (which is a repeat of Exhibit 17–5 for your convenience). First, trace the $101,000 and $57,000 cash amounts on the balance sheet in Exhibit 17–10 to the bottom part of the cash flow statement in Exhibit 17–11. You see that the beginning and ending cash amounts come from the balance sheets. Now let's compute the cash flows from operating activities.

Computing the Cash Amounts of Operating Activities

Cash Collections from Customers Collections can be computed by converting sales revenue (an accrual-basis amount) to the cash basis. Capilano Ltd.'s income statement (Exhibit 17–9) reports sales of $682,000. Exhibit 17–10 shows that Accounts Receivable increased from $192,000 at the beginning of the year to $224,000 at year

EXHIBIT 17–9   Income Statement

CAPILANO LTD.
Income Statement
For the Year Ended December 31, 2010
(amounts in thousands)

Revenues and gains:		
Sales revenue	$682	
Interest revenue	29	
Dividend revenue	22	
Gain on sale of property, plant, and equipment,		
and intangible assets	19	
Total revenues and gains		$752
Expenses:		
Cost of goods sold	360	
Salaries expense	134	
Amortization expense	43	
Other operating expenses	41	
Interest expense	38	
Total expenses		616
Net income before income taxes		136
Income tax expense		36
Net income		$100

EXHIBIT 17–10 Comparative Balance Sheet

CAPILANO LTD.
Comparative Balance Sheet
December 31, 2010 and 2009
(amounts in thousands)

Assets	2010	2009	Increase (Decrease)	
Current				
Cash	$ 57	$ 101	$ (44)	
Accounts receivable	224	192	32	Changes in current assets—**Operating**
Interest receivable	8	3	5	
Inventory	323	330	(7)	
Prepaid expenses	18	17	1	
Long-term receivable from another company	26	—	26	Changes in noncurrent assets—**Investing**
Property, plant, and equipment, net of amortization	1,087	525	562	
Total	$1,743	$1,168	$575	
Liabilities				Changes in current liabilities—**Operating**
Current				
Accounts payable	$ 220	$ 137	$ 83	and change in current portion of long-term debt—**Financing**
Salaries payable	6	12	(6)	
Accrued liabilities	5	7	(2)	
Long-term debt	384	185	199	Changes in most long-term liabilities and contributed capital—**Financing**
Shareholders' Equity				
Common shares	861	619	242	
Retained earnings	267	208	59	Change due to net income—
Total	$1,743	$1,168	$575	**Operating** and change due to dividends—**Financing**

end, a $32,000 increase. Based on those amounts, Cash Collections equals $650,000, as shown in the Accounts Receivable T-account:

Accounts Receivable

Beginning balance	192,000	Collections	650,000
Sales	682,000		
Ending balance	224,000		

Another explanation: Accounts Receivable increased by $32,000, so Capilano Ltd. must have received $32,000 less cash than sales revenue for the period.

The following equation shows another way to compute cash collections from customers:

Accounts Receivable

Beginning + balance	Sales	− Collections	= Ending balance
$192,000	+ $682,000	− X	= $224,000
		−X	= $224,000 − $192,000 − $682,000
		X	= $650,000

A decrease in Accounts Receivable would mean that the company received more cash than the amount of sales revenue. This computation is summarized as the first item in Exhibit 17–12 on page 943.

LEARNING TIPS

Remember that each account contains four basic elements:

> Beginning Balance
> + Increases
> − Decreases
> = Ending Balance

Apply this relationship to Accounts Receivable for Capilano Ltd. Compute collections.

Beg. A/R	$192,000
+ Sales	682,000
− Collections*	?
= Ending Balance	$224,000

*Collections = $650,000

CAPILANO LTD.
Cash Flow Statement
For the Year Ended December 31, 2010

Cash flows from operating activities		(In thousands)	
Receipts:			
Collections from customers		$ 650	
Interest received on notes receivable		24	
Dividends received on investments in shares		22	
Total cash receipts			$ 696
Payments:			
To suppliers for merchandise for resale		(270)	
To suppliers for operating expenses		(44)	
To employees		(140)	
For interest		(38)	
For income tax		(36)	
Total cash payments			(528)
Net cash inflow from operating activities			168
Cash flows from investing activities			
Acquisition of property, plant, and equipment,			
and intangible assets		(735)	
Loan to another company		(26)	
Cash received from selling property, plant,			
and equipment, and intangible assets		149	
Net cash outflow from investing activities			(612)
Cash flows from financing activities			
Cash received from issuing common shares		242	
Cash received from issuing long-term debt		226	
Payment of long-term debt*		(27)	
Payment of dividends		(41)	
Net cash inflow from financing activities			400
Net increase (decrease) in cash and cash equivalents			(44)
Cash and cash equivalents at beginning of 2010			101
Cash and cash equivalents at end of 2010			$ 57

*This would also include the current portion of long-term debt payable, which is NIL in this case.

All collections of receivables are computed in the same way. In our example, Capilano Ltd.'s income statement, Exhibit 17–9, reports interest revenue of $29,000. Interest Receivable's balance in Exhibit 17–10 increased $5,000. Cash receipts of interest must be $24,000 (Interest Revenue of $29,000 minus the $5,000 increase in Interest Receivable). Exhibit 17–12 on page 943 summarizes this computation.

Payments to Suppliers This computation includes two parts, payments for inventory related to Cost of Goods Sold and payments for operating expenses.

Payments for inventory are computed by converting cost of goods sold to the cash basis. We must analyze the Inventory and Accounts Payable accounts. To "analyze" an account means to explain each amount in the account. For companies that purchase inventory on short-term notes payable, we must also analyze Short-Term Notes Payable in the same manner as Accounts Payable. The computation of Capilano Ltd.'s cash payments for inventory is given by this analysis of the T-accounts (again, we are using Exhibits 17–9 and 17–10 for our numbers):

LEARNING TIPS

An *increase* in Inventory indicates more inventory has been purchased than sold. A *decrease* in Inventory indicates that purchases are less than COGS. A *decrease* in Accounts Payable indicates that payments for inventory were greater than purchases. An *increase* in Accounts Payable indicates that payments for inventory were less than purchases.

Inventory				Accounts Payable			
Beg. Inventory	330,000	Cost of goods		Payments for		Beg. bal.	137,000
Purchases	353,000	sold	360,000	inventory	270,000	Purchases	353,000
End. Inventory	323,000					End. bal.	220,000

The first equation details the activity in the Inventory account to compute Purchases, as follows:

Inventory

Beginning inventory	+ Purchases	− Cost of goods sold	= Ending inventory
$330,000	+ X	− $360,000	= $323,000
	X		= $323,000 − $330,000 + $360,000
	X		= $353,000

Now we can insert the purchases figure into Accounts Payable to compute the amount of cash paid for inventory, as follows:

Accounts Payable

Beginning balance	+ Purchases	− Payments for inventory	= Ending balance
$137,000	+ $353,000	− X	= $220,000
		− X	= $220,000 − $137,000 − $353,000
		X	= $270,000

Beginning and ending inventory amounts come from the balance sheet, and Cost of Goods Sold comes from the income statement. Exhibit 17–12 on page 943 shows the general approach to compute the payments to suppliers of inventory (fourth item).

Payments for inventory appear in the Accounts Payable account, but we must first work through the Inventory account to calculate payments to suppliers of inventory.

Payments for Operating Expenses Payments for operating expenses other than interest and income tax can be computed as "plug figures," or differences, by analyzing Prepaid Expenses and Accrued Liabilities, as follows for Capilano Ltd. (again, all numbers are taken from Exhibits 17–9 and 17–10). The assumption here is that all prepaid items, such as rent, insurance, and advertising or all accrued liabilities, such as entertainment, telephone, and utilities, flow through the one Other Operating Expenses account.

Prepaid Expenses			Accrued Liabilities			Operating Expenses (other than Salaries, Wages, and Amortization)	
Beg. bal. 17,000	Expiration of prepaid		Payments 7,000	Beg. bal. 7,000		Accrual of expense at year end 5,000	
Payments 18,000	expense 17,000			Accrual of expense at year end 5,000		Expiration of prepaid expense 17,000	
End. bal. 18,000				End. bal. 5,000		Payments 19,000	
						End. bal. 41,000	

Total payments for operating expenses = $44,000
$18,000 + $7,000 + $19,000 = $44,000

The following equations show another way to calculate payments for operating expenses.

Prepaid Expenses

Beginning balance	+ Payments	− Expiration of prepaid expense	= Ending balance
$17,000	+ X	− $17,000	= $18,000
	X		= $18,000 − $17,000 + $17,000
	X		= $18,000

Accrued Liabilities

Beginning balance	+	Accrual of expense at year end	−	Payments	=	Ending balance
$7,000	+	$5,000	−	X	=	$5,000
				−X	=	$5,000 − $7,000 − $5,000
				X	=	$7,000

Operating Expenses

Accrual of expense at year end	+	Expiration of prepaid expense	+	Payments	=	Ending balance
$5,000	+	$17,000	+	X	=	$41,000
				X	=	$41,000 − $5,000 − $17,000
				X	=	$19,000

The expense total for operating expenses is $41,000. Once we remove the prepaid expirations and the expense accruals, the remaining balance must be the cash payments for expenses.

Payments to Employees Companies keep separate accounts for salaries, wages, and other forms of employee compensation. It is convenient to combine all compensation amounts into one account. Capilano Ltd.'s calculation adjusts Salaries Expense for the change in Salaries Payable, as shown in the following T-account:

Salaries and Wages Payable

		Beginning balance	12,000
Payments to employees	140,000	Salaries expense	134,000
		Ending balance	6,000

Salaries and Wages Payable

Beginning balance	+	Salaries expense	−	Payments	=	Ending balance
$12,000	+	$134,000	−	X	=	$6,000
				−X	=	$6,000 − $12,000 − $134,000
				X	=	$140,000

Exhibit 17–12 summarizes this computation under Payments to Employees.

Payments of Interest and Income Tax In our example, the expense and payment amount is the same for interest and income tax. Therefore, no analysis is required to determine the payment amount—we can use the expense amounts on the income statement for the cash flow statement. However, if the expense and the payment differ, the payment can be computed by analyzing the related liability or prepayment account. The payment computation follows the pattern illustrated for payments to employees; Exhibit 17–12 summarizes the procedure for interest and income tax.

Exhibit 17–12 shows how to compute operating cash flows under the direct method.

Computing the Cash Amounts of Investing Activities

Investing activities affect long-term asset accounts, such as Property, Plant, and Equipment, intangible assets, Investments, and Notes Receivable. Cash flows from investing activities can be computed by analyzing these accounts. The income statement and beginning and ending balance sheets provide the data.

Acquisitions and Sales of Tangible and Intangible Assets Companies keep separate accounts for Land, Buildings, Equipment, and other tangible and intangible assets. It is helpful to combine these accounts into a single summary for computing the cash flows from acquisitions and sales of these assets. Also, we often subtract accumulated amortization from the assets' cost and work with a net figure for

LEARNING TIPS

Increases and decreases in other payables (Salary Payable, Interest Payable, and Income Tax Payable) are treated in the same way as increases and decreases in Accounts Payable and Accrued Liabilities. A *decrease* in the payable indicates that payments for salaries/interest/income taxes were greater than the expense. The decrease is added to the expense. An *increase* in the payable indicates that payments for salaries/interest/income taxes were less than the expense. The increase is *deducted* from the expense.

KEY POINT

Changes in asset accounts, other than those used to compute cash flow from operating activities, are investing activities. An increase in an asset represents a cash outflow; a decrease in an asset represents a cash inflow.

Cash Receipts and Payments	From the Income Statement (Exhibit 17–9)	From the Balance Sheet (Exhibit 17–10)	
CASH RECEIPTS			
From customers	Sales Revenue	+ Decrease in Accounts Receivable	
		− Increase in Accounts Receivable	
Of interest	Interest Revenue	+ Decrease in Interest Receivable	
		− Increase in Interest Receivable	
Of dividends	Dividend Revenue	+ Decrease in Dividends Receivable	
		− Increase in Dividends Receivable	
CASH PAYMENTS			
To suppliers of inventory	Cost of Goods Sold	+ Increase in Inventory	+ Decrease in Accounts Payable
		− Decrease in Inventory	− Increase in Accounts Payable
To suppliers of other items	Operating Expense	+ Increase in Prepaids	+ Decrease in Accrued Liabilities
		− Decrease in Prepaids	− Increase in Accrued Liabilities
To employees	Salaries (Wages) Expense	+ Decrease in Salaries (Wages) Payable	
		− Increase in Salaries (Wages) Payable	
For interest	Interest Expense	+ Decrease in Interest Payable	
		− Increase in Interest Payable	
For income tax	Income Tax Expense	+ Decrease in Income Tax Payable	
		− Increase in Income Tax Payable	

Source: Suggestion of Barbara Gerrity

property, plant, and equipment, and amortizable intangible assets. This approach allows us to work with a single total for tangible and intangible assets.

To illustrate, observe that Capilano Ltd.'s balance sheet (Exhibit 17–10) reports beginning property, plant, and equipment, net of amortization, of $525,000 and an ending net amount of $1,087,000. The income statement in Exhibit 17–9 shows amortization of $43,000 and a $19,000 gain on sale of property, plant, and equipment. Further, the acquisitions are $735,000, an amount provided by the accounting records. How much are the proceeds from the sale of property, plant, and equipment? First, we must compute the book value of property, plant, and equipment sold as follows:

> **KEY POINT**
>
> Proceeds from the sale of an asset need not equal the asset's book value. Remember:
>
> Book value + Gain = Proceeds
>
> Book value − Loss = Proceeds
>
> The book value information comes from the balance sheet, the gain or loss from the income statement.

Property, Plant, and Equipment (net)

Beginning balance (net)	525,000	Amortization	43,000
Acquisitions	735,000	Book value of assets sold	130,000
Ending balance (net)	1,087,000		

Property, Plant, and Equipment, Net

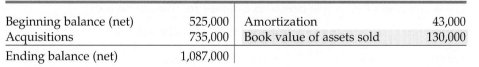

Beginning balance	+ Acquisitions	− Amortization	− Book value of assets sold	= Ending balance
$525,000	+ $735,000	− $43,000	− X	= $1,087,000
			−X	= $1,087,000 − $525,000 − $735,000 + $43,000
			X	= $130,000

Now we can compute the proceeds from the sale of property, plant, and equipment as follows:

$$
\begin{aligned}
\text{Sale proceeds} &= \text{Book value of assets sold} + \text{Gain} - \text{Loss} \\
&= \$130,000 + \$19,000 - \$0 \\
&= \$149,000
\end{aligned}
$$

Trace the sale proceeds of $149,000 to the cash flow statement in Exhibit 17–11. If the sale had resulted in a loss of $6,000, the sale proceeds would be $124,000 ($130,000 − $6,000), and the cash flow statement would report $124,000 as a cash receipt from this investing activity.

Acquisitions and Sales of Long-Term Investments, and Long-Term Loans and Loan Collections   The cash amounts of long-term investment and loan transactions can be computed in the manner illustrated for property, plant, and equipment, and intangible assets. Investments are easier to analyze, because there is no amortization to account for, as shown by the following T-account:

Investments

Beginning balance*	xxx		
Purchases**	xxx	Cost of investments sold	xxx
Ending balance*	xxx		

*From the balance sheet
**From the accounting records, used to create the cash flow statement

Long-Term Investments (amounts assumed for illustration only)

Beginning balance	+ Purchases	− Cost of investments sold	= Ending balance
$200,000	+ $100,000	− X	= $280,000
		− X	= $280,000 − $200,000 − $100,000
		X	= $20,000

$$
\begin{aligned}
\text{Sale proceeds} &= \text{Cost of investments sold} + \text{Gain} - \text{Loss} \\
&= \$20,000 + \$6,000 - \$0 \\
&= \$26,000
\end{aligned}
$$

Loan transactions follow the pattern described on pages 938–940 for collections from customers. New loans made increase the receivable and decrease the amount of cash. Collections decrease the receivable and increase the amount of cash, as follows:

Loans and Notes Receivable (Long-Term)

Beginning balance*	xxx		
New loans made**	xxx	Collections	xxx
Ending balance*	xxx		

*From the balance sheet
**From the accounting records, used to create the cash flow statement

Loans and Notes Receivable (amounts assumed for illustration only)

Beginning balance	+ New loans made	− Collections	= Ending balance
$180,000	+ $20,000	− X	= $60,000
		− X	= $60,000 − $180,000 − $20,000
		X	= $140,000

Computing the Cash Amounts of Financing Activities

Financing activities affect the long-term liability and shareholders' equity accounts, such as Notes Payable, Bonds Payable, Long-Term Debt, Common Shares, and Retained Earnings. To compute the cash flow amounts, analyze these accounts.

Issuances and Payments of Long-Term Debt Notes Payable, Bonds Payable, and Long-Term Debt accounts are related to borrowing, a financing activity. Their balances come from the balance sheet. If either the amount of new issuances or the amount of the payments is known, the other amount can be computed. New debt issuances totalled $226,000 for Capilano Ltd. as provided by the accounting records. Debt payments are computed from the Long-Term Debt T-account, using amounts from Capilano Ltd.'s balance sheet, Exhibit 17–10:

Long-Term Debt

		Beginning balance	185,000
Payments	27,000	Issuance of new debt	226,000
		Ending balance	384,000

Long-Term Debt

Beginning balance	+	Issuance of new debt	−	Payments of debt	=	Ending balance
$185,000	+	$226,000	−	X	=	$384,000
				$-X$	=	$384,000 − $185,000 − $226,000
				X	=	$27,000

Issuances and Repurchases of Shares These financing activities are computed from the various share accounts. It is convenient to work with a single summary account for shares. Using data from Exhibits 17–10 and 17–11, we have:

Common Shares

		Beginning balance	619,000
Retirements of shares	0	Issuance of new shares	242,000
		Ending balance	861,000

Common Shares

Beginning balance	+	Issuance of new shares	−	Retirements of shares	=	Ending balance
$619,000	+	$242,000	−	X	=	$861,000
				$-X$	=	$861,000 − $619,000 − $242,000
				X	=	$0

Dividend Payments If the amount of the dividends is not given elsewhere (for example, in a statement of retained earnings), it can be computed as follows:

Retained Earnings

		Beginning balance	208,000
Dividend declaration	41,000	Net income	100,000
		Ending balance	267,000

Dividends Payable

		Beginning balance	0
Dividend payments	41,000	Dividend declaration	41,000
		Ending balance	0

LEARNING TIPS

How are you able to tell, by referring to the balance sheet, if the amount of dividends paid is different from the dividends declared? If there is not a Dividend Payable account (or no change in the Dividend Payable account), then the dividends declared are equal to the dividends paid.

First, we must compute dividend declarations by analyzing Retained Earnings. Then we can solve for dividend payments with the Dividends Payable account. Capilano Ltd. has no Dividends Payable account, so dividend payments are the same as declarations. The following computations show how to compute Capilano Ltd.'s dividend payments.

Retained Earnings

Beginning balance	+	Net income	−	Dividend declarations	=	Ending balance
$208,000	+	$100,000	−	X	=	$267,000
				−X	=	$267,000 − $208,000 − $100,000
				X	=	$41,000

Noncash Investing and Financing Activities

Companies make investments that do not require cash. For example, they may issue a note payable to buy land, or they may pay off a loan by issuing shares. Our examples thus far included none of these transactions.

Suppose Capilano Ltd. issued common shares with a stated value of $730,000 to acquire a warehouse. Capilano Ltd. would make this journal entry:

Warehouse...	730,000	
Common Shares		730,000

Since this transaction has no net effect on the cash flow statement, Paragraph 1540.48 of the *CICA Handbook* requires that noncash investing and financing activities be disclosed elsewhere in the financial statements in a way that provides all the relevant information about these investing and financing activities. This can be done in a note to the financial statements in a summary as illustrated in Exhibit 17–13.

When there is a cash component to a transaction, it is appropriate to show only the net effect of the transaction on the cash flow statement. For example, if the purchase of the building had been for common shares of $700,000 and for cash of $30,000, it would be appropriate to show only the net effect on cash of $30,000 and the other components of the transaction in the notes to the financial statements.

EXHIBIT 17–13 Noncash Investing and Financing Activities (All Amounts Assumed for Illustration Only)

Noncash investing and financing activities	Thousands
Acquisition of building by issuing common shares..	$ 730
Acquisition of land by issuing note payable	172
Payment of long-term debt by transferring investments to the creditor	250
Acquisition of equipment by issuing short-term note payable......................	89
Total noncash investing and financing activities...	$1,241

Measuring Cash Adequacy: Free Cash Flow

So far, we have focused on cash flows from operating, investing, and financing activities. Some investors want to know how much cash a company can "free up" for new opportunities. **Free cash flow** is the amount of cash available from operations after paying for planned investments in long-term assets. Free cash flow can be computed as follows:

$$\text{Free cash flow} = \begin{matrix}\text{Net cash provided} \\ \text{by operating} \\ \text{activities}\end{matrix} - \begin{matrix}\text{Cash payments planned for} \\ \text{investments in property, plant,} \\ \text{equipment, and other long-term assets}\end{matrix}$$

PepsiCo, Inc. uses free cash flow to manage its operations. Suppose PepsiCo expects net cash provided by operations of $2.9 billion. Assume PepsiCo plans to spend $2.3 billion to modernize its bottling factories. In this case, PepsiCo's free cash flow would be $0.6 billion ($2.9 billion − $2.3 billion). If a good investment opportunity comes along, PepsiCo should have $0.6 billion to invest in the opportunity. Shell Oil Company also uses free-cash-flow analysis. A large amount of free cash flow is preferable because it means a lot of cash is available for new investments.

DID YOU GET IT?

MyAccountingLab

To check your understanding of the material in this Learning Objective, complete these questions. The solutions appear on MyAccountingLab so you can check your progress.

7. Symphonie Limited reported the following current-asset and current-liability amounts at year end

	December 31, 2010	December 31, 2009
Current assets		
Cash and cash equivalents	$38,000	$ 6,000
Accounts receivable	44,000	46,000
Inventories	68,000	62,000
Prepaid expenses	2,000	6,000
Current liabilities		
Notes payable (for inventory purchases)	$22,000	$14,000
Accounts payable	48,000	38,000
Accrued liabilities	14,000	18,000
Income and other taxes payable	22,000	20,000

Use this information to answer the following questions about the company:

i. Compute collections from customers during 2010. Sales totalled $240,000 and all sales were on credit.

ii. Compute payments for inventory during 2010, assuming the change in Accounts Payable is due to inventory. Cost of goods sold was $140,000.

iii. Compute payments for income taxes during 2010. Income tax expense for 2010 was $20,000.

iv. Compute payments for prepaid expenses during 2010. Prepaid expenses of $8,000 expired during 2010.

8. Brown Corp. reported the following (amounts in thousands):

Retirement of Brown Corp. preferred shares	$ 90
Sale of bonds issued by Blue Ltd.	224
Payment of interest on mortgage note to bank	22
Purchase of land	316
Payment of income taxes	76
Sale of Brown Corp. common shares	210
Collection of long-term note receivable	126
Payment of dividends	300

a. What is Brown Corp.'s net change in cash from investing activities?

b. Categorize the other items.

9. Refer to the Brown Corp. data in the previous question. What is Brown Corp.'s net change in cash from financing activities?

The Cash Flow Statement: The Indirect Method

A company that formats operating activities by the direct method may also wish to report a conversion or a reconciliation from net income to net cash inflow (or outflow) from operating activities. This conversion shows how the company's net income is related to net cash flow from operating activities. Exhibit 17–14 shows the reconciliation for Capilano Ltd.

 **EXHIBIT 17–14** Converting Net Income from the Accrual Basis to the Cash Basis

CAPILANO LTD.
Reconciliation of Net Income to Net Cash Inflow from
Operating Activities
For the Year Ended December 31, 2010
(In thousands)

Net income		$100
Add (subtract) items that affect net income and cash flow differently:		
Amortization	$ 43	
Gain on sale of property, plant, and equipment, and intangible assets....	(19)	
Increase in accounts receivable...	(32)	
Increase in interest receivable	(5)	
Decrease in inventory	7	
Increase in prepaid expenses	(1)	
Increase in accounts payable...	83	
Decrease in salaries payable...	(6)	
Decrease in accrued liabilities..	(2)	68
Net cash inflow from operating activities..............................		$168

The end result—net cash inflow from operating activities of $168,000—is the same as the result we derived earlier under the *direct* method (see Exhibit 17–11). The reconciliation is also the same as the *indirect* method of computing operating cash flows. We now turn to the indirect method.

The indirect method starts with net income from the income statement and reconciles to operating cash flows. For example, the operating activities section from the December 31, 2008 consolidated statement of cash flows of CCL Industries Inc., one of Canada's leading packagers of consumer goods, follows:

	(in thousands)
Net earnings	$ 47,986
Items not requiring cash:	
Depreciation and amortization	85,144
Goodwill impairment loss	31,386
Executive compensation	2,028
Future income taxes	6,495
Restructuring and other items, net of tax	1,965
Gain on sale of property, plant, and equipment	(1,464)
Net change in noncash working capital	42,808
Cash provided by operating activities	$216,348

The indirect method shows the link between net income and cash flow from operations better than the direct method. Many companies use the indirect method for that reason. The main drawback of the indirect method is that it does not report the detailed operating cash flows—collections from customers and other cash receipts, payments to suppliers, payments to employees, and payments for interest and taxes. Although the Accounting Stardards Board prefers the direct method, the vast majority of Canadian companies use the indirect method.

These two methods (direct and indirect) of preparing the cash flow statement affect only the operating activities section of the statement. No difference exists for investing activities or financing activities.

Exhibit 17–15 is Capilano Ltd.'s cash flow statement prepared by the indirect method. Only the operating section of the statement differs from the direct-method format in Exhibit 17–11. The new items Ⓐ, Ⓑ, and Ⓒ are keyed to their explanations, which are discussed below. For ease of reference, we repeat Capilano Ltd.'s income statement and balance sheet here as Exhibits 17–16 and 17–17.

KEY POINT

These two methods (direct and indirect) of preparing the cash flow statement affect only the operating activities section of the statement. No difference exists for investing activities or financing activities.

| EXHIBIT 17–15 | Cash Flow Statement (Indirect Method for Operating Activities) |

CAPILANO LTD.
Cash Flow Statement
For the Year Ended December 31, 2010

	(in thousands)	
Cash flows from operating activities		
Net income		$100
Add (subtract) items that affect		
net income and cash flow differently:		
Ⓐ Amortization	$ 43	
Ⓑ Gain on sale of property, plant, and equipment,		
and intangible assets	(19)	
Increase in accounts receivable	(32)	
Increase in interest receivable	(5)	
Ⓒ Decrease in inventory	7	
Increase in prepaid expenses	(1)	
Increase in accounts payable	83	
Decrease in salaries payable	(6)	
Decrease in accrued liabilities	(2)	68
Net cash inflow from operating activities		168
Cash flows from investing activities		
Acquisition of property, plant, and equipment, and		
intangible assets	(735)	
Loan to another company	(26)	
Cash received from selling property, plant, and		
equipment, and intangible assets	149	
Net cash outflow from investing activities		(612)
Cash flows from financing activities		
Cash received from issuing common shares	242	
Cash received from issuing long-term debt	226	
Payment of long-term debt	(27)	
Payment of dividends	(41)	
Net cash inflow from financing activities		400
Net increase (decrease) in cash and cash equivalents		(44)
Cash and cash equivalents at beginning of 2010		101
Cash and cash equivalents at end of 2010		$ 57

From Exhibit 17–11

EXHIBIT 17–16 Income Statement

CAPILANO LTD.
Income Statement
For the Year Ended December 31, 2010
(amounts in thousands)

Revenues and gains:		
Sales revenue	$682	
Interest revenue	29	
Dividend revenue	22	
Gain on sale of property, plant, and equipment, and intangible assets	19	
Total revenues and gains		$752
Expenses:		
Cost of goods sold	360	
Salaries expense	134	
Amortization expense	43	
Other operating expenses	41	
Interest expense	38	
Total expenses		616
Net income before income taxes		136
Income tax expense		36
Net income		$100

EXHIBIT 17–17 Comparative Balance Sheet

CAPILANO LTD.
Comparative Balance Sheet
December 31, 2010 and 2009
(amounts in thousands)

Assets	2010	2009	Increase (Decrease)	
Current				
Cash	$ 57	$ 101	$ (44)	
Accounts receivable	224	192	32	⎫
Interest receivable	8	3	5	⎬ Changes in current
Inventory	323	330	(7)	assets—**Operating**
Prepaid expenses	18	17	1	⎭
Long-term receivable from another company	26	—	26	⎫ Changes in noncurrent
Property, plant, and equipment, net of amortization	1,087	525	562	⎬ assets—**Investing**
Total	$1,743	$1,168	$575	
Liabilities				Changes in current
Current				liabilities—**Operating**
Accounts payable	$ 220	$ 137	$ 83	⎫ and change in current
Salaries payable	6	12	(6)	⎬ portion of long-term
Accrued liabilities	5	7	(2)	⎭ debt—**Financing**
Long-term debt	384	185	199	⎫
				⎬ Changes in most long-term
				liabilities and contri-
Shareholders' Equity				buted capital—**Financing**
Common shares	861	619	242	⎭
Retained earnings	267	208	59	⎫ Change due to net
Total	$1,743	$1,168	$575	income—**Operating** and change due to dividends—**Financing**

Logic Behind the Indirect Method

The indirect-method cash flow statement begins with accrual-basis net income, from the income statement. Additions and subtractions follow. These are labelled "Add (subtract) items that affect net income and cash flow differently." We discuss these items in the following sections. Refer to Exhibit 17–15.

Amortization Expenses These expenses are added back to net income to compute cash flow from operations. Let's see why.

Amortization is recorded as follows:

Amortization Expense....................................	43,000	
Accumulated Amortization.................		43,000

This entry neither debits nor credits Cash because amortization has no cash effect. However, amortization expense is deducted from revenues to compute income. Therefore, in going from net income to cash flows from operations, we add amortization back to net income. The addback cancels the earlier deduction.

The following example should help clarify this practice: Suppose a company had only two transactions during the period, a $5,000 cash sale and amortization expense of $1,000. Net income is $4,000 ($5,000 − $1,000). But cash flow from operations is $5,000. To go from net income ($4,000) to cash flow ($5,000), we must add back the amortization amount of $1,000.

An example of a revenue that does not provide cash is equity-method investment revenue. We learned about equity-method investment revenue in Chapter 16, pages 884–885.

Gains and Losses on the Sale of Assets Sales of property, plant, and equipment and of intangible assets are investing activities on the cash flow statement. Recall that Capilano Ltd. sold equipment with a book value of $130,000 for $149,000, producing a gain of $19,000. The $19,000 gain is reported on the income statement and is therefore included in net income. The cash receipt from the sale is $149,000, and that is what we report on the cash flow statement. The $149,000 of cash received also includes the $19,000 gain on the sale. To avoid counting the gain twice, we need to remove the gain from income and report the cash receipt of $149,000 in the investing activities section of the cash flow statement. Starting with net income, we subtract the gain. This deduction removes the gain's earlier effect on income. The sale of property, plant, and equipment and of intangible assets is reported as a $149,000 cash receipt from an investing activity, as shown in Exhibit 17–15.

A loss on the sale of property, plant, and equipment and of intangible assets is also an adjustment to net income on the cash flow statement. A loss is *added back* to income to compute cash flow from operations. The cash received from selling the property, plant, and equipment and intangible assets is reported under investing activities on the cash flow statement.

> **All expenses with no cash effects, such as accruals, are added back to net income on the cash flow statement.**
>
> **Likewise, revenues that do not provide cash, such as accrued income, are subtracted from net income.**
>
> **These items are added and subtracted by calculating differences in current assets and current liabilities between the opening and closing amounts.**

Changes in the Current Asset and Current Liability Accounts© Most current assets and current liabilities result from operating activities. Changes in the current accounts are reported as adjustments to net income on the cash flow statement. The following rules apply:

1. **An increase in a current asset other than cash is subtracted from net income to compute cash flow from operations.** Suppose a company makes a sale.

Income is increased by the sale amount. However, collection of less than the full amount increases Accounts Receivable. For example, Exhibit 17–17 reports that Capilano Ltd.'s Accounts Receivable increased by $32,000 during 2010. To compute the impact of revenue on Capilano Ltd.'s cash flows, we must subtract the $32,000 increase in Accounts Receivable from net income in Exhibit 17–15. The reason is this: We have *not* collected this $32,000 in cash. The same logic applies to the other current assets. If they increase during the period, subtract the increase from net income.

Remember this:[2]

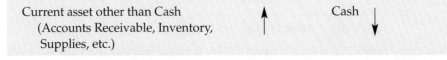

Current asset other than Cash
    (Accounts Receivable, Inventory,
      Supplies, etc.)   ↑   Cash ↓

2. **A *decrease* in a current asset other than cash is added to net income.** Suppose Capilano Ltd.'s Accounts Receivable balance decreased by $8,000 during the period. Cash receipts cause Accounts Receivable to decrease and Cash to increase, so decreases in Accounts Receivable and the other current assets are *added* to net income.

Symbolically,

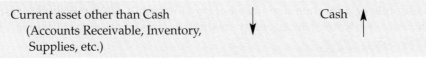

Current asset other than Cash
    (Accounts Receivable, Inventory,
      Supplies, etc.)   ↓   Cash ↑

3. **A *decrease* in a current liability is subtracted from net income.** The payment of a current liability decreases both Cash and the current liability, so decreases in current liabilities are subtracted from net income. For example, in Exhibit 17–15, the $2,000 decrease in Accrued Liabilities is *subtracted* from net income to compute net cash inflow from operating activities.

Current liability
    (Accounts Payable, Salaries Payable,
      Unearned Sales Revenue, etc.) ↓   Cash ↓

4. **An increase in a current liability is added to net income.** Capilano Ltd.'s Accounts Payable increased during the year. This increase can occur only if cash is not spent to pay this liability, which means that cash payments are less than the related expense. As a result, we have more cash on hand. Thus, increases in current liabilities are *added* to net income.

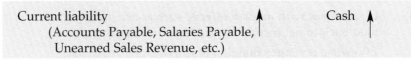

Current liability
    (Accounts Payable, Salaries Payable,
      Unearned Sales Revenue, etc.) ↑   Cash ↑

Computing net cash inflow or net cash outflow from *operating* activities by the indirect method takes a path that is very different from the direct-method computation. However, both methods arrive at the same amount of net cash flow from operating activities, as shown in Exhibits 17–11 and 17–15: both report a net cash inflow of $168,000.

Exhibit 17–18 summarizes the adjustments needed to convert net income to net cash inflow (or net cash outflow) from operating activities by the indirect method.

If you are studying *only* the indirect method for operating cash flows, please turn to pages 935–937 and pages 942–946 for coverage of investing and financing activities.

---

[2] The authors thank Mari S. duToit for suggesting these displays.

Add (subtract) items that affect net income and cash flow differently

Net Income
+ **Amortization**
+ **Loss on disposal or exchange of long-term asset or early extinguishment of debt**
− **Gain on disposal of long-term asset or early extinguishment of debt**
+ **Decrease in current asset other than cash**
− **Increase in current asset other than cash**
+ **Increase in current liability***
− **Decrease in current liability***

Net cash inflow (or outflow) from operating activities

* Short-term notes payable for general borrowing and current portion of long-term debt, are related to *financing* activities, not to operating activities; however, for simplicity, we treat short-term amounts as operating activities.

Source: We thank Barbara Gerrity and Jean Marie Hudson for suggesting this exhibit.

Using Cash Flow Information in Investment and Credit Analysis

It is clear that cash flows are important to a company's survival. A cash shortage is usually the most pressing problem of a struggling organization. Abundant cash allows a company to expand, invest in research and development, and hire the best employees. How, then, do investors (and their representatives, financial analysts) and creditors use cash flow information for decision making?

Neither cash flow data, net income information, balance sheet figures, nor the financial statement notes tell investors all they need to know about a company. Decision making is much more complex than inserting a few numbers into a simple formula. To decide whether to invest in a company's shares, investors analyze:

- A company's financial statements
- Articles in the financial press
- Data about the company's industry
- Predictions about the world economy

To evaluate a loan request, a bank loan officer may interview a company's top managers to decide whether they are trustworthy and whether their projections for the future of the company are reasonable. Both investors and creditors are interested mainly in a company's future. They want to make predictions about a company's future net income and future cash flows.

It has been said that cash-flow data help to spot losers better than winners. This is often true. When a company's business is booming, profits are high and cash flows are usually improving. In almost all cases, a negative cash flow from operations warrants investigation. A cash downturn in a *single* year is not necessarily a danger signal. But negative cash flows for two *consecutive* years may lead to bankruptcy. Without cash flow from operations, a business simply cannot survive.

You may ask, "Can't the business raise money by issuing shares or by borrowing?" The answer is no, because if operations cannot generate enough cash, then investors will not buy the company's shares. Bankers will not lend it money. *Over the long run, if a company cannot generate cash from operations, it is doomed.*

DID YOU GET IT?

To check your understanding of the material in this Learning Objective, complete these questions. The solutions appear on MyAccountingLab so you can check your progress.

10. The information listed below is taken from the financial statements of Vista Corp. for the year ended December 31, 2010, when net income is $150. All amounts are in thousands of dollars:

	Dec. 31, 2010	Jan. 1, 2010
Cash	$45	$15
Accounts Receivable	12	18
Inventory	66	48
Accounts Payable	20	9
Wages Payable	24	39

Compute cash flow from operating activities using the indirect method.

11. Examine Capilano Ltd.'s cash flow statement, Exhibit 17–15, and answer these questions:

a. Does Capilano Ltd. appear to be growing or shrinking? How can you tell?

b. Where did most of Capilano Ltd.'s cash for expansion come from?

c. Suppose Accounts Receivable decreased by $80,000 (instead of increasing by $32,000) during the current year. What would Capilano Ltd.'s cash flow from operating activities be?

The Impact on the Cash Flow Statement of International Financial Reporting Standards (IFRS)

As we saw earlier in this chapter under GAAP for private enterprises, receipts of interest and dividends, and payments of interest are operating activities. Payment of dividends is a financing activity. Under IFRS, a company may choose to classify receipts of interest and dividends as either operating or investing activities. Similarly, a company may choose to report payments of interest and dividends as either operating or financing activities. Once a company chooses its accounting policy, it must apply the policy consistently to all similar transactions. Under IFRS, there is no preference for the direct or indirect method of reporting cash flows from operating activities; either method is acceptable.

Under GAAP for private enterprises, the statement showing cash inflows and outflows is called the *Cash Flow Statement*; under IFRS, it is called the *Statement of Cash Flows*. However, this is a very minor difference as both sets of standards allow some flexibility in naming the statements. In practice, *Cash Flow Statement* and *Statement of Cash Flows* are used interchangeably.

OBJECTIVE 6

Describe the impact on the cash flow statement of international financial reporting standards (IFRS)

DID YOU GET IT?

To check your understanding of the material in this Learning Objective, complete these questions. The solutions appear on MyAccountingLab so you can check your progress.

12. Under IFRS, what options does an entity have for classifying cash inflows from interest and dividends on the statement of cash flows? How does this differ from GAAP for private enterprises?

13. Under IFRS, what options does an entity have for classifying cash payments of interest and dividends on the statement of cash flows? How does this differ from GAAP for private enterprises?

As we conclude this chapter, we return to our opening questions: What is the cash flow statement, and what information does it show that the other financial statements do not show? What are operating, investing, and financing activities, and are they equally important to a company's continued success? How do the direct and indirect methods of calculating cash flows from operations differ? How do you calculate the amounts that appear on the cash flow statement? How do investors and creditors use cash flow and related information? These questions were answered throughout this chapter, and the following Decision Guidelines feature provides investors and creditors with a few suggestions on how to use cash flow information for decision making.

DECISION GUIDELINES

Investors' and Creditors' Use of Cash Flow and Related Information

INVESTORS

Question	Financial Statement	What to Look For
Where is most of the company's cash coming from?	Cash flow statement	Operating activities → Good sign Investing activities → Bad sign Financing activities → Neutral sign
Do high sales and profits mean the company is generating more cash?	Cash flow statement	Usually, but cash flows from *operating* activities must be the main source of cash for long-term success.
If sales and profits are low, how is the company generating cash?	Cash flow statement	If *investing* activities are generating the cash, the business may be in trouble because it is selling its long-term assets. If *financing* activities are generating the cash, that cannot go on forever. Sooner or later, creditors will demand cash flow from operating activities.
Is the cash and cash equivalents balance large enough to provide for expansion?	Balance sheet	The cash and cash equivalents balance should be steady (if cash is reinvested regularly) or growing over time. If not, the company may be stagnant or in trouble.

CREDITORS

Question	Financial Statement	What to Look For
Can the business pay its debts?	Income statement	Increasing net income over time.
	Cash flow statement	Cash flows from operating activities should be the main source of cash.
	Balance sheet	Current ratio, quick ratio, debt ratio

Prepare the 2010 cash flow statement for Valemont Corporation, using the indirect method to report cash flows from operating activities.

Name: Valemont Corporation
Fiscal Period: Year ended December 31, 2010

Transaction data for 2010

Amortization expense	$ 40,000	Payment of cash dividends...............................	$ 72,000
Issuance of long-term note payable to borrow cash	28,000	Net income	104,000
Issuance of common shares for cash.................................	76,000	Purchase of long-term investment............................	32,000
Cash received from sale of building..........................	296,000	Issuance of long-term note payable to purchase patent	148,000
Repurchase of own shares	20,000		
Loss on sale of building.........	8,000	Issuance of common shares to retire $52,000 of bonds	52,000
Purchase of equipment..........	392,000		

For the indirect method, calculate the dollar change in all *non cash* current asset and current liability accounts.

		December 31,	
		2010	**2009**
Current assets			
	Cash and cash equivalents	$ 76,000	$ 12,000
$(4,000)	Accounts receivable..	88,000	92,000
12,000	Inventories...	136,000	124,000
(8,000)	Prepaid expenses	4,000	12,000
Current liabilities			
$16,000	Notes payable (for inventory purchases)...............................	$ 44,000	$ 28,000
20,000	Accounts payable	96,000	76,000
(8,000)	Accrued liabilities..	28,000	36,000
0	Income and other taxes payable...	40,000	40,000

SOLUTION

VALEMONT CORPORATION
Cash Flow Statement
For the Year Ended December 31, 2010

Cash flows from operating activities

Net income...		$104,000
Add (subtract) items that affect net income and		
cash flow differently:		
Amortization	$ 40,000	
Loss on sale of building	8,000	
Decrease in accounts receivable........................	4,000	
Increase in inventories	(12,000)	
Decrease in prepaid expenses	8,000	
Increase in notes payable, short-term	16,000	
Increase in accounts payable............................	20,000	
Decrease in accrued liabilities.........................	(8,000)	76,000
Net cash inflow from operating activities.................		180,000

Cash flows from investing activities

Purchase of equipment...	(392,000)	
Sale of building	296,000	
Purchase of long-term investment	(32,000)	
Net cash outflow from investing activities....................		(128,000)

Cash flows from financing activities

Issuance of long-term note payable	28,000	
Issuance of common shares...	76,000	
Payment of cash dividends	(72,000)	
Repurchase of Valemont Corporation common shares.....	(20,000)	
Net cash inflow from financing activities		12,000
Net increase in cash and cash equivalents		$ 64,000
Cash and cash equivalents at beginning of 2010.....................		12,000
Cash and cash equivalents at end of 2010		$ 76,000

In the notes to the financial statements:

1. During the year, the company issued a long-term note payable in the amount of $148,000 in payment for a patent.
2. During the year, the company issued common shares in the amount of $52,000 to retire bonds payable in the same amount.

The title must include the name of the company, "Cash Flow Statement," and the specific period of time covered. There are three sections: Cash flows from operating, investing, and financing activities.

For the indirect method, always begin with accrual-basis net income from the income statement (or from data given in this case).

Add back noncash items: amortization and losses; subtract gains

Reflect changes in current assets and liabilities as follows:
Current asset increases—deduct
Current asset decreases—add
Current liability increases—add
Current liability decreases—subtract

For cash flows from investing activities, look for activities that have a cash impact on long-term asset accounts. Brackets indicate cash outflows (purchases).

For cash flows from financing activities, look for activities that have a cash impact on short-term debt accounts, long-term liability accounts, and equity accounts. Brackets indicate cash outflows.

The end result should equal the December 31, 2010 balance sheet amount of cash and cash equivalents, given as part of Current assets. If it does not, there is an error in the cash flow statement.

CHAPTER 17 APPENDIX
The Spreadsheet Approach to Preparing the Cash Flow Statement

The body of this chapter discusses the uses of the cash flow statement in decision making and shows how to prepare the statement by using T-accounts. The T-account approach works well as a learning device, especially for simple situations. In practice, however, most companies face complex situations. In these cases, a spreadsheet can help accountants prepare the cash flow statement.

The basic task in preparing the cash flow statement is to account for all cash effects of transactions that took the business from its beginning financial position to its ending financial position. Like the T-account approach, the spreadsheet approach helps accountants identify the cash effects of all the period's transactions. The spreadsheet starts with the beginning balance sheet and concludes with the ending balance sheet. Two middle columns—one for debit amounts and the other for credit amounts—complete the spreadsheet. These columns, labelled Transaction Analysis, contain the data for the cash flow statement. Exhibit 17A–1 presents the basic framework of the spreadsheet. Accountants can prepare the cash flow statement directly from the lower part of the spreadsheet (Panel B in Exhibit 17A–1). The advantage of the spreadsheet is that it organizes all relevant data for the statement's preparation in one place. All the exhibits in this Appendix are based on the Capilano Ltd. data presented earlier in the chapter in Exhibit 17–8 on page 934 and repeated in this Appendix on the next page.

The spreadsheet can be used with either the direct method or the indirect method for operating activities. This Appendix will demonstrate the spreadsheet using the indirect method. As with the T-account approach, cash flows from investing activities and cash flows from financing activities are unaffected by the method used for operating activities.

EXHIBIT 17A–1 Spreadsheet for Preparing the Cash Flow Statement (data are assumed for illustration; amounts in thousands)

CAPILANO LTD.
Cash Flow Statement
For the Year Ended December 31, 2010

	Balances	Transaction Analysis		Balances
	Jan. 1, 2010	Debit	Credit	Dec. 31, 2010
PANEL A—Account Titles				
Cash....................................	84		40	44
Accounts receivable, etc..................	192	32		224
PANEL B—Cash Flow Statement				
Cash flows from operating activities:				
Cash flows from investing activities:			32	
Cash flows from financing activities:				
Net increase or decrease in cash.........		40		

Preparing the Spreadsheet—Indirect Method for Operating Activities

The indirect method shows the reconciliation from net income to net cash inflow (or net cash outflow) from operating activities. Exhibit 17A–2 on page 960 is the spreadsheet for preparing the cash flow statement by the indirect method.

The Capilano Ltd. data for analyzing operating activities come from the income statement (Exhibit 17–16 on page 950) and the comparative balance sheet (Exhibit 17–17 on page 950). The data are reproduced below. The analysis of investing activities and financing activities uses the information presented in Exhibit 17–8 and below.

OBJECTIVE A1
Prepare a spreadsheet for the cash flow statement—indirect method

Transaction Analysis on the Spreadsheet

For your convenience, set out below are the net income amount from Exhibit 17–16 and the changes in current assets and current liabilities from Exhibit 17–17, as well as some of the information presented in Exhibit 17–8.

Operating Activities:

(a) Net income, $100,000.

(b) Amortization, $43,000.

(c) Proceeds from sale of property, plant, and equipment, and intangible assets, $149,000, including a $19,000 gain.

(d) Increase in accounts receivable, $32,000.

(e) Increase in interest receivable, $5,000.

(f) Decrease in inventory, $7,000.

(g) Increase in prepaid expenses, $1,000.

(h) Increase in accounts payable, $83,000.

(i) Decrease in salaries payable, $6,000.

(j) Decrease in accrued liabilities, $2,000.

Investing Activities:

(k) Cash payments to acquire property, plant, and equipment, and intangible assets, $735,000.

(l) Loan to another company, $26,000.

Financing Activities:

(m) Cash received from issuing common shares, $242,000.

(n) Cash received from issuing long-term note payable, $226,000.

(o) Payment of long-term debt, $27,000.

(p) Declaration and payment of cash dividends, $41,000.

Transaction Analysis under the Indirect Method

Refer to Exhibit 17A–2 on page 960. Only balance sheet accounts appear on the spreadsheet. There are no income statement accounts. Only the *balance* of net income or net loss is used on the spreadsheet.

Transaction (a), net income, is the first operating cash inflow. Net income is entered on the spreadsheet as a debit to net income under cash flows from operating activities and a credit to Retained Earnings. Next, list the additions to, and subtractions from, net income.

Transaction (b), amortization, is debited to Amortization on the cash flow statement section and credited to Property, Plant, and Equipment, Net of Amortization.

Transaction (c) is the gain on the sale of property, plant, and equipment, and intangible assets. The $19,000 gain on the sale is entered as a credit to Gain on sale of property, plant, and equipment under operating cash flows—a subtraction

CAPILANO LTD.
Spreadsheet for Cash Flow Statement (Indirect Method)
For the Year Ended December 31, 2010
(Amounts in thousands)

	Balances	Transaction Analysis		Balances
Panel A: Balance Sheet	**Jan. 1, 2010**	**Debit**	**Credit**	**Dec. 31, 2010**
Cash	101		(q) 44	57
Accounts receivable	192	(d) 32		224
Interest receivable	3	(e) 5		8
Inventory	330		(f) 7	323
Prepaid expenses	17	(g) 1		18
Long-term receivable from another company	—	(l) 26		26
Property, plant, and equipment, net of	525	(k) 735	(b) 43	
amortization			(c) 130	1,087
Totals	1,168			1,743
Accounts payable	137		(h) 83	220
Salaries payable	12	(i) 6		6
Accrued liabilities	7	(j) 2		5
Long-term debt	185	(o) 27	(n) 226	384
Common shares	619		(m) 242	861
Retained earnings	208	(p) 41	(a) 100	267
Totals	1,168	875	875	1,743

Panel B: Cash Flow Statement				
Cash flows from operating activities				
Net income		(a) 100		
Add (subtract) items that affect net income and cash flow differently:				
Amortization		(b) 43		
Gain on sale of property, plant, and equipment, and intangible assets			(c) 19	
Increase in accounts receivable			(d) 32	
Increase in interest receivable			(e) 5	
Decrease in inventory		(f) 7		
Increase in prepaid expenses			(g) 1	
Increase in accounts payable		(h) 83		
Decrease in salaries payable			(i) 6	
Decrease in accrued liabilities			(j) 2	
Cash flows from investing activities				
Acquisition of property, plant, and equipment, and intangible assets			(k) 735	
Cash received from selling property, plant, and equipment, and intangible assets		(c) 149		
Loan to another company			(l) 26	
Cash flows from financing activities				
Cash received from issuing common shares		(m) 242		
Cash received from issuing long-term debt		(n) 226		
Payment of long-term debt			(o) 27	
Payment of dividends			(p) 41	
		850	894	
Net decrease in cash		(q) 44	—	
Totals		894	894	

from net income. This credit removes the $19,000 amount of the gain from cash flow from operations because the cash proceeds from the sale were not $19,000. The cash proceeds were $149,000, so this amount is entered on the spreadsheet as a debit under investing activities. Entry (c) is completed by crediting the property, plant, and equipment's book value of $130,000 ($149,000 – $19,000) to the Property, Plant, and Equipment, Net of Amortization account on the balance sheet section.

Transactions (d) through (j) reconcile net income to cash flows from operations for increases and decreases in the current assets other than Cash and for increases and decreases in the current liabilities. Entry (d) debits Accounts Receivable for its $32,000 increase during the year. This decrease in cash flows is credited to Increase in accounts receivable under operating cash flows. Entries (e) and (g) are similar for Interest Receivable and Prepaid Expenses.

Transaction (k) records the purchase of property, plant, and equipment and of intangible assets, while entry (l) records the loan of funds to another company; both of these are investing activities.

Transaction (m) is the issuance of common shares for cash while entry (n) records the issuance of long-term debt for cash.

Transaction (o) records the repayment of long-term debt while entry (p) is for the payment of dividends. Entries (m) to (p) are financing activities.

Transaction (q) is the final item in Exhibit 17A–2, the Net Decrease in Cash—a credit to Cash and a debit to Net decrease in cash. Amount (q) is your check figure, so if Panel B equals the change in cash from the comparative balance sheets, you have likely completed the spreadsheet correctly. To prepare the cash flow statement from the spreadsheet, the accountant merely transfers the data from Panel B of the spreadsheet to the cash flow statement, adding subtotals for the three categories of activities.

Noncash Investing and Financing Activities on the Spreadsheet   Noncash investing and financing activities can also be analyzed on the spreadsheet. Because these types of transactions include both a financing activity and an investing activity, they require two spreadsheet entries. For example, suppose Capilano Ltd. purchased a building by issuing common shares for $640,000. Exhibit 17A–3 illustrates the transaction analysis of this noncash investing and financing activity. Observe that Cash is unaffected.

Spreadsheet entry (t1) records the purchase of the building, and entry (t2) records the issuance of the shares. The order of the entries is unimportant.

EXHIBIT 17A–3 Noncash Investing and Financing Activities on the Spreadsheet

CAPILANO LTD.
Spreadsheet for the Cash Flow Statement
For the Year Ended December 31, 2010
(Amounts in Thousands)

	Balances	Transaction Analysis		Balances
Panel A: Account Titles	Jan. 1, 2010	Debit	Credit	Dec. 31, 2010
Cash				
Accounts receivable				
Building...	1,300,000	(t1) 640,000		1,940,000
Common shares...	1,780,000		(t2) 640,000	2,420,000
Panel B: Cash Flow Statement				
Noncash investing and financing transactions:				
Purchase of building by issuing common shares		(t2) 640,000	(t1) 640,000	

Summary

1. **Identify the purposes of the cash flow statement.** The *cash flow statement* reports a business's cash receipts, cash payments, and change in cash for the accounting period. It shows *why* cash increased or decreased during the period. A required financial statement, it gives a different view of the business from that given by accrual-basis statements. The cash flow statement aids in the prediction of future cash flows and evaluation of management decisions. Cash includes cash on hand, cash in the bank, and *cash equivalents* such as liquid short-term investments.

2. **Identify cash flows from operating, investing, and financing activities.** The cash flow statement reports *operating activities, investing activities,* and *financing activities.* Operating activities create revenues and expenses in the entity's major line of business. Investing activities affect the long-term assets. Financing activities obtain from investors and creditors the cash needed to launch and sustain the business. Each of these sections of the cash flow statement includes cash receipts and cash payments. The statement must agree with the change in cash reported on the comparative balance sheet. In addition, *noncash investing and financing activities* are reported in the notes to the financial statements.

3. **Prepare a cash flow statement by the direct method.** Two formats can be used to report *operating* activities—the direct method and the indirect method. Examples of items that the *direct method* reports include collections from customers and receipts of interest and dividends, minus cash payments to suppliers, payments to employees, and payments for interest and income taxes. Investing cash flows and financing cash flows are unaffected by the method used to report operating activities.

4. **Compute the cash effects of a wide variety of business transactions.** The analysis of T-accounts aids the computation of the cash effects of business transactions. The information needed comes from the balance sheet, the income statement, the statement of earnings, and the related accounts. *Free cash flow* is the amount of cash available for new opportunities, calculated as cash available from operations after paying for planned investments in long-term assets.

5. **Prepare a cash flow statement by the indirect method.** The *indirect method* starts with net income and reconciles net income to cash flow from operations. Although the Accounting Standards Board permits both the direct and the indirect method, it prefers the direct method. However, the indirect method is still much more widely used in Canada.

6. **Describe the impact on the cash flow statement of international financial reporting standards (IFRS).** IFRS provide companies with some alternatives for classifying both the receipt and payment of interest and dividends on the statement of cash flows. Specifically, the receipt of interest and dividends may be recorded as either operating or investing activities, while the payment of interest and dividends may be recorded as either operating or financing activities. Once the company chooses an accounting policy from these choices, however, it must apply the policy consistently to all transactions of a similar nature.

A1. **Chapter 17 Appendix: Prepare a spreadsheet for the cash flow statement—indirect method.** The chapter showed how to use T-accounts to prepare the cash flow statement. The Appendix shows how to use a spreadsheet, with operating activities reported using the indirect method.

SELF-STUDY QUESTIONS

1. The income statement and the balance sheet (*p. 927*)
   a. Report the cash effects of transactions
   b. Fail to report why cash changed during the period
   c. Report the sources and uses of cash during the period
   d. Are divided into operating, investing, and financing activities

2. The purpose of the cash flow statement is to (*p. 928*)
   a. Predict future cash flows
   b. Evaluate management decisions
   c. Determine the ability to pay liabilities and dividends
   d. Do all the above

3. A successful company's major source of cash should be (*p. 930*)
   a. Operating activities
   b. Investing activities

   c. Financing activities
   d. A combination of the above

4. Dividends paid to shareholders are usually reported on the cash flow statement as a(n) (*pp. 930–931*)
   a. Operating activity
   b. Investing activity
   c. Financing activity
   d. Combination of the above

5. Which of the following items appears on a cash flow statement prepared by the direct method? (*p. 935*)
   a. Amortization expense
   b. Decrease in accounts receivable
   c. Loss on sale of property, plant, and equipment, and intangible assets
   d. Cash payments to suppliers

6. Falcon Lake Copy Centre had accounts receivable of $40,000 at the beginning of the year and $50,000 at year end. Revenue for the year totalled $150,000. How much cash did Falcon Lake Copy Centre collect from customers? (pp. 938–940)

   a. $160,000
   b. $190,000
   c. $200,000
   d. $140,000

7. Windemere Ltd. sold a long-term investment for $200,000; the selling price included a loss of $10,000. The cash flow from investing activities will show (p. 944)

   a. An increase of $200,000
   b. An increase of $190,000
   c. A decrease of $210,000
   d. None of the above

8. Redtail Corp. borrowed $50,000, issued common shares for $20,000, and paid dividends of $15,000. What was Redtail Corp.'s net cash provided (used) by financing activities? (pp. 944–946)

   a. $0
   b. $55,000
   c. $(15,000)
   d. $70,000

9. In preparing a cash flow statement by the indirect method, the accountant will treat an increase in inventory as a(n) (pp. 951–953)

   a. Increase in investment cash flows
   b. Decrease in investment cash flows
   c. Decrease in operating cash flows
   d. Increase in operating cash flows

10. Net income is $20,000, and amortization is $6,000. In addition, the sale of property, plant, and equipment generated a $4,000 gain. Current assets other than cash increased by $6,000, and current liabilities increased by $8,000. What was the amount of cash flow from operations using the indirect method? (pp. 948–953)

   a. $32,000
   b. $24,000
   c. $20,000
   d. $36,000

ACCOUNTING VOCABULARY

Cash equivalents (p. 928)
Cash flow statement (p. 927)
Cash flows (p. 927)
Direct method (p. 932)
Financing activity (p. 930)

Free cash flow (p. 946)
Indirect method (p. 932)
Investing activity (p. 930)
Operating activity (p. 929)

SIMILAR ACCOUNTING TERMS

Cash flows	Cash receipts and cash payments
Cash flow statement	Statement of cash flows; Statement of changes in financial position
Cash payments	Disbursements
Cash receipts	Proceeds

Assignment Material

QUESTIONS

1. What information does the cash flow statement report that is not shown on the balance sheet, the income statement, or the statement of retained earnings?

2. Identify four purposes of the cash flow statement.

3. Identify and briefly describe the three types of activities that are reported on the cash flow statement.

4. How is the cash flow statement dated and why?

5. What is the check figure for the cash flow statement? In other words, which figure do you check to make sure you've done your work correctly? Where is it obtained, and how is it used?

6. What is the most important source of cash for most successful companies?

7. How can cash decrease during a year when income is high? How can cash increase when income is low? How can investors and creditors learn these facts about the company?

8. Fort Inc. prepares its cash flow statement using the *direct* method for operating activities. Identify the section of Fort Inc.'s cash flow statement where the results of each of the following transactions will appear. If the transaction does not appear on the cash flow statement, give the reason.

    a. Cash 14,000
           Note Payable, Long-Term   14,000
    b. Salary Payable 7,300
           Cash   7,300
    c. Cash 28,400
           Sales Revenue   28,400
    d. Amortization Expense.............. 6,500
           Patent   6,500
    e. Accounts Payable...................... 1,400
           Cash   1,400

9. Why is amortization expense *not* reported on a cash flow statement that reports operating activities by the direct method? Why and how are these expenses reported on a statement prepared by the indirect method?

10. Winford Distributing Corp. collected cash of $102,000 from customers and $8,000 interest on notes receivable. Cash payments included $28,000 to employees, $18,000 to suppliers, $11,000 as dividends to shareholders, and $10,000 as a long-term loan to another company. How much was Winford Distributing Corp.'s net cash inflow from operating activities?

11. Summarize the major cash receipts and cash payments in the three categories of activities that appear on the cash flow statement prepared by the direct method.

12. Nelson Inc. recorded salary expense of $54,000 during a year when the balance of Salary Payable decreased from $8,000 to $2,000. How much cash did Nelson Inc. pay to employees during the year? Where on the cash flow statement should Nelson Inc. report this item?

13. Trail Corporation's beginning Property, Plant, and Equipment balance, net of accumulated amortization, was $200,000, and the ending amount was $180,000. Trail Corporation recorded amortization of $35,000 and sold property, plant, and equipment with a book value of $10,000. How much cash did Trail Corporation pay to purchase property, plant, and equipment during the period? Where on the cash flow statement should Trail Corporation report this item?

14. How should issuance of a note payable to purchase land be reported in the financial statements? Identify three other transactions that fall into this same category.

15. What is free cash flow, and how is it calculated?

16. Which format of the cash flow statement gives a clearer description of the individual cash flows from operating activities? Which format better shows the relationship between net income and operating cash flow?

17. An investment that cost $75,000 was sold for $80,000, resulting in a $5,000 gain. Show how to report this transaction on a cash flow statement prepared by the indirect method.

18. Using the indirect method, identify the cash effects of net increases and net decreases in current assets other than cash. What are the cash effects of net increases and net decreases in current liabilities?

19. Midland Corporation earned net income of $45,000 and had amortization expense of $12,000. Also, noncash current assets decreased by $9,000, and current liabilities decreased by $6,000. Using the indirect method, what was Midland Corporation's net cash flow from operating activities?

20. What is the difference between the direct method and the indirect method of reporting investing activities and financing activities?

21. Greenwood Corp. reports operating activities by the direct method. Does this method show the relationship between net income and cash flow from operations? If so, state how. If not, how can Greenwood Corp. satisfy this purpose of the cash flow statement?

STARTERS

Starter 17–1 Describe how the cash flow statement helps investors and creditors perform each of the following functions:

1. Predict future cash flows.
2. Evaluate management decisions.
3. Predict the ability to make debt payments to lenders and pay dividends to shareholders.
4. Show the relationship of net income to cash flow.

Purposes of the cash flow statement

①

Starter 17–2 Answer these questions about the cash flow statement.

a. List the categories of cash flows in order of importance.
b. What is the "check figure" for the statement of cash flows? Where do you get this check figure?
c. What is the first dollar amount to report for the direct method?
d. What is the first dollar amount to report for the indirect method?

Classifying cash flow items

①

Starter 17–3 Gillam Health Labs Inc. began 2010 with cash of $65,000. During the year, Gillam earned service revenue of $650,000 and collected $660,000 from customers. Expenses for the year totalled $470,000, of which Gillam paid $460,000 in cash to suppliers and employees. Gillam also paid $150,000 to purchase equipment and paid a cash dividend of $40,000 to its shareholders during 2010.

Prepare the company's cash flow statement for the year ended December 31, 2010. Format operating activities by the direct method.

Preparing a cash flow statement—direct method

③

Net increase in cash $10,000

Starter 17–4 (Starter 17–5 is an alternate.) Napanee Resources Inc. has assembled the following data for the year ended June 30, 2010.

Payment of dividends....................................	$ 12,000
Cash received from issuing shares...............	40,000
Collections from customers..........................	400,000
Cash received from sale of land....................	120,000
Payments to suppliers...................................	220,000
Purchase of equipment	80,000
Payments to employees	140,000
Payment of note payable	60,000

Prepare the *operating* activities section of Napanee's cash flow statement for the year ended June 30, 2010. Napanee uses the direct method for operating cash flows.

Computing operating cash flows—direct method

③

Net cash provided $40,000

Starter 17–5 Use the data in Starter 17–4 to prepare Napanee Resources Inc.'s cash flow statement for the year ended June 30, 2010. Napanee uses the *direct* method for operating activities. Use Exhibit 17–11 page 940, as a guide, but you may stop after determining the net increase (or decrease) in cash.

Preparing a cash flow statement—direct method

③

Net increase in cash $48,000

Starter 17–6 Milton Toys Ltd. had the following comparative balance sheet:

Computing operating cash flows—direct method

③ ④

a. Collections from customers $402,000

MILTON TOYS LTD.
Comparative Balance Sheet
December 31, 2010 and 2009

Assets	2010	2009	Liabilities	2010	2009
Current			Current		
Cash.....................................	$ 57,000	$ 48,000	Accounts payable......	$ 141,000	$ 126,000
Accounts receivable	162,000	144,000	Salary payable	69,000	63,000
Inventory	240,000	232,000	Accrued liabilities	24,000	33,000
Prepaid expenses...............	9,000	6,000	Long-term notes		
			payable	198,000	204,000
Long-term investments..........	225,000	270,000	**Shareholders' Equity**		
Property and			Common shares......	120,000	111,000
equipment, net..................	675,000	575,000	Retained earnings...	816,000	738,000
Total	$1,368,000	$1,275,000	Total..............................	$1,368,000	$1,275,000

Compute for Milton Toys Ltd:

a. Collections from customers during 2010. Sales totalled $420,000.
b. Payments for inventory during 2010, assuming the change in Accounts Payable is due to inventory. Cost of good sold was $240,000.

Computing financing cash flows

④

c. Dividends $42,000

Starter 17–7 Use the Milton Toys Ltd. data in Starter 17–6 to compute

a. New borrowing or payment of long-term note payable, with Milton having only one long-term note payable transaction during the year.
b. Issuance of common shares, with Milton having only one common share transaction during the year.
c. Payment of cash dividends. Net income for the year ended December 31, 2010 was $120,000.

Computing investing and financing cash flows

④

a. Acquisitions $16,500

Starter 17–8 Truro Media Corporation had the following income statement and balance sheet for 2010:

TRURO MEDIA CORPORATION
Income Statement
For the Year Ended December 31, 2010

Service revenue..	$120,000
Amortization expense	9,000
Other expenses	81,000
Net income	$ 30,000

TRURO MEDIA CORPORATION
Comparative Balance Sheet
December 31, 2010 and 2009

Assets	2010	2009	Liabilities	2010	2009
Current:			Current:		
Cash............................	$ 7,500	$ 6,000	Accounts payable	$ 12,000	$ 9,000
Accounts receivable..	15,000	9,000	Long-term notes		
Equipment, net	112,500	105,000	payable	15,000	18,000
			Shareholders' equity		
			Common shares........	33,000	30,000
			Retained earnings.....	75,000	63,000
	$135,000	$120,000		$135,000	$120,000

Compute for Truro during 2010:

a. Acquisition of equipment. Truro sold no equipment during the year.
b. Payment of a long-term note payable. During the year, Truro issued a $7,500 note payable.

Identifying items for reporting cash flows from operations— indirect method

⑤

a. O+
j. O–

Starter 17–9 Pillar Corporation is preparing its cash flow statement by the *indirect* method. The company has the following items for you to consider in preparing the statement. Identify each item as

- Operating activity—addition to net income (O+), or subtraction from net income (O−)
- Investing activity (I)
- Financing activity (F)
- Activity that is not used to prepare the cash flow statement (N)

Answer by placing the appropriate symbol in the blank space.

_____ a. Loss on sale of land
_____ b. Amortization expense
_____ c. Increase in inventory
_____ d. Decrease in accounts receivable
_____ e. Purchase of equipment
_____ f. Increase in accounts payable

_____ g. Payment of dividends
_____ h. Decrease in accrued liabilities
_____ i. Issuance of common shares
_____ j. Gain on sale of building

Starter 17–10 Urgent Printers reported the following data for 2010:

Computing cash flows from operating activities—indirect method

⑤

Net cash provided $61,000

> **Income Statement**
> Net income... $63,000
> Amortization expense 10,000
> **Balance sheet**
> Increase in Accounts Receivable 7,000
> Decrease in Accounts Payable 5,000

Compute Urgent Printers' net cash provided by operating activities, using the indirect method.

Starter 17–11 Howard's Gourmet Shops earned net income of $88,000, which included amortization of $16,500. Howard's paid $132,000 for a building and borrowed $66,000 on a long-term note payable. How much did Howard's cash balance increase or decrease during the year?

Computing a cash increase or decrease—indirect method

⑤

Increased $38,500

Starter 17–12 (Starter 17–13 is an alternate.) Dryden Resources Inc. accountants have assembled the following data for the year ended June 30, 2010.

Computing operating cash flows—indirect method

⑤

Net cash provided $80,000

Payment of dividends	$12,000	Net income	$120,000
Cash receipt from issuance		Purchase of equipment..............	80,000
of common shares.....................	40,000	Decrease in current liabilities	10,000
Increase in current		Payment of note payable...........	60,000
assets other than cash...............	60,000	Cash receipt from sale of land...	120,000
Repurchase of Dryden shares.....	10,000	Amortization expense................	30,000

Prepare the *operating* activities section of Dryden Resources Inc.'s cash flow statement for the year ended June 30, 2010. Dryden uses the *indirect* method for operating cash flows.

Starter 17–13 Use the data in Starter 17–12 to prepare Dryden Resources Inc.'s cash flow statement for the year ended June 30, 2010. Dryden uses the *indirect* method for operating activities. Use Exhibit 17–15 as a guide, but you may stop after determining the net increase (or decrease) in cash.

Preparing a cash flow statement—indirect method

⑤

Net increase in cash $78,000

Starter 17–14 Latham Company expects the following for 2010:

- Net cash provided by operating activities of $240,000
- Net cash provided by financing activities of $96,000
- Net cash used for investing activities of $128,000 (no sales of long-term assets)

How much free cash flow does Latham Company expect for 2010?

Free cash flow

④

Free cash flow $112,000

EXERCISES

MyAccountingLab | All questions in this section appear in MyAccountingLab.

Exercise 17–1

Keremeos Properties Ltd., a real estate developer, has experienced ten years of growth in net income. Nevertheless, the business is facing bankruptcy. Creditors are calling all Keremeos Properties Ltd.'s outstanding loans for immediate payment, and the cash is simply not available. Where did Keremeos Properties Ltd. go wrong? Managers placed too much emphasis on net income and gave too little attention to cash flows.

Identifying the purposes of the cash flow statement

①

Required

Write a brief memo, in your own words, to explain for Keremeos Properties Ltd. managers the purposes of the cash flow statement.

Exercise 17–2

Suppose Whiteshell Inc.'s cash flow statement showed a net cash outflow from operations of $12,000,000.

Using a cash flow statement

①

Required

1. Suggest possible reasons for the cash outflow from operations.
2. What is the main danger signal this situation reveals?
3. Suppose Whiteshell Inc. has two more years with the cash flows mentioned above. What is likely to happen to the company?

Distinguishing among operating, investing, and financing activities

(2)

Exercise 17–3

Describe operating activities, investing activities, and financing activities. For each category, give an example of (a) a cash receipt and (b) a cash payment.

Identifying activities for the cash flow statement

(2)

a. NIF
h. I–
s. O+

Exercise 17–4

Identify each of the following transactions as an operating activity (O), an investing activity (I), a financing activity (F), a noncash investing and financing activity (NIF), or a transaction that is not reported on the cash flow statement (N). For each cash flow, indicate whether the item increases (+) or decreases (–) cash. Assume the direct method is used to report cash flows from operating activities.

____ a. Acquisition of a building by issuance of common shares

____ b. Accrual of salaries expense

____ c. Issuance of common shares for cash

____ d. Payment of accounts payable

____ e. Issuance of preferred shares for cash

____ f. Acquisition of equipment by issuance of note payable

____ g. Payment of long-term debt

____ h. Purchase of long-term investment

____ i. Payment of wages to employees

____ j. Collection of cash interest

____ k. Cash sale of land

____ l. Distribution of stock dividend

____ m. Payment of cash dividend

____ n. Sale of long-term investment

____ o. Amortization of equipment

____ p. Repurchase of common shares

____ q. Issuance of long-term note payable to borrow cash

____ r. Amortization of bond discount

____ s. Collection of accounts receivable

Classifying transactions for the cash flow statement

(2)

a. Investing
i. Operating
m. Operating

Exercise 17–5

Indicate in which category (operating, investing, or financing) or noncash investing and financing, if at all, each of the following transactions would be reported on a cash flow statement prepared by the *direct* method.

a.	Land	185,000	
	Cash		185,000
b.	Dividends Payable	40,000	
	Cash		40,000
c.	Furniture and Fixtures	43,000	
	Note Payable, Short-Term		43,000
d.	Salaries Expense	19,000	
	Cash		19,000
e.	Equipment	137,000	
	Cash		137,000
f.	Cash	125,000	
	Long-Term Investment in Bonds		125,000
g.	Bonds Payable	80,000	
	Cash		80,000

h. Building..	210,000	
Note Payable, Long-Term		210,000
i. Cash	25,000	
Accounts Receivable...		25,000
j. Accounts Payable..	39,000	
Cash...		39,000
k. Cash	140,000	
Common Shares		140,000
l. Common Shares...	36,000	
Cash...		36,000
m. Cash	8,000	
Interest Revenue..		8,000

Exercise 17–6

Computing cash flows from operating activities—direct method

③

Net cash inflow from operating activities $52,000

The accounting records of BKC Auto Parts Ltd. reveal the following:

Acquisition of land	$ 89,000	Loss on sale of land	$ 12,000
Amortization..............................	40,000	Net income.................................	78,000
Cash sales..................................	78,000	Payment of accounts payable...	110,000
Collection of accounts		Payment of dividends...............	25,000
receivable	186,000	Payment of income tax.............	16,000
Collection of dividend revenue..	4,000	Payment of interest...................	14,000
Decrease in current liabilities...	52,000	Payment of salaries	
Increase in current assets		and wages	76,000
other than cash	48,000		

Required

Compute cash flows from operating activities by the direct method. Use the format of the operating activities section of Exhibit 17–11.

Exercise 17–7

Identifying items for the cash flow statement—direct method

③

Selected accounts of Acorn Storage Centres show the following:

Accounts Receivable

Beginning balance	27,000	Cash receipts from customers	354,000
Service revenue	360,000		
Ending balance	33,000		

Land

Beginning balance	570,000	
Acquisitions	81,000	
Ending balance	651,000	

Long-Term Debt

Payments	207,000	Beginning balance	819,000
		Issuance of debt for cash	249,000
		Ending balance	861,000

Required

For each account, identify the item or items that should appear on a cash flow statement prepared by the direct method. Also, state each item's amount and where to report the item.

Exercise 17–8

Preparing a cash flow statement—direct method

③

3. Net increase in cash $60,000

Tech Arts Ltd. began 2010 with cash of $112,000. During the year, the company earned service revenue of $2,400,000 and collected $2,360,000 from clients. Expenses for the year totalled $1,760,000, of which the company paid $1,640,000 in cash to employees and $60,000 in cash for supplies. Tech Arts Ltd. also paid $480,000 to purchase computer equipment and paid a cash dividend of $120,000 to its shareholders during 2010.

Required

1. Compute net income for the year.
2. Determine the cash balance at the end of the year.
3. Prepare the company's cash flow statement for the year. Format operating activities by the direct method.

Preparing the cash flow
statement—direct method

③

Net cash from
operating $188,000;
investing $(182,000);
financing $14,000

Exercise 17–9

The income statement and additional data of Yellowpoint Consulting Ltd. follow:

YELLOWPOINT CONSULTING LTD.
Income Statement
For the Year Ended September 30, 2010

Revenues		
Consulting revenue		$548,000
Expenses		
Salaries expense	$296,000	
Amortization expense	58,000	
Rent expense	24,000	
Office supplies expense	6,000	
Insurance expense	4,000	
Interest expense	4,000	
Income tax expense	36,000	428,000
Net income		$120,000

Additional data:

a. Collections from clients were $14,000 more than revenues.
b. Increase in cash balance, $20,000.
c. Payments to employees are $8,000 less than salaries expense.
d. Interest expense and income tax expense equal their cash amounts.
e. Acquisition of property, plant, and equipment is $232,000. Of this amount, $202,000 was paid in cash, $30,000 by signing a long-term note payable.
f. Cash received from sale of land, $20,000.
g. Cash received from issuance of common shares, $84,000.
h. Payment of long-term note payable, $40,000.
i. Payment of cash dividends, $30,000.
j. Payments for rent and insurance were equal to expense.
k. Payment for office supplies was $12,000 more than expense.

Prepare Yellowpoint Consulting Ltd.'s cash flow statement by the direct method and the note to the financial statements giving the summary of noncash investing and financing activities. Evaluate Yellowpoint's cash flow for the year. Mention all three categories of cash flows and the reason for your evaluation.

Computing amounts for the cash
flow statement—direct method

③ ④

a. $104,000

Exercise 17–10

Compute the following items for the cash flow statement:

a. Beginning and ending Accounts Receivable are $25,000 and $21,000, respectively. Credit sales for the period total $100,000. How much are cash collections?
b. Cost of goods sold is $80,000. Beginning Inventory balance is $20,000, and ending Inventory balance is $16,000. Beginning and ending Accounts Payable are $12,000 and $8,000, respectively. How much are cash payments for inventory?

Computing investing and
financing amounts for the
cash flow statement

④

a. $45,000

Exercise 17–11

Compute the following items for the cash flow statement:

a. Beginning and ending Retained Earnings are $120,000 and $160,000, respectively. Net income for the period is $150,000, and stock dividends are $65,000. How much are cash dividend payments?

b. Beginning and ending Property, Plant, and Equipment, net, are $320,000 and $365,000, respectively. Amortization for the period is $36,000, and acquisitions of new property, plant, and equipment, are $104,000. Property, plant, and equipment was sold at an $8,000 loss. What was the amount of the cash receipt from the sale?

Exercise 17–12

Computing cash flows from operating activities—indirect method

⑤

Cash outflows from operating activities $(24,000)

The accounting records of Provence Corporation reveal the following:

Acquisition of land	$ 444,000	Increase in current assets		
Amortization	156,000	other than cash	$252,000	
Cash sales	108,000	Loss on sale of land	60,000	
Collection of accounts		Net income	288,000	
receivable	1,116,000	Payment of accounts payable ...	576,000	
Collection of dividend		Payment of dividends	84,000	
revenue	108,000	Payment of income tax	96,000	
Decrease in current		Payment of interest	192,000	
liabilities	276,000	Payment of salaries and wages .	432,000	

Compute cash flows from operating activities by the indirect method. Use the format of the operating activities section of Exhibit 17–15. Then evaluate Provence Corporation's operating cash flows as strong or weak.

Exercise 17–13

Classifying transactions for the cash flow statement

③ ⑤

Two transactions of LRT Logistics Inc. are recorded as follows:

a. Cash	80,000	
Accumulated Amortization—Computer Equipment	830,000	
Computer Equipment		870,000
Gain on Sale of Computer Equipment		40,000
b. Land	2,900,000	
Cash		1,300,000
Note Payable		1,600,000

Required

1. Indicate where, how, and in what amount to report these transactions on the cash flow statement and accompanying schedule of noncash investing and financing activities. Are they cash inflows or outflows? LRT Logistics Inc. reports cash flows from operating activities by the *direct* method.

2. Repeat Requirement 1, assuming that LRT Logistics Inc. reports cash flows from operating activities by the *indirect* method.

Exercise 17–14

Preparing the cash flow statement by the indirect method

⑤

Net cash flow from operating $188,000; investing $(182,000); financing $14,000

Use the income statement of Yellowpoint Consulting Ltd. in Exercise 17–9, plus these additional data during fiscal year 2010:

a. Acquisition of computer equipment was $232,000. Of this amount, $202,000 was paid in cash, $30,000 by signing a long-term note payable. Yellowpoint Consulting Ltd. sold no computer equipment during fiscal year 2010.
b. Cash received from sale of land, $20,000.
c. Cash received from issuance of common shares, $84,000.
d. Payment of long-term note payable, $40,000.
e. Payment of dividends, $30,000.
f. Change in cash balance, $?.

g. From the comparative balance sheet:

YELLOWPOINT CONSULTING LTD.
Comparative Balance Sheet (partial)
September 30, 2010 and 2009

	2010	2009
Current assets:		
Cash	$ 56,000	$ 36,000
Accounts receivable........................	130,000	144,000
Office supplies..............................	18,000	6,000
Prepaid expenses	10,000	10,000
Current liabilities:		
Accounts payable...........................	$ 68,000	$ 56,000
Accrued liabilities..........................	38,000	42,000

Required

1. Prepare Yellowpoint Consulting Ltd.'s cash flow statement for the year ended September 30, 2010 using the indirect method.

2. Evaluate Yellowpoint Consulting Ltd.'s cash flows for the year. In your evaluation, mention all three categories of cash flows, and give the reason for your evaluation.

Exercise 17–15

Computing cash flows from operating activities— indirect method

⑤

Net cash outflow from operating activities $21,000

Belleville Printing Ltd.'s year end is February 28. The accounting records of Belleville Printing Ltd. at March 31, 2010 include the selected accounts shown below.

Cash

Mar. 1	75,000	Dividend	24,000
Collections	126,000	Payments	138,000
Mar. 31	39,000		

Accounts Receivable

Mar. 1	54,000		
Sales	228,000	Collections	126,000
Mar. 31	156,000		

Inventory

Mar. 1	57,000		
Purchases	111,000	Cost of sales	108,000
Mar. 31	60,000		

Equipment

Mar. 1	279,000		
Mar. 31	279,000		

Accumulated Amortization—Equipment

		Mar. 1	78,000
		Amortization	9,000
		Mar. 31	87,000

Accounts Payable

		Mar. 1	42,000
Payments	96,000	Purchases	111,000
		Mar. 31	57,000

Accrued Liabilities

		Mar. 1	27,000
Payments	42,000	Expenses	33,000
		Mar. 31	18,000

Retained Earnings

Quarterly		Mar. 1	192,000
dividend	24,000	Net income	69,000
		Mar. 31	237,000

Required

Compute Belleville Printing Ltd.'s net cash inflow or outflow from operating activities during March 2010. Use the *indirect* method. Does Belleville Printing Ltd. have trouble collecting receivables or selling inventory? How can you tell?

Exercise 17-16

Interpreting a cash flow statement—indirect method
(5)

Consider three independent cases for the cash flow data of Rennie Recreation Products Inc.:

	Case A	Case B	Case C
Cash flows from operating activities:			
Net income	$ 120,000	$ 120,000	$ 120,000
Amortization	44,000	44,000	44,000
Increase in current assets	(4,000)	(28,000)	(76,000)
Decrease in current liabilities	0	(32,000)	(24,000)
	160,000	104,000	64,000
Cash flows from investing activities:			
Acquisition of property, plant, and equipment	(364,000)	(364,000)	(364,000)
Sales of property, plant, and equipment	16,000	16,000	388,000
	(348,000)	(348,000)	24,000
Cash flows from financing activities:			
New borrowing	200,000	416,000	64,000
Payment of debt	(36,000)	(116,000)	(84,000)
	164,000	300,000	(20,000)
Net increase (decrease) in cash	$(24,000)	$ 56,000	$ 68,000

Required   For each case, identify from the cash flow statement how Rennie Recreation Products Inc. generated the cash to acquire new property, plant, and equipment.

Exercise 17-17

Preparing the cash flow statement under IFRS— direct method

(6)

Net cash from operating $39,500; investing $(45,500); financing $11,000

The income statement and additional data of Raincoast Consulting Ltd. follow:

RAINCOAST CONSULTING LTD.
Income Statement
For the Year Ended December 31, 2011

Revenues:		
Consulting revenue		$137,000
Expenses:		
Salaries expense	$74,000	
Amortization expense	14,500	
Rent expense	6,000	
Office supplies expense	1,500	
Insurance expense	1,000	
Interest expense	1,000	
Income tax expense	9,000	107,000
Net income		$ 30,000

Additional data:

a. Collections from clients are $3,500 more than revenues.
b. Increase in cash balance, $5,000.
c. Payments to employees are $2,000 less than salaries expense.
d. Interest expense and income tax expense equal their cash amounts.
e. Acquisition of property, plant, and equipment is $58,000. Of this amount, $50,500 is paid in cash, $7,500 by signing a long-term note payable.
f. Cash received from sale of land, $5,000.
g. Cash received from issuance of common shares, $21,000.
h. Payment of long-term note payable, $10,000.
i. Payment of cash dividends, $7,500.
j. Payments for rent and insurance are equal to expense.
k. Payment for office supplies is $3,000 more than expense.
l. Opening cash balance, $8,000.

Required

Assume Raincoast Consulting Ltd. has adopted IFRS and elects to classify as operating activities all cash inflows and outflows for interest and dividends. Prepare Raincoast Consulting Ltd.'s cash flow statement by the direct method for operating activities, and a note to the financial statements providing a summary of noncash investing and financing activities.

SERIAL EXERCISE

This exercise continues the Haupt Consulting Corporation situation from Chapter 16. You can complete the following exercise without having done the previous Serial Exercises.

Preparing the cash flow
statement—indirect
method
⑤

Net cash from
operating $39,000;
investing $(83,000);
financing $40,000

Exercise 17–18

Suppose, at December 31, 2011, Haupt Consulting Corporation has the following comparative balance sheet.

HAUPT CONSULTING CORPORATION
Comparative Balance Sheet
December 31, 2011 and 2010

	2011	2010
Current assets		
Cash	$ 5,000	$ 8,100
Accounts receivable	2,200	1,700
Supplies	420	300
Equipment	10,000	2,000
Furniture	3,600	3,600
Building	55,000	—
Less: accumulated amortization	(2,753)	(93)
Land	20,000	—
Total assets	$93,467	$15,607
Current liabilities		
Accounts payable	$ 350	$ 3,900
Salary payable	2,500	—
Long-term liabilities		
Notes payable	40,000	—
Shareholders' equity		
Common shares	20,000	10,000
Retained earnings	30,617	1,707
Total liabilities and shareholders' equity	$93,467	$15,607

Additional information: Haupt Consulting Corporation declared and paid $10,000 in dividends during 2011. Net income for the year ended December 31, 2011 was $38,910.

Required

Using this information, prepare the cash flow statement for Haupt Consulting Corporation using the indirect method for operating activities.

CHALLENGE EXERCISE

Exercise 17–19

Canadian Tire Corporation, Limited's cash flow statement for the years ended January 3, 2009 and December 29, 2007 is reproduced below:

Analyzing an actual company's cash flow statement

① ② ③ ⑤

5. Accumulated amortization $32.7 million

CANADIAN TIRE CORPORATION, LIMITED
Consolidated Cash Flow Statement (adapted)

For the Years Ended (Dollars in millions)	January 3 2009	December 29 2007
Cash generated from (used for):		
Operating activities		
Net earnings	$ 374.2	$ 411.7
Items not affecting cash		
Amortization of property and equipment	228.9	206.9
Net provision for loans receivable	87.3	81.4
Gain on disposals of property and equipment	(7.8)	(17.4)
Changes in fair value of derivative instruments	55.6	(2.2)
Future income taxes	(42.1)	(11.2)
Other	(106.8)	(140.5)
Cash generated from operations	589.3	528.7
Changes in other working capital components	(406.9)	(467.1)
Cash generated from operating activities	182.4	61.6
Investing activities		
Additions to property and equipment	(436.9)	(587.7)
Investment in loans receivable	(140.5)	(296.5)
Long-term receivables and other assets	(27.2)	20.8
Purchases of stores	(36.5)	(11.4)
Proceeds on disposition of property and equipment	240.1	30.0
Securitization of loans receivable	(31.7)	(420.1)
Other	(23.8)	5.6
Cash used for investing activities	(456.5)	(1,259.3)
Financing activities		
Net change in deposits	1,024.1	113.1
Issuance of long-term debt	0.1	300.9
Dividends	(66.4)	(58.8)
Class A Non-Voting Share transactions, net	7.0	0.2
Repayment of long-term debt	(156.2)	(4.5)
Cash generated from financing activities	808.6	350.9
Cash generated in the year	534.5	(846.8)
Cash and cash equivalents, beginning of year	(105.5)	741.3
Cash and cash equivalents, end of year	$ 429.0	$ (105.5)

Required

1. Which format did Canadian Tire Corporation, Limited use for reporting cash flows from operating activities?

2. What was Canadian Tire's largest source of cash during the year ended January 3, 2009? During the year ended December 29, 2007?

3. What was Canadian Tire's largest use of cash during the year ended January 3, 2009? During the year ended December 29, 2007?

4. The operating activities section of the statement lists (in millions of dollars) "Changes in other working capital components $(406.9)." This amount includes in part:

Accounts receivable..............................	$(104.8)
Accounts payable and other	(104.6)

Did these accounts' balances increase or decrease during the year ended January 3, 2009? How can you tell?

5. During the year ended January 3, 2009, Canadian Tire sold property, plant, and equipment. Assume that the cost was $200.0 (million). Journalize the sale of the property, plant, and equipment, and calculate the accumulated amortization for the assets disposed of.

6. Why are Canadian Tire's year ends shown as January 3, 2009 and December 29, 2007?

BEYOND THE NUMBERS

Using cash flow data to evaluate an investment

① ②

Beyond the Numbers 17–1

Hill Ltd. and Genoway Inc. are asking you to recommend their shares to your clients. Hill Ltd. and Genoway Inc. earn about the same net income and have similar financial positions, so your decision depends on their cash flow statements, summarized as follows:

	Hill Ltd.		Genoway Inc.	
Net cash inflows from operating activities......................................		$ 90,000		$50,000
Net cash inflows (outflows) from investing activities:				
Purchase of property, plant, and equipment.......................	$(100,000)		$(20,000)	
Sale of property, plant, and equipment.......................	10,000	(90,000)	40,000	20,000
Net cash inflows (outflows) from financing activities:				
Issuance of common shares....	30,000		—	
Issuance of long-term debt	—		80,000	
Repayment of long-term debt	—	30,000	(120,000)	(40,000)
Net increase in cash.........................		$ 30,000		$30,000

Based on their cash flows, which company looks better? Give your reasons.

ETHICAL ISSUE

Belland Travel Ltd. is experiencing a bad year. Net income is only $60,000. Also, two important clients are falling behind in their payments to Belland Travel Ltd., and the agency's accounts receivable are increasing dramatically. The company desperately needs a loan. The company's board of directors is considering ways to put the best face on the company's financial statements. The company's bank closely examines cash flow from operations. Trent Belland, a director, suggests reclassifying as long term the receivables from the slow-paying clients. He explains to the other members of the board that removing the $40,000 rise in accounts receivable will increase net cash inflow from operations. This approach will increase the company's cash balance and may help Belland Travel Ltd. get the loan.

Required

1. Using only the amounts given, compute net cash inflow from operations both without and with the reclassification of the receivables. Which reporting makes Belland Travel Ltd. look better?

2. Where else in Belland's cash flow statement will the reclassification of the receivable be reported? What cash flow effect will this item report? What effect would the reclassification have on *overall* cash flow from all activities?

3. Under what condition would the reclassification of the receivables be ethical? Unethical?

PROBLEMS (GROUP A)

MyAccountingLab | All questions in this section appear in MyAccountingLab.

Problem 17–1A

Using cash flow information to evaluate performance

Top managers of Upland Communications Corp. are reviewing company performance for 2010. The income statement reports an 18 percent increase in net income, which is excellent. The balance sheet shows modest increases in assets, liabilities, and shareholders' equity. The assets with the largest increases are plant and equipment because the company is halfway through an expansion program. No other assets and no liabilities are increasing dramatically. A summarized version of the cash flow statement reports the following:

Net cash inflow from operating activities	$1,240,000
Net cash outflow from investing activities	(1,140,000)
Net cash inflow from financing activities	380,000
Increase in cash during 2010	$ 480,000

Required Write a memo to give top managers of Upland Communications Corp. your assessment of 2010 and your outlook for the future. Focus on the information content of the cash flow data.

Problem 17–2A

Preparing the cash flow statement—direct method ② ③

1. Net cash from operating $(240,000), investing $307,800, financing $601,200

Charlton Products Ltd. accountants have developed the following data from the company's accounting records for the year ended July 31, 2010:

a. Salaries expense, $631,800.
b. Cash payments to purchase property, plant, and equipment, $1,035,000.
c. Proceeds from issuance of long-term debt, $264,600.
d. Payments of long-term debt, $112,800.
e. Proceeds from sale of property, plant, and equipment, $358,200.
f. Interest revenue, $72,600.
g. Cash receipt of dividend revenue on investments in shares, $16,200.
h. Payments to suppliers, $4,129,800.
i. Interest expense and payments, $226,800.
j. Cost of goods sold, $2,886,600.
k. Collection of interest revenue, $70,200.
l. Acquisition of equipment by issuing short-term note payable, $213,000.
m. Payment of salaries, $804,000.

n. Credit sales, $3,648,600.
o. Income tax expense and payments, $338,400.
p. Amortization expense, $309,600.
q. Collections on accounts receivable, $4,038,600.
r. Collection of long-term notes receivable, $446,400.
s. Proceeds from sale of investments, $538,200.
t. Payment of long-term debt by issuing preferred shares, $900,000.
u. Cash sales, $1,134,000.
v. Proceeds from issuance of common shares, $689,400.
w. Payment of cash dividends, $240,000.
x. Cash balance: July 31, 2009—$454,800
            July 31, 2010—$?

Required

1. Prepare Charlton Products Ltd.'s cash flow statement for the year ended July 31, 2010. Follow the format of Exhibit 17–11, but do *not* show amounts in thousands. Include a note to the financial statements giving a summary of noncash investing and financing activities.

2. Evaluate 2010 in terms of cash flow. Give your reasons.

Excel Spreadsheet Template

The 2010 comparative balance sheet and income statement of Sherbrooke Group Inc. follow:

Preparing the cash flow statement—direct method
② ③ ④

1. Net cash from operating $666,000, investing $(526,000), financing $(249,000)

SHERBROOKE GROUP INC.
Comparative Balance Sheet
December 31, 2010 and 2009

	2010	2009
Current assets		
Cash and cash equivalents................................	$ 47,000	$ 156,000
Accounts receivable	415,000	431,000
Interest receivable	6,000	9,000
Inventories...	993,000	899,000
Prepaid expenses...	17,000	22,000
Plant and equipment, net	1,009,000	937,000
Land	401,000	100,000
Total assets..	$2,888,000	$2,554,000
Current liabilities		
Accounts payable	$ 114,000	$ 179,000
Interest payable	63,000	67,000
Salaries payable	71,000	14,000
Other accrued liabilities	181,000	187,000
Income tax payable	73,000	38,000
Long-term liabilities		
Notes payable	450,000	650,000
Shareholders' equity		
Common shares..	1,411,000	1,223,000
Retained earnings...	525,000	196,000
Total liabilities and shareholders' equity	$2,888,000	$2,554,000

SHERBROOKE GROUP INC.
Income Statement
For the Year Ended December 31, 2010

Revenues:		
Sales revenue		$4,380,000
Interest revenue..		17,000
Total revenues..		4,397,000
Expenses:		
Cost of goods sold...	$1,952,000	
Salaries expense...	814,000	
Amortization expense...	153,000	
Other operating expenses	497,000	
Interest expense	246,000	
Income tax expense...	169,000	
Total expenses..		3,831,000
Net income..		$ 566,000

Sherbrooke Group had no noncash investing and financing transactions during 2010. During the year, there were no sales of land or plant and equipment, no issuances of notes payable, and no repurchase of common shares.

Required

1. Prepare the 2010 cash flow statement, formatting operating activities by the direct method.

2. Evaluate the 2010 cash flow for this company.

Problem 17–4A

Use the Sherbrooke Group Inc. data from Problem 17–3A.

Required

1. Prepare the 2010 cash flow statement by the *indirect* method. If your instructor also assigned Problem 17–3A, prepare only the operating activities section.
2. Evaluate the 2010 cash flow for this company.

Problem 17–5A

Accountants for Clarke Confectionary Ltd. have assembled the following data for the year ended December 31, 2010:

	December 31,	
	2010	2009
Current accounts (all result from operations)		
Current assets		
Cash and cash equivalents	$ 9,050	$ 8,700
Accounts receivable......................................	17,025	18,425
Inventories..	29,625	24,125
Prepaid expenses	800	525
Current liabilities		
Notes payable (for inventory purchases)....	7,575	9,200
Accounts payable..	18,025	16,875
Income tax payable.......................................	1,475	1,950
Accrued liabilities	12,075	5,800

Transaction data for 2010:

Acquisition of building by issuing long-term note payable...........................	$33,000	Issuance of preferred shares for cash	$14,050
		Net income.................................	12,625
Acquisition of equipment.........	18,500	Payment of cash dividends	10,700
Acquisition of long-term		Payment of long-term debt.......	16,950
investment	11,200	Payment of long-term debt	
Amortization expense...............	5,075	by issuing common	
Collection of loan......................	2,575	shares......................................	22,350
Gain on sale of investment.......	875	Sale of long-term	
Issuance of long-term debt		investment	5,550
to borrow cash........................	17,750	Stock dividends..........................	3,150

Required

Prepare Clarke Confectionary Ltd.'s cash flow statement, using the *indirect* method to report operating activities. Include a note regarding noncash investing and financing activities.

Problem 17–6A

The comparative balance sheet of Brees Distributing Corp. at December 31, 2010 reported the following:

	December 31,	
	2010	2009
Current assets		
Cash and cash equivalents............................	$ 16,800	$175,000
Accounts receivable......................................	518,000	410,200
Inventories	722,400	742,000
Prepaid expenses..	58,800	51,800
Current liabilities		
Notes payable (for inventory purchases) ...	128,800	0
Accounts payable..	467,600	392,000
Accrued liabilities	200,200	235,200
Income tax payable.......................................	154,000	200,200

Excel Spreadsheet Template

Preparing the cash flow statement—indirect method

(2) (3) (5)

1. Net cash from operating $666,000, investing $(526,000), financing $(249,000)

Preparing the cash flow statement—indirect method

(2) (5)

Net cash from operating $17,775, investing $(21,575), financing $4,150

Excel Spreadsheet Template

Preparing the cash flow statement—indirect method

(2) (5)

1. Net cash from operating $813,400, investing $(2,380,000), financing $1,408,400

Brees Distributing Corp.'s transactions during 2010 included the following:

Amortization expense	$ 224,000	Net income	$561,400
Cash acquisition of building	1,624,000	Payment of cash dividends	238,000
Cash acquisition of equipment	1,260,000	Retirement of bonds payable by issuing common shares	560,000
Issuance of common shares for cash	1,198,400	Sale of long-term investment	504,000
Issuance of long-term note payable to borrow cash	448,000	Stock dividend	182,000

Required

1. Prepare Brees Distributing Corp.'s cash flow statement for the year ended December 31, 2010. Use the *indirect* method to report cash flows from operating activities. Report non-cash financing activities in a note to the financial statements.

2. Evaluate Brees Distributing Corp.'s cash flows for the year. Mention all three categories of cash flows, and give the reason for your evaluation.

Preparing the cash flow statement—direct and indirect methods

③ ⑤

1. Net cash from operating $74,100, investing $(51,500), financing $(34,500)

Problem 17–7A

To prepare the cash flow statement, accountants for Dalhousie Sales Ltd. have summarized 2010 activity in two accounts as follows:

Cash

Beginning balance	87,100	Payments of operating expenses	46,100
Sale of common shares	80,800	Payment of long-term debt	78,900
Receipts of dividends	7,900	Repurchase of common shares	30,400
Sale of investments	28,400	Payment of income tax	6,000
Receipts of interest	22,200	Payments on accounts payable	101,600
Collections from customers	307,000	Payments of dividends	6,000
		Payments of salaries and wages	67,500
		Payments of interest	41,800
		Purchase of equipment	79,900
Ending balance	75,200		

Common Shares

Repurchase of common shares	30,400	Beginning balance	103,500
		Issuance for cash	80,800
		Issuance to acquire land	75,000
		Issuance to retire long-term debt	21,100
		Ending balance	250,000

Dalhousie Sales Ltd.'s 2010 income statement and selected balance sheet data follow:

DALHOUSIE SALES LTD.
Income Statement
For the Year Ended December 31, 2010

Revenues and gains:		
Sales revenue		$317,000
Interest revenue		22,200
Dividend revenue		7,900
Gain on sale of investments		700
Total revenues and gains		347,800
Expenses:		
Cost of goods sold	$103,600	
Salaries and wages expense	66,800	
Amortization expense	10,900	
Other operating expenses	44,700	
Interest expense	44,100	
Income tax expense	9,200	
Total expenses		279,300
Net income		$ 68,500

DALHOUSIE SALES LTD.
Balance Sheet Data
For the Year Ended December 31, 2010

	Increase (Decrease)
Current assets	
Cash and cash equivalents	$?
Accounts receivable	10,000
Inventories	5,700
Prepaid expenses	(1,900)
Investments	(27,700)
Plant and equipment, net	69,000
Land	75,000
Current liabilities	
Accounts payable	$ 7,700
Interest payable	2,300
Salaries payable	(700)
Other accrued liabilities	(3,300)
Income tax payable	3,200
Long-term debt	(100,000)
Common shares	146,500
Retained earnings	62,500

Required

1. Prepare Dalhousie Sales Ltd.'s cash flow statement for the year ended December 31, 2010 using the *direct* method to report operating activities. Also prepare a note to the financial statements summarizing the noncash investing and financing activities.

2. Prepare a schedule showing cash flows from operating activities using the *indirect* method. All activity in the current accounts results from operations.

Preparing the cash flow
statement—direct and indirect
methods

1. Net cash from
operating $487,200,
investing $(25,600),
financing $(264,800)

Problem 17–8A

Mill Bay Inc.'s comparative balance sheet at September 30, 2010 and its 2010 income statement are shown below.

MILL BAY INC.
Balance Sheet
September 30, 2010 and 2009

	2010	2009
Current assets		
Cash	$ 389,600	$ 192,800
Accounts receivable	335,200	328,000
Interest receivable	32,800	22,400
Inventories	973,600	935,200
Prepaid expenses	68,800	74,400
Long-term investments	408,800	110,400
Plant and equipment, net	1,055,200	832,800
Land	376,800	594,400
	$3,640,800	$3,090,400
Current liabilities		
Notes payable, short-term	$ 80,000	$ 0
Accounts payable	494,400	562,400
Income tax payable	94,400	92,800
Accrued liabilities	143,200	232,800
Interest payable	36,000	25,600
Salaries payable	12,000	8,800
Long-term note payable	984,000	1,051,200
Common shares	1,087,200	672,000
Retained earnings	709,600	444,800
	$3,640,800	$3,090,400

MILL BAY INC.
Income Statement
For the Year Ended September 30, 2010

Sales revenue		$2,936,800
Cost of goods sold		1,292,000
Gross margin		1,644,800
Operating expenses:		
Amortization	$ 68,000	
Salaries	507,200	
Other	236,800	812,000
Operating income		832,800
Other revenues and expenses:		
Revenues and gains:		
Interest	58,400	
Gain on sale of land	87,200	145,600
		978,400
Interest expense		108,000
Income before income taxes		870,400
Income tax expense		171,200
Net income		$ 699,200

Other information for the year ended September 30, 2010:

a. Acquired equipment by issuing long-term note payable, $178,400, and paying $32,000 cash.
b. Paid long-term note payable, $245,600.
c. Received $415,200 cash for issuance of common shares.
d. Paid cash dividends, $434,400.
e. Acquired equipment by issuing short-term note payable, $80,000.

Required

1. Prepare Mill Bay Inc.'s cash flow statement for the year ended September 30, 2010 using the *direct* method to report operating activities. Also prepare a note to the financial statements giving a summary of noncash investing and financing activities. All current accounts, except short-term notes payable, result from operating transactions.

2. Prepare a supplementary schedule showing the cash flows from operating activities using the *indirect* method.

Problem 17–9A

Distinguishing among operating (indirect method), investing, and financing activities; computing the cash effects of a wide variety of business transactions

Indicate whether or not each of the items below would be shown on a cash flow statement, with operating activities reported using the indirect method. Indicate whether the adjustment is added to, deducted from, or has no effect on the cash flow statement. If the transaction affects the cash flow statement, state whether it relates to operating activities, investing activities, or financing activities. Provide the reason for your answer.

a. The payment of interest on long-term debt.
b. The declaration and distribution of a common stock dividend.
c. A decrease in accounts payable.
d. The sale of office equipment for its book value.
e. The borrowing of funds for future expansion through the sale of bonds.
f. A gain on the sale of property, plant, and equipment.
g. The purchase of equipment in exchange for common shares.
h. Amortization expense—buildings.
i. A decrease in merchandise inventory.
j. An increase in prepaid expenses.
k. Amortization of the premium on bonds payable.
l. An increase in a money market fund investment.

Problem 17–10A

The financial statements for Fieldgate Corp. for the year ended December 31, 2010 are as follows:

Distinguishing among operating, investing, and financing activities; using the financial statements to compute the cash effects of a wide variety of business transactions; preparing a cash flow statement by the indirect method

1. Net cash from operating $586,000, investing $(204,000), financing $(430,000)

FIELDGATE CORP.
Balance Sheet
December 31, 2010 and 2009

	2010	2009
Assets		
Cash	$ 10,000	$ 18,000
Investment in money market fund	0	40,000
Accounts receivable	189,000	175,000
Merchandise inventory	280,000	610,000
Prepaid expenses	30,000	23,000
Plant and equipment	1,798,000	1,654,000
Less accumulated amortization	(180,000)	(120,000)
Land	400,000	0
Goodwill	90,000	100,000
Total assets	$2,617,000	$2,500,000
Liabilities		
Accounts payable	$ 176,000	$ 120,000
Salaries payable	110,000	100,000
Loan payable	350,000	400,000
Total liabilities	636,000	620,000
Shareholders' equity		
Preferred shares	500,000	500,000
Common shares	1,000,000	500,000
Retained earnings	481,000	880,000
Total shareholders' equity	1,981,000	1,880,000
Total liabilities and shareholders' equity	$2,617,000	$2,500,000

FIELDGATE CORP.
Income Statement
For the Year Ended December 31, 2010

Net sales..	$1,600,000
Cost of goods sold	840,000
Gross margin	760,000
Operating expenses:	
Selling expenses...	350,000
Administrative expenses...	250,000
Interest expense	40,000
Total operating expenses..	640,000
Operating income...	120,000
Income taxes..	39,000
Net income	$ 81,000

Additional information:

a. The administrative expenses included:
   Amortization expense on plant and equipment, $120,000.
   Writedown of goodwill, $10,000.
b. Sold equipment for its book value. The equipment cost $430,000 and had been amortized for $60,000.
c. Purchased additional equipment in December for $574,000.
d. Issued common shares for land valued at $400,000.
e. Declared and paid cash dividends: Preferred, $230,000; Common, $250,000.
f. Sold 10,000 common shares for $10.00 per share.
g. Paid $90,000 (of which $40,000 was interest) on the loans.

Required

1. Prepare a cash flow statement for Fieldgate Corp. for the year ended December 31, 2010 using the *indirect* method. The investment in the money market fund is a cash equivalent.

2. Did the company improve its cash position in 2010? Give your reasons.

Preparing the cash flow statement under IFRS—direct method

(6)

1. Net cash from operating $(33,200), investing $131,400, financing $124,800

Problem 17–11A

Crystal Products Ltd.'s accountants have developed the following data from the company's accounting records for the year ended December 31, 2011:

a. Salaries expense, $210,600.
b. Cash payments to purchase property, plant, and equipment, $345,000.
c. Proceeds from issuance of long-term debt, $88,200.
d. Payments of long-term debt, $37,600.
e. Proceeds from sale of property, plant, and equipment, $119,400.
f. Interest revenue, $24,200.
g. Cash receipt of dividend revenue on investments in shares, $5,400.
h. Payments to suppliers, $1,376,600.
i. Interest expense and payments, $75,600.
j. Cost of goods sold, $962,200.
k. Collection of interest revenue, $23,400.
l. Acquisition of equipment by issuing short-term note payable, $71,000.
m. Payment of salaries, $268,000.
n. Credit sales, $1,216,200.
o. Income tax expense and payments, $112,800.

p. Amortization expense, $103,200.
q. Collections on accounts receivable, $1,346,200.
r. Collection of long-term notes receivable, $148,800.
s. Proceeds from sale of investments, $179,400.
t. Payment of long-term debt by issuing preferred shares, $300,000.
u. Cash sales, $378,000.
v. Proceeds from issuance of common shares, $229,800.
w. Payment of cash dividends, $80,000.
x. Cash balance:
   December 31, 2010—$151,600
   December 31, 2011—$?

Required Assume that Crystal Products Ltd. has adopted IFRS and elected to classify cash inflows from interest and dividends as investing activities, and cash outflows for the payment of interest and dividends as financing activities. Prepare Crystal's cash flow statement for the year ended December 31, 2011 reporting operating activities by the direct method. Include a note to the financial statements providing a summary of noncash investing and financing activities.

*Problem 17–12A

Skeena Manufacturing Corp.'s comparative balance sheet at September 30, 2010 and 2009, and its income statement for the year ended September 30, 2010, are shown below.

Preparing the spreadsheet for the cash flow statement—indirect method

(A1)

Transaction analysis debit total Panel A $61,175

SKEENA MANUFACTURING CORP.
Comparative Balance Sheet
September 30, 2010 and 2009

	2010	2009
Current assets		
Cash..........	$ 14,470	$ 4,400
Accounts receivable.........	11,475	11,000
Interest receivable.........	1,025	700
Inventories.........	30,425	29,225
Prepaid expenses.........	2,150	2,325
Long-term investments.........	26,350	4,525
Plant and equipment, net.........	23,875	12,425
Land.........	16,450	23,250
Total assets.........	$126,220	$87,850
Current liabilities		
Notes payable, short-term.........	$ 5,500	$ 0
Accounts payable.........	17,950	17,575
Income tax payable.........	5,450	6,150
Accrued liabilities.........	5,775	7,275
Interest payable.........	1,125	800
Salaries payable.........	375	275
Notes payable, long-term.........	17,225	15,325
Shareholders' equity		
Common shares.........	35,525	22,550
Retained earnings.........	37,295	17,900
Total liabilities and shareholders' equity.........	$126,220	$87,850

SKEENA MANUFACTURING CORP.
Income Statement
For the Year Ended September 30, 2010

Revenues and gains:		
Sales.........		$93,900
Gain on sale of land.........		2,725
Interest revenue.........		1,825
Total revenues and gains.........		98,450
Expenses:		
Cost of goods sold.........	$40,375	
Salaries expense.........	15,850	
Other operating expenses.........	7,400	
Income tax expense.........	4,600	
Interest expense.........	3,375	
Amortization expense.........	2,125	
Total expenses.........		73,725
Net income.........		$24,725

---

*This Problem refers to topics covered in the Chapter 17 Appendix.

Transaction data for the year ended September 30, 2010 are as follows:

a. Acquired long-term investments for cash, $21,825.
b. Sold land for cash, $9,525, including a $2,725 gain.
c. Acquired equipment by issuing a long-term note payable, $8,075.
d. Paid a long-term note payable, $6,175.
e. Received $12,975 cash for issuance of common shares.
f. Paid cash dividends, $5,330.
g. Acquired equipment by issuing short-term note payable, $5,500.

Required

Prepare Skeena Manufacturing Corp.'s spreadsheet for the cash flow statement for the year ended September 30, 2010 using the *indirect* method to report operating activities. Include on the spreadsheet the noncash investing and financing activities.

PROBLEMS (GROUP B)

MyAccountingLab All questions in this section appear in MyAccountingLab.

Using cash flow information to evaluate performance

①

Problem 17–1B

Top managers of Speedy Delivery Ltd. are reviewing company performance for 2010. The income statement reports a 20-percent increase in net income over 2009. However, most of the net income increase resulted from an unusual gain of $60,000 on the sale of equipment. The cash proceeds were $180,000. The balance sheet shows a large increase in receivables. The cash flow statement, in summarized form, reports the following:

Net cash outflow from operating activities	$(330,000)
Net cash inflow from investing activities	300,000
Net cash inflow from financing activities	150,000
Increase in cash during 2010	$ 120,000

Required

Write a memo to give the managers of Speedy Delivery Ltd. your assessment of 2010 operations and your outlook for the future. Focus on the information content of the cash flow data.

Preparing the cash flow statement—direct method

② ③

Problem 17–2B

Accountants for Renovation Builders' Supply Ltd. have developed the following data from the company's accounting records for the year ended April 30, 2010:

a. Credit sales, $728,125.
b. Income tax expense and payments, $47,375.
c. Cash payments to acquire property, plant, and equipment, $49,250.
d. Cost of goods sold, $478,250.
e. Cash received from issuance of long-term debt, $85,000.
f. Payment of cash dividends, $60,500.
g. Collection of interest, $34,250.
h. Acquisition of equipment by issuing short-term note payable, $20,500.
i. Payment of salaries, $109,500.
j. Cash received from sale of property, plant, and equipment, $28,000, including an $8,500 loss.
k. Collections on accounts receivable, $578,250.
l. Interest revenue, $4,750.
m. Cash receipt of dividend revenue on investment in shares, $5,125.
n. Payments to suppliers, $460,625.
o. Cash sales, $214,875.
p. Amortization expense, $78,500.
q. Cash received from issuance of short-term debt, $49,500.
r. Payments of long-term debt, $62,500.
s. Interest expense and payments, $16,625.
t. Salaries expense, $119,125.
u. Collections of notes receivable, $35,000.

v. Cash received from sale of investments, $11,375, including $2,500 gain.

w. Payment of short-term note payable by issuing long-term note payable, $78,750.

x. Cash balance: May 1, 2009—$99,125
April 30, 2010—$?

Required

1. Prepare Renovation Builders' Supply Ltd.'s cash flow statement for the year ended April 30, 2010. Follow the format of Exhibit 17–11, but do *not* show amounts in thousands. Include a note regarding the noncash investing and financing activities.

2. Evaluate 2010 from a cash flow standpoint. Give your reasons.

Problem 17–3B

The 2010 comparative income statement and balance sheet of Garries Ltd. follow:

Excel Spreadsheet Template

Preparing the cash flow statement—direct method
(2)(3)(4)

GARRIES LTD.
Income Statement
For the Year Ended December 31, 2010

Revenues:		
Sales revenue		$257,000
Interest revenue		13,600
Total revenues		270,600
Expenses:		
Cost of goods sold	$76,600	
Salaries expense	27,800	
Amortization expense	4,000	
Other operating expenses	10,500	
Interest expense	16,600	
Income tax expense	27,800	
Total expenses		163,300
Net income		$107,300

GARRIES LTD.
Comparative Balance Sheet
December 31, 2010 and 2009

	2010	2009
Current assets		
Cash and cash equivalents	$ 7,200	$ 6,300
Accounts receivable	31,600	26,900
Interest receivable	1,900	700
Inventories	53,600	57,200
Prepaid expenses	2,500	1,900
Plant and equipment, net	66,500	49,400
Land	83,000	54,000
Total assets	$246,300	$196,400
Current liabilities		
Accounts payable	$ 31,400	$ 28,800
Interest payable	4,400	4,900
Salaries payable	3,100	6,600
Other accrued liabilities	13,700	16,000
Income tax payable	8,900	7,700
Long-term liabilities		
Notes payable	85,000	95,000
Shareholders' equity		
Common shares	58,300	34,700
Retained earnings	41,500	2,700
Total liabilities and shareholders' equity	$246,300	$196,400

Garries Ltd. had no noncash financing and investing transactions during 2010. During the year, there were no sales of land or plant and equipment, and no issuances of notes payable.

Required

1. Prepare the 2010 cash flow statement, formatting operating activities by the direct method.
2. Evaluate the 2010 cash flow for this company.

Problem 17–4B

Use the Garries Ltd. data from Problem 17–3B.

Excel Spreadsheet Template

Preparing the cash flow statement—indirect method
② ③ ⑤

Required

1. Prepare the 2010 cash flow statement by the indirect method. If your instructor also assigned Problem 17–3B, prepare only the operating activities section of the statement.
2. Evaluate the 2010 cash flow for this company.

Preparing the cash flow statement—indirect method
② ⑤

Problem 17–5B

Humber Ltd.'s accountants have assembled the following data for the year ended December 31, 2010:

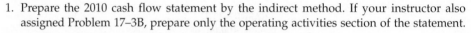

	December 31, 2010	December 31, 2009
Current accounts (all result from operations)		
Current assets		
Cash and cash equivalents	$ 75,500	$ 56,750
Accounts receivable	174,250	155,500
Inventories	271,500	212,500
Prepaid expenses	13,250	10,250
Current liabilities		
Notes payable (for inventory purchases)	56,500	45,750
Accounts payable	132,250	139,500
Income tax payable	96,500	41,750
Accrued liabilities	38,750	68,000

Transaction data for 2010:

Acquisition of building	$325,750	Issuance of long-term note payable to borrow cash	$ 36,000
Acquisition of land by issuing long-term note payable	267,500	Loss on sale of equipment	16,750
Acquisition of long-term investment	79,000	Net income	199,000
Amortization expense	60,250	Payment of cash dividends	90,750
Collection of loan	71,750	Repurchase and retirement of common shares	65,750
Issuance of common shares for cash	103,000	Retirement of bonds payable by issuing common shares	137,500
Stock dividends	79,500	Sale of equipment for cash	145,000

Required

Prepare Humber Ltd.'s cash flow statement, using the *indirect* method to report operating activities. Note any additional disclosures that are required.

Problem 17–6B

The comparative balance sheet of Westwind Outfitters Ltd. at March 31, 2010 reported the following:

Excel Spreadsheet Template

Preparing the cash flow statement—indirect method

2 5

	March 31,	
	2010	**2009**
Current assets		
Cash and cash equivalents.............................	$ 49,000	$ 420,000
Accounts receivable	2,443,000	1,519,000
Inventories	4,424,000	4,242,000
Prepaid expenses..	133,000	119,000
Current liabilities		
Notes payable (for inventory purchases)	280,000	280,000
Accounts payable..	2,093,000	1,757,000
Accrued liabilities	749,000	777,000
Income tax payable	560,000	329,000

Westwind Outfitters Ltd.'s transactions during the year ended March 31, 2010, included the following:

Acquisition of land by issuing note payable..............	$5,320,000	Repurchase of common shares for cash	$ 910,000
Amortization expense................	770,000	Issuance of long-term note payable to borrow cash.........	3,500,000
Cash acquisition of building.................................	3,780,000	Net income.................................	7,280,000
Cash acquisition of equipment...............................	5,509,000	Payment of cash dividends	2,100,000
		Sale of long-term investment	959,000

Required

1. Prepare Westwind Outfitters Ltd.'s cash flow statement for the year ended March 31, 2010, using the *indirect* method to report cash flows from operating activities. Report noncash investing and financing activities in a schedule that will be part of the notes to the financial statements.

2. Evaluate Westwind Outfitters Ltd.'s cash flows for the year. Mention all three categories of cash flows, and give the reason for your evaluation.

Problem 17–7B

To prepare the cash flow statement, accountants for Jennings Inc. have summarized activity for the year 2010 in two accounts as follows:

Preparing the cash flow statement—direct and indirect methods

3 5

Cash

Beginning balance	64,320	Payments on accounts payable	447,720
Collection of loan	39,600	Payments of dividends	32,640
Sale of investment	31,440	Payments of salaries and wages	172,560
Receipts of interest	39,120	Payments of interest	56,280
Collections from customers	814,440	Purchase of equipment	37,680
Issuance of common shares	33,360	Payments of operating expenses	41,160
Receipts of dividends	5,400	Payment of long-term debt	73,560
		Repurchase of common shares	20,280
		Payment of income tax	22,680
Ending balance	123,120		

Common Shares

Repurchase of shares	20,280	Beginning balance	101,280
		Issuance for cash	33,360
		Issuance to acquire land	97,320
		Issuance to retire long-term debt	22,800
		Ending balance	234,480

Jennings Inc.'s income statement and selected balance sheet data follow:

JENNINGS INC.
Income Statement
For the Year Ended December 31, 2010

Revenues:		
Sales revenue		$847,560
Interest revenue		39,120
Dividend revenue		5,400
Total revenues		892,080
Expenses and losses:		
Cost of goods sold	$420,720	
Salaries and wages expense	180,960	
Amortization expense	29,160	
Other operating expenses	52,920	
Interest expense	58,560	
Income tax expense	19,440	
Loss on sale of investments	3,720	
Total expenses		765,480
Net income		$126,600

JENNINGS INC.
Balance Sheet Data
For the Year Ended December 31, 2010

	Increase (Decrease)
Current assets	
Cash and cash equivalents	$?
Accounts receivable	33,120
Inventories	(14,160)
Prepaid expenses	720
Loan receivable	(39,600)
Long-term investments	(35,160)
Plant and equipment, net	8,520
Land	97,320
Current liabilities	
Accounts payable	$(41,160)
Interest payable	2,280
Salaries payable	8,400
Other accrued liabilities	12,480
Income tax payable	(3,240)
Long-term debt	(96,360)
Common shares	133,200
Retained earnings	93,960

Required

1. Prepare the cash flow statement of Jennings Inc. for the year ended December 31, 2010 using the *direct* method to report operating activities. Also prepare a summary of noncash investing and financing activities that will be part of a note to the financial statements.

2. Use the data from Jennings Inc.'s 2010 income statement and the selected balance sheet data to prepare a supplementary schedule showing cash flows from operating activities by the *indirect* method. All activity in the current accounts results from operations.

Problem 17–8B

Rare Antiques Ltd.'s comparative balance sheet at June 30, 2010 and its 2010 income statement are as follows:

Preparing the cash flow statement—direct and indirect methods

③ ④ ⑤

RARE ANTIQUES LTD.
Balance Sheet
June 30, 2010 and 2009

	2010	2009
Current assets		
Cash..	$ 188,000	$ 43,000
Accounts receivable	370,000	241,500
Interest receivable	14,500	18,000
Inventories	343,000	301,000
Prepaid expenses..	18,500	14,000
Long-term investment	50,500	26,000
Plant and equipment, net	422,500	368,000
Land...	212,000	480,000
	$1,619,000	$1,491,500
Current liabilities		
Notes payable, short-term		
(for general borrowing)..	$ 67,000	$ 90,500
Accounts payable	234,500	201,500
Income tax payable	69,000	72,500
Accrued liabilities	41,000	48,500
Interest payable	18,500	14,500
Salaries payable..	4,500	13,000
Long-term note payable	237,000	470,500
Common shares...	319,500	256,000
Retained earnings...	628,000	324,500
	$1,619,000	$1,491,500

RARE ANTIQUES LTD.
Income Statement
For the Year Ended June 30, 2010

Net sales...		$1,327,000
Cost of goods sold		402,000
Gross margin..		925,000
Operating expenses:		
Salaries expense...	$194,000	
Amortization expense	27,000	
Other expenses	210,000	431,000
Operating income..		494,000
Other revenues and expenses:		
Revenues and gains:		
Interest revenue..		53,000
Expenses and losses:		
Interest expense...	(30,500)	
Loss on sale of land	(33,500)	(64,000)
Income before income taxes...................................		483,000
Income tax expense		49,500
Net income		$ 433,500

Other information for the year ended June 30, 2010:

a. Acquired equipment by issuing a long-term note payable, $56,500, and paying $25,000 cash.
b. Purchased a long-term investment for cash.
c. Received cash for issuance of common shares, $40,000.
d. Only cash dividends were issued during the year.
e. Paid short-term note payable by issuing common shares.

Required

1. Prepare the cash flow statement of Rare Antiques Ltd. for the year ended June 30, 2010, using the *direct* method to report operating activities. Also prepare a note to the financial statements providing a summary of noncash investing and financing activities. All current accounts, except short-term notes payable, result from operating transactions.

2. Prepare a supplementary schedule showing cash flows from operations by the *indirect* method.

Distinguishing among operating (indirect method), investing, and financing activities; computing the cash effects of a wide variety of business transactions

Problem 17–9B

Indicate whether or not each of items below would be shown on a cash flow statement that reports operating activities by the indirect method, and provide the reason for your answer.
    Indicate whether the adjustment is added to, deducted from, or has no effect on the cash flow statement. If the transaction affects the cash flow statement, state whether it relates to operating activities, investing activities, or financing activities.

a. A loss on the sale of property, plant, and equipment
b. Amortization expense—equipment
c. An increase in merchandise inventory
d. A decrease in prepaid expenses
e. Amortization of the discount on bonds payable
f. The receipt of interest on long-term investments
g. The declaration and distribution of a common stock dividend
h. An increase in trade accounts payable
i. The purchase of office equipment
j. The borrowing of funds for future expansion through the sale of bonds
k. Amortization of intangible assets
l. The purchase of land in exchange for common shares

Distinguishing among operating, investing, and financing activities; using the financial statements to compute the cash effects of a wide variety of business transactions; preparing a cash flow statement by the indirect method

Problem 17–10B

Airdrie Sales Corp. had the financial statements for the year ended December 31 shown below.

AIRDRIE SALES CORP. Income Statement For the Year Ended December 31, 2010	
Net sales	$267,000
Cost of goods sold	120,000
Gross margin	147,000
Operating expenses	
Selling expenses	73,800
Administrative expenses	43,500
Interest expense	8,700
Total operating expenses	126,000
Operating income	21,000
Income taxes	8,400
Net income	$12,600

AIRDRIE SALES CORP.
Balance Sheet
December 31, 2010 and 2009

	2010	2009
Assets		
Cash...	$ 6,000	$ 27,600
Investments in money-market funds.............................	1,500	4,500
Accounts receivable	2,700	34,200
Merchandise inventory	45,900	107,815
Prepaid expenses..	3,600	2,850
Plant and equipment	285,600	235,535
Less accumulated amortization.................................	(24,000)	(15,000)
Land	90,000	0
Goodwill..	18,000	22,500
Total assets	$429,300	$420,000
Liabilities		
Accounts payable...	$ 21,300	$ 22,500
Salaries payable...	24,000	21,000
Loans payable...	84,000	99,000
Total liabilities...	129,300	142,500
Shareholders' equity		
Common shares...	165,000	150,000
Retained earnings...	135,000	127,500
Total shareholders' equity	300,000	277,500
Total liabilities and shareholders' equity.............................	$429,300	$420,000

Additional information:

a. The Administrative expenses included:
   Amortization expense on plant and equipment = $24,000
   Writedown of goodwill = 4,500
b. Sold equipment for its net book value. The equipment cost $34,685 and had been amortized for $15,000.
c. Purchased additional equipment for $84,750.
d. Exchanged common shares for land valued at $90,000.
e. Declared and paid cash dividends on common shares, $5,100.
f. Repurchased common shares for $75,000.
g. Paid $23,700 (of which $8,700 was interest) on the loans.

Required

1. Prepare a cash flow statement for Airdrie Sales Corp. for the year ended December 31, 2010 using the *indirect* method. Consider the investments in money market funds to be a cash equivalent.

2. Comment on the results indicated by the cash flow statement.

Problem 17–11B

Accountants for Home Services Builders' Supply Ltd. have developed the following data from the company's accounting records for the year ended December 31, 2011.

Preparing the cash flow statement under IFRS—direct method

⑥

a. Credit sales, $291,950.
b. Income tax expense and payments, $18,950.
c. Cash payments to acquire property, plant, and equipment, $19,700.
d. Cost of goods sold, $191,300.
e. Cash received from issuance of long-term debt, $34,000.
f. Payment of cash dividends, $24,200.
g. Collection of interest, $13,700.
h. Acquisition of equipment by issuing short-term note payable, $8,200.
i. Payment of salaries, $43,800.
j. Cash received from sale of property, plant, and equipment, $11,200, including a $3,400 loss.

k. Collections on accounts receivable, $231,300.
l. Interest revenue, $1,900.
m. Cash receipt of dividend revenue on investment in shares, $2,050.
n. Payments to suppliers, $184,250.
o. Cash sales, $85,950.
p. Amortization expense, $31,400.
q. Cash received from issuance of short-term debt, $19,800.
r. Payments of long-term debt, $25,000.

s. Interest expense and payments, $6,650.
t. Salaries expense, $47,650.
u. Collections of notes receivable, $14,000.
v. Cash received from sale of investments, $4,550, including $1,000 gain.
w. Payment of short-term note payable by issuing long-term note payable, $31,500.
x. Cash balance: December 31, 2010—$39,650
    December 31, 2011—$?

Required

Assume that Home Services Builders' Supply Ltd. has adopted IFRS and elected to classify cash inflows from interest and dividends as investing activities, and cash outflows for the payment of interest and dividends as financing activities. Prepare Home's cash flow statement for the year ended December 31, 2011, reporting operating activities by the direct method. Include a note to the financial statements giving a summary of noncash investing and financing activities.

Preparing the spreadsheet for the cash flow statement—indirect method

A1

*Problem 17–12B

The 2010 and 2009 comparative balance sheet and the 2010 income statement of Sundowner Tools Ltd. follow. Sundowner had no noncash investing and financing transactions during 2010.

SUNDOWNER TOOLS LTD.
Comparative Balance Sheet
December 31, 2010 and 2009

	December 31, 2010	December 31, 2009
Current assets		
Cash and cash equivalents	$ 86,400	$ 46,800
Accounts receivable	133,500	129,300
Interest receivable	1,800	2,700
Inventories	291,900	269,700
Prepaid expenses	5,100	6,600
Property, plant, and equipment:		
Plant and equipment, net	302,700	281,100
Land	105,300	30,000
Total assets	$926,700	$766,200
Current liabilities		
Accounts payable	$ 49,200	$ 53,700
Interest payable	18,900	20,100
Salaries payable	9,600	4,200
Other accrued liabilities	54,300	56,100
Income tax payable	18,900	11,400
Long-term liabilities:		
Notes payable	165,000	195,000
Shareholders' equity		
Common shares	393,300	366,900
Retained earnings	217,500	58,800
Total liabilities and shareholders' equity	$926,700	$766,200

*This Problem refers to topics covered in the Chapter 17 Appendix.

SUNDOWNER TOOLS LTD.
Income Statement
For the Year Ended December 31, 2010

Revenues:		
Sales revenue...		$1,374,000
Interest revenue		35,100
Total revenues		1,409,100
Expenses:		
Cost of goods sold.....................................	$615,600	
Salaries expense...	229,200	
Amortization expense.................................	45,900	
Other operating expenses...........................	149,100	
Interest expense	73,800	
Income tax expense....................................	50,700	
Total expenses		1,164,300
Net income...		$ 244,800

Transaction data for the year ended December 31, 2010 are as follows:

a. Bought land for cash, $75,300.
b. Bought equipment for cash, $67,500.
c. Paid $30,000 on notes payable.
d. Paid dividends in cash, $86,100.
e. Issued common shares for cash, $26,400.

Required

Prepare the spreadsheet for the 2010 cash flow statement. Format cash flows from operating activities by the *indirect* method.

CHALLENGE PROBLEMS

Problem 17–1C

Both the Accounting Standards Board (AcSB) in Canada and the Financial Accounting Standards Board (FASB) in the United States prefer the direct method of preparing the operating activities portion of the cash flow statement. Yet most companies use the indirect method when preparing their cash flow statement.

Distinguishing between the direct method and indirect method

③ ⑤

Required

Discuss why you think companies use the indirect method when the direct method is the method preferred by the standard-setting bodies.

Problem 17–2C

Initially, the *CICA Handbook* did not require financial statements to include information about noncash investing and financing activities. The financial statements reported only changes in working capital (defined as current assets less current liabilities) and so transactions such as the use of long-term debt to purchase property, plant, and equipment, or conversion of debt into equity were excluded.

Accounting for noncash financing and investing activities

④

Required

Discuss the present *CICA Handbook*'s requirements with respect to disclosure of noncash financing and investing decisions, and explain why you think the required disclosure does or does not benefit users.

Extending Your Knowledge

DECISION PROBLEMS

Preparing and using the cash flow statement to evaluate operations

4 5

1. Net cash from operating $60,000, investing $(66,500), financing $(18,500)

Decision Problem 1

The 2010 comparative income statement and the 2010 comparative balance sheet of Eclipse Golf Inc. have just been distributed at a meeting of the company's board of directors.

In discussing the company's results of operations and year-end financial position, the members of the board of directors raise a fundamental question: Why is the cash balance so low? This question is especially puzzling to the board members because 2010 showed record profits. As the controller of the company, you must answer the question.

ECLIPSE GOLF INC.
Comparative Income Statement
For the Years Ended December 31, 2010 and 2009
(amounts in thousands)

	2010	2009
Revenues and gains:		
Sales revenue...	$222.0	$155.0
Gain on sale of equipment (sale price, $17.5)..	—	9.0
Total revenues and gains............................	222.0	164.0
Expenses and losses:		
Cost of goods sold..	110.5	81.0
Salaries expense...	24.0	14.0
Amortization expense.....................................	28.5	16.5
Interest expense	6.5	10.0
Loss on sale of land (sale price, $30.5)..........	—	17.5
Total expenses and losses...........................	169.5	139.0
Net income...	$ 52.5	$ 25.0

ECLIPSE GOLF INC.
Comparative Balance Sheet
December 31, 2010 and 2009
(amounts in thousands)

Assets	2010	2009
Cash	$ 6.5	$ 31.5
Accounts receivable, net......................................	46.0	30.5
Inventories	97.0	90.5
Property, plant, and equipment, net..................	74.0	30.5
Patents, net...	88.5	94.0
Total assets	$312.0	$277.0

Liabilities and Shareholders' Equity		
Notes payable, short-term		
(for general borrowing)...................................	$ 16.0	$ 50.5
Accounts payable...	31.5	28.0
Accrued liabilities...	6.0	8.5
Notes payable, long-term	73.5	81.5
Common shares	74.5	30.5
Retained earnings	110.5	78.0
Total liabilities and shareholders' equity......	$312.0	$277.0

Required

1. Prepare a cash flow statement for 2010 in the format that best shows the relationship between net income and operating cash flow. The company sold no capital assets or long-term investments and issued no notes payable during 2010. The changes in all current accounts except short-term notes payable arose from operations. There were no noncash financing and investing transactions during the year. Show all amounts in thousands. Amortization expense on the patent was $5,500.

2. Answer the board members' question: Why is the cash balance so low? In explaining the business's cash flows, identify two significant cash receipts that occurred during 2009 but not in 2010. Also point out the two largest cash payments during 2010.

3. Considering net income and the company's cash flows during 2010, was it a good year or a bad year for Eclipse Golf Inc.? Give your reasons.

Decision Problem 2

Using the cash flow statement to evaluate a company's operations

The cash flow statement, in the not-too-distant past, included information in only two categories: sources of funds and uses of funds. Funds were usually defined as working capital (current assets minus current liabilities). The present-day statement provides information about cash flows from operating activities, investing activities, and financing activities. The earlier statement permitted the information to be about changes in working capital or in cash, while today's cash flow statement deals specifically with information about flows in cash and cash equivalents.

Required

1. Explain why you think the present-day cash flow statement, with its disclosure of the three different kinds of activities, is or is not an improvement over the earlier model that showed only sources and uses of funds.

2. Is information about cash flows more informative to users than information about working capital flows?

3. Briefly explain why comparative balance sheets and a cash flow statement are more informative than just comparative balance sheets.

FINANCIAL STATEMENT CASES

Financial Statement Case 1

Using the cash flow statement

Canadian Western Bank's (CWB) Consolidated Statements of Cash Flow appear in Appendix A. Use these statements along with the other material in Appendix A to answer the following questions.

1. By which method of reporting does CWB report net cash flows from operations? How can you tell?

2. Did CWB improve its cash position in fiscal 2008? If so, by how much? If not, by how much did it decline?

3. By how much did CWB's cash from operations increase or decrease in fiscal 2008? Why is it important for cash from operating activities to be a positive number?

4. What were the major investing activities during fiscal 2008? Financing activities?

5. Was CWB expanding or contracting in fiscal 2008? Support your answer with specific references to the financial statements.

Financial Statement Case 2

Using the cash flow statement

Sun-Rype Products Ltd.'s Statements of Cash Flows appear in Appendix B. Use these statements along with the other material in Appendix B to answer the following questions.

1. By which method of reporting does Sun-Rype report net cash flows from operations? How can you tell?

2. Did Sun-Rype improve its cash position in 2008? If so, by how much?

3. Sun-Rype reports items differently in the operating section than the method described in the chapter. Explain.

4. Explain the cause for the large outflow of property, plant, and equipment, and discuss.

5. Was Sun-Rype expanding or contracting in 2008? Support your answer with specific references to the financial statements.

18 Financial Statement Analysis

What is financial statement analysis, and why is it important?

What are horizontal and vertical analysis?

How do you calculate and use standard financial ratios?

These questions and others are answered in this chapter. And the Decision Guidelines at the end of this chapter will provide the answers in a useful summary.

LEARNING OBJECTIVES

1 Perform a horizontal analysis of financial statements

2 Perform a vertical analysis of financial statements

3 Prepare and use common-size financial statements

4 Compute the standard financial ratios

5 Describe the impact on financial statement analysis of international financial reporting standards (IFRS)

Winpak Ltd., based in Winnipeg, is a Canadian success story. We will examine Winpak's financial statements throughout this chapter.

Winpak manufactures and sells high-quality packaging materials and innovative packaging machines. Customers use Winpak packaging for perishable foods, beverages, pharmaceuticals, and medical applications. Most Winpak products are sold in the United States and Canada. Customers include Proctor & Gamble, McCain Foods Limited, High Liner Foods Inc., and Maple Leaf Foods.

Winpak's sales have grown steadily over the past 10 years. The company targets an annual growth rate of 6 to 9 percent, and this was exceeded in 2008. Gross margin declined in 2007 but rebounded in 2008. The main reason for the increase in gross margin in 2008 was "enhanced manufacturing performance as well as the overall reduction in labor and overhead unit costs resulting from greater volumes and the efficiencies gained as a result of the capital investments of recent years."

During 2006 and 2007, Winpak's management invested $75 million in capital projects such as plant and equipment. In 2008, such investment was reduced to about $15 million. "As a result, the considerable start-up and development costs experienced in 2007 were curtailed in 2008 and production management was better able to focus on refining manufacturing processes and improving efficiencies."

The future looks bright for Winpak's cash flows. "During 2009, the Company will utilize its cash resources on hand and generate sufficient additional cash resources to fund its investing and financing activities, including the repayment of all the long-term debt, barring any unforeseen circumstances."

Source: Winpak Ltd.'s 2008 Annual Report, Management's Discussion and Analysis section, p. 3.

As the opening vignette illustrates, managers rely on accounting information to make business decisions. Investors and creditors also rely on accounting information. Often they want to compare two or more similar companies. The way to compare companies of different sizes is to use *standard* measures. Throughout this book, we have discussed financial ratios, such as the current ratio, inventory turnover, and return on shareholders' equity. These ratios are standard measures that enable investors to compare companies of similar sizes or different sizes, or companies that operate in the same or different industries. Managers use the ratios to monitor operations and to help make business decisions. In this chapter, we discuss most of the basic ratios and related measures that managers use to run a company. Investors and lenders use the same tools to search for good investments and loan prospects. The information value of these ratios is one reason accounting is called the "language of business."

The Objectives of Financial Statement Analysis

Financial statement analysis focuses on techniques used by internal managers and by analysts external to the organization. A major source of their information is the annual report. Annual reports usually contain:

1. The basic financial statements: balance sheet, income statement, statement of retained earnings, and cash flow statement, and the notes to the financial statements, including a statement of significant accounting policies;
2. Comparative financial information for at least the prior year;
3. The auditor's report;
4. Management's discussion and analysis (MD&A) of the past financial results and expectations for the future;
5. A management report; and
6. Other financial and nonfinancial information about the company, such as information relating to environmental affairs.

More and more companies have web pages on the Internet where they place information about the company, ranging from its annual reports to its products and news releases.

Exhibit 18–1 shows graphical data taken from the 2008 annual report of Winpak Ltd. Management uses the graphical data to show how the company performed over the 10 years ended December 28, 2008.

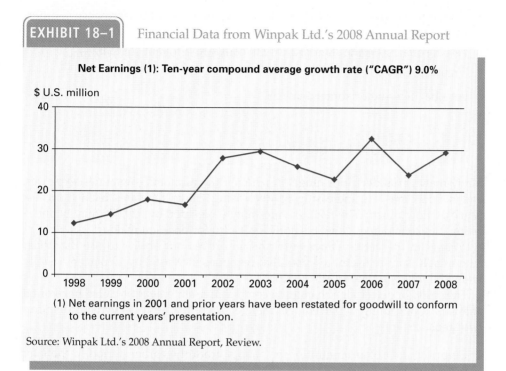

EXHIBIT 18–1 Financial Data from Winpak Ltd.'s 2008 Annual Report

Net Earnings (1): Ten-year compound average growth rate ("CAGR") 9.0%

(1) Net earnings in 2001 and prior years have been restated for goodwill to conform to the current years' presentation.

Source: Winpak Ltd.'s 2008 Annual Report, Review.

Investors who purchase a company's shares expect to receive dividends and hope the shares' value will increase. Creditors make loans with the expectation of receiving cash for the interest and principal. Both groups bear the risk they will not receive their expected returns. They use financial statement analysis to (1) predict the amount of expected returns and (2) assess the risks associated with those returns.

Creditors generally expect to receive specific fixed amounts and have the first claim on a company's assets, so they are most concerned with assessing short-term liquidity and long-term solvency. **Short-term liquidity** is an organization's ability to meet current payments as they become due. **Long-term solvency** is the ability to generate enough cash to pay long-term debts as they mature.

In contrast, *investors* are more concerned with profitability, dividends, and future share prices. Why? Because dividends and future share prices depend on profitable operations. Creditors also assess profitability because profitable operations are the company's prime source of cash to repay loans.

However, investors and creditors cannot evaluate a company by looking at only one year's data. This is why most financial statements cover at least two periods. This chapter illustrates some of the analytical tools for charting a company's progress over time.

How can we decide what we really think about Winpak's performance? We need some way to analyze a company's performance

- From year to year
- Compared with a competing company
- Compared with the company's industry

Then, we can better judge the company's situation now and predict what might happen in the near future.

Methods of Analysis

There are three main ways to analyze financial statements:

- Horizontal analysis provides year-to-year comparison of performance in different periods.
- Vertical analysis is the standard way to compare different companies.
- Financial ratios.

Let's begin with horizontal analysis.

OBJECTIVE 1
Perform a horizontal analysis of financial statements

Horizontal Analysis

Many managerial decisions hinge on whether the numbers—revenues, expenses, and net income—are increasing or decreasing. Have revenues risen from last year? By how much? The fact revenues may have risen by $20,000 may be interesting, but considered alone it is not very useful for decision making. The *percentage change* in the net revenues over time improves our ability to use the dollar amounts. It is more useful to know that revenues increased by 20 percent than to know that revenues increased by $20,000.

The study of percentage changes in comparative statements is called **horizontal analysis**. Computing a percentage change in comparative statements requires two steps:

1. Compute the dollar amount of the change from the earlier period to the later period.
2. Divide the dollar amount of the change by the earlier-period amount and multiply by 100. We call the earlier period the base period.

Horizontal analysis is illustrated for Winpak Ltd.:

| | (U.S. dollar amounts in millions) | | Increase (Decrease) | |
	2008	2007	Amount	Percent
Sales	$512	$466	$46	9.9
Net earnings	29	24	5	20.8

The percentage change in Winpak's sales during 2008 is computed as follows:

Step 1. Compute the dollar amount of change in sales during 2008.

2008		2007		Increase
$512	−	$466	=	$46

Step 2. Divide the dollar amount of change by the base-period amount and multiply by 100 to compute the percentage change during the later period.

$$\text{Percentage change} = \frac{\text{Dollar amount of change}}{\text{Base-year amount}} = \frac{\$46}{\$466} \times 100 = 9.9 \text{ percent}$$

During 2008, Winpak's sales (revenues) increased by 9.9 percent.

Detailed horizontal analyses of a comparative income statement and a comparative balance sheet are shown in the two right-hand columns of Exhibits 18–2 and 18–3. The comparative income statement shows that sales increased by $46 million, or 9.9 percent, during 2008. Cost of goods sold (cost of sales) and expenses

KEY POINT

Horizontal analysis often involves a percentage change, calculated as:

$$\frac{\$ \text{ change}}{\text{Base year } \$} \times 100 = \% \text{ change}$$

It is important to use both dollar changes and percentage changes in horizontal analysis. The dollar increase may be growing, but the percentage change may be growing less because the base is greater each year.

EXHIBIT 18–2 | Comparative Income Statement—Horizontal Analysis

WINPAK LTD.
Consolidated Statements of Income (adapted)
For the Years Ended December 28, 2008, and December 30, 2007
(U.S. dollar amounts in millions except per-share amounts)

	2008	2007	Increase (Decrease) Amount	Increase (Decrease) Percent
Sales	$512	$466	$46	9.9%
Cost of sales	379	356	23	6.5
Gross margin	133	110	23	20.9
Expenses				
Selling, general, & administrative	75	65	10	15.4
Research and technical	11	10	1	10.0
Pre-production	1	1	0	0
Earnings from operations	46	34	12	35.3
Interest	1	2	(1)	(50.0)
Earnings before income taxes and noncontrolling interest	45	32	13	40.6
Provision for income taxes	16	8	8	100.0
Noncontrolling interest	0	0	0	0
Net earnings	$ 29	$ 24	$ 5	20.8
Earnings per share (basic and fully diluted)	$0.45	$0.37	$0.08	21.6

increased by a lesser amount ($34 million or 7.9 percent), so that earnings from operations increased by $12 million, or 35.3 percent.

The comparative balance sheet in Exhibit 18–3 shows that there was a change between 2007 and 2008. Total assets decreased by $25 million, or 5.7 percent, while total liabilities decreased by $12 million, or 10.1 percent. The increase in retained earnings was $22 million, or 9.6 percent.

Trend Percentages

Trend percentages are a form of horizontal analysis. Trends are important indicators of the direction a business is taking. How have sales changed over a five-year period? What trend does gross margin show? These questions can be answered by analyzing trend percentages over a recent period, such as the most recent five years or 10 years. To gain a realistic view of the company, it is often necessary to examine more than just a two- or three-year period.

Trend percentages are computed by selecting a base year. The base-year amounts are set to 100 percent. The amounts for each following year are expressed as a percent of the base amount. To compute trend percentages, divide each item for following years by the base-year amount and multiply by 100 percent.

KEY POINT

Trend percentages indicate the change between a base year and any later year:

$$\text{Trend \%} = \frac{\text{Any year \$}}{\text{Base-year \$}} \times 100\%$$

To calculate the % change from the base year, subtract 100% from the trend %.
For example, sales increased 30% from 2004 to 2008
(130% − 100%).

$$\text{Trend \%} = \frac{\text{Any year \$}}{\text{Base-year \$}} \times 100 \%$$

EXHIBIT 18–3   Comparative Balance Sheet—Horizontal Analysis

WINPAK LTD.
Consolidated Balance Sheet (adapted)
December 28, 2008, and December 30, 2007
(U.S. dollar amounts in millions)

			Increase (Decrease)	
	2008	**2007**	**Amount**	**Percent**
Assets				
Current assets:				
Cash..	$ 20	$ —	$ 20	100.0%
Accounts receivable	63	57	6	10.5
Income taxes receivable	—	6	(6)	(100.0)
Inventory	68	75	(7)	(9.3)
Prepaid expenses............................	2	2	0	0
Future income taxes........................	3	3	0	0
	157*	143	14	9.8
Property, plant, and equipment	227	263	(36)	(13.7)
Other assets, intangible assets,				
and goodwill....................................	33	35	(2)	(5.7)
Total assets..	$417	$442*	$(25)	(5.7)
Liabilities and Shareholders' Equity				
Current liabilities:				
Bank indebtedness (unsecured)....	$ —	$ 5	$ (5)	(100.0)%
Accounts payable and				
accrued liabilities	33	38	(5)	(13.2)
Income taxes payable	2	—	2	100.0
	35	43	(8)	(18.6)
Noncurrent liabilities:				
Long-term debt................................	17	22	(5)	(22.7)
Deferred credits..............................	11	13	(2)	(15.4)
Future income taxes........................	28	29	(1)	(3.4)
Postretirement benefits...................	2	2	0	0
Noncontrolling interest	14	11	3	27.3
	72	77	(5)	(6.5)
Total liabilities......................................	107	119*	(12)	(10.1)
Shareholders' equity:				
Common shares.............................	29	29	0	0
Retained earnings	250	228	22	9.6
Accumulated other				
comprehensive income..............	31	65	(34)	(52.3)
Total shareholders' equity	310	323*	(13)	(4.0)
Total liabilities and				
shareholders' equity	$417	$442	$(25)	(5.7)

Percentage changes are typically not computed for shifts from a negative amount to a positive amount, and vice versa.

* Slight differences are due to rounding.

Note: A decrease from any number to zero is a decrease of 100 percent. We will treat an increase from zero to any positive number as an increase of 100 percent.

KEY POINT

The Amount column of the Increase (Decrease) analysis of Exhibit 18–3 totals $(25) million. There are no equal sign lines on the Percent column. This column will never total (5.7)% because a separate percentage has been calculated for each item, as is always done in horizontal analysis.

Winpak showed sales and earnings from operations for the past five years as follows:

	(Amounts in millions)				
	2008	**2007**	**2006**	**2005**	**2004**
Sales	$512	$466	$447	$437	$393
Earnings from operations	46	34	49	35	44
Net earnings	29	24	33	23	26

We want trend percentages for a four-year period, 2004 through 2008. We use 2004 as the base year. Trend percentages for sales are computed by dividing each sales amount by the 2004 amount of $393 million. Likewise, dividing each year's earnings from operations amount by the base-year amount, $44 million, yields the trend percentages for earnings from operations. The same steps are done for net earnings. The resulting trend percentages follow (2004, the base year = 100%):

	2008	2007	2006	2005	2004
Sales	130%	119%	114%	111%	100%
Earnings from operations	105	77	111	80	100
Net earnings	112	92	127	88	100

Winpak's sales have trended upward from 2004; 2008 sales are 130 percent of 2004 sales. Earnings from operations have trended upward from 2004. Net earnings also followed the same upwards trend, from $26 million in 2004 to $29 million in 2008; 2008's net earnings were 112 percent of 2004's net earnings. Sales, earnings from operations, and net earnings have all trended upwards. However, earnings from operations and net earnings have been up and down over the five-year period. Further analysis would need to be completed to confirm whether the trend is expected to continue upward.

You can perform a trend analysis on any item you consider important. Trend analysis is widely used to help predict the future.

DID YOU GET IT?

MyAccountingLab

To check your understanding of the material in this Learning Objective, complete these questions. The solutions appear on MyAccountingLab so you can check your progress.

1. Perform a horizontal analysis of the comparative income statement of Umoja Inc. State whether 2010 was a good year or a bad year and give your reasons.

UMOJA INC.
Comparative Income Statement
For the Years Ended December 31, 2010 and 2009

	2010	2009
Net sales	$275,000	$225,000
Expenses:		
Cost of goods sold	194,000	165,000
Engineering, selling, and administrative expenses	54,000	48,000
Interest expense	5,000	5,000
Income tax expense	9,000	3,000
Other expense (income)	1,000	(1,000)
Total expenses	263,000	220,000
Net income	$ 12,000	$ 5,000

2. Suppose Umoja Inc. reported the following revenues and net income amounts:

(in thousands)	2010	2009	2008	2007
Revenues (net sales)	$275,000	$225,000	$210,000	$200,000
Net income	12,000	5,000	6,000	3,000

a. Show Umoja Inc.'s trend percentages for revenues and net income. Use 2007 as the base year.
b. Which measure increased faster between 2007 and 2010?

Vertical Analysis

As we have seen, horizontal analysis and trend percentages highlight changes in an item over time. However, no single technique provides a complete picture of a business. Another way to analyze a company is called vertical analysis.

Vertical analysis of a financial statement reveals the relationship of each statement item to a base, which is the 100 percent figure. For example, when an income statement for a merchandising company is subjected to vertical analysis, net sales is usually the base. Every other item on the income statement is then reported as a percentage of that base. Suppose under normal conditions a company's gross margin is 70 percent of net sales. A drop in gross margin to 60 percent of net sales may cause the company to report a net loss on the income statement. Management, investors, and creditors view a large decline in gross margin with alarm. Exhibit 18–4 shows the vertical analysis of Winpak's income statement as a percentage of sales. In this case,

$$\text{Vertical analysis \%} = \frac{\text{Each income statement item}}{\text{Sales}} \times 100\%$$

EXHIBIT 18–4   Comparative Income Statement—Vertical Analysis

WINPAK LTD.
Consolidated Statement of Income (adapted)
For the Years Ended December 28, 2008 and December 30, 2007
(U.S. dollar amounts in millions)

	2008		2007	
	Amount	Percent*	Amount	Percent*
Sales	$ 512	100.0%	$ 466	100.0%
Cost of sales	379	74.0	356	76.4
Gross margin..	133	26.0	110	23.6
Expenses:				
Selling, general, & administrative	75	14.7	65	14.0
Research and technical	11	2.1	10	2.1
Pre-production...	1	0.2	1	0.2
Earnings from operations	46	9.0	34	7.3
Interest...	1	0.2	2	0.4
Earnings before income taxes and				
noncontrolling interest............................	45	8.8	32	6.9
Provision for income taxes..........................	16	3.1	8	1.7
Noncontrolling interest................................	0	0	0	0
Net earnings...	$ 29	5.7	$ 24	5.1
Earnings per share (basic and				
fully diluted)...	$0.45		$0.37	

* Some percentages were rounded up or down in order to reconcile the total.

The 2008 comparative income statement (Exhibit 18–4) reports that cost of sales decreased from 76.4 percent of sales in 2007 to 74.0 percent of sales in 2008. Note that earnings from operations increased from 7.3 percent of sales in 2007 to 9.0 percent of sales in 2008.

The vertical analysis of Winpak's balance sheet (Exhibit 18–5) shows that non-current liabilities decreased from 17.5 percent of total assets in 2007 to 17.3 percent of total assets in 2008. Shareholders' equity increased from 72.9 percent of total assets in 2007 to 74.3 percent in 2008. Both of these are good signs; the company is reducing its long-term debt (5 percent in 2007 to 4.1 percent in 2008) and is profitable (retained earnings went from 51.6 percent in 2007 to 60.0 percent in 2008).

EXHIBIT 18–5 Comparative Balance Sheet—Vertical Analysis

WINPAK LTD.
Consolidated Balance Sheet (adapted)
December 28, 2008, and December 30, 2007
(U.S. dollar amounts in millions)

	2008		2007	
	Amount	Percent*	Amount	Percent*
Assets				
Current assets:				
Cash..	$ 20	4.8%	$ —	—
Accounts receivable.............................	63	15.1	57	12.9
Income tax receivable	—	—	6	1.4
Inventory..	68	16.3	75	17.0
Prepaid expenses...................................	2	0.5	2	0.5
Future income taxes..............................	3	0.7	3	0.7
	156	37.4	143	32.5
Property, plant, and equipment	227	54.4	263	59.5
Other assets, intangible assets,				
and goodwill....................................	34	8.2	35	8.0
Total assets	$417	100.0%	$442	100.0%
Liabilities and Shareholders' Equity				
Current liabilities:				
Bank indebtedness (unsecured)...............	$ —	—	$ 5	1.1%
Accounts payable and				
accrued liabilities	33	7.9%	38	8.6
Income taxes payable	2	0.5	—	—
	35	8.4	43	9.7
Noncurrent liabilities:				
Long-term debt......................................	17	4.1	22	5.0
Deferred credits....................................	11	2.6	13	2.9
Future income taxes..............................	28	6.7	29	6.6
Post-retirement benefits	2	0.5	2	0.5
Noncontrolling interest	14	3.4	11	2.5
	72	17.3	77	17.5
Total liabilities	107	25.7	120	27.2
Shareholders' equity:				
Common shares......................................	29	7.0	29	6.6
Retained earnings..................................	250	60.0	228	51.6
Accumulated other				
comprehensive income.......................	31	7.3	65	14.7
Total shareholders' equity	310	74.3	322	72.9
Total liabilities and				
shareholders' equity	$417	100.0%	$442	100.0%

* Some percentages were rounded up or down in order to reconcile to the total.

DID YOU GET IT?

To check your understanding of the material in this Learning Objective, complete this question. The solution appears on MyAccountingLab so you can check your progress.

3. Refer to the Umoja Inc. information in Did You Get It? Question 1. Perform a vertical analysis of the comparative income statement. Was 2010 a good year or a bad year? Give your reasons.

Common-Size Statements

Horizontal analysis and vertical analysis provide useful data about a company. As we have seen, Winpak's percentages depict a successful company. But the Winpak data apply only to one business.

To compare one company to another we can use a common-size statement. A **common-size statement** reports only percentages—the same percentages that appear in a vertical analysis. For example, Winpak's common-size income statement comes directly from the percentages in Exhibit 18–4.

On a common-size income statement, each item is expressed as a percentage of the net sales amount (or the revenues amount for a service company). Net sales (or revenues) is the *common size* to which we relate the statement's other amounts. In the balance sheet, the *common size* is total assets *or* the sum of total liabilities and shareholders' equity. A common-size statement eases the comparison of different companies because their amounts are stated as percentages.

Common-size statements may identify the need for corrective action. Exhibit 18–6 is the common-size analysis of current assets taken from Exhibit 18–5. Exhibit 18–6 shows that inventory has decreased from 17.0 percent of total assets in 2007 to 16.3 percent of total assets in 2008. Exhibit 18–5 shows that current liabilities have decreased from 9.7 percent of total assets in 2007 to 8.4 percent in 2008. Exhibit 18–6 shows that current assets have increased from 32.4 percent of total assets in 2007 to 37.4 percent of total assets in 2008. Common-size statements provide information useful for analyzing the cash position and current assets, as we just saw.

EXHIBIT 18–6 | Common-Size Analysis of Current Assets

WINPAK LTD.
Common-Size Analysis of Current Assets
December 28, 2008, and December 30, 2007

	Percent of Total Assets	
	2008	2007
Current assets:		
Cash	4.8%	0%
Accounts receivable	15.1	12.9
Inventory	16.3	17.0
Other (includes income tax receivable, future income taxes and prepaid expenses)	1.2	2.6
Total current assets	37.4%	32.5%

Percent of Total Assets

Total Current Assets 37.4%

Other current assets 6.0%
Accounts receivable 15.1%
Inventory 16.3%
Other long-term assets and deferred charges 8.2%
Property, plant, and equipment 54.4%

2008

Total Current Assets 32.5%

Other current assets 2.6%
Accounts receivable 12.9%
Inventory 17.0%
Other long-term assets and deferred charges 8.0%
Property, plant, and equipment 59.5%

2007

Benchmarking

Benchmarking is the practice of comparing a company's performance with that of other leading companies. There are two main types of benchmarks in financial statement analysis.

Benchmarking Against Another Company

A company's financial statements show past results and help investors predict future performance. Still, that knowledge is limited to that one company. We may learn that gross margin and net income have increased. This information is helpful, but it does not consider how other companies in the same industry have fared over the same period. Have competitors profited even more? Is there an industry-wide increase in net income? Managers, investors, creditors, and other interested parties need to know how one company compares with other companies in the same line of business. For example, in its fiscal year ended February 28, 2009, Research in Motion spent $684.7 million on research and development or 6.2 percent of revenue, compared to $359.8 million, or 6.0 percent of revenue, in fiscal 2008. For the year ended December 31, 2008, Google spent $2,793.2 million, or 13.0 percent of revenue, on research and development. Ballard Power Systems spent $37.2 million (U.S. dollars), or 62.4 percent, of its revenues on research and development for the year ended December 31, 2008. These companies are heavily involved in research as they are at the cutting edge in their industries; other companies likely spend less, and some spend nothing on research and development.

In the Internet service industry, Google Inc. and YAHOO! Inc. increased both revenue and profit. Google's total revenue increased from $3.2 billion in 2004 to $21.8 billion in 2008. YAHOO's increased from $3.6 billion in 2004 to $7.2 billion in 2008. Exhibit 18–7 gives the common-size income statement of Google Inc. compared to that of YAHOO! Inc. Analysts at RBC Dominion Securities, ScotiaMcLeod,

---

EXHIBIT 18–7 Common-Size Income Statement of Google Inc. Compared with YAHOO! Inc.

	Google Inc.	YAHOO! Inc.
Revenues	100.0%	100.0%
Cost of revenues	39.6	41.9
Gross margin	60.4	58.1
Sales and marketing expense	8.9	21.7
General and administrative expense	8.3	9.8
Research and development expense	12.8	16.9
Other expense (income)	3.5	0.2
Income before income taxes	26.9	9.5
Income tax expense	7.5	3.6
Net income	19.4%	5.9%

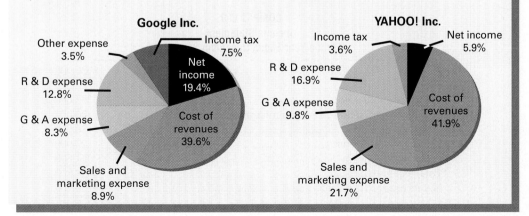

Google Inc.

- Other expense 3.5%
- Income tax 7.5%
- Net income 19.4%
- R & D expense 12.8%
- G & A expense 8.3%
- Cost of revenues 39.6%
- Sales and marketing expense 8.9%

YAHOO! Inc.

- Income tax 3.6%
- Net income 5.9%
- R & D expense 16.9%
- G & A expense 9.8%
- Cost of revenues 41.9%
- Sales and marketing expense 21.7%

and other financial services firms specialize in a particular industry. For example, ScotiaMcLeod has health-care specialists, paper and forest products specialists, and so on. Specialists compare a company with others in the same industry. Exhibit 18–7 shows that YAHOO! Inc. compares favourably with a key competitor, Google Inc. Since the two companies compete in the same industry, YAHOO! serves as an ideal benchmark for Google. YAHOO!'s net income is 5.9 percent of revenue while Google's net income is 19.4 percent. YAHOO! is much less profitable than Google.

Benchmarking Against the Industry Average

The industry average can also serve as a useful benchmark for evaluating a company. An industry comparison would show how Google is performing compared with the industry. *Annual Statement Studies*, published by The Risk Management Association, provides common-size statements for most industries. To compare Google Inc. to the industry average, simply insert the industry-average common-size income statement in place of YAHOO! Inc., shown in Exhibit 18–7.

Information Sources

Financial analysts draw their information from various sources. Annual and quarterly reports offer readers a good look at an individual business's operations. Publicly held companies must, in addition, submit annual reports that are more detailed to the provincial securities commission in each province where they are listed on a stock exchange (for example, the Ontario Securities Commission for the Toronto Stock Exchange). Business publications such as the daily and weekend editions of *The National Post* and the daily *Globe and Mail* Report on Business carry information about individual companies and Canadian industries. The Globe Information Services, with its online services like globeinvestor.com, and the Financial Post DataGroup provide data on public companies and industries in Canada. Credit agencies, like Dun & Bradstreet Canada, for example, offer industry averages as part of their financial service.

DID YOU GET IT?

To check your understanding of the material in this Learning Objective, complete this question. The solution appears on MyAccountingLab so you can check your progress.

4. Refer to the vertical analysis of Umoja Inc. performed in Did You Get It? Question 3. Suppose Compet Ltd. is a competitor of Umoja Inc. in the same industry. Use the Compet Ltd. information given below to create its common-size income statement. How do the results of Umoja Inc. compare with those of Compet Ltd.?

COMPET LTD.
Income Statement
For the Year Ended December 31, 2010

Net sales	$580,000
Expenses:	
Cost of goods sold	395,000
Engineering, selling, and administrative expenses	100,000
Interest expense	30,000
Income tax expense	23,000
Other expense (income)	1,800
Total expenses	549,800
Net income	$ 30,200

Using Ratios to Make Decisions

OBJECTIVE ④
Compute the standard financial ratios

An important part of financial analysis is the calculation and interpretation of ratios. A ratio is a useful way to show the relationship of one number to another. For example, if the balance sheet shows current assets of $100,000 and current liabilities of $25,000, the ratio of current assets to current liabilities is $100,000 to $25,000. We simplify this numerical expression to the ratio of 4 to 1, which may also be written 4:1 and 4/1. Other acceptable ways of expressing this ratio include "current assets are 400 percent of current liabilities," "the business has four dollars in current assets for every one dollar in current liabilities," or simply, "the current ratio is 4.0."

Online financial databases, such as LexisNexis, Financial Post DataGroup, and Globe Information Services, offer quarterly financial figures for hundreds of public corporations going back as much as 10 years. Assume that you wanted to compare some companies' recent earnings histories. You might have the computer compare the companies on the basis of the rate of return on shareholders' equity. The computer could then give you the names of the 20 companies with the highest return on equity.

A manager, a lender, or a financial analyst may use any ratio that is relevant to a particular decision. Many companies include ratios in a special section of their annual report. The ratios we discuss in this chapter may be classified as follows:

1. Measuring ability to pay current liabilities
2. Measuring ability to sell inventory and collect receivables
3. Measuring ability to pay long-term debt
4. Measuring profitability
5. Analyzing shares as an investment

KEY POINT

Horizontal and vertical analyses were our first attempt at using data for decision making. We now learn to use ratios, which help even more in analyzing the financial statements. How do we assess a ratio? We must consider prior years, industry averages, budgeted ratios, and so on—only then does a ratio have meaning.

Measuring Ability to Pay Current Liabilities

Working capital is defined by the following equation:

$$\text{Working capital} = \text{Current assets} - \text{Current liabilities}$$

Working capital measures the ability to meet short-term obligations with current assets. The working capital amount considered alone, however, does not give a complete picture of the entity's working capital position. Consider two companies with equal working capital.

	Company A	Company B
Current assets	$100,000	$200,000
Less current liabilities	50,000	150,000
Working capital	$ 50,000	$ 50,000
Working capital as a percent of current liabilities	100%	33%

Both companies have working capital of $50,000, but Company A's working capital is as large as its current liabilities. Company B's working capital, on the other hand, is only one-third as large as its current liabilities. Which business has the better working-capital position? Company A, because its working capital is a higher percentage of current assets and current liabilities. Two decision tools based on working capital data are the *current ratio* and the *acid-test ratio*.

Current Ratio The most common ratio using current asset and current liability data is the **current ratio**, which is total current assets divided by total current liabilities. We introduced the current ratio in Chapter 4 (p. 182). Recall the makeup of current assets and current liabilities. Current assets consist of cash, short-term investments, net receivables, inventory, and prepaid expenses. Current liabilities include accounts payable, short-term notes payable, unearned revenues, and all types of accrued liabilities. The current ratio measures the company's ability to pay current liabilities with current assets.

Exhibits 18–8 and 18–9 give the comparative income statement and balance sheet of Sofawerks Furniture Inc., respectively. The current ratios of Sofawerks Furniture Inc. at December 31, 2010 and 2009 appear below, along with the average for the retail furniture industry, a benchmark for evaluating Sofawerks Furniture Inc.'s ratios.

EXHIBIT 18–8   Comparative Income Statement

SOFAWERKS FURNITURE INC.
Comparative Income Statement
For the Years Ended December 31, 2010 and 2009

	2010	2009
Net sales	$858,000	$803,000
Cost of goods sold	513,000	509,000
Gross margin	345,000	294,000
Operating expenses:		
Selling expenses	116,000	104,000
General expenses	118,000	123,000
Total operating expenses	234,000	227,000
Income from operations	111,000	67,000
Interest revenue	4,000	—
Less interest expense	34,000	24,000
Income before income taxes	81,000	43,000
Income tax expense	33,000	17,000
Net income	$ 48,000	$ 26,000

	Formula	Current Ratio of Sofawerks Furniture Inc. 2010	Current Ratio of Sofawerks Furniture Inc. 2009	Retail Furniture Industry Average
Current ratio =	$\dfrac{\text{Current assets}}{\text{Current liabilities}}$	$\dfrac{\$272,000}{\$152,000} = 1.79$	$\dfrac{\$246,000}{\$136,000} = 1.81$	1.68

The current ratio decreased slightly during 2010. A high current ratio indicates a strong financial position and that the business has sufficient liquid assets to maintain normal business operations. Compare Sofawerks Furniture Inc.'s current ratio of 1.79 with the 1.68 average for the retail furniture industry and with current ratios of some actual companies.

EXHIBIT 18–9 | Comparative Balance Sheet

SOFAWERKS FURNITURE INC.
Comparative Balance Sheet
December 31, 2010 and 2009

Assets	2010	2009
Current assets:		
Cash	$ 39,000	$ 42,000
Accounts receivable, net	114,000	85,000
Inventories	113,000	111,000
Prepaid expenses	6,000	8,000
Total current assets	272,000	246,000
Long-term investments	18,000	9,000
Property, plant, and equipment, net	507,000	399,000
Total assets	$797,000	$654,000
Liabilities		
Current liabilities:		
Notes payable	$ 42,000	$ 27,000
Accounts payable	83,000	78,000
Accrued liabilities	27,000	31,000
Total current liabilities	152,000	136,000
Long-term debt	289,000	198,000
Total liabilities	441,000	334,000
Shareholders' Equity		
Common shares	186,000	186,000
Retained earnings	170,000	134,000
Total shareholders' equity	356,000	320,000
Total liabilities and shareholders' equity	$797,000	$654,000

Company	Current Ratio
Canadian Tire Corporation, Limited (Merchandising)	1.99
Research in Motion (Communication devices)	2.29
Molson Coors Brewing Company (Brewery)	1.12
Suncor Energy Inc. (Oil and gas)	0.92

What is an acceptable current ratio? The answer to this question depends on the nature of the business. The current ratio should generally exceed 1.0, while the norm for most companies is around 1.50. Sofawerks Furniture Inc.'s current ratio in excess of 1.75 is within the range of those values. In most industries, a current ratio of 2.0 is considered very good. The companies listed above are typical of their industries; note that they range from 0.92 to 2.29.

Acid-Test Ratio

The **acid-test** (or **quick**) **ratio** tells us whether the entity could pay all its current liabilities if they came due immediately. We saw in Chapter 9 (p. 469) that the higher the acid-test ratio, the better able the business is to pay its current liabilities. That is, could the company pass this *acid test*? To do so, the company would have to convert its most liquid assets to cash.

To compute the acid-test ratio, we add cash, short-term investments, and net current receivables (accounts and notes receivable, net of allowances) and divide by total current liabilities. Inventory and prepaid expenses are *not* included in the acid-test computations because a business may not be able to convert them to cash immediately to pay current liabilities. The acid-test ratio measures liquidity using a narrower asset base than the current ratio does.

Sofawerks Furniture Inc.'s acid-test ratios for 2010 and 2009 are as follows:

Formula	Acid-Test Ratio of Sofawerks Furniture Inc. 2010	Acid-Test Ratio of Sofawerks Furniture Inc. 2009	Retail Furniture Industry Average
Acid-test ratio = $\dfrac{\text{Cash + Short-term investments + Net current receivables}}{\text{Current liabilities}}$	$\dfrac{\$39,000 + \$0 + \$114,000}{\$152,000} = 1.01$	$\dfrac{\$42,000 + \$0 + \$85,000}{\$136,000} = 0.93$	0.60

The company's acid-test ratio improved considerably during 2010 and is significantly better than the industry average. Compare Sofawerks Furniture Inc.'s 1.01 acid-test ratio with the acid-test ratios of some well-known companies:

Company	Acid-Test Ratio
Canadian Tire Corporation, Limited (Merchandising)	1.47
Research in Motion (Communication devices)	1.79
Molson Coors Brewing Company (Brewery)	0.86
Suncor Energy Inc. (Oil and gas)	0.63

The norm ranges from 0.20 to 1.00 as reported by Robert Morris Associates. An acid-test ratio of 0.90 to 1.00 is considered good in most industries. Note the range for the companies listed is from a low of 0.63 to a high of 1.79.

Measuring the Ability to Sell Inventory and Collect Receivables

The ability to sell inventory and collect receivables is fundamental to business success. Recall the operating cycle of a merchandiser: cash to inventory to receivables and back to cash. (If you need to, refer to the discussion of the operating cycle in Chapter 5, p. 227.) This section discusses three ratios that measure the ability to sell inventory and collect receivables.

Inventory Turnover Companies generally seek to achieve the quickest possible return on their investments. A return on an investment in inventory—usually a substantial amount—is no exception. The faster inventory sells, the sooner the business creates accounts receivable, and the sooner it collects cash.

Inventory turnover measures the number of times a company sells its average level of inventory during a year. It is also used as a measure of the efficiency of a company in managing its inventory. We introduced inventory turnover in Chapter 5, pages 248–249. A high rate of turnover indicates ease in selling inventory; a low turnover indicates slower sales and may indicate difficulty in selling. Of course, there is a relationship between turnover and the product; Zellers will have a higher rate of turnover than a company such as Finning International Inc. of Vancouver, which sells heavy equipment. A value of 6 means that the company sold its average level of inventory six times during the year. A business also strives for the *most profitable* rate of inventory turnover, not necessarily the *highest* rate.

To compute inventory turnover, we divide cost of goods sold by the average inventory for the period. We use the cost of goods sold—not sales—because both cost of goods sold and inventory are stated *at cost*. Sales at *retail* are not comparable to inventory at *cost*.

LEARNING TIPS

Another helpful way to analyze inventory is to compare the inventory turnover days:

$$\frac{365}{\text{Inventory turnover}}$$

The calculation for Sofawerks Furniture Inc. for 2010 would be

$$\frac{365}{4.58} = 80 \text{ days}$$

It took the company approximately 80 days to sell all the items in inventory.

Sofawerks Furniture Inc.'s inventory turnover for 2010 is

Formula	Inventory Turnover of Sofawerks Furniture Inc.		Retail Furniture Industry Average
Inventory turnover = $\dfrac{\text{Cost of goods sold}}{\text{Average inventory}}$	$\dfrac{\$513,000}{(\$111,000 + \$113,000)/2}$ =	4.58 times	2.70 times

Cost of goods sold appears in the income statement (Exhibit 18–8). Average inventory is calculated by averaging the beginning inventory, $111,000, and ending inventory, $113,000, from Exhibit 18–9. If inventory levels vary greatly from month to month, compute the average by adding the 12 monthly balances and dividing this sum by 12.

Inventory turnover varies widely with the nature of the business. Companies that remove natural gas from the ground hold their inventory for a very short period of time and have an average turnover of 30. Sofawerks Furniture Inc.'s turnover of 4.58 times a year is high for its industry, which has an average turnover of 2.70. Sofawerks Furniture Inc.'s high inventory turnover results from its policy of keeping little inventory on hand. The company takes customer orders and has its suppliers ship directly to customers.

KEY POINT

The accounts receivable turnover helps measure the effectiveness and efficiency of credit collections.

Accounts-Receivable Turnover   **Accounts-receivable turnover** measures the ability to collect cash from credit customers. It is also used as a measure of the efficiency of a company to manage its cash collections. The higher the ratio is, the faster are the cash collections. However, a receivable turnover that is too high may indicate that credit is too tight, causing the loss of sales to good customers.

To compute the accounts-receivable turnover, we divide net credit sales by average net accounts receivable. The resulting ratio indicates how many times during the year the average level of receivables was turned into cash.

Sofawerks Furniture Inc.'s accounts-receivable turnover ratio for 2010 is computed as follows:

KEY POINT

Recall that net accounts receivable is computed by subtracting the allowance for doubtful accounts from the accounts receivable total.

Formula	Accounts Receivable Turnover of Sofawerks Furniture Inc.	Retail Furniture Industry Average
Accounts-receivable turnover = $\dfrac{\text{Net credit sales}}{\text{Average net accounts receivable}}$	$\dfrac{\$858,000}{(\$85,000 + \$114,000)/2}$ = 8.62 times	22.2 times

The net credit sales figure comes from the income statement. Sofawerks Furniture Inc. makes all sales on credit. (If a company makes both cash and credit sales, this ratio is best computed using only net *credit* sales.) Average net accounts receivable is calculated by adding the beginning net accounts receivable balance ($85,000) and the ending balance ($114,000), then dividing by 2. If accounts receivable balances exhibit a seasonal pattern, compute the average using the 12 monthly balances.

KEY POINT

If a company makes both cash and credit sales, use net credit sales when calculating accounts receivable turnover.

Sofawerks Furniture Inc.'s accounts-receivable turnover of 8.62 times is much lower than the industry average. Why the difference? Sofawerks is a home-town store that sells to local people who tend to pay their bills over a period of time. Many larger furniture stores sell their receivables to other companies called *factors*. This practice keeps receivables low and receivable turnover high. But companies that factor (sell) their receivables receive less than face value for the receivables.

Days' Sales in Receivables   The **days'-sales-in-receivables** ratio measures the ability to collect receivables. This ratio tells us how many days' credit sales remain in Accounts Receivable. Recall from Chapter 9 (p. 470) that days' sales in receivables indicates how many days it takes to collect the average level of receivables. To compute the ratio, we can follow a two-step process.

First, divide net sales by 365 days to calculate average sales for one day.

Second, divide this average day's sales amount into the average net accounts receivable.

The data to compute this ratio for Sofawerks Furniture Inc. for 2010 are taken from the income statement and the balance sheet (Exhibits 18–8 and 18–9).

Formulas	Days' Sales in Accounts Receivable of Sofawerks Furniture Inc. for 2010	Retail Furniture Industry Average
Days' Sales in Average Accounts Receivable:		
1. One day's sales $= \dfrac{\text{Net sales}}{365 \text{ days}}$	$\dfrac{\$858{,}000}{365 \text{ days}} = \$2{,}351$	
2. Day's sales in average accounts receivable $= \dfrac{\text{Average net accounts receivable}}{\text{One day's sales}}$	$\dfrac{(\$85{,}000+\$114{,}000)/2}{\$2{,}351} = 42 \text{ days}$	16 days

Days' sales in average receivables can also be computed in a single step: $\$99{,}500 \div (\$858{,}000 \div 365 \text{ days}) = 42$ days.

Sofawerks Furniture Inc.'s ratio tells us that 42 days' sales remained in average accounts receivable during the year, or that it takes 42 days to collect receivables. The company will increase its cash inflow if it can decrease this ratio. Ways to do this include offering discounts for early payments, tightening credit policies to disallow slow-paying customers, and using more aggressive collection procedures. The days' sales in receivables is higher (worse) than the industry average because the company collects its own receivables. Other furniture stores may sell their receivables or carry fewer days' sales in receivables. Sofawerks Furniture Inc. remains competitive because of the personal relationship with customers. Without their good paying habits, the company's cash flow would suffer.

Measuring the Ability to Pay Long-Term Debt

The ratios discussed so far give us insight into current assets and current liabilities. They help us measure the ability to sell inventory, collect receivables, and pay current liabilities. Most businesses also have long-term debt. Two key indicators of a business's ability to pay long-term liabilities are the *debt ratio* and *times-interest-earned ratio*.

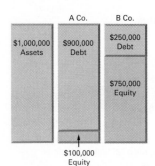

Debt Ratio   Suppose you are a loan officer at a bank and you are evaluating loan applications from two companies with equal sales and equal total assets of $1,000,000. Both A Co. and B Co. have asked to borrow $500,000 and have agreed to repay the loan over a five-year period. A Co. already owes $900,000 to another bank. B Co. owes only $250,000. Other things being equal, you would be more likely to lend money to B Co. because B Co. owes less money than A Co. owes. This relationship between total liabilities and total assets—called the **debt ratio**—shows the proportion of the company's assets that it has financed with debt. We introduced the debt ratio in Chapter 4, page 183. If the debt ratio is 0.90, as shown for A Co., then debt has been used to finance most of the assets. A debt ratio of 0.50 means that the company has borrowed to finance half its assets; the owners have financed the other half. The higher the debt ratio is, the higher the strain of paying interest each year and the principal amount at maturity.

Creditors view a high debt ratio with caution. To help protect themselves, creditors generally charge higher interest rates on new borrowings to companies with an already-high debt ratio.

Sofawerks Furniture Inc.'s debt ratios at the end of 2010 and 2009 are as follows:

Formula	Debt Ratio of Sofawerks Furniture Inc.		Retail Furniture Industry Average
	2010	2009	
Debt ratio = $\dfrac{\text{Total liabilities}}{\text{Total assets}}$	$\dfrac{\$441,000}{\$797,000}$ = 0.55	$\dfrac{\$334,000}{\$654,000}$ = 0.51	0.61

Sofawerks Furniture Inc. expanded operations by financing the purchase of buildings and fixtures through borrowing, which is common. This expansion explains the company's increased debt ratio. Even after the increase in 2010, the company's debt is not very high. The average debt ratio for most companies ranges around 0.57 to 0.67, with relatively little variation from company to company. Sofawerks Furniture Inc.'s 0.55 debt ratio indicates a fairly low-risk debt position in comparison with the retail furniture industry average of 0.61.

The *equity ratio* provides complementary information to the debt ratio. By dividing total shareholders's equity by total assets, the equity ratio provides investors with the amount of assets financed by the owners of the company. The debt ratio and the equity ratio give lenders and investors an indication of how the company is financed.

Times-Interest-Earned Ratio   The debt ratio indicates nothing about the ability to pay interest expense. Analysts use a second ratio—the **times-interest-earned ratio**—to relate income to interest expense. This ratio is sometimes called the *interest-coverage ratio*. It measures the number of times that operating income can cover interest expense. A high interest-coverage ratio indicates ease in paying interest expense; a low value suggests difficulty.

Calculation of Sofawerks Furniture Inc.'s times-interest-earned ratios follow:

Formula	Times-Interest-Earned Ratio of Sofawerks Furniture Inc.		Retail Furniture Industry Average
	2010	2009	
Times-interest-earned ratio = $\dfrac{\text{Income from operations}}{\text{Interest expense}}$	$\dfrac{\$111,000}{\$34,000}$ = 3.26 times	$\dfrac{\$67,000}{\$24,000}$ = 2.79 times	2.00 times

The company's times-interest-earned ratio increased in 2010. This is a favourable sign about the company, especially since the company's liabilities rose substantially during the year. Sofawerks Furniture Inc.'s new buildings and fixtures, we conclude, have earned more in operating income than they have cost the business in interest expense. The company's times-interest-earned ratio of 3.26 is much better than the 2.00 average for furniture retailers. The norm for businesses, as reported by Robert Morris Associates, falls in the range of 2.00 to 3.00 for most companies. Based on its debt ratio and times-interest-earned ratio, Sofawerks Furniture Inc. appears to have little difficulty *servicing its debt*, that is, paying its liabilities.

What makes a corporation with a lot of debt a more risky loan prospect than one with a lot of equity? For a corporation with a lot of debt, interest on debt is contractual and must be paid; it is not discretionary. If interest on debt is not paid, creditors can force the company into bankruptcy. With equity, dividends are discretionary and do not have to be declared.

Measuring Profitability

The fundamental goal of business is to earn a profit. Ratios that measure profitability are reported in the business press, on business TV, by investment services, and in annual reports. We examine four profitability measures.

Rate of Return on Net Sales In business, the term *return* is used broadly as a measure of profitability. Consider a ratio called the **rate of return on net sales** or, simply *return on sales*. (The word *net* is usually omitted for convenience, even though net sales is used to compute the ratio.) It is also called the *profit margin*. This ratio shows the percentage of each sales dollar earned as net income. The rate-of-return-on-sales ratios for Sofawerks Furniture Inc. follow:

| Formula | | Rate of Return on Sales of Sofawerks Furniture Inc. | | Retail Furniture Industry Average |
		2010	2009	
Rate of return on net sales	$= \dfrac{\text{Net income}}{\text{Net sales}}$	$\dfrac{\$48,000}{\$858,000} = 0.056$	$\dfrac{\$26,000}{\$803,000} = 0.032$	0.008

Companies strive for a high rate of return on sales. The higher the rate of return, the more sales dollars are providing profit. The increase in Sofawerks Furniture Inc.'s return on sales is significant and identifies the company as more successful than the average furniture store. Compare Sofawerks Furniture Inc.'s rate of return on sales to the rates of some leading companies in other industries:

Company	Rate of Return on Sales
Brick Brewing Co. Limited (Brewery)...	(0.250)
Sobeys Inc. (Grocery chain)	0.018
TransCanada Corporation (Oil and gas utility)	0.197
Loblaw Companies Limited	0.018

As these numbers indicate, the rate of return on sales varies widely from industry to industry.

Rate of Return on Total Assets The **rate of return on total assets** or, simply, *return on assets* measures success in using assets to earn a profit. We first discussed rate of return on total assets in Chapter 13, page 740. Two groups finance a company's assets. Creditors have lent money to the company, and they earn interest on this money. Shareholders have invested in shares, and their rate of return is the company's net income.

The sum of interest expense and net income is thus the return to the two groups that have financed the company's assets. Computation of the rate of return on total assets for Sofawerks Furniture Inc. follows:

Formula		Rate of Return on Total Assets of Sofawerks Furniture Inc.	Retail Furniture Industry Average
Rate of return on total assets	$= \dfrac{\text{Net Income} + \text{Interest expense}}{\text{Average total assets}}$	$\dfrac{\$48,000 + \$34,000}{(\$797,000 + \$654,000)/2} = 0.113$	0.078

Net income and interest expense are taken from the income statement (Exhibit 18–8). Average total assets is the average of beginning and ending total

KEY POINT

The denominator for rate of return on total assets is average total assets. Income is earned throughout the year. For the denominator to be stated for the same time period as the numerator, an average of assets for the year is used.

KEY POINT

The rate of return on total assets tells those who finance the assets, both creditors and owners, the level of return the company earned for each dollar invested in the assets. A return of 0.113, or 11.3 percent, indicates that the company earned $0.113 for each dollar invested in assets.

assets from the comparative balance sheet (Exhibit 18–9). Compare Sofawerks Furniture Inc.'s rate of return on assets to the rates of some other companies:

Company	Rate of Return on Assets
Brick Brewing Co. Limited (Brewery)...	(0.262)
Sobeys Inc. (Grocery chain)	0.060
TransCanada Corporation (Oil and gas utility)	0.038
Loblaw Companies Limited	0.039

Rate of Return on Common Shareholders' Equity   A popular measure of profitability is the **rate of return on common shareholders' equity**, often shortened to **return on shareholders' equity**, or simply, **return on equity**. We examined this ratio in detail in Chapter 13, page 741.

This ratio shows the relationship between net income and common shareholders' investment in the company—how much income is earned for every dollar invested by the common shareholders. To compute this ratio, we first subtract preferred dividends from net income. The remainder is net income available to the common shareholders. Then divide net income available to common shareholders by the average common shareholders' equity during the year. The 2010 rate of return on common shareholders' equity for Sofawerks Furniture Inc. follows:

KEY POINT

> Return on shareholders' equity measures how much income is earned for every $1 invested by the *common* shareholders (both contributed capital and retained earnings).

Formula	Rate of Return on Common Shareholders' Equity of Sofawerks Furniture Inc.	Retail Furniture Industry Average
$\text{Rate of return on common shareholders' equity} = \dfrac{\text{Net income} - \text{Preferred dividends}}{\text{Average common shareholders' equity}}$	$\dfrac{\$48,000 - \$0}{(\$356,000 + \$320,000)/2} = 0.142$	0.121

Average equity is the average of the beginning and ending balances [($356,000 + $320,000)/2 = $338,000]. Common shareholders' equity is equal to total equity minus preferred equity.

Observe that Sofawerks Furniture Inc.'s return on equity, 0.142, is higher than its return on assets, 0.113. This difference results from borrowing at one rate—say, 8 percent—and investing the funds to earn a higher rate, such as the firm's 14.2 percent return on shareholders' equity. This practice is called **trading on the equity**, or using **leverage**. It is directly related to the debt ratio. The higher the debt ratio, the higher the leverage. Companies that finance operations with debt are said to *leverage* their positions.

Leverage usually increases profitability, but not always. Leverage can have a negative impact on profitability. If revenues drop, debt and interest expense must still be paid. Therefore, leverage is a double-edged sword, increasing profits during good times but compounding losses during bad times. Compare Sofawerks Furniture Inc.'s rate of return on common shareholder's equity with rates of other companies. We have used the same companies as for the previous illustration:

Company	Rate of Return on Common Shareholders' Equity
Brick Brewing Co. Limited (Brewery).................	(0.360)
Sobeys Inc. (Grocery chain)	0.105
TransCanada Corporation (Oil and gas utility)	0.113
Loblaw Companies Limited	0.093

Sofawerks Furniture Inc. is more profitable than all of these leading companies. A return on equity of 15 to 20 percent year after year is considered excellent in most industries.

Earnings per Common Share   *Earnings per common share* or, simply, **earnings per share (EPS)** is perhaps the most widely quoted of all financial statistics. It was introduced in Chapter 14, page 783. While GAAP for private enterprises do not require that corporations disclose EPS figures on the income statement or in a note to the financial statements, many corporations do provide this information because investors and financial analysts use it to assess a corporation's profitability. EPS is the amount of net income per *common* share. Earnings per share is computed by dividing net income available to common shareholders by the weighted average number of common shares outstanding during the year. Preferred dividends are subtracted from net income because the preferred shareholders have a prior claim to their dividends. If the company has bonds or preferred shares that are convertible into common shares, the company must also disclose fully diluted earnings per share. Sofawerks Furniture Inc. has no preferred shares outstanding and so has no preferred dividends. Computations of the firm's EPS for 2010 and 2009 follow (the company had 10,000 common shares outstanding throughout 2009 and 2010):

	Formula	Earnings per Share of Sofawerks Furniture Inc.	
		2010	**2009**
Earnings per common share (EPS) $=$	$\dfrac{\text{Net income} - \text{Preferred dividends}}{\text{Weighted average number of common shares outstanding}}$	$\dfrac{\$48,000 - \$0}{10,000} = \$4.80$	$\dfrac{\$26,000 - \$0}{10,000} = \$2.60$

Sofawerks Furniture Inc.'s EPS increased 85 percent from 2009 to 2010. Its shareholders should not expect such a large boost in EPS every year. Most companies strive to increase EPS by 10 to 15 percent annually, and strong companies do so. However, even the most successful companies have an occasional bad year.

Analyzing Shares as an Investment

Investors purchase shares to earn a return on their investment. This return consists of two parts: (1) gains (or losses) from selling the shares at a price that is different from the investors' purchase price, and (2) dividends, the periodic distributions to shareholders. The ratios we examine in this section help analysts evaluate investments in shares.

Price/Earnings Ratio   The **price/earnings (P/E) ratio** is the ratio of the market price of a common share to the company's earnings per share. The P/E ratio appears on Internet sites giving stock information, such as that of the Toronto Stock Exchange, as well as in the stock listings of newspapers. The P/E ratio plays an important part in evaluating decisions to buy, hold, and sell shares. It indicates the market price of $1.00 of earnings. If earnings are negative, the P/E ratio is not applicable.

The calculations for the P/E ratios of Sofawerks Furniture Inc. follow. The market price of its common shares was $50.00 at the end of 2010 and $35.00 at the end of 2009. These prices can be obtained from such sources as financial publications, a stockbroker, the Internet, or some other source outside the accounting records of the company.

Formula		Price/Earnings Ratio of Sofawerks Furniture Inc.	
		2010	2009
Price/ earnings ratio	= Market price per common share / Earnings per share	$\dfrac{\$50.00}{\$4.80} = 10.4$	$\dfrac{\$35.00}{\$2.60} = 13.5$

Given Sofawerks Furniture Inc.'s 2010 P/E ratio of 10.4, we would say that the company's shares are selling at 10.4 times earnings. The decline from the 2009 P/E ratio of 13.5 is not a cause for alarm because the market price of the shares is not under Sofawerks Furniture Inc.'s control. Net income is more controllable, and it increased during 2010. Like most other ratios, P/E ratios vary from industry to industry. P/E ratios may range from 8.90 for ATCO Ltd., the Calgary-based conglomerate, to 12.88 for the Canadian National Railway Company (CN Rail), to negative earnings for MDS Inc., the health-care company, for which the P/E ratio would not be applicable.

The higher a share's P/E ratio, the higher its *downside risk*—the risk that the share's market price will fall. Some investors interpret a sharp increase in a share's P/E ratio as a signal to sell the shares.

Dividend Yield　The **dividend yield** is the ratio of dividends per share to the share's market price. This ratio measures the percentage of a share's market value that is returned annually as dividends, an important concern of shareholders. *Preferred shareholders*, who invest primarily to receive dividends, pay special attention to this ratio.[1]

Sofawerks Furniture Inc. paid annual cash dividends of $1.20 per share in 2010 and $1.00 in 2009 and market prices of the company's common shares were $50.00 in 2010 and $35.00 in 2009. Calculation of the company's dividend yields on common shares is as follows:

Formula		Dividend Yield on Common Shares of Sofawerks Furniture Inc.	
		2010	2009
Dividend yield on common shares	= Dividend per common share / Market price per common share	$\dfrac{\$1.20}{\$50.00} = 0.024$ or 2.4%	$\dfrac{\$1.00}{\$35.00} = 0.029$ or 2.9%

Investors who buy Sofawerks Furniture Inc.'s common shares for $50.00 can expect to receive almost 2.5 percent of their investment annually in the form of cash dividends. Dividend yields vary widely, from more than 5.0 percent for older established firms (for example, BCE Inc. at 6.15 percent and TELUS at 5.51 percent) down to a range of 0 to 4 percent for growth-oriented companies (for example, EnCana Corporation, the energy company, at 3.04 percent and ClubLink Corporation, the golf course developer and owner, at 4.07 percent). Sofawerks Furniture Inc.'s dividend yield places the company just below the first group.

Book Value per Common Share　**Book value per common share** is simply common shareholders' equity divided by the number of common shares outstanding. Common shareholders' equity equals total shareholders' equity less preferred equity including cumulative preferred dividends. Sofawerks Furniture Inc. has no

---

[1] Dividend yields may be calculated for both preferred shares and common shares.

preferred shares outstanding. Calculations of its book value per common share ratios are as follows:

Formula	Book Value per Common Share of Sofawerks Furniture Inc.	
	2010	**2009**
Book value per common share $=$ $\dfrac{\text{Total shareholders' equity} - \text{Preferred equity}}{\text{Number of common shares outstanding}}$	$\dfrac{\$356{,}000 - \$0}{10{,}000} = \$35.60$	$\dfrac{\$320{,}000 - \$0}{10{,}000} = \$32.00$

Recall that 10,000 common shares were outstanding at the end of the years 2009 and 2010.

Book value indicates the recorded accounting amount for each common share outstanding. Many experts argue that book value is not useful for investment analysis. Recall from Chapter 13, page 739, that book value depends on historical costs, while market value depends on investors' outlook for dividends and an increase in the share's market price. Book value bears no relationship to market value and provides little information beyond shareholders' equity reported on the balance sheet. However, some investors base their investment decisions on book value. For example, some investors rank shares on the basis of the ratio of market price to book value. To these investors, the lower the ratio, the lower the risk, and the more attractive the shares. These investors who focus on the balance sheet are called "value" investors (Warren Buffet is an example), as contrasted with "growth" investors, who focus more on trends in a company's net income.

Limitations of Financial Analysis

Business decisions are made in a world of uncertainty. As useful as ratios may be, they do have limitations. When a physician reads a thermometer, 39°C indicates that something is wrong with the patient, but the temperature alone does not indicate what the problem is or how to cure it. The same is true of ratios.

In financial analysis, a sudden drop in a company's current ratio signals that *something* is wrong, but this change does not identify the problem or show how to correct it. The business manager and users of the financial statements must analyze the figures that go into the ratio to determine whether current assets have decreased, current liabilities have increased, or both. If current assets have dropped, is the problem a cash shortage? Are accounts receivable down? Are inventories too low? Is the condition temporary? This process can be shown in a figure:

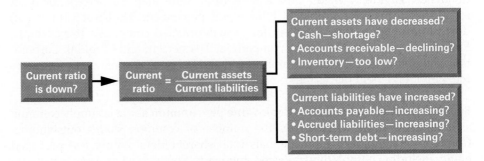

By analyzing the individual items that make up the ratio, managers can determine how to solve the problem and users of the financial statements can determine whether the company is a good investment or credit risk. The managers and users of the financial statements must evaluate data on all ratios in the light of other information about the company and about its particular line of business, such as increased competition or a slowdown in the economy.

Legislation, international affairs, competition, scandals, and many other factors can turn profits into losses, and vice versa. To be most useful, ratios should also be analyzed over a period of years to take into account a representative group of these factors. Any one year, or even any two years, may not be representative of the company's performance over the long term.

Efficient Markets, Management Action, and Investor Decisions

An **efficient capital market** is one in which the market prices reflect the impact of all information available to the public. Market efficiency means that managers cannot fool the market with accounting gimmicks. If the information is available, the market as a whole can translate accounting data into a "fair" price for the company's shares.

Suppose you are the president of CompSys Ltd. Reported earnings per share are $4.00 and the share price is $40.00—so the P/E ratio is 10. You believe the corporation's shares are underpriced in comparison with other companies in your industry. To correct this situation you are considering changing from accelerated to straight-line amortization. The accounting change will increase earnings per share to $5.00. Will the shares then rise to $50.00? Probably not. The share price will likely remain at $40.00 because the market can understand that the change in amortization method, not improved operations, caused earnings to increase.

In an efficient market, the search for "underpriced" shares is fruitless unless the investor has relevant private information. Moreover, it is unlawful to invest based on *insider* information—information that is available only to corporate management.

Users of financial statements should be aware of potential problems in companies they might want to invest in or lend money to. Users of a company's financial statements should also consider the following issues when evaluating the company.

Nonfinancial Data

There is more to analyzing financial statements than performing horizontal and vertical analyses and computing the standard ratios. The nonquantitative parts of the annual report may hold more important information than the financial statements. For example, the president's letter may describe a turnover of top managers. The management's discussion and analysis will reveal management's opinion of the year's results. And the auditor's report may indicate a major problem with the company. Let's consider each of these parts of a corporate annual report.

President's Letter to the Shareholders   The president of the company gives his or her view of the year's results and outlines the direction top management is charting for the company. The December 31, 2008 annual report of Loblaw Companies Limited described the reason for the 42.1 percent increase in operating income. Net earnings and basic net earnings per common share increased by $215 million and $0.79 in 2008 respectively compared to 2007, a 66-percent increase. A shift in top management or a major change in the company's direction is important to investors.

Management's Discussion and Analysis (MD&A)   MD&A was discussed earlier in this chapter. The people who know the most about a company are its executives. For this reason, the shareholders want to know what management thinks about the company's net income (or net loss), cash flows, and financial position. The MD&A section of the annual report discusses *why* net income was up or down, how the company invested the shareholders' money, and plans for future spending. Through the MD&A, investors may learn of the company's plan to discontinue a product line or to expand into new markets. These forward-looking data are not permitted in the historical financial statements, which are based on past transactions.

Auditor's Report   Both the president's letter and the MD&A express the views of corporate insiders. The financial statements are also produced by the management of the company. These people naturally want to describe the company in a favourable light. Therefore, all the information coming from the company could be slanted to make the company look good.

Investors are aware of the possibility for management bias in the financial statements. For this reason, the various provincial securities acts require that all financial statements of public corporations be audited by independent accountants. The auditors are not employees of the companies they audit, so they can be objective. After auditing the Winpak Ltd. financial statements, PricewaterhouseCoopers (PwC), an international accounting firm, issued its professional opinion on the Winpak statements. PwC stated that the Winpak statements agreed with Canadian generally accepted accounting principles. This is how investors in Canada and other developed countries gain assurance that they can rely on a company's financial statements. If the survival of Winpak were in doubt, PwC would ensure that the notes to the financial statements would alert investors to the difficulty.

Appearing just before the Auditor's Report is the Management's Report to the Shareholders, in which management acknowledges its responsibility for the financial information presented in the financial statements. Management also highlights that an independent audit has been completed and directs shareholders to the Auditor's Report.

Look for Red Flags When Analyzing Financial Statements

Recent accounting scandals highlight the importance of *red flags* that may signal financial trouble. The following conditions may reveal that the company is too risky.

- **Movement of Sales, Inventory, and Receivables.** Sales, receivables, and inventory generally move together. Increased sales lead to higher receivables and require more inventory to meet demand. Strange movements among sales, inventory, and receivables may indicate trouble.

- **Earnings Problems.** Has net income decreased significantly for several years in a row? Has income turned into a loss? Most companies cannot survive consecutive annual losses.

- **Decreased Cash Flow.** Cash flow validates net income. Is cash flow from operations consistently lower than net income? Are the sales of property, plant, and equipment assets a major source of cash? If so, the company may face a cash shortage.

- **Too Much Debt.** How does the company's debt ratio compare with that of major competitors and with the industry average? If the debt ratio is too high, the company may be unable to pay its debts.

- **Inability to Collect Receivables.** Are days' sales in receivables growing faster than for other companies in the industry? A cash shortage may be looming.

- **Buildup of Inventories.** Is inventory turnover too slow? If so, the company may be unable to sell goods, or it may be overstating inventory. Recall from the cost-of-goods-sold model that one of the easiest ways to overstate net income is to overstate ending inventory.

To check your understanding of the material in this Learning Objective, complete these questions. The solutions appear on MyAccountingLab so you can check your progress.

5. a) Suppose JMT Ltd. has a current ratio of 2.00 and an acid-test ratio of only 0.70. Which account explains the big difference between these two measures of ability to pay current liabilities? Explain.

   b) If JMT Ltd. has 42 days' sales in receivables, is this good or bad? Explain.

6. For an average company, rank the three rates of return from highest to lowest. Sofawerks Furniture Inc., the company examined in the chapter, is typical.

7. Big Bend Picture Frames Inc. has asked you to determine whether the company's ability to pay its current liabilities and total liabilities has improved or deteriorated during 2010. To answer this question, you gather the following data:

	2010	2009
Cash	$ 50,000	$ 47,000
Short-term investments	27,000	—
Net receivables	128,000	124,000
Inventory	237,000	272,000
Total assets	480,000	490,000
Total current liabilities	295,000	202,000
Long-term note payable	44,000	56,000
Income from operations	170,000	168,000
Interest expense	46,000	33,000

Compute the following ratios for 2010 and 2009:

a) Current ratio

b) Acid-test ratio

c) Debt ratio

d) Times-interest-earned ratio

The Impact on Financial Statement Analysis of International Financial Reporting Standards (IFRS)

OBJECTIVE ⑤

Describe the impact on financial statement analysis of international financial reporting standards (IFRS)

The tools and procedures for analyzing financial statements remain the same whether financial information is reported and presented under GAAP for private enterprises or under IFRS. This is the case because financial analysis involves determining relationships between various components of the financial statements to determine the company's current financial position and to predict future performance. While the numbers in the financial statements under GAAP for private enterprises and IFRS will usually differ, the procedures for analyzing the relationships among the reported numbers remain unchanged.

However, when conducting their investigation, financial analysts and investors must be aware of the limitations of financial statements and adjust for these as appropriate. For example, under GAAP for private enterprises, land and buildings are carried at their historical cost. In their evaluation, analysts may substitute an approximate market value for land and buildings to make predictions. The values for these items in an IFRS balance sheet may already reflect the market values.

A bigger issue stemming from the change in accounting standards from GAAP for private enterprises to IFRS is the resulting change in ratios and how these differences impact financial covenants [promises or conditions]. For example, most loan agreements include a number of covenants, or conditions, in which the borrower agrees to do certain things and not to do other things, for example agreeing to maintain a minimum current ratio of 1.5:1. For the most part, these covenants were agreed upon based on the financial results of statements prepared under GAAP for private enterprises. However, the covenants might not be maintained if the financial statements are prepared under IFRS and some financial-statement amounts change. The reported income and the value of certain assets and liabilities will depend to some extent on the set of standards used—GAAP for private enterprises or IFRS. Given this situation, lenders and borrowers should renegotiate covenants ahead of time to avoid unintentional defaults arising simply from the adoption of a different set of accounting standards.

DID YOU GET IT?

To check your understanding of the material in this Learning Objective, complete this question. The solution appears on MyAccountingLab so you can check your progress.

8. Are there procedural differences when analyzing financial statements prepared under GAAP for private enterprises and financial statements prepared under IFRS? Why or why not?

As we conclude this chapter, we return to our opening questions: What is financial statement analysis, and why is it important? What are horizontal and vertical analysis? How do you calculate and use standard financial ratios? These questions were answered in the course of this chapter. Managers, owners, investors, and creditors all use financial ratios to measure an entity's progress. The Decision Guidelines summarize the most widely used ratios.

DECISION GUIDELINES — Using Ratios in Financial Statement Analysis

Ratio	Computation	Information Provided
Measuring the company's ability to pay current liabilities (liquidity):		
1. Current ratio	$\dfrac{\text{Current assets}}{\text{Current liabilities}}$	Measures ability to pay liabilities with current assets.
2. Acid-test (quick) ratio	$\dfrac{\text{Cash + Short-term investments + Net current receivables}}{\text{Current liabilities}}$	Shows ability to pay all current liabilities if they come due immediately.
Measuring the company's ability to sell inventory and collect receivables (efficiency):		
3. Inventory turnover	$\dfrac{\text{Cost of goods sold}}{\text{Average inventory}}$	Indicates saleability of inventory—the number of times a company sells its average amount of inventory during a year.
4. Accounts-receivable turnover	$\dfrac{\text{Net credit sales}}{\text{Average net accounts receivable}}$	Measures ability to collect cash from credit customers.
5. Days' sales in receivables	$\dfrac{\text{Average net accounts receivable}}{\text{One day's sales}}$	Shows how many days' sales remain in Accounts Receivable—how many days it takes to collect the average level of receivables.
Measuring the company's ability to pay long-term debt:		
6. Debt ratio	$\dfrac{\text{Total liabilities}}{\text{Total assets}}$	Indicates percentage of assets financed with debt.
7. Times-interest-earned ratio	$\dfrac{\text{Income from operations}}{\text{Interest expense}}$	Measures the number of times operating income can cover interest expense.

Ratio	Computation	Information Provided
Measuring the company's profitability:		
8. Rate of return on net sales (profit margin)	$\dfrac{\text{Net income}}{\text{Net sales}}$	Shows the percentage of each sales dollar earned as net income.
9. Rate of return on total assets	$\dfrac{\text{Net income} + \text{Interest expense}}{\text{Average total assets}}$	Measures how profitably a company uses its assets.
10. Rate of return on common shareholders' equity	$\dfrac{\text{Net income} - \text{Preferred dividends}}{\text{Average common shareholders' equity}}$	Gauges how much income is earned for each dollar invested by common shareholders.
11. Earnings per common share	$\dfrac{\text{Net income} - \text{Preferred dividends}}{\text{Weighted average number of common shares outstanding}}$	Gives the amount of earnings earned for each of the company's common shares.
Analyzing the company's shares as an investment:		
12. Price/earnings ratio	$\dfrac{\text{Market price per common share}}{\text{Earnings per share}}$	Indicates the market price of $1 of earnings.
13. Dividend yield	$\dfrac{\text{Annual dividends per common (or preferred) share}}{\text{Market price per common (or preferred) share}}$	Shows the percentage of the market price of each share returned as dividends to shareholders each period.
14. Book value per common share	$\dfrac{\text{Total shareholders' equity} - \text{Preferred equity}}{\text{Number of common shares outstanding}}$	Indicates the recorded accounting amount for each common share outstanding.

Summary Problem for Your Review

Kool Duds Inc., which operates a chain of clothing stores, reported these figures:

KOOL DUDS INC.
Five-Year Selected Financial Data
For the Years Ended January 31,

(Dollar amounts in thousands)	2010	2009	2008	2007	2006
Operating Results					
Net sales	$2,960	$2,519	$1,934	$1,587	$1,252
Cost of goods sold	1,856	1,496	1,188	1,007	814
Interest expense (net)	4	4	1	3	3
Income from operations	340	371	237	163	126
Income taxes	129	141	92	65	52
Net income	211	230	145	98	74
Cash dividends	44	41	30	23	18
Financial Position					
Merchandise inventory	366	314	247	243	193
Total assets	1,379	1,147	777	579	481
Working capital	355	236	579	129	434
Current ratio	2.06:1	1.71:1	1.39:1	1.69:1	1.70:1
Shareholders' equity	888	678	466	338	276
Average number of common shares outstanding (in thousands)	144	142	142	141	145

Name: Kool Duds Inc.
Fiscal Period: The fiscal years 2006 to 2010

Required

Compute the following ratios for 2007 through 2010, and evaluate Kool Duds Inc.'s operating results. Are operating results strong or weak? Did they improve or deteriorate during the four-year period?

1. Gross margin percentage
2. Rate of return on net sales
3. Earnings per share
4. Inventory turnover
5. Times-interest-earned ratio
6. Rate of return on shareholders' equity

SOLUTION

Remember to use the previous year's inventory balance when calculating average inventory in the inventory turnover ratio. Use the previous year's shareholders' equity when calculating average shareholders' equity in the rate of return on shareholders' equity.

	2010	2009	2008	2007
1. Gross margin percentage	$\dfrac{\$2,960 - \$1,856}{\$2,960}$	$\dfrac{\$2,519 - \$1,496}{\$2,519}$	$\dfrac{\$1,934 - \$1,188}{\$1,934}$	$\dfrac{\$1,587 - \$1,007}{\$1,587}$
	$= 37.3\%$	$= 40.6\%$	$= 38.6\%$	$= 36.5\%$
2. Rate of return on net sales	$\dfrac{\$211}{\$2,960} = 7.1\%$	$\dfrac{\$230}{\$2,519} = 9.1\%$	$\dfrac{\$145}{\$1,934} = 7.5\%$	$\dfrac{\$98}{\$1,587} = 6.2\%$
3. Earnings per share	$\dfrac{\$211}{144} = \$1.47$	$\dfrac{\$230}{142} = \$1.62$	$\dfrac{\$145}{142} = \$1.02$	$\dfrac{\$98}{141} = \$0.70$
4. Inventory turnover	$\dfrac{\$1,856}{(\$366 + \$314)/2}$	$\dfrac{\$1,496}{(\$314 + \$247)/2}$	$\dfrac{\$1,188}{(\$247 + \$243)/2}$	$\dfrac{\$1,007}{(\$243 + \$193)/2}$
	$= 5.5$ times	$= 5.3$ times	$= 4.8$ times	$= 4.6$ times
5. Times-interest-earned ratio	$\dfrac{\$340}{\$4} = 85$ times	$\dfrac{\$371}{\$4} = 93$ times	$\dfrac{\$237}{\$1} = 237$ times	$\dfrac{\$163}{\$3} = 54$ times
6. Rate of return on shareholders' equity	$\dfrac{\$211}{(\$888 + \$678)/2}$	$\dfrac{\$230}{(\$678 + \$466)/2}$	$\dfrac{\$145}{(\$466 + \$338)/2}$	$\dfrac{\$98}{(\$338 + \$276)/2}$
	$= 26.9\%$	$= 40.2\%$	$= 36.1\%$	$= 31.9\%$

For the six ratios calculated, the higher the ratio, the better. Ratios that increase each year are a positive trend and indicate good news. Remember to evaluate all ratios along with other information about the company. One ratio will not tell the complete story.

Evaluation: During this four-year period, Kool Duds Inc.'s operating results were outstanding. Operating results improved, with all ratio values higher in 2010 than in 2007 except return on shareholders' equity. Moreover, all the performance measures indicate high levels of income and return to investors.

Summary

1. **Perform a horizontal analysis of financial statements.** Banks lend money, investors buy shares, and managers run businesses on the basis of the analysis of accounting information. *Horizontal analysis* is the study of percentage changes in financial statement items from one period to the next. To compute these percentage changes, (1) calculate the dollar amount of the change from the base (earlier) period to the later period, and (2) divide the dollar amount of change by the base-period amount and multiply by 100. *Trend percentages* are a form of horizontal analysis.

2. **Perform a vertical analysis of financial statements.** *Vertical analysis* of a financial statement reveals the relationship of each statement item to a specified base, which is the 100 percent figure. On an income statement, net sales (or revenues) is usually the base. On a balance sheet, total assets is usually the base.

3. **Prepare and use common-size financial statements.** A form of vertical analysis, *common-size statements* report only percentages, not dollar amounts. Common-size statements ease the comparison of different companies and may signal the need for corrective action. *Benchmarking* is the practice of comparing a company's performance with that of other companies, usually in the same industry.

4. **Compute the standard financial ratios.** An important part of financial analysis is the calculation and interpretation of financial ratios. A ratio expresses the relationship of one item to another. The most important financial ratios measure a company's ability to pay current liabilities (current ratio, acid-test ratio); its ability to sell inventory and collect receivables (inventory turnover, accounts-receivable turnover, days' sales in receivables); its ability to pay long-term debt (debt ratio, times-interest-earned ratio); its profitability (rate of return on net sales, rate of return on total assets, rate of return on common shareholders' equity, earnings per common share); and its value as an investment (price/earnings ratio, dividend yield, book value per common share).

5. **Describe the impact on financial statement analysis of international financial reporting standards (IFRS).** The numbers in the financial statements prepared under GAAP for private enterprises and IFRS will usually differ. However, the procedures for analyzing the relationships among the reported numbers are the same. Debt covenants and other contractual arrangements may be affected by the numbers reported under the different sets of standards. Therefore, covenants should be checked and renegotiated if necessary to avoid unintentional defaults arising from the adoption of IFRS.

SELF-STUDY QUESTIONS

Test your understanding of the chapter by marking the best answer for each of the following questions:

1. Net income for PJ Ltd. was $240,000 in 2008, $210,000 in 2009, and $252,000 in 2010. The change from 2009 to 2010 is a(n) (*p. 1002*)
   a. Increase of 5 percent
   b. Increase of 20 percent
   c. Decrease of 10 percent
   d. Decrease of 12.5 percent

2. Vertical analysis of a financial statement shows (*p. 1006*)
   a. Trend percentages
   b. The percentage change in an item from period to period
   c. The relationship of an item to a base amount on the statement
   d. Net income expressed as a percentage of shareholders' equity

3. Common-size statements are useful for comparing (*p. 1008*)
   a. Changes in the makeup of assets from period to period
   b. Different companies

   c. A company to its industry
   d. All of the above

4. Benchmarking allows a user of the financial statements of a company to (*pp. 1009–1010*)
   a. Compare the performance of the company against that of its key competitors
   b. Compare the performance of the company against best practices
   c. Compare the performance of the company against average performance
   d. Do all of the above

5. The following figures were taken from the 2010 balance sheet of Plateau Golf Academy Ltd. Cash is $10,000, net accounts receivable amount to $22,000, inventory is $55,000, prepaid expenses total $3,000, and current liabilities are $40,000. What is the acid-test ratio? (*pp. 1013–1014*)
   a. 0.25
   b. 0.80
   c. 2.18
   d. 2.25

6. Inventory turnover is computed by dividing (p. 1015)
   a. Sales revenue by average inventory
   b. Cost of goods sold by average inventory
   c. Credit sales by average inventory
   d. Average inventory by cost of goods sold

7. Garnet Motors Ltd. is experiencing a severe cash shortage because of its inability to collect accounts receivable. The decision tool most likely to help identify the appropriate corrective action is the (p. 1016)
   a. Acid-test ratio
   b. Inventory turnover
   c. Times-interest-earned ratio
   d. Day's sales in receivables

8. Analysis of Sanjay Corp.'s financial statements over five years reveals that sales are growing steadily, the debt ratio is higher than the industry average and is increasing, interest coverage is decreasing, return on total assets is declining, and earnings per common share is decreasing. Considered together, these ratios suggest that (pp. 1016–1020)
   a. Sanjay Corp. should pursue collections of receivables more vigourously
   b. Competition is taking sales away from Sanjay Corp.
   c. Sanjay Corp. is in a declining industry
   d. The company's debt burden is hurting profitability

9. Which of the following is most likely to be true? (pp. 1018–1019)
   a. Return on common equity exceeds return on total assets.
   b. Return on total assets exceeds return on common equity.
   c. Return on total assets equals return on common equity.
   d. None of the above is true.

10. How are financial ratios used in decision making? (pp. 1022–1023)
   a. They remove the uncertainty of the business environment.
   b. They give clear signals about the appropriate action to take.
   c. They can help identify the reasons for success and failure in business, but decision making requires information beyond the ratios.
   d. They are not useful because decision making is too complex.

ACCOUNTING VOCABULARY

SIMILAR ACCOUNTING TERMS

Acid-test ratio	Quick ratio
Current ratio	Working-capital ratio
Leverage	Trading on the equity
Earnings per share	Earnings per common share
Rate of return on common shareholders' equity	Return on shareholders' equity; Return on equity
Rate of return on net sales	Return on sales; Profit margin
Rate of return on total assets	Return on assets
Times-interest-earned ratio	Interest-coverage ratio

Assignment Material

QUESTIONS

1. Identify three groups of users of accounting information and the decisions they base on accounting data.

2. Name the three broad categories of analytical tools that are based on accounting information.

3. Briefly describe horizontal analysis. How do decision makers use this analytical tool?

4. What is vertical analysis and what is its purpose?

5. What is the purpose of common-size statements?

6. What is benchmarking? Give an example of its use.

7. Why are ratios an important tool of financial analysis? Give an example of an important financial ratio.

8. Identify two ratios used to measure a company's ability to pay current liabilities. Show how they are computed.

9. Why is the acid-test ratio given that name?

10. What does the inventory-turnover ratio measure?

11. Suppose the days'-sales-in-receivables ratio of Marshall Ltd. increased from 33 days at January 1 to 45 days at December 31. Is this a good sign or a bad sign about the company? What might Marshall Ltd. management do in response to this change?

12. Patel Inc.'s debt ratio has increased from 0.40 to 0.75. Identify a decision maker to whom this increase is important, and state how the increase affects this party's decisions about the company.

13. Which ratio measures the *effect of debt* on (a) financial position (the balance sheet) and (b) the company's ability to pay interest expense (the income statement)?

14. Your Market Ltd. is a chain of grocery stores and Dynamo Inc. is a computer manufacturer. Which company is likely to have the higher (a) current ratio, (b) inventory turnover, (c) rate of return on sales? Give your reasons.

15. Identify four ratios used to measure a company's profitability. Show how to compute these ratios and state what information each ratio provides.

16. Recently, the price/earnings ratio of WestJet Airlines was 10.18, and the price/earnings ratio of the Bank of Nova Scotia was 15.26. Which company did the stock market favour? Explain.

17. Recently, TransCanada Corporation paid cash dividends of $2.54 per share when the market price of the company's shares was $35.00 per share. What was the dividend yield on TransCanada's shares? What does dividend yield measure?

18. Hold all other factors constant and indicate whether each of the following situations generally signals good or bad news about a company. Explain your answer.
   a. Increase in return on sales
   b. Decrease in earnings per share
   c. Increase in price/earnings ratio
   d. Increase in book value per share
   e. Increase in current ratio
   f. Decrease in inventory turnover
   g. Increase in debt ratio
   h. Decrease in interest-coverage ratio

19. Explain how an investor might use book value per share in making an investment decision.

20. Describe how decision makers use ratio data. What are the limitations of ratios?

Starter 18–1 Sun-Rype Products Ltd. reported the following on its 2008 comparative income statement:

(in millions)	2008	2007	2006
Net sales..................................	$125.4	$135.1	$130.6
Cost of sales............................	111.3	93.3	85.3

Perform a horizontal analysis of revenues, cost of sales, and gross margin, both in dollar amounts and in percentages, for 2008 and 2007.

Starter 18–2 Sun-Rype Products Ltd. reported the following revenues and net income amounts:

(in millions)	2008	2007	2006	2005
Net sales	$125.4	$135.1	$130.6	$125.4
Net income..	(11.7)	4.6	7.3	6.5

1. Show Sun-Rype's trend percentages for revenues and net income. Use 2005 as the base year.
2. Which measure declined faster between 2006 and 2008?

Starter 18–3 Sporting Goods Inc. reported the following amounts on its balance sheet at December 31, 2010.

	2010
Cash and receivables	$24,000
Inventory	19,000
Property, plant, and equipment, net.....................................	48,000
Total assets..	$91,000

Perform a vertical analysis of the company's assets at the end of 2010.

Starter 18–4 Compare P-Mart Corp. and Sellers Inc. by converting their income statements to common size.

(in thousands)	P-Mart Corp.	Sellers Inc.
Net sales	$18,978	$39,072
Cost of goods sold	11,570	28,202
Other expenses	6,228	8,994
Net income..	$ 1,180	$ 1,876

Which company earns more net income? Which company's net income is a higher percentage of its net sales?

Use the following data for Starters 18–5 through 18–9. Nesters Corp., a home-improvement-store chain, reported these summarized figures (in millions):

NESTERS CORP.
Income Statement
For the Year Ended December 31, 2010

Net sales...	$61.6
Cost of goods sold..	42.4
Interest expense	0.4
All other expenses..	15.0
Net income	$ 3.8

NESTERS CORP.
Balance Sheet
December 31

	2010	2009		2010	2009
Cash	$ 2.8	$ 1.6	Total current liabilities...	$ 8.8	$ 7.2
Short-term investments	0.4	0.6	Long-term liabilities	8.6	8.4
Accounts receivable............	0.2	0.4	Total liabilities	17.4	15.6
Inventory..............................	9.2	8.0	Common shares..............	5.2	4.8
Other current assets............	0.8	0.6	Retained earnings	15.4	11.8
Total current assets	13.4	11.2	Total equity	20.6	16.6
All other assets....................	24.6	21.0	Total liabilities		
Total assets..........................	$38.0	$32.2	and equity	$38.0	$32.2

Starter 18–5 Use the Nesters Corp. balance sheet data given above.

1. Compute the company's current ratio at December 31, 2010 and 2009.
2. Did Nesters Corp.'s current ratio value improve, deteriorate, or hold steady during 2010?

Evaluating a company's current ratio
④
1. 2010 current ratio 1.52

Starter 18–6 Use the Nesters Corp. data to compute the following (amounts in millions):

a. The rate of inventory turnover for 2010.
b. Days' sales in average receivables during 2010. All sales are made on account. Round dollar amounts to three decimal places.

Computing inventory turnover and days' sales in receivables
④
a. 4.9 times

Starter 18–7 Use the financial statements of Nesters Corp.

1. Compute the debt ratio at December 31, 2010.
2. Is Nesters Corp.'s ability to pay its liabilities strong or weak? Explain your reasoning.

Measuring ability to pay liabilities
④
1. 0.46

Starter 18–8 Use the financial statements of Nesters Corp. given above.

1. Compute these profitability measures for 2010:
   a. Rate of return on net sales.
   b. Rate of return on total assets. Interest expense for 2010 was $0.4 million.
   c. Rate of return on common shareholders' equity.
2. Are these rates of return strong or weak? Explain.

Measuring profitability
④
a. 6.2%

Starter 18–9 Use the financial statements of Nesters Corp., plus the following item (in millions):

Number of common shares outstanding 0.8

1. Compute earnings per share (EPS) for Nesters Corp. Round to the nearest cent.
2. Compute Nesters Corp.'s price/earnings ratio. The price of a Nesters Corp. common share is $133.00.

Computing EPS and the price/earnings ratio
④
1. $4.75

Starter 18–10 A skeleton of Crocco Ltd.'s income statement appears as follows:

Income Statement

Net sales	$3,600
Cost of goods sold	(a)
Selling and administrative expenses ..	855
Interest expenses	(b)
Other expenses	75
Income before taxes	500
Income tax expenses..............................	(c)
Net income...	$ (d)

Using ratio data to reconstruct an income statement
④
(d) Net income $342

Use the following ratio data to complete Crocco Ltd.'s income statement:

a. Inventory turnover was 5.50 (beginning inventory was $395, ending inventory was $375).
b. Rate of return on sales is 0.095.

Starter 18–11 A skeleton of Crocco Ltd.'s balance sheet appears as follows:

Balance Sheet

Cash	$ 25	Total current liabilities	$1,050
Receivables	(a)	Long-term note payable	(e)
Inventories	375	Other long-term liabilities	410
Prepaid expenses	(b)		
Total current assets	(c)		
Property, plant, and equipment, net	(d)		
Other assets	1,075	Shareholders' equity	1,200
Total assets	$3,400	Total liabilities and equity	$ (f)

Use the following ratio data to complete Crocco Ltd.'s balance sheet:

a. Current ratio is 0.70.
b. Acid-test ratio is 0.30.

EXERCISES

Exercise 18–1

Compute the dollar change and the percentage change in Light Year Ltd.'s working capital each year during 2009 and 2010. Is this trend favourable or unfavourable?

	2010	2009	2008
Total current assets	$92,500	$87,000	$78,750
Total current liabilities	39,000	34,750	42,500

Exercise 18–2

Prepare a horizontal analysis of the comparative income statement of Cobbler Shoes Inc. Round percentage changes to the nearest one-tenth percent (three decimal places).

Why was the percentage increase in net income higher than that in total revenue during 2010?

COBBLER SHOES INC.
Comparative Income Statement
For the Years Ended December 31, 2010 and 2009

	2010	2009
Net sales	$533,000	$465,000
Expenses		
Cost of goods sold	235,000	202,000
Selling and general expenses	140,000	135,000
Interest expense	10,000	6,000
Wages expense	51,000	41,000
Total expenses	436,000	384,000
Net income	$ 97,000	$ 81,000

Exercise 18–3

Compute trend percentages for Ceder Inc.'s net sales and net income for the following five-year period, using 2006 as the base year:

	2010	2009	2008	2007	2006
		(Amounts in thousands)			
Net sales	$1,625	$1,463	$1,375	$1,200	$1,304
Net income	149	131	100	80	105

Which measure grew more during the period, net sales or net income? By what percentage did net sales and net income grow from 2006 to 2010?

Exercise 18–4

Teranishi Corp. has requested that you perform a vertical analysis of its balance sheet. Determine the component percentages of its assets, liabilities, and shareholders' equity.

Vertical analysis of a balance sheet

(2)

Total current assets are 26.2% of total assets

TERANISHI CORP.
Balance Sheet
December 31, 2010

Assets

Total current assets	$109,000
Property, plant, and equipment, net	267,000
Other assets..	40,000
Total assets...	$416,000

Liabilities

Total current liabilities...	$ 85,000
Long-term debt..	156,000
Total liabilities...	241,000

Shareholders' Equity

Total shareholders' equity	175,000
Total liabilities and shareholders' equity.............................	$416,000

Excel Spreadsheet Template

Exercise 18–5

Prepare a comparative common-size income statement for Cobbler Shoes Inc. using the 2010 and 2009 data of Exercise 18–2 and rounding percentages to one-tenth of a percent (three decimal places).

Preparing a common-size income statement

(3)

2010 net income is 18.2% of net sales.

Exercise 18–6

Prepare a common-size analysis to compare the asset composition of Stentor Inc. and Sefton Ltd. (amounts in millions).

Common-size analysis of assets

(3)

Cash and equiv. as % of total assets: Stentor Inc. 4.2%, Sefton Ltd. 1.9%

Assets	Stentor Inc.	Sefton Ltd.
Current assets:		
Cash and equivalents..	$ 462	$ 372
Short-term investments	—	804
Accounts receivable, net..	2,898	882
Inventories..	2,082	5,380
Other current assets	408	134
Total current assets	5,850	7,572
Property, plant, and equipment, net..............................	4,660	11,280
Goodwill and other intangibles	206	226
Other assets...	302	540
Total assets	$11,018	$19,618

To which company are *current assets* more important? Which company places more emphasis on its *property, plant, and equipment*?

Exercise 18–7

Excel Spreadsheet Template

Computing five ratios

④

a. 1.54

The financial statements of Baca Bay Ltd. include the following items:

	2010	2009
Balance sheet		
Cash	$ 11,500	$ 14,500
Short-term investments	6,500	10,500
Net receivables	39,000	35,000
Inventory	45,500	38,500
Prepaid expenses	3,500	3,500
Total current assets	$106,000	$102,000
Total current liabilities	$ 69,000	$ 46,000
Income statement		
Net credit sales	$248,500	
Cost of goods sold	138,500	

Required

Compute the following ratios for 2010: (a) current ratio, (b) acid-test ratio, (c) inventory turnover, (d) accounts receivable turnover, and (e) days' sales in average receivables.

Exercise 18–8

Analyzing the ability to pay current liabilities

④

a. 2010: 1.98
  2009: 1.84

Gambier Plumbing Products Ltd. has requested that you determine whether the company's ability to pay its current liabilities and long-term debt has improved or deteriorated during 2010. To answer this question, compute the following ratios for 2010 and 2009: (a) current ratio, (b) acid-test ratio, (c) debt ratio, and (d) times-interest-earned ratio. Summarize the results of your analysis in a written report.

	2010	2009
Cash	$ 13,000	$ 25,500
Short-term investments	15,000	—
Net receivables	59,500	65,500
Inventory	120,000	135,000
Prepaid expenses	7,000	5,500
Total assets	275,000	260,000
Total current liabilities	108,500	126,000
Total liabilities	137,000	143,000
Income from operations	99,000	82,500
Interest expense	20,500	21,000

Exercise 18–9

Analyzing profitability

④

EPS: 2010 $0.34
   2009 $0.71

Compute four ratios that measure the ability to earn profits for GoodEarth Farm Supplies Ltd., whose comparative income statement appears below. Additional data follow.

GOODEARTH FARM SUPPLIES LTD.
Comparative Income Statement
For the Years Ended December 31, 2010 and 2009

	2010	2009
Net sales	$195,000	$174,000
Cost of goods sold	101,500	91,750
Gross margin	93,500	82,250
Selling and general expenses	50,200	40,000
Income from operations	43,300	42,250
Interest expense	25,400	12,050
Income before income tax	17,900	30,200
Income tax expense	4,475	7,550
Net income	$ 13,425	$ 22,650

Additional data

	2010	2009
a. Average total assets..	$230,000	$222,000
b. Average common shareholders' equity.............................	102,000	98,000
c. Preferred dividends..	5,000	5,000
d. Number of common shares outstanding	25,000	25,000

Did the company's operating performance improve or deteriorate during 2010?

Exercise 18–10

Evaluate the common shares of Spyware Software Inc. as an investment. Specifically, use the three share ratios to determine whether the shares have increased or decreased in attractiveness during the past year.

Evaluating shares as an investment
④
Dividend yield:
2010 3.9%
2009 3.3%

	2010	2009
Net income	$ 32,000	$ 26,000
Dividends (25% for preferred shares)	19,000	13,000
Common shareholders' equity at year end (75,000 shares).....	275,000	255,000
Preferred shareholders' equity at year end	50,000	50,000
Market price per common share at year end	$ 4.83	$ 3.89

Exercise 18–11

Homburg Invest Inc. is an international real estate investment and development company headquartered in Halifax, Nova Scotia. For the year ended December 31, 2008, Homburg prepared two sets of financial statements—one in accordance with Canadian GAAP in place at that time (similar to GAAP for private enterprises), the other in accordance with international financial reporting standards (IFRS).

Computing ratios under GAAP and IFRS
⑤
1. (a) Under GAAP, 0.39
2. (a) Under IFRS, 0.62

Excerpts from Homburg Invest Inc.'s Canadian GAAP-based financial statements and IFRS-based financial statements appear below.

GAAP-Based Financial Statements:
(Notice that the listing of assets and liabilities is in an order different from Canadian GAAP.)

HOMBURG INVEST INC.
Consolidated Balance Sheet

($ amounts in thousands)	December 31 2008	December 31 2007
Assets		
Investment properties	$3,310,317	$2,939,960
Development properties	360,562	293,955
Long term investments	40,086	39,562
Intangible assests	110,067	100,619
Goodwill..		33,036
Restricted cash..	25,969	27,704
Cash..	16,359	17,927
Receivables and other	138,397	78,845
Currency guarantee receivable	28,165	
	$4,029,922	$3,531,608
Liabilities		
Long term debt..	$2,952,124	$2,094,122
Accounts payable and other liabilities	268,796	579,373
Construction financing...	102,433	66,393
Future income taxes..	129,097	110,578
Intangible liabilities	15,429	12,234
Liabilities of discontinued operations	28,903	28,903
Derivative instrument liability	19,427	
	3,516,209	2,891,603
Shareholders' equity	513,713	640,005
	$4,029,922	$3,531,608

HOMBURG INVEST INC.
Consolidated Statement of Earnings (Loss)
For the Year Ended December 31

($ amounts in thousands)	2008	2007
Property revenue	$ 309,579	$207,331
Sale of properties developed for resale	191,260	229,139
Dividend income and distributions	2,992	2,011
Gain on fair value increase in investments		938
Other income	1,849	3,857
Foreign exchange gain		18,305
Gain on derivative instrument		2,303
Gain on sale of assests	443	2,051
	506,123	465,935
Property operating expenses	84,421	45,173
Cost of sale of properties developed for resale	142,841	147,677
Interest on long term debt	154,899	106,818
Interest and financing costs	11,916	13,053
Depreciation and amortization	62,860	39,278
General and administrative	23,956	11,051
Stock based compensation	307	5,288
Foreign exchange loss	19,656	
Loss on derivative instruments	18,542	
Goodwill impairment loss	63,456	
Loss on fair value decrease in investments	23,133	
	605,987	368,338
Earnings (loss) before income taxes	(99,864)	97,597
Total income taxes (recovery)	(3,781)	16,270
Net earnings (loss) from continuing operations	(96,083)	81,327
Net loss from discontinued operations		(2,159)
Net earnings (loss)	$(96,083)	$ 79,168

IFRS-Based Financial Statements:

HOMBURG INVEST INC.
Consolidated Balance Sheet

($ amounts in thousands)	December 31 2008	December 31 2007
Assets		
Non-current assets		
Investment properties	$3,549,744	$3,304,880
Development properties	224,285	126,522
Currency guarantee receivable	28,165	
Goodwill		48,594
Investments	40,086	39,562
Restricted cash	25,969	27,704
	3,868,249	3,547,262
Current assets		
Cash	16,359	17,927
Construction properties being developed for resale	194,638	225,596
Receivables and other	65,390	26,694
	276,387	270,217
Total assets	$4,144,636	$3,817,479
Equity and Liabilities		
Total equity	$ 606,768	$ 886,271
Non-current liabilities		
Long term debt	2,901,348	1,910,668
Derivatives	19,427	
Deferred tax liabilities	143,930	145,559
Other liabilities	29,727	28,602
	3,094,432	2,084,829

(Continued on next page)

(Continued from previous page)

Current liabilities

Accounts payable and other	255,585	561,122
Income taxes payable	5,739	6,507
Liabilities of discontinued operations	28,903	28,903
Construction financing	102,433	66,393
Current portion of long term debt	50,776	183,454
	443,436	846,379
Total liabilities	3,537,868	2,931,208
Total equity and liabilities	$4,144,636	$3,817,479

HOMBURG INVEST INC.
Consolidated Income Statement
For the Year Ended December 31

($ amounts in thousands)	2008	2007
Property revenue	$310,466	$211,025
Sales of properties developed for resale	186,350	191,139
Total revenues	496,816	402,164
Property operating expenses	88,414	51,854
Cost of sale of properties developed for resale	143,131	131,677
	231,545	183,531
Gross income from operations	265,271	218,633
General and administrative	(23,956)	(11,051)
Stock based compensation	(307)	(5,288)
Other income, net	1,849	3,857
Dividend income and distributions	2,992	2,011
Net adjustment to fair value of investment properties	(286,060)	55,757
Gain on sale of investment properties	443	924
Goodwill impairment loss	(48,594)	
Net adjustment to fair value of held-for-trading financial assets	(23,133)	938
Net adjustment to fair value of derivative financial instruments	(18,542)	2,303
Interest expense	(166,815)	(119,871)
Exchange differences, net	(19,656)	18,305
Income (loss) before income taxes	(316,508)	166,518
Total income taxes (recovery)	(39,855)	23,864
Net income (loss) from continuing operations	(276,653)	142,654
Net loss from discontinued operations		(2,159)
Net income (loss)	$(276,653)	$140,495

Notice that the presentation of the financial statements differs somewhat, as well as some of the recorded balances. These differences arise because Canadian GAAP and IFRS currently measure certain transactions differently. However, the focus of this question is the potential impact on ratios. Differences in the ratios may require lenders and borrowers to renegotiate financial covenants as a result of the standards used to prepare the financial statements.

Required

1. Compute the following ratios for 2008 based on Homburg's financial statements prepared in accordance with GAAP. For the purpose of this exercise, assume that "cash" and "receivables and other assets" are current assets, and that "accounts payable and other liabilities," "construction financing," and "liabilities of discontinued operations" are current liabilities. Include both "interest on long term debt" and "interest and financing costs" in your computations for part d.

    a. Current ratio   b. Acid-test ratio   c. Debt ratio   d. Rate of return on total assets

2. Compute the same ratios as in question 1 for 2008 based on Homburg's IFRS financial statements.

SERIAL EXERCISE

This exercise continues the Haupt Consulting Corporation situation from Chapter 17. You can complete the following exercise without having done the previous Serial Exercises.

Computing six ratios

④

(a) 2.67

Exercise 18–12

Suppose, at December 31, 2011, Haupt Consulting Corporation has the following balance sheet.

HAUPT CONSULTING CORPORATION
Balance Sheet
December 31, 2011

Current assets:	
Cash..	$ 5,000
Accounts receivable..	2,200
Supplies..	420
Equipment	10,000
Furniture	3,600
Building...	55,000
Less accumulated amortization.......................................	(2,753)
Land	20,000
Total assets...	$93,467
Current liabilities:	
Accounts payable	$ 350
Salary payable...	2,500
Long-term liabilities:	
Notes payable...	40,000
Shareholders' equity:	
Common shares	20,000
Retained earnings...	30,617
Total liabilities and shareholders' equity........................	$93,467

Additional information: Haupt Consulting Corporation incurred interest expense of $2,400 during 2011. Net income for the year ended December 31, 2011, was $38,910. The market price of Haupt Consulting Corporation's 1,500 common shares is $50.00 per share on December 31, 2011.

Required

Using this information, calculate the following ratios for Haupt Consulting Corporation:

a. Current ratio

b. Debt ratio

c. Earnings per share

d. Price/earnings ratio

e. Rate of return on total assets

f. Rate of return on common shareholders' equity

CHALLENGE EXERCISES

Using ratio data to reconstruct a real company's income statement

② ③ ④

Net income $4,586 mil.

Exercise 18–13

The following data (dollar amounts in millions) are from the financial statements of The Brewhouse Income Trust, a large Canadian craft brewery.

	Dollars in Millions
Average unitholders'/shareholders' equity	$18,710
Interest expense...	$ 560
Preferred shares..	0
Operating income as a percent of sales	10.9%
Rate of return on sales..	7.53%
Rate of return on shareholders' equity	24.51%
Income tax rate	24.58%

Required

Complete the following condensed income statement. Report amounts to the nearest million dollars:

Sales	$?
Operating expenses...	?
Operating income..	?
Interest expense	?
Pretax income..	?
Income tax expense	?
Net income	$?

Exercise 18–14

The following data (dollar amounts in thousands) are from the financial statements of Wilmas Movers Ltd.

Using ratio data to reconstruct a company's balance sheet
② ③ ④
Total assets $52,799 thou.

Total liabilities	$29,204
Preferred shares..	0
Total current assets	$24,498
Accumulated amortization	$ 7,854
Debt ratio...	55.312%
Current ratio..	1.75:1

Required

Complete the following condensed balance sheet. Report amounts to the nearest thousand dollars:

Current assets...		$?
Property, plant, and equipment	$?	
Less accumulated amortization	?	?
Total assets..		$?
Current liabilities..		$?
Long-term liabilities..		?
Shareholders' equity		?
Total liabilities and shareholders' equity......		$?

BEYOND THE NUMBERS

Beyond the Numbers 18–1

Understanding the components of accounting ratios
④

Consider the following business situations.

1. Teresa Chan has asked you about the shares of a particular company. She finds them attractive because they have a high dividend yield relative to another company's shares that she is also considering. Explain to her the meaning of the ratio and the danger of making a decision based on it alone. Suggest other information (ratios) Teresa should consider as she makes the investment decision.

2. Saskatoon Plumbing Supplies Ltd.'s owners are concerned because the number of days' sales in receivables has increased over the previous two years. Explain why the ratio might have increased.

Beyond the Numbers 18–2

Moe Sahota is the controller of Jupiter Ltd., whose year end is December 31. Sahota prepares cheques for suppliers in December and posts them to the appropriate accounts in that month. However, he holds on to the cheques and mails them to the suppliers in January. What financial ratio(s) are most affected by the action? What is Sahota's purpose in undertaking the activity?

ETHICAL ISSUE

Harrison Outfitters Inc.'s (HOI) long-term debt agreements make certain demands on the business. For example, HOI may not repurchase company shares in excess of the balance of Retained Earnings. Long-term debt may not exceed shareholders' equity, and the current ratio may not fall below 1.60. If HOI fails to meet these requirements, the company's lenders have the authority to take over management of the corporation.

Changes in consumer demand have made it hard for HOI to sell its products. Current liabilities have mounted faster than current assets, causing the current ratio to fall to 1.45. Prior to releasing financial statements, HOI management is scrambling to improve the current ratio. The controller points out that an equity investment can be classified as either long term or short term, depending on management's intention. By deciding to convert an investment to cash within one year, HOI can classify the investment as short term (a current asset). On the controller's recommendation, HOI's board of directors votes to reclassify the long-term equity investments as short-term equity investments.

Required

1. What effect will reclassifying the investment have on the current ratio? Is Harrison Outfitters Inc.'s financial position stronger as a result of reclassifying the investment?

2. Shortly after releasing the financial statements, sales improve and so, then, does the current ratio. As a result, HOI management decides not to sell the investments it had reclassified as short term. Accordingly, the company reclassifies the investments as long term. Has management behaved unethically? Give your reason.

PROBLEMS (GROUP A)

MyAccountingLab All questions in this section appear in MyAccountingLab.

Problem 18–1A

Net sales, net income, and common shareholders' equity for Naturah Products Ltd. for a six-year period follow:

	2010	2009	2008	2007	2006	2005
			(Amounts in thousands)			
Net sales	$1,806	$1,782	$1,606	$1,704	$1,638	$1,588
Net income	144	120	90	126	100	96
Ending common shareholders' equity	906	860	772	684	628	600

Required

1. Compute trend percentages for 2006 through 2010, using 2005 as the base year.

2. Compute the rate of return on average common shareholders' equity for 2006 through 2010, rounding to three decimal places. In this industry, rates of 12 percent are average, rates above 15 percent are considered good, and rates above 20 percent are viewed as outstanding.

3. How does Naturah Products Ltd.'s return on common shareholders' equity compare with the industry's?

Problem 18–2A

Common-size statements, analysis of profitability, and comparison with the industry

② ③ ④

Net income 15.9% of net sales

Lucint Ltd. has asked for your help in comparing the company's profit performance and financial position with the computer services industry average. The manager has given you the company's income statement and balance sheet, and also the following industry average data for computer services companies:

LUCINT LTD. Income Statement Compared with Industry Average For the Year Ended December 31, 2010		
	Lucint Ltd.	Industry Average
Net sales...............................	$425,625	100.0%
Cost of goods sold................	250,375	53.2
Gross margin.........................	175,250	46.8
Operating expenses.............	87,300	21.3
Operating income................	87,950	25.5
Other expenses....................	20,500	5.2
Net income	$ 67,450	20.3%

LUCINT LTD. Balance Sheet Compared with Industry Average December 31, 2010		
	Lucint Ltd.	Industry Average
Current assets.........................	$162,750	62.5%
Property and equip., net.......	85,250	35.2
Other assets	6,000	2.3
Total assets.............................	$254,000	100.0%
Current liabilities...................	$112,500	42.5%
Long-term liabilities..............	62,500	32.5
Shareholders' equity..............	79,000	25.0
Total liabilities and shareholders' equity..........	$254,000	100.0%

Required

1. Prepare a two-column common-size income statement and a two-column common-size balance sheet for Lucint Ltd. The first column of each statement should present Lucint Ltd.'s common-size statement, and the second column should show the industry averages.

2. For the profitability analysis, compute Lucint Ltd.'s (a) ratio of gross margin to net sales, (b) ratio of operating income to net sales, and (c) ratio of net income to net sales. Compare these figures to the industry averages. Is Lucint Ltd.'s profit performance better or worse than the industry average?

3. For the analysis of financial position, compute Lucint Ltd.'s (a) ratio of current assets to total assets, and (b) ratio of shareholders' equity to total assets. Compare these ratios to the industry averages. Is Lucint Ltd.'s financial position better or worse than the industry averages?

Problem 18–3A

Effects of business transactions on selected ratios

④

1. Current ratio 1.71

Financial statement data of Hartmann Supplies Ltd. include the following items:

Cash..	$ 68,000
Accounts receivable, net	97,500
Inventories	129,000
Prepaid expenses..	6,000
Total assets..	625,000
Short-term notes payable...	39,000
Accounts payable..	109,500
Accrued liabilities	27,000
Long-term liabilities	204,000
Net income..	103,000
Number of common shares outstanding...................	50,000 shares

Required

1. Compute Hartmann Supplies Ltd.'s current ratio, debt ratio, and earnings per share.

2. Compute each of the three ratios after evaluating the effect of each transaction that follows. Consider each transaction *separately*.

   a. Purchased merchandise of $33,000 on account, debiting Inventory.
   b. Paid long-term liabilities, $40,000.

c. Declared, but did not pay, a $30,000 cash dividend on common shares.

d. Borrowed $50,000 on a long-term note payable.

e. Issued 10,000 common shares at the beginning of the year, receiving cash of $140,000.

f. Received cash on account, $25,000.

g. Paid short-term notes payable, $30,000.

Use the following format for your answers:

Requirement 1		Current Ratio	Debt Ratio	Earnings per Share

Requirement 2	Transaction (letter)	Current Ratio	Debt Ratio	Earnings per Share

Using ratios to evaluate a share investment
④
1. a. 2010, 2.45
2009, 2.07

Problem 18–4A

Comparative financial statement data of Main Street Antiques Ltd. appear below:

MAIN STREET ANTIQUES LTD.
Comparative Income Statement
For the Years Ended December 31, 2010 and 2009

	2010	2009
Net sales	$311,850	$297,000
Cost of goods sold	148,850	147,000
Gross margin	163,000	150,000
Operating expenses	79,250	77,000
Income from operations	83,750	73,000
Interest expense	12,500	14,000
Income before income tax	71,250	59,000
Income tax expense	17,850	14,600
Net income	$ 53,400	$ 44,400

MAIN STREET ANTIQUES LTD.
Comparative Balance Sheet
December 31, 2010 and 2009
(selected 2008 amounts given for computation of ratios)

	2010	2009	2008
Current assets:			
Cash	$ 27,500	$ 25,000	
Current receivables, net	67,500	62,500	$ 52,500
Inventories	127,500	117,500	95,000
Prepaid expenses	5,000	4,000	
Total current assets	227,500	209,000	
Property, plant, and equipment, net	100,500	98,000	
Total assets	$328,000	$307,000	295,500
Total current liabilities	$ 93,000	$100,725	
Long-term liabilities	117,500	127,500	
Total liabilities	210,500	228,225	
Preferred shares, $1.25	5,000	5,000	
Common shares	50,000	37,500	17,500
Retained earnings	62,500	36,275	25,000
Total liabilities and shareholders' equity	$328,000	$307,000	

Other information:

a. Market price of Main Street Antiques Ltd. common shares: $24.00 at December 31, 2010 and $12.00 at December 31, 2009.

b. Common shares outstanding: 10,000 during 2010 and 7,500 during 2009. There are 1,000 preferred shares outstanding at December 31, 2010 and 2009.

c. All sales are on credit.

Required

1. Compute the following ratios for 2010 and 2009:

a. Current ratio
b. Inventory turnover
c. Accounts-receivable turnover
d. Times-interest-earned ratio
e. Return on assets

f. Return on common shareholders' equity
g. Earnings per common share
h. Price/earnings ratio
i. Book value per common share at year end

2. Decide (a) whether Main Street Antiques Ltd.'s financial position improved or deteriorated during 2010, and (b) whether the investment attractiveness of its common shares appears to have increased or decreased.

3. How will what you have learned in this problem help you evaluate an investment?

Problem 18–5A

Incomplete and adapted versions of the financial statements of Excelsor Ltd. follow (amounts in thousands).

Using ratio data to complete a set of financial statements

④

Net income $4,954 thou.

EXCELSOR LTD.
Income Statement
For the Year Ended May 31, 2010

Net sales	$30,718
Cost of goods sold	(a)
Gross margin	(b)
Selling and general expenses	9,654
Other expense (income)	1,130
Income before income tax	(c)
Income tax expense (25%)	(d)
Net income	$ (e)

EXCELSOR LTD.
Comparative Balance Sheet
May 31, 2010 and 2009

Assets	2010	2009
Current:		
Cash	$ (f)	$ 300
Short-term investments	1,852	1,630
Receivables, net	4,224	3,726
Inventories	1,300	1,046
Prepaid expenses	(g)	168
Total current assets	(h)	6,870
Property, plant, and equipment, net	22,354	19,248
Total assets	$ (i)	$26,118
Liabilities		
Current liabilities	$ 9,270	$ 7,434
Long-term liabilities	(j)	15,964
Total liabilities	(k)	23,398
Shareholders' Equity		
Common shareholders' equity	(l)	2,720
Total liabilities and shareholders' equity	$ (m)	$26,118

Ratio data:

a. Current ratio at May 31, 2010 is 0.9276.
b. Inventory turnover for the year ended May 31, 2010 is 11.362.
c. Debt ratio at May 31, 2010 is 0.7521.

Required

Complete the financial statements. Start with the income statement, then go to the cash flow statement. Complete the balance sheet last.

Excel Spreadsheet Template

Using ratios to decide between two share investments

④

a. Stagers 1.86, Wesbuild 1.52

Problem 18–6A

Assume you are purchasing an investment and have decided to invest in a company in the home renovation business. Suppose you have narrowed the choice to Stagers Ltd. and Wesbuild Homes Ltd. You have assembled the following selected data:

Selected income statement data for current year

	Stagers Ltd.	Wesbuild Homes Ltd.
Net sales (all on credit)	$323,050	$231,875
Cost of goods sold	187,700	154,250
Income from operations...	87,500	48,750
Interest expense..	15,000	2,500
Net income...	75,000	36,550

Selected balance sheet and market price data at end of current year

	Stagers Ltd.	Wesbuild Homes Ltd.
Current assets:		
Cash	$ 17,250	$ 18,500
Short-term investments..	11,500	9,750
Current receivables, net...	32,300	26,100
Inventories	60,950	55,775
Prepaid expenses	2,000	1,250
Total current assets..	$124,000	$111,375
Total assets..	$210,000	$169,000
Total current liabilities	66,750	73,500
Total liabilities	82,500	68,500
Preferred shares: $3.00 (250 shares)...................................	12,500	
Common shares (4,000 shares)..		15,000
Common shares (7,000 shares)..	17,500	
Total shareholders' equity	127,500	100,500
Market price per common share...	$ 10.00	$ 10.00

Selected balance sheet data at beginning of current year

	Stagers Ltd.	Wesbuild Homes Ltd.
Current receivables, net..	$ 30,250	$ 16,000
Inventories..	52,500	52,500
Total assets	240,000	192,500
Preferred shareholders' equity, $3.00 (250 shares)	12,500	—
Common shares (4,000 shares)...		15,000
Common shares (7,000 shares)...	17,500	
Total shareholders' equity	90,000	87,500

Your investment strategy is to purchase the shares of companies that have low price/earnings ratios but appear to be in good shape financially. Assume you have analyzed all other factors, and your decision depends on the results of the ratio analysis to be performed.

Required

Compute the following ratios for both companies for the current year and decide which company's shares better fits your investment strategy:

a. Current ratio
b. Acid-test ratio
c. Inventory turnover
d. Day's sales in average receivables
e. Debt ratio
f. Times-interest-earned ratio

g. Return on net sales
h. Return on total assets
i. Return on common shareholders' equity
j. Earnings per common share
k. Book value per common share
l. Price/earnings ratio

Problem 18–7A

Cranberry Products Ltd.'s financial statements for the year ended December 31, 2010, are shown below.

Preparing a horizontal analysis of a financial statement, computing the standard financial ratios used for decision making, using ratios in decision making

2. a. 8.9:1

CRANBERRY PRODUCTS LTD.
Income Statement
For the Year Ended December 31, 2010

Net sales..	$945,000
Cost of goods sold	610,000
Gross margin	335,000
Operating expenses:	
Selling expenses..	128,200
Administrative expenses...	78,000
Interest expense...	22,000
Total operating expenses..	228,200
Operating income...	106,800
Income taxes (25%)...	26,700
Net income...	$ 80,100

CRANBERRY PRODUCTS LTD.
Statement of Retained Earnings
For the Year Ended December 31, 2010

Retained earnings, January 1, 2010.....................................		$162,000
Add net income for 2010		80,100
		242,100
Less dividends: Preferred...	$15,000	
Common..	9,000	24,000
Retained earnings, December 31, 2010..............................		$218,100

CRANBERRY PRODUCTS LTD.
Balance Sheet
December 31, 2010 and 2009

	2010	2009
Assets		
Cash	$102,000	$ 45,000
Accounts receivable	84,000	92,000
Merchandise inventory	102,000	118,000
Prepaid expenses	8,000	6,000
Property, plant, and equipment	498,000	474,000
Less accumulated amortization	(106,000)	(70,000)
Goodwill	40,000	40,000
Total assets	$728,000	$705,000
Liabilities		
Accounts payable	$ 30,100	$ 43,000
Notes payable (due in 30 days)	3,000	10,000
Mortgage payable (secured by the equipment)	68,800	130,000
Total liabilities	101,900	183,000
Shareholders' equity		
Preferred shares (1,200 shares, $10.00)		
callable at $210.00 per share	240,000	240,000
Common shares		
(2010—12,000 shares; 2009—6,000 shares)	168,000	120,000
Retained earnings	218,100	162,000
Total shareholders' equity	626,100	522,000
Total liabilities and shareholders' equity	$728,000	$705,000

Required

1. Perform a horizontal analysis of the comparative balance sheets. Comment on the analysis.

2. Calculate each of the following ratios for the year ended December 31, 2010. The industry standards are provided in parentheses for some of the ratios.

   a. Current ratio (3:1)
   b. Acid-test ratio
   c. Inventory turnover
   d. Days' sales in receivables
   e. Debt ratio (0.50)
   f. Times-interest-earned ratio
   g. Rate of return on net sales

   h. Rate of return on total assets
   i. Rate of return on common shareholders' equity
   j. Price/earnings ratio—the market price per share is $30.00 at year end, when dividends were paid (5.0)
   k. Dividend yield (5%)

3. Comment on your calculations for Cranberry Products Ltd. in Requirement 2. Include comments for those ratios for which industry standards were provided (items a, e, j, and k).

Problem 18–8A

Preparing a vertical analysis of a financial statement, computing the standard financial ratios used for decision making, using ratios in decision making

2. a. 0.50:1

Battleford Ltd.'s financial statements for the year ended December 31, 2010 are shown below; the financial statements and additional information are in thousands of dollars.

BATTLEFORD LTD.
Balance Sheet
December 31, 2010

Assets

Cash..	$ 32.0
Accounts receivable.......................	76.8
Inventory.......................................	110.4
Prepaid expenses...........................	16.0
Long-term investments................	364.8
Property, plant, and	
equipment (net).........................	390.0
Total assets.................................	$990.0

Liabilities

Accounts payable...........................	$175.0
Salaries payable.............................	14.0
Dividends payable.........................	30.0
Bonds payable	379.0
Total liabilities...........................	598.0

Shareholders' Equity

Common shares (10,000 shares)...	180.0
Retained earnings	212.0
Total shareholders' equity	392.0
Total liabilities and	
shareholders' equity	$990.0

BATTLEFORD LTD.
Income Statement
For the Year Ended December 31, 2010

Sales...	$960.0
Cost of goods sold	500.0
Gross margin...............................	460.0
Operating expenses:	
Selling expense........................	181.2
Administrative	
expenses.............................	141.2
Interest expense	10.0
Total operating expenses....	332.4
Operating income.......................	127.6
Income taxes...............................	44.6
Net income	$ 83.0

Account Balances, January 1, 2010:

Total assets....................................	$924.0
Accounts receivable	56.0
Inventory	58.0
Retained earnings........................	159.0

Required

1. Prepare a vertical analysis of the income statement. The industry standards are gross margin of 35 percent and net income of 12 percent. Comment on the results.
2. Calculate each of the following for December 31, 2010 (industry standards are shown in parentheses for some items):

   a. Acid-test ratio (0.54:1)
   b. Inventory turnover (4.0 times)
   c. Days' sales in receivables (50 days)
   d. Debt ratio (55 percent)
   e. Rate of return on total assets (12 percent)
   f. Rate of return on shareholders' equity
   g. Earnings per share
   h. Price/earnings ratio (market price is $70.00 per share)
   i. Dividend yield

3. Comment on the ratios in Requirement 2 for which an industry standard was provided (items a to e).
4. Battleford Ltd. has a policy of increasing purchases (all on credit) in the final month of the year to achieve inventory levels that are 50 percent higher than required. Thus, the inventory balance of $110,400 at December 31, 2010 is 50 percent higher than it would be normally. This is done to ensure that the company has adequate inventory for the new year. Management is concerned about the effects this policy may have on the acid-test ratio and inventory turnover. Calculate what these ratios would have been without the policy and comment on the results.

PROBLEMS (GROUP B)

MyAccountingLab | All questions in this section appear in MyAccountingLab.

Problem 18–1B

Net sales, net income, and total assets for Cahall Holdings Ltd. for a six-year period follow.

	2010	2009	2008	2007	2006	2005
			(Amounts in thousands)			
Net sales..............................	$804	$762	$662	$714	$616	$604
Net income	112	92	60	82	68	58
Total assets	654	610	522	508	462	410

Required

1. Compute trend percentages for 2006 through 2010. Use 2005 as the base year.
2. Compute the return on net sales for 2006 through 2010, rounding to three decimal places. In this industry, rates above 8 percent are considered good, and rates above 10 percent are viewed as outstanding.
3. How does Cahall Holdings Ltd.'s return on net sales compare to the industry's?

Problem 18–2B

Top managers of Gimley Steel Fabricators Inc., a specialty steel fabricating company, have asked for your help in comparing the company's profit performance and financial position with the average for the steel fabricating industry. The accountant has given you the company's income statement and balance sheet, and also the average data for the steel fabricating industry (amounts in millions).

GIMLEY STEEL FABRICATORS INC.
Income Statement
Compared with Industry Average
For the Year Ended December 31, 2010

	Gimley Steel Fabricators Inc.	Industry Average
Net sales..................................	$29.2	100.0%
Cost of goods sold	17.6	65.9
Gross margin..........................	11.6	34.1
Operating expenses..............	8.4	28.1
Operating income................	3.2	6.0
Other expenses.....................	0.2	0.4
Net income	$ 3.0	5.6%

GIMLEY STEEL FABRICATORS INC.
Balance Sheet
Compared with Industry Average
December 31, 2010

	Gimley Steel Fabricators Inc.	Industry Average
Current assets	$10.4	66.6%
Property, plant, equip., net...	8.0	32.3
Other assets	0.2	1.1
Total assets............................	$18.6	100.0%
Current liabilities..................	$ 6.2	35.6%
Long-term liabilities.............	5.2	19.0
Shareholders' equity	7.2	45.4
Total liabilities and shareholders' equity.........	$18.6	100.0%

Required

1. Prepare a two-column common-size income statement and a two-column common-size balance sheet for Gimley Steel Fabricators Inc. The first column of each statement should present Gimley Steel Fabricators Inc.'s common-size statement, and the second column should show the industry averages.
2. For the profitability analysis, compare Gimley Steel Fabricators Inc.'s (a) ratio of gross margin to net sales, (b) ratio of operating income (loss) to net sales, and (c) ratio of net income (loss) to net sales. Compare these figures with the industry averages. Is Gimley Steel Fabricators Inc.'s profit performance better or worse than the average for the industry?
3. For the analysis of financial position, compare Gimley Steel Fabricators Inc.'s (a) ratio of current assets to total assets and (b) ratio of shareholders' equity to total assets. Compare these ratios with the industry averages. Is Gimley Steel Fabricators Inc.'s financial position better or worse than the average for the industry?

Problem 18–3B

Effects of business transactions on selected ratios ④

Financial statement data of Shaw Supplies Inc. as at December 31, 2010 include the following items:

Cash	$ 53,000
Accounts receivable, net	127,000
Inventories	251,000
Prepaid expenses	10,000
Total assets	922,000
Short-term notes payable	80,000
Accounts payable	91,000
Accrued liabilities	64,000
Long-term liabilities	248,000
Net income	147,000
Number of common shares outstanding	24,000 shares

Required

1. Compute Shaw Supplies Inc.'s current ratio, debt ratio, and earnings per share. Round all ratios to two decimal places.
2. Compute each of the three ratios after evaluating the effect of each transaction that follows. Consider each transaction *separately*.
   a. Borrowed $50,000 on a long-term note payable.
   b. Issued 12,000 common shares on January 2, 2011, receiving cash of $180,000.
   c. Received cash on account, $9,000.
   d. Paid short-term notes payable, $50,000.
   e. Purchased merchandise costing $62,000 on account, debiting Inventory.
   f. Paid long-term liabilities, $31,000.
   g. Declared, but did not pay, a $20,000 cash dividend on the common shares.

Use the following format for your answers:

Requirement 1		Current Ratio	Debt Ratio	Earnings per Share

Requirement 2	Transaction (letter)	Current Ratio	Debt Ratio	Earnings per Share

Problem 18–4B

Using ratios to evaluate a share investment ④

Comparative financial statement data of Olympic Hardware Ltd. are as follows:

OLYMPIC HARDWARE LTD.
Comparative Income Statement
For the Years Ended December 31, 2010 and 2009

	2010	2009
Net sales	$351,500	$310,000
Cost of goods sold	201,000	155,000
Gross margin	150,500	155,000
Operating expenses	65,000	71,000
Income from operations	85,500	84,000
Interest expense	26,000	20,000
Income before income tax	59,500	64,000
Income tax expense	19,000	22,500
Net income	$ 40,500	$ 41,500

OLYMPIC HARDWARE LTD.
Comparative Balance Sheet
December 31, 2010 and 2009
(Selected 2008 amounts given for computation of ratios)

	2010	2009	2008
Current assets:			
Cash	$ 21,000	$ 25,000	
Current receivables, net	116,000	80,500	$ 62,500
Inventories	149,000	137,000	86,000
Prepaid expenses	6,000	9,000	
Total current assets	292,000	251,500	
Property, plant, and equipment, net	154,500	143,500	
Total assets	$446,500	$395,000	351,500
Total current liabilities	$141,000	$138,500	
Long-term liabilities	114,500	121,000	
Total liabilities	255,500	259,500	
Preferred shares, $1.50	30,000	30,000	
Common shares	75,000	60,000	60,000
Retained earnings	86,000	45,500	19,000
Total liabilities and shareholders' equity	$446,500	$395,000	

Other information:

a. Market price of Olympic Hardware Ltd. common shares: $19.00 at December 31, 2010 and $31.00 at December 31, 2009.

b. Weighted-average number of common shares outstanding: 15,000 during 2010 and 12,000 during 2009.

c. There are 2,000 preferred shares outstanding.

d. All sales are on credit.

Required

1. Compute the following ratios for 2010 and 2009:
   a. Current ratio
   b. Inventory turnover
   c. Accounts receivable turnover
   d. Times-interest-earned ratio
   e. Return on assets
   f. Return on common shareholders' equity
   g. Earnings per common share
   h. Price/earnings ratio
   i. Book value per common share at year end

2. Decide (a) whether Olympic Hardware Ltd.'s ability to pay its debts and to sell inventory improved or deteriorated during 2010 and (b) whether the investment attractiveness of its common shares appears to have increased or decreased.

3. How will what you have learned in this problem help you evaluate an investment?

Using ratio data to complete
a set of financial statements

④

Problem 18–5B

Incomplete and adapted versions of the financial statements of Tasker Concrete Ltd. follow (amounts in thousands).

Ratio data:

a. Current ratio at December 31, 2010 is 0.7547.
b. Inventory turnover for 2010 was 5.284.
c. Debt ratio at December 31, 2010 is 0.5906.

TASKER CONCRETE LTD.
Comparative Balance Sheet
December 31, 2010 and 2009

Assets	2010	2009
Current:		
Cash..	$ (f)	$ 2,528
Short-term investments.................................	1,702	1,702
Receivables, net...	3,600	2,984
Inventories...	2,428	2,196
Prepaid expenses...	(g)	204
Total current assets.......................................	(h)	9,614
Property, plant, and equipment, net...............	19,632	17,336
Total assets..	$ (i)	$26,950
Liabilities		
Current liabilities...	$14,204	$11,684
Long-term liabilities.......................................	(j)	4,416
Total liabilities..	(k)	16,100
Shareholders' Equity		
Common shareholders' equity.........................	(l)	10,850
Total liabilities and shareholders' equity.........	$ (m)	$26,950

TASKER CONCRETE LTD.
Income Statement
For the Year Ended December 31, 2010

Net sales..	$32,548
Cost of goods sold...	(a)
Gross margin..	(b)
Selling and general expenses...................................	13,624
Other expense (income)...	480
Income before income tax..	(c)
Income tax expense (35%)..	(d)
Net income...	$ (e)

TASKER CONCRETE LTD.
Cash Flow Statement
For the Year Ended December 31, 2010

Net cash inflow from operating activities......................	$ 6,640
Net cash outflow from investing activities.....................	(2,420)
Net cash outflow from financing activities.....................	(4,094)
Net increase (decrease) in cash during 2010.................	$ (n)

Required

Complete the financial statements. Start with the income statement. Then go to the cash flow statement. Complete the balance sheet last.

Problem 18–6B

Assume that you are purchasing shares in a company in the variety store and gas bar supply business. Suppose you have narrowed the choice to Rubin Trading Ltd. and Hyska Ltd. and have assembled the following data:

Excel Spreadsheet Template

Using ratios to decide between two share investments

④

Selected income statement data for the year ended December 31, 2010

	Rubin Trading Ltd.	Hyska Ltd.
Net sales (all on credit)	$1,060,000	$1,246,000
Cost of goods sold	602,000	722,000
Income from operations	166,000	202,000
Interest expense	30,000	10,000
Net income	82,000	124,000

Selected balance sheet and market price data for the year ended December 31, 2010

	Rubin Trading Ltd.	Hyska Ltd.
Current assets:		
Cash	$ 134,000	$ 110,000
Short-term investments	0	24,000
Current receivables, net	312,000	392,000
Inventories	424,000	448,000
Prepaid expenses	24,000	28,000
Total current assets	$ 894,000	$1,002,000
Total assets	$2,070,000	$2,244,000
Total current liabilities	748,000	800,000
Total liabilities	1,444,000	1,408,000
Preferred shares, $10.00 (300 shares)	60,000	
Common shares (75,000 shares)		450,000
Common shares (10,000 shares)	100,000	
Total shareholders' equity	626,000	836,000
Market price per common share	$ 84.00	$ 56.00

Selected balance sheet data at January 1, 2010

	Rubin Trading Ltd.	Hyska Ltd.
Current receivables, net	$ 330,000	$ 280,000
Inventories	448,000	420,000
Total assets	1,970,000	1,720,000
Preferred shareholders' equity, $10.00 (300 shares)	60,000	
Common shares (75,000 shares)		450,000
Common shares (10,000 shares)	100,000	
Total shareholders' equity	560,000	720,000

Your investment strategy is to purchase the shares of companies that have low price/earnings ratios but appear to be in good shape financially. Assume you have analyzed all other factors, and your decision depends on the results of the ratio analysis to be performed.

Required

Compute the following ratios for both companies for the current year and decide which company's shares better fit your investment strategy:

a. Current ratio
b. Acid-test ratio
c. Inventory turnover
d. Days' sales in average receivables
e. Debt ratio
f. Times-interest-earned ratio
g. Return on net sales
h. Return on total assets
i. Return on common shareholders' equity
j. Earnings per common share
k. Book value per common share
l. Price/earnings ratio

Preparing a horizontal analysis of a financial statement, computing the standard financial ratios used for decision making, using ratios in decision making

① ④

Sarah Hardware Inc.'s financial statements for the year ended December 31, 2010 are shown below.

SARAH HARDWARE INC.
Income Statement
For the Year Ended December 31, 2010

Net sales...	$230,000
Cost of goods sold...	120,000
Gross margin..	110,000
Operating expenses:	
Selling expenses...	40,000
Administrative expenses...	23,000
Interest expense...	6,000
Total operating expenses...	69,000
Operating income...	41,000
Income taxes (35%)...	14,350
Net income...	$ 26,650

SARAH HARDWARE INC.
Statement of Retained Earnings
For the Year Ended December 31, 2010

Retained earnings, January 1, 2010		$ 48,100
Add net income for 2010...		26,650
		74,750
Less dividends: Preferred	$16,000	
Common	13,150	29,150
Retained earnings, December 31, 2010		$ 45,600

SARAH HARDWARE INC.
Balance Sheet
December 31, 2010 and 2009

	2010	2009
Assets		
Cash	$ 21,600	$ 15,600
Accounts receivable...	20,000	21,000
Merchandise inventory	38,000	42,000
Prepaid expenses	1,000	1,500
Property, plant, and equipment...........................	170,000	157,000
Less accumulated amortization........................	(34,000)	(24,000)
Goodwill	15,000	15,000
Total assets...	$231,600	$228,100
Liabilities		
Accounts payable..	$ 15,000	$ 18,500
Notes payable (due in 30 days)............................	2,000	3,500
Mortgage payable (secured by the equipment).............	40,000	45,000
Total liabilities...	57,000	67,000
Shareholders' equity		
Preferred shares (8,000 shares; $2.00,		
callable at $15.00 per share)............................	48,000	48,000
Common shares		
(2010—12,000 shares; 2009—8,000 shares)	81,000	65,000
Retained earnings	45,600	48,100
Total shareholders' equity.................................	174,600	161,100
Total liabilities and shareholders' equity	$231,600	$228,100

Required

1. Perform a horizontal analysis of the comparative balance sheets. Comment on the analysis.

2. Calculate each of the following ratios for the year ended December 31, 2010. The industry standards are provided in parentheses for some of the ratios.
   a. Current ratio (2:1)
   b. Acid-test ratio
   c. Inventory turnover
   d. Days' sales in receivables
   e. Debt ratio (0.47)
   f. Times-interest-earned ratio
   g. Rate of return on net sales
   h. Rate of return on total assets
   i. Rate of return on common shareholders' equity
   j. Price/earnings ratio—the market price per share is $9.00 at year end, when dividends were paid (14.0)
   k. Dividend yield (4%)

3. Comment on your calculations for Sarah Hardware Inc. Include comments for those ratios for which industry standards were provided (items a, e, j, and k).

Preparing a vertical analysis of a financial statement, computing the standard financial ratios used for decision making, using ratios in decision making

② ④

Problem 18–8B

Cornwall EduProducts Inc. provides wholesale and retail school products to the lower B.C. mainland. The company's financial statements for the year ending June 30, 2010 are shown below. The financial statements and additional information are in thousands of dollars.

CORNWALL EDUPRODUCTS INC. Balance Sheet June 30, 2010		CORNWALL EDUPRODUCTS INC. Income Statement For the Year Ended June 30, 2010	
Assets			
Cash	$ 20.0	Sales	$536.0
Accounts receivable	36.8	Cost of goods sold	320.8
Inventory	100.4	Gross margin	215.2
Prepaid expenses	4.0		
Property, plant, and equipment (net)	320.0	Operating expenses:	
Long-term investments	150.0	Selling expense	30.0
Total assets	$631.2	Administrative expenses	35.2
Liabilities		Interest expense	16.0
Accounts payable	$ 70.0	Total operating	
Salaries payable	16.8	expenses	81.2
Dividends payable	20.0	Operating income	134.0
Bonds payable	240.0	Income taxes	47.0
Total liabilities	346.8	Net income	$ 87.0
Shareholders' equity			
Common shares		**Account Balances, July 1, 2009:**	
(5,000 shares)	140.0	Total assets	$650.0
Retained earnings	144.4	Accounts receivable	28.4
Total shareholders' equity	284.4	Inventory	129.2
Total liabilities and shareholders' equity	$631.2	Retained earnings	97.4

Required

1. Prepare a vertical analysis of the income statement. The industry standards are gross margin of 45 percent and net income of 15 percent. Comment on the results.

2. Calculate each of the following for June 30, 2010 (industry standards are shown in parentheses for some items):
   a. Acid-test ratio (1:1)
   b. Inventory turnover (3.0 times)
   c. Days' sales in receivables (50 days)
   d. Debt ratio (0.40)
   e. Rate of return on total assets (12%)
   f. Rate of return on shareholders' equity
   g. Earnings per share
   h. Price/earnings ratio (market price is $60.00 per share)
   i. Dividend yield

3. Comment on the ratios in Requirement 2 for which an industry standard was provided (items a to e).

4. Cornwall EduProducts Inc. has a policy of increasing purchases (all on credit) in the final month of the year to achieve inventory levels that are 100 percent higher than required. Thus, the inventory balance of $100,400 at June 30, 2010 is more than twice as high as it would be normally. This is done to provide an inventory cushion prior to the start of the fall school term. Management is concerned about the effects this policy may have on the acid-test ratio and inventory turnover. Calculate what these ratios would have been without the policy (i.e., reduce opening inventory by $64,600 and closing inventory by $50,200) and comment on the results.

CHALLENGE PROBLEMS

Problem 18–1C

Using horizontal analysis to assess whether a company is using improper accounting practices

(1)

Recently newspapers carried stories about a company that fired three top executives for management fraud. The three had been using improper accounting practices to overstate profits. The improper practices included improperly recording assets on the company's balance sheet, overstating sales, and understating cost of goods sold by inflating inventory numbers. When inventory got out of line, the executives would debit property, plant, and equipment and credit inventory to further hide their fraud.

The company had been growing at a very rapid pace, outdistancing its competitors. However, there were warning signals or "red flags" that revealed that all was not well with the company and that suggested that the books might have been "cooked" in order to report the rapid growth. For example, sales, which were almost all on credit, grew much faster than did accounts receivable when these balances on the company's financial statements were compared with industry data. Inventory turnover was lower than that of competitors while sales were unusually low relative to property, plant, and equipment. A final "red flag" was that management bonuses were tied to sales increases.

Required

1. Which items would be misstated in a horizontal analysis of the company's income statement? Which items would be misstated in a horizontal analysis of the company's balance sheet? Indicate the direction of the misstatement.

2. Why do you think the issue of management bonuses is considered a "red flag"?

Problem 18–2C

Understanding the impact of improper accounting practices on the financial statements of a company

(4)

You are a senior staff member of a public accounting firm, and you have been asked by one of the firm's partners to discuss the impact of improper accounting practices on the financial statements of a company to new junior staff accountants. Using the information given in Problem 18–1C, use the following questions to frame your comments to the new juniors.

Required

1. Sales grew faster than receivables. Would this situation create an unusually high or unusually low accounts receivable turnover?

2. Why was the fact that sales grew faster than receivables relative to other companies in the industry a "red flag"?

3. Explain why inventory turnover was too low.

4. Why was the fact that inventory turnover was low relative to other companies a "red flag"?

5. Compare the company's receivables turnover with inventory turnover. Does the comparison suggest a "red flag"? If so, what is it?

Extending Your Knowledge

DECISION PROBLEM

Identifying action to cut losses
and establish profitability

② ④

Suppose you manage Wally's SportsWorld Inc., a ski and snowboard store, which lost money during the past year. Before you can set the business on a successful course, you must first analyze the company and industry data for the current year in an effort to learn what is wrong. The data appear below.

Required

On the basis of your analysis of these figures, suggest three courses of action Wally's SportsWorld Inc. should take to reduce its losses and establish profitable operations. Give your reasons for each suggestion.

Wally's SportsWorld Inc. Income Statement Data

	Wally's SportsWorld Inc.	Industry Average
Net sales	100.0%	100.0%
Cost of sales	(61.2)	(55.4)
Gross margin	38.8	44.6
Operating expense	(40.2)	(38.6)
Operating income (loss)	(1.4)	6.0
Interest expense	(3.1)	(1.2)
Other revenue	0.8	0.4
Income (loss) before income tax	(3.7)	5.2
Income tax (expense) saving	1.3	(1.8)
Net income (loss)	(2.4)%	3.4%

Wally's SportsWorld Inc. Balance Sheet Data

	Wally's SportsWorld Inc.	Industry Average
Cash and short-term investments	0.2%	8.0%
Accounts receivable	20.0	15.5
Inventory	67.1	57.5
Prepaid expenses	0.5	0.6
Total current assets	87.8	81.6
Property, plant, and equipment, net	10.2	14.4
Other assets	2.0	4.0
Total assets	100.0%	100.0%
Bank loan, 6%	18.0%	14.0%
Notes payable, short-term, 8%	6.0	0.0
Accounts payable	18.2	22.3
Accrued liabilities	6.9	8.4
Total current liabilities	49.1	44.7
Long-term debt, 8%	16.0	14.0
Total liabilities	65.1	58.7
Common shareholders' equity	34.9	41.3
Total liabilities and shareholders' equity	100.0%	100.0%

FINANCIAL STATEMENT CASE

Sun-Rype Products Ltd's annual report is in Appendix B. Sun-Rype's website (http://ir.sunrype.com/phoenix.zhtml?c=70705&p=irol-financial) gives a Five-Year Historical Review, with data for the fiscal years ended December 31, 2004 to December 31, 2008. Portions of the Five-Year Historical Review are reproduced below.

Measuring profitability and analyzing shares as an investment

④

SUN-RYPE PRODUCTS LTD.
Five-Year Historical Review
For the Years Ended December 31
(dollar amounts in thousands except per share amounts)

Operating Results	2008	2007	2006[1]	2005[1]	2004[1]
Net sales	$ 125,368	$135,134	$130,622	$125,411	$115,214
Gross profit[2]	$ 14,091	$ 41,836	$ 45,309	$ 44,228	$ 39,241
Gross profit %[2]	11.2%	31.0%	34.7%	35.3%	34.1%
Selling, general, & administrative expenses ("SG&A")	$ 29,053	$ 28,538	$ 30,476	$ 30,205	$ 27,539
Other[3]	—	$ 2,190	$ 241	$ 60	$ (691)
Amortization[2]	$ 2,288	$ 4,186	$ 3,858	$ 3,898	$ 3,358
Earnings (loss) before interest and income taxes ("EBIT")	$(17,250)	$ 6,922	$ 10,734	$ 10,065	$ 9,035
Interest Expense	$879	$ 148	$ 42	$ 39	$ 86
Earnings (loss) before income taxes ("EBT")	$(18,129)	$ 6,774	$ 10,692	$ 10,026	$ 8,949
Income taxes (recovery)	$ (6,456)	$ 2,138	$ 3,426	$ 3,502	$ 3,098
Net earnings (loss)	$(11,673)	$ 4,636	$ 7,266	$ 6,524	$ 5,851
Financial Ratios					
Net earnings (loss) as % of net sales	(9.3)%	3.4%	5.6%	5.2%	5.1%
After-tax return on average equity	(33.4)%	11.7%	16.8%	14.3%	14.4%
After-tax return on average assets	(17.9)%	8.0%	11.4%	10.1%	10.0%
Pre-tax (EBIT) return on average invested capital	(35.1)%	17.3%	24.5%	21.7%	21.9%
Current ratio	1.6	2.1	1.7	2.6	2.3
Debit-to-equity ratio	1.0	0.0	0.0	0.0	0.0
Per Share Information					
Average shares outstanding (thousands)	10,828	10,828	10,828	10,828	10,817
Earnings/share	$ (1.08)	$ 0.43	$ 0.67	$ 0.60	$ 0.54
Cash flow/share	$ (0.75)	$ 0.89	$ 1.03	$ 1.01	$ 0.83
Book value/share	$ 2.68	$ 3.79	$ 3.51	$ 4.46	$ 3.98
Share price—high	$ 11.70	$ 14.00	$ 14.14	$ 12.60	$ 13.00
Share price—low	$ 4.94	$ 11.03	$ 10.95	$ 10.36	$ 7.90
Share price—close	$ 5.79	$ 11.50	$ 13.10	$ 12.10	$ 10.95

[1] Certain of the comparative figures for 2004–2006 have been changed to conform to the classifications used in 2007.
[2] Gross profit and amortization in 2008 are affected by the adoption of new accounting standards. This change has not been reflected in 2004—2007 amounts.
[3] Other includes gains and losses on capital dispositions and foreign exchange gains and losses.

Prospective investors should note that this information has been extracted from Sun-Rype's audited annual financial statements and may not give a complete profile of Sun-Rype. The review includes non-GAAP financial measures that do not have a standardized meaning prescribed by Canadian generally accepted accounting principles and therefore may not be comparable to similar measures presented by other companies. It should be read in conjunction with Management's Discussion and Analysis, as well as the audited financial statements and the accompanying notes for the years, which are available for viewing on the Canadian Securities Administrators' website (www.sedar.com) and on Sun-Rype's website (www.sunrype.com).

Required

1. Using the Five-Year Historical Review, perform a four-year trend analysis of
   a. Net sales
   b. Income from continuing operations (EBIT)
   c. Basic earnings per common share
   Start with 2005 and end with 2008; use 2004 as the base year.

2. Evaluate Sun-Rype Products Ltd.'s profitability trend during this four-year period.

Comprehensive Problem for Part Four

ANALYZING A COMPANY FOR ITS INVESTMENT POTENTIAL

In its 2008 annual report, Loblaw Companies Limited included a five-year summary of its operating and financial record (the most recent eight years are presented below). Loblaw Companies Limited operates a range of stores across Canada. One of Loblaw Companies Limited's best-known products is the "President's Choice" line of products.

Analyze the company's Operating and Financial Record for the fiscal years 2001 to 2008 to decide whether to invest in the common shares of Loblaw Companies Limited. Include the following sections in your analysis and fully explain your final decision:

- Trend analysis (use 2001 as the base year). Analyses for sales, net earnings (loss), total assets, shareholders' equity, and fixed asset investment are suggested.
- Profitability analysis. Returns on sales, assets, and equity, and EPS would be key.
- Measuring ability to pay liabilities and debt. Debt ratio and interest coverage would be important to include.

LOBLAW COMPANIES LIMITED
Eight-Year Operating and Financial Record[1,6]

	2008[2]	2007	2006	2005	2004	2003[2]	2002	2001
($ millions)								
Sales[4]	30,802	29,384	28,640	27,801	26,209	25,220	23,082	21,468
Operating income	1,046	736	289	1,401	1,652	1,467	1,671	1,451
Interest expense	263	252	259	252	239	196	161	158
Net earnings (loss)	545	330	(219)	746	968	845	728	563
Financial position								
Working capital[5]	730	58	338	539	290	356	320	290
Fixed assets	8,045	7,953	8,055	7,785	7,113	6,390	5,557	4,931
Goodwill	807	806	794	1,587	1,621	1,607	1,599	1,599
Total assets	13,985	13,674	13,486	13,761	12,949	12,113	11,047	10,025
Net debt[3]	3,287	3,728	3,891	3,901	3,828	3,707	2,932	2,699
Shareholders' equity	5,830	5,545	5,441	5,886	5,414	4,690	4,082	3,569
Cash flow								
Cash flows from operating activities	989	1,245	1,180	1,489	1,443	1,032	998	818
Free cash flow[3]	(49)	402	70	103	(24)	—	—	—
Fixed asset purchases	750	613	937	1,156	1,258	1,271	1,079	1,108
Per Common Share ($)								
Basic net earnings	1.99	1.20	(0.80)	2.72	3.53	3.07	2.64	2.04
Dividend rate at year end	0.84	0.84	0.84	0.84	0.76	0.60	0.48	0.40
Cash flows from operating activities	3.61	4.55	4.31	5.43	5.26	3.75	3.61	2.96
Capital investment	2.74	2.24	3.42	4.22	4.59	4.62	3.91	4.01
Book value	21.26	20.22	19.85	21.48	19.74	17.07	14.79	12.92
Market value at year end	35.23	34.07	48.79	56.37	72.02	67.85	54.00	51.85
Shares outstanding (millions)	274	274	274	274	274	275	276	276

[1]For financial definitions and ratios refer to the Glossary of Terms on page 83 of the 2008 Annual Report.
[2]2008 and 2003 were 53-week years.
[3]See Non-GAAP Financial Measures on page 33 of the 2008 Annual Report.
[4]During 2006, the Company implemented Emerging Issues Committee Abstract 156, "Accounting by a Vendor for Consideration Given to a Customer (Including a Reseller of the Vendor's Products)" on a retroactive basis. Accordingly certain sales incentives paid to independent franchisees, associates, and independent accounts for prior years have been reclassified between sales and cost of sales, selling, and administrative expenses.
[5]Certain prior year information has been reclassified to conform with current year presentation. Prior to 2007, security deposits were presented as cash and cash equivalents and short-term investments, and are now included in other assets on the consolidated balance sheets. Prior to 2007, the unrealized equity forwards liability was presented as other long-term liabilities, and is now included in accounts payable and accrued liabilities. See note 1 of the 2008 consolidated financial statements for more information.
[6]In 2008, the Company adopted Canadian Institute of Chartered Accountants ("CICA") Section 3031 "Inventories" without restatement of prior periods. In 2007, the Company implemented CICA Section 3855 "Financial Instruments – Recognition and Measurement," CICA Section 3865 "Hedges," CICA Section "1530 – Comprehensive Income," and CICA Section 3251 "Equity" without restatement of prior periods. In 2005, the Company adopted Accounting Guideline 15 "Consolidation of Variable Interest Entities," without restatement of prior periods.

WINNING THE

WEST

CWB | CANADIAN WESTERN BANK GROUP
BANK · TRUST · INSURANCE

2008 ANNUAL REPORT

FINANCIAL STATEMENTS

MANAGEMENT'S RESPONSIBILITY FOR FINANCIAL REPORTING

The consolidated financial statements of Canadian Western Bank and related financial information presented in this annual report have been prepared by management, who are responsible for the integrity and fair presentation of the information presented, which includes the consolidated financial statements, Management's Discussion and Analysis (MD&A) and other information. The consolidated financial statements were prepared in accordance with Canadian generally accepted accounting principles, including the requirements of the Bank Act and related rules and regulations issued by the Office of the Superintendent of Financial Institutions Canada. The MD&A has been prepared in accordance with the requirements of securities regulators, including National Instrument 51-102 of the Canadian Securities Administrators (CSA).

The consolidated financial statements, MD&A and related financial information reflect amounts which must, of necessity, be based on informed estimates and judgments of management with appropriate consideration to materiality. The financial information presented elsewhere in this annual report is fairly presented and consistent with that in the consolidated financial statements.

Management has designed the accounting system and related internal controls, and supporting procedures are maintained to provide reasonable assurance that financial records are complete and accurate, assets are safeguarded and the Bank is in compliance with all regulatory requirements. These supporting procedures include the careful selection and training of qualified staff, defined division of responsibilities and accountability for performance, and the written communication of policies and guidelines of business conduct and risk management throughout the Bank.

We, as the Bank's Chief Executive Officer and Chief Financial Officer, will certify Canadian Western Bank's annual filings with the CSA as required by Multilateral Instrument 52-109 (Certification of Disclosure in Issuers' Annual and Interim Filings).

The system of internal controls is also supported by the internal audit department, which carries out periodic inspections of all aspects of the Bank's operations. The Chief Internal Auditor has full and free access to the Audit Committee and to the external auditors.

The Audit Committee, appointed by the Board of Directors, is comprised entirely of independent directors who are not officers or employees of the Bank. The Committee is responsible for reviewing the financial statements and annual report, including management's discussion and analysis of operations and financial condition, and recommending them to the Board of Directors for approval. Other key responsibilities of the Audit Committee include meeting with management, the Chief Internal Auditor and the external auditors to discuss the effectiveness of certain internal controls over the financial reporting process and the planning and results of the external audit. The Committee also meets regularly with the Chief Internal Auditor and the external auditors without management present.

The Conduct Review Committee, appointed by the Board of Directors, is composed of directors who are not officers or employees of the Bank. Their responsibilities include reviewing related party transactions and reporting to the Board of Directors those transactions which may have a material impact on the Bank.

The Office of the Superintendent of Financial Institutions Canada, at least once a year, makes such examination and inquiry into the affairs of the Bank and its federally regulated subsidiaries as is deemed necessary or expedient to satisfy that the provisions of the relevant Acts, having reference to the safety of the depositors and policyholders, are being duly observed and that the Bank is in a sound financial condition.

KPMG LLP, the independent auditors appointed by the shareholders of the Bank, have performed an audit of the consolidated financial statements and their report follows. The external auditors have full and free access to, and meet periodically with, the Audit Committee to discuss their audit and matters arising therefrom.

Larry M. Pollock
President and Chief Executive Officer

November 24, 2008

Tracey C. Ball, FCA
Executive Vice President and Chief Financial Officer

AUDITORS' REPORT

TO THE SHAREHOLDERS OF CANADIAN WESTERN BANK

We have audited the Consolidated Balance Sheet of Canadian Western Bank as at October 31, 2008 and the Consolidated Statements of Income, Comprehensive Income, Changes in Shareholders' Equity and Cash Flow for the year then ended. These consolidated financial statements are the responsibility of the Bank's management. Our responsibility is to express an opinion on these consolidated financial statements based on our audit.

We conducted our audit in accordance with Canadian generally accepted auditing standards. Those standards require that we plan and perform an audit to obtain reasonable assurance whether the financial statements are free of material misstatement. An audit includes examining, on a test basis, evidence supporting the amounts and disclosures in the financial statements. An audit also includes assessing the accounting principles used and significant estimates made by management, as well as evaluating the overall financial statement presentation.

In our opinion, these consolidated financial statements present fairly, in all material respects, the financial position of the Bank as at October 31, 2008 and the results of its operations and its cash flow for the year then ended in accordance with Canadian generally accepted accounting principles.

The consolidated financial statements as at October 31, 2007 and for the year then ended were audited by other auditors, who expressed an opinion without reservation on these statements in their report dated November 30, 2007.

KPMG LLP

KPMG LLP
Chartered Accountants
Edmonton, Alberta

November 24, 2008

CONSOLIDATED BALANCE SHEETS

FOR THE YEAR ENDED OCTOBER 31
($ thousands)

		2008	2007
Assets			
Cash Resources			
Cash and non-interest bearing deposits with financial institutions		$ 8,988	$ 6,446
Deposits with regulated financial institutions	(Note 3)	464,193	405,122
Cheques and other items in transit		18,992	1,122
		492,173	412,690
Securities	(Note 4)		
Issued or guaranteed by Canada		347,777	630,396
Issued or guaranteed by a province or municipality		452,045	251,418
Other securities		429,142	459,812
		1,228,964	1,341,626
Securities Purchased Under Resale Agreements	(Note 5)	77,000	206,925
Loans	(Note 6)		
Residential mortgages		2,134,327	1,780,442
Other loans		6,565,280	5,688,160
		8,699,607	7,468,602
Allowance for credit losses	(Note 7)	(75,538)	(63,022)
		8,624,069	7,405,580
Other			
Land, buildings and equipment	(Note 8)	31,893	25,736
Goodwill	(Note 9)	6,933	6,933
Intangible assets	(Note 9)	2,155	2,681
Insurance related	(Note 10)	52,943	51,744
Derivative related	(Note 11)	9,980	1,496
Other assets	(Note 12)	74,622	69,629
		178,526	158,219
Total Assets		$ 10,600,732	$ 9,525,040
Liabilities and Shareholders' Equity			
Deposits	(Note 13)		
Payable on demand		$ 383,083	$ 376,488
Payable after notice		2,010,039	1,843,799
Payable on a fixed date		6,747,597	5,931,631
Deposit from Canadian Western Bank Capital Trust	(Note 14)	105,000	105,000
		9,245,719	8,256,918
Other			
Cheques and other items in transit		29,036	22,177
Insurance related	(Note 15)	134,769	124,480
Derivative related	(Note 11)	163	1,307
Other liabilities	(Note 16)	136,897	134,665
		300,865	282,629
Subordinated Debentures			
Conventional	(Note 17)	375,000	390,000
Shareholders' Equity			
Retained earnings		448,203	372,739
Accumulated other comprehensive income (loss)		(5,203)	(5,931)
Capital stock	(Note 18)	221,914	219,004
Contributed surplus		14,234	9,681
		679,148	595,493
Total Liabilities and Shareholders' Equity		$ 10,600,732	$ 9,525,040
Contingent Liabilities and Commitments	(Note 20)		

Jack C. Donald
Chairman

Larry M. Pollock
President and Chief Executive Officer

CONSOLIDATED STATEMENTS OF INCOME

FOR THE YEAR ENDED OCTOBER 31

($ thousands, except per share amounts)

		2008	2007
Interest Income			
Loans		$ 491,991	$ 439,668
Securities		52,929	45,590
Deposits with regulated financial institutions		17,847	13,677
		562,767	498,935
Interest Expense			
Deposits		317,554	275,840
Subordinated debentures		22,267	17,846
		339,821	293,686
Net Interest Income		222,946	205,249
Provision for Credit Losses	(Note 7)	12,000	10,200
Net Interest Income after Provision for Credit Losses		210,946	195,049
Other Income			
Credit related		26,998	22,426
Insurance, net	(Note 21)	15,866	15,263
Trust services		13,299	14,943
Retail services		7,689	7,290
Gains on sale of securities		4,725	438
Foreign exchange gains		1,225	2,159
Other		438	302
		70,240	62,821
Net Interest and Other Income		281,186	257,870
Non-Interest Expenses			
Salaries and employee benefits		87,660	76,506
Premises and equipment		22,360	20,239
Other expenses		23,145	22,780
Provincial capital taxes		2,001	2,409
		135,166	121,934
Net Income before Provision for Income Taxes		146,020	135,936
Provision for Income Taxes	(Note 24)	44,001	39,654
Net Income		$ 102,019	$ 96,282
Earnings Per Common Share	(Note 25)		
Basic		$ 1.61	$ 1.54
Diluted		1.58	1.50

CONSOLIDATED STATEMENTS OF CHANGES IN SHAREHOLDERS' EQUITY

FOR THE YEAR ENDED OCTOBER 31
($ thousands)

		2008	2007
Retained Earnings			
Balance at beginning of year	$	372,739	$ 297,675
Net income		102,019	96,282
Dividends		(26,555)	(21,218)
Balance at end of year		448,203	372,739
Accumulated Other Comprehensive Income (Loss)			
Balance at beginning of year		(5,931)	(1,494)
Other comprehensive income (loss)		728	(4,437)
Balance at end of year		(5,203)	(5,931)
Total retained earnings and accumulated other comprehensive income		443,000	366,808
Capital Stock	(Note 18)		
Balance at beginning of year		219,004	215,349
Issued on exercise of employee stock options		1,646	2,464
Transferred from contributed surplus on the exercise or exchange of options		1,264	1,191
Balance at end of year		221,914	219,004
Contributed Surplus			
Balance at beginning of year		9,681	6,340
Amortization of fair value of employee stock options	(Note 19)	5,817	4,532
Transferred to contributed surplus on the exercise or exchange of options		(1,264)	(1,191)
Balance at end of year		14,234	9,681
Total Shareholders' Equity	$	679,148	$ 595,493

CONSOLIDATED STATEMENTS OF COMPREHENSIVE INCOME

FOR THE YEAR ENDED OCTOBER 31
($ thousands)

		2008	2007
Net Income	$	102,019	$ 96,282
Other Comprehensive Income (Loss), net of tax			
Available-for-sale securities			
Losses from change in fair value[1]		(2,631)	(5,544)
Reclassification to other income[2]		(3,271)	(295)
		(5,902)	(5,839)
Derivatives designated as cash flow hedges			
Gains (losses) from change in fair value[3]		9,341	(403)
Reclassification to net interest income[4]		(1,773)	1,805
Reclassification to other liabilities for derivatives terminated prior to maturity[5]		(938)	—
		6,630	1,402
		728	(4,437)
Comprehensive Income for the Year	$	102,747	$ 91,845

(1) Net of income tax benefit of $1,170 (2007 – tax benefit of $2,720).
(2) Net of income tax benefit of $1,454 (2007 – tax benefit of $144).
(3) Net of income tax expense of $4,104 (2007 – tax benefit of $197).
(4) Net of income tax benefit of $775 (2007 – tax expense of $882).
(5) Net of income tax benefit of $429 (2007 – $nil).

CONSOLIDATED STATEMENTS OF CASH FLOW

FOR THE YEAR ENDED OCTOBER 31
($ thousands)

		2008	2007
Cash Flows from Operating Activities			
Net income		$ 102,019	$ 96,282
Adjustments to determine net cash flows:			
Provision for credit losses		12,000	10,200
Depreciation and amortization		6,896	6,017
Future income taxes, net		276	1,387
Gain on sale of securities, net		(4,725)	(438)
Accrued interest receivable and payable, net		2,719	13,287
Current income taxes payable, net		(454)	(1,777)
Amortization of fair value of employee stock options		5,817	4,532
Other items, net		(5,164)	13,183
		119,384	142,673
Cash Flows from Financing Activities			
Deposits, net		988,801	1,965,953
Debentures issued	(Note 17)	50,000	195,000
Debentures redeemed	(Note 17)	(65,000)	(3,126)
Common shares issued	(Note 18)	1,646	2,464
Dividends		(26,555)	(21,218)
		948,892	2,139,073
Cash Flows from Investing Activities			
Interest bearing deposits with regulated financial institutions, net		(57,057)	(55,550)
Securities, purchased		(2,609,432)	(2,860,204)
Securities, sales proceeds		1,303,698	960,350
Securities, matured		1,421,159	1,437,710
Securities purchased under resale agreements, net		129,925	(197,925)
Loans, net		(1,230,489)	(1,633,943)
Land, buildings and equipment		(12,527)	(7,012)
		(1,054,723)	(2,356,574)
Change in Cash and Cash Equivalents		13,553	(74,828)
Cash and Cash Equivalents at Beginning of Year		(14,609)	60,219
Cash and Cash Equivalents at End of Year *		$ (1,056)	$ (14,609)
***** Represented by:			
Cash and non-interest bearing deposits with financial institutions		$ 8,988	$ 6,446
Cheques and other items in transit (included in Cash Resources)		18,992	1,122
Cheques and other items in transit (included in Other Liabilities)		(29,036)	(22,177)
Cash and Cash Equivalents at End of Year		$ (1,056)	$ (14,609)
Supplemental Disclosure of Cash Flow Information			
Amount of interest paid in the year		$ 336,106	$ 267,963
Amount of income taxes paid in the year		44,179	40,044

NOTES TO CONSOLIDATED FINANCIAL STATEMENTS

OCTOBER 31, 2008

($ thousands, except per share amounts)

1. BASIS OF PRESENTATION

These consolidated financial statements of Canadian Western Bank (CWB or the Bank) have been prepared in accordance with subsection 308 (4) of the Bank Act, which states that, except as otherwise specified by the Office of the Superintendent of Financial Institutions Canada (OSFI), the financial statements are to be prepared in accordance with Canadian generally accepted accounting principles (GAAP). The significant accounting policies used in the preparation of these financial statements, including the accounting requirements of OSFI, are summarized below and in the following notes. These accounting policies conform, in all material respects, to Canadian GAAP.

The preparation of financial statements in conformity with Canadian GAAP requires management to make estimates and assumptions that affect the reported amounts of assets and liabilities and the disclosure of contingent assets and liabilities at the date of the financial statements as well as the reported amount of revenues and expenses during the year. Key areas of estimation where management has made subjective judgments, often as a result of matters that are inherently uncertain, include those relating to the allowance for credit losses, fair value of financial instruments, goodwill and intangible assets, provision for unpaid claims and adjustment expenses, future income tax asset and liability, other than temporary impairment of securities and fair value of employee stock options. Therefore, actual results could differ from these estimates.

a) Basis of Consolidation

The consolidated financial statements include the assets, liabilities and results of operations of the Bank and all of its subsidiaries, after the elimination of intercompany transactions and balances. Subsidiaries are defined as corporations whose operations are controlled by the Bank and are corporations in which the Bank is the beneficial owner. See Note 34 for details of the subsidiaries and affiliate.

b) Business Combinations

Business acquisitions are accounted for using the purchase method.

c) Translation of Foreign Currencies

Assets and liabilities denominated in foreign currencies are translated into Canadian dollars at rates prevailing at the balance sheet date. Revenues and expenses in foreign currencies are translated at the average exchange rates prevailing during the year. Realized and unrealized gains and losses on foreign currency positions are included in other income, except for unrealized foreign exchange gains and losses on available-for-sale securities that are included in other comprehensive income.

d) Specific Accounting Policies

To facilitate a better understanding of the Bank's consolidated financial statements, the significant accounting policies are disclosed in the notes, where applicable, with related financial disclosures by major caption:

Note	Topic
2	Financial instruments
3	Cash resources
4	Securities
5	Securities purchased under resale agreements and securities purchased under reverse resale agreements
6	Loans
7	Allowance for credit losses
8	Land, buildings and equipment
9	Goodwill and intangible assets
10	Insurance related other assets
11	Derivative financial instruments
12	Other assets
13	Deposits
14	Trust capital securities
15	Insurance related other liabilities
16	Other liabilities
17	Subordinated debentures
18	Capital stock
19	Share incentive plan
20	Contingent liabilities and commitments
21	Insurance operations
22	Disclosures on rate regulation
23	Employee future benefits
24	Income taxes

Note	Topic
25	Earnings per common share
26	Trust assets under administration
27	Related party transactions
28	Interest rate sensitivity
29	Fair value of financial instruments
30	Risk management
31	Capital management
32	Segmented information
33	Subsequent event
34	Subsidiaries and affiliate

e) **Change in Accounting Policies**

Effective November 1, 2007, the Bank adopted new accounting standards issued by the Canadian Institute of Chartered Accountants (CICA): *Financial Instruments – Disclosure and Presentation* and *Capital Disclosures.* The new standards require additional disclosures regarding financial instruments and capital management practices. As a result of adopting these standards, new or enhanced disclosure is provided in Note 2 Financial Instruments, Note 6 Loans and Note 31 Capital Management.

In addition, as permitted by the CICA, certain of the required disclosure is provided in the Management's Discussion and Analysis (MD&A). The relevant MD&A sections are identified by shading and shaded areas form an integral part of these audited consolidated financial statements.

f) **Future Accounting Changes**

International Financial Reporting Standards

The CICA will transition Canadian GAAP for publicly accountable entities to International Financial Reporting Standards (IFRS). The Bank's consolidated financial statements will be prepared in accordance with IFRS for the fiscal year commencing November 1, 2011.

The Bank has embarked on a project to identify and evaluate the impact of the implementation of IFRS on the consolidated financial statements and to develop a plan to complete the transition. The impact of the transition to IFRS on the Bank's consolidated financial statements is not yet determinable. Additional information on the Bank's transition plan and the expected impact of the transition will be provided commencing in the quarterly reports for 2009, the third fiscal year prior to transition.

2. FINANCIAL INSTRUMENTS

As a financial institution, most of the Bank's balance sheet is comprised of financial instruments and the majority of net income results from gains, losses, income and expenses related to the same.

Financial instrument assets include cash resources, securities, securities purchased under resale agreements, loans and derivative financial instruments. Financial instrument liabilities include deposits, securities purchased under reverse resale agreements, derivative financial instruments and subordinated debentures.

The use of financial instruments exposes the Bank to credit, liquidity and market risks. A discussion of how these are managed can be found in the Risk Management section of the 2008 Annual Report beginning on page 54.

Income and expenses are classified as to source, either securities or loans for income, and deposits or subordinated debentures for expense. Gains on the sale of securities, net, are shown separately in other income.

3. CASH RESOURCES

Cash resources have been designated as available-for-sale and are reported on the balance sheet at fair value with changes in fair value reported in other comprehensive income, net of income taxes.

Included in deposits with regulated financial institutions are available-for-sale financial instruments reported on the consolidated balance sheets at the fair value of $459,875 (2007 – $362,849), which is $940 higher (2007 – $1,070 lower) than amortized cost.

4. SECURITIES

Securities have been designated as available-for-sale, are accounted for at settlement date and reported on the balance sheet at fair value with changes in fair value reported in other comprehensive income, net of income taxes.

Securities are purchased with the original intention to hold the securities to maturity or until market conditions render alternative investments more attractive. If an impairment in value is other than temporary, any write-down to net realizable value is reported in the consolidated statements of income. Gains and losses realized on disposal of securities and adjustments to record any other than temporary impairment in value are included in other income. Amortization of premiums and discounts are reported in interest income from securities in the consolidated statements of income.

Securities designated as held-for-trading, which are purchased for resale over a short period of time, are carried at fair value. Gains and losses realized on disposal and adjustments to fair value are reported in other income in the consolidated statements of income in the period during which they occur. There were no securities designated as held-for-trading at any time during 2007 and 2008.

The analysis of securities at carrying value, by type and maturity, is as follows:

	Maturities				2008 Total Carrying Value	2007 Total Carrying Value
	Within 1 Year	Over 1 to 3 Years	Over 3 to 5 Years	Over 5 Years		
Securities issued or guaranteed by						
Canada	$ 246,395	$ 91,116	$ 10,266	$ –	$ 347,777	$ 630,396
A province or municipality	135,770	260,642	53,442	2,191	452,045	251,418
Other debt securities	59,745	62,471	35,464	11,027	168,707	236,255
Equity securities						
Preferred shares	43,352	49,023	137,684	26,173	256,232	221,878
Other equity	–	–	–	4,203[2]	4,203	1,679
Total[1]	$ 485,262	$ 463,252	$ 236,856	$ 43,594	$ 1,228,964	$ 1,341,626

(1) All securities have been designated as available-for-sale.
(2) Includes securities with no specific maturity.

The analysis of unrealized gains and losses on securities reflected on the balance sheet is as follows:

	2008				2007			
	Amortized Cost	Unrealized Gains	Unrealized Losses	Fair Value	Amortized Cost	Unrealized Gains	Unrealized Losses	Fair Value
Securities issued or guaranteed by								
Canada	$ 346,360	$ 1,417	$ –	$ 347,777	$ 630,270	$ 415	$ 289	$ 630,396
A province or municipality	450,831	1,442	228	452,045	251,432	260	274	251,418
Other debt securities	170,665	686	2,644	168,707	237,958	160	1,863	236,255
Equity securities								
Preferred shares	274,061	–	17,829	256,232	227,331	34	5,487	221,878
Other equity	5,802	49	1,648	4,203	2,850	–	1,171	1,679
Total	$ 1,247,719	$ 3,594	$ 22,349	$ 1,228,964	$ 1,349,841	$ 869	$ 9,084	$ 1,341,626

The securities portfolio is primarily comprised of high quality debt instruments and preferred shares that are not held for trading purposes and are typically held until maturity. Fluctuations in value are generally attributed to changes in interest rates, market spreads and shifts in the interest rate curve. Unrealized losses at year-end are considered to be temporary in nature.

5. **SECURITIES PURCHASED UNDER RESALE AGREEMENTS AND SECURITIES PURCHASED UNDER REVERSE RESALE AGREEMENTS**

Securities purchased under resale agreements represent a purchase of Government of Canada securities by the Bank effected with a simultaneous agreement to sell them back at a specified price on a future date, which is generally short term. The difference between the cost of the purchase and the predetermined proceeds to be received on a resale agreement is recorded as securities interest income.

Securities purchased under reverse resale agreements represent a sale of Government of Canada securities by the Bank effected with a simultaneous agreement to buy them back at a specified price on a future date, which is generally short term. The difference between the proceeds of the sale and the predetermined cost to be paid on a resale agreement is recorded as deposit interest expense. There were no reverse resale agreements outstanding at year-end.

Securities purchased under resale agreements have been designated as available-for-sale and are reported on the consolidated balance sheets at fair value with changes in fair value reported in other comprehensive income, net of income taxes.

Interest earned or paid is recorded in interest income or expense as earned.

6. LOANS

Loans are recorded at amortized cost and are stated net of unearned income, unamortized premiums and an allowance for credit losses (Note 7).

Interest income is recorded using the effective interest method, except for loans classified as impaired. Loans are determined to be impaired when payments are contractually past due 90 days, or where the Bank has taken realization proceedings, or where the Bank is of the opinion that the loan should be regarded as impaired. An exception may be made where management determines that the loan is well secured and in the process of collection and the collection efforts are reasonably expected to result in either repayment of the loan or restoring it to a current status within 180 days from the date the payment went in arrears. All loans are classified as impaired when a payment is 180 days in arrears other than loans guaranteed or insured for both principal and interest by the Canadian government, the provinces or a Canadian government agency. These loans are classified as impaired when payment is 365 days in arrears.

Impairment is measured as the difference between the carrying value of the loan at the time it is classified as impaired and the present value of the expected cash flows (estimated realizable amount), using the interest rate inherent in the loan at the date the loan is classified as impaired. When the amounts and timing of future cash flows cannot be reliably estimated, either the fair value of the security underlying the loan, net of any expected realization costs, or the current market price for the loan may be used to measure the estimated realizable amount. At the time a loan is classified as impaired, interest income will cease to be recognized in accordance with the loan agreement, and any uncollected but accrued interest will be added to the carrying value of the loan, together with any unamortized premiums, discounts or loan fees. Subsequent payments received on an impaired loan are recorded as a reduction of the recorded investment in the loan. Impaired loans are returned to performing status when the timely collection of both principal and interest is reasonably assured and all delinquent principal and interest payments are brought current and all charges for loan impairment have been reversed.

Loan fees, net of directly related costs, are amortized to interest income over the expected term of the loan. Premiums paid on the acquisition of loan portfolios are amortized to interest income over the expected term of the loans.

Outstanding gross loans and impaired loans, net of allowances for credit losses, are as follows:

| | 2008 | | | | 2007 | | | |
	Gross Amount	Gross Impaired Amount	Specific Allowance	Net Impaired Loans	Gross Amount	Gross Impaired Amount	Specific Allowance	Net Impaired Loans
Consumer and personal	$1,288,160	$ 11,462	$ 305	$ 11,157	$1,062,898	$ 2,878	$ 351	$ 2,527
Real estate[1][3]	3,673,158	51,909	2,948	48,961	2,887,822	1,098	896	202
Industrial	1,391,287	20,456	5,647	14,809	1,325,431	11,261	2,550	8,711
Commercial	2,347,002	7,809	6,111	1,698	2,192,451	5,867	3,617	2,250
Total	$8,699,607	$ 91,636	$ 15,011	76,625	$7,468,602	$ 21,104	$ 7,414	13,690
General allowance[2]				(60,527)				(55,608)
Net impaired loans after general allowance				$ 16,098				$ (41,918)

(1) Multi-family residential mortgages are presented as real estate loans in this table.
(2) The general allowance for credit risk is available for the total loan portfolio.
(3) Foreclosed real estate assets with a carrying value of $901 (2007 – $nil) are held for sale. Foreclosed real estate assets are generally liquidated quickly to repay the outstanding loan.

Outstanding impaired loans, net of allowance for credit losses, by provincial location of security, are as follows:

| | 2008 | | | 2007 | | |
	Gross Impaired Amount	Specific Allowance	Net Impaired Loans	Gross Impaired Amount	Specific Allowance	Net Impaired Loans
Alberta	$ 48,436	$ 9,204	$ 39,232	$ 9,163	$ 3,927	$ 5,236
British Columbia	40,656	4,626	36,030	8,864	2,013	6,851
Saskatchewan	2,155	792	1,363	3,061	1,458	1,603
Manitoba	389	389	–	16	16	–
Total	$ 91,636	$ 15,011	76,625	$ 21,104	$ 7,414	13,690
General allowance[1]			(60,527)			(55,608)
Net impaired loans after general allowance			$ 16,098			$ (41,918)

(1) The general allowance for credit risk is not allocated by province.

During the year, interest recognized as income on impaired loans totaled $360 (2007 – $414).

Gross impaired loans exclude certain past due loans, which are loans where payment of interest or principal is contractually in arrears but which are not classified as impaired. Details of such past due loans that have not been included in the gross impaired amount are as follows:

As at October 31, 2008	1 – 30 days		31 – 60 days		61 – 90 days		More than 90 days		Total
Residential mortgages	$ 7,217	$	8,550	$	347	$	–	$	16,114
Other loans	11,732		4,010		342		–		16,084
	$ 18,949	$	12,560	$	689	$	–	$	32,198

Certain process changes were required to compile the above information and comparative figures are not available.

7. ALLOWANCE FOR CREDIT LOSSES

An allowance for credit losses is maintained which, in the Bank's opinion, is adequate to absorb credit related losses in its loan portfolio. The adequacy of the allowance for credit losses is reviewed at least quarterly. The allowance for credit losses is deducted from the outstanding loan balance.

The allowance for credit losses consists of specific provisions and the general allowance for credit risk. Specific provisions include all the accumulated provisions for losses on identified impaired loans required to reduce the carrying value of those loans to their estimated realizable amount. The general allowance for credit risk includes provisions for losses inherent in the portfolio that are not presently identifiable by management of the Bank on an account-by-account basis. The general allowance for credit risk is established by taking into consideration historical trends in the loss experience during economic cycles, the current portfolio profile, estimated losses for the current phase of the economic cycle and historical experience in the industry.

Actual write-offs, net of recoveries, are deducted from the allowance for credit losses. The provision for credit losses in the consolidated statements of income is charged with an amount sufficient to keep the balance in the allowance for credit losses adequate to absorb all credit related losses.

The following table shows the changes in the allowance for credit losses during the year:

| | 2008 | | | | 2007 | | |
	Specific Allowance	General Allowance for Credit Losses	Total		Specific Allowance	General Allowance for Credit Losses	Total
Balance at beginning of year	$ 7,414	$ 55,608	$ 63,022	$	5,484	$ 48,037	$ 53,521
Provision for credit losses	7,081	4,919	12,000		2,629	7,571	10,200
Write-offs	(2,577)	–	(2,577)		(786)	–	(786)
Recoveries	3,093	–	3,093		87	–	87
Balance at end of year	$ 15,011	$ 60,527	$ 75,538	$	7,414	$ 55,608	$ 63,022

8. LAND, BUILDINGS AND EQUIPMENT

Land is carried at cost. Buildings, equipment and furniture, and leasehold improvements are carried at cost less accumulated depreciation and amortization. Depreciation and amortization are calculated primarily using the straight-line method over the estimated useful life of the asset, as follows: buildings – 20 years, equipment and furniture – three to five years, and leasehold improvements – term of the lease. Gains and losses on disposal are recorded in other income in the year of disposal. Land, building and equipment, if no longer in use or considered impaired, are written down to the fair value.

Operating leases primarily comprise branch and office premises and are not capitalized. Total costs, including free rent periods and step-rent increases, are expensed on a straight-line basis over the lease term.

	Cost	Accumulated Depreciation and Amortization	2008 Net Book Value	2007 Net Book Value
Land	$ 2,783	$ –	$ 2,783	$ 2,783
Buildings	5,337	3,090	2,247	1,669
Computer equipment	25,490	19,897	5,593	5,688
Office equipment and furniture	15,776	10,450	5,326	4,521
Leasehold improvements	28,165	12,221	15,944	11,075
Total	$ 77,551	$ 45,658	$ 31,893	$ 25,736

Depreciation and amortization for the year amounted to $6,370 (2007 – $5,474).

9. GOODWILL AND INTANGIBLE ASSETS

Goodwill is the excess of the purchase price paid for the acquisition of a subsidiary over the fair value of the net assets acquired, including identifiable intangible assets. Goodwill and other intangibles with an indefinite life are not amortized, but are subject to a fair value impairment test at least annually. Other intangibles with a finite life are amortized to the statement of income over their expected lives not exceeding 10 years. These intangible assets are tested for impairment whenever circumstances indicate that the carrying amount may not be recoverable. Any impairment of goodwill or other intangible assets will be charged to the consolidated statement of income in the period of impairment.

	Cost	Accumulated Amortization	2008 Net Book Value	2007 Net Book Value
Goodwill	$ 6,933	$ –	$ 6,933	$ 6,933
Identifiable intangible assets				
Customer relationships	3,950	2,115	1,835	2,305
Trademark	300	–	300	300
Others	330	310	20	76
	4,580	2,425	2,155	2,681
Total	$ 11,513	$ 2,425	$ 9,088	$ 9,614

Amortization of customer relationships and other intangible assets for the year amounted to $526 (2007 – $543). The trademark has an indefinite life and is not subject to amortization. Goodwill includes $3,679 related to the banking and trust segment and $3,254 related to the insurance segment. There were no writedowns of goodwill or intangible assets due to impairment.

10. INSURANCE RELATED OTHER ASSETS

	2008	2007
Instalment premiums receivable	$ 24,333	$ 22,803
Reinsurers' share of unpaid claims and adjustment expenses	11,561	10,915
Deferred policy acquisition costs	8,924	8,626
Recoverable on unpaid claims	6,939	7,257
Due from reinsurers	1,186	2,143
Total	$ 52,943	$ 51,744

11. DERIVATIVE FINANCIAL INSTRUMENTS

Interest rate, foreign exchange and equity contracts such as futures, options, swaps, floors and rate locks are entered into for risk management purposes in accordance with the Bank's asset liability management policies. It is the Bank's policy not to utilize derivative financial instruments for trading or speculative purposes. Interest rate swaps and floors are primarily used to reduce the impact of fluctuating interest rates. Equity contracts are used to economically offset the return paid to depositors on certain deposit products that are linked to a stock index. Foreign exchange contracts are only used for the purposes of meeting needs of clients or day-to-day business.

The Bank designates certain derivative financial instruments as either a hedge of the fair value of recognized assets or liabilities or firm commitments (fair value hedges), or a hedge of highly probable future cash flows attributable to a recognized asset or liability or a forecasted transaction (cash flow hedges). The Bank has designated all interest rate swaps as cash flow hedges. On an ongoing basis, the Bank assesses whether the derivatives that are used in hedging transactions are effective in offsetting changes in fair values or cash flows of the hedged items.

Certain derivatives embedded in other financial instruments, such as the return on fixed term deposits that are linked to a stock index, are treated as separate derivatives when their economic characteristics and risks are not closely related to those of the host contract and the combined contract is not carried at fair value. Embedded derivatives identified in contracts entered into after November 1, 2002 have been separated from the host contract and are recorded at fair value.

Interest income received or interest expense paid on derivative financial instruments is accounted for on the accrual basis and recognized as interest income or expense, as appropriate, over the term of the hedge contract. Premiums on purchased contracts are amortized to interest expense over the term of the contract. Accrued interest receivable and payable and deferred gains and losses for these contracts are recorded in other assets or liabilities as appropriate. Realized and unrealized gains or losses associated with derivative instruments, which have been terminated or cease to be effective prior to maturity, are deferred under other assets or other liabilities, as appropriate, and amortized into income over the original hedged period. In the event a designated hedged item is terminated or eliminated prior to the termination of the related derivative instrument, any realized or unrealized gain or loss on such derivative instrument is recognized in other income.

Derivative financial instruments are recorded on the balance sheet at fair value as either other assets or other liabilities with changes in fair value related to the effective portion of cash flow interest rate hedges recorded in other comprehensive income, net of income taxes. Changes in fair value related to the ineffective portion of cash flow hedges and all other derivative financial instruments are reported in other income on the consolidated statement of income.

The Bank enters into derivative financial instruments for risk management purposes. Derivative financial instruments are financial contracts whose value is derived from an underlying interest rate, foreign exchange rate, equity or commodity instrument or index.

Derivative financial instruments primarily used by the Bank include:

· interest rate swaps, which are agreements where two counterparties exchange a series of payments based on different interest rates applied to a notional amount;

· equity swap contracts, which are agreements where one counterparty agrees to pay or receive from the other cash flows based on changes in the value of an equity index as well as a designated interest rate applied to a notional amount; and

· foreign exchange forwards and futures, which are contractual obligations to exchange one currency for another at a specified price for settlement at a predetermined future date.

Interest rate swaps and other instruments are used as hedging devices to control interest rate risk. The Bank enters into these interest rate derivative instruments only for its own account and does not act as an intermediary in this market. The credit risk is limited to the amount of any adverse change in interest rates applied on the notional contract amount should the counterparty default. Equity contracts are used to offset the return paid to depositors on certain deposit products where the return is linked to a stock index. The credit risk is limited to the average return on an equity index, applied on the notional contract amount should the counterparty default. The principal amounts are not exchanged and, hence, are not at risk. The Asset Liability Committee (ALCO) of the Bank establishes and monitors approved counterparties (including an assessment of credit worthiness) and maximum notional limits. Approved counterparties are limited to rated financial institutions or their associated parent/affiliate with a minimum rating of A high or equivalent.

Foreign exchange transactions are undertaken only for the purposes of meeting the needs of clients and of day-to-day business. Foreign exchange markets are not speculated in by taking a trading position in currencies. Maximum exposure limits are established and monitored by ALCO and are defined by allowable unhedged amounts. The position is managed within the allowable target range by spot and forward transactions or other hedging techniques. Exposure to foreign exchange risk is not material to the Bank's overall financial position.

The following table summarizes the derivative financial instrument portfolio and the related credit risk. Notional amounts represent the amount to which a rate or price is applied in order to calculate the exchange of cash flows. The notional amounts are not recorded on the consolidated balance sheets. They represent the volume of outstanding transactions and do not represent the potential gain or loss associated with the market risk or credit risk of such instruments. The replacement cost represents the cost of replacing, at current market rates, all contracts with a positive fair value. The future credit exposure represents the potential for future changes in value and is based on a formula prescribed by OSFI. The credit risk equivalent is the sum of the future credit exposure and the replacement cost. The risk-weighted balance represents the credit risk equivalent weighted according to the credit worthiness of the counterparty as prescribed by OSFI. Additional discussion of OSFI's capital adequacy requirements is provided on page 42 of Management's Discussion and Analysis.

	2008					2007				
	Notional Amount	Replace-ment Cost	Future Credit Exposure	Credit Risk Equivalent	Risk-Weighted Balance	Notional Amount	Replace-ment Cost	Future Credit Exposure	Credit Risk Equivalent	Risk-Weighted Balance
Interest rate swaps	$ 593,000	$ 9,978	$ 1,825	$ 11,803	$ 2,361	$ 482,000	$ 946	$ 1,010	$ 1,956	$ 391
Equity contracts	4,400	–	304	304	61	6,000	515	480	995	199
Foreign exchange contracts	2,600	2	26	28	14	3,405	35	34	68	14
Total	$ 600,000	$ 9,980	$ 2,155	$ 12,135	$ 2,436	$ 491,405	$ 1,496	$ 1,524	$ 3,019	$ 604

The following table shows the derivative financial instruments split between those contracts that have a positive fair value (favourable contracts) and those that have a negative fair value (unfavourable contracts).

	2008				2007			
	Favourable Contracts		Unfavourable Contracts		Favourable Contracts		Unfavourable Contracts	
	Notional Amount	Fair Value	Notional Amount	Fair Value	Notional Amount	Fair Value	Notional Amount	Fair Value
Interest rate swaps	$ 593,000	$ 9,978	$ –	$ –	$ 273,000	$ 946	$ 209,000	$ (498)
Equity contracts	–	–	4,400	(139)	6,000	515	–	–
Foreign exchange contracts	1,300	2	1,300	(175)	2,594	35	811	(63)
Embedded derivatives in equity linked deposits	n/a	151	n/a	–	n/a	–	n/a	(746)
Other forecasted transactions	–	–	–	–	–	–	–	–
Total	$ 594,300	$ 10,131	$ 5,700	$ (314)	$ 281,594	$ 1,496	$ 209,811	$ (1,307)

The aggregate contractual or notional amount of the derivative financial instruments on hand, the extent to which instruments are favourable or unfavourable and, thus, the aggregate fair values of these financial assets and liabilities can fluctuate significantly from time to time. The average fair values of the derivative financial instruments on hand during the year are set out in the following table.

	2008	2007
Favourable derivative financial instruments (assets)	$ 4,094	$ 867
Unfavourable derivative financial instruments (liabilities)	$ 322	$ 1,124

The following table summarizes maturities of derivative financial instruments and weighted average interest rates paid and received on contracts.

	2008				2007			
	Maturity				Maturity			
	1 Year or Less		More than 1 Year		1 Year or Less		More than 1 Year	
	Notional Amount	Contractual Interest Rate	Notional Amount	Contractual Interest Rate	Notional Amount	Contractual Interest Rate	Notional Amount	Contractual Interest Rate
Interest Rate Contracts								
Interest rate swaps – receive fixed amounts[1]	$ 228,000	2.98%	$ 365,000	2.89%	$ 394,000	4.82%	$ 88,000	4.83%
Equity Contracts[2]	2,400		2,000		1,600		4,400	
Foreign Exchange Contracts[3]	2,600		–		3,405		–	
Total	$ 233,000		$ 367,000		$ 399,005		$ 92,400	

(1) The Bank pays floating interest amounts based on the one-month (30-day) Canadian Bankers' Acceptance rate. Interest rate swaps mature between December 2008 and January 2013.
(2) The Bank receives amounts based on the specified equity index and pays amounts based on the one-month (30-day) Canadian Bankers' Acceptance rate. Equity contracts mature between February 2009 and March 2011.
(3) The contractual interest rate is not meaningful for foreign exchange contracts. Foreign exchange contracts mature between January 2009 and May 2009.

During the year, a net unrealized after tax gain of $9,341 (2007 – $403 after tax loss) was recorded in other comprehensive income for changes in fair value of the effective portion of derivatives designated as cash flow hedges and $nil (2007 – $nil) was recorded in other income for changes in fair value of the ineffective portion of derivatives classified as cash flow hedges. Amounts accumulated in other comprehensive income are reclassified to net income in the same period that interest on certain floating rate loans (i.e. the hedged items) affect income. A net gain after tax of $1,773 (2007 – $1,805 net loss after tax) was reclassified to net income. During the year, $938 after tax (2007 – $nil) was reclassified to other liabilities for derivatives terminated prior to maturity and the deferred balance will be amortized into net income over the original hedged period. A net gain of $2,432 (2007 – $68 net loss) after tax recorded in accumulated other comprehensive income (loss) as at October 31 is expected to be reclassified to net income in the next 12 months and will offset variable cash flows from floating rate loans.

There were no forecasted transactions that failed to occur.

12. OTHER ASSETS

		2008	2007
Accrued interest receivable		$ 40,241	$ 39,245
Future income tax asset	(Note 24)	16,142	16,944
Financing costs[1]		4,636	4,667
Accounts receivable		6,004	3,550
Prepaid expenses		3,520	2,589
Taxes receivable		1,259	–
Other		2,820	2,634
Total		$ 74,622	$ 69,629

(1) Amortization for the year amounted to $1,037 (2007 – $839).

13. DEPOSITS

Deposits are accounted for on an amortized cost basis. Costs relating to the issuance of fixed term deposits are amortized over the expected life of the deposit using the effective interest method.

	Individuals	Business and Government	Financial Institutions	2008 Total
Payable on demand	$ 16,071	$ 367,012	$ –	$ 383,083
Payable after notice	732,630	1,277,409	–	2,010,039
Payable on a fixed date	4,601,439	2,136,158	10,000	6,747,597
Deposit from CWB Capital Trust[1]	–	105,000	–	105,000
Total	$ 5,350,140	$ 3,885,579	$ 10,000	$ 9,245,719

	Individuals	Business and Government	Financial Institutions	2007 Total
Payable on demand	$ 15,873	$ 360,615	$ –	$ 376,488
Payable after notice	788,199	1,055,600	–	1,843,799
Payable on a fixed date	3,909,616	2,012,015	10,000	5,931,631
Deposit from CWB Capital Trust[1]	–	105,000	–	105,000
Total	$ 4,713,688	$ 3,533,230	$ 10,000	$ 8,256,918

(1) The senior deposit note of $105 million from CWB Capital Trust is reflected as a Business and Government deposit payable on a fixed date. This senior deposit note bears interest at an annual rate of 6.199% until December 31, 2016 and, thereafter, at the CDOR 180-day Bankers' Acceptance rate plus 2.55%. This note is redeemable at the Bank's option, in whole or in part, on and after December 31, 2011, or earlier in certain specified circumstances, both subject to the approval of OSFI. Each one thousand dollars of WesTS principal is convertible at any time into 40 non-cumulative redeemable CWB First Preferred Shares Series 1 of the Bank at the option of CWB Capital Trust. CWB Capital Trust will exercise this conversion right in circumstances in which holders of CWB Capital Trust Capital Securities Series 1 (WesTS) exercise their holder exchange rights. See Note 14 for more information on WesTS and CWB Capital Trust.

14. TRUST CAPITAL SECURITIES

In 2006, the Bank arranged for the issuance of innovative capital instruments, CWB Capital Trust Capital Securities Series 1 (WesTS), through Canadian Western Bank Capital Trust (CWB Capital Trust), a special purpose entity. CWB Capital Trust, an open-end trust, issued non-voting WesTS and the proceeds were used to purchase a senior deposit note from CWB.

Canadian Institute of Chartered Accountants (CICA) Accounting Guideline (AcG-15) provides a framework for identifying Variable Interest Entities ("VIEs") and requires the consolidation of a VIE if the Bank is the primary beneficiary of the VIE. The only special purpose entity in which the Bank participates is CWB Capital Trust. Although CWB owns the unit holder's equity and voting control of CWB Capital Trust through Special Trust Securities, the Bank is not exposed to the majority of any CWB Capital Trust losses and is, therefore, not the primary beneficiary under AcG-15. Accordingly, CWB does not consolidate CWB Capital Trust and the WesTS issued by CWB Capital Trust are not reported on the consolidated balance sheets, but the senior deposit note is reported in deposits (see Note 13) and interest expense is recognized on the senior deposit note.

Holders of WesTS are eligible to receive semi-annual non-cumulative fixed cash distributions. No cash distributions will be payable by CWB Capital Trust on WesTS if CWB fails to declare regular dividends on its preferred shares or, if no preferred shares are outstanding, on its common shares. In this case, the net distributable funds of CWB Capital Trust will be distributed to the Bank as holder of the residual interest in CWB Capital Trust.

Should CWB Capital Trust fail to pay the semi-annual distributions in full, CWB has contractually agreed not to declare dividends of any kind on any of the preferred or common shares for a specified period of time.

The following information presents the outstanding WesTS:

Issuance date	August 31, 2006
Distribution dates	June 30, December 31
Annual yield	6.199%
Earliest date redeemable at the option of the issuer	December 31, 2011
Earliest date exchangeable at the option of the holder	Anytime
Trust capital securities outstanding	105,000
Principal amount	$105,000

The significant terms and conditions of the WesTS are

1) Subject to the approval of OSFI, CWB Capital Trust may, in whole (but not in part), on the redemption date specified above, and on any distribution date thereafter, redeem the WesTS without the consent of the holders.

2) Subject to the approval of OSFI, upon occurrence of a special event as defined, prior to the redemption date specified above, CWB Capital Trust may redeem all, but not part, of the WesTS without the consent of the holders.

3) The WesTS may be redeemed for cash equivalent to (i) the early redemption price if the redemption occurs prior to December 31, 2016 or (ii) the redemption price if the redemption occurs on or after December 31, 2016. Redemption price refers to an amount equal to one thousand dollars plus the unpaid distributions to the redemption date. Early redemption price refers to an amount equal to the greater of (i) the redemption price and (ii) the price calculated to provide an annual yield, equal to the yield on a Government of Canada bond issued on the redemption date with a maturity date of December 31, 2016, plus 0.50%.

4) Holders of WesTS may, at any time, exchange each one thousand dollars of principal for 40 First Preferred Shares Series 1 of the Bank. CWB's First Preferred Shares Series 1 pay semi-annual non-cumulative cash dividends with an annual yield of 4.00% and will be redeemable at the option of the Bank, with OSFI approval, on or after December 31, 2011, but not at the option of the holders. This exchange right will be effected through the conversion by CWB Capital Trust of the corresponding amount of the deposit note of the Bank. The WesTS exchanged for the Bank's First Preferred Shares Series 1 will be cancelled by CWB Capital Trust.

5) Each WesTS will be exchanged automatically without the consent of the holders for 40 non-cumulative redeemable CWB First Preferred Shares Series 2 upon occurrence of any one of the following events: (i) proceedings are commenced for the winding up of the Bank, (ii) OSFI takes control of the Bank, (iii) the Bank has a Tier 1 capital ratio of less than 5% or Total capital ratio of less than 8%, or (iv) OSFI has directed the Bank to increase its capital or provide additional liquidity and the Bank elects such automatic exchange or the Bank fails to comply with such direction. Following the occurrence of an automatic exchange, the Bank would hold all of the Special Trust Securities and all of the WesTS, and the primary asset of CWB Capital Trust would continue to be the senior deposit note. The Bank's First Preferred Shares Series 2 pay semi-annual non-cumulative cash dividends with an annual yield of 5.25% and will be redeemable at the option of the Bank, with OSFI approval, on or after December 31, 2011, but not at the option of the holders.

6) For regulatory capital purposes, WesTS are included in Tier 1 capital to a maximum of 15% of net Tier 1 capital with the remainder included in Tier 2 capital. All of the outstanding WesTS amount are currently included in Tier 1 capital.

7) The non-cumulative cash distribution on the WesTS will be 6.199% paid semi-annually until December 31, 2016 and, thereafter, at CDOR 180-day Bankers' Acceptance rate plus 2.55%.

15. **INSURANCE RELATED OTHER LIABILITIES**

	2008	2007
Unpaid claims and adjustment expenses	$ 76,176	$ 68,561
Unearned premiums	56,799	54,537
Due to insurance companies and policyholders	987	558
Unearned reinsurance commissions	807	824
Total	$ 134,769	$ 124,480

16. OTHER LIABILITIES

		2008		2007
Accrued interest payable	$	101,584	$	97,869
Accounts payable		24,895		26,265
Taxes payable		5,260		4,455
Deferred revenue		2,485		2,570
Leasehold inducements		1,373		1,588
Future income tax liability (Note 24)		1,300		1,550
Other		–		368
Total	$	136,897	$	134,665

17. SUBORDINATED DEBENTURES

Financing costs relating to the issuance of subordinated debentures are amortized over the expected life of the related subordinated debenture using the effective interest method.

Each of the following qualifies as a bank debenture under the Bank Act and is subordinate in right of payment to all deposit liabilities. All redemptions are subject to the approval of OSFI.

Interest Rate	Maturity Date	Earliest Date Redeemable by CWB at Par		2008		2007
5.550%[1]	November 19, 2014	November 20, 2009	$	60,000	$	60,000
5.426%[2]	November 21, 2015	November 22, 2010		70,000		70,000
5.070%[3]	March 21, 2017	March 22, 2012		120,000		120,000
5.571%[4]	March 21, 2022	March 22, 2017		75,000		75,000
5.950%[5]	June 27, 2018	June 27, 2013		50,000		–
5.660%[6]	July 7, 2013	July 8, 2008		–		30,000
5.960%[6]	October 24, 2013	October 25, 2008		–		35,000
			$	375,000	$	390,000

(1) These conventional debentures have a 10-year term with a fixed interest rate for the first five years. Thereafter, the interest rate will be reset quarterly at the Canadian dollar CDOR 90-day Bankers' Acceptance rate plus 160 basis points.

(2) These conventional debentures have a 10-year term with a fixed interest rate for the first five years. Thereafter, the interest rate will be reset quarterly at the Canadian dollar CDOR 90-day Bankers' Acceptance rate plus 180 basis points.

(3) These conventional debentures have a 10-year term with a fixed interest rate for the first five years. Thereafter, the interest rate will be reset quarterly at the Canadian dollar CDOR 90-day Bankers' Acceptance rate plus 155 basis points. Of the $125,000 debentures issued, $5,000 were acquired by Canadian Direct Insurance Incorporated, a wholly owned subsidiary, and have been eliminated on consolidation.

(4) These conventional debentures have a 15-year term with a fixed interest rate for the first 10 years. Thereafter, the interest rate will be reset quarterly at the Canadian dollar CDOR 90-day Bankers' Acceptance rate plus 180 basis points.

(5) These conventional debentures have a 10-year term with a fixed interest rate for the first five years. Thereafter, the interest rate will be reset quarterly at the Canadian dollar CDOR 90-day Bankers' Acceptance rate plus 302 basis points.

(6) These conventional debentures had a 10-year term with a fixed interest rate for the first five years and were redeemed by the Bank at face value on July 8 and October 25, 2008, respectively.

18. CAPITAL STOCK

Authorized:

An unlimited number of common shares without nominal or par value;

33,964,324 class A shares without nominal or par value; and

25,000,000 first preferred shares without nominal or par value, issuable in series, of which 4,200,000 first preferred shares Series 1 and 4,200,000 first preferred shares Series 2 have been reserved (see Note 14).

Issued and fully paid:

	2008		2007	
	Number of Shares	Amount	Number of Shares	Amount
Common Shares				
Outstanding at beginning of year	62,836,189 $	219,004	61,936,260 $	215,349
Issued on exercise or exchange of options	620,953	1,646	899,929	2,464
Transferred from contributed surplus on exercise or exchange of options	–	1,264	–	1,191
Outstanding at end of year	63,457,142 $	221,914	62,836,189 $	219,004

The Bank is prohibited by the Bank Act from declaring any dividends on common shares when the Bank is or would be placed, as a result of the declaration, in contravention of the capital adequacy and liquidity regulations or any regulatory directives issued under the Act. In addition, should CWB Capital Trust fail to pay the semi-annual distributions in full on the CWB Capital Trust Securities Series 1 (see Note 14), the Bank has contractually agreed to not declare dividends on any of its common and preferred shares for a specified period of time. These limitations do not restrict the current level of dividends.

19. SHARE INCENTIVE PLAN

The fair value based method has been adopted to account for stock options granted to employees on or after November 1, 2002. The estimated fair value is recognized over the applicable vesting period as an increase to both salary expense and contributed surplus. In accordance with GAAP, no expense is recognized for options granted prior to November 1, 2002. When options are exercised, the proceeds received and the applicable amount, if any, in contributed surplus are credited to capital stock.

The Bank has authorized 5,505,404 common shares (2007 – 5,176,357) for issuance under the share incentive plan. Of the amount authorized, options exercisable into 5,204,882 shares (2007 – 4,911,277) are issued and outstanding. The options generally vest within three years and are exercisable at a fixed price equal to the average of the market price on the day of and the four days preceding the grant date. All options expire within eight years of date of grant. Outstanding options expire on dates ranging from December 2008 to September 2013.

The details of, and changes in, the issued and outstanding options follow:

	2008		2007	
	Number of Options	Weighted Average Exercise Price	Number of Options	Weighted Average Exercise Price
Options				
Balance at beginning of year	4,911,277 $	16.96	5,030,040 $	13.07
Granted	1,249,032	28.39	1,118,000	25.49
Exercised or exchanged	(838,177)	8.98	(1,122,863)	7.61
Forfeited	(117,250)	24.26	(113,900)	20.98
Balance at end of year	5,204,882 $	20.83	4,911,277 $	16.96
Exercisable at end of year	1,870,500 $	13.10	1,656,077 $	9.30

Further details relating to stock options outstanding and exercisable follow:

Range of Exercise Prices	Options Outstanding				Options Exercisable		
	Number of Options	Weighted Average Remaining Contractual Life (years)		Weighted Average Exercise Price	Number of Options		Weighted Average Exercise Price
$10.00 to $10.84	863,800	0.7	$	10.08	863,800	$	10.08
$11.18 to $17.58	1,052,700	1.8		15.77	1,006,700		15.69
$19.16 to $21.46	1,068,290	3.1		21.45	–		–
$22.29 to $26.38	1,640,500	3.8		25.68	–		–
$28.11 to $31.18	579,592	4.1		31.15	–		–
Total	5,204,882	2.8	$	20.83	1,870,500	$	13.10

The terms of the share incentive plan allow the holders of vested options a cashless settlement alternative whereby the option holder can either (a) elect to receive shares by delivering cash to the Bank in the amount of the option exercise price or (b) elect to receive the number of shares equivalent to the excess of the market value of the shares under option, determined at the exercise date, over the exercise price. Of the 838,177 (2007 – 1,122,863) options exercised or exchanged, option holders exchanged the rights to 651,727 (2007 – 796,213) options and received 434,503 (2007 – 572,777) shares in return under the cashless settlement alternative.

Salary expense of $5,817 (2007 – $4,532) was recognized relating to the estimated fair value of options granted since November 1, 2002. The fair value of options granted was estimated using a binomial option pricing model with the following variables and assumptions: (i) risk-free interest rate of 3.8% (2007 – 4.2%), (ii) expected option life of 4.0 (2007 – 4.0) years, (iii) expected volatility of 23% (2007 – 19%), and (iv) expected dividends of 1.49% (2007 – 1.31%). The weighted average fair value of options granted was estimated at $5.84 (2007 – $4.94) per share.

During the year, $1,264 (2007 – $1,191) was transferred from contributed surplus to share capital, representing the estimated fair value recognized for 804,177 (2007 – 795,863) options granted after November 1, 2002 and exercised during the year.

20. CONTINGENT LIABILITIES AND COMMITMENTS

a) Credit Instruments

In the normal course of business, the Bank enters into various commitments and has contingent liabilities which are not reflected in the consolidated balance sheets. These items are reported below and are expressed in terms of the contractual amount of the related commitment.

	2008		2007
Credit Instruments			
Guarantees and standby letters of credit	$ 232,649	$	202,194
Commitments to extend credit	3,190,420		2,367,215
Total	$ 3,423,069	$	2,569,409

Guarantees and standby letters of credit represent the Bank's obligation to make payments to third parties when a customer is unable to make required payments or meet other contractual obligations. These instruments carry the same credit risk, recourse and collateral security requirements as loans extended to customers and generally have a term that does not exceed one year. Losses, if any, resulting from these transactions are not expected to be material.

Commitments to extend credit to customers also arise in the normal course of business and include undrawn availability under lines of credit and commercial operating loans of $931,957 (2007 – $800,301) and recently authorized but unfunded loan commitments of $2,258,463 (2007 – $1,566,915). In the majority of instances, availability of undrawn commercial commitments is subject to the borrower meeting specified financial tests or other covenants regarding completion or satisfaction of certain conditions precedent. It is also usual practice to include the right to review and withhold funding in the event of a material adverse change in the financial condition of the borrower. From a liquidity perspective, undrawn credit authorizations will be funded over time, with draws in many cases extending over a period of months. In some instances, authorizations are never advanced or may be reduced because of changing requirements. Revolving credit authorizations are subject to repayment which, on a pooled basis, also decreases liquidity risk.

b) Lease Commitments

The Bank has obligations under long-term non-cancellable operating leases for the rental of premises. Minimum future lease commitments for each of the five succeeding years and thereafter are as follows:

2009	$	8,036
2010		7,931
2011		7,678
2012		7,355
2013		7,334
2014 and thereafter		28,873
Total	$	67,207

c) Guarantees

A guarantee is defined as a contract that contingently requires the guarantor to make payments to a third party based on i) changes in an underlying economic characteristic that is related to an asset, liability or equity security of the guaranteed party, ii) failure of another party to perform under an obligating agreement, or iii) failure of another third party to pay indebtedness when due.

Significant guarantees provided to third parties include guarantees and standby letters of credit as discussed above.

In the ordinary course of business, the Bank enters into contractual arrangements under which the Bank may agree to indemnify the other party. Under these agreements, the Bank may be required to compensate counterparties for costs incurred as a result of various contingencies, such as changes in laws and regulations and litigation claims. A maximum potential liability cannot be identified as the terms of these arrangements vary and generally no predetermined amounts or limits are identified. The likelihood of occurrence of contingent events that would trigger payment under these arrangements is either remote or difficult to predict and, in the past, payments under these arrangements have been insignificant.

The Bank issues personal and business credit cards through an agreement with a third party card issuer. The Bank has indemnified the card issuer from loss if there is a default on the issuer's collection of the business credit card balances. The Bank has provided no indemnification relating to the personal or reward credit card balances. The issuance of business credit cards and establishment of business credit card limits are approved by the Bank and subject to the same credit assessment, approval and monitoring as the extension of direct loans. At year-end, the total approved business credit card limit was $11,503 (2007 – $9,728), and the balance outstanding was $2,778 (2007 – $2,238).

No amounts are reflected in the consolidated financial statements related to these guarantees and indemnifications.

d) Legal Proceedings

In the ordinary course of business, the Bank and its subsidiaries are party to legal proceedings. Based on current knowledge, the Bank does not expect the outcome of any of these proceedings to have a material effect on the consolidated financial position or results of operations.

21. INSURANCE OPERATIONS

Premiums Earned and Deferred Policy Acquisition Costs

Insurance premiums are included in other income on a daily pro rata basis over the terms of the underlying insurance policies. Unearned premiums represent the portion of premiums written that relate to the unexpired term of the policies in force and are included in other liabilities.

Policy acquisition costs are those expenses incurred in the acquisition of insurance business. Acquisition costs comprise advertising and marketing expenses, insurance advisor salaries and benefits, premium taxes and other expenses directly attributable to the production of business. Policy acquisition costs related to unearned premiums are only deferred, and included in other assets, to the extent that they are expected to be recovered from unearned premiums and are amortized to income over the periods in which the premiums are earned. If the unearned premiums are not sufficient to pay expected claims and expenses (including policy maintenance expenses and unamortized policy acquisition costs), a premium deficiency is said to exist. Anticipated investment income is considered in determining whether a premium deficiency exists. Premium deficiencies are recognized by writing down the deferred policy acquisition cost asset.

Unpaid Claims and Adjustment Expenses

The provision for unpaid claims represents the amounts needed to provide for the estimated ultimate expected cost of settling claims related to insured events (both reported and unreported) that have occurred on or before each balance sheet date. The provision for adjustment expenses represents the estimated ultimate expected costs of investigating, resolving and processing these claims. These provisions are included in other liabilities and their computation takes into account the time value of money using discount rates based on projected investment income from the assets supporting the provisions.

All provisions are periodically reviewed and evaluated in light of emerging claims experience and changing circumstances. The resulting changes in estimates of the ultimate liability are recorded as incurred claims in the current period.

Reinsurance Ceded
Earned premiums and claims expenses are recorded net of amounts ceded to, and recoverable from, reinsurers. Estimates of amounts recoverable from reinsurers on unpaid claims and adjustment expenses are recorded in other assets and are estimated in a manner consistent with the liabilities associated with the reinsured policies.

a) **Insurance Revenues, Net**
Insurance revenues, net reported in other income on the consolidated statements of income is presented net of claims, adjustment expenses and policy acquisition costs.

	2008	2007
Net earned premiums	$ 97,943	$ 94,914
Commissions and processing fees	2,876	2,751
Net claims and adjustment expenses	(64,380)	(62,391)
Policy acquisition costs	(20,573)	(20,011)
Insurance revenues, net	$ 15,866	$ 15,263

b) **Unpaid Claims and Adjustment Expenses**

(i) Nature of Unpaid Claims
The establishment of the provision for unpaid claims and adjustment expenses and the related reinsurers' share is based on known facts and interpretation of circumstances and is, therefore, a complex and dynamic process influenced by a large variety of factors. These factors include experience with similar cases and historical trends involving claim payment patterns, loss payments, pending levels of unpaid claims, product mix or concentration, claims severity, and claims frequency patterns.

Other factors include the continually evolving and changing regulatory and legal environment, actuarial studies, professional experience and expertise of the claims department personnel and independent adjusters retained to handle individual claims, quality of the data used for projection purposes, existing claims management practices, including claims handling and settlement practices, effect of inflationary trends on future claims settlement costs, investment rates of return, court decisions, economic conditions and public attitudes. In addition, time can be a critical part of the provision determination since, the longer the span between the incidence of a loss and the payment or settlement of the claim, the more variable the ultimate settlement amount can be. Accordingly, short-tailed claims, such as property claims, tend to be more reasonably predictable than long-tailed claims, such as liability claims.

Consequently, the establishment of the provision for unpaid claims and adjustment expenses relies on the judgment and opinions of a large number of individuals, on historical precedent and trends, on prevailing legal, economic, social and regulatory trends and on expectations as to future developments. The process of determining the provisions necessarily involves risks that the actual results will deviate, perhaps substantially, from the best estimates made.

(ii) Provision for Unpaid Claims and Adjustment Expenses
An annual evaluation of the adequacy of unpaid claims is completed at the end of each financial year. This evaluation includes a re-estimation of the liability for unpaid claims relating to each preceding financial year compared to the liability that was originally established. The results of this comparison and the changes in the provision for unpaid claims and adjustment expenses follow:

	2008	2007
Unpaid claims and adjustment expenses, net, beginning of year	$ 50,389	$ 40,561
Claims incurred		
In the current year	67,457	62,406
In prior periods	(3,077)	(15)
Claims paid during the year	(57,093)	(52,563)
Unpaid claims and adjustment expenses, net, end of year	57,676	50,389
Reinsurers' share of unpaid claims and adjustment expenses	11,561	10,915
Recoverable on unpaid claims	6,939	7,257
Unpaid claims and adjustment expenses, net, end of year	$ 76,176	$ 68,561

The provision for unpaid claims and adjustment expenses and related reinsurance recoveries are discounted using rates based on the projected investment income from the assets supporting the provisions, and reflecting the estimated timing of payments and recoveries. The investment rate of return used for all cash flow periods and all lines of business was 4.1% (2007 – 4.3%). However, that rate was reduced by a 1% (2007 – 1%) provision for adverse deviation in discounting the provision for unpaid claims and adjustment expenses and related reinsurance recoveries. The impact of this provision for adverse deviation results in an increase of $850 (2007 – $821) in unpaid claims and adjustment expenses and related reinsurance recoveries.

Policy balances, included in insurance related other assets and other liabilities, analyzed by major lines of business are as follows:

	2008		2007	
	Automobile	Home	Automobile	Home
Unpaid claims and adjustment expenses	$ 64,181	$ 11,995	$ 59,379	$ 9,182
Reinsurers' share of unpaid claims and adjustment expenses	11,561	–	10,904	11
Unearned premiums	40,886	15,913	40,741	13,796

c) Underwriting Policy and Reinsurance Ceded

Reinsurance contracts with coverage up to maximum policy limits are entered into to protect against losses in excess of certain amounts that may arise from automobile, personal property and liability claims.

Reinsurance with a limit of $180,000 (2007 – $180,000) is obtained to protect against certain catastrophic losses. Retention on catastrophic events and property and liability risks is generally $1,000 (2007 – $1,000). Retentions are further reduced by quota share reinsurance and, for the British Columbia automobile insurance product, by the underlying mandatory coverage provided by the provincially governed Crown corporation. Due to the geographic concentration of the business, management believes earthquakes and windstorms are its most significant exposure to catastrophic losses. Utilizing sophisticated computer modelling techniques developed by independent consultants to quantify the estimated exposure to such losses, management believes there is sufficient catastrophe reinsurance protection.

There was no quota share agreement in effect for the past two years. The previous quota share agreement, ceding 10% of gross retention, expired October 31, 2006.

At October 31, 2008, $11,561 (2007 – $10,915) of unpaid claims and adjustment expenses were recorded as recoverable from reinsurers. Failure of a reinsurer to honour its obligation could result in losses. The financial condition of reinsurers is regularly evaluated to minimize the exposure to significant losses from reinsurer insolvency.

The amounts shown in other income are net of the following amounts relating to reinsurance ceded to other insurance companies:

	2008	2007
Premiums earned reduced by	$ 6,849	$ 7,057
Claims incurred reduced by	2,987	1,466

22. DISCLOSURES ON RATE REGULATION

Canadian Direct Insurance Incorporated (Canadian Direct), a wholly owned subsidiary, is licensed under insurance legislation in the provinces in which it conducts business. Automobile insurance is a compulsory product and is subject to different regulations across the provinces in Canada, including those with respect to rate setting. Rate setting mechanisms vary across the provinces, but they generally fall under three categories: "use and file", "file and use" and "file and approve". Under "use and file", rates are filed following use. Under "file and use", insurers file their rates with the relevant authorities and wait for a prescribed period of time and then implement the proposed rates. Under "file and approve", insurers must wait for specific approval of filed rates before they may be used.

The authorities that regulate automobile insurance rates, in the provinces in which Canadian Direct is writing that business, are listed below. Automobile direct written premiums in these provinces totaled $71,300 in 2008 (2007 – $71,700) and represented 100% (2007 – 100%) of direct automobile premiums written.

Province	Rate Filing	Regulatory Authority
Alberta	File and approve or File and use	Alberta Automobile Insurance Rate Board
British Columbia	File and use	British Columbia Utilities Commission

Relevant regulatory authorities may, in some circumstances, require retroactive rate adjustments, which could result in a regulatory asset or liability. At October 31, 2008, there was no regulatory asset or liability.

23. EMPLOYEE FUTURE BENEFITS

All employee future benefits are accounted for on an accrual basis. The Bank's contributions to the group retirement savings plan and employee share purchase plan totaled $6,183 (2007 – $4,876).

24. INCOME TAXES

The Bank follows the asset and liability method of accounting for income taxes whereby current income taxes are recognized for the estimated income taxes payable for the current year. Future tax assets and liabilities represent the cumulative amount of tax applicable to temporary differences between the carrying amount of the assets and liabilities, and their values for tax purposes. Future tax assets and liabilities are measured using enacted or substantively enacted tax rates expected to apply to taxable income in the years in which those temporary differences are expected to be recovered or settled. Changes in future income taxes related to a change in tax rates are recognized in income in the period of the tax rate change. All future income tax assets are expected to be realized in the normal course of operations.

The provision for income taxes consists of the following:

	2008	2007
Consolidated statements of income		
Current	$ 43,725	$ 38,267
Future	276	1,387
	44,001	39,654
Shareholders' equity		
Future income tax expense related to:		
Unrealized losses on available-for-sale securities	(2,624)	(2,864)
Gains on derivatives designated as cash flow hedges	2,900	685
	276	(2,179)
Total	$ 44,277	$ 37,475

A reconciliation of the statutory tax rates and income tax that would be payable at these rates to the effective income tax rates and provision for income taxes that is reported in the consolidated statements of income follows:

	2008		2007	
Combined Canadian federal and provincial income taxes				
and statutory tax rate	$ 44,536	30.5%	$ 44,832	33.0%
Increase (decrease) arising from:				
Tax-exempt income	(3,579)	(2.5)	(4,124)	(3.0)
Stock-based compensation	1,774	1.2	1,486	1.1
Future federal and provincial tax rate reductions[1]	999	0.7	–	–
Income tax recovery	–	–	(3,495)	(2.6)
Other	271	0.2	955	0.7
Provision for income taxes and effective tax rate	$ 44,001	30.1%	$ 39,654	29.2%

(1) Future federal and provincial tax rate reductions represent the revaluation of future income tax assets to reflect corporate income tax rate reductions enacted for accounting purposes.

Future income tax balances are comprised of the following:

	2008	2007
Net future income tax assets		
Allowance for credit losses	$ 16,103	$ 16,235
Other temporary differences	39	709
	$ 16,142	$ 16,944
Net future income tax liabilities		
Intangible assets	$ 742	$ 923
Allowance for credit losses	(845)	(729)
Other temporary differences	1,403	1,356
	$ 1,300	$ 1,550

The Bank has approximately $11,140 (2007 – $11,140) of capital losses that are available to apply against future capital gains and have no expiry date. The tax benefit of these losses has not been recognized in the consolidated financial statements.

25. EARNINGS PER COMMON SHARE

Basic earnings per common share is calculated based on the average number of common shares outstanding during the year. Diluted earnings per share is calculated based on the treasury stock method, which assumes that any proceeds from the exercise of in-the-money stock options would be used to purchase the Bank's common shares at the average market price during the year.

The calculation of earnings per common share follows:

	2008	2007
Numerator		
Net income - basic and diluted	$ 102,019	$ 96,282
Denominator		
Weighted average of common shares outstanding - basic	63,214,117	62,354,101
Dilutive instruments:		
Employee stock options[1]	1,227,017	1,897,449
Weighted average number of common shares outstanding - diluted	64,441,134	64,251,550
Earnings per Common Share		
Basic	$ 1.61	$ 1.54
Diluted	1.58	1.50

(1) At October 31, the denominator excludes 3,334,382 (2007 – 365,000) employee stock options with an average adjusted exercise price of $27.45 (2007 – $31.38) where the exercise price, adjusted for unrecognized stock-based compensation, is greater than the average market price.

26. TRUST ASSETS UNDER ADMINISTRATION

Trust assets under administration of $4,347,723 (2007 – $4,283,900) represent the fair value of assets held for personal and corporate clients, administered by subsidiaries, and are kept separate from the subsidiaries' own assets. Trust assets under administration are not reflected in the consolidated balance sheets and relate to the banking and trust segment.

27. RELATED PARTY TRANSACTIONS

The Bank makes loans, primarily residential mortgages, to its officers and employees at various preferred rates and terms. The total amount outstanding for these types of loans is $64,836 (2007 – $56,045). The Bank offers deposits, primarily fixed term deposits to its officers, employees and their immediate family at preferred rates. The total amount outstanding for these types of deposits is $127,219 (2007 – $102,776).

28. INTEREST RATE SENSITIVITY

The Bank is exposed to interest rate risk as a result of a difference, or gap, between the maturity or repricing behaviour of interest sensitive assets and liabilities. The interest rate gap is managed by forecasting core balance trends. The repricing profile of these assets and liabilities has been incorporated in the table following showing the gap position at October 31 for select time intervals. Figures in brackets represent an excess of liabilities over assets or a negative gap position.

ASSET LIABILITY GAP POSITIONS
($ millions)

October 31, 2008	Floating Rate and Within 1 Month	1 to 3 Months	3 Months to 1 Year	Total Within 1 Year	1 Year to 5 Years	More than 5 Years	Non-Interest Sensitive	Total
Assets								
Cash resources and securities	$ 176	$ 220	$ 339	$ 735	$ 921	$ 46	$ 18	$ 1,720
Loans	4,964	484	774	6,222	2,461	95	(77)	8,701
Other assets	–	–	–	–	–	–	179	179
Derivative financial instruments[1]	–	80	150	230	367	–	–	597
Total	5,140	784	1,263	7,187	3,749	141	120	11,197
Liabilities and Equity								
Deposits	3,472	883	1,967	6,322	2,832	105	(14)	9,245
Other liabilities	3	6	25	34	33	9	225	301
Debentures	–	–	–	–	300	75	–	375
Shareholders' equity	–	–	–	–	–	–	679	679
Derivative financial instruments[1]	597	–	–	597	–	–	–	597
Total	4,072	889	1,992	6,953	3,165	189	890	11,197
Interest Rate Sensitive Gap	$ 1,068	$ (105)	$ (729)	$ 234	$ 584	$ (48)	$ (770)	$ –
Cumulative Gap	$ 1,068	$ 963	$ 234	$ 234	$ 818	$ 770	$ –	$ –
Cumulative Gap as a Percentage of Total Assets	9.5%	8.6%	2.1%	2.1%	7.3%	6.9%	–	–
October 31, 2007								
Total assets	$ 4,377	$ 552	$ 1,868	$ 6,797	$ 2,921	$ 195	$ 100	$ 10,013
Total liabilities and equity	4,013	692	1,666	6,371	2,638	194	810	10,013
Interest Rate Sensitive Gap	$ 364	$ (140)	$ 202	$ 426	$ 283	$ 1	$ (710)	$ –
Cumulative Gap	$ 364	$ 224	$ 426	$ 426	$ 709	$ 710	$ –	$ –
Cumulative Gap as a Percentage of Total Assets	3.6%	2.2%	4.3%	4.3%	7.1%	7.1%	–	–

(1) Derivative financial instruments are included in this table at the notional amount.
(2) Accrued interest is excluded in calculating interest sensitive assets and liabilities.
(3) Potential prepayments of fixed rate loans and early redemption of redeemable fixed term deposits have not been estimated. Redemptions of fixed term deposits where depositors have this option are not expected to be material. The majority of fixed rate loans, mortgages and leases are either closed or carry prepayment penalties.

The effective, weighted average interest rates for each class of financial asset and liability are shown below.

WEIGHTED AVERAGE EFFECTIVE INTEREST RATES
(%)

October 31, 2008	Floating Rate and Within 1 Month	1 to 3 Months	3 Months to 1 Year	Total Within 1 Year	1 Year to 5 Years	More than 5 Years	Total
Assets							
Cash resources and securities	2.7%	3.0%	3.2%	3.0%	4.4%	5.8%	3.8%
Loans	4.8	4.7	6.2	5.0	6.1	5.9	5.3
Derivative financial instruments	–	4.1	3.7	3.8	3.5	–	3.6
Total	4.7	4.2	5.1	4.8	5.4	5.8	5.0
Liabilities							
Deposits	2.1	3.6	4.0	2.9	4.2	6.4	3.3
Debentures	–	–	–	–	5.4	5.6	5.4
Derivative financial instruments	2.9	–	–	2.9	–	–	2.9
Total	2.2	3.6	4.0	2.9	4.2	5.7	3.4
Interest Rate Sensitive Gap	2.5%	0.6%	1.1%	1.9%	1.2%	0.1%	1.6%
October 31, 2007							
Total assets	6.6%	5.2%	5.2%	6.1%	5.9%	5.7%	6.0%
Total liabilities	3.9	4.4	4.3	4.1	4.2	5.6	4.1
Interest Rate Sensitive Gap	2.7%	0.8%	0.9%	2.0%	1.7%	0.1%	1.9%

Based on the current interest rate gap position, it is estimated that a one-percentage point increase in all interest rates would increase net interest income by approximately 4.8% (2007 – 2.5%) and decrease other comprehensive income by $19,982, net of tax. A one-percentage point decrease in all interest rates would decrease net interest income and increase other comprehensive income by a similar amount. Information on the estimated change in other comprehensive income at October 2007 is not readily available.

29. FAIR VALUE OF FINANCIAL INSTRUMENTS

The fair value of a financial instrument on initial recognition is the value of the consideration given or received. Subsequent to initial recognition, financial instruments measured at fair value that are quoted in active markets are based on bid prices for financial assets and offer prices for financial liabilities. For certain securities and derivative financial instruments where an active market does not exist, fair values are determined using valuation techniques that refer to observable market data, including discounted cash flow analysis, option pricing models and other valuation techniques commonly used by market participants. The fair value of financial assets recorded on the consolidated balance sheets at fair value (cash, securities, securities purchased under resale agreements and derivatives) was determined using published market prices quoted in active markets for 92% (2007 – 87%) of the portfolio and estimated using a valuation technique based on observable market data for 8% (2007 – 13%) of the portfolio. The fair value of liabilities recorded on the consolidated balance sheets at fair value (derivatives) was determined using a valuation technique based on observable market data.

Fair value represents the estimated consideration that would be agreed upon in a current transaction between knowledgeable, willing parties who are under no compulsion to act. The fair value of a financial instrument on initial recognition is normally the transaction price (i.e. the value of the consideration given or received). Subsequent to initial recognition, financial instruments measured at fair value on the consolidated balance sheets that are quoted in active markets are based on bid prices for financial assets and offer prices for financial liabilities. For certain securities and derivative financial instruments where an active market does not exist, fair values are determined using valuation techniques that refer to observable market data, including discounted cash flow analysis, option pricing models and other valuation techniques commonly used by market participants.

Several of the Bank's significant financial instruments, such as loans and deposits, lack an available trading market as they are not typically exchanged. Therefore, these instruments have been valued assuming they will not be sold, using present value or other suitable techniques and are not necessarily representative of the amounts realizable in an immediate settlement of the instrument.

Changes in interest rates are the main cause of changes in the fair value of the Bank's financial instruments. The carrying value of loans, deposits and subordinated debentures are not adjusted to reflect increases or decreases in fair value due to interest rate changes as the Bank's intention is to realize their value over time by holding them to maturity.

The table below sets out the fair values of financial instruments (including certain derivatives) using the valuation methods and assumptions referred to below the table. The table does not include assets and liabilities that are not considered financial instruments.

	2008			2007		
	Book Value	Fair Value	Fair Value Over (Under) Book Value	Book Value	Fair Value	Fair Value Over (Under) Book Value
Assets						
Cash resources (Note 3)	$ 492,173	$ 492,173	$ –	$ 412,690	$ 412,690	$ –
Securities (Note 4)	1,228,964	1,228,964	–	1,341,626	1,341,626	–
Securities purchased under resale agreements	77,000	77,000	–	206,925	206,925	–
Loans[1]	8,700,672	8,635,811	(64,861)	7,406,733	7,325,340	(81,393)
Other assets[2]	82,782	82,782	–	77,573	77,573	–
Derivative related	9,980	9,980	–	1,496	1,496	–
Liabilities						
Deposits[1]	9,258,776	9,247,017	(11,759)	8,256,918	8,219,463	(37,455)
Other liabilities[3]	232,678	232,678	–	215,798	215,798	–
Subordinated debentures	375,000	387,774	12,774	390,000	386,690	(3,310)
Derivative related	163	163	–	1,307	1,307	–

(1) Loans and deposits exclude deferred premiums and deferred revenue, which are not financial instruments.
(2) Other assets exclude land, buildings and equipment, goodwill and other intangible assets, reinsurers' share of unpaid claims and adjustment expenses, future income tax asset, prepaid and deferred expenses, financing costs and other items that are not financial instruments.
(3) Other liabilities exclude future income tax liability, deferred revenue, unearned insurance premiums and other items that are not financial instruments.
(4) For further information on interest rates associated with financial assets and liabilities, including derivative instruments, refer to Note 28.

The methods and assumptions used to estimate the fair values of financial instruments are as follows:

· cash resources and securities are reported on the consolidated balance sheets at the fair value disclosed in Notes 3 and 4. These values are based on quoted market prices, if available. Where a quoted market price is not readily available, other valuation techniques are based on observable market rates used to estimate fair value;

· loans reflect changes in the general level of interest rates that have occurred since the loans were originated and are net of the allowance for credit losses. For floating rate loans, fair value is assumed to be equal to book value as the interest rates on these loans automatically reprice to market. For all other loans, fair value is estimated by discounting the expected future cash flows of these loans at current market rates for loans with similar terms and risks;

· other assets and other liabilities, with the exception of derivative financial instruments, are assumed to approximate their carrying value, due to their short-term nature;

· for derivative financial instruments where an active market does not exist, fair values are determined using valuation techniques that refer to observable market data, including discounted cash flow analysis, option pricing models and other valuation techniques commonly used by market participants;

· deposits with no stated maturity are assumed to be equal to their carrying values. The estimated fair values of fixed rate deposits are determined by discounting the contractual cash flows at current market rates for deposits of similar terms; and

· the fair values of subordinated debentures are determined by reference to current market prices for debt with similar terms and risks.

Fair values are based on management's best estimates based on market conditions and pricing policies at a certain point in time. The estimates are subjective and involve particular assumptions and matters of judgment and, as such, may not be reflective of future fair values.

30. RISK MANAGEMENT

As part of the Bank's risk management practices, the risks that are significant to the business are identified, monitored and controlled. The most significant risks include credit risk, liquidity risk, market risk, insurance risk, operational risk and litigation risk. The nature of these risks and how they are managed is provided in the commentary on pages 54 to 57 of the MD&A.

As permitted by the CICA, certain of the risk management disclosure related to risks inherent with financial instruments is in the Management Discussion & Analysis (MD&A). The relevant MD&A sections are identified by shading and the shaded areas form an integral part of these audited consolidated financial statements.

Information on specific measures of risk, including the allowance for credit losses, derivative financial instruments, interest rate sensitivity, fair value of financial instruments and liability for unpaid claims are included elsewhere in these notes to the consolidated financial statements.

31. CAPITAL MANAGEMENT

OSFI requires banks to measure capital adequacy in accordance with instructions for determining risk-adjusted capital and risk-weighted assets, including off-balance sheet commitments. Based on the deemed credit risk of each type of asset, a weighting of 0% to 150% is assigned. As an example, a loan that is fully insured by the Canada Mortgage and Housing Corporation (CMHC) is applied a risk weighting of 0% as the Bank's risk of loss is nil, while uninsured commercial loans are assigned a risk weighting of 100% to reflect the higher level of risk associated with this type of asset. The ratio of regulatory capital to risk-weighted assets is calculated and compared to OSFI's standards for Canadian financial institutions. Off-balance sheet assets, such as the notional amount of derivatives and some credit commitments, are included in the calculation of risk-weighted assets and both the credit risk equivalent and the risk-weight calculations are prescribed by OSFI. As Canadian Direct is subject to separate OSFI capital requirements specific to insurance companies, the Bank's investment in CDI is deducted from total capital and CDI's assets are excluded from the calculation of risk-weighted assets.

Current regulatory guidelines require banks to maintain a minimum ratio of capital to risk-weighted assets and off-balance sheet items of 8%, of which 4% must be core capital (Tier 1) and the remainder supplementary capital (Tier 2). However, OSFI has established that Canadian banks need to maintain a minimum total capital adequacy ratio of 10% with a Tier 1 ratio of not less than 7%. CWB's Tier 1 capital is comprised of common shareholders' equity and innovative capital (to a regulatory maximum of 15% of net Tier 1 capital), while Tier 2 capital includes subordinated debentures (to the regulatory maximum amount of 50% of net Tier 1 capital), the inclusion of the general allowance for credit losses (to the regulatory maximum) and any innovative capital not included in Tier 1.

Capital funds are managed in accordance with policies and plans that are regularly reviewed and approved by the Board of Directors and take into account forecasted capital needs and markets. The goal is to maintain adequate regulatory capital to be considered well capitalized, protect customer deposits and provide capacity for internally generated growth and strategic opportunities that do not otherwise require accessing the public capital markets, all while providing a satisfactory return for shareholders.

The Bank has a share incentive plan that is provided to officers and employees who are in a position to materially impact the longer term financial success of the Bank as measured by share price appreciation and dividend yield. Note 19 to the consolidated financial statements details the number of shares under options outstanding, the weighted average exercise price and the amounts exercisable at year-end.

Basel II Capital Adequacy Accord

Effective November 1, 2007, the Office of the Superintendent of Financial Institutions (OSFI) required Canadian financial institutions to manage and report regulatory capital in accordance with a new capital management framework, commonly called Basel II. Basel II introduced several significant changes to the risk-weighting of assets and the calculation of regulatory capital. The Bank has implemented the standardized approach to calculating risk-weighted assets for both credit and operational risk. Changes for CWB under Basel II include a reclassification into lower risk-weight categories for residential mortgages and loans to small- to medium-sized enterprises, as well as a new capital requirement related to operational risk.

Basel II had a modest positive impact on the overall required level of regulatory capital for CWB. New procedures and system enhancements were developed to conform to the new framework, including the formalization of internal capital adequacy assessment processes.

During the year, the Bank complied with all internal and external capital requirements.

CAPITAL STRUCTURE AND REGULATORY RATIOS AT YEAR-END

($ thousands)

	2008[1]	2007
Tier 1 Capital		
Retained earnings	$ 448,203	$ 372,739
Accumulated other comprehensive income, net of tax[2]	(6,973)	(1,741)
Capital stock	221,914	219,004
Contributed surplus	14,234	9,681
Innovative capital instrument[3]	105,000	105,000
Less goodwill of subsidiaries[7]	(6,933)	(3,679)
Total	775,445	701,004
Tier 2 Capital		
General allowance for credit losses (Tier A)[4]	60,527	55,627
Subordinated debentures (Tier B)[5]	380,000	350,502
Total	440,527	406,129
Less investment in insurance subsidiary	(47,700)	(47,864)
Total Regulatory Capital	$ 1,168,272	$ 1,059,269
Regulatory Capital to Risk-Weighted Assets		
Tier 1 capital	8.9%	9.1%
Tier 2 capital	5.1%	5.3%
Less investment in insurance subsidiary	(0.5)%	(0.7)%
Total Regulatory Capital Adequacy Ratio	13.5%	13.7%
Assets to Regulatory Capital Multiple[6]	9.2	9.1

(1) Regulatory capital and capital ratios are calculated in accordance with the requirements of the Office of the Superintendent of Financial Institutions. Beginning in 2008, capital is managed and reported in accordance with the requirements of the Basel II Capital Adequacy Accord (Basel II). Prior year ratios have been calculated using the previous framework.
(2) Accumulated other comprehensive income related to unrealized losses on certain available-for-sale equity securities, net of tax, reduces Tier 1 capital.
(3) Innovative capital may be included in Tier 1 capital to a maximum of 15% of net Tier 1 capital. Any excess innovative capital outstanding is included in Tier 2B capital.
(4) Banks are allowed to include their general allowance for credit losses up to a prescribed percentage of risk-weighted assets in Tier 2A capital. At October 31, 2008, the Bank's general allowance represented 0.70% (2007 – 0.72%) of risk-weighted assets.
(5) Tier 2B capital may be included in Tier 2 capital to a maximum of 50% of net Tier 1 capital. Any excess Tier 2B capital is included in capital as net Tier 1 capital increases. At October 31, 2008, $nil (2007 – $44,498) of subordinated debentures exceed the Tier 2B threshold and are available for inclusion in the future.
(6) Total assets plus off-balance sheet credit instruments, such as letters of credit and guarantees, less goodwill divided by regulatory capital.
(7) Beginning in 2008 with Basel II, goodwill related to the Bank's trust and insurance subsidiaries is deducted from Tier 1 capital. Prior to 2008, goodwill related to the insurance subsidiary was deducted from total capital.

32. SEGMENTED INFORMATION

The Bank operates principally in two industry segments – banking and trust, and insurance. These two segments differ in products and services but are both within the same geographic region.

The banking and trust segment provides services to personal clients and small- to medium-sized commercial business clients primarily in Western Canada. The insurance segment provides home and automobile insurance to individuals in Alberta and British Columbia.

	Banking and Trust		Insurance		Total	
	2008	2007	2008	2007	2008	2007
Net interest income (teb)[1]	$ 222,837	$ 205,867	$ 5,780	$ 4,792	$ 228,617	$ 210,659
Less teb adjustment	5,191	5,023	480	387	5,671	5,410
Net interest income per financial statements	217,646	200,844	5,300	4,405	222,946	205,249
Other income[2]	54,338	47,506	15,902	15,315	70,240	62,821
Total revenues	271,984	248,350	21,202	19,720	293,186	268,070
Provision for credit losses	12,000	10,200	–	–	12,000	10,200
Non-interest expenses[3]	125,748	113,456	9,418	8,478	135,166	121,934
Provision for income taxes	40,589	36,185	3,412	3,469	44,001	39,654
Net Income[5]	$ 93,647	$ 88,509	$ 8,372	$ 7,773	$ 102,019	$ 96,282
Total Average Assets ($ millions)[4]	$ 9,747	$ 8,014	$ 184	$ 164	$ 9,931	$ 8,178

(1) Taxable Equivalent Basis (teb) - Most banks analyze revenue on a taxable equivalent basis to permit uniform measurement and comparison of net interest income. Net interest income (as presented in the consolidated statements of income) includes tax-exempt income on certain securities. Since this income is not taxable, the rate of interest or dividends received is significantly lower than would apply to a loan or security of the same amount. The adjustment to taxable equivalent basis increases interest income and the provision for income taxes to what they would have been had the tax-exempt securities been taxed at the statutory rate. The taxable equivalent basis does not have a standardized meaning prescribed by GAAP and, therefore, may not be comparable to similar measures presented by other banks.
(2) Other income for the insurance segment is presented net of claims, adjustment costs and policy acquisition costs (see Note 21) and also includes the gain on the sale of securities.
(3) Amortization of intangible assets of $276 (2007 – $293) is included in the banking and trust segment and $250 (2007 – $250) in the insurance segment. Amortization of land, buildings and equipment total $5,040 (2007 – $4,365) for the banking and trust segment and $1,330 (2007 – $1,109) for the insurance segment while additions amounted to $10,552 (2007 – $6,010) for the banking and trust segment and $1,975 (2007 – $1,002) for the insurance segment. Goodwill of $3,679 (2007 – $3,679) is allocated to the banking and trust segment and $3,254 (2007 – $3,254) to the insurance segment.
(4) Assets are disclosed on an average daily balance basis as this measure is most relevant to a financial institution and is the measure reviewed by management.
(5) Transactions between the segments are reported at the exchange amount, which approximates fair market value.

33. SUBSEQUENT EVENT

On December 1, 2008, the Bank acquired 72.5% ownership of Adroit Investment Management Ltd. with an effective date of November 1, 2008. Adroit Investment Management Ltd. is an Edmonton, Alberta based firm specializing in wealth management for individuals, corporations and institutional clients.

34. SUBSIDIARIES AND AFFILIATE

CANADIAN WESTERN BANK SUBSIDIARIES[1]
(annexed in accordance with subsection 308(3) of the Bank Act)
OCTOBER 31, 2008

	Address of Head Office	Carrying Value of Voting Shares Owned by the Bank[2]
Canadian Direct Insurance Incorporated	Suite 600, 750 Cambie Street Vancouver, British Columbia	$ 50,820
Canadian Western Trust Company	Suite 2300, 10303 Jasper Avenue Edmonton, Alberta	45,879
Valiant Trust Company	Suite 310, 606 4th St. S.W. Calgary, Alberta	13,982
Canadian Western Financial Ltd.	Suite 2300, 10303 Jasper Avenue Edmonton, Alberta	1,334
Canadian Western Bank Capital Trust[3]	Suite 2300, 10303 Jasper Avenue Edmonton, Alberta	1,000

(1) The Bank owns 100% of the voting shares of each entity.
(2) The carrying value of voting shares is stated at the Bank's equity in the subsidiaries.
(3) In accordance with accounting standards, this entity is not consolidated as the Bank is not the primary beneficiary.

ANNUAL REPORT
For the Year Ended December 31, 2008

Auditors' Report

To the Shareholders of Sun-Rype Products Ltd.

We have audited the balance sheets of Sun-Rype Products Ltd. as at December 31, 2008 and 2007 and the statements of operations, comprehensive income, retained earnings and cash flows for the years then ended. These financial statements are the responsibility of the Company's management. Our responsibility is to express an opinion on these financial statements based on our audits.

We conducted our audits in accordance with Canadian generally accepted auditing standards. Those standards require that we plan and perform an audit to obtain reasonable assurance whether the financial statements are free of material misstatement. An audit includes examining, on a test basis, evidence supporting the amounts and disclosures in the financial statements. An audit also includes assessing the accounting principles used and significant estimates made by management, as well as evaluating the overall financial statement presentation.

In our opinion, these financial statements present fairly, in all material respects, the financial position of the Company as at December 31, 2008 and 2007 and the results of its operations and its cash flows for the years then ended in accordance with Canadian generally accepted accounting principles.

Deloitte & Touche LLP

Chartered Accountants
Vancouver, British Columbia
February 23, 2009

Sun-Rype Products Ltd.
Balance Sheets
As at December 31
(in thousands of dollars)

	2008	2007
Assets		
Current		
Cash	$ 625	$ 2,687
Accounts receivable	11,830	7,392
Unrealized foreign exchange gain on derivatives	718	-
Income taxes recoverable	6,987	818
Inventories (note 3)	27,778	17,304
Prepaid expenses	554	381
Future income taxes (note 4)	-	435
	48,492	29,017
Property, plant and equipment (note 5)	25,130	27,867
	$ 73,622	$ 56,884
Liabilities and Shareholders' Equity		
Current		
Bank operating loan (note 6)	$ 12,554	$ -
Promissory note payable (note 7)	400	500
Accounts payable and accrued liabilities	15,229	12,688
Unrealized foreign exchange loss on derivatives	-	460
Future income taxes (note 4)	11	-
Current portion, obligation under capital leases (note 8)	97	-
Current portion, long-term obligations (note 9)	220	321
Current portion, long-term debt (note 10)	1,500	-
	30,011	13,969
Obligation under capital leases (note 8)	395	-
Long-term obligations (note 9)	145	744
Long-term debt (note 10)	12,750	-
Future income taxes (note 4)	1,343	1,148
	44,644	15,861
Shareholders' equity		
Share capital and contributed surplus (note 11)	18,698	18,698
Retained earnings	10,280	22,325
	28,978	41,023
	$ 73,622	$ 56,884

Commitments, guarantees and contingencies (note 16)

Approved by the Board of Directors

_____
D. Selman, Director

_____
D. Souter, Director

See accompanying notes to financial statements

Sun-Rype Products Ltd.
Statements of Operations and Comprehensive Income
For the years ended December 31
(in thousands of dollars, except per share amounts)

	2008	2007
Net sales (note 12)	$ 125,368	$ 135,134
Cost of sales (note 13)	111,277	93,298
Gross profit	14,091	41,836
Expenses		
Selling, general, and administrative	29,053	28,538
Amortization	2,288	4,186
Interest	879	148
Loss on disposal of property, plant and equipment	-	213
Foreign exchange loss	-	1,977
	32,220	35,062
Earnings (loss) before income taxes	(18,129)	6,774
Income taxes (note 4)	(6,456)	2,138
Net earnings (loss) and comprehensive income (loss)	$ (11,673)	$ 4,636
Earnings (loss) per share		
Basic and diluted	$ (1.08)	$ 0.43

See accompanying notes to financial statements

Sun-Rype Products Ltd.
Statements of Retained Earnings
For the years ended December 31
(in thousands of dollars)

	2008	2007
Retained earnings, beginning of year, as previously reported	$ 22,325	$ 19,310
Adoption of new accounting standards (note 2)	61	-
Retained earnings, beginning of year, as restated	22,386	19,310
Net earnings (loss)	(11,673)	4,636
Dividends paid	(433)	(1,621)
Retained earnings, end of year	$ 10,280	$ 22,325

See accompanying notes to financial statements

Sun-Rype Products Ltd.
Statements of Cash Flows
For the years ended December 31
(in thousands of dollars)

	2008	2007
Cash provided by (used in):		
Operating activities		
Net earnings (loss)	$ (11,673)	$ 4,636
Non-cash items:		
Deferred compensation (recovery)	(241)	168
Amortization	4,470	4,186
Loss on disposal of property, plant and equipment	-	213
Unrealized foreign exchange loss (gain)	(1,294)	784
Future income taxes	609	(310)
	(8,129)	9,677
Changes in non-cash working capital items (note 15)	(18,690)	913
	(26,819)	10,590
Financing activities		
Bank operating loan advances	27,554	-
Repayment of long-term debt	(750)	-
Reduction of obligation under capital leases	(79)	-
Reduction of long-term obligations	(459)	(232)
Dividends paid	(433)	(1,621)
	25,833	(1,853)
Investing activities		
Proceeds on disposal of property, plant and equipment	39	98
Payments for property, plant and equipment	(1,231)	(7,358)
	(1,192)	(7,260)
Effect of exchange rate changes on cash position	116	(324)
Increase (decrease) in cash position	(2,178)	1,153
Cash, beginning of year	2,687	1,534
Cash, end of year	$ 625	$ 2,687

Supplemental cash flow information   (note 15)

See accompanying notes to financial statements

1. SIGNIFICANT ACCOUNTING POLICIES

Basis of presentation

The financial statements of Sun-Rype Products Ltd. (the "Company") have been prepared in accordance with Canadian generally accepted accounting principles ("Canadian GAAP") and reflect the following significant accounting policies:

(a) Measurement uncertainty

The presentation of financial statements in conformity with Canadian GAAP requires management to make estimates and assumptions that affect the reported amounts of assets and liabilities at the date of the financial statements and the reported amounts of revenues and expenses disclosed during reporting periods. Significant areas that involve estimates include provisions for uncollectible accounts receivable, the amortization rate and estimated useful life of property, plant and equipment, provisions for sales returns and allowances, provisions for obsolete inventory, and impairment of long-lived assets. The actual amounts could differ from those estimates.

(b) Inventories

Raw materials and supplies are recorded at the lower of cost, determined on a weighted average basis, and net realizable value, being the estimated selling price of finished goods less the estimated costs of completion of the finished goods. Minor parts and supplies are included in inventory at the lower of cost, determined on a weighted average basis, and replacement cost.

Finished goods are recorded at the lower of cost and net realizable value. Finished goods include the cost of direct labour, direct materials and variable and fixed overhead related to production, including amortization, applied at a standard rate, which approximates actual costs.

(c) Property, plant and equipment

Property, plant and equipment, including major spares, are recorded at cost, net of investment tax credits. The Company uses the straight-line method of recording amortization over the estimated useful lives of the property, plant and equipment as follows:

Buildings	10 - 20 years
Equipment - Processing	5 - 10 years
- Other	3 - 5 years

(d) Impairment of long-lived assets

The Company regularly compares the carrying value of long-lived assets to the estimated undiscounted future cash flows that may be generated from future use and eventual disposition of those assets. The Company records an impairment loss in the period when it is determined that the carrying amount of the asset exceeds the undiscounted estimate of future cash flows from the asset. The impairment loss is measured as the difference between the carrying amount and estimated fair value of the asset.

1.   SIGNIFICANT ACCOUNTING POLICIES (continued)

(e) Asset retirement obligations

The Company recognizes legal obligations associated with the retirement of property, plant and equipment that result from its acquisition, construction or normal operations. These obligations are recorded at fair value and subsequently adjusted for the accretion of discount and any changes in the underlying cash flows. The asset retirement cost is capitalized as part of the cost of the related asset, and amortized to earnings over the remaining life of the asset. Other than as described in Note 16, the Company has determined that it has no material asset retirement obligations at December 31, 2008.

(f) Revenue recognition

Sales are recognized upon the transfer of risk and title to finished goods to customers, which typically occurs upon shipment and when collectibility of proceeds is reasonably assured. The Company deducts from gross sales all payments to customers related to pricing discounts, returns and allowances, certain sales and marketing discounts, promotion funds, co-operative advertising, coupons and product listing fees.

(g) Marketing and product launch costs

The Company expenses new product marketing and launch costs as incurred.

(h) Long-term incentive plan

The Company maintains a long-term incentive plan ("LTIP") that is more fully described in Note 9. A portion of the LTIP liability will vary with the market price of the Company's common shares.

The Company recognizes the LTIP compensation expense when earned and throughout the deferral period to the extent that the fair value of the performance units earned has changed. Should any amounts be forfeited due to future circumstances, these amounts will be accounted for in the period in which the forfeiture is confirmed.

(i) Research and development

The Company incurs costs for activities that relate to research and development of new products. Research costs are expensed as they are incurred. Development costs are also expensed as incurred unless they meet all the criteria for deferral under Canadian GAAP and their recovery is reasonably assured. To date no amounts have been capitalized. Investment tax credits arising from research and development activities are deducted from the related costs and are accordingly included in the determination of earnings when there is reasonable assurance that the credits will be realized.

(j) Income taxes

The Company uses the liability method of accounting for income taxes. Under this method, temporary differences arising from the tax basis of an asset or liability and the corresponding carrying amount on the balance sheet are used to calculate future income tax assets or liabilities. Future income tax assets or liabilities are calculated using tax rates anticipated to be in effect in the periods that the temporary differences are expected to reverse. The effect of a change in income tax rates on future income tax assets and liabilities is recognized in income in the period the change is substantively enacted.

1. SIGNIFICANT ACCOUNTING POLICIES (continued)

(k) Financial instruments

The Company's financial instruments are classified into one of the following categories: held for trading, held-to-maturity investments, loans and receivables, available-for-sale financial assets, and other financial liabilities. The classification determines the accounting treatment of the instrument. The classification is determined by the Company when the financial instrument is initially recorded, based on the underlying purpose of the instrument.

The Company's financial assets and financial liabilities are classified and measured as follows:

Financial Instrument	Category	Measurement
Cash	Held for trading	Fair value
Accounts receivable	Loans and receivables	Amortized cost
Currency contracts	Held for trading	Fair value
Bank operating loan	Held for trading	Fair value
Promissory note payable	Other financial liabilities	Amortized cost
Accounts payable	Other financial liabilities	Amortized cost
Long-term obligations	Other financial liabilities	Amortized cost
Long-term debt	Other financial liabilities	Amortized cost

(l) Foreign currency translation

Transactions denominated in foreign currencies are translated into Canadian dollars at the exchange rate prevailing at the time of each transaction. At the balance sheet date, monetary assets and liabilities denominated in a foreign currency are translated at the period end rate of exchange. Exchange gains and losses arising on translation or settlement of foreign currency-denominated items are included in the determination of net income for the current period.

(m) Foreign exchange forward contracts

The Company periodically enters into foreign exchange forward contracts to manage foreign exchange risk associated with anticipated future purchases denominated in foreign currencies. Realized and unrealized gains and losses resulting from changes in the market value of these contracts are recorded as foreign exhange gain or loss each period unless they meet specified criteria to qualify as hedging instruments under Canadian GAAP. If these contracts meet the criteria for hedging instruments, any unrealized gains or losses are deferred and recognized in earnings when the related hedged transaction is recognized in earnings.

(n) Earnings per share

Basic earnings per share is calculated by dividing the net earnings available to common shareholders by the weighted average number of common shares outstanding during the year. Diluted earnings per share is calculated using the treasury stock method, which assumes that any outstanding stock option grants are exercised, if dilutive, and the assumed proceeds are used to purchase the Company's common shares at the average market price during the year.

2. ADOPTION OF NEW ACCOUNTING STANDARDS

(a) Inventories

Effective January 1, 2008, the Company adopted CICA Handbook Section 3031 "Inventories" without restatement of the results of operations of prior periods. As a result of the adoption of this Section, the Company's inventory accounting policy has been changed as follows:

Raw materials and supplies are recorded at the lower of cost, determined on a weighted average basis, and net realizable value, being the estimated selling price of finished goods less the estimated costs of completion of the finished goods. Under the previous policy raw materials and supplies were recorded at the lower of cost, determined on a weighted average basis, and replacement cost.

Finished goods are recorded at the lower of cost and net realizable value. Finished goods include the cost of direct labour, direct materials and variable and fixed overhead related to production, including amortization, applied at a standard rate, which approximates actual costs. Under the previous policy, fixed overhead costs related to production were considered a period cost and, as such, were not included as a component of inventory but were expensed in the period they were incurred.

As a result of the requirement for adoption of this Section, management undertook a review of its accounting for parts and supplies included in inventories for financial statement purposes. From this review management determined that major equipment spares were more appropriately classified as property, plant and equipment, and amortized in accordance with the Company's accounting policy for property, plant and equipment. As a result, the Company's inventory accounting policy has been changed as follows:

Minor parts and supplies are included in inventory at the lower of cost, determined on a weighted average basis, and replacement cost. Major replacement parts and spares are included in property, plant and equipment. Under the previous policy all parts and supplies were included in inventory and recorded at the lower of cost, determined on a weighted average basis, and replacement cost.

As a result of these changes in accounting policy, the following adjustments have been made at January 1, 2008:

(in thousands of dollars)		
Inventories decreased by	$	(228)
Property, plant and equipment increased by		321
Future income tax asset reduced by		(32)
Retained earnings increased by		61

2. ADOPTION OF NEW ACCOUNTING STANDARDS (continued)

(b) Capital disclosures and financial instruments – disclosures and presentation

Effective January 1, 2008, the Company adopted CICA Handbook Section 1535 "Capital Disclosures"; Section 3862 "Financial Instruments – Disclosures"; and Section 3863 "Financial Instruments – Presentation".

(i) Section 1535 establishes guidelines for the disclosure of information on the Company's capital and how it is managed. This enhanced disclosure enables users to evaluate the Company's objectives, policies and processes for managing capital. See Note 17.

(ii) Sections 3862 and 3863 replaced the existing Section 3861 "Financial Instruments – Disclosure and Presentation." Section 3862 requires enhanced disclosure on the nature and extent of financial instrument risks and how the Company manages those risks. Section 3863 carries forward the existing presentation requirements and provides additional guidance for the classification of financial instruments. See Note 18.

Future accounting and reporting changes

Goodwill and Intangible Assets

In February 2008, the Canadian Institute of Chartered Accountants issued Section 3064, "Goodwill And Intangible Assets", replacing Section 3062, "Goodwill And Other Intangible Assets", and Section 3450, "Research and Development Costs". This Section establishes standards for the recognition, measurement, presentation and disclosure of goodwill subsequent to its initial recognition and for intangible assets. The new Section will be applicable to financial statements for fiscal years beginning on or after October 1, 2008. Accordingly, the Company will adopt the new standards for its fiscal year beginning January 1, 2009. The adoption of this Section is not expected to have a material impact on the Company's financial statements.

3. INVENTORIES

(in thousands of dollars)	2008	2007
Raw materials and supplies	$ 16,633	$ 13,412
Finished goods	11,145	3,892
	$ 27,778	$ 17,304

Sun-Rype Products Ltd.
Notes to Financial Statements
For the years ended December 31, 2008 and 2007

4. INCOME TAXES

The income tax provision differs from the amount that would be computed by applying the combined federal and provincial statutory income tax rates as a result of the following:

(in thousands of dollars)	2008	2007
Statutory income tax rates	30.4%	33.8%
Income tax expense (recovery) at statutory rates	$ (5,511)	$ 2,292
Effect on income taxes of:		
Non-deductible expenses	24	28
Tax rate changes, including differences in rates applying to tax loss carry-back	(896)	(118)
Other	(73)	(64)
Effective income tax expense (recovery)	$ (6,456)	$ 2,138

The income tax expense (recovery) consists of the following:

(in thousands of dollars)	2008	2007
Current income tax expense (recovery)	$ (7,065)	$ 2,448
Future income tax expense (recovery)	609	(310)
	$ (6,456)	$ 2,138

The future income tax balances are recorded as follows:

(in thousands of dollars)	2008	2007
Future income tax assets – current	$ -	$ 435
Future income tax liabilities – current	(11)	-
Future income tax liabilities – long-term	(1,343)	(1,148)
Net future income tax liability	$ (1,354)	$ (713)

Significant components of future income tax assets and liabilities include:

(in thousands of dollars)	2008	2007
Accrued liabilities	$ 158	$ 711
Obligations under capital leases	135	-
Losses and other deductions	90	14
Future income tax assets	383	725
Property, plant and equipment	(1,535)	(1,360)
Other	(202)	(78)
Future income tax liabilities	(1,737)	(1,438)
Net future income tax liability	$ (1,354)	$ (713)

5. PROPERTY, PLANT AND EQUIPMENT

(in thousands of dollars)	2008		
	Cost	Accumulated Amortization	Net Book Value
Land	$ 170	$ -	$ 170
Buildings	16,643	13,293	3,350
Processing equipment	51,860	32,229	19,631
Other equipment	8,522	6,543	1,979
	$ 77,195	$ 52,065	$ 25,130

	2007		
	Cost	Accumulated Amortization	Net Book Value
Land	$ 170	$ -	$ 170
Buildings	16,624	12,572	4,052
Processing equipment	50,384	28,560	21,824
Other equipment	7,775	5,954	1,821
	$ 74,953	$ 47,086	$ 27,867

Included in processing equipment at December 31, 2008, is construction in progress with a cost of $0.1 million that has not been amortized (December 31, 2007 - $0.7 million).

6. BANK OPERATING LOAN

The Company maintains a $20.0 million standby operating line of credit with a Canadian bank, which bears interest at the bank's prime lending rate plus 1% (December 31, 2008 – 4.5%). This facility is secured as described in note 10.

7. PROMISSORY NOTE PAYABLE

The promissory note payable is due on demand, is secured by a letter of credit and bears interest at the bank prime rate plus 0.25% (December 31, 2008 – 3.75%). Subsequent to December 31, 2008, the promissory note was repaid.

8. OBLIGATION UNDER CAPITAL LEASES

The Company has acquired equipment through capital leases that bear interest at a weighted average rate of 4.64% and require payments to the lease expiry dates as follows:

(in thousands of dollars)	2008
Years ending December 31:	
2009	$ 118
2010	118
2011	118
2012	118
2013	76
Total minimum lease payments	548
Less amount representing interest	56
Balance of the obligation	492
Current portion	97
Long-term portion	$ 395

Included in property, plant and equipment at December 31, 2008, are leased assets with a cost of $0.6 million (December 31, 2007 - nil) and accumulated amortization of $0.1 million (December 31, 2007 - nil). Interest on capital leases of $18,500 is included in interest expense in 2008 (2007 - nil).

9. LONG-TERM OBLIGATIONS

(in thousands of dollars)	2008	2007
Deferred management compensation	$ 148	$ 298
Long-term incentive plan	217	767
Total	365	1,065
Current portion	220	321
Long-term portion	$ 145	$ 744

Deferred management compensation

Under the terms of employment agreements with certain senior officers, the Company has provided for compensation to be paid to the individuals at the date they cease their employment. No compensation expense relating to these employment agreements was recorded in 2008 or 2007. Subsequent to December 31, 2008, the remaining deferred management compensation was paid.

9. LONG-TERM OBLIGATIONS (continued)

Long-term Incentive Plan ("LTIP")

In 2005 the Company's board of directors adopted an LTIP for its senior officers that entitles these officers to earn awards that will be confirmed during the two-year period following the year in which the awards are earned. The LTIP awards are comprised of a combination of cash and performance units. A performance unit is a notional unit, equivalent in value to the average trading price of the Company's common shares for the previous 20 trading days. At the termination of employment, the performance units are settled in cash.

No compensation expense was recorded in 2008 as performance units were not awarded (2007 – $0.2). Revaluation of the performance units resulted in an expense recovery of $0.2 million in 2008 (2007 – $0.1 million). As at December 31, 2008, 37,428 performance units have been granted under the plan. Subsequent to December 31, 2008, 12,067 performance units were settled in cash as a result of terminations of employment.

10. LONG-TERM DEBT

(in thousands of dollars)	2008
Bank loan repayable at $125,000 per month plus interest at the bank's prime lending rate plus 1% (December 31, 2008 – 4.5%)	$ 14,250
Current portion	1,500
Long-term portion	$ 12,750

The Company has a further $5.0 million committed revolving financing facility bearing interest at the bank's prime lending rate plus 1% available for future capital expenditures.

These facilities and the bank operating loan (note 6) are secured by a general assignment of accounts receivable, inventories and demand debentures creating a fixed and floating charge over all Company assets.

Principal repayments due for the remaining term of the long-term debt are as follows:

Year	Amount (in thousands of dollars)
2009	$ 1,500
2010	1,500
2011	1,500
2012	1,500
2013	1,500
2014 and thereafter	6,750
	$ 14,250

11. SHARE CAPITAL AND CONTRIBUTED SURPLUS

Authorized

100,000,000 common shares fully participating and without par value

Issued and fully paid capital

(in thousands of dollars)	2008	2007
10,827,600 Common shares	$ 17,756	$ 17,756
Contributed surplus	942	942
	$ 18,698	$ 18,698

Earnings per share

The weighted average number of common shares outstanding in 2008 and 2007, on a basic and diluted basis, was 10,827,600.

Employee share purchase plan

The Company has an employee share purchase plan ("ESPP") enabling eligible employees to acquire publicly traded Company common shares through payroll deductions with financial assistance provided by the Company. Eligible employees may contribute a monthly amount not to exceed 7% of salary, and the Company contributes a further 35% of the employee contribution. All funds and equity shares held by the administrator pursuant to the ESPP are held for the account of the individual employee. The Company's 2008 contributions of $0.2 million to the ESPP are included in selling, general and administrative expense (2007 - $0.2 million).

12. CUSTOMER CONCENTRATION

The Company's customers consist mainly of Canadian grocery stores, mass merchandisers and club stores. Net sales to three customers, individually representing more than 10% of net sales, are as follows:

(in thousands of dollars)	2008	2007
Net sales	$ 68,079	$ 71,237
Percentage of total net sales	54.3%	52.7%

13. COST OF SALES

(in thousands of dollars)	2008	2007
Cost of inventories expensed	$ 107,442	$ 93,298
Write-down of inventories	1,653	-
Amortization	2,182	-
	$ 111,277	$ 93,298

Sun-Rype Products Ltd.
Notes to Financial Statements
For the years ended December 31, 2008 and 2007

14. POST-EMPLOYMENT BENEFITS

The Company maintains a defined contribution (money purchase) pension plan for substantially all of its salaried employees. The Company's 2008 contributions of $0.3 million to the plan are included in selling, general and administrative expense (2007 - $0.3 million).

15. SUPPLEMENTAL CASH FLOW INFORMATION

(in thousands of dollars)	2008	2007
Changes in non-cash working capital items:		
Accounts receivable	$ (4,439)	$ 5,284
Inventories	(10,350)	1,404
Prepaid expenses	(173)	-
Promissory note payable	(100)	(100)
Accounts payable and accrued liabilities	2,541	(4,623)
Income taxes	(6,169)	(1,052)
	$ (18,690)	$ 913
Cash flows during the year resulting from:		
Payment of interest	$ 879	$ 148
Payment (recovery) of income taxes	$ (896)	$ 3,503

Non-cash transactions:

During 2008, the Company repaid $15.0 million of bank operating loan advances with proceeds from the issuance of long-term debt (2007 – nil).

During 2008, the Company acquired property, plant and equipment for $0.6 million directly financed through capital leases (2007 – nil).

At December 31, 2008, accounts payable and accrued liabilities includes nil for unpaid property, plant and equipment purchases (2007 - $0.1 million).

16. COMMITMENTS, GUARANTEES AND CONTINGENCIES

(a) The Company has entered into operating lease and rental commitments for equipment and office space for the next five years as follows:

Year	Amount (in thousands of dollars)
2009	$ 144
2010	131
2011	80
2012	63
2013	3

(b) Under the terms of a processing and filling systems agreement expiring December 31, 2012, the Company is contingently liable for annual rental payments of $0.8 million should the Company's purchase of annual volumes of beverage packaging materials not meet certain minimum thresholds. Based on historical purchase levels these rental payments would only be payable in the event of a dramatic decline in market demand.

16. COMMITMENTS, GUARANTEES AND CONTINGENCIES (continued)

(c) In the normal course of business, the Company enters into commitments to purchase certain minimum quantities of raw materials, primarily in US dollars. At December 31, 2008, the Company has commitments to purchase approximately $4.0 million of these materials in 2009 and $0.2 million in 2010.

(d) The Company periodically enters into foreign exchange forward purchase contracts to manage foreign exchange risk associated with anticipated future purchases and contractual commitments denominated in foreign currencies. At December 31, 2008, the Company had currency contracts outstanding that allow the Company to purchase USD$5 million at an average exchange rate of 1.0743 should the spot rate be above the rates on the individual contracts, while requiring the Company to purchase US dollars at an average exchange rate of 1.0383 should the spot rate be below the rates on the individual contracts. At December 31, 2008, the Company has recorded an unrealized foreign exchange gain of $0.7 million to reflect the fair value of these currency contracts.

(e) The Company is subject to regulations that require the handling and disposal of asbestos that is contained in a certain property in a special manner if the property undergoes major renovations or demolition. Otherwise, the Company is not required to remove the asbestos from the property. The Company has determined that there is an indeterminate settlement date for this asset retirement obligation because the range of time over which the Company may settle the obligation cannot be estimated. Therefore, the Company cannot reasonably estimate the fair value of the liability. The Company will recognize a liability in the period in which sufficient information is available to reasonably estimate its fair value.

17. CAPITAL MANAGEMENT

The Company's objectives when managing capital are:

(i)   To safeguard the Company's ability to continue as a going concern, so that it can continue to provide returns for shareholders and benefits for other stakeholders, and

(ii)   To maintain a flexible capital structure which optimizes the cost of capital at acceptable risk.

The Company includes shareholders' equity, lease financing, and bank financing in the definition of capital. The Company sets the amount of its capital structure in proportion to risk. The Company manages the capital structure and makes adjustments to it in light of changes in economic conditions and the risk characteristics of the underlying assets. In order to maintain or adjust the capital structure, the Company may adjust the amount of dividends paid to shareholders, purchase shares for cancellation pursuant to normal course issuer bids, issue new shares, issue new debt, or issue new debt to replace existing debt with different characteristics.

17. CAPITAL MANAGEMENT (continued)

During 2008, the Company's capital strategy was changed from prior periods such that certain investments in property, plant and equipment, and other assets will be considered for financing with long-term capital. Previously all investments in property, plant and equipment, and other assets were financed with working capital, using temporary bank overdraft financing as needed. During 2008, the Company acquired equipment using capital lease financing (note 8).

The Company's credit facilities are reviewed annually in order to make sure that sufficient funds are available to meet its financial needs. During 2008, the Company revised its financing and replaced temporary bank financing with long-term debt (note 10).

The Company uses temporary bank financing during the year as cash flows are required by its cyclical production schedule (note 6).

Under its bank credit facilities (notes 6 and 10), the Company is required to comply with certain financial covenants regarding current ratio and total liabilities to tangible net worth ratio. At December 31, 2008, the Company is in compliance with these financial covenants.

18. FINANCIAL RISK MANAGEMENT

The Company's financial instruments are exposed to certain financial risks, including currency risk, credit risk, liquidity risk, and interest rate risk.

(a) Currency risk

The Company is exposed to the financial risk related to the fluctuations of foreign exchange rates. The Company has customers in Canada and the United States and a significant portion of its purchases are incurred in US dollars. A significant change in the currency exchange rate of the Canadian dollar relative to the US dollar could have a material effect on the Company's results of operations, financial position and cash flows. Foreign currency risk is managed in accordance with the Company's treasury policy, the objective of which is to mitigate the impact of foreign exchange rate fluctuations on the Company's results of operations, financial position and cash flows. Under this policy the Company enters into foreign exchange forward purchase contracts to manage foreign exchange risk associated with anticipated future purchases. The policy prohibits speculative foreign exchange transactions.

The fair value of foreign exchange forward purchase contracts is determined using exchange rates available on the balance sheet date.

At December 31, 2008, the Company is exposed to currency risk through the following assets and liabilities denominated in US dollars:

(in thousands of dollars)	2008	2007
Cash	$ 625	$ 1,846
Accounts receivable	1,296	276
US dollar currency contracts asset (liability)	718	(460)
Accounts payable and accrued liabilities	(3,544)	(1,681)
Net exposure	$ (905)	$ (19)

18. FINANCIAL RISK MANAGEMENT (continued)

(a) Currency risk (continued)

Based on the above net exposure at December 31, 2008, and assuming all other variables remain constant, a 10% depreciation or appreciation of the Canadian dollar against the US dollar would result in a decrease or increase of $0.1 million in the Company's net earnings.

(b) Credit risk

Credit risk is the risk of an unexpected loss if a customer or a third party to a financial instrument fails to meet its contractual obligations.

The Company's cash equivalents are held through large Canadian financial institutions.

As at December 31, 2008, the Company is exposed to credit risk through the following assets:

(in thousands of dollars)	2008	2007
Trade receivables	$ 11,438	$ 6,876
Other receivables	392	516
Net credit risk	$ 11,830	$ 7,392

The Company maintains credit policies that include a review of a counter party's financial condition, measurement of credit exposure and monitoring of concentration of exposure to any one customer or counter party. At December 31, 2008, 81% of trade receivables are due from ten customers (2007 - 81%).

Of the trade receivables outstanding at December 31, 2008, 97% are not due, and 3% are between 30 and 90 days overdue. Outstanding amounts totalling less than $0.1 million are considered impaired in that there is doubt about ultimate collection of the amounts due to the length of time the amounts have been outstanding. An allowance has been made to fully provide for the possible non-collection of these amounts.

The Company's other receivables include GST and investment tax credits due from the Federal Government of Canada.

(c) Liquidity risk

Liquidity risk is the risk that the Company will not be able to meet its financial obligations as they fall due. The Company manages liquidity risk by maintaining financial forecasts as well as long-term operating and strategic plans. Managing liquidity requires monitoring of projected cash inflows and outflows using forecasts of the Company's financial position to ensure adequate and efficient use of cash resources. The appropriate liquidity level is established based on historical volatility and seasonal requirements, as well as planned investments and the debt maturity requirements.

The Company's bank operating loan and promissory note payable are due on demand.

Accounts payable and accrued liabilities are generally due within 60 days. The current portions of employee future benefits, obligation under capital leases and bank loans are due within 12 months.

18. FINANCIAL RISK MANAGEMENT (continued)

(d) Interest rate risk

Interest rate risk is the risk that the fair value or future cash flows of a financial instrument will fluctuate because of changes in market interest rates.

As at December 31, 2008, the Company is exposed to interest rate risk through the following liabilities:

(in thousands of dollars)	2008	2007
Bank operating loan	$ 12,554	$ -
Promissory note payable	400	500
Long-term debt	14,250	-
	$ 27,204	$ 500

The Company's bank operating loan, promissory note payable, and long-term debt bear interest based on the bank's prime borrowing rate. Based on the above exposure at December 31, 2008, and assuming all other variables remain constant, a one hundred basis point increase or decrease of the bank prime borrowing rate would result in an decrease or increase of $0.2 million in the Company's net earnings.

19. SEGMENTED INFORMATION

The Company has one reportable operating segment, the processing, packaging and marketing of food products. The Company's assets are located in Canada and substantially all of the Company's net sales are in Canada.

20. RELATED PARTY TRANSACTIONS

The Company has entered into the following transactions with companies that are controlled by a director and shareholder of the Company who controls 48.5% of the Company's outstanding common shares:

(a) In the normal course of business, the Company sells products to a related company that is a major food retailer in western Canada. Sales to this retailer are less than 10% of the Company's net sales. These transactions are recorded at the exchange amounts, which are the amounts agreed upon between the related parties, and are consistent with transactions with non-related customers.

(b) In February 2009, the Company entered into a management agreement with a related company under which the Company will receive administrative, advisory and executive services for a period of three years beginning January 1, 2009, for an annual fee of $0.6 million. Included in selling, general and administrative expense for 2008 is $0.1 million for services provided prior to commencement of the term of the agreement. These transactions are recorded at the exchange amounts, which are the amounts agreed upon between the related parties.

21. COMPARATIVE FIGURES

Certain items in the comparative figures have been reclassified in the financial statements.

Appendix C

Standard Setting in Canada

How are accounting standards developed and monitored? In Canada, there are two bodies that have been given regulatory control over standard setting.

The Accounting Standards Oversight Council (ACSOC) is an independent volunteer body that, among other duties, oversees and provides input on the activities of the Accounting Standards Board. ACSOC consists of up to 25 business, government, and academic leaders. The Council assists the Accounting Standards Board in setting high-quality accounting standards for all Canadian enterprises.

The Accounting Standards Board (AcSB) is the body that develops and establishes standards and guidance governing financial accounting and reporting in the private sector in Canada. As the standard-setter for the private sector in Canada, the AcSB determines the format and content of financial statements, and strives to ensure that the information within them is relevant, reliable, understandable, and comparable.

Beginning in 2011, publicly accountable companies in Canada will follow international financial reporting standards (IFRS). These financial reporting standards have been developed and approved by the International Accounting Standards Board (IASB), of which Canada is a member.

The accounting standards established by the AcSB are the primary source of generally accepted accounting principles (GAAP) in Canada. The *CICA Handbook— Accounting* produced by the Canadian Institute of Chartered Accountants (CICA) contains accounting standards that apply to all types of profit-oriented enterprises and not-for-profit organizations in Canada.

The Objective of Financial Reporting

The basic objective of financial reporting is to provide information that is useful in making investment and lending decisions. Accounting information can be useful in decision making only if it is *understandable, relevant, reliable* and *comparable*.

Accounting information must be *understandable* to users if they are to be able to use it. *Relevant* information is useful in making predictions and for evaluating past performance—that is, the information has feedback value. For example, Canadian Tire Corporation, Limited's disclosure of the profitability of each of its lines of business is relevant for investor evaluations of the company. To be relevant, information must be timely. *Reliable* information is free from significant error—that is, it has validity. Also, it is free from the bias of a particular viewpoint—that is, it is verifiable and neutral. *Comparable* information can be compared from period to period to help investors and creditors assess the entity's progress through time. These characteristics combine to shape the assumptions and principles that comprise GAAP. Exhibit C-1 on the next page summarizes the assumptions, principles and constraints that accounting has developed to provide useful information for decision making.

Assumptions, Principles, and Financial Statements	Quick Summary	Text Reference
Assumptions		
Economic-entity assumption	Accounting draws a boundary around each organization to be accounted for.	Chapter 1
Going-concern assumption	Accountants assume the business will continue operating for the foreseeable future.	Chapter 1
Stable-monetary-unit assumption	Accounting information is expressed primarily in monetary terms.	Chapter 1
Time period assumption	Ensures that accounting information is reported at regular intervals.	Chapter 3
Cost/benefit constraint	The benefits of the information produced should exceed the costs of producing the information.	Chapter 1
Materiality constraint	Accountants consider the materiality of an amount when making disclosure decisions.	Chapters 1 and 6
Principles, Criteria, and Characteristics		
Reliability (objectivity) characteristic	Accounting records and statements are based on the most reliable data available	Chapter 1
Consistency (comparability) characteristic	Businesses should use the same accounting methods from period to period.	Chapter 6
Recognition criteria: For Revenues	Tell accountants when to record revenue (only after it has been earned) and the amount of revenue to record (the cash value of what has been received).	Chapter 3
For Expenses (includes the matching objective)	Direct accountants to (1) identify all expenses incurred during the period, (2) measure the expenses, and (3) match the expenses against the revenues earned during the period. The goal is to measure net income.	Chapter 3
Measurement: Cost Basis Other Bases (used in limited circumstances	Assets and services, revenues and expenses are recorded at their actual historical cost.	Chapter 1
Disclosure principle	A company's financial statements should report enough information for outsiders to make informed decisions about the company.	Chapter 6
Financial Statements		
Balance sheet	Assets = Liabilities + Owners' Equity at a point in time (for proprietorships and partnerships). Assets = Liabilities + Shareholders' Equity at a point in time (for corporations).	Chapters 1 and 13
Income statement	Revenues and gains − Expenses and losses = Net income or net loss for the period	Chapters 1 and 14
Cash flow statement	Cash receipts − Cash payments = Increase or decrease in cash during the period, grouped under operating, investing, and financing activities	Chapters 1 and 17
Statement of owner's equity	Beginning owner's equity + Net income (or − Net loss) − Withdrawals = Ending owner's equity	Chapter 1
Statement of retained earnings	Beginning retained earnings + Net income (or − Net loss) − Dividends = Ending retained earnings	Chapter 14

Appendix D

Present-Value Tables and Future-Value Tables

This appendix provides present-value tables (more complete than those appearing in Chapter 15) and future-value tables.

Table D-1 *Present Value of $1*

	Present Value										
Periods	**1%**	**2%**	**3%**	**4%**	**5%**	**6%**	**7%**	**8%**	**9%**	**10%**	**12%**
1	0.990	0.980	0.971	0.962	0.952	0.943	0.935	0.926	0.917	0.909	0.893
2	0.980	0.961	0.943	0.925	0.907	0.890	0.873	0.857	0.842	0.826	0.797
3	0.971	0.942	0.915	0.889	0.864	0.840	0.816	0.794	0.772	0.751	0.712
4	0.961	0.924	0.888	0.855	0.823	0.792	0.763	0.735	0.708	0.683	0.636
5	0.951	0.906	0.883	0.822	0.784	0.747	0.713	0.681	0.650	0.621	0.567
6	0.942	0.888	0.837	0.790	0.746	0.705	0.666	0.630	0.596	0.564	0.507
7	0.933	0.871	0.813	0.760	0.711	0.665	0.623	0.583	0.547	0.513	0.452
8	0.923	0.853	0.789	0.731	0.677	0.627	0.582	0.540	0.502	0.467	0.404
9	0.914	0.837	0.766	0.703	0.645	0.592	0.544	0.500	0.460	0.424	0.361
10	0.905	0.820	0.744	0.676	0.614	0.558	0.508	0.463	0.422	0.386	0.322
11	0.896	0.804	0.722	0.650	0.585	0.527	0.475	0.429	0.388	0.350	0.287
12	0.887	0.788	0.701	0.625	0.557	0.497	0.444	0.397	0.356	0.319	0.257
13	0.879	0.773	0.681	0.601	0.530	0.469	0.415	0.368	0.326	0.290	0.229
14	0.870	0.758	0.661	0.577	0.505	0.442	0.388	0.340	0.299	0.263	0.205
15	0.861	0.743	0.642	0.555	0.481	0.417	0.362	0.315	0.275	0.239	0.183
16	0.853	0.728	0.623	0.534	0.458	0.394	0.339	0.292	0.252	0.218	0.163
17	0.844	0.714	0.605	0.513	0.436	0.371	0.317	0.270	0.231	0.198	0.146
18	0.836	0.700	0.587	0.494	0.416	0.350	0.296	0.250	0.212	0.180	0.130
19	0.828	0.686	0.570	0.475	0.396	0.331	0.277	0.232	0.194	0.164	0.116
20	0.820	0.673	0.554	0.456	0.377	0.312	0.258	0.215	0.178	0.149	0.104
21	0.811	0.660	0.538	0.439	0.359	0.294	0.242	0.199	0.164	0.135	0.093
22	0.803	0.647	0.522	0.422	0.342	0.278	0.226	0.184	0.150	0.123	0.083
23	0.795	0.634	0.507	0.406	0.326	0.262	0.211	0.170	0.138	0.112	0.074
24	0.788	0.622	0.492	0.390	0.310	0.247	0.197	0.158	0.126	0.102	0.066
25	0.780	0.610	0.478	0.375	0.295	0.233	0.184	0.146	0.116	0.092	0.059
26	0.772	0.598	0.464	0.361	0.281	0.220	0.172	0.135	0.106	0.084	0.053
27	0.764	0.586	0.450	0.347	0.268	0.207	0.161	0.125	0.098	0.076	0.047
28	0.757	0.574	0.437	0.333	0.255	0.196	0.150	0.116	0.090	0.069	0.042
29	0.749	0.563	0.424	0.321	0.243	0.185	0.141	0.107	0.082	0.063	0.037
30	0.742	0.552	0.412	0.308	0.231	0.174	0.131	0.099	0.075	0.057	0.033
40	0.672	0.453	0.307	0.208	0.142	0.097	0.067	0.046	0.032	0.022	0.011
50	0.608	0.372	0.228	0.141	0.087	0.054	0.034	0.021	0.013	0.009	0.003

Table D-1 (cont'd)

Periods	Present Value										
	14%	15%	16%	18%	20%	25%	30%	35%	40%	45%	50%
1	0.877	0.870	0.862	0.847	0.833	0.800	0.769	0.741	0.714	0.690	0.667
2	0.769	0.756	0.743	0.718	0.694	0.640	0.592	0.549	0.510	0.476	0.444
3	0.675	0.658	0.641	0.609	0.579	0.512	0.455	0.406	0.364	0.328	0.296
4	0.592	0.572	0.552	0.516	0.482	0.410	0.350	0.301	0.260	0.226	0.198
5	0.519	0.497	0.476	0.437	0.402	0.328	0.269	0.223	0.186	0.156	0.132
6	0.456	0.432	0.410	0.370	0.335	0.262	0.207	0.165	0.133	0.108	0.088
7	0.400	0.376	0.354	0.314	0.279	0.210	0.159	0.122	0.095	0.074	0.059
8	0.351	0.327	0.305	0.266	0.233	0.168	0.123	0.091	0.068	0.051	0.039
9	0.308	0.284	0.263	0.225	0.194	0.134	0.094	0.067	0.048	0.035	0.026
10	0.270	0.247	0.227	0.191	0.162	0.107	0.073	0.050	0.035	0.024	0.017
11	0.237	0.215	0.195	0.162	0.135	0.086	0.056	0.037	0.025	0.017	0.012
12	0.208	0.187	0.168	0.137	0.112	0.069	0.043	0.027	0.018	0.012	0.008
13	0.182	0.163	0.145	0.116	0.093	0.055	0.033	0.020	0.013	0.008	0.005
14	0.160	0.141	0.125	0.099	0.078	0.044	0.025	0.015	0.009	0.006	0.003
15	0.140	0.123	0.108	0.084	0.065	0.035	0.020	0.011	0.006	0.004	0.002
16	0.123	0.107	0.093	0.071	0.054	0.028	0.015	0.008	0.005	0.003	0.002
17	0.108	0.093	0.080	0.060	0.045	0.023	0.012	0.006	0.003	0.002	0.001
18	0.095	0.081	0.069	0.051	0.038	0.018	0.009	0.005	0.002	0.001	0.001
19	0.083	0.070	0.060	0.043	0.031	0.014	0.007	0.003	0.002	0.001	
20	0.073	0.061	0.051	0.037	0.026	0.012	0.005	0.002	0.001	0.001	
21	0.064	0.053	0.044	0.031	0.022	0.009	0.004	0.002	0.001		
22	0.056	0.046	0.038	0.026	0.018	0.007	0.003	0.001	0.001		
23	0.049	0.040	0.033	0.022	0.015	0.006	0.002	0.001			
24	0.043	0.035	0.028	0.019	0.013	0.005	0.002	0.001			
25	0.038	0.030	0.024	0.016	0.010	0.004	0.001	0.001			
26	0.033	0.026	0.021	0.014	0.009	0.003	0.001				
27	0.029	0.023	0.018	0.011	0.007	0.002	0.001				
28	0.026	0.020	0.016	0.010	0.006	0.002	0.001				
29	0.022	0.017	0.014	0.008	0.005	0.002					
30	0.020	0.015	0.012	0.007	0.004	0.001					
40	0.005	0.004	0.003	0.001	0.001						
50	0.001	0.001	0.001								

Table D-2 *Present Value of Annuity $1*

Periods	1%	2%	3%	4%	5%	6%	7%	8%	9%	10%	12%
					Present Value						
1	0.990	0.980	0.971	0.962	0.952	0.943	0.935	0.926	0.917	0.909	0.893
2	1.970	1.942	1.913	1.886	1.859	1.833	1.808	1.783	1.759	1.736	1.690
3	2.941	2.884	2.829	2.775	2.723	2.673	2.624	2.577	2.531	2.487	2.402
4	3.902	3.808	3.717	3.630	3.546	3.465	3.387	3.312	3.240	3.170	3.037
5	4.853	4.713	4.580	4.452	4.329	4.212	4.100	3.993	3.890	3.791	3.605
6	5.795	5.601	5.417	5.242	5.076	4.917	4.767	4.623	4.486	4.355	4.111
7	6.728	6.472	6.230	6.002	5.786	5.582	5.389	5.206	5.033	4.868	4.564
8	7.652	7.325	7.020	6.733	6.463	6.210	5.971	5.747	5.535	5.335	4.968
9	8.566	8.162	7.786	7.435	7.108	6.802	6.515	6.247	5.995	5.759	5.328
10	9.471	8.983	8.530	8.111	7.722	7.360	7.024	6.710	6.418	6.145	5.650
11	10.368	9.787	9.253	8.760	8.306	7.887	7.499	7.139	6.805	6.495	5.938
12	11.255	10.575	9.954	9.385	8.863	8.384	7.943	7.536	7.161	6.814	6.194
13	12.134	11.348	10.635	9.986	9.394	8.853	8.358	7.904	7.487	7.103	6.424
14	13.004	12.106	11.296	10.563	9.899	9.295	8.745	8.244	7.786	7.367	6.628
15	13.865	12.849	11.938	11.118	10.380	9.712	9.108	8.559	8.061	7.606	6.811
16	14.718	13.578	12.561	11.652	10.838	10.106	9.447	8.851	8.313	7.824	6.974
17	15.562	14.292	13.166	12.166	11.274	10.477	9.763	9.122	8.544	8.022	7.120
18	16.398	14.992	13.754	12.659	11.690	10.828	10.059	9.372	8.756	8.201	7.250
19	17.226	15.678	14.324	13.134	12.085	11.158	10.336	9.604	8.950	8.365	7.366
20	18.046	16.351	14.878	13.590	12.462	11.470	10.594	9.818	9.129	8.514	7.469
21	18.857	17.011	15.415	14.029	12.821	11.764	10.836	10.017	9.292	8.649	7.562
22	19.660	17.658	15.937	14.451	13.163	12.042	11.061	10.201	9.442	8.772	7.645
23	20.456	18.292	16.444	14.857	13.489	12.303	11.272	10.371	9.580	8.883	7.718
24	21.243	18.914	16.936	15.247	13.799	12.550	11.469	10.529	9.707	8.985	7.784
25	22.023	19.523	17.413	15.622	14.094	12.783	11.654	10.675	9.823	9.077	7.843
26	22.795	20.121	17.877	15.983	14.375	13.003	11.826	10.810	9.929	9.161	7.896
27	23.560	20.707	18.327	16.330	14.643	13.211	11.987	10.935	10.027	9.237	7.943
28	24.316	21.281	18.764	16.663	14.898	13.406	12.137	11.051	10.116	9.307	7.984
29	25.066	21.844	19.189	16.984	15.141	13.591	12.278	11.158	10.198	9.370	8.022
30	25.808	22.396	19.600	17.292	15.373	13.765	12.409	11.258	10.274	9.427	8.055
40	32.835	27.355	23.115	19.793	17.159	15.046	13.332	11.925	10.757	9.779	8.244
50	39.196	31.424	25.730	21.482	18.256	15.762	13.801	12.234	10.962	9.915	8.305

Table D-2   *(cont'd)*

Periods	14%	15%	16%	18%	Present Value 20%	25%	30%	35%	40%	45%	50%
1	0.877	0.870	0.862	0.847	0.833	0.800	0.769	0.741	0.714	0.690	0.667
2	1.647	1.626	1.605	1.566	1.528	1.440	1.361	1.289	1.224	1.165	1.111
3	2.322	2.283	2.246	2.174	2.106	1.952	1.816	1.696	1.589	1.493	1.407
4	2.914	2.855	2.798	2.690	2.589	2.362	2.166	1.997	1.849	1.720	1.605
5	3.433	3.352	3.274	3.127	2.991	2.689	2.436	2.220	2.035	1.876	1.737
6	3.889	3.784	3.685	3.498	3.326	2.951	2.643	2.385	2.168	1.983	1.824
7	4.288	4.160	4.039	3.812	3.605	3.161	2.802	2.508	2.263	2.057	1.883
8	4.639	4.487	4.344	4.078	3.837	3.329	2.925	2.598	2.331	2.109	1.922
9	4.946	4.772	4.607	4.303	4.031	3.463	3.019	2.665	2.379	2.144	1.948
10	5.216	5.019	4.833	4.494	4.192	3.571	3.092	2.715	2.414	2.168	1.965
11	5.453	5.234	5.029	4.656	4.327	3.656	3.147	2.752	2.438	2.185	1.977
12	5.660	5.421	5.197	4.793	4.439	3.725	3.190	2.779	2.456	2.197	1.985
13	5.842	5.583	5.342	4.910	4.533	3.780	3.223	2.799	2.469	2.204	1.990
14	6.002	5.724	5.468	5.008	4.611	3.824	3.249	2.814	2.478	2.210	1.993
15	6.142	5.847	5.575	5.092	4.675	3.859	3.268	2.825	2.484	2.214	1.995
16	6.265	5.954	5.669	5.162	4.730	3.887	3.283	2.834	2.489	2.216	1.997
17	6.373	6.047	5.749	5.222	4.775	3.910	3.295	2.840	2.492	2.218	1.998
18	6.467	6.128	5.818	5.273	4.812	3.928	3.304	2.844	2.494	2.219	1.999
19	6.550	6.198	5.877	5.316	4.844	3.942	3.311	2.848	2.496	2.220	1.999
20	6.623	6.259	5.929	5.353	4.870	3.954	3.316	2.850	2.497	2.221	1.999
21	6.687	6.312	5.973	5.384	4.891	3.963	3.320	2.852	2.498	2.221	2.000
22	6.743	6.359	6.011	5.410	4.909	3.970	3.323	2.853	2.498	2.222	2.000
23	6.792	6.399	6.044	5.432	4.925	3.976	3.325	2.854	2.499	2.222	2.000
24	6.835	6.434	6.073	5.451	4.937	3.981	3.327	2.855	2.499	2.222	2.000
25	6.873	6.464	6.097	5.467	4.948	3.985	3.329	2.856	2.499	2.222	2.000
26	6.906	6.491	6.118	5.480	4.956	3.988	3.330	2.856	2.500	2.222	2.000
27	6.935	6.514	6.136	5.492	4.964	3.990	3.331	2.856	2.500	2.222	2.000
28	6.961	6.534	6.152	5.502	4.970	3.992	3.331	2.857	2.500	2.222	2.000
29	6.983	6.551	6.166	5.510	4.975	3.994	3.332	2.857	2.500	2.222	2.000
30	7.003	6.566	6.177	5.517	4.979	3.995	3.332	2.857	2.500	2.222	2.000
40	7.105	6.642	6.234	5.548	4.997	3.999	3.333	2.857	2.500	2.222	2.000
50	7.133	6.661	6.246	5.554	4.999	4.000	3.333	2.857	2.500	2.222	2.000

Table D-3 *Future Value of $1*

							Future Value						
Periods	1%	2%	3%	4%	5%	6%	7%	8%	9%	10%	12%	14%	15%
1	1.010	1.020	1.030	1.040	1.050	1.060	1.070	1.080	1.090	1.100	1.120	1.140	1.150
2	1.020	1.040	1.061	1.082	1.103	1.124	1.145	1.166	1.188	1.210	1.254	1.300	1.323
3	1.030	1.061	1.093	1.125	1.158	1.191	1.225	1.260	1.295	1.331	1.405	1.482	1.521
4	1.041	1.082	1.126	1.170	1.216	1.262	1.311	1.360	1.412	1.464	1.574	1.689	1.749
5	1.051	1.104	1.159	1.217	1.276	1.338	1.403	1.469	1.539	1.611	1.762	1.925	2.011
6	1.062	1.126	1.194	1.265	1.340	1.419	1.501	1.587	1.677	1.772	1.974	2.195	2.313
7	1.072	1.149	1.230	1.316	1.407	1.501	1.606	1.714	1.828	1.949	2.211	2.502	2.660
8	1.083	1.172	1.267	1.369	1.477	1.594	1.718	1.851	1.993	2.144	2.476	2.853	3.059
9	1.094	1.195	1.305	1.423	1.551	1.689	1.838	1.999	2.172	2.358	2.773	3.252	3.518
10	1.105	1.219	1.344	1.480	1.629	1.791	1.967	2.159	2.367	2.594	3.106	3.707	4.046
11	1.116	1.243	1.384	1.539	1.710	1.898	2.105	2.332	2.580	2.853	3.479	4.226	4.652
12	1.127	1.268	1.426	1.601	1.796	2.012	2.252	2.518	2.813	3.138	3.896	4.818	5.350
13	1.138	1.294	1.469	1.665	1.886	2.133	2.410	2.720	3.066	3.452	4.363	5.492	6.153
14	1.149	1.319	1.513	1.732	1.980	2.261	2.579	2.937	3.342	3.798	4.887	6.261	7.076
15	1.161	1.346	1.558	1.801	2.079	2.397	2.759	3.172	3.642	4.177	5.474	7.138	8.137
16	1.173	1.373	1.605	1.873	2.183	2.540	2.952	3.426	3.970	4.595	6.130	8.137	9.358
17	1.184	1.400	1.653	1.948	2.292	2.693	3.159	3.700	4.328	5.054	6.866	9.276	10.76
18	1.196	1.428	1.702	2.026	2.407	2.854	3.380	3.996	4.717	5.560	7.690	10.58	12.38
19	1.208	1.457	1.754	2.107	2.527	3.026	3.617	4.316	5.142	6.116	8.613	12.06	14.23
20	1.220	1.486	1.806	2.191	2.653	3.207	3.870	4.661	5.604	6.728	9.646	13.74	16.37
21	1.232	1.516	1.860	2.279	2.786	3.400	4.141	5.034	6.109	7.400	10.80	15.67	18.82
22	1.245	1.546	1.916	2.370	2.925	3.604	4.430	5.437	6.659	8.140	12.10	17.86	21.64
23	1.257	1.577	1.974	2.465	3.072	3.820	4.741	5.871	7.258	8.954	13.55	20.36	24.89
24	1.270	1.608	2.033	2.563	3.225	4.049	5.072	6.341	7.911	9.850	15.18	23.21	28.63
25	1.282	1.641	2.094	2.666	3.386	4.292	5.427	6.848	8.623	10.83	17.00	26.46	32.92
26	1.295	1.673	2.157	2.772	3.556	4.549	5.807	7.396	9.399	11.92	19.04	30.17	37.86
27	1.308	1.707	2.221	2.883	3.733	4.822	6.214	7.988	10.25	13.11	21.32	34.39	43.54
28	1.321	1.741	2.288	2.999	3.920	5.112	6.649	8.627	11.17	14.42	23.88	39.20	50.07
29	1.335	1.776	2.357	3.119	4.116	5.418	7.114	9.317	12.17	15.86	26.75	44.69	57.58
30	1.348	1.811	2.427	3.243	4.322	5.743	7.612	10.06	13.27	17.45	29.96	50.95	66.21
40	1.489	2.208	3.262	4.801	7.040	10.29	14.97	21.72	31.41	45.26	93.05	188.9	267.9
50	1.645	2.692	4.384	7.107	11.47	18.42	29.46	46.90	74.36	117.4	289.0	700.2	1,084

Table D-4 *Future Value of Annuity of $1*

Periods	Future Value												
	1%	2%	3%	4%	5%	6%	7%	8%	9%	10%	12%	14%	15%
1	1.000	1.000	1.000	1.000	1.000	1.000	1.000	1.000	1.000	1.000	1.000	1.000	1.000
2	2.010	2.020	2.030	2.040	2.050	2.060	2.070	2.080	2.090	2.100	2.120	2.140	2.150
3	3.030	3.060	3.091	3.122	3.153	3.184	3.215	3.246	3.278	3.310	3.374	3.440	3.473
4	4.060	4.122	4.184	4.246	4.310	4.375	4.440	4.506	4.573	4.641	4.779	4.921	4.993
5	5.101	5.204	5.309	5.416	5.526	5.637	5.751	5.867	5.985	6.105	6.353	6.610	6.742
6	6.152	6.308	6.468	6.633	6.802	6.975	7.153	7.336	7.523	7.716	8.115	8.536	8.754
7	7.214	7.434	7.662	7.898	8.142	8.394	8.654	8.923	9.200	9.487	10.09	10.73	11.07
8	8.286	8.583	8.892	9.214	9.549	9.897	10.26	10.64	11.03	11.44	12.30	13.23	13.73
9	9.369	9.755	10.16	10.58	11.03	11.49	11.98	12.49	13.02	13.58	14.78	16.09	16.79
10	10.46	10.95	11.46	12.01	12.58	13.18	13.82	14.49	15.19	15.94	17.55	19.34	20.30
11	11.57	12.17	12.81	13.49	14.21	14.97	15.78	16.65	17.56	18.53	20.65	23.04	24.35
12	12.68	13.41	14.19	15.03	15.92	16.87	17.89	18.98	20.14	21.38	24.13	27.27	29.00
13	13.81	14.68	15.62	16.63	17.71	18.88	20.14	21.50	22.95	24.52	28.03	32.09	34.35
14	14.95	15.97	17.09	18.29	19.60	21.02	22.55	24.21	26.02	27.98	32.39	37.58	40.50
15	16.10	17.29	18.60	20.02	21.58	23.28	25.13	27.15	29.36	31.77	37.28	43.84	47.58
16	17.26	18.64	20.16	21.82	23.66	25.67	27.89	30.32	33.00	35.95	42.75	50.98	55.72
17	18.43	20.01	21.76	23.70	25.84	28.21	30.84	33.75	36.97	40.54	48.88	59.12	65.08
18	19.61	21.41	23.41	25.65	28.13	30.91	34.00	37.45	41.30	45.60	55.75	68.39	75.84
19	20.81	22.84	25.12	27.67	30.54	33.76	37.38	41.45	46.02	51.16	63.44	78.97	88.21
20	22.02	24.30	26.87	29.78	33.07	36.79	41.00	45.76	51.16	57.28	72.05	91.02	102.4
21	23.24	25.78	28.68	31.97	35.72	39.99	44.87	50.42	56.76	64.00	81.70	104.8	118.8
22	24.47	27.30	30.54	34.25	38.51	43.39	49.01	55.46	62.87	71.40	92.50	120.4	137.6
23	25.72	28.85	32.45	36.62	41.43	47.00	53.44	60.89	69.53	79.54	104.6	138.3	159.3
24	26.97	30.42	34.43	39.08	44.50	50.82	58.18	66.76	76.79	88.50	118.2	158.7	184.2
25	28.24	32.03	36.46	41.65	47.73	54.86	63.25	73.11	84.70	98.35	133.3	181.9	212.8
26	29.53	33.67	38.55	44.31	51.11	59.16	68.68	79.95	93.32	109.2	150.3	208.3	245.7
27	30.82	35.34	40.71	47.08	54.67	63.71	74.48	87.35	102.7	121.1	169.4	238.5	283.6
28	32.13	37.05	42.93	49.97	58.40	68.53	80.70	95.34	113.0	134.2	190.7	272.9	327.1
29	33.45	38.79	45.22	52.97	62.32	73.64	87.35	104.0	124.1	148.6	214.6	312.1	377.2
30	34.78	40.57	47.58	56.08	66.44	79.06	94.46	113.3	136.3	164.5	241.3	356.8	434.7
40	48.89	60.40	75.40	95.03	120.8	154.8	199.6	259.1	337.9	442.6	767.1	1,342	1,779
50	64.46	84.58	112.8	152.7	209.3	290.3	406.5	573.8	815.1	1,164	2,400	4,995	7,218

Appendix E

Typical Charts of Accounts for Different Types of Businesses (For Businesses Discussed in Chapters 1–12).

SERVICE PROPRIETORSHIP

ASSETS

Cash
Accounts Receivable
Allowance for
  Doubtful Accounts
Notes Receivable,
  Short-Term
Goods and Services Tax
  Recoverable
Interest Receivable
Supplies
Prepaid Rent
Prepaid Insurance
Notes Receivable,
  Long-Term
Land
Furniture
Accumulated
  Amortization—
  Furniture
Equipment
Accumulated
  Amortization—
  Equipment
Building
Accumulated
  Amortization—
  Building

LIABILITIES

Accounts Payable
Notes Payable, Short-Term
Salaries Payable
Wages Payable
Goods and Services Tax
  Payable
Employee Income Tax
  Payable
Employment Insurance
  Payable
Canada Pension Plan
  Payable
Quebec Pension Plan
  Payable
Employee Benefits Payable
Interest Payable
Unearned Service Revenue
Notes Payable, Long-
  Term

OWNER'S EQUITY

Owner, Capital
Owner, Withdrawals

Revenues and Gains

Service Revenue
Interest Revenue
Gain on Sale of Land
  (or Furniture,
  Equipment, or
  Building)

Expenses and Losses

Salaries Expense
Wages Expense
Employee Benefits
  Expense
Insurance Expense for
  Employees
Rent Expense
Insurance Expense
Supplies Expense
Bad-Debt Expense
Amortization Expense—
  Furniture
Amortization Expense—
  Equipment
Amortization Expense—
  Building
Property Tax Expense
Interest Expense
Miscellaneous Expense
Loss on Sale (or Exchange)
  of Land (Furniture,
  Equipment, or Buildings)

SERVICE PARTNERSHIP

Same as Service Proprietorship, except for Owners' Equity:

OWNERS' EQUITY

Partner 1, Capital
Partner 2, Capital
Partner N, Capital
Partner 1, Withdrawals
Partner 2, Withdrawals
Partner N, Withdrawals

MERCHANDISING CORPORATION

ASSETS	LIABILITIES	SHAREHOLDERS' EQUITY	

ASSETS

Cash
Short-Term Investments
Fair-Value Valuation
   Allowance
Allowance for Doubtful
   Accounts
Notes Receivable,
   Short-Term
Goods and Services Tax
   Recoverable
Interest Receivable
Inventory
Supplies
Prepaid Rent
Prepaid Insurance
Notes Receivable,
   Long-Term
Investment Subject to
   Significant Influence
Long-Term Investments
Other Receivables,
   Long-Term
Land
Land Improvements
Accumulated
   Amortization—Land
   Improvements
Furniture and Fixtures
Accumulated
   Amortization—
   Furniture and Fixtures
Equipment
Accumulated
   Amortization—
   Equipment
Buildings
Accumulated
   Amortization—Buildings
Organization Costs
Franchises
Patents
Leaseholds
Goodwill

LIABILITIES

Accounts Payable
Notes Payable, Short-
   Term
Current Portion of
   Bonds Payable
Salaries Payable
Wages Payable
Goods and Services Tax
   Payable
Employee Income Tax
   Payable
Employment Insurance
   Payable
Canada Pension Plan
   Payable
Quebec Pension Plan
   Payable
Employee Benefits
   Payable
Interest Payable
Income Tax Payable
Unearned Service
   Revenue
Notes Payable, Long-Term
Bonds Payable
Lease Liability

Non-Controlling Interest

SHAREHOLDERS' EQUITY

Common Shares
Retained Earnings
Dividends

Revenues and Gains

Sales Revenue
Interest Revenue
Dividend Revenue
Equity-Method
   Investment Revenue
Gain on Sale of
   Investments
Unrealized Gain on Short-
   Term Investments
Gain on Sale of Land
   (Furniture and Fixtures,
   Equipment, or Building)
Discontinued
   Operations—Gain

Expenses and Losses

Cost of Goods Sold
Salaries Expense
Wages Expense
Commission Expense
Payroll Benefits Expense
Insurance Expense for
   Employees
Rent Expense
Insurance Expense
Supplies Expense
Bad-Debt Expense
Amortization Expense—
   Land Improvements
Amortization Expense—
   Furniture and Fixtures
Amortization Expense—
   Equipment
Amortization Expense—
   Buildings
Incorporation Expense
Amortization Expense—
   Franchises
Amortization Expense—
   Leaseholds
Income Tax Expense
Loss on Writedown of
   Goodwill
Loss on Sale of
   Investments
Unrealized Loss on Short-
   Term Investments
Loss on Sale (or
   Exchange) of Land (or
   Furniture and Fixtures,
   Equipment, or
   Buildings)
Discontinued
   Operations—Loss

MANUFACTURING CORPORATION

Same as Merchandising Corporation, except for Assets and Certain Expenses:

ASSETS

Inventories:
   Materials Inventory
   Work in Progress Inventory
   Finished Goods Inventory
Factory Wages
Factory Overhead

EXPENSES (CONTRA EXPENSES IF CREDIT BALANCE)

Overhead Production Volume Variance
Direct Materials Price Variance
Direct Materials Efficiency Variance
Direct Labour Price Variance
Direct Labour Efficiency Variance
Overhead Flexible Budget Variance

Glossary

Accounts receivable turnover Ratio of net credit sales to average net accounts receivable. Measures ability to collect cash from credit customers (p. 1015).

Acid-test ratio Ratio of the sum of cash plus short-term investments plus net current receivables to current liabilities. Tells whether the entity could pay all its current liabilities if they came due immediately. Also called the quick ratio (p. 1013).

Appropriations Restriction of retained earnings that is recorded by a formal journal entry (p. 789).

Articles of incorporation The document issued by the federal or provincial government giving the incorporators permission to form a corporation (p. 720).

Authorization of shares Provision in a corporation's articles of incorporation that permits a corporation to sell a certain number of shares of stock (p. 722).

Benchmarking Comparison of current performance with some standard. The standard often is the performance level of a leading outside organization (p. 1009).

Board of directors Group elected by the shareholders to set policy for a corporation and to appoint its officers (p. 722).

Bond A formal agreement in which a lender loans money to a borrower, who agrees to repay the money loaned at a future date and agrees to pay interest regularly over the life of the bond (p. 814).

Bonds payable Groups of notes payable (bonds) issued to multiple lenders called bondholders (p. 814).

Book value Amount of shareholders' equity on the company's books for each share of its stock (p. 739).

Book value per common share Common shareholders' equity divided by the number of common shares outstanding (p. 1021).

Bylaws Constitution for governing a corporation (p. 722).

Callable bonds Bonds that the issuer may call or pay off at a specified price whenever the issuer wants (p. 832).

Capital lease Lease agreement that substantially transfers all the benefits and risks of ownership from the lessor to the lessee (p. 837).

Cash equivalents Highly liquid short-term investments that can be converted into cash with little delay (p. 928).

Cash flow statement Reports cash receipts and cash payments classified according to the entity's major activities: operating, investing, and financing (p. 926).

Cash flows Cash receipts and cash payments (disbursements) (p. 927).

Chairperson (of board) Elected person on a corporation's board of directors; usually the most powerful person in the corporation (p. 722).

Common-size statement A financial statement that reports only percentages (no dollar amounts); a type of vertical analysis (p. 1008).

Common shares The most basic form of share capital. In describing a corporation, the common shareholders are the owners of the business (p. 724).

Consolidated statements Financial statements of the parent company plus those of majority-owned subsidiaries as if the combination were a single legal entity (p. 888).

Contract interest rate Interest rate that determines the amount of cash interest the borrower pays and the investor receives each year. Also called the stated interest rate (p. 818).

Contributed capital A corporation's capital from investments by the shareholders. Also called share capital or capital stock (p. 724).

Controlling interest Ownership of more than 50 percent of an investee company's voting shares (p. 886).

Convertible bonds (or notes) Bonds (or notes) that may be converted into the common shares of the issuing company at the option of the investor (p. 833).

Convertible preferred shares Preferred shares that may be exchanged by the preferred shareholders, if they choose, for another class of shares in the corporation (p. 731).

Cumulative preferred shares Preferred shares whose owners must receive all dividends in arrears before the corporation pays dividends to the common shareholders (p. 737).

Current ratio Current assets divided by current liabilities. Measures the ability to pay current liabilities from current assets (p. 1012).

Days' sales in receivables Ratio of average net accounts receivable to one day's sales. Tells how many days' sales remain in Accounts Receivable awaiting collection (p. 1016).

Debenture Unsecured bond, backed only by the good faith of the issuer (p. 816).

Debt ratio Ratio of total liabilities to total assets. Tells the proportion of a company's assets that it has financed with debt (p. 1016).

Deficit Debit balance in the retained earnings account (p. 725).

Direct method Format of the operating activities section of the cash flow statement that shows cash receipts from and cash payments for operating activities (p. 932).

Discount Amount of bond's issue price under its maturity (par) value (p. 816).

Dissolution Ending of a partnership (p. 672).

Dividend yield Ratio of dividends per share to the share's market price per share. Tells the percentage of a share's market value that the company pays to shareholders as dividends (p. 1021).

Dividends Distributions by a corporation to its shareholders (p. 725).

Double taxation Corporations pay their own income taxes on corporate income. Then, the shareholders pay personal income tax on the cash dividends that they receive from corporations (p. 721).

Earnings per share (EPS) Amount of a company's net income per outstanding common share (pp. 783, 1020).

Effective-interest amortization (of a bond) Amortization method in which a different amount of amortization expense is assigned to each year (or period) of the bond's life. The amount of amortization expense is the same percentage of a bond's carrying value for every period over a bond's life (p. 825).

Effective interest rate Another name for market interest rate (p. 818).

Efficient capital market One in which the market prices fully reflect the impact of all information available to the public (p. 1023).

Equity method for Investments The method used to account for investments in which the investor generally has 20 to 50 percent of the investor's voting shares and can significantly influence the decisions of the investee. The investment account is debited for ownership in the investee's net income and credited for ownership in the investee's dividends (p. 884).

Face value Another name for maturity value of a bond (p. 816).

Fair-value method The method of accounting for held-for-trading shares that values them at their fair, or market, value on the year-end balance sheet date. Any gain or loss resulting from the change in fair value is recognized in net income for the period in which it arises, and fair value becomes the new carrying value of the shares (p. 877).

Financing activity Activity that obtains the funds from investors and creditors needed to launch and sustain the business; a section of the cash flow statement (p. 930).

Foreign-currency exchange rate The measure of one currency against another currency (p. 897).

Foreign-currency transaction gain The gain that occurs when a cash payment is less than the related account payable or a cash receipt is greater than the related account receivable due to a change in exchange rate between the transaction date and the payment date (p. 898).

Foreign-currency transaction loss The loss that occurs when a cash payment is greater than the related account payable or a cash receipt is less than the related account receivable due to a change in exchange rate between the transaction date and the payment date (p. 898).

Free cash flow The amount of cash available from operations after paying for planned investments in plant, equipment, and other long-term assets (p. 946).

General partnership A form of partnership in which each partner is an owner of the business, with all the privileges and risks of ownership (p. 676).

Hedging A way to protect oneself from losing money in a foreign-currency transaction by engaging in a counterbalancing foreign-currency transaction (p. 900).

Horizontal analysis Study of percentage changes in comparative financial statements (p. 1002).

Income trust (or investment trust) A portfolio of assets designed to provide safety of principal and a regular fixed income (p. 774).

Indirect method Format of the operating activities section of the cash flow statement that starts with net income and shows the reconciliation from net income to operating cash flows. Also called the reconciliation method (p. 932).

Inventory turnover Ratio of cost of goods sold to average inventory. Measures the number of times a company sells its average level of inventory during a year (p. 1014).

Investing activity Activity that increases and decreases the long-term assets available to the business; a section of the cash flow statement (p. 930).

Lease Agreement in which the tenant (lessee) agrees to make rent payments to the property owner (lessor) in exchange for the exclusive use of the asset (p. 836).

Lessee Tenant in a lease agreement (p. 836).

Lessor Property owner in a lease agreement (p. 836).

Leverage Another name for trading on the equity (p. 1019).

Limited liability No personal obligation of a shareholder for corporation debts. The most that a shareholder can lose on an investment in a corporation's shares is the cost of the investment (p. 721).

Limited liability partnership (LLP) A partnership in which each partner's personal liability for the business's debts is limited to a certain dollar amount (p. 677).

Limited partnership A partnership with at lease two classes of partners: a general partner and limited partners (p. 676).

Liquidation The process of going out of business by selling the entity's assets and paying its liabilities. The final step in liquidation of a business is the distribution of any remaining cash to the owners (p. 692).

Long-term solvency The ability to generate enough cash to pay long-term debts as they mature (p. 1001).

Majority Interest Another name for controlling interest (p. 886).

Market interest rate Interest rate that investors demand in order to loan their money. Also called the effective interest rate (p. 818).

Market value Price for which a person could buy or sell a share (p. 738).

Market-value method Another name for the fair-value method of accounting for held-for-trading investments in shares (p. 877).

Maturity date The date on which the borrower must pay the principal amount to the lender (p. 816).

Maturity value A bond issued at par that has no discount or premium (p. 816).

Mortgage Borrower's promise to transfer the legal title to certain assets to the lender if the debt is not paid on schedule (p. 816).

Mutual agency Every partner can bind the business to a contract within the scope of the partnership's regular business operations (p. 674).

Non-controlling interest A subsidiary company's equity that is held by shareholders other than the parent company. Also called minority interest (p. 891).

No-par-value shares Shares that do not have a value assigned to them by the articles of incorporation (p. 728).

Off-balance-sheet financing Acquisition of assets or services whose resulting debt is not reported on the balance sheet (p. 839).

Operating activity Activity that creates revenue or expense in the entity's major line of business. A section of the cash flow statement. Operating activities affect the income statement (p. 929).

Operating lease Usually a short-term or cancelable rental agreement (p. 836).

Organization costs The costs of organizing a corporation, including legal fees, and charges by promoters for selling the shares. Organization cost is an intangible asset (p. 733).

Outstanding shares Shares in the hands of a shareholder (p. 723).

Par value Another name for maturity value of a bond (p. 816).

Parent company An investor company that generally owns more than 50 percent of the voting shares of a subsidiary company (p. 886).

Partnership An unincorporated business with two or more owners (p. 672).

Partnership agreement Agreement that is the contract between partners specifying such items as the name, location, and nature of the business; the name, capital investment, and duties of each partner; and the method of sharing profits and losses by the partners (p. 673).

Preferred shares Shares of stock that gives its owners certain advantages over common shareholders, such as the priority to receive dividends before the common shareholders and the priority to receive assets before the common shareholders if the corporation liquidates (p. 729).

Premium Excess of bond's issue price over its maturity (par) value (p. 816).

Present value Amount a person would invest now to receive a greater amount at a future date (p. 817).

President Chief operating officer in charge of managing the day-to-day operations of a corporation (p. 722).

Price/earnings (P/E) ratio Ratio of the market price of a common share to the company's earnings per share. Measures the value that the stock market places on $1 of a company's earnings (p. 1020).

Principal value Another name for maturity value of a bond (p. 816).

Quick ratio Another name for the acid-test ratio (p. 1013).

Rate of return on common shareholders' equity Net income minus preferred dividends, divided by average common shareholders' equity. A measure of profitability. Also called return on common shareholders' equity (pp. 741, 1019).

Rate of return on net sales Ratio of net income to net sales. A measure of profitability. Also called return on sales (p. 1018).

Rate of return on total assets The sum of net income plus interest expense divided by average total assets. This ratio measures the success a company has in using its assets to earn income for the persons who finance the business. Also called return on assets (pp. 740, 1018).

Repurchase of own shares A corporation may repurchase its own shares that it has issued previously (p. 774).

Retained earnings A corporation's capital that is earned through profitable operation of the business (p. 724).

Return on assets Another name for rate of return on total assets (p. 740).

Return on equity Another name for rate of return on common shareholders' equity (pp. 741, 1019).

Return on shareholders' equity Another name for rate of return on common shareholders' equity (p. 1019).

Secured bond A bond that gives the bondholder the right to take specified assets of the issuer if the issuer fails to pay principal or interest (p. 816).

Segment of the business A significant part of a company (p. 782).

Serial bond Bond that matures in installments over a period of time (p. 816).

Shareholder A person who owns shares in a corporation (p. 720).

Shareholders' equity Owners' equity of a corporation (p. 724).

Shares Units into which the owners' equity of a corporation is divided (p. 720).

Short-term liquidity Ability to meet current payments as they come due (p. 1001).

Stated interest rate Another name for the contract interest rate (p. 818).

Stated value Another name for par value, an arbitrary amount assigned to a share of stock (p. 728).

Statement of equity (statement of shareholders' equity) Presents changes in all components of equity (p. 787).

Stock Shares into which the owners' equity of a corporation is divided (p. 720).

Stock dividend (or share dividend) A proportional distribution by a corporation of its own shares to its shareholders (p. 769).

Stock split An increase in the number of authorized and outstanding shares coupled with a proportionate reduction in the book value of each share (p. 772).

Straight-line (SL) amortization Amortization method in which an equal amount of amortization expense is assigned to each year (or period) of asset use (p. 823).

Strong currency A currency that is rising relative to other nations' currencies (p. 898).

Subsidiary An investee company in which a parent company owns more than 50 percent of the voting shares (p. 886).

Term bonds Bonds that all mature at the same time for a particular issue (p. 816).

Times-interest-earned ratio Ratio of income from operations to interest expenses. Measures the number of times that operating income can cover interest expense. Also called the interest-coverage ratio (p. 1017).

Trading on the equity Earning more income on borrowed money than the related expense, thereby increasing the earnings for the owners of the business (pp. 836, 1019).

Unlimited personal liability When a partnership (or a proprietorship) cannot pay its debts with business assets, the partners (or the proprietor) must use personal assets to meet the debt (p. 674).

Vertical analysis Analysis of a financial statement that reveals the relationship of each statement item to the total, which is 100 percent (p. 1006).

Weak currency A currency that is falling relative to other nations' currencies (p. 898).

Working capital Current assets minus current liabilities; measures a business's ability to meet its short-term obligations with its current assets (p. 1011).

Index